REVIEW OF RESEARCH IN EDUCATION

Review of Research in Education is published annually on behalf of the American Educational Research Association, 1430 K St., NW, Suite 1200, Washington, DC 20005, by SAGE Publications, 2455 Teller Road, Thousand Oaks, CA 91320. Send address changes to AERA Membership Department, 1430 K St., NW, Suite 1200, Washington, DC 20005.

Member Information: American Educational Research Association (AERA) member inquiries, member renewal requests, changes of address, and membership subscription inquiries should be addressed to the AERA Membership Department, 1430 K St., NW, Suite 1200, Washington, DC 20005; fax 202-238-3250; e-mail: members@aera.net. AERA annual membership dues are $180 (Regular Members), $150 (Affiliate Members), $110 (International Affiliates), and $55 (Graduate Students and Student Affiliates). **Claims:** Claims for undelivered copies must be made no later than six months following month of publication. Beyond six months and at the request of the American Educational Research Association, the publisher will supply missing copies when losses have been sustained in transit and when the reserve stock permits.

Subscription Information: All non-member subscription inquiries, orders, back-issue requests, claims, and renewals should be addressed to SAGE Publications, 2455 Teller Road, Thousand Oaks, CA 91320; telephone (800) 818-SAGE (7243) and (805) 499-0721; fax: (805) 375-1700; e-mail: journals@sagepub.com; http://www.sagepublications .com. **Subscription Price:** Institutions: $321; Individuals: $64. For all customers outside the Americas, please visit http://www.sagepub.co.uk/customercare.nav for information. **Claims:** Claims for undelivered copies must be made no later than six months following month of publication. The publisher will supply missing copies when losses have been sustained in transit and when the reserve stock will permit.

Abstracting and Indexing: Please visit http://rre.aera.net and, under the "More about this journal" menu on the right-hand side, click on the Abstracting/Indexing link to view a full list of databases in which this journal is indexed.

Copyright Permission: Permission requests to photocopy or otherwise reproduce copyrighted material owned by the American Educational Research Association should be submitted by accessing the Copyright Clearance Center's Rightslink˚ service through the journal's website at http://rre.aera.net. Permission may also be requested by contacting the Copyright Clearance Center via its website at http://www.copyright.com, or via e-mail at info@copyright.com.

Advertising and Reprints: Current advertising rates and specifications may be obtained by contacting the advertising coordinator in the Thousand Oaks office at (805) 410-7763 or by sending an e-mail to advertising@sagepub.com. To order reprints, please e-mail reprint@ sagepub.com. Acceptance of advertising in this journal in no way implies endorsement of the advertised product or service by SAGE or the journal's affiliated society(ies). No endorsement is intended or implied. SAGE reserves the right to reject any advertising it deems as inappropriate for this journal.

Change of Address: Six weeks' advance notice must be given when notifying of change of address. Please send old address label along with the new address to ensure proper identification. Please specify name of journal.

International Standard Serial Number ISSN 0091-732X
International Standard Book Number ISBN 978-1-4739-2671-4 (Vol. 39, 2015, paper)
Manufactured in the United States of America. First printing, March 2015.
Copyright © 2015 by the American Educational Research Association. All rights reserved.

REVIEW OF RESEARCH IN EDUCATION

Teacher Assessment and the Assessment of Students With Diverse Learning Needs

Volume 39, 2015

Jamal Abedi, Editor
Christian Faltis, Editor
University of California, Davis

Review of Research in Education

Teacher Assessment and the Assessment of Students With Diverse Learning Needs

Volume 39

EDITORS

JAMAL ABEDI
University of California, Davis

CHRISTIAN FALTIS
University of California, Davis

AMERICAN EDUCATIONAL RESEARCH ASSOCIATION

Tel: 202-238-3200 Fax: 202-238-3250
http://www.aera.net/pubs

FELICE J. LEVINE
Executive Director

JOHN NEIKIRK
Director of Publications

Contents

Cover image © Tonyvictor | Dreamstime.com

Introduction

Teacher Assessment and the Assessment of Students With Diverse Learning Needs

Jamal Abedi
Christian Faltis
University of California, Davis

Assessment outcomes are used in many high-stakes decisions concerning students, teachers, and schools, including for accountability purposes (Darling-Hammond, 2004). For students, decisions regarding promotion, graduation, and curriculum are often made based on the results of assessments. Teachers also use information from assessments to enhance student learning. Assessments of teachers are used for improvement and personnel decisions regarding pay and advancement. For schools, sanction decisions are made based on student performance at mandatory state and district assessments. Clearly, assessments play an integral role in instruction, placement, promotion, and efforts to ensure that students and teachers receive the support they need for success.

At the same time, serious consequences can result from all of these assessments if they are not constructed and used properly. In particular, the use of assessment outcomes for high-stakes decision making is especially pronounced for students with special needs, such as English language learners (ELLs/ELs)[1] and students with disabilities (SWDs). For example, the process of initial identification, classification, and reclassification of ELL students is based extensively on the results of a single English language proficiency (ELP) test administered at a single time. If, for any reason, these test results are not dependable due to unreliable or invalid tests, it can jeopardize a student's academic path. An ELL student who is improperly classified as fluent English proficient may miss the opportunity to receive English language development services, and therefore may not receive the academic support necessary for success. Similarly, an ELL student at the lower level of English proficiency may mistakenly be classified as a student with learning or reading disabilities, which can also prevent him or her from receiving the appropriate support for his or her specific language

Review of Research in Education
March 2015, Vol. 39, pp. vii–xiv
DOI: 10.3102/0091732X14558995
© 2015 AERA. http://rre.aera.net

needs. Therefore, caution must be exercised when making high-stakes decisions based on assessments that may have questionable content and psychometric properties.

The purpose of this volume is to bring awareness to specific considerations necessary in the use of high-stakes assessments, particularly for students with diverse learning needs and for teachers. In addition, this volume attempts to shed light on the decisions made based on the results of assessments and explores the implications of using high-stakes assessments for students with special needs. The volume includes exemplary chapters addressing major issues in the content and psychometric characteristics of assessments for both students with diverse learning needs and for teachers.

ASSESSMENT OF STUDENTS WITH DIVERSE LEARNING NEEDS

Although there are many groups of students who could potentially be labeled as students with diverse learning needs, the primary focus of this volume is on ELLs and SWDs (Shimoni, Barrington, Wilde, & Henwood, 2013). For these students to succeed, it is imperative that their specific academic needs be recognized and addressed.[2] ELLs and SWDs need additional attention in the areas that can impede their academic progress, such as limited English proficiency or their disabilities. To be fair to these students, it is essential to make instruction and assessments accessible for them so they may fully demonstrate what they know, and what they are able to do academically. For example, unnecessary linguistic complexity of content-based assessments (e.g., mathematics and science) can unfairly affect the academic performance of ELLs, particularly those at the lower level of English proficiency, as well as students with reading or learning disabilities. Many ELL students may possess the content knowledge being assessed but may not be at the level of English proficiency needed to understand the complex linguistic structure of the test items, and therefore, the items block students from showing knowledge of the focal construct. Accordingly, the performance gap between ELLs and their native English-speaking peers due to unnecessary linguistic complexity of test items is a serious equity issue in assessment that must be addressed properly (Abedi, in press; Solano-Flores, 2008).

Similarly, many SWDs can perform at the same level as their peers if assessments are made accessible to them by controlling for sources of construct-irrelevant factors in their assessments. Issues such as fatigue and frustration due to the presentation of a large number of test items, crowded pages, and complex tables and charts can affect the performance of SWDs. Therefore, assessments must be constructed to focus on student knowledge and aptitude, while controlling for these inhibiting distractions (Ketterlin-Geller, 2008).

A NEW GENERATION OF ASSESSMENTS

Attention to the assessment of students with diverse learning needs is of paramount importance as the nation moves toward the development and implementation of a new generation of assessments. Currently, many states across the nation are implementing major changes to their assessment and accountability systems. The Race-To-The-Top College and Career Readiness standards-based assessment system, currently under development by two consortia of states, the Smarter Balanced Assessment Consortium (Smarter Balanced) and the Partnership for Assessment of Readiness for College and Career (PARCC), present a historical juncture to address issues related to the content and psychometric characteristics of the assessment of students with diverse learning needs. The issues identified by research in assessment and accountability systems must be addressed in the new generation of assessment systems as they will have a substantial impact on the validity of the interpretation of test scores for students with diverse learning needs.

TEACHER ASSESSMENTS

Assessment outcomes for teachers in both cognitive (e.g., teacher's content knowledge of subject areas) and noncognitive domains (e.g., teacher's level of motivation and engagement and other psychological factors) provide valuable information in understanding teachers' instructional strategies and students' performance in school. As Gitomer and Zisk (Chapter 1 in this volume) have indicated, teachers need to have deep knowledge and understanding of the content they are teaching, but the literature lacks specifics on how teachers should and actually do apply their knowledge during teaching. Moreover, much of the literature on teacher knowledge omits attention to the kinds of pedagogical language knowledge teachers need to have when teaching content to ELs (Faltis & Valdés, in press). Although there are different instruments that are commonly used for measuring teacher's content knowledge and attention to academic language (e.g., Performance Assessment for California Teachers) and for measuring teacher effectiveness, there is a need for research to judge the content and psychometric quality of these instruments (Tretter, Brown, Bush, Saderholm, & Holmes, 2013). Furthermore, research on the impact of teachers' cognitive and noncognitive assessment outcomes on student performance is scarce.

VOLUME OVERVIEW

Chapter 1 of this volume by Drew Gitomer and Robert Zisk focuses on the development of assessments of teacher knowledge. The chapter not only discusses assessments that serve licensing functions but also focuses on broader issues, including advances in assessment design and new ideas for promoting teacher knowledge and effectiveness. Gitomer and Zisk also discuss the domain-general rules of pedagogy, including knowledge of child development, classroom management, teaching methods, and classroom assessment. The authors distinguish between the domain-general pedagogical knowledge from the pedagogical content knowledge that provides the foundation for the assessment of pedagogical content knowledge. The authors acknowledge that limited information is available about the outcomes of and research into these content validation processes. Furthermore, they indicate that by understanding the relationships among these measures of teacher content knowledge, a more developed understanding of the nature and use of teacher knowledge can be articulated in carrying out the work of teaching.

In Chapter 2, Ayesha Madni, Eva Baker, Kirby Chow, Girlie Delacruz, and Noelle Griffin present the literature on the assessment of teachers' social psychological factors, as well as common strategies for assessing these variables. The authors suggest that the assessment of social psychological constructs for teachers might be useful in assigning and representing competent teachers in classrooms where they could model and incite appropriate student behaviors. The chapter examines various social psychological teacher factors such as motivation, intra- and interpersonal skills, and how these variables affect teacher effectiveness. The authors discuss teacher motivation as broken down into beliefs, efficacy, expectations, attribution, and goal orientation. They find that teacher efficacy, intrapersonal skills, and goal orientation can positively affect teacher beliefs about teaching and their instructional practices. The authors indicate that some teachers tend to underestimate the academic ability of students from lower income families or minority groups. The chapter also discusses technical quality issues of measurement, validity models, and the role of technology in measuring social psychological variables.

Chapter 3 by Kip Téllez and Eduardo Mosqueda discusses teachers' knowledge and skills as they relate to language learners and language assessments. The chapter begins with a discussion of the challenges with assessing ELLs in nondominant languages and the need to create accurate assessment tools. The authors also describe the misdiagnosis of ELLs who are placed into special needs classes and question whether the assessment is related to the students' language knowledge at the time of the assessment or other learning issues. They offer suggestions for more accurate assessments of ELLs. For example, the authors indicate that the Bilingual Verbal Ability Test helps identify ELLs who are academically skilled when all other linguistic capacity tests fail to recognize these talents. Next, the chapter discusses the issues related to teacher preparedness with dealing with ELLs. Based on the literature presented, the authors indicate that bilingual teachers who knew the home language of their ELL students were more accurate than English-only teachers for assessing their ELLs' academic abilities. The chapter also highlights a major concern that low income and minority students will continue to be underserved in schools and concludes with a note about the realities of testing ELLs and the potential that these populations may continue to be underserved due to the fact that a majority of ELLs attend underfunded schools that enroll few English speakers from other ethnic groups (Gifford & Valdés, 2006; Powers, 2014)

Chapter 4 by Timothy Boals, Dorry Kenyon, Alissa Blair, Elizabeth Cranley, Carsten Wilmes, and Laura Wright presents a comprehensive literature review on the concept and construct of ELP assessments. This chapter examines the ELP test design and the evolution of the ELP assessment. The authors examine the literature on the merits and shortcomings of ELP test design and testing as they have evolved over time. In the first section of the chapter the authors explain the role of language testing in its broader historical and policy context. In the second section the authors examine the evolving construct and operationalization of academic English, and use the ACCESS for ELLs as an example of how the conceptualization of academic language is operationalized in the design, development, administration, and use of a large-scale ELP assessment. This section also examines the issues of accessibility and accommodations in large-scale ELP testing. In the final section of this chapter the authors explore expanded conceptualizations of ELP assessment in the era of College and Career Readiness standards and conclude with recommendations for future research.

Chapter 5 by Suzanne Lane and Brian Leventhal presents a comprehensive review of the literature on psychometric issues in the assessment of ELLs and SWDs. The chapter is structured in four sections. The first section presents general concepts in the assessment of ELLs and SWDs, such as the inclusion of ELLs and SWDs in large-scale assessments, validity issues in the assessment of ELLs and SWDs, the concept and application of test accommodations in assessment of these students, and a discussion of psychometric challenges, which includes issues related to the validity and fairness of assessing ELLs and SWDs. The second section presents a comprehensive literature review on the efficacy of test accommodations and modifications for SWDs and ELLs. The third section examines the extent to which the psychometric properties (e.g., reliability and score precision, internal structure evidence, external structure evidence, and evidence of equating) of a test are invariant across groups of students. The authors indicate that the establishment of measurement invariance for ELLs and SWDs is required to make valid and fair score interpretations for these students and for group comparisons. The chapter concludes with the presentation of issues related to growth measures for ELLs and SWDs. The authors explain the challenges and goals of the assessment consortia to address these issues by designing better tests and by providing accommodations that are more effective in making assessments more accessible to students without altering the focal construct.

Chapter 6 by Stephen Sireci and Molly Faulkner-Bond presents a thorough discussion of the validity of assessments for ELLs. Acknowledging the complex nature of assessing the knowledge, skills, and abilities of ELLs, the authors discuss how a validation framework for evaluating the inferences derived from ELLs' test performance can be developed. Since accommodations used for ELLs play a major role in the validity of assessments for these students, the authors present a review of the literature on the effectiveness and validity of accommodations used for ELLs and how construct-irrelevant sources due to inappropriate use of accommodations can affect the validity of assessments. The authors include a discussion of the most common accommodations provided to ELLs and the level of improvement in ELL student performance due to the use of these accommodations. The authors then discuss best practices that test developers can use to promote more valid assessments of ELLs, as well as future directions for research and practice in assessment and accommodations for ELLs.

Chapter 7 by Alison Bailey and Patricia Carroll presents a comprehensive view of current language assessment policies and practices for ELL students and discusses relevant research studies to evaluate their technical quality. The authors discuss a system with four main components to determine students who should and those who should not receive services under Title III of the No Child Left Behind Act. The first component of the system involves administration of a home language survey to identify potential ELL students. In the second phase of the system, screening tools or placement tests are used to determine ELL status and instructional placement. The third phase involves monitoring English language progress and proficiency with classroom assessment approaches for instructional purposes and for annual accountability of the student's English language progress and level of proficiency as measured by an ELP assessment. In the last phase, ELL students are evaluated based on their level of English proficiency for reclassification as English proficient and exit from ELL programming based on the state and local district formulas. The authors also discuss validity concerns regarding the criteria used in the different phases of the system. The authors examine the intersection of language assessment and academic content assessment in terms of their purposeful interpretation and use (including accommodation use) by educators in decision making at the federal, state, and local levels. Bailey and Carroll conclude by providing recommendations for further research that focuses on improving the ELL assessment system to validly identify students who should receive services under Title III of No Child Left Behind with its focus on ELL language support.

Chapter 8 by Ryan Kettler provides a broad review of research on the role of testing adaptations as well as examples of item modifications and testing accommodations. The chapter begins by introducing the role of testing adaptations in the accessibility of tests for a diverse population of students. The chapter documents the substantial research that has been completed on testing adaptations, along with critical findings. Based on the summary of research presented, the chapter recommends reexamination of the methods that are used to answer questions about the appropriateness of testing adaptations. The final section of the chapter introduces a new practice and research paradigm that recognizes the many related variables that must be considered to draw sophisticated inferences from achievement test scores.

Chapter 9 by Martha Thurlow and Rebecca Kopriva describes the concept and application of accessibility and accommodations in the assessment of special needs student populations. The primary focus of this chapter is on large-scale content assessments used at the state and national levels and the direct implications that these assessments have on students' academic career, and on district and state policies and practices. The chapter provides a history of the push for assessment accessibility and accommodations in national and state assessments particularly in the new generation of assessments. The authors explain the dramatic shifts that have occurred in the participation of ELLs and SWDs in national and state assessments, and the legal basis for many of the changes in inclusion, accessibility, and accommodations. The authors then discuss the foundational assumptions and research findings regarding accessibility and accommodations for SWDs and ELLs, and the implications for district and classroom assessments.

Chapter 10 by Randy Bennett focuses on the transition of educational assessments from a paper-based to an electronic format. The author indicates that this transition is not a simple change of assessment presentation but is a more substantive process and involves major restructuring in the content, construct, and presentation of the assessment items. The chapter begins by describing the different developmental stages associated with the evolution of assessment programs, including the new generation of assessments being created by PARCC and Smarter Balanced. The author then discusses innovations made possible by electronic learning environments. In this section, the author presents some of the advanced features that the Common Core State Assessment consortia are actively incorporating in the new assessments.

ACKNOWLEDGMENTS

The editors wish to express their appreciation to individuals who made this work possible. First, we would like to thank the authors for their great contribution to this volume. We are also grateful to the consulting editors and all the outside reviewers for their time and the valuable suggestions and advice they provided to the authors. Special thanks to Kelsey Krausen, our editorial assistant, who performed an extraordinary job of managing the various tasks related to the volume. She communicated so gracefully with authors, consulting editors, and reviewers and kept everyone on track. She also provided excellent suggestions for revisions of this introduction and different chapters of the volume. We also wish to thank Felice Levine, AERA Executive Director; John Neikirk, AERA Director of Publication; and other members of the AERA Publication Committee for their guidance and support. Last, we want to express our gratitude to Sara Sarver, the project editor at Sage, for her efforts toward publication of this work.

NOTES

[1]In this volume, the terms *English learner* (EL) and *English language learner* (ELL) have been used interchangeably. Some authors prefer the term *EL* and some *ELL*. We left the decision of which term to use to the authors.

[2]It must be noted that although assessment issues for ELLs and SWDs are discussed in this volume in tandem, this should not imply any association between these two groups of students.

REFERENCES

Abedi, J. (in press). Language issues in item-development. In S. Lane, M. S. Raymond, & T. M. Haladyna (Eds.), *Handbook of test development* (2nd ed.). Florence, KY: Routledge.

Darling-Hammond, L. (2004). Standards, accountability, and school reform. *Teachers College Record, 106,* 1047–1085.

Faltis, C., & Valdés, G. (in press). Preparing teachers to teach in and advocate for linguistically diverse classrooms: A vade mecum for teacher educators. In D. Gitomer & C. Bell (Eds.), *The handbook of research on teaching* (5th ed.). Washington, DC: American Educational Research Association.

Gifford, B. R., & Valdés, G. (2006). The linguistic isolation of Hispanic students in California's public schools: The challenge of reintegration. *Yearbook of the National Society for the Study of Education, 105,* 125–154.

Ketterlin-Geller, L. (2008). Testing students with special needs: A model for understanding the interaction between assessment and student characteristics in a universally designed environment. *Educational Measurement: Issues and Practice, 27*(3), 3–16.

Powers, J. (2014, September 15). Race, ethnicity, and poverty factor into the re-segregation of Arizona's schools. *Arizona Education News.* Retrieved from http://azednews.com/2014/09/15/race-ethnicity-poverty-factor-into-the-re-segregation-of-arizonas-schools

Shimoni, R., Barrington, G., Wilde, R., & Henwood, S. (2013). Addressing the needs of diverse distributed students. *International Review of Research in Open and Distance Learning, 14,* 134–157.

Solano-Flores, G. (2008). Who is given tests in what language, by whom, when, and where? The need for probabilistic views of language in the testing of English language learners. *Educational Researcher, 37,* 189–199.

Tretter, T. R., Brown, S. L., Bush, W. S., Saderholm, J. C., & Holmes, V. (2013). Valid and reliable science content assessment for science teachers. *Journal of Science Teacher Education, 24,* 269–295.

Chapter 1

Knowing What Teachers Know

DREW H. GITOMER
ROBERT C. ZISK
Rutgers, the State University of New Jersey

That teachers need to have deep knowledge has been an article of faith among philosophers, educators, and policymakers tracing back to Socrates. But the specifics of what teachers ought to know and how they can make use of knowledge during teaching continue to evolve (Biesta & Burbules, 2003) and are related to underlying conceptions of the role of teachers and the teaching profession that have evolved in the United States across its entire history (see Kafka, in press, for a review of the history of teaching in the United States).

Coupled with these changing ideas about what teachers need to know has been the educational authority's interest in assessing and warranting teachers' and prospective teachers' knowledge. Thirty years ago, in the last explicit treatment of teacher testing in *Review of Research in Education*, Haney, Madaus, and Kreitzer (1987) provided accounts of teacher assessments that were introduced as early as colonial times. The chapter remains an important critique of teacher testing by focusing on the use and social implications of such tests and on the ways in which teacher assessment might be improved.

Although some of the concerns that Haney et al. (1987) raised 30 years ago are still germane today, there have been substantial changes as well. Not only have assessments that serve a regulatory function (e.g., licensure) evolved, but an intensive scholarly focus, during the last 30 years in particular, has produced a broad literature that attempts to conceptualize and empirically examine the knowledge base of teachers (e.g., Ball, Thames, & Phelps, 2008; Grimmett & MacKinnon, 1992; Shulman, 1987).

Review of Research in Education
March 2015, Vol. 39, pp. 1–53
DOI: 10.3102/0091732X14557001
© 2015 AERA. http://rre.aera.net

Haney et al. (1987) note that from colonial times through the first half of the 19th century, examinations of teachers were essentially oral interviews that were conducted by local officials and that focused on moral fitness, classroom/student management, and fundamental literacies. Over the course of the 19th century, counties and states attempted to impose more control on localities, partly due to the finding that those conducting the interviews were often ill-equipped to evaluate the examinees' responses and partly because of increasing state interest in public education. Conducting oral interviews continued to be the dominant form of assessment during this transitional period of control. As the 20th century unfolded, however, written objective tests became more common as the science and practice of standardized assessment first emerged.

In the 1930s, the Cooperative Test Service, an agency of the American Council on Education (ACE), developed objective tests in more than 40 subject areas at the senior high school and junior college levels. It was these tests that largely formed the basis for the development by the ACE of the National Teacher Examination (NTE)— the first national assessment for teachers (Haney et al., 1987). Given the national scope of these assessments and the fact that these were the first tests for teachers with any significant research base and scholarly record, it is at this point in time that we begin to focus the current analysis.

The current chapter focuses on philosophical and scientific developments in the assessment of teacher knowledge. Although we give attention to assessments that serve licensing functions, our goal is not to update the implications of regulatory assessments within a policy context. Nor do we limit the use of teacher assessments to only regulatory functions. Instead we focus on how conceptions of teaching and teacher development, together with research on teacher knowledge and advances in assessment design and related technologies, have led to new ideas about what teachers need to know, how to assess that knowledge, and how such information can serve a multiplicity of purposes.

It is important that we clarify how the chapter, as a review of the assessment of teacher knowledge, is organized. The goal is to provide an overview of major developments in the assessment of teacher knowledge and to illustrate those developments with representative and significant efforts. We made evaluative judgments of importance based on their presence in practice, their contributions to policy, and/or their contributions to the research base on teacher assessment. Our judgments are subjective in some sense, and we try to provide our rationale for including these illustrations as demonstrations of major developments. However, by no means is this a comprehensive review of every assessment of teacher knowledge that has been developed.

This chapter is also not intended to be a comprehensive review of all of the work that has been carried out in two areas that have shaped these assessments: (1) research that focuses on the nature of teacher knowledge across disciplines; and (2) contexts and policy initiatives that have influenced the nature of teacher assessment. In both cases we illustrate our points with relevant research and policy efforts that have shaped the directions of assessments, but our intent is not to be exhaustive in the reviews of all relevant research and policy.

We conducted our literature review for this chapter by first searching for all relevant papers that addressed teacher knowledge. Search terms included the following: teacher knowledge, conceptions of teacher knowledge, teacher-enacted knowledge, teacher practical knowledge, assessments of teacher knowledge, content knowledge for teaching (CKT), content knowledge for teaching and CKT by subject areas, pedagogical content knowledge (PCK), pedagogical content knowledge and PCK by subject areas, assessments of content knowledge for teaching, CKT validation, assessments of PCK, PCK validation, core teaching practices, and high-leverage practices. We then selected from this very broad literature articles and examples that we judged to have had significant influence and impact on assessments of teacher knowledge and used these examples to support the conceptual argument and framework of the chapter.

Given the scope of the entire volume, we conducted a more focused search on assessments of teacher knowledge with respect to English language learners (ELLs). That search did not yield much, as the knowledge base for what teachers need to know to teach ELLs is also limited (Faltis & Valdés, in press). Therefore, we do not focus much of the chapter's attention explicitly on ELL teacher assessments but instead provide at the conclusion of the chapter some discussion about the state of the field and future directions.

We organize the chapter using the validity framework described in the 2001 landmark publication by National Academies Press, *Knowing What Students Know* (National Research Council, 2001a). Key points, applicable to assessments of teacher knowledge, include the following:

1. Educational assessments have been inadequate largely because they were based on impoverished views of cognition.
2. Assessments can be thought of as having three components—a model of cognition (what we are trying to measure), a model of observation (how we collect evidence), and a model of interpretation (how we make sense of the evidence).
3. Building off a long history, the validity of assessments must be considered in terms of how scores are interpreted and used within particular contexts for particular purposes.

This chapter uses and builds on this framework to review the past 75 years of teacher assessment by considering four different assessment foci, described in Table 1, beginning with the assessments embedded within the first national assessment system for teachers, the NTE. We review the models of cognition, observation, and interpretation that undergird each of the major teacher assessment foci. We also review the nature and evidence of the validity arguments for the assessments that underlie each of the foci.

It is important to recognize that these foci are not temporally bound or linear in their development. Although it is true that the emergence of the four foci largely developed in sequence over time, assessments of basic skills and content knowledge,

TABLE 1
Major Foci in the Assessment of Teacher Knowledge

Focus	Underlying Premise	Sample Assessments	Interpretation	Use(s)
Teacher as educated professional	Teachers should have a general set of intellectual competencies.	National Teacher Examination Core Battery (General Knowledge, Communication Skills, Professional Knowledge); Praxis I	Test scores indicate extent to which teachers have fundamental knowledge that is critical for teachers to know.	Licensure
Teacher as content knowledge professional	Teachers should understand the specific subject-matter content they will teach.	Praxis II; state-specific content licensure assessments	Test scores indicate extent to which teachers have fundamental knowledge of the subject(s) they will teach.	Licensure
Teacher as content knowledge for teaching professional	Teachers should understand both the subject-matter content and how to teach that content.	Content knowledge for teaching (CKT) assessments (Mathematics Knowledge for Teaching [MKT]); National Board for Professional Teaching Standards (NBPTS) Assessment Center	Test scores indicate extent to which teachers hold subject-matter knowledge in ways needed to successfully teach.	Research into teaching; professional development; potential uses: teacher education; licensure; advanced certification
Teacher as knowledge-rich practitioner	Teachers draw on content as they carry out teaching practices.	NBPTS portfolios; high-leverage practices; core practices	Test scores indicate extent to which teachers have the ability to carry out integrated teaching practices that call on different forms of knowledge relevant to teaching.	Research into teaching; professional development; potential uses: teacher education; licensure; advanced certification

which were the initial foci of teacher assessment, remain the dominant forms of consequential assessments for teachers. Thus, any historical trajectories represent developments in theory and assessment design but do not describe historical transitions in assessment implementation.

The four foci are characterized by assessment tasks that increasingly approximate teaching practice. The first two foci have very tenuous connections to teaching practice, as they simply hold that certain types of knowledge are prerequisite to competent teaching. Yet these foci assiduously avoid claiming that greater amounts of knowledge beyond the licensure standard imply better teaching. These tests are designed as minimum competency tests only.

The more recent CKT focus makes a much stronger claim about its relationship to teaching. Each assessment task is designed to tap knowledge that is called for in carrying out the work of teaching (Ball et al., 2008). The most recent focus goes even further and attempts to assess the enactment of teacher knowledge in the carrying out of teaching practices. Although this latter focus has not yet resulted in substantial deployment of assessments, promising work that is likely to influence the future of teacher knowledge assessment is moving forward.

We limit our discussion of assessment to structured tasks that ask test takers to provide specific types of evidence and for which there are clear expectations for what constitutes a quality response. In all of these tasks, test takers are specifically asked to demonstrate their knowledge. An incorrect or poor-quality response is taken as negative evidence of an individual's knowledge.

The implication of this stance is that we do not consider tasks as assessments of teaching that occur in more naturalistic/nonstructured settings. So, for example, we do not include teacher observations of everyday teaching as a source of evidence about teacher knowledge. This is based on the reasoning that although one may draw inferences about a teacher's knowledge based on some demonstration of skilled teaching performance, a lack of demonstration does not necessarily give information about the teacher's knowledge. For example, if a teacher is leading an effective discussion and asking productive questions, it might be reasonable to infer that a teacher has a certain command of both the content of the discussion and the ways of engaging students in the content. However, a poor discussion may be caused by a myriad of reasons (e.g., classroom management) that have nothing to do with whether or not a teacher knows the content or even principles that are associated with effective discussions. Such naturalistic observations are also not a very efficient and direct method for capturing teacher knowledge. Therefore, we examine only assessment models that ask the teacher to explicitly respond to a prompt that is designed to assess a particular aspect of teacher knowledge.

HISTORICAL PERSPECTIVES ON TEACHER KNOWLEDGE

Conceptions of teacher knowledge—what teachers should know—have developed, and continue to develop, from multiple influences including philosophical and psychological views on the nature of knowledge, philosophical and political perspectives on the purposes and nature of teaching, sociopolitical demands, and research on teaching.

We begin this discussion by considering a long-standing dialogue that has concerned both philosophers and psychologists in terms of what constitutes knowledge. Specifically, how do we make sense of the distinction between *knowing that* and *knowing how?* Fantl (2014) summarizes much of the historical philosophical debate that harkens back to the ancient Greek philosophers' reference to *epistêmê* (knowledge) and *technê* (craft or art). Even then, the boundaries had not been clear, as Fantl references the Plato argument that to "live a good life, we ultimately need knowledge in the forms of virtue." Yet philosophers have debated whether Plato meant that a virtuous life requires only knowledge of what is virtuous or that it also requires knowledge of how to live virtuously.

The extent to which *knowing that* and *knowing how* are independent constructs has also been the subject of substantial philosophical treatment. Using an example such as riding a bicycle makes apparent the difficulty in resolving the debate. One can imagine a young person who rides a bicycle quite skillfully, yet cannot articulate accurately any of the actions that contribute to successful riding. One can also imagine an elderly, infirm engineer who can describe in exquisite detail how to ride a bicycle. Yet, because of physical limitations, the engineer cannot actually ride the bicycle. Which of these individuals knows *how* to ride a bicycle?

Ryle (1946) presents a view that is useful for considering the assessment foci described in this chapter. He argues that the distinction between *knowing that* and *knowing how* is not particularly productive. Rather, the useful distinction is between theoretical and practical knowledge. Practical knowledge is that which results in *intelligent behavior.* He makes the distinction "between the museum-possession and the workshop-possession of knowledge. A silly person can be stocked with information, yet never know how to answer the particular question" (p. 16).

Cognitive psychologists, and later researchers in artificial intelligence, reconsidered the *knowing that/knowing how* distinction in terms of declarative and procedural knowledge. Chi and Ohlsson (2005) summarize declarative knowledge as descriptive and use-independent, embodying concepts, principles, ideas, schemas, and theories. Procedural knowledge, in contrast, is prescriptive and use-specific and consists of associations among goals, situations, and actions. Substantial research in a variety of domains attempted to develop psychological models that connected and described the transformation of declarative knowledge into procedural knowledge (e.g., Anderson, 1976; Kintsch, 1998; Rumelhart & Norman, 1978). As declarative knowledge becomes proceduralized, access to the declarative knowledge may be lost. The skilled performer may have little ability to describe the actions he/she undertook in executing that performance.

The foregoing distinction is important in two ways. First, philosophical treatments of teaching have certainly focused on knowledge that can be considered practical or procedural. The focus has been dominated by what teachers do or ought to do. However, this stands in stark contrast to dominant forms of assessment that have focused on the declarative or theoretical. The second important feature is that the assessment foci we describe in this chapter show an increasing approximation to knowledge as practice.

Considerations of what teachers should know must be made in light of conceptions of the nature and role of teaching in helping students learn. On one hand, philosophical conceptions have been far-ranging and have often viewed teaching as a set of interactions in which the teacher's role is to facilitate learning through questioning and feedback and by providing experiences that spur students' thinking and build on the knowledge they already possess. This vision is quite distant from the primarily didactic instruction that has been the hallmark of most American educational practice (e.g., Goodlad, 1984). These philosophical views are similarly inconsistent with the dominant teacher and student assessment practices during the past century. The underlying premise that has guided instructional and assessment practice has been that the teacher holds knowledge and, primarily through lecture and instructional materials, transmits content to students (e.g., Goodlad, 1984).

The perspective that teaching is both interactive and facilitating has deep roots in history. Mintz (2007) discusses Socrates's view of pedagogy as *midwifery*, in which the role of the teacher is to create the proper conditions for birth (learning) to occur. Furthermore, the importance of the relation between the midwife and the mother is analogous to the relation of student and teacher, and the match between the student and teacher is critical to the quality of the educational experience.

In *Emile*, Rousseau (1979) articulates the role of the teacher as one who guides rather than tells:

It is a question of guidance rather than instruction. He must not give precepts, he must let the scholar find them out for himself. . . . The teacher's art consists in this: To turn the child's attention from trivial details and to guide his thoughts continually towards relations of importance which he will one day need to know, that he may judge rightly of good and evil in human society.

John Dewey, perhaps the most influential philosopher guiding progressive education, actually says little about the role of the teacher in learning. Biesta and Stengel (in press) present Dewey's teaching view as follows:

The teacher is therefore not the "guide on the side" but the designer of "a vital and personal experiencing." The teacher cannot make growth happen but *can* "determine the medium" that makes growth possible. S/he can do that as the member of the group "having the riper and fuller experience and the greater insight into the possibilities of continuous development found in a suggested project."

Although Dewey has shifted the focus of educational attention from the act of teaching to the fact of children's lives, it does not mean that there is no authoritative task for the teacher.

It is no longer a question of how the teacher is to instruct or how the pupil is to study. The problem is to find what conditions must be fulfilled in order that study and learning will naturally and necessarily take place, what conditions must be present so that pupils will make the responses which cannot help having learning as their consequence. The pupil's mind is no longer to be on study or learning. It is given to doing the things that the situation calls for, while learning is the result. The method of the teacher, on the other hand, becomes a matter of finding the conditions which call out self-educative activity, or learning, and of cooperating with the activities of the pupils so that they have learning as their consequence. (Boydston, 1984, p. 267)

Interestingly, the view of interaction and facilitation has not been the dominant form of instruction. Instead, it has been much more didactic. And as we will see, until recently, teacher assessments paid little mind to these views of pedagogy and instead focused on explicit knowledge held by the teacher. One alternative theoretical position does stand out as supporting didactic instruction—Skinner's (1965) theory of positive reinforcement.

In addition to the *how* of teaching, there have been substantial consideration and tensions regarding what ought to be taught. Certainly, in the past century or so, we have seen a variety of imperatives that, at times, can be contested but can also coexist. In the United States, early views of the purposes of teaching, even through the early part of the 20th century, focused on morality and citizenship. Education's primary purpose was to acculturate students. Kafka (in press) notes, "Teachers were to instill in their students the values of hard work, respect for authority, and loyalty to God, family, and country."

The long-standing focus on cultivating citizenship, democratic, and social values through education is captured in an edited volume by Ravitch and Viteritti (2001). Noddings's (2005) work on caring addresses the role of schooling in helping students develop in ways that go beyond academic goals. However, what those values are and how they ought to be developed within a diverse community have always been contested terrain. One only has to look at the now discredited attempts to "civilize the Indians" (*Official Report of the Nineteenth Annual Conference of Charities and Correction*; Prucha, 1892/1973) to understand how terms like *citizenship* have been politicized and used for less than noble purposes. Debates about addressing the educational needs of students from the nondominant culture persist and include considerations of race, language, gender, and sexuality (e.g., August & Hakuta, 1997; Freire, 1970; Gay, 2010).

Other views of educational purposes are much more concerned with a core set of academic skills and knowledge as the basis for becoming a fully functioning member of society. Of course, the precise definition of what constitutes the core has long been a matter of debate, but various specifications have been offered by scholars and organizations. Hirsch (1988) lays out a common core of knowledge that should be held by all individuals in our society. Paideia (National Paideia Center, 2014) is an organization that has built schools and curricula around the idea that a body of core content should be integrated with critical thinking skills and activities. And, of course, the educational standards movement, including the current Common Core effort (National Governors Association Center for Best Practices & Council for Chief State School Officers, 2010), represents attempts by states and subject-matter organizations to articulate expectations for what students should learn. The definition of core knowledge is certainly subject to evolution and includes more modern specifications described in far-ranging articulations that include works by Hirsch (1988) and National Paideia Center (2014) and, more recently, broad standards documents such as the Common Core State Standards (National Governors Association Center for Best Practices & Council for Chief State School Officers, 2010) and the Next Generation Science Standards (NGSS Lead States, 2013).

FOCUS 1—TEACHER AS EDUCATED PROFESSIONAL

Assessments built on the teacher as educated professional focus were introduced in March 1940 when 3,726 teacher candidates took the first NTE in 23 testing centers across the country. One year before, the ACE appointed a National Committee on Teacher Examinations comprised of primarily state and large district school superintendents and deans or presidents of teacher colleges. The goals were to support superintendents in selecting new teachers and to provide teacher preparation institutions with national information so that they could better gauge the selectivity of their own institutions (see A. J. Wilson, 1985).

The Cognitive Model for Teacher as Educated Professional

The National Committee viewed teaching ability within the larger frame of factor theories of intelligence and cognitive abilities that was the dominant perspective on testing at the time. Charles Spearman explored the correlations among different ability measures and identified the general factor of intelligence, g, along with specific factors. Louis Thurstone, using factor analytic methods, pursued the idea of multiple factors of human abilities (see Carroll, 1993). This overarching view considered human abilities, both general and specific, as sets of traits that were applied across contexts. Specific traits were not only judged to be systematically related to other traits (the general factor) but also deemed to measure something unique (the specific factor).

Within this frame, teaching ability was viewed as a complex set of intellectual factors. The ACE, under the direction of Ben Wood, also immediately recognized that all teaching could not be assessed through standardized objective tests of knowledge:

Common sense has long told us . . . that objective examinations do not and cannot measure the total subtle complex which we call teaching ability. When we are concerned with a complex that includes such fundamentally different factors as intelligence, general culture, professional information, special subject-matter mastery, moral character, interest in children, emotional stability, personality, physical health and energy, etc., it is, or ought to be obvious that no one type of measurement, such as the examination, can be an adequate basis for selection or eligibility ranking. (ACE, 1940, p. 3)

Wood went on to argue that despite the fact that only a subset of information could be assessed using extant testing procedures, such tests could still contribute to selection processes by providing comparable measures that were not compromised by the varying standards operating across institutions that prepared teachers. He dismissed the criticism that Messick (1989) would later label *construct under-representation* by noting:

> To neglect examinations of intelligence, general culture, and professional information because they do not also measure personality, moral character, interest in children, and other important factors that determine teaching ability, would be as illogical as to neglect the use of the clinical thermometer and stethoscope because they do not measure a thousand other important diagnostic factors…The validity of the examinations should be judged by the accuracy with which they measure, not the total complex of teaching ability, but those parts which they are designed to measure, namely intelligence (linguistic and quantitative), general and special cultures of the types judged desirable by the teacher-selecting authorities, and professional information. (ACE, 1940, p. 4)

Wood's position, in the field of teacher licensure, has remained relatively unaltered. Although there is a recognition that teaching involves a complex set of abilities, licensure tests have been designed and defended as only measuring a subset of those skills (National Research Council, 2001b). Furthermore, licensure tests are positioned as tests that should never be used alone and that should be only one part of a larger licensure/selection process. However, those who have developed and used licensure tests have rarely described the details of other elements of that process.

Thus, the first generation of these assessments was based on an assumption that every teacher has a "certain minimum of intelligence, culture, and professional preparation" (A. J. Wilson, 1985, p. 20). In fact, Wood had developed these kinds of assessments and administered them to all college graduates as a marker of general educational quality, examining differences in performance across different fields. Thus, the focus on teaching was simply an extension of this earlier development of educational accountability measures.

For Wood, intelligence was operationalized as being able to reason, comprehend, and express oneself in English. Culture was defined as knowing current social problems, history and social studies, science, fine arts, literature, and mathematics. Professional information included knowledge of education and social policy, child development and educational psychology, guidance, individual and group analysis, and either elementary or secondary school methods. There was also an assumption that there is specific content knowledge that general elementary teachers and subject-specific teachers should have. Developed in 1940, this underlying cognitive model was the foundation of teacher testing for the next 60 years. Up until the NTE transitioned over to Praxis™ during the latter half of the 1990s (S. M. Wilson & Youngs, 2005), it consisted of three primary components in its core battery: communication skills, general knowledge, and professional knowledge.

One major development that did occur during these 60 years was the introduction of basic skills tests for teachers. Amid the general concern for educational performance in the United States (The National Commission on Excellence in Education, 1983) and the perceived low standards of teacher education institutions (see Levine, 2006), states began to implement policies that mandated that teachers demonstrate basic competency in reading, writing, and mathematics in order to be licensed. In addition to using state-specific tests, multiple states used these basic skills tests, which included the Pre-Professional Skills Test (later called Praxis I° and as of 2013 called the Praxis Core Academic Skills for Educators Test; Educational Testing Service [ETS], 2014b). Still in use today, these tests are basic literacy tests that are not tied to a theory of teaching. They were simply developed to assure the public that teachers were minimally competent in the basic skills of reading, writing, and mathematics.

The Evidence Model for Teacher as Educated Professional

In almost all cases, the evidence for assessments in this focus was developed through responses to multiple-choice items, though some writing assessments asked candidates to write short essays. The first versions of the NTE asked candidates to select the best option choice from among five choices. Several examples from the first NTE administration (Flanagan, 1941) are presented in Appendix A. The first test was extraordinarily lengthy. The common examination was 480 minutes, plus optional elementary/subject-specific tests. The time allowed to complete each part of the test was as follows: *intelligence*, 120 minutes; *general culture*, 180 minutes; *professional information*, 120 minutes; and *contemporary affairs*, 60 minutes. Ninety minutes were allowed to complete any of the optional elementary/subject-specific tests. Testing time was shortened such that the common examination was about 3 hours long by 1951 (Humphry, 1966). The NTE maintained the five-option multiple-choice items for its entire existence.

Basic skills tests generally collected the same type of evidence through multiple-choice exams. Both the California Basic Educational Skills Test™ (Pearson Education, Inc., 2014) and the Praxis I° used five-option multiple-choice items, although the more recent versions also include essays to assess writing. More recent versions of the ETS tests include a range of selected-response item formats.

Assessments in this focal category were obviously developed as paper-and-pencil tests, and some are still offered in that format. However, many tests are now delivered in computerized modes as well, though they are designed to ask the same content and are scored in the same manner. From the test developer's perspective, there is no difference between administrative modes (e.g., ETS, 2014a).

The Interpretive Model for Teacher as Educated Professional

Scores on these assessments were simply transformations of number of items correct to scaled scores. The original scaled scores on the NTE ranged from 0 to 100 with the mean set at 50 (Flanagan, 1941). The tests were designed to yield internally consistent measures. As psychometric methods advanced, processes such as test equating were used to ensure comparability across administrations. Over the years, the scales underwent some modifications and did not try to emulate the intelligence test scales that informed their original design. However, the basic transformation of items correct to scaled scores continued.

The most important interpretation for any of these assessments, as with any licensure test, is how an individual score compares with a passing standard. Because licensure testing is the province of the states, each state sets its own passing standard for a test using one of a number of common methods described in the rich literature on standard setting (e.g., Cizek & Bunch, 2007; Hambleton & Pitoniak, 2006).

The first score reports provided individuals with tabular and graphical representations of scores for each subtest. Each score was compared to several reference groups: an expected average for all individuals with an average intelligence score, the average of all candidates from that administration, and score levels designated to be superior and exceptional (scaled scores of 70 and 80, respectively; Flanagan, 1941). Percentages of individuals from the two groups selecting each response are presented along with the items in Appendix A.

Research Findings for Teacher as Educated Professional

Research on these assessments most often focused on the distribution of test scores across different population groups of interest. Even the earliest reports presented subtest scores for men and women, intended subject areas and grade levels, educational degrees, and prior teaching experience (Flanagan, 1941).

One of the most important and consistent findings has been that basic skills tests produce disparate impact. African American and Latino teacher candidates typically pass these tests at much lower rates than do White candidates. Disparate impact has been assailed as keeping otherwise qualified individuals from entering teaching (e.g., Bennett, McWhorter, & Kuykendall, 2006). Other research has contended that basic skills tests are, in fact, identifying individuals who are likely to have substantial difficulty in mastering the subject content necessary to pass licensure tests in specific content areas (Gitomer, Brown, & Bonett, 2011).

Disparate impact has led to lawsuits over the years, including one brought against California's basic skills test, California Basic Educational Skills Test, in *Association of Mexican American Educators v. State of California* (1996). In this case and others, the use of the tests has generally been upheld. Pullin (2001) provides a detailed review of legal considerations across licensure tests generally.

Another line of research has focused on attempting to establish a relationship between scores on these tests and student outcomes. Findings have been inconsistent, and when significant statistical relationships have been observed, they have generally been quite modest (National Research Council, 2001b).

FOCUS 2—TEACHER AS CONTENT KNOWLEDGE PROFESSIONAL

Whereas subject-specific tests were optional when the NTE first was introduced, during the 1980s, these content-specific tests increasingly became the key requirement for teacher certification and remain so to the present day. These tests predominantly focus on knowledge of content that is judged to be the content that is addressed in the subject and grade(s) for which the test is intended (e.g., high school chemistry, middle school social studies).

This focus was driven by a set of key policy considerations that described the importance of both knowing content and knowing how to teach that content. Knowledge of content and knowledge of how to teach content have had very different trajectories in terms of the development of assessments for teachers. It is for this reason that we treat the corresponding assessments as two separate foci.

The Cognitive Model for Teacher as Content Knowledge Professional

Concerns about educational performance in the United States and implications for future economic success were raised in a number of significant publications during the 1980s. *A Nation at Risk* (The National Commission on Excellence in Education, 1983) presented a broad range of apprehensions about education, with a particular focus on the inadequate preparation of teachers to meet ever-changing demands in a rapidly transforming global environment:

> The teacher preparation curriculum is weighted heavily with courses in "educational methods" at the expense of courses in subjects to be taught. A survey of 1,350 institutions training teachers indicated that 41 percent of the time of elementary school teacher candidates is spent in education courses, which reduces the amount of time available for subject matter courses. (The National Commission of Excellence in Education, p. 30)

A Nation at Risk led to a set of policy documents focused on a new vision of teaching and teacher preparation that concentrated on what teachers need to know and do. *A Nation Prepared* (Carnegie Task Force on Teaching as a Profession, 1986), followed by the Interstate New Teacher Assessment and Support Consortium (InTASC) standards (Council of Chief State School Officers, 1992) and the National Board for Professional Teaching Standards (1989), stressed the importance of teachers knowing their subject matter, as well as how to teach it. The importance of content knowledge was later codified into law through the 1998 amendment to Title II of the Higher Education Act (1998) requiring teacher preparation institutions to report on how well teachers do on licensure tests and then through the Elementary and Secondary Education Act (ESEA) of 2002 (No Child Left Behind; ESEA, 2002), in which teachers were required to be highly qualified by virtue of, in large part, demonstrating subject-matter knowledge through content tests. A set of research reviews that included recommendations for improving teacher preparation has continued to strengthen the argument for teachers having strong content knowledge, as well as knowing how to teach that content (e.g., Darling-Hammond & Bransford, 2007; National Research Council, 2010; S. M. Wilson, Floden, & Ferrini-Mundy, 2002).

Coinciding with these policy initiatives was the emergence of a cognitive psychology that emphasized the importance of domain-specific knowledge in the acquisition of skill (e.g., Chase & Simon, 1973; Chi, 1978; Chomsky, 1988; Norman & Rumelhart, 1975; Schank & Abelson, 1977; Wellman & Gelman, 1997). This work challenged the previously dominant view that expertise was simply a matter of intelligence or intellectual processing capacity and development. Rather, the learning and (re)structuring of content knowledge were shown to result in more sophisticated reasoning and problem solving. For example, Wellman and Gelman, among others, challenged the traditional developmental stage model of Piaget by demonstrating that children, with sufficient familiarity in a domain, could demonstrate more advanced reasoning than a traditional Piagetian stage theory would suggest. Thus, the policy focus on content knowledge was certainly consistent with the dominant learning theories of the time.

But what specific content did teachers need to know? Here, too, *A Nation at Risk* played a substantial role. The National Education Goals Panel (National Council on Education Standards and Testing, 1992; National Education Goals Panel, 1993) called for clear and ambitious content standards for K–12 education. The response was that professional organizations and almost all states (Council of Chief State School Officers, 2000) developed detailed standards describing what students should know across grade levels and subject areas (e.g., National Council for the Social Studies, 1994; National Council of Teachers of English & the International Reading Association, 1996; National Council of Teachers of Mathematics, 1989; National Research Council, 1996).

Another body of content has also been included as part of the professional content knowledge of teachers. This body of knowledge consists of domain-general rules of pedagogy, including knowledge of child development, classroom management, teaching methods, and classroom assessment (Voss, Kunter, & Baumert, 2011). Because it is not tied to subject-matter content, we distinguish this domain-general pedagogical knowledge from the PCK that provides the foundation for the assessment of CKT discussed in the next section.

Content specifications for teacher tests are typically derived from state and disciplinary standards. Then, through a set of test validation processes, committees of educators are asked to judge the relevance of the test specifications and the tests themselves to what teachers should know (Educational Testing Service, 2005). There is limited information available about the outcomes of and research into these content validation processes (National Research Council, 2001b). Researchers have raised cautions about validation procedures by arguing that just because a test measures aspects of the intended domain, it does not imply that the full domain is represented by the test (Shepard, 1993) and that validation methods have a strong confirmation bias (Moss, 1998).

The Evidence Model for Teacher as Content Knowledge Professional

Administering multiple-choice items has been the dominant method of collecting evidence about teachers' content knowledge. However, there are a number of assessments that also include constructed-response items. An example of standards and an assessment item in English and mathematics, respectively, from the California Educator Credentialing Examinations (CSET; California Subject Examinations for Teachers'; Pearson Education, Inc., 2014) are presented in Table 2. These assessments were originally all paper-and-pencil administrations but now also are delivered via computer.

TABLE 2

California Subject Examination for Teachers (CSET): Sample Subject Matter Requirements (SMRs) and Questions

SMR	Question
English Language Arts (ELA): Language, Linguistics, and Literacy (SMR Domain 2)	2. Which of the following statements accurately describes a significant effect that the Great Vowel Shift had on the English language?
0001 Human Language Structures (SMR 2.1) a. Demonstrate knowledge of the nature of human language, differences among languages, the universality of linguistic structures, and language change across time, locale, and communities b. Demonstrate knowledge of word analysis, including sound patterns (phonology) and inflection, derivation, compounding, roots and affixes (morphology) c. Demonstrate knowledge of sentence structures (syntax), word and sentence meanings (semantics), and language function in communicative context (pragmatics)	A. English vowel sounds no longer corresponded to French vowel sounds. B. Regional variations of vowel sounds emerged within England as well as in Scotland and Wales. C. Vowel sounds used by speakers in British colonies differed from vowel sounds used in Great Britain. D. The spelling of certain vowel sounds no longer corresponded to the pronunciation of those sounds.
Mathematics: Number and Quantity (SMR Domain 1)	3. Three numbers, x, y, and z, have a sum of 871. The ratio $x{:}y$ is 4:5 and the ratio $y{:}z$ is 3:8. Which of the following is the value of y?
0001 The Real and Complex Number Systems (SMR 1.1) a. Demonstrate knowledge of the properties of the real number system and of its subsets b. Perform operations and recognize equivalent expressions using various representations of real numbers (e.g., fractions, decimals, exponents) c. Solve real-world and mathematical problems using numerical and algebraic expressions and equations d. Apply proportional relationships to model and solve real-world and mathematical problems e. Reason quantitatively and use units to solve problems (i.e., dimensional analysis) f. Perform operations on complex numbers and represent complex numbers and their operations on the complex plane	A. 134 B. 156 C. 195 D. 201

Note. To view other SMRs and questions for the CSET, see http://www.ctcexams.nesinc.com/about_CSET.asp. To view preparation materials for the Praxis® tests, see http://www.ets.org/praxis/prepare/materials?WT.ac=praxishome_prepare_121126

While the delivery mode may differ, tests are designed to include the same content and are scored in the same manner. From the test developer's perspective, there is no difference between administration modes (e.g., Educational Testing Service, 2014a).

Individual tests are typically allotted several hours for administration, and students can complete tests more quickly in a computer-based environment because they need not wait for the testing time period to be completed. Depending on licensing requirements, individual candidates may need to take multiple content tests.

The Interpretive Model for Teacher as Content Knowledge Professional

In the case of traditional content tests used for licensure, it is almost certainly true that the domain of teaching knowledge, as expressed in documents such as the InTASC and National Board for Professional Teaching Standards (NBPTS), as well as in disciplinary standards, is underrepresented (e.g., American Federation of Teachers, 2012). The deep and integrated levels of understanding that are articulated in standards documents can be underrepresented in two ways.

The first type of underrepresentation concerns the nature of the items on the tests. As described in critiques of student assessments, and equally germane to teacher assessments, traditional tests "have theoretical roots in the differential and behaviorist traditions" (National Research Council, 2001b, p. 60). The richer cognitive models described in the standards are not well assessed through the traditional testing approaches evident in teacher licensure assessments.

The second form of underrepresentation involves the requirements for passing the test as defined by the passing standard. As described in the previous section, each state sets its own passing standard for a test using one of a number of common methods described in the rich literature on standard setting (e.g., Cizek & Bunch, 2007; Hambleton & Pitoniak, 2006). Teacher licensure tests that assess content frequently have been criticized for having passing standards that are very minimal and that result in extremely high passing rates (Crowe, Allen, & Coble, 2013; U.S. Department of Education, Office of Postsecondary Education, 2011). Thus, even if a test contains a large set of items that would be considered rigorous, if only a relatively small proportion of correct items is needed to meet the passing standard, then successful candidates will not have demonstrated mastery of the tested domain.

As with other licensure tests, these content tests typically involve a transformation from a raw score to a scaled score, which is then compared with the passing standard to determine a candidate's success. Scaled scores beyond passing status may or may not be reported to users, depending on existing policies. Often subscores reflecting subdomains that the test is designed to assess will be reported as well, though the validity of reporting these scores has been questioned due to the unreliability of scores based on small numbers of items (Sinharay, 2010).

Research Findings for Teacher as Content Knowledge Professional

Three primary research directions around teacher content tests have been pursued. The first has been to examine the content skill of individuals who take the teacher licensure tests and how that has varied across different demographic groups of individuals and over time. Such studies have been used to attempt to characterize the teaching force. For example, annual reports about licensure test results by content area are produced by the U.S. Department of Education, Office of Postsecondary Education (2011). Gitomer and Qi (2010) reported on the distribution of test scores for a number of Praxis content tests over a period of time in which there was an increase in accountability pressure from No Child Left Behind (Elementary and Secondary Education Act, 2001). They observed very high passing rates across tests, with the median score well above the passing standard across states. Additionally, they found little change in scores across years for those who passed the exams. They also observed very substantial differences between the scores of those who passed and those who did not. Finally, they concluded that the primary function of the tests is to identify a relatively small set of individuals who have very limited content knowledge. The use of the tests is not designed to make finer distinctions above these relatively low passing standards.

A second research direction focuses on how the wide use of content tests can both affect, and inform us about, the shape of the teaching pool. For example, Angrist and Guryan (2007) examined teaching employment patterns associated with increasing test demands. They found that increased use of tests led to higher wages but also dissuaded some higher ability individuals from entering teaching. They also concluded that Hispanic candidates were less likely to teach in states with increased licensure test requirements. Fuller and Ladd (2012) found that teachers in lower elementary grades had weaker licensure test scores than those in upper grades. Goldhaber, Lavery, and Theobald (2014) found that students with more educational disadvantage (e.g., free/reduced-price lunch status, underrepresented minority, low prior academic performance) have teachers with lower licensure scores. Furthermore, Gitomer, Latham, and Ziomek (1999) found that because passing rates for African American candidates were substantially lower than those for White candidates, policies that simply raised passing standards on licensure tests would likely lead to greater adverse impact. Goldhaber (2007) also argued that raising passing scores would reduce the teaching pool without having material effects on educational quality.

The third research direction has looked at relationships among licensure test scores and important educational outcomes, most especially student achievement. In general, findings have been mixed. Clotfelter, Ladd, and Vigdor (2007) found small but positive relationships between teacher test scores and student achievement in mathematics and reading, with mathematics effects substantially larger. Goldhaber (2007) found small but significant relationships between teacher scores and student achievement. However, Buddin and Zamarro (2008) found no significant relationship between teacher and student measures. As summarized in National Research Council (2001b), these studies and effect sizes must be treated cautiously. Even with more sophisticated methodologies employed in the studies reported here, there are still issues of the assignment of students to classroom teachers and the nature of both teacher and student tests that can influence the results of these studies.

FOCUS 3—TEACHER AS CONTENT KNOWLEDGE FOR TEACHING PROFESSIONAL

A new generation of teacher knowledge assessments has gradually emerged over the last two decades. These assessments are predicated on the idea that teachers' knowledge of content is situated in the practice of teaching, and knowledge is held in ways that support instruction and learning. This knowledge, however, is not separate from content knowledge; instead, it is assumed to rely heavily on the integration of content knowledge and pedagogical knowledge. This has led to both large-scale assessments and significant programs of research. Nevertheless, even as conceptions of both teaching and testing have evolved to support this focus, the dominant forms of teacher testing remain rooted in the first two foci. CKT assessments remain largely the province of research efforts. For ease of presentation, we label all assessment efforts in this category as CKT, even if they were originally discussed as PCK measures.

The Cognitive Model for Teacher as CKT Professional

During the 1980s, the same policy initiatives described in the previous section set the stage for addressing CKT. Consequently, research on teacher knowledge broadened considerably, influenced by the larger emergence of the cognitive sciences and a focus on situated cognition. From this perspective, knowledge moved from being conceived of as a stable trait of individuals to a set of understandings inextricably associated with specific contexts. For example, there were classic cross-cultural and developmental studies of individuals who demonstrated very powerful understanding of complex ideas within particular contexts even though they would not evidence such understanding on formal assessments of the underlying constructs (e.g., Cole & Scribner, 1974; Lave, 1988; Rogoff & Waddell, 1982).

The foundation of this focus is *pedagogical content knowledge*, introduced by Lee Shulman (1986, 1987). In his 1985 American Educational Research Association address, Shulman described the ever-changing movements in classifying teacher knowledge from general knowledge to content knowledge. He acknowledged that these movements identified important aspects of teaching such as classroom organization and knowledge of the content one is teaching; however, he pointed out that they miss an important aspect of knowledge—how teachers transform their content knowledge into lessons and are able to teach the content that they know to those who do not yet understand it. According to Shulman (1986), this knowledge answers the question, "How do teachers decide what to teach, how to represent it, how to question students about it, and how to deal with problems of misunderstanding?" (p. 8). In essence, this knowledge is the knowledge that enables teachers to conduct the actions necessary to teach a particular subject.

The idea of PCK built on research that was focusing on teachers' use of knowledge in the practice of teaching. For example, Elbaz (1983) studied Canadian English teachers through a series of observations and interviews in an effort to identify a teacher's "practical knowledge," or the knowledge that teachers employ when teaching. Through this work, Elbaz developed a framework for the practical knowledge for teaching that encompassed five domains: knowledge of self, knowledge of the social content, knowledge of subject matter, knowledge of curriculum development, and knowledge of instruction. Through observation, Elbaz noted, "Practical knowledge encompasses first hand experience of students' learning styles, interests, needs, strengths and difficulties, and a repertoire of instructional techniques and classroom management skills" (p. 5).

Leinhardt and Greeno (1986) analyzed how expert and novice teachers carried out common teaching activities (e.g., homework, guided practice) in mathematics. For each, they developed action schema and planning nets, common representations used by cognitive psychologists at the time. These flow diagrams specified the conditions necessary to execute an action and the potential consequences of each action. For example, if a teacher is explaining the relationship among a set of concepts, the prerequisite condition would be that the component concepts are understood. Or, a teacher might take an action with the intent that the action engages the students and moves the lesson forward. Leinhardt and Greeno concluded that teachers use their knowledge of lesson structure and subject matter to successfully carry out these complex plans.

Shulman (1987) broke down the knowledge that informed teaching into seven distinct types of knowledge: general pedagogical knowledge; content knowledge; knowledge of the curriculum; knowledge of learners and their characteristics; knowledge of the educational context; knowledge of educational ends, purposes, and values; and, finally, PCK. It is important to note that by identifying these domains that contribute to the work of teaching, Shulman acknowledges previous movements in the identification of teacher knowledge and emphasizes the importance of general teacher knowledge and content knowledge in carrying out the work of teaching. However, it is the final domain of teacher knowledge identified by Shulman, *pedagogical content knowledge*, that is at the heart of the CKT focus in the study of teacher knowledge. Shulman (1986) conceptualized PCK as comprising the following:

For the most regularly taught topics in one's subject area, the most useful forms of representation of those ideas, the most powerful analogies, illustrations, examples, explanations, and demonstrations—in a word, the ways of representing and formulating the subject that make it comprehensible to others . . . Pedagogical content knowledge also includes an understanding of what makes the learning of specific topics easy or difficult: the conceptions and preconceptions that students of different ages and backgrounds bring with them to the learning of those most frequently taught topics and lessons. (p. 9)

Shulman (1987) further defined PCK as representing, "The blending of content and pedagogy into an understanding of how particular topics, problems, or issues are organized, represented, and adapted to the diverse interests and abilities of learners and presented for instruction" (p. 8).

Since Shulman first developed the notion of PCK, many attempts have been made to elaborate the construct across different domains (Ball et al., 2008). For example,

Magnusson, Krajcik, and Borko (1999) defined PCK in science as a unique domain of teacher knowledge that is "a transformation of several types of knowledge for teaching, including subject matter knowledge" (p. 95). Magnusson et al. stated that teachers' PCK is influenced by their subject-matter knowledge and beliefs, their pedagogical knowledge and beliefs, and their knowledge and beliefs about the educational context.

By observing teachers in the United Kingdom teaching mathematics in the upper and lower primary grades, Rowland, Huckstep, and Thwaites (2005) identified a "knowledge quartet," or the four types of knowledge that teachers use in practice: foundational knowledge, transformative knowledge, connection knowledge, and contingency knowledge. At the heart of their framework is the foundational knowledge that teachers have gained "in the academy," such as content knowledge and knowledge of teaching methods. Building from this foundation is transformative knowledge, which is the knowledge that enables teachers to transform content knowledge and knowledge of teaching methods into a lesson in which they teach the content; connection knowledge, which enables teachers to make connections drawn by the teacher during the lesson and enables the sequencing of instructional topics both locally (in the lesson) and globally (throughout the curriculum); and contingency knowledge, which enables teachers to deviate from the planned lesson or to respond to students' ideas. What resulted was a framework of PCK that includes four components: subject matter for instructional purposes, students' understanding of the subject matter, media for instruction in the subject matter, and instructional processes for the subject matter.

Pedagogical content knowledge has been substantially elaborated over the years in domain-specific treatments. Some examples include van Driel, Verloop, and de Vos (1998), Abell (2007), Baxter and Lederman (1999), and Gess-Newsome and Lederman (1999) in science; Döhrmann, Kaiser, and Blömeke (2012) and Ma (1999) in mathematics; Grossman (1990, 1991) and Howey and Grossman (1989) in English language arts (ELA); Monte-Sano and Budano (2013), S. M. Wilson and Wineburg (1988, 1993), and Leinhardt (1993) in history; and Neiss (2005) in multiple subject areas for integrating technology into instruction.

Though definitions of PCK have varied across research efforts, there are several principles that characterize the range of PCK definitions (van Driel et al., 1998). First, PCK is centered on specific topics and domains. Well-developed PCK in mathematics does not imply well-developed PCK in other content areas. Second, although PCK relies heavily on content knowledge, it is specifically concerned with the teaching of a subject. A mathematician, for example, who has never taught may have a large subject-matter knowledge base but may not have well-developed PCK. Finally, all definitions of PCK are in terms of practices that comprise the work of teaching.

More recently, Ball et al. (2008) sought to clarify what constitutes teaching specific content knowledge and developed the construct of *content knowledge for teaching*. Although they acknowledge that the work of Shulman and others in developing the concept of PCK was critical to advancing the study of teacher knowledge, they point out that PCK is still inadequately understood and that the domain as a whole is underdeveloped. First, they point to the many differing definitions of PCK as hindering the development of a precise definition of the construct. Second, possibly as a consequence of the lack of definition, few studies have attempted to measure PCK in teachers in an effort to validate the construct.

To better identify the content knowledge specific to teaching, Ball et al. (2008) called on their work with the Mathematics Knowledge for Teaching (MKT) project, which sought to better understand the knowledge teachers need to have and what they need to be able to do in order to effectively carry out the work of teaching mathematics (Ball, Hill, & Bass, 2005). In this study, the authors looked specifically at the work of teaching and tried to first identify what a teacher needs to do in the classroom when teaching a specific subject. Then they identified the knowledge needed to carry out the tasks of teaching. Through this work, they distinguished among the types of content knowledge used in teaching a subject: the shared or common content knowledge used in many professions (common content knowledge), the content knowledge specifically used in teaching (specialized content knowledge), and PCK. Overall, they defined CKT as the knowledge that directly links the work of teaching and the content knowledge that is required to do that work (Ball et al., 2008). For international comparisons of teacher knowledge of mathematics, Tatto et al. (2008) and Krauss, Baumert, and Blum (2008) divided the domain of teacher knowledge into content knowledge and PCK. Gitomer, Phelps, Weren, Howell, and Croft (2014) built on this work to develop a set of tasks of teaching for the domains of mathematics and ELA that are designed to be general at the highest level but then articulated at more specific levels (see Table 3). The successful execution of each task of teaching requires knowledge of content that is structured in ways particular to teaching.

Ball et al. (2008) further elaborated the construct with the idea of specialized content knowledge. This special set of knowledge is described as content knowledge beyond that of what a well-educated adult should know. It is the knowledge that enables teachers to carry out everyday tasks of teaching such as presenting ideas, responding to "why" questions, linking representations to underlying ideas, and modifying tasks to make them easier or harder (Ball et al., 2008). For example, teachers need to understand the underlying structure of a mathematical algorithm for teaching purposes (e.g., why division of fractions can be carried out with an invert and multiply algorithm), whereas the typical user of the algorithm need not have such knowledge.

Kersting, Givvin, Sotelo, and Stigler (2010) introduced the concept of *usable knowledge* by designing classroom video analysis tasks to which teachers needed to respond. They divide the domain into four subdomains: mathematical content, student thinking, suggestions for improvement, and depth of interpretation.

Although the development of the construct of *pedagogical content knowledge* by Shulman and others and the development of the construct of *content knowledge for teaching* by Ball and colleagues have led to somewhat different definitions of the

TABLE 3
Tasks of Teaching Requiring Content Knowledge for Teaching

Task of Teaching	Mathematics Examples	ELA Examples
1. Anticipating student challenges, misconceptions, partial misconceptions, alternate conceptions, strengths, interests, capabilities, and background knowledge	• Anticipating student challenges in reasoning about and doing mathematics due to the interplay of content demands and students' understanding • Anticipating likely misconceptions, partial conceptions, and alternate conceptions about particular mathematics content and practices	• Anticipating the impact of limited English language proficiency on students' comprehension of text and speech and on their written and spoken expression • Anticipating how students' background knowledge, life experiences, and cultural background can interact with new ELA concepts, texts, resources, and processes
2. Evaluating student ideas evident in work, talk, actions, and interactions	• Evaluating student work, talk, and actions in order to identify conceptions in mathematics, including incorrect or partial conceptions • Evaluating non-standard responses for evidence of mathematical understanding and in terms of efficiency, validity, and generalizability	• Evaluating student work, talk, and actions for evidence of strengths and weaknesses in reading, writing, speaking, and listening • Evaluating discussion among groups of students for evidence of understanding ELA concepts, texts, and processes
3. Explaining concepts, procedures, representations, models, examples, definitions, and hypotheses	• Explaining mathematical concepts or why a mathematical idea is "true" • Interpreting a particular representation in multiple ways to further understanding	• Explaining literary or language concepts, using definitions, examples, and analogies when appropriate • Explaining processes of reading, including why certain processes are appropriate for particular texts and/or tasks
4. Creating and adapting resources for instruction (examples, models, representations, explanations, definitions, hypotheses, procedures)	• Creating and adapting examples that support particular mathematical strategies or to address particular student questions, misconceptions, or challenges with content • Adapting student-generated conjectures to support instructional purposes	• Creating and adapting examples or model texts to introduce a concept or to demonstrate a literary technique or a reading, writing, or speaking strategy • Creating and adapting analogies to support student understanding of ELA concepts, texts, and processes

(continued)

TABLE 3 (CONTINUED)

Task of Teaching	Mathematics Examples	ELA Examples
5. Evaluating and selecting resources for instruction (examples, models, representations, explanations, definitions, hypotheses, procedures)	• Evaluating and selecting representations or models that support multiple interpretations • Evaluating and selecting explanations of mathematical concepts for potential to support mathematical learning or in terms of validity, generalizability, or explanatory power	• Evaluating and selecting examples to develop understanding of a concept, literary technique, or literacy strategy, or to address particular student questions, misconceptions, or challenges with content • Evaluating and selecting procedures for writing or working with text
6. Developing questions, activities, tasks, and problems to elicit student thinking	• Creating or adapting questions, activities, tasks, or problems that demonstrate desired mathematical characteristics • Creating or adapting classes of problems that address the same mathematical concept or that systematically vary in difficulty and complexity	• Creating or adapting prompts or questions with the potential to elicit productive student writing • Developing questions, activities, or tasks to elicit evidence that students have a particular literary understanding or skill
7. Evaluating and selecting student activities (questions, problems) to elicit student thinking	• Evaluating and selecting questions, activities, or tasks to elicit evidence that students have a particular mathematical understanding or skill • Evaluating and selecting problems that support particular mathematical strategies and practices	• Evaluating and selecting questions, activities, or tasks to elicit discussion about a specific text or literary concept • Evaluating and selecting questions, activities, or tasks to support the development of a particular literary understanding or skill
8. Doing the work of the student curriculum	• Doing the work that will be demanded of the students as part of the intended curriculum	• Doing the work that will be demanded of the students as part of the intended curriculum

Note. ELA = English language arts.
Source. Gitomer, Phelps, Weren, Howell, and Croft (2014).

knowledge that teachers use while teaching, the driving force behind the CKT focus is clear: Teachers have and employ a distinct set of content and professional knowledge when engaging in the work of teaching. This knowledge enables them to carry out the routine tasks of teaching and to help students better understand the content that is being taught. Although this knowledge may be specific to teaching, it is strongly dependent on the common content knowledge of the subject. In fact, Krauss, Baumert, et al. (2008) report a series of factor analytic studies that generally supports the argument that many of these subtler theoretical distinctions are not supported through empirical analysis.

This transformation in the characterization of teachers' content knowledge has led to major policy documents that have shaped some new types of teaching assessments. Perhaps the most significant policy development is the establishment of the NBPTS documents. Each set of disciplinary and student age-band standards elaborates on one of the NBPTS core propositions: *Teachers know the subjects they teach and how to teach those subjects to students* (National Board for Professional Teaching Standards, 1989). The InTASC standards, developed in 1992 and updated in 2011 (Council of Chief State School Officers, 1992, 2011) have also been influential in the development of a range of teacher assessments. Most of the assessments grounded in the NBPTS and InTASC standards have focused on measures of teacher practice (e.g., portfolios) and are not addressed in this chapter as knowledge measures. However, these standards have also driven the development of the NBPTS assessment center, which was a large-scale attempt at assessing CKT.

The Evidence Model for Teacher as CKT Professional

At the heart of the definitions of both PCK and CKT is that the knowledge defined by the constructs enables teachers to carry out the work of teaching. Because of this, traditional content knowledge assessments do not capture evidence of a teacher's CKT. Instead, CKT assessments must be grounded in the work of teaching so that judgments can be made regarding a teacher's professional content knowledge. The first large-scale standardized assessments in this area were those of the NBPTS. Since then, a broad range of assessment methods has been used to collect evidence of PCK across domains.

The NBPTS assessment consists of two components: the portfolio, which samples classroom practice directly through videos and artifacts, and the assessment center, which is designed to assess PCK through a set of constructed-response items. The items of a given year's assessment center are instances of an item category that has specific targets. A sample set of specifications for each of the item categories for one of the certifications (Middle Childhood Generalist [i.e., upper elementary self-contained classrooms]) is presented in Appendix B. Each response is scored on the basis of an item-level rubric, and those scores then contribute to the overall NBPTS assessment score (National Board for Professional Teaching Standards, 2013).

A relatively broad array of assessment tasks, including multiple-choice items, interviews, cognitive study tasks such as card-sorting, and constructed-response items, has been used to collect evidence of CKT (Baxter & Lederman, 1999). In most cases, stimuli have been verbal descriptions of a teaching scenario.

However, some recent work has used video stimuli (e.g., Kersting, 2008; Kersting et al., 2010). Examinees are presented with a classroom video segment and asked to analyze, in writing, how the teacher and the student(s) interacted around the mathematical content.

In one of the most cited attempts to measure CKT, Hill, Schilling, and Ball (2004) developed a set of assessment items that would allow them to draw inferences about teachers' CKT, specifically in the area of mathematics. These items were meant to measure common content knowledge and the specialized content knowledge that teachers use specifically when teaching. To develop the items, Hill et al. drew on the work of high-quality classroom instruction and analyzed curricular materials, student work, and personal experience in the classroom. The result of this work was a set of items meant to assess MKT.

The initial items were developed for K–6 teachers and were classified into three content areas: number concepts; operations; and patterns, functions, and algebra. For the first two content areas, separate items were developed to measure knowledge of content and knowledge of students and content. For the third content area, only items measuring knowledge of content were developed (Hill et al., 2004). After administering the assessment to more than 1,500 teachers, they found evidence of multiple factors, aligned with both content areas and type of knowledge being assessed.

Another effort to measure teachers' content-specific knowledge was the COACTIV study (Baumert et al., 2010), in which teachers of students who took the 2003–2004 Program for International Student Assessment (PISA) were given assessments of both their CKT and their common content knowledge (Krauss, Brunner, et al., 2008). The items in this study were similar to the items developed by Hill et al. (2004) in that they were paper-and-pencil items meant to address scenarios specific to teaching. However, these items differed somewhat in that they were constructed-response items and addressed specific tasks of teaching, including knowledge of multiple solution paths, knowledge of alternative student ideas, and knowledge of instructional strategies. Using the framework developed by Ball et al. (2008), the second two item types would fall under PCK (specifically, knowledge of content and students, and knowledge of content and teaching), but the first item type, knowledge of multiple solution paths, would fall into the specialized content knowledge domain. Regardless of the domains that each question type addresses, the design of the assessment is clear: to address teacher-specific knowledge by grounding the assessment items in the work of teaching. The international Teacher Education and Development Study in Mathematics (TEDS-M) also used primarily multiple-choice items to estimate content knowledge and CKT for teachers in different countries (Blömeke, Houang, & Suhl, 2011).

Related work has been done to assess CKT in the area of reading. Phelps and Schilling (2004) set out to develop an assessment of teachers' content knowledge for

FIGURE 1
Sample Mathematics Single-Selection Multiple-Choice Item

Ms. Hupman is teaching an introductory lesson on exponents. She wants to give her students a quick problem at the end of class to check their proficiency in evaluating simple exponential expressions. Of the following expressions, which would be <u>least</u> useful in assessing student proficiency in evaluating simple exponential expressions?

○ 3^3

○ 2^3

○ 2^2

○ All of these are equally useful in assessing student proficiency in evaluating simple exponential expressions.

Note. The correct answer is 2^2. The relevant task of teaching is: Creating problems or questions to elicit student mathematical thinking, justifications, or explanations.

teaching elementary-level reading, resulting in a series of survey items to assess teachers' content knowledge, knowledge of content and students, and knowledge of teaching and content in reading. Further work to assess content knowledge for teaching reading includes the use of the *Language and Reading Concept* assessment that is based on required components of the Reading First legislation that was designed to improve reading skills in students enrolled in high-poverty and low-achieving schools. The assessment focuses on content knowledge and knowledge of teaching the content in five areas defined by the legislation: phonemic awareness, phonics, fluency, vocabulary, and reading comprehension (Carlisle, Correnti, Phelps, & Zeng, 2009). Kucan, Hapgood, and Palincsar (2011) also developed a constructed-response assessment designed to assess teachers' specialized knowledge for comprehension instruction. This assessment provides teachers with a passage and then asks them to state the main idea of the passage, to highlight any text features that may prove difficult for students, and then to analyze a student response about the text.

One large-scale research project (Gitomer et al., 2014) in the assessment of CKT was a part of the Measures of Effective Teaching project (Bill and Melinda Gates Foundation, 2011). In this project, the researchers set out to develop a set of CKT assessments in the areas of ELA and mathematics. The Measures of Effective Teaching study drew teachers from districts across the country and across grades 4–9. Because CKT is dependent on content knowledge and knowledge of the wide range of content taught across grade levels and districts, separate assessments were developed for grades 4–6 ELA, 7–8 ELA, 4–5 mathematics, 6–8 mathematics, and grade 9 algebra. The researchers developed assessments comprised of selected-response and constructed-response items that built on the tasks of teaching framework described in Table 3. An example from mathematics is presented in Figure 1.

FIGURE 2
Sample English Language Arts Table Item

Ms. Rice begins a unit on memoir writing by reading a passage from a literary model. She then asks students to complete a warm-up activity to help them generate ideas for their own writing.

For each assignment, indicate whether or not it will help students focus their brainstorming on generating a memoir.

	Will help focus brainstorming	Will not help focus brainstorming
Write a poem about the ways you have changed, using the form "I used to be…but now I am…"		
Write a sequence of sentences describing some of your experiences, beginning each sentence with the phrase "I remember."		
Write a few adjectives that describe your personality.		
Write down some of your favorite foods and describe what you like about them.		

Note. Correct answers are: Will, Will, Will not, Will not. The relevant task of teaching is: Evaluating and selecting questions to elicit productive student writing.

The mathematics item in Figure 1 does not ask the teachers to simply solve exponential expressions, which would draw on common content knowledge, but instead asks teachers to use their knowledge to identify which exponential expressions would tell them that the student knows how to work with exponents. Similarly, in the ELA item presented in Figure 2, teachers have to select the activities that will help students focus their brainstorming on a specific topic. Common content knowledge alone would not be sufficient to answer such items successfully.

The Interpretive Model for Teacher as CKT Professional

Scores on these assessments are typically reports of the number of questions the teacher answered correctly when compared to the correct answer for the given item. However, some studies use more sophisticated psychometric models, including item response theory (Blömeke et al., 2011; Hill, Ball, Blunk, Goffney, & Rowan, 2007).

For many of these assessment questions, the best answer cannot simply be justified through an appeal to the content (e.g., 2 + 2 = 4). Rather, appropriate answers rely on professional judgment of appropriate actions to take given a particular instructional context (see Hill et al., 2004; Gitomer et al., 2014).

For the NBPTS assessments and other constructed-response measures (e.g., Kersting et al., 2010), standardized rubrics are typically developed and then rated by human judges who have been trained on the scoring criteria. Each item receives a score, and these are then weighted in computing a total certification score. Scores are provided for each of the four dimensions that define the domain. Some recent explorations in using automated techniques to interpret written responses show promising levels of reliability (Kersting, Sherin, & Stigler, 2014).

For some assessments of PCK, score interpretations based on performance on items corresponding to individual domains are provided. For example, on the MKT Assessment, there are items corresponding to common content knowledge and items corresponding to knowledge of content and students.

Research Findings for Teacher as CKT Professional

Probably because the assessment work in this focus has primarily been a research enterprise rather than a tool for teacher selection, the body of research is far more developed than for the other two foci. These assessments have been largely designed to help understand teacher knowledge and its relationship to practice at a fairly deep level.

The research in this focus can be organized into several broad categories. One body of work has attempted to establish the construct of CKT through factor analytic studies and measures of psychometric quality. A second body of work has explored the relationship of CKT scores to measures associated with the practice and effectiveness of teaching. A third body of research has examined differences in performance and reasoning on these items for individuals with differing amounts of expertise in teaching. The final research question has focused on the distribution of teacher CKT across schools differing in socioeconomic and achievement characteristics.

Examinations of the factor structure of assessments demonstrate consistently that CKT items measure something distinct from content knowledge measures, though the measures are highly correlated (Blömeke et al., 2011; Krauss, Baumert, et al., 2008; Schilling, Blunk, & Hill, 2007). Initial results from the MKT project indicated that it was possible to use a paper-and-pencil test to measure teaching-specific content knowledge. Although a general factor for overall performance on the items accounted for a large portion of the variance on individual items, common content knowledge and specialized content knowledge were distinguishable second-order factors. Similarly, in reading, Phelps (2009) found that measures of content knowledge in reading call on specialized knowledge of language, text structures, and reading processes that is different from common reading ability.

This may not be all that surprising, as it becomes clear that individuals draw on subject content knowledge when they are asked to solve CKT problems aloud (Gitomer et al., 2014; Hill, Ball, & Schilling, 2008). Hill's work (Hill, Blunk, et al., 2008; Schilling et al., 2007) illustrates the difficulty of finding factor analytic support for further distinction of constructs within the larger domain of CKT.

A number of studies have examined the relationship of CKT scores to other measures. Hill, Rowan, and Ball (2005) found that higher scores on the MKT measure were associated with greater gains in mathematics for first- and third-grade students.

Hill, Umland, Litke, and Kapitula (2012) and Hill, Blunk, et al. (2008) observed a strong relationship between MKT scores and the quality of instruction in mathematics as measured by a mathematics-specific observation protocol. The relationship to student achievement was less consistent.

Gitomer et al. (2014) studied the reasoning on assessment items in mathematics and ELA by teachers who varied in their scores on CKT assessments that were taken one year prior and included these items. They found substantial evidence that observed reasoning patterns for both correct and incorrect responses were consistent with the anticipated reasoning built into the design of the assessment items and that the quality of reasoning was associated with scores on the assessments.

Kersting's work (Kersting et al., 2010; Kersting, Givvin, Thompson, Santagata, & Stigler, 2012) examines the relationship of scores on their video analysis measures of knowledge to the MKT measures and to measures of classroom practice and student learning. The focus for all of this work was in the area of fractions, and teachers of students in grades 5–7 participated. They found that their video analysis scores were related to MKT scores and that the strongest dimension correlation was with mathematical content. They also observed a strong relationship with instructional practice as measured by an instrument the researchers developed. Finally, they found a significant relationship between video analysis scores and student learning of fractions. On further examination, only one dimension, *Suggestions for Improvement*, was associated with student learning. This is the dimension that captures teachers' suggestions for improving the instruction in the video interactions they observed.

A number of studies have compared groups with known characteristics that would be expected to show different levels of competence on CKT assessments. As part of the COACTIV study, Krauss, Baumert, et al. (2008) compared teachers who taught students who were on track to attend a university at the end of their secondary education (academic track) with teachers who taught students who were on the vocational track (nonacademic track). To teach in the academic track, teachers must essentially major in mathematics, whereas those who plan to teach in the nonacademic track have a more varied education. On each of the question types, the academic-track teachers scored significantly higher than the nonacademic-track teachers. Together with the correlation between scores on the CK items and the CKT items (.60), these findings provided additional support for the connection between content knowledge and PCK. Hill, Dean, and Goffney (2007) also found different patterns of performance and reasoning among those with different teaching and mathematics backgrounds.

In addition to testing teachers with different training, the COACTIV study tested teachers in content areas other than mathematics to develop an argument as to the validity of the construct of teacher-specific content knowledge (Krauss, Baumert, et al., 2008). University mathematics majors, high school academic-track mathematics students, and academic-track biology and chemistry teachers were all given the same PCK assessment. As expected, the biology and chemistry teachers who have neither the content knowledge nor the teaching experience in mathematics scored low on both the CK items and the CKT items, and the high school mathematics students scored low on the CKT items. Those who taught mathematics in both academic and nonacademic tracks scored higher on both the CK and CKT items. One interesting result, however, was the high CKT scores of the university mathematics majors. Although this result supports the idea that content knowledge plays an important part in teacher-specific knowledge, it does not necessarily suggest that any mathematics major has the knowledge and the ability to teach. One possibility is that those with strong mathematics backgrounds are able to use that knowledge to reason through CKT assessment items.

Buschang, Chung, Delacruz, and Baker (2012) addressed this possibility by administering several assessments meant to measure both content knowledge and PCK for the teaching of mathematics, including the MKT Assessment and the Student Response Assessment (SRA), which asked test takers to evaluate student responses to questions. These assessments were administered to mathematics content experts (those with a PhD in mathematics and no K–12 teaching experience), expert teachers (teachers who either held a National Board certification or had experience in training teachers), and novice teachers. The SRA was specifically developed to assess the PCK needed to assess student work. On the MKT Assessment, the content experts and the expert teachers performed similarly, and both groups performed significantly better than the novice teachers. However, on the SRA, a task that is typical to the everyday work of teaching, the content experts performed poorly compared to the expert and novice teachers. This suggests that performance on the MKT Assessment is sensitive to content knowledge but that content knowledge alone is not enough to perform well on tasks that occur in the work of teaching, such as the SRA.

As with other measures of content knowledge, teachers higher in CKT tend to teach in classrooms that have fewer minority and poor students and that have higher levels of prior achievement. Hill et al. (2005) and Hill and Lubienski (2007) found that teachers of students with higher proportions of low-socioeconomic status and minority students had lower scores on the MKT Assessment.

FOCUS 4—TEACHER AS KNOWLEDGE-RICH PRACTITIONER

The last focus, teacher as knowledge-rich practitioner, is nascent. There is a small but growing literature that provides the basis for these kinds of assessments, and there are no systematic research studies that have explored the measurement characteristics of these assessments. Yet this articulation of knowledge use in practice represents a natural progression from the CKT efforts in moving from conceptions of knowledge from *knowing that* to *knowing how*.

The Cognitive Model for Teacher as Knowledge-Rich Practitioner

This focus of assessing teacher knowledge is predicated on the idea that content knowledge and CKT underlie the teacher's ability to effectively engage in critical practices of teaching. The primary motivation behind the knowledge-rich practitioner focus is the idea that teaching is a practice-based profession and that there are core component practices (Grossman, Hammerness, & McDonald, 2009; Grossman & McDonald, 2008) that are "agnostic with respect to various models of teaching" (Grossman & McDonald, 2008, p. 186)—that is, whether a particular model of teaching is more didactic or constructivist or whether the model is in mathematics or social studies, and so on. The particular execution of those components, however, will shift with different models of teaching.

Ball and colleagues have designated these key practices as *high-leverage practices*. Ball, Sleep, Boerst, and Bass (2009) defined these high-leverage practices as follows:

Practices in which the proficient enactment by a teacher is likely to lead to comparatively large advances in student learning . . . They include activities of teaching that are essential to the work and that are used frequently, ones that have significant power for teachers' effectiveness with pupils. (pp. 460–461)

A fundamental idea in this focus is that by focusing on practice, knowledge is studied as it is enacted (Grossman et al., 2009; Lampert, 2010). Ball and Forzani (2009) discuss a shift from knowledge to practice that is "entailed by the work" (p. 503). Teachers represent their knowledge of practice in terms of common structures or schema that they apply in situations that call for specific practices. Thus, a goal of teacher education is to help teachers develop such situated knowledge.

As the knowledge-rich practitioner focus places emphasis on developing situated knowledge during preservice teacher education, recent efforts have begun to discuss how teacher education must shift and be reconceptualized in response to the most recent practice-based focus (see Forzani, 2014; McDonald, Kazemi, & Kavanagh, 2013; Zeichner, 2012). Other efforts, such as Lampert et al. (2013), have been aimed at designing teacher education experiences that provide opportunities for preservice teachers to practice and develop the ability to carry out these practices.

Though the practices are general at an abstract level, how they develop in particular content areas is unique. A discussion around literature is different from one in physics in terms of the nature of evidence and warrants and common discourse norms, for example. Thus, the development of high-leverage or core practices is being carried out in specific domains including ELA (Hatch & Grossman, 2009), history (Fogo, 2014), science (Janssen, Westbroek, & Doyle, 2014; Windschitl, Thompson, Braaten, & Stroupe, 2012), mathematics (Boerst, Sleep, Ball, & Bass, 2011; Franke et al., 2009; TeachingWorks, 2014b), foreign language (Hlas & Hlas, 2012; Troyan, Davin, & Donato, 2013), social justice (McDonald, 2010), and culturally responsive pedagogical practices (Ladson-Billings, 1995) in mathematics (Waddell, 2014).

The Evidence Model for Teacher as Knowledge-Rich Practitioner

At this point in time, the evidence models are, at most, in a state of design. There are a number of potentially interesting methods for capturing evidence and frameworks for considering how such evidence might be developed.

One of the earliest forerunners of this kind of effort was portfolio assessments of teaching that included entries that involved evidence of practice in the form of brief classroom videos or instructional artifacts such as classroom assignments or tests. The most prominent of these efforts was associated with NBPTS. Teachers were also required to present detailed commentary around the classroom evidence. Each portfolio task, in essence, asked teachers to carry out some limited set of what would become known as core practices. For example, a portfolio might ask teachers to lead a discussion or analyze student work (National Research Council, 2008).

Parallel work led by Grossman and Ball focuses on breaking down, or decomposing (Grossman et al., 2009), the complex act of teaching into constituent parts that can be closely examined. Much of this work has referenced teacher education, but it is equally applicable to assessment and has been discussed by Moss (2010). The challenge is to create simulated task structures that are constrained in ways that focus attention on a particular practice. The structures are rich enough that they do elicit evidence that draws on knowledge and skill in executing an important teaching practice. But the tasks are constrained in ways that do not fully approximate teaching. The focus is on a particular task (e.g., leading a discussion, planning a lesson, or providing an explanation of an important concept), but the task does not require coordinating all of these components or dealing with the various competing considerations (e.g., student behavior) that teachers face in an actual classroom.

Moss (2010) describes six elements that characterize this type of assessment work in a teacher education program. First, high-leverage practices are identified and decomposed in ways that allow them to be studied and developed. Second, learning and assessment activities are designed so that they become increasingly complex and call on greater skill of the developing teacher. Third, there is a need to develop a common analytic language to interpret performance on these activities. Fourth, there is attention given to the general and immediate contexts of task design that make for effective prompts. Fifth, annotated exemplars of practice are necessary in order to give meaning to any verbal or other descriptions of the practice. Sixth, descriptions of the learning trajectories or progressions of these practices are essential.

Because these practices are enacted, the performance needs to be captured in ways that are different from traditional assessments. For certain practices, video may be an appropriate way to capture evidence. For other practices (e.g., planning), the evidence may take the form of written artifacts. One interesting possibility involves the use of simulated environments in which the preservice teacher interacts with the simulation. Dieker, Straub, Hughes, Hynes, and Hardin (2014) have developed a system that uses avatars that respond to a student in a teacher education program to develop specific competencies, including classroom management. Human actors control the avatars at this point, but in the long term, it may be possible for intelligently designed systems to drive significant parts of the interaction.

Given that assessment systems are not yet designed, there is no literature that addresses the interpretive or research dimensions of this focus. However, given what Moss (2010) identified as a shared language for guiding and analyzing practice, it would be most natural for a central interpretive component to be some type of scoring system that relied on human judgment guided by a scoring protocol.

The knowledge-rich practitioner model has been developed in the context of teacher education. Therefore, natural places for assessment use would be in the context of developing and certifying the performance of beginning teachers. These assessments, assuming they continue to develop, would be used by teacher preparation institutions. However, there are early efforts to build out these assessments for the purpose of licensure (TeachingWorks, 2014a).

A DESIGN FRAMEWORK FOR ASSESSING TEACHER KNOWLEDGE

The broad foci of assessing teacher knowledge described in this chapter have been loosely coupled enterprises. Yet, underlying each focus are either explicit or implicit cognitive models for what students should know, what teachers should know, and the role of teachers in instruction. Also, whether explicit or implicit, these foci have relied on assumptions that teacher knowledge is associated with effective instruction and student outcomes. Only the CKT and knowledge-rich practitioner foci make strong theoretical linkages to those outcomes.

In this concluding section, we present a general design framework that can guide both the development and validation of assessments of teacher knowledge. We then suggest ways in which current knowledge about the teaching of ELLs can form the foundation of knowledge assessments for ELL teaching.

The design framework builds from the evidence-centered design (ECD) approach developed by Bob Mislevy and colleagues (e.g., Mislevy & Haertel, 2006). ECD is an effort to bring formal design principles to the development of assessments and begins with a conceptual assessment framework that consists of three major components. The first, the *student model*, is a detailed specification of the concepts, skills, and relationships that represent the target domain of the assessment. Though ECD uses the term *student model* generically, for the present purposes we will apply this conception to teachers. The second component, the *task model*, describes the kinds of assessment tasks and assessment environments that are used to collect evidence of understanding with respect to the concepts, skills, and relationships articulated in the student model. The third component, the *evidence model*, specifies the procedures for interpreting and scoring the evidence.

We propose a design framework in Figure 3 that supports the design of teacher knowledge assessments broadly but that is specifically intended to support the design of assessments of teacher knowledge within the CKT and knowledge-rich practitioner domains. The top of the figure represents the teacher model and includes three constituent components. The first box represents a set of learning targets for the students who are being taught. So, for example, it could represent the various concepts and skills that students in fourth grade mathematics should have. The second box represents what a teacher needs to have with regard to the content knowledge about the domain that includes all the student targets, but other content knowledge is likely to be included as well. For example, Ball et al. (2008) describe *horizon content*

FIGURE 3
Design Framework for Assessment and Validation of Teacher Knowledge

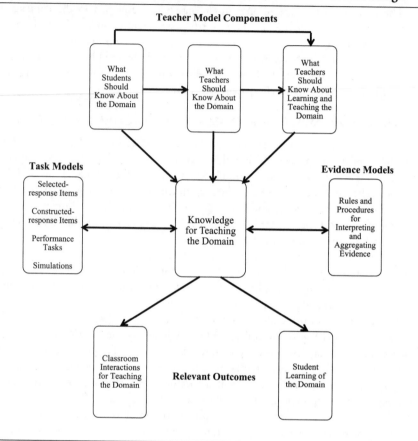

knowledge as the knowledge of content that students will encounter in later (as well as earlier) grades. As noted earlier, they also describe the construct of specialized content knowledge. The box on the right describes the knowledge needed to effectively carry out tasks of teaching, examples of which are presented in Table 3. This component of the model would include, for example, knowledge of the kinds of representations that will help students learn a concept or the ways in which students may have difficulty in grasping an idea.

Together, these three components describe the target domain of teacher knowledge, represented in the middle of the figure. At the left center of the figure are task models. Task models are evidence-capturing devices. For example, multiple-choice questions ask examinees to select from a set of given options. The choice an examinee selects is intended to provide evidence of quality of understanding of some aspect of the teacher model. Other tasks that have been used in teacher assessment include shorter and longer written responses as well as performance tasks such as those used in the NBPTS portfolio. The work of Kersting and others described earlier provides other kinds of task models. Different task models may be more or less effective at providing evidence about different aspects of the teacher model.

We can use this framework to design assessments that address different foci of teacher knowledge, each deemed necessary to effectively carry out any task of teaching. Table 4 presents several examples of the types of assessment tasks that might be developed to assess different aspects of the teacher model. For example, if the target task of teaching is anticipating students' challenges and conceptions about a particular concept, then we can imagine one kind of assessment task that asks teachers about their direct knowledge of that concept. An assessment of CKT might pose questions that directly inquire about the kinds of conceptions and conceptual difficulties that students are likely to have. Finally, assessment tasks that are designed to call on specific types of CKT can be developed to collect evidence about a teacher's ability to enact practices, such as carrying out a discussion.

The box on the right center represents the evidence model that interprets and aggregates performance on these kinds of tasks into assessment scores. The evidence model includes such things as the answer key for multiple-choice tasks, scoring rubrics for tasks that require more qualitative interpretation, and scoring models (e.g., item response theory) that are used to develop scores that estimate a teacher's proficiency with respect to teacher knowledge.

Ultimately, it is important to validate the inferences that are made on the basis of an assessment score. The process of developing a validity argument is described by Kane (2006) and includes establishing evidence that the scores mean what they are intended to mean. Articulating a design process provides a detailed specification that can then be evaluated. Another key aspect of Kane's and other validity frameworks (e.g., Messick, 1989) is to evaluate the relationship between scores on an assessment and other outcomes that are theorized as being related to those scores.

In the case of teacher knowledge measures of CKT and practice, we establish the hypothesis that teachers who know more will engage in more effective teaching practice and also will have a greater effect on student learning. These hypotheses can be investigated directly by observing and scoring the quality of classroom interactions or evaluating measures of student learning based on some type of assessments of student knowledge and growth. Support for the validity of the assessments is achieved to the extent that there is a positive and systematic relationship between scores on these different measures.

IMPLICATIONS FOR ASSESSING KNOWLEDGE FOR TEACHERS OF ENGLISH LANGUAGE LEARNERS

How might we use such a design framework for the assessment of teacher knowledge with respect to teachers of ELLs, an area that has received minimal attention? There is a great deal of work that lays the foundation for what such assessment efforts might look like.

TABLE 4

Framework (With Examples) Connecting Different Forms of Teacher Knowledge to Tasks of Teaching

Task of Teaching	Content Knowledge	Content Knowledge for Teaching	Knowledge Through Enactment
Anticipating student challenges, misconceptions, partial misconceptions, alternate conceptions, strengths, interests, capabilities, and background knowledge	What do teachers need to know about domain content?	What do teachers need to know about the teaching of content?	What do teachers need to know or be able to do to enact content?
Mathematics example: Anticipating student challenges in proportional reasoning due to the interplay of content demands and students' understanding	Proportional reasoning Fractions	Common conceptual challenges students face in proportional reasoning Instructional resources to highlight and support resolution of challenges	Creating classroom interactions (e.g., discussions) to address challenges Using resources effectively to address challenges
ELA example: Anticipating how students' background knowledge, life experiences, and cultural background can interact with the ELA concept of character development	Fiction Literary techniques Character development	Questions that help students connect their own experiences to the writing task Exemplars that model how authors use their own backgrounds in developing their characters	Using exemplars and models that help students see potential connections between their own lives and character development Supporting classroom discussion that helps students explore strategies for character development

Note. ELA = English language arts.

The first step must be to lay out the teacher model that specifies what constellation of knowledge and skills is important for teachers to have in order to teach these students. There are very useful reports and papers that attempt to lay out what such teachers should know and be able to do, but there is currently no professional consensus on this among teacher educators (Faltis & Valdés, in press). However, important ideas about what students need to know and what teachers need to do to help students learn have been offered by the National Literacy Panel on Language-Minority Children and Youth (August & Shanahan, 2006), August and Hakuta (1997), and others. Implications for what teachers need to know and be able to do are summarized both by Faltis and Valdés (in press) as well as by the National Research Council (2010). This panel identified six areas on which there was some consensus:

- understanding of the complexity of the reading process for English-language learners;
- competence at explicit instruction in vocabulary, the development of oral proficiency;
- content instruction that focuses on learning from text, understanding and producing academic language, genre differentiation, and academic writing;
- understanding of home-school differences in interaction patterns or styles and individual differences among the wide range of English-language learners; and
- understanding of the ways language and reading interact, the skills that transfer into English, and how to facilitate that transfer; and understanding of the context in which second-language learners develop as readers. (National Research Council, 2010, p. 90)

de Jong and Harper (2005) also provide a related framework for what teachers need to know about teaching ELLs. Teachers must:

- acquire specific knowledge and skills related to the language and culture of their students;
- understand the process of sound language acquisition and acculturation;
- understand how bilingual processes are manifested in ELL oral and literacy development and how they can build on students' resources;
- understand the difficulties that ELLs may face when they are trying to learn content through a language over which they have no control (this entails a basic knowledge of the structure of the English language by the teacher);
- have a cultural awareness, particularly of the culturally-based assumptions regarding learning and literacy; and
- understand the language demands of their subject area.

Turkan, de Oliveira, Lee, and Phelps (2014) have built on this work to theorize about the specialized knowledge involved in teaching content to ELLs. They propose the idea of *disciplinary linguistic knowledge* as an understanding of the discourse of particular disciplines and having the knowledge to engage students in such discourse. They focus on the particular linguistic challenges that ELLs face in learning academic content and the teacher knowledge needed to help students overcome those challenges.

As noted by Faltis and Valdés (in press), much of this theorizing has a very limited empirical basis. The development of assessments based on such theories, together with a validation effort, offers the opportunity to strengthen the empirical basis for the knowledge teachers need to support learning for ELLs.

The outlines of what teachers need to know, such as those presented above, begin to lay out the teacher model that would be the basis for such assessments. However, much more specificity of concepts and skills that teachers should know needs to be developed for a more complete and productive teacher model. Once the model is articulated, then corresponding task and evidence models can be designed. These models certainly would overlap with the models we have described elsewhere in the chapter.

The validation effort would then examine relationships of scores on assessments of knowledge for teachers of ELLs with measures of classroom practice and interactions, and with student outcomes including, but not limited to, academic learning. For example, it may also be useful to understand student attitudes and motivations and to examine their social interactions in and out of school. Exactly what would be considered relevant evidence depends on the student model that contributes to the teacher model (what students should learn) and the hypothesized relationship of teacher knowledge and practice to aspects of the student model.

For example, one might reasonably hypothesize that effective teachers of ELLs know a good bit about linguistic moves that will support student learning of content. We could also imagine CKT assessments that involve knowledge of these linguistic moves with respect to challenges that ELLs face. We could also imagine practice-based assessments—for example, simulations that require teachers to enact such knowledge in order to be successful. To the extent that there are positive relationships between scores on assessments like these with desired student outcomes, there is validity support not only for the assessment but also for the theory that underlies it—namely, that CKT and the enactment of linguistic moves is important for the teaching of ELLs.

CONCLUDING COMMENTS

Bringing together much more developed theories of teacher knowledge with advances in assessment design provides an opportunity to develop measures of teacher knowledge that have value far more than simply being used for certification. Such assessments, precisely because they are rooted in practice, have the potential to dramatically influence how teachers are prepared and supported throughout their careers. Obviously, substantial design work needs to be carried out to use assessments of teacher knowledge with different purposes from what they have been traditionally used for. Finally, having measures of knowledge that are based on strong and explicit theories of practice provides rich opportunities to test and revise the assumptions that guide our theories of how teachers learn and how they help students learn.

APPENDIX A

Sample Items, First National Teacher Examination Administration

(Note: Percentages of individuals from the two groups selecting each response are presented after each response.)

English Comprehension, Part II

Slade was a matchless marksman with a navy revolver. One morning at Rocky Ridge when he was feeling comfortable he saw a man approaching who had offended him some days before. "Gentlemen," said Slade, drawing, "it is a good twenty-yard shot— I'll clip the third button on his coat!" Which he did. The bystanders admired it. And they all attended the funeral, too.

7.   Slade may be best described as

1.   humorous. (3%, 0%)
2.   cold-blooded. (44%, 70%)
3.   revengeful. (34%, 19%)
4.   playful. (8%, 7%)
5.   daring. (11%, 3%)
     Omitted (0%, 1%) *not reached* (0%, 0%)

8.   The passage achieves its effect chiefly by means of

1.   suspense. (13%, 10%)
2.   exaggeration. (5%, 0%)
3.   direct quotation. (20%, 3%)
4.   matter-of-fact treatment. (60%, 86%)
5.   detailed description. (2%, 0%)
     Omitted (0%, 1%) *not reached* (0%, 0%)

English Expression, Punctuation

All the childrens art classes were represented in the exhibit, and the class which had done the best work received a prize.

7.   1.   No punctuation necessary (10%, 1%)
     2.   Children's. (56%, 84%)
     3.   Childrens'. (27%, 15%)
          Omitted (5%, 0%) *not reached* (2%, 0%)

General Culture, Part I, Current Social Problems

60. In the past 50 years, man in the Western world has gained most in

1. health. (52%, 97%)
2. native intelligence. (6%, 0%)
3. emotional stability. (4%, 0%)
4. security of employment. (6%, 1%)
5. stability of government. (14%, 2%)
     Omitted (0%, 0%) *not reached* (18%, 0%)

General Culture, Part III, Literature

70. The poet who "sounded his barbaric yawp over the roofs of the world," yet brought a new freedom and flexibility to poetry, was

1. T. S. Eliot. (4%, 4%)
2. Emerson. (6%, 0%)
3. Edgar Lee Masters. (4%, 0%)
4. Edwin Markham. (4%, 0%)
5. Walt Whitman. (55%, 95%)
     Omitted (21%, 1%) *not reached* (6%, 0%)

General Culture, Part IV, Science

60. The physical discomfort produced by a warm, badly ventilated room full of people is due mainly to

1. lack of sufficient oxygen. (24%, 13%)
2. accumulated carbon dioxide. (24%, 15%)
3. poisonous vapors from people's bodies. (4%, 1%)
4. accumulated water vapor. (28%, 68%)
5. the very low humidity of the air. (12%, 3%)
     Omitted (0%, 0%) *not reached* (8%, 0%)

General Culture, Part V, Fine Arts

76. What modern painters are largely responsible for the revival of mural painting today?

1. English (5%, 0%)
2. German (2%, 2%)
3. Italian (12%, 3%)
4. Mexican (53%, 91%)
5. French (8%, 1%)
     Omitted (16%, 3%) *not reached* (4%, 0%)

General Culture, Part VI, Mathematics

21. The positive square root of ¼ is
   1.   ½. (54%, 100%)
   2.   2. (4%, 0%)
   3.   1√2. (6%, 0%)
   4.   ⅛. (4%, 0%)
   5.   1/16 (19%, 0%)
        Omitted (12%, 0%) *not reached* (1%, 0%)

Professional Information, Part I, Education and Social Policy

43. Substantial modifications in the high school curriculum have been necessary since the World War to allow for

   1.   expansion of the college preparatory curriculum. (14%, 5%)
   2.   the presence in high school of many persons with slight aptitude for book learning. (61%, 88%)
   3.   studies on a more difficult level, necessitated by better preparation in the grades. (3%, 3%)
   4.   emphasis on cultural rather than vocational subjects because of decreased employment opportunities. (5%, 2%)
   5.   consolidation of rural high schools. (10%, 2%)
        Omitted (7%, 0%) *not reached* (0%, 0%)

Professional Information, Part II, Child Development and Educational Psychology

55. Six-year-old children differ most from 10-year-olds in which one of the following respects?

   1.   Fine-muscle control (48%, 80%)
   2.   Large-muscle control (8%, 3%)
   3.   Visual acuity (3%, 2%)
   4.   Auditory acuity (1%, 0%)
   5.   Metabolic rate (20%, 13%)
        Omitted (14%, 2%) *not reached* (6%, 0%)

Professional Information, Part III, Guidance and Individual and Group Analysis

26. It is a basic assumption of experts in vocational guidance that

   1.   interest in an occupation is the best evidence of future success in that occupation. (10%, 0%)
   2.   vocational aptitudes cannot be measured objectively. (4%, 2%)
   3.   pupils need assistance in estimating their own abilities, aptitudes, and interests. (84%, 98%)

4. there is one, and only one, occupation for which each individual is ideally suited. (0%, 0%)
5. vocational and educational guidance should be kept entirely separate. (1%, 0%)
    Omitted (1%, 0%) *not reached* (0%, 0%)

Professional Information, Part IV, Secondary School Methods

1. The primary function of the recitation should be to

    1. give individual attention to the slower pupils. (1%, 0%)
    2. discover the pupils who have not assimilated previous lessons. (6%, 2%)
    3. discover the extent to which the individual pupils are able to recall material read. (1%, 0%)
    4. develop understanding through group discussion. (74%, 90%)
    5. improve the ability of the pupils to present material orally. (17%, 7%)
        Omitted (1%, 1%) *not reached* (0%, 0%)

APPENDIX B

National Board for Professional Teaching Standards (NBPTS)
Middle Childhood: Generalist
Assessment at a Glance (p. 4)

Assessment Center Exercises

This assessment is composed of six exercises that examine content knowledge specified in the NBPTS Standards. You are given up to 30 minutes to respond to each exercise.

Following is a description of each assessment exercise.

Exercise 1: Supporting Reading Skills	In this exercise, you demonstrate your ability to analyze and interpret a transcript of a student's oral reading of a given reading passage to identify one strength and one weakness in the student's oral reading. You are also asked to identify and justify appropriate strategies to support the identified student's ongoing reading development.
Exercise 2: Analyzing Student Work	In this exercise, you demonstrate your ability to identify mathematical misconceptions/errors in a given student's work, to identify concepts/skills necessary for student understanding of the math problem, and to provide appropriate strategies with a rationale to assist the student's understanding of the identified concepts or skills.

(continued)

APPENDIX B (CONTINUED)

Exercise 3: Knowledge of Science	In this exercise, you demonstrate your ability to identify and understand fundamental concepts and principles in science. You are asked to respond to a student's inquiry about a real-world phenomenon by identifying scientific concepts and principles that are related to the real-world phenomenon. You are also asked to describe an appropriate learning experience with a rationale that will provide student understanding of a concept/principle that relates to the real-world phenomenon.
Exercise 4: Social Studies	In this exercise, you demonstrate your ability to identify and interpret social studies/history information within a given graphic. You are asked to identify a cause-and-effect relationship based on the information in the given graphic and to identify a specific historic event related to the cause-and-effect relationship. You are also asked to describe a learning experience/activity that develops student understanding of a real-world connection related to the identified cause-and-effect relationship.
Exercise 5: Health and Wellness	In this exercise, you demonstrate your ability to identify a developmentally appropriate goal and learning activity to promote students' knowledge and skills related to a given health and wellness topic and enable them to transfer their knowledge and skills. You are also asked to explain how the learning activity would support the goal and promote students' knowledge and skills related to the health and wellness topic.
Exercise 6: Integrating the Arts	In this exercise, you demonstrate your ability to use the arts to develop student understanding of concepts in another discipline. You are asked to identify concepts in a given subject area and describe an arts-focused learning experience that will establish a connection for students' understanding of an identified concept and provide multiple paths of access for student learning of that concept. You are asked to justify how the arts-focused learning experience will enable students to develop a deeper or broader appreciation of the arts.

NOTE

This study was supported in part by the National Science Foundation, through Grant DRL-1222777. Additionally, we would like to thank the editors and reviewers for their very helpful feedback. We are also grateful to Sean Smith of Horizon Research, Inc., and our research group at Rutgers Graduate School of Education for their very useful comments. Finally, we thank Colleen McDermott for all her support in the preparation of the chapter.

REFERENCES

Abell, S. K. (2007). Research on science teacher knowledge. In S. K. Abell & N. G. Lederman (Eds.), *Handbook of research on science education* (pp. 3–28). Mahwah, NJ: Lawrence Erlbaum.

American Council on Education. (1940). *Report of the first annual administration of the National Teacher Examinations and announcement of the 1941 examinations.* New York, NY: Author.

American Federation of Teachers. (2012). *Raising the bar: Aligning and elevating teacher preparation and the teaching profession* (A report of the American Federation of Teachers Teacher Preparation Task Force). Washington, DC: Author. Retrieved from http://www.highered.nysed.gov/raisingthebar2012.pdf

Anderson, J. R. (1976). *Language, memory, and thought.* Hillsdale, NJ: Lawrence Erlbaum.

Angrist, J. D., & Guryan, J. (2007). Does teacher testing raise teacher quality? Evidence from state certification requirements. *Economics of Education Review, 27,* 483–503. doi:10.1016/j.econedurev.2007.03.002

Association of Mexican American Educators v. State of Cal. (1996). 937 F. Supp. 1397, N.D. Cal.

August, D., & Hakuta, K. (Eds.). (1997). *Improving schooling for language-minority children: A research agenda.* Washington, DC: National Academies Press. Retrieved from http://www.nap.edu/openbook.php?isbn=0309054974

August, D., & Shanahan, T. (Eds.). (2006). *Developing literacy in second-language learners: Report of the National Literacy Panel on Language-Minority Children and Youth* (Executive summary). Mahwah, NJ: Lawrence Erlbaum. Retrieved from http://www.bilingualeducation.org/pdfs/PROP2272.pdf

Ball, D. L., & Forzani, F. M. (2009). The work of teaching and the challenge for teacher education. *Journal of Teacher Education, 60,* 497–511. doi:10.1177/0022487109348479

Ball, D. L., Hill, H. C., & Bass, H. (2005). Knowing mathematics for teaching: Who knows mathematics well enough to teach third grade, and how can we decide? *American Educator, 29,* 14–46. Retrieved from http://www.aft.org/pdfs/americaneducator/fall2005/BallF05.pdf

Ball, D. L., Sleep, L., Boerst, T., & Bass, H. (2009). Combining the development of practice and the practice of development in teacher education. *Elementary School Journal, 109,* 458–476. doi:10.1086/596996

Ball, D. L., Thames, M. H., & Phelps, G. C. (2008). Content knowledge for teaching: What makes it special? *Journal of Teacher Education, 59,* 389–407. doi:10.1177/0022487108324554

Baumert, J., Kunter, M., Blum, W., Brunner, M., Voss, T., Jordan, A., . . .Tsai, Y.-M. (2010). Teachers' mathematical knowledge, cognitive activation in the classroom, and student progress. *American Educational Research Journal, 47,* 133–180. doi:10.3102/0002831209345157

Baxter, J. A., & Lederman, N. G. (1999). Assessment and measurement of pedagogical content knowledge. In J. Gess-Newsome & N. G. Lederman (Eds.), *Examining pedagogical content knowledge: The construct and its implications for science education* (pp. 147–161). Dordrecht, Netherlands: Kluwer Academic.

Bennett, C. I., McWhorter, L. M., & Kuykendall, J. A. (2006). Will I ever teach? Latino and African American students' perspectives on PRAXIS I. *American Educational Research Journal, 43,* 531–575. doi:10.3102/00028312043003531

Biesta, G. J. J., & Burbules, N. C. (2003). *Pragmatism and educational research.* Latham, MD: Rowman & Littlefield.

Biesta, G. J. J., & Stengel, B. (in press). Thinking philosophically about teaching: Illuminating issues and (re)framing research. In D. H. Gitomer & C. A. Bell (Eds.), *Handbook of research on teaching* (5th ed.). Washington, DC: American Educational Research Association.

Bill and Melinda Gates Foundation. (2011). *Learning about teaching: Initial findings from the Measures of Effective Teaching project* (MET Project Research Paper). Seattle, WA: Author. Retrieved from https://docs.gatesfoundation.org/Documents/preliminary-findings-research-paper.pdf

Blömeke, S., Houang, R., & Suhl, U. (2011). TEDS-M: Diagnosing teacher knowledge by applying multidimensional item response theory and multi-group models. *IERI Monograph Series: Issues and Methodologies in Large-Scale Assessments, 4,* 109–126. Retrieved from http://www.ierinstitute.org/fileadmin/Documents/IERI_Monograph/IERI_Monograph_Volume_04_Chapter_5.pdf

Boerst, T. A., Sleep, L., Ball, D. L., & Bass, H. (2011). Preparing teachers to lead mathematics discussions. *Teachers College Record, 113,* 2844–2877. Retrieved from https://www.tcrecord.org/Content.asp?ContentID=16496

Boydston, J. A. (Ed.). (1984). *John Dewey: The later works, 1925–1953: Vol. 3. 1927–1928: Essays, reviews, miscellany, and "impressions of Soviet Russia."* Carbondale: Southern Illinois University.

Buddin, R., & Zamarro, G. (2008). *Teacher quality, teacher licensure tests, and student achievement* (RAND Working Paper No. WR-555-IES). Santa Monica, CA: RAND Corporation. Retrieved from http://www.rand.org/content/dam/rand/pubs/working_papers/2008/RAND_WR555.pdf

Buschang, R. E., Chung, G. K. W. K., Delacruz, G. C., & Baker, E. L. (2012). *Validating measures of algebra teacher subject matter knowledge and pedagogical content knowledge* (CRESST Report No. 820). Los Angeles: National Center for Research on Evaluation, Standards, & Student Testing, UCLA.

Carlisle, J. F., Correnti, R., Phelps, G., & Zeng, J. (2009). Exploration of the contribution of teachers' knowledge about reading to their students' improvement in reading. *Reading and Writing, 22,* 457–486. doi:10.1007/s11145-009-9165-y

Carnegie Task Force on Teaching as a Profession. (1986). *A nation prepared: Teachers for the 21st century* (The report of the Task Force on Teaching as a Profession). Hyattsville, MD: Carnegie Forum on Education and the Economy.

Carroll, J. B. (1993). *Human cognitive abilities: A survey of factor-analytic studies.* New York, NY: Cambridge University Press. Retrieved from http://steinhardtapps.es.its.nyu.edu/create/courses/2174/reading/Carroll_1.pdf

Chase, W. G., & Simon, H. A. (1973). The mind's eye in chess. In W. G. Chase (Ed.), *Visual information processing* (pp. 215–281). New York, NY: Academic Press.

Chi, M. T. H. (1978). Knowledge structure and memory development. In R. S. Siegler (Ed.), *Children's thinking: What develops?* (pp. 73–96). Hillsdale, NJ: Lawrence Erlbaum.

Chi, M. T. H., & Ohlsson, S. (2005). Complex declarative learning. In K. J. Holyoak & R. G. Morrison (Eds.), *Cambridge handbook of thinking and reasoning* (pp. 371–400). New York, NY: Cambridge University Press. Retrieved from http://chilab.asu.edu/papers/Handbook_Chapter_with_Din.pdf

Chomsky, N. (1988). *Language and problems of knowledge.* Cambridge: MIT Press.

Cizek, G. J., & Bunch, M. B. (2007). *Standard setting: A guide to establishing and evaluating performance standards on tests.* London, England: Sage.

Clotfelter, C. T., Ladd, H. F., & Vigdor, J. L. (2007). *How and why do teacher credentials matter for student achievement?* (NBER Working Paper No. 12828). Cambridge, MA: National Bureau of Economic Research. doi:10.3386/w12828

Cole, M., & Scribner, S. (1974). *Culture and thought: A psychological introduction.* New York, NY: John Wiley.

Council of Chief State School Officers. (1992). *Model standards for beginning teacher licensing and development: A resource for state dialogue.* Washington, DC: Author. Retrieved from http://thesciencenetwork.org/docs/BrainsRUs/Model%20Standards%20for%20Beg%20Teaching_Paliokas.pdf

Council of Chief State School Officers. (2000). *Key state education policies on K–12 education: 2000: Results from the 2000 policies and practices survey, state departments of education.* Washington, DC: Author. Retrieved from http://www.personal.psu.edu/dgm122/epfp/KeyState2000.PDF

Council of Chief State School Officers. (2011). *InTASC model core teaching standards: A resource for state dialogue.* Washington, DC: Author. Retrieved from http://www.ccsso.org/Documents/2011/InTASC_Model_Core_Teaching_Standards_2011.pdf

Crowe, E., Allen, M., & Coble, C. (2013). *Outcomes, measures, and data systems: A paper prepared for the CAEP Commission on Standards and Performance Reporting.* Retrieved from http://caepnet.files.wordpress.com/2012/12/caep-paper-final-1-19-2013.pdf

Darling-Hammond, L., & Bransford, J. (Eds.). (2007). *Preparing teachers for a changing world: What teachers should learn and be able to do.* San Francisco, CA: Jossey-Bass.

de Jong, E. J., & Harper, C. A. (2005). Preparing mainstream teachers for English-language learners: Is being a good teacher good enough? *Teacher Education Quarterly, 32,* 101–124. Retrieved from http://www.teqjournal.org/backvols/2005/32_2/13dejong&harper.pdf

Dieker, L. A., Straub, C. L., Hughes, C. E., Hynes, M. C., & Hardin, S. (2014). Learning from virtual students. *Educational Leadership, 71*(8), 54–58.

Döhrmann, M., Kaiser, G., & Blömeke, S. (2012). The conceptualisation of mathematics competencies in the international teacher education study TEDS-M. *ZDM: International Journal on Mathematics Education, 44,* 325–340. doi:10.1007/s11858-012-0432-z

Educational Testing Service. (2005). *Validity for licensing tests: A brief orientation.* Princeton, NJ: Author. Retrieved from http://www.ets.org/s/praxis/pdf/validity.pdf

Educational Testing Service. (2014a). *Frequently asked questions about the Praxis™ series tests.* Princeton, NJ: Author. Retrieved from https://www.ets.org/praxis/faq_test_takers/

Educational Testing Service. (2014b). *Praxis® core academic skills for educators (core) test content and structure.* Princeton, NJ: Author. Retrieved from https://www.ets.org/praxis/about/core/content/

Elbaz, F. (1983). *Teacher thinking: A study of practical knowledge.* London, England: Croom Helm.

Elementary and Secondary Education Act of 2002, Pub. L. No. 107-110, 115 Stat. 1425 (2002).

Faltis, C. J., & Valdés, G. (in press). Preparing teachers for teaching in and advocating for linguistically diverse classrooms: A vade mecum for teacher educators. In D. H. Gitomer & C. A. Bell (Eds.), *Handbook of research on teaching* (5th ed.). Washington, DC: American Educational Research Association.

Fantl, J. (2014). Knowledge how. In E. N. Zalta (Ed.), *The Stanford encyclopedia of philosophy.* Retrieved from http://plato.stanford.edu/archives/spr2014/entries/knowledge-how/

Flanagan, J. C. (1941). An analysis of the results from the first annual edition of the National Teacher Examinations. *Journal of Experimental Education, 9,* 237–250. Retrieved from http://www.jstor.org/stable/20150668

Fogo, B. (2014). Core practices for teaching history: The results of a Delphi panel survey. *Theory & Research in Social Education, 42,* 151–196. doi:10.1080/00933104.2014.902781

Forzani, F. M. (2014). Understanding core practices and practice-based teacher education: Learning from the past. *Journal of Teacher Education, 65,* 357–368. doi:10.1177/0022487114533800

Franke, M., Webb, N., Chan, A., Ing, M., Freund, D., & Battey, D. (2009). Teacher questioning to elicit students' mathematical thinking in elementary school classrooms. *Journal of Teacher Education, 60,* 380–392. doi:10.1177/0022487109339906

Freire, P. (1970). *Pedagogy of the oppressed.* New York, NY: Bloomsbury.

Fuller, S. C., & Ladd, H. F. (2012). *School based accountability and the distribution of teacher quality among grades in elementary school* (CALDER Working Paper No. 75). Washington, DC: Center for the Analysis of Longitudinal Data in Education Research, American Institutes for Research. Retrieved from http://www.caldercenter.org/publications/upload/wp75.pdf

Gay, G. (2010). *Culturally responsive teaching: Theory, research, and practice* (2nd ed.). New York, NY: Teachers College Press.

Gess-Newsome, J., & Lederman, N. G. (Eds.). (1999). *Examining pedagogical content knowledge: The construct and its implications for science education.* Dordrecht, Netherlands: Kluwer Academic.

Gitomer, D. H., Brown, T. L., & Bonett, J. (2011). Useful signal or unnecessary obstacle? The role of basic skills tests in teacher preparation. *Journal of Teacher Education, 62,* 431–445. doi:10.1177/0022487111412785

Gitomer, D. H., Latham, A. S., & Ziomek, R. (1999). *The academic quality of prospective teachers: The impact of admissions and licensure testing* (ETS Teaching & Learning Report Series, ETS RR-03-25). Princeton, NJ: Educational Testing Service. Retrieved from http://www.ets.org/Media/Research/pdf/RR-03-35.pdf

Gitomer, D. H., Phelps, G., Weren, B., Howell, H., & Croft, A. J. (2014). Evidence on the validity of content knowledge for teaching assessments. In T. J. Kane, K. A. Kerr, & R. C. Pianta (Eds.), *Designing teacher evaluation systems: New guidance from the Measures of Effective Teaching project* (pp. 493–528). San Francisco, CA: Jossey-Bass.

Gitomer, D. H., & Qi, Y. (2010). *Score trends for Praxis II.* Washington, DC: U. S. Department of Education, Office of Planning, Evaluation, and Policy Development, Policy and Program Studies Service.

Goldhaber, D. (2007). Everyone's doing it, but what does teacher testing tell us about teacher effectiveness? *Journal of Human Resources, 42*(4), 765–794. doi:10.3368/jhr.XLII.4.765

Goldhaber, D., Lavery, L., & Theobald, R. (2014). *Uneven playing field? Assessing the inequity of teacher characteristics and measured performance across students* (CEDR Working Paper No. 2014-4). Seattle: Center for Education Data & Research, University of Washington. Retrieved from http://www.cedr.us/papers/working/CEDR%20WP%202014-4.pdf

Goodlad, J. I. (1984). *A place called school.* New York, NY: McGraw-Hill.

Grimmett, P. P., & MacKinnon, A. M. (1992). Craft knowledge and the education of teachers. *Review of Research in Education, 18,* 385–456. doi:10.3102/0091732X018001385

Grossman, P. L. (1990). *The making of a teacher: Teacher knowledge and teacher education.* New York, NY: Teachers College Press.

Grossman, P. L. (1991). What are we talking about anyhow: Subject matter knowledge for secondary English teachers. In J. Brophy (Ed.), *Advances in research on teaching: Vol. 2: Subject matter knowledge* (pp. 245–264). Greenwich, CT: JAI Press.

Grossman, P., Hammerness, K., & McDonald, M. (2009). Redefining teaching: Re-imagining teacher education. *Teachers and Teaching: Theory and Practice, 15,* 273–290. doi:10.1080/13540600902875340

Grossman, P., & McDonald, M. (2008). Back to the future: Directions for research in teaching and teacher education. *Educational Research Journal, 45,* 184–205. doi:10.3102/0002831207312906

Hambleton, R. K., & Pitoniak, M. J. (2006). Setting performance standards. In R. L. Brennan (Ed.), *Educational measurement* (4th ed., pp. 433–470). Westport, CT: Praeger.

Haney, W., Madaus, G., & Kreitzer, A. (1987). Charms talismanic: Testing teachers for the improvement of American education. *Review of Research in Education, 14,* 169–238. doi: 10.3102/0091732X014001169

Hatch, T., & Grossman, P. (2009). Learning to look beyond the boundaries of representation: Using technology to examine teaching (Overview for a digital exhibition: Learning from the practice of teaching). *Journal of Teacher Education, 60,* 70–85. doi:10.1177/0022487108328533

Hill, H. C., Ball, D. L., Blunk, M., Goffney, I. M., & Rowan, B. (2007). Validating the ecological assumption: The relationship of measure scores to classroom teaching and student learning. *Measurement: Interdisciplinary Research and Perspectives, 5,* 107–117. doi:10.1080/15366360701487138

Hill, H. C., Ball, D. L., & Schilling, S. G. (2008). Unpacking pedagogical content knowledge: Conceptualizing and measuring teachers' topic-specific knowledge of students. *Journal for Research in Mathematics Education, 39*, 372–400. Retrieved from http://www.ugr.es/~pflores/2008_9/Master_Conocim/textos%20JP/[1]_Hill-Ball-Schilling-JRME2008-07.pdf

Hill, H. C., Blunk, M. L., Charalambous, C. Y., Lewis, J. M., Phelps, G. C., Sleep, L., & Ball, D. L. (2008). Mathematical knowledge for teaching and the mathematical quality of instruction: An exploratory study. *Cognition and Instruction, 26*, 430–511. doi:10.1080/07370000802177235

Hill, H. C., Dean, C., & Goffney, I. M. (2007). Assessing elemental and structural validity: Data from teachers, non-teachers, and mathematicians. *Measurement: Interdisciplinary Research and Perspectives, 5*(2–3), 81–92. doi:10.1080/15366360701486999

Hill, H. C., & Lubienski, S. T. (2007). Teachers' mathematics knowledge for teaching and school context: A study of California teachers. *Educational Policy, 21*, 747–768. doi:10.1177/0895904807307061

Hill, H. C., Rowan, B., & Ball, D. L. (2005). Effects of teachers' mathematical knowledge for teaching on student achievement. *American Educational Research Journal, 42*, 371–406. doi:10.3102/00028312042002371

Hill, H. C., Schilling, S. G., & Ball, D. L. (2004). Developing measures of teachers' mathematics knowledge for teaching. *Elementary School Journal, 105*, 11–30. doi:10.1086/428763

Hill, H. C., Umland, K., Litke, E., & Kapitula, L. R. (2012). Teacher quality and quality teaching: Examining the relationship of a teacher assessment to practice. *American Journal of Education, 118*, 489–519. doi:10.1086/666380

Hirsch, E. D., Jr. (1988). *Cultural literacy: What every American needs to know.* New York, NY: Random House.

Hlas, A. C., & Hlas, C. S. (2012). A review of high-leverage teaching practices: Making connections between mathematics and foreign languages. *Foreign Language Annals, 45*(Suppl. 1), s76–s97. doi:10.1111/j.1944-9720.2012.01180.x

Howey, K. R., & Grossman, P. L. (1989). A study in contrast: Sources of pedagogical content knowledge for secondary English. *Journal of Teacher Education, 40*(5), 24–31. doi:10.1177/002248718904000504

Humphry, B. J. (1966). *Report concerning the National Teacher Examinations* (ETS Confidential). Princeton, NJ: Educational Testing Service.

Janssen, F., Westbroek, H., & Doyle, W. (2014). The practical turn in teacher education: Designing a preparation sequence for core practice frames. *Journal of Teacher Education, 65*, 195–206. doi:10.1177/0022487113518584

Kafka, J. (in press). In search of a grand narrative on the history of teaching. In D. H. Gitomer & C. A. Bell (Eds.), *Handbook of research on teaching* (5th ed.). Washington, DC: American Educational Research Association.

Kane, M. (2006). Validation. In R. L. Brennan (Ed.), *Educational measurement* (4th ed., pp. 17–64). New York, NY: Macmillan.

Kersting, N. (2008). Using video clips as item prompts to measure teachers' knowledge of teaching mathematics. *Educational and Psychological Measurement, 68*, 845–861. doi:10.1177/0013164407313369

Kersting, N. B., Givvin, K., Sotelo, F., & Stigler, J. W. (2010). Teachers' analyses of classroom video predict student learning of mathematics: Further explorations of a novel measure of teacher knowledge. *Journal of Teacher Education, 61*, 172–181. doi:10.1177/0022487109347875

Kersting, N. B., Givvin, K. B., Thompson, B., Santagata, R., & Stigler, J. (2012). Developing measures of usable knowledge: Teachers' analyses of mathematics classroom videos predict teaching quality and student learning. *American Educational Research Journal, 49*, 568–590. doi:10.3102/0002831212437853

Kersting, N. B., Sherin, B. L., & Stigler, J. W. (2014). Automated scoring of teachers' open-ended responses to video prompts: Bringing the classroom-video-analysis assessment to scale. *Educational and Psychological Measurement.* Advance online publication. doi:10.1177/0013164414521634

Kintsch, W. (1998). *Comprehension.* Cambridge, England: Cambridge University Press.

Krauss, S., Baumert, J., & Blum, W. (2008). Secondary mathematics teachers' pedagogical content knowledge and content knowledge: Validation of the COACTIV constructs. *ZDM: International Journal of Mathematics Education, 40,* 873–892. doi:10.1007/s11858-008-0141-9

Krauss, S., Brunner, M., Kunter, M., Baumert, J., Neubrand, M., Blum, W., & Jordan, A. (2008). Pedagogical content knowledge and content knowledge of secondary mathematics teachers. *Journal of Educational Psychology, 100,* 716–725. doi:10.1037/0022-0663.100.3.716

Kucan, L., Hapgood, S., & Palincsar, A. S. (2011). Teachers' specialized knowledge for supporting student comprehension in text-based discussions. *Elementary School Journal, 112,* 61–82. doi:10.1086/660689

Ladson-Billings, G. (1995). Toward a theory of culturally relevant pedagogy. *American Educational Research Journal, 32,* 465–491. doi:10.3102/00028312032003465

Lampert, M. (2010). Learning teaching in, from, and for practice: What do we mean? *Journal of Teacher Education, 61*(1–2), 21–34. doi:10.1177/0022487109347321

Lampert, M., Franke, M. L., Kazemi, E., Ghousseini, H., Turrou, A. C., Beasley, H., . . . Crowe, K. (2013). Keeping it complex using rehearsals to support novice teacher learning of ambitious teaching. *Journal of Teacher Education, 64,* 226–243. doi:10.1177/0022487112473837

Lave, J. (1988). *Cognition in practice: Mind, mathematics and culture in everyday life.* Cambridge, England: Cambridge University Press.

Leinhardt, G. (1993). Weaving instructional explanations in history. *British Journal of Educational Psychology, 63,* 46–74. doi:10.1111/j.2044-8279.1993.tb01041.x

Leinhardt, G., & Greeno, J. (1986). The cognitive skill of teaching. *Journal of Educational Psychology, 78,* 75–95. doi:10.1037/0022-0663.78.2.75

Levine, A. (2006). *Educating school teachers.* Washington, DC: The Education Schools Project. Retrieved from http://www.edschools.org/pdf/Educating_Teachers_Report.pdf

Ma, L. (1999). *Knowing and teaching elementary mathematics: Teachers' understanding of fundamental mathematics in China and the United States.* Mahwah, NJ: Lawrence Erlbaum.

Magnusson, S., Krajcik, J., & Borko, H. (1999). Nature, sources and development of pedagogical content knowledge for science teaching. In J. Gess-Newsome & N. G. Lederman (Eds.), *Examining pedagogical content knowledge: The construct and its implications for science education* (pp. 95–132). Dordrecht, Netherlands: Kluwer Academic.

McDonald, M. A. (2010). Social justice teacher education and the case for enacting high-leverage practices. *Teacher Education and Practice, 23,* 452–455.

McDonald, M., Kazemi, E., & Kavanagh, S. S. (2013). Core practices and pedagogies of teacher education: A call for a common language and collective activity. *Journal of Teacher Education, 64,* 378–386. doi:10.1177/0022487113493807

Messick, S. (1989). Validity. In R. Linn (Ed.), *Educational measurement* (3rd ed., pp. 13–100). Washington, DC: American Council on Education.

Mintz, A. (2007). The midwife as matchmaker: Socrates and relational pedagogy. In B. Stengel (Ed.), *Philosophy of education yearbook* (pp. 91–99). Urbana, IL: Philosophy of Education Society. Retrieved from http://www.academia.edu/171605/The_Midwife_as_Matchmaker_Socrates_and_Relational_Pedagogy

Mislevy, R. J., & Haertel, G. D. (2006). Implications of evidence-centered design for educational testing. *Educational Measurement: Issues and Practice, 25*(4), 6–20. doi:10.1111/j.1745-3992.2006.00075.x

Monte-Sano, C., & Budano, C. (2013). Developing and enacting pedagogical content knowledge for teaching history: An exploration of two novice teachers' growth over three years. *Journal of the Learning Sciences, 22*, 171–211. doi:10.1080/10508406.2012.742016

Moss, P. A. (1998). Rethinking validity in the assessment of teaching. In N. Lyons & G. Grant (Eds.), *With portfolio in hand: Portfolios in teaching and teacher education* (pp. 202–219). New York, NY: Teachers College Press.

Moss, P. A. (2010). Thinking systemically about assessment practice. In M. Kennedy (Ed.), *Teacher assessment and the quest for teacher quality: A handbook* (pp. 355–374). San Francisco, CA: Jossey-Bass.

National Board for Professional Teaching Standards. (1989). *What teachers should know and be able to do*. Arlington, VA: Author. Retrieved from http://www.nbpts.org/sites/default/files/documents/certificates/what_teachers_should_know.pdf

National Board for Professional Teaching Standards. (2013). *Middle childhood/generalist: Assessment at a glance*. Washington, DC: Author. Retrieved from http://www.nbpts.org/sites/default/files/documents/certificates/Aaag/MC_GEN_AssessAtaGlance_Final.pdf

The National Commission on Excellence in Education. (1983). *A nation at risk: The imperative for educational reform* (A report to the nation and the Secretary of Education, U.S. Department of Education). Washington, DC: U.S. Department of Education. Retrieved from http://datacenter.spps.org/uploads/sotw_a_nation_at_risk_1983.pdf

National Council for the Social Studies. (1994). *Expectations of excellence: Curriculum standards for social studies*. Washington, DC: Author. Retrieved from http://files.eric.ed.gov/fulltext/ED378131.pdf

National Council of Teachers of English & the International Reading Association. (1996). *Standards for the English language arts*. Urbana, IL: National Council of Teachers of English.

National Council of Teachers of Mathematics. (1989). *Curriculum and evaluation standards for school mathematics*. Reston, VA: Author.

National Council on Education Standards and Testing. (1992). *Raising standards for American education: A report to Congress, the Secretary of Education, the National Education Goals Panel, and the American people*. Washington, DC: U.S. Government Printing Office. Retrieved from http://files.eric.ed.gov/fulltext/ED338721.pdf

National Education Goals Panel. (1993). *The National Education Goals Report: Building a nation of learners: Vol. 1. The national report*. Washington, DC: Author. Retrieved from http://files.eric.ed.gov/fulltext/ED360394.pdf

National Governors Association Center for Best Practices & Council of Chief State School Officers. (2010). *Common core state standards*. Washington, DC: Author.

National Paideia Center. (2014). *The Paideia principles*. Asheville, NC: Author. Retrieved from http://www.paideia.org/about-paideia/philosophy/

National Research Council. (1996). *National science education standards*. Washington, DC: National Academies Press. Retrieved from http://www.nap.edu/openbook.php?record_id=4962&page=R1

National Research Council. (2001a). *Knowing what students know: The science and design of educational assessment* (J. Pellegrino, N. Chudowsky, & R. Glaser, Eds.). Washington, DC: National Academies Press. Retrieved from http://www.nap.edu/openbook.php?isbn=0309072727

National Research Council. (2001b). *Testing teacher candidates: The role of licensure tests in improving teacher quality*. (K. J. Mitchell, D. Z. Robinson, B. S. Plake, K. T. Knowles, Eds.). Committee on Assessment and Teacher Quality, Center for Education. Board on Testing and Assessment. Washington, DC: National Academies Press. Retrieved from http://www.nap.edu/openbook.php?record_id=10090

National Research Council. (2008). *Assessing accomplished teaching: Advanced-level certification programs* (M. D. Hakel, J. A. Koenig, & S. W. Elliott, Eds.). Washington, DC: National Academies Press.

National Research Council. (2010). *Preparing teachers: Building evidence for sound policy.* Washington, DC: National Academies Press. Retrieved from http://www.nap.edu/openbook.php?record_id=12882

Neiss, M. L. (2005). Preparing teachers to teach science and mathematics with technology: Developing a technology pedagogical content knowledge. *Teaching and Teacher Education, 21,* 509–523. doi:10.1016/j.tate.2005.03.006

NGSS Lead States. (2013). *Next generation science standards: For states, by states.* Washington, DC: National Academies Press.

Noddings, N. (2005). *The challenge to care in schools* (2nd ed.). New York, NY: Teachers College Press.

Norman, D. A., & Rumelhart, D. E. (1975). Reference and comprehension. In D. A. Norman, D. E. Rumelhart, & the LNR Research Group (Eds.), *Explorations in cognition* (pp. 65–87). San Francisco, CA: W. H. Freeman.

Pearson Education, Inc. (2014). California Educator Credentialing Examinations: California Basic Educational Skills Test™ (CBEST®). Amherst, MA: Author. Retrieved from http://www.ctcexams.nesinc.com/about_CBEST.asp

Phelps, G. (2009). Just knowing how to read isn't enough! Assessing knowledge for teaching reading. *Educational Assessment, Evaluation and Accountability, 21,* 137–154. doi:10.1007/s11092-009-9070-6

Phelps, G., & Schilling, S. (2004). Developing measures of content knowledge for teaching reading. *Elementary School Journal, 105,* 31–48. doi:10.1086/428764

Prucha, F. P. (Ed.). (1973). Official report of the Nineteenth Annual Conference of Charities and Correction. In *Americanizing the American Indians: Writings by the "friends of the Indian": 1880–1900* (pp. 260–271). Cambridge, MA: Harvard University Press. Retrieved from http://historymatters.gmu.edu/d/4929/ (Original work published 1892)

Pullin, D. C. (2001). Key questions in implementing teacher testing and licensing. *Journal of Law & Education, 30,* 383–429.

Ravitch, D., & Viteritti, J. P. (Eds.). (2001). *Making good citizens: Education and civil society.* Binghamton, NY: Vail-Ballou Press.

Rogoff, B., & Waddell, K. J. (1982). Memory for information organized in a scene by children from two cultures. *Child Development, 53,* 1224–1228. Retrieved from http://www-pmhs2.stjohns.k12.fl.us/higginj/0DBE8052-0118C716.4/Memory%20for%20Information%20Organized%20in%20a%20Scene%20by%20Children%20fro.pdf

Rousseau, J.-J. (1979). *Emile* or *on education* [The Project Gutenberg EBook version]. New York, NY: Basic Books. Retrieved from http://www.gutenberg.org/cache/epub/5427/pg5427.html

Rowland, T., Huckstep, P., & Thwaites, A. (2005). Elementary teachers' mathematics subject knowledge: The knowledge quartet and the case of Naomi. *Journal of Mathematics Teacher Education, 8,* 255–281. doi:10.1007/s10857-005-0853-5

Rumelhart, D. E., & Norman, D. A. (1978). Accretion, tuning and restructuring: Three modes of learning. In J. W. Cotton & R. Klatzky (Eds.), *Semantic factors in cognition* (pp. 37–53). Hillsdale, NJ: Lawrence Erlbaum.

Ryle, G. (1946). Knowing how and knowing that: The presidential address. *Proceedings of the Aristotelian Society, 46,* 1–16. Retrieved from http://www.jstor.org/stable/4544405

Schank, R. C., & Abelson, R. P. (1977). *Scripts, plans, goals, and understanding: An inquiry into human knowledge structures.* Hillsdale, NJ: Lawrence Erlbaum.

Schilling, S. G., Blunk, M., & Hill, H. C. (2007). Test validation and the MKT measures: Generalizations and conclusions. *Measurement: Interdisciplinary Research and Perspectives, 5,* 118–127. doi:10.1080/15366360701487146

Shepard, L. (1993). Evaluating test validity. *Review of Research in Education, 19,* 405–450. doi:10.3102/0091732X019001405

Shulman, L. (1986). Paradigms and research programs for the study of teaching. In M. C. Wittrock (Ed.), *Handbook of research on teaching* (3rd ed., pp. 3–36). New York, NY: Macmillan.

Shulman, L. (1987). Knowledge and teaching: Foundations of the new reform. *Harvard Educational Review, 57,* 1–22.

Sinharay, S. (2010). How often do subscores have added value? Results from operational and simulated data. *Journal of Educational Measurement, 47,* 150–174. doi:10.1111/j.1745-3984.2010.00106.x

Skinner, B. F. (1965, October 16). Why teachers fail. *The Saturday Review,* pp. 80–81. Retrieved from http://www.isac.psc.br/wp-content/uploads/skinner/Skinner_(1965)_Why_teacher_fail.pdf

Tatto, M., Schwille, J., Senk, S., Ingvarson, L., Peck, R., & Rowley, G. (2008). *Teacher Education and Development Study in Mathematics (TEDS-M): Policy, practice, and readiness to teach primary and secondary mathematics. Conceptual framework.* East Lansing: College of Education, Michigan State University.

TeachingWorks. (2014a). *Assessments.* Retrieved from http://www.teachingworks.org/work-of-teaching/assessments

TeachingWorks. (2014b). *High-leverage practices.* Retrieved from http://www.teachingworks.org/work-of-teaching/high-leverage-practices

Troyan, F. J., Davin, K. J., & Donato, R. (2013). Exploring a practice-based approach to foreign language teacher preparation: A work in progress. *Canadian Modern Language Review, 69,* 154–180. doi:10.3138/cmlr.1523

Turkan, S., de Oliveira, L., Lee, O., & Phelps, G. (2014). Proposing a knowledge base for teaching academic content to English language learners: Disciplinary linguistic knowledge. *Teachers College Record, 116*(4). Retrieved from https://www.tcrecord.org/Content.asp?ContentID=17361

U.S. Department of Education, Office of Postsecondary Education. (2011). *Preparing and credentialing the nation's teachers: The Secretary's eighth report on teacher quality based on data provided for 2008, 2009 and 2010.* Washington, DC: Author. Retrieved from http://title2.ed.gov/Public/TitleIIReport11.pdf

van Driel, J. H., Verloop, N., & de Vos, W. (1998). Developing science teachers' pedagogical content knowledge. *Journal of Research in Science Teaching, 35,* 673–695. doi:10.1002/(SICI)1098-2736(199808)35:6<673::AID-TEA5>3.0.CO;2-J

Voss, T., Kunter, M., & Baumert, J. (2011). Assessing teacher candidates' general pedagogical/psychological knowledge: Test construction and validation. *Journal of Educational Psychology, 103,* 952–969. doi:10.1037/a0025125

Waddell, L. R. (2014). Using culturally ambitious teaching practices to support urban mathematics teaching and learning. *Journal of Praxis in Multicultural Education, 8*(2). doi:10.9741/2161-2978.1069

Wellman, H. M., & Gelman, S. A. (1997). Knowledge acquisition in foundational domains. In D. Kuhn & R. S. Siegler (Eds.), *Handbook of child psychology* (Vol. 2, pp. 523–573). New York, NY: John Wiley. doi:10.1002/9780470147658

Wilson, A. J. (1985, April). *Knowledge for teachers: The origin of the National Teachers Examinations Program.* Paper presented at the annual meeting of the American Educational Research Association, Chicago, IL. Retrieved from http://files.eric.ed.gov/fulltext/ED262049.pdf

Wilson, S. M., Floden, R. E., & Ferrini-Mundy, J. (2002). Teacher preparation research: An insider's view from the outside. *Journal of Teacher Education, 53,* 190–204. doi:10.1177/0022487102053003002

Wilson, S. M., & Wineburg, S. S. (1988). Peering at history through different lenses: The role of disciplinary perspectives in teaching history. *Teachers College Record, 89,* 525–539. Retrieved from https://www.tcrecord.org/Content.asp?ContentID=540

Wilson, S. M., & Wineburg, S. S. (1993). Wrinkles in time and place: Using performance-based exercises to assess the knowledge of history teachers. *American Educational Research Journal, 30*(4), 729–769. doi:10.3102/00028312030004729

Wilson, S. M., & Youngs, P. (2005). Research on accountability processes in teacher education. In M. Cochran-Smith & K. M. Zeichner (Eds.), *Studying teacher education: The report of the AERA panel on research and teacher education* (pp. 591–644). Mahwah, NJ: Lawrence Erlbaum.

Windschitl, M., Thompson, J., Braaten, M., & Stroupe, D. (2012). Proposing a core set of instructional practices and tools for teachers of science. *Science Education, 96*, 878–903. doi:10.1002/sce.21027

Zeichner, K. (2012). The turn once again toward practice-based teacher education. *Journal of Teacher Education, 63*, 376–382. doi:10.1177/0022487112445789

Chapter 2

Assessment of Teachers From a Social Psychological Perspective

AYESHA MADNI
EVA L. BAKER
National Center for Research on Evaluation, Standards, and Student Testing (CRESST)

KIRBY A. CHOW
Society for Research in Child Development/American Association for the Advancement of Science

GIRLIE C. DELACRUZ
NOELLE C. GRIFFIN
National Center for Research on Evaluation, Standards, and Student Testing (CRESST)

Evaluating teachers has always been controversial, in part because inferences about their behaviors based on student performance are drawn in situations where they do not have full control of who they teach, students' prior knowledge, and amounts of time needed in order to adapt teaching to individual differences (E. L. Baker, 2014). Over the years, more process-oriented approaches to teacher evaluation have used judgments of the quality of classroom artifacts, observation of teachers' classroom behavior using high inference judgments, and even the neatness of the room and blinds. Needless to say, a more scientific and defensible approach is desirable. Moreover, poor teacher evaluation systems may hurt not only teachers but, inadvertently, students as well (Popham, 2013). But teacher evaluation is a necessity. In addition to their competency in assisting students to learn the content and skills expected in schools, teachers serve many other roles. They can be attentive to individual students' needs, recognize and respond to their cultural differences, and provide support and model desirable behaviors. Many of these behaviors can be combined in the category of noncognitive factors or summarized by the term *social psychological perspectives and behaviors.*

The focus of this chapter is on the description and assessment of teachers' social psychological factors, using the scientific literature as a base. Research on teachers'

Review of Research in Education
March 2015, Vol. 39, pp. 54–86
DOI: 10.3102/0091732X14558203
© 2015 AERA. http://rre.aera.net

social psychological domains has an ultimate goal of populating classrooms with competent people who can model and incite behaviors that assist students in their own learning. Social psychological based activities may include teachers' showing that they care for students' well-being; managing classrooms to keep interest, fairness, and effort at the fore; intervening in situations that may hurt students, such as bullying; and all the while focusing on helping students achieve learning goals. Clearly there are cognitive components of these behaviors. However, this chapter will examine, not exhaustively, key topics in the teacher social psychological literature; methods used to determine teachers' status on variables, in this domain; and their association and impact in a variety of settings.

One useful word at the outset about student outcomes is appropriate here, as they are increasingly proposed as the ultimate dependent measures used to judge teacher effectiveness. Even in the relatively well-studied areas of teaching content and skills, there is considerable contention about the utility of student test performance as a major component of teacher evaluation. For instance, there is great and vocal disagreement about the design, utility, and fairness of cognitive or subject matter examinations (E. L. Baker et al., 2010; Gordon Commission on the Future of Assessment in Education, 2013). Periodic efforts to redesign and refocus these assessments have occurred (see, e.g., MET Project, 2012). Nonetheless, whatever their form, there is an abiding belief that teachers should be responsible for student performance. Without debating the details and merits of the belief, the claim has been made that teachers' social psychological behaviors are important and should be considered in their evaluation. That said, the question is how?

Since the early 1990s, with the passage of the Improving America's Schools Act (1994), social psychological concerns have broken through the policy barrier, although weakly and dependent upon archival data. With regard to students, there are three major threads: (a) noncognitive behaviors that signal their overall attitudes toward school, such as absences and tardiness, and (b) socioemotional perspectives that can be partially developed through educators' efforts, that is, a sense of balance, tolerance for other viewpoints and people, teamwork, and exploratory behaviors. Educators and parents have legitimate concerns about the boundaries and appropriateness of schools' prerogatives with regard to social psychological goals and outcomes, especially in connection to the roles and responsibilities of the family. The third major thread includes social psychological processes that support instrumentally cognitive learning by students. Since the 1990s, school goals have been operationalized as standards to be shared within and, most recently, among states. Although all three threads combine into a strong argument for research attention, our emphasis will be on the factors that contribute to student cognitive learning. For example, extensive lines of research have considered cultural interactions, including conscious and unconscious stereotyping (Dijksterhuis & Nordgren, 2006), experienced by all of us. Our review includes this range for context but will concentrate on teacher factors that are potentially influential on a student's own behaviors and accomplishments. We include empirical studies from the past 10 years, drawn from peer related journals, with the exception of older conceptual or seminal works included in books, edited books, or other study reports.[1]

CLASSIFICATION OF TEACHER SOCIAL PSYCHOLOGICAL PERSPECTIVES

Although not mutually exclusive and often intercorrelated, teacher social psychological factors are conceptualized here on a dimension moving from traits or tendencies that are relatively impervious to change, such as global temperament, specific personality variables, and long-held predispositions on one hand, and those attitudes and behaviors that are susceptible to change, even if taking a long period. Although many of these factors could have relevancy for all teachers, such as "responsibility," other variables may be especially applicable in classroom settings, for instance, "ability to motivate others." We will consider the range between persistent to malleable social and psychological factors.

PERSONALITY

Relatively intransigent factors, those that characterize the routine reactions and responses of the individual, are called personality variables. According to Olver and Mooradian (2003), the bulk of personality variables derive from the five-factor model (FFM). Personality traits are enduring dispositions that lead to consistent patterns of self-perception and behaviors with others in various environments. The FFM organizes individual personality traits into five broad categories. These five dimensions include Conscientiousness (i.e., responsible, dependable), Emotional Stability (i.e., calm under pressure, not neurotic), Extraversion (i.e., outgoing, assertive), Agreeableness (i.e., cooperative, loyal), and Openness to Experience (i.e., curious, imaginative). Multiple meta-analyses have shown consistent relationships between personality and performance in various domains (e.g., Barrick, Mount, & Judge, 2001; Hurtz & Donovan, 2000). The FFM is commonly measured using self-report Likert-type scales such as John, Donahue, and Kentle's (1991) Big 5 Inventory, Goldberg's (1999) International Personality Item Pool, and Costa and McCrae's (1992) NEO Personality Inventory–Revised. The NEO Personality Inventory–Revised is one of the most widely used measures of the FFM, and it has 6-year test-retest reliability ranging from .63 to .83; strong consensual validity between self-, peer, and spouse reports; and good convergent validity with other personality and well-being measures (Costa & McCrae, 1992).

Two interesting perspectives may be considered in the light of teachers and their personality. First, personality attributes may count explicitly during the accession process, that is, in teachers' interviews for school positions. The ability to display an appropriately extraverted (enthusiastic and outgoing) style, complemented by agreeableness and conscientiousness, is desirable for teachers in a variety of settings, in addition, of course, to mastery of subject matter, knowledge of human development, and pedagogical skills. In times of teacher shortage, these factors remain desirable but may have less weight in selection. Second, some of these variables may not be "traits," which are exhibited in all or most situations, but may vary by the state in which teachers find themselves. For example, a teacher might be very responsible about planning instruction and giving assignments but less consistent about grading student responses promptly. In an elementary or other intact classroom, teachers may be responsible for a wide range of content. As a result, teachers' exhibitions of behaviors may vary with their confidence in their own mastery of the subject matter. In any case, in the work we have undertaken, we are focusing on operational definitions of teacher attitudes, predispositions, and practices, as well as those that may imply developmental courses of action. Simply describing teachers is probably not the straightest path toward a quality educational system.

The target variables of this review also coincide with the deeper learning competencies identified as crucial for students to succeed in 21st-century jobs and civic life (Herman & Linn, 2013; O'Neil, Perez, & Baker, 2014; Webb, 2007). At the heart of the summary term *deeper learning* is a set of competencies that students must master in order to develop a keen understanding of academic content, achieve at high levels, and apply their knowledge to problems in the classroom and on the job. These include mastery of core academic content, ability to think critically and solve complex problems, ability to work collaboratively, communicating effectively, learning how to learn, and developing adaptive academic mindsets. These competencies also connect to the teacher variables discussed in this review. Before delving into a select review of our target constructs, we turn to one of the main factors that influence teachers' ability to guide students and their learning as well as their own teaching process: motivation.

TEACHER MOTIVATION

Motivation is considered a noncognitive factor that significantly influences performance. It is often referred to as the inner drive or force that sustains and directs our goal-directed behavior. Thus, motivation is a precursor for choosing and performing many other processes effectively, including, but not limited to, mastering content, thinking critically, problem solving, collaborating, and communicating. The indicators of motivated behavior include active choice, persistence, and mental effort or performance. Essentially, when individuals choose to do one thing as opposed to another, they are exhibiting active choice. Persistence involves individuals continuing to pursue a goal or task in the face of challenges and difficulty. Mental effort involves the amount of energy, thought, and involvement a person puts into a task.

In this section, we will address various variables and models that have been posited to underlie motivation. Rueda et al. (2010) describe the roots of motivation as comprising four major components: Interest, Self-Efficacy, Attribution, and Achievement Goals. As one reads the chapter, it will become obvious that even as we attempt to define, describe, and illustrate these aspects, inevitably one of these factors implicates the others. They are intertwined, and though defined as separate constructs, they most always co-occur. As a result, discussions focused on one factor will typically involve other perspectives, either of the self or of the self in various contexts. Let us consider some of the factors described by Rueda et al. Interest is defined as present when individuals seek and value what they learn. Self-efficacy broadly construed means that individuals perceive themselves as capable of success at particular tasks. Attribution is in play when appropriate inferences are drawn about success; students believe that their effort will lead to success and do not attribute failure to their own innate capability, luck, or other uncontrollable factors. Students who possess achievement goals with a mastery orientation in contrast to a performance orientation will be motivated to work because their goal is to understand a concept, context, or process rather than to compete with others.

One long-standing perspective on motivation and how an individual's choice, persistence, and performance can be explained is the expectancy-value model (Wigfield & Eccles, 2000; Appendix A). This model is well researched, and in a general sense it explains the beliefs individuals have about how well they will do on an activity (i.e., expectancy) and the extent to which they value the activity. From this perspective, individuals construct motivational beliefs through social cognitive processes, grounded in larger social and cultural contexts. This model is similar to Bandura's (1986) social cognitive theory, which posits the model of triadic reciprocity or reciprocal causation. The model of reciprocal causation postulates that individual factors as part of the person (e.g., self-efficacy), environmental factors (e.g., classroom environment, teacher expectations, etc.), and behavioral factors (e.g., behavioral indicators or manifestations) mutually influence each other to produce motivated behavior and performance.

Essentially, a student might perceive a peer successfully engaging in a certain task (i.e., behavioral factors). This observation is likely to influence positively the students' sense of efficacy (i.e., individual factors) with respect to completing the same task. The student, in turn, choses to persist and to exert mental effort with respect to completing the task (i.e., behavioral factors). A teacher observes the same student performing the task (i.e., behavioral factors) and changes his/her expectations (i.e., environmental factors) with respect to how well the student can perform. In considering teachers, we are therefore interested in the extent to which they themselves have high values or measures in these areas as well as their ability to communicate and transform students so that they are able to exhibit similar components in their behaviors.

Recent research has suggested that teachers suffer from motivational problems more than other professional groups (de Jesus & Lens, 2005). More important, a teacher's level of motivation influences his or her own behaviors as well as the behavior and motivational beliefs of students (Bandura, 1986). Thus, it is important to understand the internal factors that most readily affect teachers' levels of motivation, their perceptions of students, and their capacity to influence student behaviors. As mentioned, the most salient factors that influence these relationships include teacher interest, teacher expectations, teacher efficacy, teacher attributions, and teacher goal orientations. These factors are considered various types of teacher beliefs or orientations.

Teacher Beliefs

A substantial body of research indicates that the beliefs that teachers hold about teaching and learning influence their instructional decisions and thereby student performance (Bohlmann & Weinstein, 2013). Teacher beliefs are broadly defined as "tacit, often unconsciously held assumptions about students, classrooms, and the academic material taught" (Kagan, 1992, p. 65). The general constructs of educational and teacher beliefs are expansive and include the study of more specific beliefs, such as epistemological beliefs (teachers' view about the nature of acquisition of knowledge), teacher efficacy (beliefs about teachers' ability to influence student performance), and attributions (beliefs about the causes of teachers' and students' performance; Pajares, 1992). These various teacher beliefs are critical to understand because they affect more specific pedagogical beliefs and instructional practices, and ultimately student outcomes. Beliefs and practices share a complex relationship in that beliefs and practices mutually affect one another. For example, if teachers have a more traditional view of education, they might believe that their role as instructor is to present information that students should store and remember. These teachers may engage in direct instructional practices and incorporate drill and practice activities. In contrast, if teachers have a more constructivist view of education, they might believe that their role is to guide discovery and model active learning. These teachers may develop a more student-centered curriculum that involves students working through authentic problems (Judson, 2006). It should be noted that both types of beliefs and practices may have positive results.

Teacher Beliefs About Intelligence

Teacher beliefs about the nature of students' intelligence have also been found to predict student performance as well as to foster certain types of teaching practices. In essence, teacher beliefs about intelligence fall into two main categories: entity (i.e., fixed) mind-set and incremental (i.e., malleable) mind-set (Dweck, 1999; Hong, Chiu, Dweck, Lin, & Wan, 1999). Teachers who tend to have an entity mind-set believe that intelligence is a fixed human attribute, that one's level of intelligence is predetermined by genetics, and that functional ability stays the same. In contrast, teachers who have an incremental mind-set believe that intelligence is a malleable human attribute, that individuals have some levels of control over their own intelligence or mental abilities, and that intelligence can be amplified through study and learning (Dweck, 1999; Hong et al., 1999).

From a student perspective, implicit theories of ability have been found to affect student learning, motivation, and achievement outcomes. When students hold an entity (or fixed) belief about intelligence, they are more likely to give up easily when faced with difficult or challenging situations (i.e., less persistent), and more likely to draw conclusions about their own ability from setbacks (Dweck, 1999, 2007). On the other hand, students with an incremental belief about intelligence are more likely to devote more effort to a learning task, to persist, and to try again in the face of failure (Hong et al., 1999).

Much of the work related to implicit theories of intelligence has focused on understanding the impact of students' implicit beliefs, whereas less research has examined teachers' mind-sets (Jones, Bryant, Snyder, & Malone, 2012). However, because teachers work closely with students during their academic learning, they have the potential to influence students' implicit theories of intelligence (Jones et al., 2012). In fact, there is empirical evidence that teachers' conceptions of intelligence affect their students' beliefs about intelligence (Pretzlik, Olsson, Nabuco, & Cruz, 2003; Watanabe, 2006), which can in turn influence students' motivation and achievement (Dweck, 1999). Teachers' mind-sets have also been found to influence their teaching practices and their self-perceptions. Teachers' endorsement of an incremental mind-set (as compared to a fixed mind-set) has been associated with higher levels of self-efficacy (i.e., teachers feeling like they can help students overcome difficulties in school) and greater likelihood of creating a classroom environment that supports students' needs for autonomy, competence, and empathy and promotion of students' intrinsic motivation (Leroy, Bressoux, Sarrazin, & Trouilloud, 2007).

Furthermore, teachers' implicit theories of intelligence are related to the types of attributions teachers make about low student achievement, expectations about students, and the type of feedback and praise they deliver to students (Mueller & Dweck, 1998; Rattan, Good, & Dweck, 2012). This train of perceptions and practices can affect student motivation and achievement. For example, holding an entity theory of math intelligence is associated with making attributions to low ability (vs. effort) and not expecting appreciable future improvement in students (Rattan et al., 2012). Teachers' holding a fixed mind-set are also more likely to praise students' intelligence (vs. effort), a practice associated with negative student behaviors, such as lower levels of task persistence, and attitudes in which "being challenged" and "learning a lot" are rejected in favor of "seeming smart" (Mueller & Dweck, 1998). In experimental studies in which undergraduate students imagined themselves in the role of a teacher, those who held an entity theory were more likely to comfort students for their supposed low ability by engaging in pedagogical practices that could reduce engagement (e.g., consoling a student for a poor grade in math by telling him/her that plenty of people have trouble in this field but go on to be very successful in other fields), as compared to those who held more of an incremental theory where expectations were maintained (Rattan et al., 2012). Rattan et al. also found that students who were exposed to these types of comfort-oriented feedback practices were more likely to feel less motivated and had lower expectations about doing well in the class.

Teachers' implicit theories of intelligence have been most commonly measured using self-report questionnaires (e.g., Dweck, 1999; Nature of Ability Beliefs Questionnaire: Leroy et al., 2007). One of the most popularly used measures is Dweck's (1999) three-item scale in which individuals rate their level of agreement (1 = *strongly disagree* to 6 = *strongly agree*) with the following statements: You have a certain amount of intelligence, and you really can't do much to change it; Your intelligence is something about you that you can't change very much; and You can learn new things, but you can't really change your basic intelligence. Evaluation of the psychometric properties of this scale has shown this scale to have strong factorial validity and reliability (e.g., Dweck, Chiu, & Hong, 1995; Levy, Stroessner, & Dweck, 1998). An alternative to this teacher report questionnaire is to use a student report measure such as the four-item Perceptions of an Environmental Entity Theory scale (e.g., My professor believes that I have a certain amount of math intelligence, and I can't really do much to change it; C. Good, Rattan, & Dweck, 2012) to assess students' perceptions of their teacher's mind-set. Self-report measures have well-known and long-standing limitations, such as social desirability (see, e.g., Podsakoff & Organ, 1986; Constantine & Ladany, 2000). They also suffer from scoring approaches that average or total responses; however, improvements in their psychometric properties have been achieved using item response theory approaches (Fraley, Waller, & Brennan, 2000).

Teacher Efficacy

Teacher efficacy encompasses a teacher's individual beliefs about his or her ability to carry out a course of action and influence student performance, engagement, and learning across various student groups, including students with learning challenges and motivational difficulties (Hoy & Spero, 2005; Tschannen-Moran & Hoy, 2001). Teacher efficacy is considered a key motivational belief influencing teachers' professional behaviors and style, and student motivation and learning (Bandura, 1977, 1986; Hoy & Spero, 2005; Klassen, Tze, Betts, & Gordon, 2011; Tschannen-Moran & Hoy, 2001; Tschannen-Moran, Hoy, & Hoy, 1998).

With regard to teacher outcomes, teacher efficacy has been shown to positively affect teacher beliefs about teaching and their instructional behaviors (Skaalvik & Skaalvik, 2007). In particular, teachers with low self-efficacy experience greater difficulties in teaching, lower levels of job satisfaction, and higher levels of job-related stress (e.g., Betoret, 2006). However, teachers with high efficacy are willing to take on more challenges and risks, and tend to be more enthusiastic and committed to their teaching practice (Tschannen-Moran & Hoy, 2001). Teachers with a high sense of efficacy also experience more job-related satisfaction, expend more effort, set goals for their practice, and display more creativity in their instruction. Together these behaviors positively influence student achievement, motivation, and sense of self-efficacy (Klassen et al., 2011; Tschannen-Moran & Hoy, 2001).

Several measures of teacher efficacy have been developed and implemented over the past 50 years. These have roots in either Rotter's social learning theory or Bandura's social cognitive theory. Among the most prominent measures based on Rotter's tradition include the 2-item Rand Measure of the 1970s, Guskey's (1984) 30-item Responsibility for Student Achievement, Rose and Medway's (1981) 28-item Teacher Locus of Control, and the Webb Efficacy Scale (Ashton, Oljenik, Crocker, & McAuliffe, 1982). Among the most prominent measures based on Bandura's tradition and his construct of self-efficacy include the Ashton vignettes (Ashton, Buhr, & Crocker, 1984), Gibson and Dembo's (1984) 30-item Teacher Efficacy Scale, Midgley, Feldlaufer, and Eccles's (1989) 5-item personal teaching efficacy measure, and Bandura's (1997) Teacher Self-Efficacy Scale. Measures have also been developed for specific domains and for multiple populations. Some of these include the Science Teaching Efficacy Belief Instrument (Enoch & Riggs, 1990), and Coladarci and Breton's (1997) 30-item instrument for measuring efficacy in the context of special education. The commonality among most of these measures is that they are either forced-choice or self-report Likert-type scales based on scenarios, statements, or vignettes.

Despite this targeted effort, teacher efficacy research is troubled by divergent conceptualizations, measurement inconsistencies, and validity and reliability concerns and has an extensive research history to address these concerns (Tschannen-Moran et al., 1998; Tschannen-Moran & Hoy, 2001; Klassen et al., 2011). The main research trajectories related to validating measures of teacher efficacy have involved improving measurement of the construct and clarifying the two-factor structure that is revealed through factor analysis of most teacher efficacy measures.

Among the reasons offered to explain measurement difficulties are a lack of conceptual clarity in that a majority of measures focus on teachers' beliefs about their control of student outcomes as opposed to their perceptions about a mediating construct, their capability to teach students. In fact, Klassen et al. (2011) reviewed 218 studies on teacher efficacy and found that approximately 50% included measures that were not consistent with the Bandurian concept of self- and collective efficacy and did not assess teachers' confidence of their own capability to carry out a course of action.

Moreover, several measures are inconsistent with the tenets of self-efficacy as they focus on capability based on past performance or outcomes that are expected to result from their performance, instead of the capability to carry out a specific task (Klassen & Chiu, 2010; Tschannen-Moran et al., 1998). Bandura (1997, 2006) clearly distinguished between self-efficacy beliefs and outcome expectancies, with the former assessing judgment of capabilities for various types of performances and the latter measuring outcomes that are expected to result from these performances. Many of the teacher efficacy measures also reveal a two-factor structure, and there are confusion and debate about the meaning of and differentiation between these two factors (Tschannen-Moran & Hoy, 2001).

To address some of the issues in the measurement of teacher efficacy, Tschannen-Moran and Hoy (2001) developed a new scale, the Ohio State Teacher Efficacy Scale (OSTES) based on Bandura's (1997) teacher self-efficacy scale. The instrument was tested in three separate studies and was reduced from 52 original items in the first study to a long form with 24 items and a short form with 12 items based on factor and reliability analyses. For Study 1, items loading from .62 to .78 were selected for further testing. For Study 2, alpha reliabilities for the three subscales (i.e., engagement, instruction, and management) ranged from .72 to .82. With respect to construct validity, total scores on the OSTES had small positive relationships with both Rand items ($r = .30$ and $.28$, $p < .01$), as well as the personal teaching efficacy factor of the Gibson and Dembo (1984) measure ($r = .48$, $p < .01$), and the general teacher efficacy factor ($r = .30$, $p < .001$). For the third study, the intercorrelations between the short and long forms for the total scale and the three subscales were high, ranging from .95 to .98. Similar to Study 2, the OSTES items were positively related to both the Rand ($r = .18$ and $.53$, $p < .01$) and Gibson and Dembo's personal teaching efficacy ($r = .64$, $p < .01$) and general teacher efficacy ($r = .16$, $p < .01$) factors. Perhaps if more modern scoring approaches were used, findings would have been stronger.

Teacher Expectations

Following the classic Rosenthal and Jacobson (1968) study, a large body of experimental and correlational research has documented the effects of teachers' expectations on student outcomes. Teacher expectations are referred to as perceptions teachers have about their students' potential and what they are able to accomplish academically. There has been debate in the field about whether teachers' expectations influence student outcomes, or whether differential outcomes indicate that teachers' perceptions are accurate. Teachers typically draw these types of conclusions about their students early in the school year, forming opinions about their students' strengths, weaknesses, and their potential for academic success (T. L. Good & Nichols, 2001; Ormrod, 2011). It is hypothesized that changes in student performance as a result of teachers' expectations occur due to direct and indirect effects. Direct effects involve differential interactions with teachers that provide different opportunities to learn. Indirect effects involve social cues that communicate differential ability (Bohlmann & Weinstein, 2013).

As mentioned, teachers' implicit beliefs about intelligence influence their expectations of students in that when they have an entity belief about intelligence, teachers make attributions to low ability, which makes them expect less future improvement from students (Rattan et al., 2012). Previous research has demonstrated that many teachers do in fact have entity views of intelligence (Dweck & Molden, 2005; Reyna, 2000). This entity attribution leads teachers to form fairly stable expectations for students' performance, thereby influencing them to treat students differently (Ormrod, 2011). For instance, when teachers have high expectations for students, they tend to present more challenging tasks, interact with students more frequently, and give more positive and specific feedback. In contrast, when teachers have low expectations for students, they tend to provide easy tasks, offer few opportunities for speaking in class, and give minimal feedback (T. L. Good & Brophy, 1994; Graham, 1990; Rosenthal, 1991). These direct and indirect influences ultimately affect students' self-expectations, motivation, and learning (Bohlmann & Weinstein, 2013).

Previous research has demonstrated that some teachers also underestimate the abilities of students who come from certain ethnic minority groups or low-income families (Tenenbaum & Ruck, 2007; Woolfolk-Hoy, Davis, & Pape, 2006). Specifically, McKown and Weinstein (2008) found that teacher expectations explained more of the year-end achievement gap between stereotyped and nonstereotyped groups in high-bias classrooms than in low-bias classrooms after controlling for prior achievement. Some recent research has also investigated teachers' expectations on a class level, examining the differences between teachers who held high versus low expectations for all of their students, and found large effect size differences in expectancy outcomes between teachers who held high versus low expectations, and positive associations between high-expectancy teachers and students' personal attributes (i.e., attitudes to schoolwork, relationships with others, and home support for school), and contrasting relationships with low-expectancy teachers and students' characteristics (Rubie-Davis, 2006, 2010).

Contextual analyses of expectancy effects have largely focused on the degree of differential treatment by teachers present in classrooms. Most of these studies have measured students' perceptions of their teacher's interactions with high- versus low-achieving students in the 30-item Teacher Treatment Inventory (Weinstein, Marshall, Sharp, & Botkin, 1987), which has demonstrated adequate internal consistency (Weinstein et al., 1987). Some studies have also used adapted versions of St. George's (1983) scale for teachers to rate students' attributes and characteristics. Observational tools to determine differential treatment by teachers have also been used. These require extensive analysis of narrative records, and ultimately yield themes as opposed to more low-inference ratings (Bohlmann & Weinstein, 2013). An example of this approach includes the Classroom Ability-Based Practices scale, which has demonstrated interrater reliability with 86% agreement and a mean kappa of 0.71.

Much past research "prompted" teachers by presenting information and certain expectations for particular students. Students were randomly identified as low or high achievers, and their classification determined teachers' subsequent behaviors and practices, as well as students' perceptions thereof. More recent research has required teachers to rank students in order of their expected achievement and also asked teachers to rate them from 1 (*poor*) to 5 (*outstanding*) for another indication of the level of expectations they held for each students' achievement (Bohlmann & Weinstein, 2013). Although research on teacher expectation has been performed in a variety of ways, a generally consistent finding across research endeavors is the predictive validity of teacher expectations as they adapt to different students (Bohlmann & Weinstein, 2013; Kuklinski & Weinstein, 2001).

Teacher Attributions

In general, an attribution is considered an explanation for a past event (i.e., an event that has already occurred). As related to the educational context, both students and teachers make attributions about the causes for academic successes and failures. Previous research has demonstrated that the attributions teachers make about their own and students' performances influence their own as well as students' emotional reactions and expectations for future performances, as well as their perceptions of self-efficacy. As such, attributions can serve as a mediating variable between teachers' expectations and student motivation and performance (Zhou & Urhahne, 2013).

Teachers typically explain students' academic success and failure by reference to three dimensions: locus (i.e., attributing the causes of an event to factors within themselves or factors outside themselves), stability (i.e., belief that the event was due to things that probably cannot change or things that can change from one time to the next), and controllability (i.e., attributing to events that they or someone else can influence and change, or things over which they have no influence). These three dimensions map onto five different causes that teachers and students use to explain student performance: ability/lack of ability, effort/lack of effort, task easiness/difficulty, and help/lack of help from teachers or parents (Brady & Woolfson, 2008; Graham & Williams, 2009; Ormrod, 2011; Weiner, 1985, 1986, 2004, 2005, 2010; Zhou & Urhahne, 2013). For instance, if a teacher attributes a students' failure to stable factors such as the student lacking the ability to complete a task successfully, the teacher is also likely to have low expectations for the student and, therefore, may not encourage the student to expend more effort or experiment with academic strategies to succeed. If a teacher, on the other hand, attributes a student's failure to lack of effort, he or she is likely to encourage the student to try by expending effort and implementing new strategies.

Current research has confirmed the mediating role of attributions in the relationship between teacher expectations and student performance, as well as the negative effects that teacher negative perceptions have on students' own attributions. Zhou and Urhahne (2013) examined the impact of teacher judgment on students' motivational patterns, and the mediating effect of attributions, and found that students whose teachers had underestimated their performance had maladaptive attribution patterns (i.e., attributed their performance to lack of ability—something internal to them that they cannot change and over which they have no influence).

Recent studies investigating teacher and student attributions and performance have measured teacher attributions using a 5-point Likert-type scale consistent with Weiner's attributions of stability and controllability, with 5 signifying *low stability* (i.e., amenable to change; and low controllability), and adaptations of Clark's (1997) vignettes and Woolfson, Grant, and Campbell's (2007) Teacher Attribution Scale. Internal reliabilities for the Clark (1997) instruments have ranged from .84 to .86 across scales (Woolfson et al., 2007). Previous research has also noted that vignette-based measures, such as adaptations of Clark's (1997) instruments, pose threats to external validity given the effort to provide simple scenarios that might not adequately depict the complexity of classroom dynamics (Brady & Woolfson, 2008). The Teacher Attribution Scale (Woolfson et al., 2007) measures teacher's attributions of locus of causality, controllability, and stability regarding learners who are experiencing difficulties using vignettes. Reliabilities for the three scales (causality, controllability, and stability) have ranged from .86 to .91.

Teacher Goal Orientation

Researchers in recent years have explored the relationship between teachers' goal orientations and associated perceptions, practices, and impacts on student perceptions and behavior. Butler (2007) proposed that achievement goal theory could provide a useful perspective for conceptualizing qualitative differences in teachers' motives for teaching, as had been previously investigated with students' motives for learning. Achievement goal theory assumes that students' perceptions, strategies, and outcomes depend on their constructed goals for their schoolwork, and thereby on what they want to achieve (Butler, 2007; Butler & Shibaz, 2008; Retelsdorf, Butler, Streblow, & Schiefele, 2010).

A preponderance of research supports the fact that when students have a mastery goal orientation, they tend to have higher efficacy, be intrinsically motivated, attribute outcomes to effort, view setbacks as opportunities for improvement, and implement strategies that facilitate mastery of learning materials. In contrast, when students are performance oriented they tend to be focused toward outperforming other students, be oriented toward grades (i.e., extrinsically motivated), favor ability attributions, view difficulty as diagnostic of low ability, experience more academically related anxiety, and engage in strategies that facilitate rote memorization as opposed to meaningful learning (Butler, 2000; Elliot, 2005; Molden & Dweck, 2000).

As teacher goal orientation is a relatively new addition to the field, there are very few established measures for the construct. Also, a vast body of research regarding the impact on teacher and student outcomes does not exist. However, similar to research examining student goal orientations, research examining teachers' goal orientation has demonstrated that teacher mastery goals are associated with higher levels of perceived teacher support and positive perceptions of instructional practices, whereas ability avoidance goals are associated with student reports of negative instructional practices and student cheating (Butler & Shibaz, 2008). With respect to teacher outcomes, Retelsdorf et al. (2010) found that teacher mastery orientation and work avoidance emerged as positive and negative predictors, respectively, of adaptive patterns of instruction and high interest in teaching and low burnout.

With respect to measurement, Midgley et al. (2000) developed a self-report measure for teachers' mastery- and performance-oriented practices. This measure has been questioned for not including all of the facets of the goal orientation construct. Butler (2007) developed the Goal Orientation for Teaching Scale where teachers rate their agreement with statements such as "I would feel that I had a successful day in school if something that happened in class made me want to learn more about teaching." Internal consistencies for this measure have ranged from .71 to .82 (Butler, 2007; Butler & Shibaz, 2008; Retelsdorf et al., 2010). Recent research has also examined and affirmed the structural validity of teacher goal orientation into mastery and performance goal orientations (Butler, 2007; Malmberg, Wanner, Nordmyr, & Little, 2004).

TEACHER INTRAPERSONAL SKILLS

Teachers' intrapersonal skills are the personal behaviors and internal thought processes that can be systematically acquired or enhanced by instruction or learning experiences and where evidence of change can be directly or indirectly inferred (E. L.

Baker, 2014). Teachers' intrapersonal competencies fall within two categories: those related to emotional capacities and those related to metacognitive capacities and self-regulation.

Emotional Capacities

There is a substantial and growing body of research on the importance of fostering students' social and emotional competencies because of its consequences for academic success and impact on lifelong learning (Zins, Bloodworth, Weissberg, & Walberg, 2007). However, less attention has been paid to understanding and supporting teachers' own social and emotional skills. This is surprising given that teachers' emotional processes (e.g., emotion regulation, ability to take the perspective and empathize with others from diverse backgrounds) and social/interpersonal skills (e.g., interacting positively with students, parents, and colleagues) are likely to influence their students' social, emotional, and academic well-being, as well as students' development of interpersonal competencies, which are a key component of 21st-century skills and the deeper learning competencies (Jennings & Greenberg, 2009).

Jennings and Greenberg (2009) proposed a prosocial classroom mediational model, which essentially highlights the importance of teachers' social and emotional competence and well-being in supporting teacher-student relationships, effective classroom management, successful social and emotional learning program implementation, and preventing teacher burnout (Appendix B). Essentially, the model explains how deficits in teacher social and emotional competence and well-being provoke what the authors refer to as a "burnout cascade," which contributes to a deteriorating classroom climate with increased troublesome student behaviors. Teachers drain emotionally in attempting to manage these types of classrooms, resorting to reactive and punitive responses that in turn do not teach self-regulation and may contribute to a self-sustaining cycle of classroom disruption (Jennings & Greenberg, 2009). In contrast, teachers who recognize students' emotions and the underlying causes of students' behaviors may also show greater concern and empathy for students and be better able to help students learn to self-regulate, thereby contributing to a positive classroom climate.

One aspect of teachers' emotional processes that has received some attention is the construct of emotional intelligence (EI). EI refers to one's ability to identify, process, and regulate emotions (Mayer, Salovey, Caruso, & Sitarenios, 2001), and is positively associated with teacher efficacy (Penrose, Perry, & Ball, 2007) and lower rates of teacher burnout (Chan, 2006).

There has been some debate over appropriate measures for assessing EI. One of the main issues is the difference between ability (i.e., performance) versus self-report measures. Brackett and Mayer (2003) examined the convergent, discriminant, and incremental validities of one widely used EI ability test measure (i.e., Mayer-Salovey-Caruso Emotional Intelligence Test [MSCEIT]) and two self-report EI measures (i.e., Emotional Quotient Inventory [EQ-I] and Self-Report EI Test [SREIT]).

The MSCEIT (Mayer, Salovey, & Caruso, 2002) has right or wrong answers based on consensus or expert scoring (Brackett & Mayer, 2003). For example, emotion perception is assessed by having individuals rate how much of a particular emotion is being expressed in faces, and emotion management is measured by asking people to select effective ways to manage emotions in hypothetical situations. In contrast, the EQ-I (Bar-On, 1997) and SREIT (Schutte et al., 1998) combine mental abilities (e.g., ability to perceive emotion) and self-reported characteristics such as optimism, and are thus considered to be "mixed models" (Brackett & Mayer, 2003, p. 1147).

In light of these differences, Brackett and Mayer (2003) found that whereas the EQ-I and SREIT self-report measures were moderately related, the MSCEIT ability measure was weakly related to the self-report measures. Furthermore, the MSCEIT proved to be distinct from the Big Five Personality Inventory. There was, however, considerable shared variance between the self-report measures and the Big Five Personality Inventory, indicating that the EI ability and self-report measures appear to assess different skills and qualities, producing different measurements for the same individual. Recent work has focused on teaching teachers and students to recognize emotion in video games and other computer environments (Griffin & Madni, 2013; Madni, Griffin, & Delacruz, 2013).

Metacognition and Self-Regulation

One prevalent model that explains metacognitive and self-regulatory processes is Zimmerman's (2008) model of self-regulation (Appendix C). This model posits that the self-regulation process contains three separate phases with corresponding cognitive processes, actions, and motivational beliefs. The first phase is the forethought phase where individuals set goals and create strategic plans for goal attainment. This phase is influenced by motivational factors such as self-efficacy, outcome expectations, task interest/value, and goal orientation. For instance, an individual is likely to set more challenging goals and be more creative with the strategies for goal attainment when he or she has higher efficacy associated with the goal being set. The second phase of Zimmerman's (2008) self-regulation process is the performance phase.

The performance phase involves individuals exhibiting self-control and self-observation as they are working toward attaining their goal. Self-control involves cognitive processes and actions such as self-instruction, engaging in learning strategies such as imagery, attention focusing, and selecting and implementing appropriate task strategies to complete target tasks. The last phase of Zimmerman's (2008) model is the self-reflection phase, which involves self-judgment and self-reaction. Self-judgment involves individuals self-evaluating their process toward goal attainment and the outcome, as well as making attributions (i.e., coming up with explanations) for goal attainment or lack thereof. For instance, if an individual attributes his or her lack of goal attainment to insufficient task strategies, then he or she is likely to adjust the strategic plan for goal attainment. Self-reaction involves how individuals feel about their outcome and process and whether they have an adaptive as opposed to a defensive reaction.

SOCIAL AND INTERPERSONAL SKILLS

Social and interpersonal skills require cognition and metacognition; however, they are applied in interpersonal situations, such as when teachers are collaborating with other teachers, when teachers are working and communicating with students, and last, when teachers are communicating and working with parents. These skills and processes do not require an extraverted personality but instead require concrete abilities to clarify goals, modify behavior, and adapt to situations and people (E. L. Baker, 2014).

Collaboration and Teamwork

Teachers' interpersonal competencies associated with student academic achievement depend in part on teachers' ability to collaborate effectively and successfully with each other. Teacher collaboration is thought to provide opportunities for teacher learning in which individuals engage in professional discourse and further develop their content, pedagogical, and experiential knowledge to improve instruction (Y. L. Goddard, Goddard, & Tschannen-Moran, 2007), thereby enhancing student outcomes.

Teacher collaboration has been studied and assessed using qualitative case study methods (e.g., Levine & Marcus, 2007), survey methods (Y. L. Goddard et al., 2007), and social network analysis (Moolenaar, 2012). Y. L. Goddard et al. (2007) conducted a large-scale naturalistic study using survey methods to test the relationship between teacher collaboration for school improvement and student achievement. They used a 6-point Likert-type scale that asked teachers to rate on a scale of 1 (*not at all*) to 6 (*very much*) "To what extent do teachers work collectively to influence these types of decisions?—planning school improvement, selecting instructional methods and activities, evaluating curriculum and programs, determining professional development needs and goals, and planning professional development activities." All items loaded onto a single factor using principal axis factor analysis and showed strong internal consistency. The authors conceptualized the level of teacher collaboration as an important aspect of a school's normative and behavioral environment. Therefore, individual teacher collaboration data were then aggregated to the school level. Results showed that even after controlling for children's academic and social background characteristics and school context, fourth-grade students in a large urban school district had higher achievement in mathematics and reading when they attended schools characterized by higher levels of teacher collaboration for school improvement. In evaluation of schools, models involving social capital have been used, and a prominent part of these is teachers' perception of their collaborative effort (Huang et al., 2007; Lee, 2010).

A social network analysis approach focuses on the pattern of social relationships among teachers, captures the multilevel nature of teacher collaboration (e.g., teachers in schools), and provides a visual representation of teacher interactions (Moolenaar, 2012). Social network analysts typically examine issues of centrality (e.g., total number of relationships a teacher maintains) and ego reciprocity (to capture the two-way nature of relationships; Moolenaar, 2012). Examples of the types of questions asked of respondents when conducting social network analysis have included the following: "During this school year, to whom in your school have you turned for advice on strategies to assist low-performing students ?" (Cole & Weiss, 2009), "To whom have you turned to for advice or information about math teaching strategies and content?" (Pitts & Spillane, 2009), "Whom do you go to for work-related advice?" and "Whom do you go to for guidance on more personal matters?" (Moolenaar, Sleegers, & Daly, 2012). Moolenaar et al. (2012) found that well-connected teacher networks were associated with strong teacher collective efficacy, which in turn supported student achievement. Thus, there is some evidence that the construct of collective efficacy may help explain the relationship between teacher collaboration and student achievement outcomes.

Collective Efficacy

Collective efficacy refers to teachers' beliefs at a school that the entire faculty as a whole is capable of organizing and executing the necessary actions to have a positive impact on its students (R. D. Goddard, Hoy, & Hoy, 2004). Collective efficacy depends on the interaction of perceived competence to perform a given task and the context in which the task will take place. With regard to teacher collective efficacy, these two components have been conceptualized in terms of group competence and task analysis (R. Goddard, 2002). Group competence refers to the capabilities the faculty brings to a teaching situation (e.g., teaching methods, skills, training, expertise), whereas task analysis refers to perceptions of constraints and opportunities due to the nature of the task (e.g., level of support provided by students' home and the community; R. Goddard, 2002). A strong sense of collective teacher efficacy enhances individual teacher's sense of efficacy and has been linked to student academic achievement (R. D. Goddard et al., 2004; Tschannen-Moran & Barr, 2004). Teachers' collective efficacy beliefs are an important construct of interest because it can be affected by educational leadership efforts to foster strong teacher relationships (Moolenaar, Daly, & Sleegers, 2011).

There are various approaches to measuring collective efficacy. One approach is to aggregate individual teacher's self-efficacy beliefs (e.g., "I have what it takes to get my students to learn") to develop a group mean of self-efficacy perceptions at a school. Another approach is to ask teachers to discuss questions as a group and arrive at a group consensus of how they view their collective efficacy. However, this method may suffer from social desirability issues affecting the validity of the assessment and may also hide the variability that exists within a group (Bandura, 1997).

A method that is more widely endorsed by researchers (R. D. Goddard et al., 2004) is to aggregate measures of individual teacher's perceptions of the group's capability by responding to statements such as "Teachers in this school have what it takes to educate students here" (p. 6). This approach aligns more closely with Bandura's (1997) stance that the collective efficacy is an "emergent organizational property" (R. D. Goddard et al., 2004, p. 7) that reflects the perceptions of teachers about a school's conjoint capability to successfully influence students (R. Goddard, 2002). Thus, the assessment of collective efficacy necessitates the combination of individual-level perceptual measures, which can be achieved through group-level (i.e., school-level) aggregates. Furthermore, R. D. Goddard (2001) showed that within-school variabilities among teachers' reports of collective efficacy were not predictive of student achievement differences between schools but rather that the use of a central tendency measure (i.e., school-level aggregates of teacher collective efficacy) was a better predictor. R. D. Goddard, Hoy, and Hoy (2000) developed a 21-item Collective Efficacy Scale, which R. Goddard (2002) later modified to develop a short form using only 12 of the original items. This abbreviated measure is more theoretically pure and parsimonious and is highly correlated with the original longer scale ($r = .983$). Furthermore, the short form has high internal consistency based on Cronbach's alpha and demonstrated predictive validity using multilevel modeling (R. Goddard, 2002). Modern practical models of school and other institutional evaluation use collective effort, efficacy, and transparency and trust as key attributes to be studied (Cai, Baker, Choi, & Buschang, 2014; Huang et al., 2007).

Collaborating With Students

High quality teacher-child relationships provide students with a supportive and emotionally secure environment. Students are better able to regulate their emotions, interact with others, and focus on academics (Pianta, 1999). Furthermore, teacher-student relationships are associated with school satisfaction, engagement, and academic and behavioral outcomes (J. A. Baker, 2006, Elias & Haynes, 2008; Hamre & Pianta, 2001; Maldonado-Carreño & Votruba-Drzal, 2011; Murray, 2009).

Methods to assess teacher-student relationships are often tied to a particular perspective (e.g., attachment, motivation, sociocultural; Davis, 2003). For example, researchers from a sociocultural perspective view relationships as "dynamic, changing, and culturally bound" (p. 225) and tend to employ qualitative methodologies such as case studies and ethnography, conducting in-depth interviews and holistic observations (Davis, 2003). In contrast, those who work within attachment theory use observational methods, checklists, and teacher-rating scales to evaluate the quality of relationships according to theoretically defined dimensions and social developmental outcomes. Clearly choice of method depends substantially on the age of the student.

Furthermore, motivation researchers are inclined to use student report for older students (e.g., Network of Relationships Inventory; Furman & Buhrmester, 1985) and teacher self-report instruments (e.g., Student-Teacher Relationship Scale; Pianta & Steinberg, 1992) to evaluate relationships based on their own set of dimensions believed to shape cognitive and academic outcomes because they view relationships as embedded in complex classroom contexts (Davis, 2003).

Collaborating With Parents

Although there is a considerable body of work on teacher-student relationships, less is known about teachers' relationships with parents. Researchers have studied the benefits of parental involvement and engagement for student educational outcomes (Fan & Chen, 2001; Minke, Sheridan, Kim, Ryoo, & Koziol, 2014; Murray, 2009), yet less is known about affective quality of parent-teacher interactions. Some qualitative studies (Angelides, Theophanous, & Leigh, 2006; Bruckman & Blanton, 2003; Miretzky, 2004) and case studies (Billman, Geddes, & Hedges, 2005) assess teachers' relationships with parents through observations, interviews, and focus groups. Such studies often highlight the challenges of developing positive relationships and true collaboration between teachers and parents, perhaps because they involve complex status relationships. Some research has implemented quantitative analyses of teacher self-report and parent self-report measures (Hughes & Kwok, 2007; Nzinga-Johnson, Baker, & Aupperlee, 2009). In studies by Herman and Baker (2003), structural models were used to document that synchronicity of teacher and parent goals influenced student performance on standardized and other content measures, although results were mediated by other factors such as attendance (Herman & Baker, 2003; Quigley, 2000).

Minke et al. (2014) findings substantiated that congruence between teachers and parents was an important factor in understanding reports of child behavior. With a more extensive set of measures, agreement on ways to support and influence positive student outcomes had effects (Minke et al., 2014). As part of this study, teachers and parents completed the Parent-Teacher Relationship Scale (Vickers & Minke, 1995), which contains two subscales and is rated on a 5-point Likert-type scale. The Joining subscale assesses the interpersonal connection between parents and teachers (e.g., "We understand each other"). The Communication-to-Other subscale evaluates the communication quality between parents and teachers (e.g., "I tell this parent/teacher when I am pleased"). The internal consistency reliabilities of this scale range from .93 to .95. These efforts to assess reliability are important because of the reputation of "softer" constructs such as collaboration that have a wide variety of definitions and hence interpretations.

Similarly, Murray (2009) examined the relationship between teacher-parent relationships and urban youth engagement and functioning. The researchers implemented the Research Assessment Package for Schools (RAPS; Connell & Wellborn, 1991), and adapted it for both parents and teachers. The RAPS is an 84-item Likert-type measure that can be used to assess student school engagement, student self-beliefs, and student perceptions of interpersonal support. Example items include "My parents are fair with me," "My teachers think what I say is important," and "My teachers don't seem to have enough time for me." The alpha reliabilities for the RAPS ranged from .65 to .84. No validity data were reported.

Taken together, the preceding findings on teacher-parent relationships suggest that these relationships predict parental involvement (Nzinga-Johnson et al., 2009) and children's engagement, motivation, functioning, and performance in school (Hughes, Luo, Kwok, & Loyd, 2008; Minke et al., 2014; Murray, 2009).

Diversity and Acceptance

Underlying teachers' ability to collaborate effectively with each other, parents, and students are their beliefs and perceptions related to diversity and acceptance. These beliefs are also of particular importance to English language learners, their teachers, and their parents. Teachers' beliefs and ability to engage in perspective taking, especially when working with diverse students and/or students from different backgrounds, are imperative given their association with how teachers interact and respond to students (Pajares, 1992). Children who are at risk of school failure (e.g., low socioeconomic status) are most affected by the quality of their relationships with teachers (Hamre & Pianta, 2001); yet marginalized students and their parents may also experience less supportive relationships with teachers (e.g., Hughes & Kwok, 2007). Part of this relationship may depend on parents' experiences with schools as students or their beliefs about institutional authority.

Teachers, however, bear strong responsibility to make these relationships work. Several existing measures in use to assess teachers' beliefs about diversity lack technical information about reliability and validity (see Brown, 2004, for review; Pohan & Aguilar, 2001). However, Brown (2004) discusses two measures that are psychometrically sound. One is the Cultural and Educational Issues Survey (CEIS; Pettus & Allain, 1999), which assesses how individuals and groups feel about social and cultural issues that have consequences for how teachers make decisions about educational services in society. The CEIS contains four demographic items and 59 opinion statements graded on a 5-point Likert-type scale. Although the scale is considered a viable instrument, it has not been widely implemented or tested.

The CEIS contains both positively and negatively worded statements. Example positively worded items include "Teachers should draw on students' experiences, cultures, and languages to make learning relevant and interesting for the students" and "A teacher should openly express dissatisfaction with a colleague who makes disparaging comments about a student's sexual orientation." Examples of negatively worded statements include "Compared to other problems, sexism is not a significant problem in the schools in the United States," and "Generally, different racial groups have different abilities to learn different school subjects and activities."

The other measure of presumed quality is the Personal and Professional Beliefs About Diversity Scale (Pohan & Aguilar, 2001), which addresses a spectrum of diversity issues including race and ethnicity, social class, gender, religion, language, and sexual orientation. This scale was specifically designed to assess varying levels of openness to a wide range of diversity topics and issues. It is a two-part open-ended survey and therefore provides the opportunity for assessment to vary widely (see Pohan & Aguilar, 2001). Example items include "There is nothing wrong with people from different racial backgrounds having/raising children," "Making all public facilities accessible to the disabled is simply too costly," "Teachers should not be expected to adjust their preferred mode of instruction to accommodate the needs of all students," and "Students and teachers would benefit from having a basic understanding of different (diverse) religions."

PSYCHOMETRIC PROPERTIES OF MEASURES

In discussing measurement of teachers' social psychological constructs, it is essential to also address the importance of technical quality as it pertains to validity. Validity has been reconceptualized over the years to focus not on the quantitative properties of the measure but on the quality of the inferences that can be drawn from results of the measures in light of their purposes. (Cai et al., 2014; Messick, 1995; O'Neil et al., 2014). This definition broadens the application of validity to measures that are not strictly psychometric in nature. The use of construct validity and quality of evidence and inference related to the purposes for which the results will be used permits the integration of alternative methods into the validity paradigm, heretofore seen as the province of quantitatively oriented analyses. Even so, there remain a number of challenges for the measurement of social, psychological, and emotional factors. For research purposes, there is always a need to vet new or replicate prior measures to determine their consistency and validity. These approaches can include refining and establishing validity of scoring approaches used for observation; the transformations of raw data into item response theory or other scales, for more precise interpretation; and clarification of contextual variables likely to influence process and outcome measures. For example, teachers' motivation or attribution behavior may be observed in a short period of time, whereas the student outcome measure, particularly of an end-of-year standardized test, is unlikely to be sensitive to relatively short or variable interventions. Second, triangulating on various instruments (current validity in the 20th century) requires careful vetting of each of the measures assumed to corroborate validity. As in practical use, research studies need to relate the inferences they draw about constructs to the purposes they explicitly describe in their hypotheses. Is the interest in the change of self-perception over time? Is the interest in the ability to translate their attributions into positive support for students? These two different questions would depend on different data to obtain valid inferences, even if the same measures were used. In reviewing the literature it seems clear that the emphasis is on reliability, such as alpha coefficients and between-rater kappa, rather than extending inferences to the purposes for which the constructs are intended to be used—in other words, their validity.

The problems of reliability come into play in the use of such measures to make decisions about people. Minimally, one would want some consistency over a short time period, as measuring traits, or "types," of personality or temperament would unlikely meet standards associated with employment law. When teacher processes are judged, such as their adaptive behavior based on student attributions, it would be important to have good measures of alternative evidence of such adaptation as well as evidence that the adaptations work as intended—that is, aligned with their purposes. Our review suggests that far more evidence is required for all elements in a validity argument, including measures of social or emotional perspective, the enacted teaching behaviors, students' process responses, and the relevance and quality of outcome measures. To date, very few investigators have taken on this stream of evidence. Our suggestion rides not on a desire for comprehensiveness but on the imperative to marshal strong arguments if the measures are intended for high-stakes use. High stakes in this regard means not only typical accountability sanctions but the consequences to the respondent of the data and decision.

In the past 10 years, a new line of research has been undertaken by researchers intending to use these and other psychological constructs for support, advice, or therapeutic recommendations. Technology, as it has expanded, has an array of tools that can be combined to draw inferences about psychological states. These approaches may involve the use of cameras, gestural sensors, electroencephalography caps to read simple neurological states, and inferences from motion patterns during an extended period. In addition, there are voice analyses used to infer anxiety or disturbance from pitch, pauses, and repetitive word choice. Some of these methods are used with everyday activities, such as the use of smart phones, whereas others rely on structured interactions and where respondent answers are analyzed for voice and text features (Rizzo et al., 2013; Stripling, 2012; Stripling, Lee, & Cohn, 2014). Whether such approaches will become, or are already, routine by web providers raises the questions of informed consent, confidentiality, and privacy. All three of these issues are highly pertinent to affective behaviors, especially when inferences will be made about individuals. Nonetheless, the benefit of these approaches is that computers, well debugged and programmed, are reliable collectors of data. The focus then shifts to validity, in particular, the evidence as collected, its use, and the inferences drawn from it. This area will be a strong domain for research, particularly in the light of wearable computing, sending signals, whether desired or not, to developers and instigating web sites.

CONCLUSIONS AND IMPLICATIONS

In this chapter, we reviewed research on teachers' social and motivational behavior. Our interest was in drawing research attention to those factors that (1) can be shaped by appropriate interventions, (2) influence teacher instructional practices, and (3) predict student motivational and performance outcomes needed in the 21st century. Our research based on our review clearly suggests two overarching categories under which the research falls: teacher motivational constructs, and teacher intrapersonal and interpersonal competencies. We have also discussed limitations of measures throughout and in a final segment of the chapter.

Discussion Related to Measures of Teacher Social Psychological Constructs

Within the area of teacher social psychological constructs, it is apparent that a majority of the research data flow from variations of self-report questionnaires, including Likert-type scales. In some cases self-reports involve parents and student report measures as well. These may be based on stimulus statements, scenarios, or vignettes related to teacher attributions; teacher efficacy; collaboration; support; and teacher expectations. Self-report teacher measures of teacher expectations have also been measured through student reports about teacher treatment, through observational tools, by "prompting" teachers with preestablished expectations, or having teachers rank students in order of expected achievement. Further refinement of the construct of teacher expectations would be useful to create more replicable and consistent measurements of the construct.

Our chapter also revealed mixed findings across constructs with respect to factorial and construct validities, and reliability. The measures of teachers' implicit theories of intelligence and teacher attributions have demonstrated appropriate psychometric properties. After a "troublesome" measurement history, it appears that a measure of teacher efficacy with stronger factorial and construct validities, and reliability has emerged (i.e., the OSTES; Tschannen-Moran & Hoy, 2001). The OSTES is nascent in the field and, therefore, needs further testing and refinement. Emerging from the field more recently is the construct of teacher goal orientation (Butler, 2007). This construct is demonstrating promise with respect to psychometric properties and influencing both teacher practice and student outcomes. However, the Midgley et al. (2000) measure has been critiqued for not including all facets of the construct. Further exploration and refinement of this construct would be a positive addition to the field of teacher motivation.

The teacher motivation constructs reviewed as part of this study also demonstrated predictive effects on salient and valued teacher perceptions and practices as well as student motivation and performance. This finding indicates that continued focus on exploring and enhancing measurement of these constructs, as part of early teacher education programs as well as later teacher training opportunities and program development, is warranted. Further refinement of these constructs would also aid in differentiating the constructs studied from each other, and in enhancing already-established models and producing new models of their interrelationships.

Technical Quality Summary and Recommendations

This chapter also determined that information related to reliability and validity information across teacher motivation constructs and measures is not consistently available in the literature. Thus, it is imperative that validation type studies are performed using measures in the anticipated structural model linking internal states to behaviors and then to desired student processes and outcomes

Measurement Related to Intrapersonal and Interpersonal Competencies

In contrast to the intrapersonal competencies, it appears that interpersonal teacher competencies have more variation with respect to different forms of measurement and research methodologies including self-report survey methods, case studies, ethnographies, in-depth interviews, holistic observations, and social network analysis. In addition, intrapersonal competencies demonstrate mixed findings with respect to the psychometric properties of certain measures. The measures of EI appear to assess different skills and qualities, producing inconsistent results. Measures for collective efficacy, on the other hand, have demonstrated high correlations across scales and high internal consistency and predictive validity. Collective efficacy may also serve as a moderating variable to explain the influence of teacher collaboration on student achievement outcomes. Teacher collaboration has been measured using survey methods and social network analysis with relevant measures producing internally consistent results, and has been found to influence higher math and reading achievement in students. Further using social network analysis to characterize what specific aspects of teacher collaboration result in positive student outcomes would provide a significant contribution to research within this area.

As evidenced by the current review, methods implemented to assess teacher-child relationships tend to be tied to a particular learning or psychological perspective and, therefore, span various qualitative and quantitative methods including ethnographies, in-depth interviews, observations, checklists, teacher rating scales, and student and teacher self-report measures. In contrast, there is minimal research and measurement history about teacher's relationships with parents. However, findings in the area indicate that teacher-parent relationships are key to parent involvement. Given these sets of results, in future studies refining measures are needed to further determine the specific facets of teacher-parent relationships that contribute to positive student outcomes. In contrast to the research on teacher-parent relationships, research on teachers' beliefs about diversity has used several measures, but some reflect only minimal reliability and validity information. As such, it would be pertinent for future scholars to perform studies evaluating and validating these measures. Such studies will be increasingly pertinent in the practical world as the demography of teachers, parents, and students changes.

Further recommendations for future studies include combining various forms of measurement to produce more robust results, thereby further solidifying constructs. Performance type assessments to determine teacher's actual level and skill with respect to relevant constructs, such as collaboration and interpersonal engagement, could aid in refining the aspects of these processes that are salient in key predictive relationships. Moreover, focusing on defining and capturing behavioral indicators of instructional practices associated with internal non-cognitive factors, such as teacher efficacy, teacher attributions, and teacher expectations, can contribute to development of new measurements for robust triangulation, assuming concurrent measures also have strong evidence. Computational modeling of such behavioral indicators can also aid in composing and refining these types of constructs.

LIMITATIONS

In conclusion, we note that certain limitations in our study influence the findings presented. First, given the span of constructs, the chapter is not exhaustive relative to each construct. This is a practical constraint. Nevertheless, we strongly believe that our careful sampling of articles for this chapter adequately portrays the state of the field. Future reviewers are encouraged to consider searching non-English journals and graduate theses and dissertations to uncover novel patterns, themes, or new avenues within the field. Since our focus was on the measurement of key noncognitive teacher factors, a detailed exploration of the strengths of relationships among the noncognitive factors and a variety of teacher and student outcomes was beyond the scope of our chapter. Consequently, we chose to focus primarily on outcomes related to teacher practice and pedagogy, and student motivation and achievement.

APPENDIX A
Expectancy-Value Model

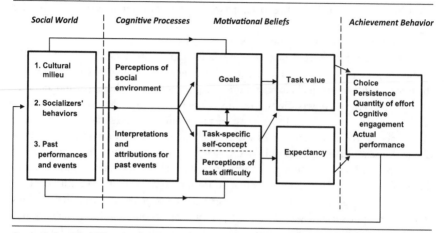

Source. Eccles, Wigfield, and colleagues' expectancy-value model of achievement motivation is described in Eccles (1984), Eccles et al. (1983), Wigfield (1999), and Wigfield and Eccles (1992). This version is redrawn from Wigfield and Eccles (2000). Used with permission.

APPENDIX B
Prosocial Classroom Mediational Model

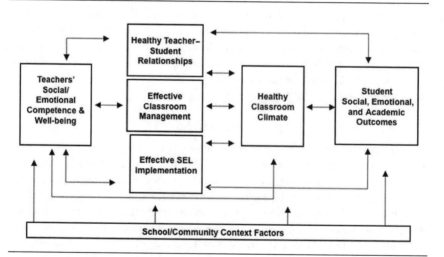

Source. Reprinted with permission from Jennings and Greenberg (2008).

APPENDIX C
Self-Regulation Model

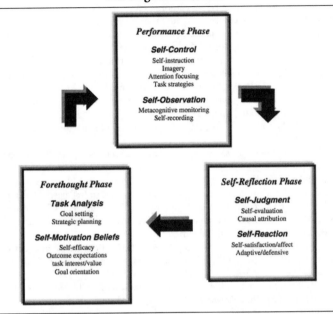

Source. Adapted from "Motivating Self-Regulated Problem Solvers" by B. J. Zimmerman and M. Campillo (2003), in J. E. Davidson and R. J. Sternberg (Eds.), *The Nature of Problem Solving.* New York: Cambridge University Press. Previously presented in this format in Zimmerman (2008). Reprinted with permission.

NOTE

The work reported herein was supported under the DARPA ENGAGE Program, N00014-12-C-0090, with funding to the National Center for Research on Evaluation, Standards, and Student Testing (CRESST). The findings and opinions expressed here do not necessarily reflect the positions or policies of the Defense Advanced Research Projects Agency, the Office of Naval Research, or the U.S. Department of Defense.

[1]We searched PsychINFO, Google Scholar, and ERIC using the following descriptors and keywords: Big Five Personality, teacher motivation, teacher beliefs, teacher EI, teacher social and emotional learning, teacher social competence, teacher empathy, teacher efficacy, teacher attributions, teacher goal orientation, teacher interest, teacher expectations, teacher interpersonal skills, teacher intrapersonal skills, teacher collaboration, collective efficacy, teacher and student relationships, parental involvement, teacher and parent relationships, teacher perceptions and diversity, and teacher perceptions and diverse students.

REFERENCES

Angelides, P., Theophanous, L., & Leigh, J. (2006). Understanding teacher–parent relationships for improving pre-primary schools in Cyprus. *Educational Review, 58,* 303–316.

Ashton, P. T., Buhr, D., & Crocker, L. (1984). Teachers' sense of efficacy: A self- or norm-referenced construct? *Florida Journal of Educational Research, 26,* 29–41.

Ashton, P. T., Oljenik, S., Crocker, L., & McAuliffe, M. (1982, April). *Measurement problems in the study of teachers' sense of efficacy.* Paper presented at the annual meeting of the American Educational Research Association, New York, NY.

Baker, E. L. (2014). Learning and assessment: Twenty-first century skills and cognitive readiness. In H. F. O' Neil, R. S. Perez, & E. L. Baker (Eds.), *Teaching and measuring cognitive readiness* (pp. 53–70). New York, NY: Springer Science+Business Media.

Baker, E. L., Barton, P. E., Darling-Hammond, L., Haertel, E., Ladd, H. F., Linn, R. L., . . . Shepard, L. A. (2010). *Problems with the use of student test scores to evaluate teachers* (EPI Briefing Paper No. 278). Washington, DC: Economic Policy Institute.

Baker, J. A. (2006). Contributions of teacher–child relationships to positive school adjustment during elementary school. *Journal of School Psychology, 44,* 211–229.

Bandura, A. (1977). Self-efficacy: Toward a unifying theory of behavioral change. *Psychological Review, 84,* 191–215.

Bandura, A. (1986). *Social foundations of thought and action* (pp. 5–107). Englewood Cliffs, NJ: Prentice Hall.

Bandura, A. (1997). *Self-efficacy: The exercise of control.* New York, NY: Freeman.

Bandura, A. (2006). Guide for constructing self-efficacy scales. In F. Pajares & T. Urdan (Eds.), *Self-efficacy beliefs of adolescents* (Vol. 5, pp. 307–337). Greenwich, CT: Information Age.

Bar-On, R. (1997). *The Emotional Quotient Inventory (EQ-i): Technical manual.* Toronto, Ontario, Canada: Multi-Health Systems.

Barrick, M. R., Mount, M. K., & Judge, T. A. (2001). Personality and performance at the beginning of the new millennium: What do we know and where do we go next? *International Journal of Selection and Assessment, 9,* 9–30.

Betoret, F. D. (2006). Stressors, self-efficacy, coping resources, and burnout among secondary school teachers in Spain. *Educational Psychology, 26,* 519–539.

Billman, N., Geddes, C., & Hedges, H. (2005). Teacher-parent partnerships: Sharing understandings and making changes. *Australian Journal of Early Childhood, 30,* 44–48.

Bohlmann, N. L., & Weinstein, R. S. (2013). Classroom context, teacher expectations, and cognitive level: Predicting children's math ability judgments. *Journal of Applied Developmental Psychology, 34,* 288–298.

Brackett, M. A., & Mayer, J. D. (2003). Convergent, discriminant, and incremental validity of competing measures of emotional intelligence. *Personality and Social Psychology Bulletin, 29,* 1147–1158.

Brady, K., & Woolfson, L. (2008). What teacher factors influence their attributions for children's difficulties in learning? *British Journal of Educational Psychology, 78,* 527–544.

Brown, K. M. (2004). Assessing preservice leaders' beliefs, attitudes, and values regarding issues of diversity, social justice, and equity: A review of existing measures. *Equity & Excellence in Education, 37,* 332–342.

Bruckman, M., & Blanton, P. W. (2003). Welfare-to-work single mothers' perspectives on parent involvement in head start: Implications for parent–teacher collaboration. *Early Childhood Education Journal, 30,* 145–150.

Butler, R. (2000). What learners want to know: The role of achievement goal orientations and associations with teachers' help-seeking: Examination of a novel approach to teacher motivation. *Journal of Educational Psychology, 99,* 241–252.

Butler, R. (2007). Teachers' achievement goal orientations and associations with teachers' help seeking: Examination of a novel approach to teacher motivation. *Journal of Educational Psychology, 99,* 241–252.

Butler, R., & Shibaz, L. (2008). Achievement goals for teaching as predictors of students' perceptions of instructional practices and students' help seeking and cheating. *Learning and Instruction, 18,* 453–467.

Cai, L., Baker, E., Choi, K., & Buschang, R. (2014, April). *CRESST functional validity model: Deriving formative and summative information from common core assessments.* Paper presented at the annual meeting of the American Educational Research Association, Symposium 46.010 "Innovative Validity Approaches for High-Quality Assessments: An Interaction," Philadelphia, PA.

Chan, D. W. (2006). Emotional intelligence and components of burnout among Chinese secondary school teachers in Hong Kong. *Teaching and Teacher Education, 22,* 1042–1054.

Clark, M. D. (1997). Teacher response to learning disability. A test of attributional principles. *Journal of Learning Disabilities, 30,* 69–79.

Coladarci, T., & Breton, W. A. (1997). Teacher efficacy, supervision, and the special education resource-room teacher. *Journal of Educational Research, 90,* 230–239.

Cole, R., & Weiss, M. (2009). Identifying organizational influentials: Methods and application using social network data. *Connections, 29*(2), 45–61.

Connell, J. P., & Wellborn, J. G. (1991). Competence, autonomy and relatedness: A motivational analysis of self-system processes. In M. Gunnar & L. A. Sroufe (Eds.), *Minnesota Symposium on Child Psychology: Vol. 23. Self processes in development* (pp. 43–77). Chicago, IL: University of Chicago Press.

Constantine, M. G., & Ladany, N. (2000). Self-report multicultural counseling competence scales: Their relation to social desirability attitudes and multicultural case conceptualization ability. *Journal of Counseling Psychology, 47,* 155–164.

Costa, P. T., & McCrae, R. R. (1992). *Revised NEO Personality Inventory (NEO PI-R) and NEO Five-Factor Inventory (NEO-FFI).* Odessa, FL: Psychological Assessment Resources.

Davis, H. A. (2003). Conceptualizing the role and influence of student-teacher relationships on children's social and cognitive development. *Educational Psychologist, 38,* 207–234.

de Jesus, S. N., & Lens, W. (2005). An integrated model for the study of teacher motivation. *Applied Psychology, 54,* 119–134.

Dijksterhuis, A., & Nordgren, L. F. (2006). A theory of unconscious thought. *Psychological Science, 1,* 95–109.

Dweck, C. S. (1999). *Self-theories: Their role in motivation, personality and development.* Philadelphia, PA: Taylor & Francis/Psychology Press.

Dweck, C. S. (2007). The perils and promises of praise. *Educational Leadership, 65*(2), 34–39.

Dweck, C. S., Chiu, C. Y., & Hong, Y. Y. (1995). Implicit theories and their role in judgments and reactions: A word from two perspectives. *Psychological Inquiry, 6,* 267–285.

Dweck, C. S., & Molden, D. C. (2005). Self-theories: Their impact on competence motivation and acquisition. In A. Elliot & C. S. Dweck (Eds.), The handbook of competence and motivation (pp. 122–140). New York, NY: Guilford.

Elias, M. J., & Haynes, N. M. (2008). Social competence, social support, and academic achievement in minority, low-income, urban elementary school children. *School Psychology Quarterly, 23,* 474–495.

Elliot, A. J. (2005). A conceptual history of the achievement goal construct. In A. J. Elliot & C. S. Dweck (Eds.), *Handbook of competence and motivation* (pp. 52–72). New York, NY: Guilford.

Enoch, L G., & Riggs, I. M. (1990). Further development of an elementary science teaching efficacy belief instrument: A preservice elementary scale. *School Science and Mathematics, 90,* 694–706.

Fan, X., & Chen, M. (2001). Parental involvement and students' academic achievement: A meta-analysis. *Educational Psychology Review, 13,* 1–22.

Fraley, R. C., Waller, N. G., & Brennan, K. A. (2000). An item-response theory analysis of self-report measures of adult attachment. *Journal of Personality and Social Psychology, 78,* 350–365.

Furman, W., & Buhrmester, D. (1985). Children's perceptions of the personal relationships in their social networks. *Developmental Psychology, 21,* 1016–1024.

Gibson, S., & Dembo, M. (1984). Teacher efficacy: A construct validation. *Journal of Educational Psychology, 76,* 569–582.

Goddard, R. (2002). A theoretical and empirical analysis of the measurement of collective efficacy: The development of a short form. *Educational and Psychological Measurement, 62,* 97–110.

Goddard, R. D. (2001). Collective efficacy: A neglected construct in the study of schools and student achievement. *Journal of Educational Psychology, 93,* 467–476.

Goddard, R. D., Hoy, W. K., & Hoy, A. W. (2000). Collective teacher efficacy: Its meaning, measure, and impact on student achievement. *American Educational Research Journal, 37,* 479–507.

Goddard, R. D., Hoy, W. K., & Hoy, A. W. (2004). Collective efficacy beliefs: Theoretical developments, empirical evidence, and future directions. *Educational Researcher, 33*(3), 3–13.

Goddard, Y. L., Goddard, R., & Tschannen-Moran, M. (2007). A theoretical and empirical investigation of teacher collaboration for school improvement and student achievement in public elementary schools. *Teachers College Record, 109,* 877–896.

Goldberg, L. R. (1999). *International Personality Item Pool: A scientific collaboratory for the development of advanced measures of personality and other individual differences.* Retrieved from http://ipip.ori.org/

Good, C., Rattan, A., & Dweck, C. S. (2012). Why do women opt out? Sense of belonging and women's representation in mathematics. *Journal of Personality and Social Psychology, 102,* 700–717.

Good, T. L., & Brophy, J. (1994). *Looking in classrooms* (6th ed). New York, NY: HarperCollins.

Good, T. L., & Nichols, S. L. (2001). Expectancy effects in the classroom: A special focus on improving the reading performance of minority students in first-grade classrooms. *Educational Psychologist, 36,* 113–126.

The Gordon Commission on the Future of Assessment in Education. (2013). *A public policy statement.* Princeton, NJ: Author. Retrieved from http://www.gordoncommission.org/rsc/pdfs/gordon_commission_public_policy_report.pdf

Graham, S. (1990). On communicating low ability in the classroom: Bad things good teachers sometimes do. In S. Graham & V. Folkes (Eds.), *Attribution theory: Applications to achievement, mental health, and interpersonal conflict* (pp. 17–36). Hillsdale, NJ: Erlbaum.

Graham, S., & Williams, C. (2009). An attributional approach to motivation in school. In K. R. Wentzel & Wigfield (Eds.), *Handbook of motivation at school* (pp. 11–34). New York: Routledge.

Griffin, N. C., & Madni, A. (April, 2013). *Integrating assessment of social and emotional learning into an early childhood science learning context.* Paper presented at the annual meeting of the American Educational Research Association, San Francisco, CA.

Guskey, T. R. (1984). The influence of change in instructional effectiveness upon the affective characteristics of teachers. *American Educational Research Journal, 21,* 245–259.

Hamre, B. K., & Pianta, R. C. (2001). Early teacher–child relationships and the trajectory of children's school outcomes through eighth grade. *Child Development, 72,* 625–638.

Herman, J. L., & Baker, E. L. (2003). *The Los Angeles Annenberg metropolitan project: Evaluation findings* (CRESST Report No. 591). Los Angeles: University of California, National Center for Research on Evaluation, Standards, and Student Testing.

Herman, J. L., & Linn, R. L. (2013). *On the road to assessing deeper learning: The status of Smarter Balanced and PARCC assessment consortia* (CRESST Report 823). Los Angeles: University of California, National Center for Research on Evaluation, Standards, and Student Testing.

Hong, Y. Y., Chiu, C. Y., Dweck, C. S., Lin, D. M. S., & Wan, W. (1999). Implicit theories, attributions, and coping: A meaning system approach. *Journal of Personality and Social Psychology, 77,* 588–599.

Hoy, A, W., & Spero, R. B. (2005). Changes in teacher efficacy during the early years of teaching: A comparison of four measures. *Teaching and Teacher Education, 21,* 343–356.

Huang, D., Miyoshi, J., La Torre, D., Marshall, A., Perez, P., & Peterson, C. (2007). *Exploring the intellectual, social and organizational capitals at LA's BEST* (CRESST Report 714). Los

Angeles: University of California, National Center for Research on Evaluation, Standards, and Student Testing.

Hughes, J., & Kwok, O. M. (2007). Influence of student-teacher and parent-teacher relationships on lower achieving readers' engagement and achievement in the primary grades. *Journal of Educational Psychology, 99*, 39–51.

Hughes, J. N., Luo, W., Kwok, O. M., & Loyd, L. K. (2008). Teacher-student support, effortful engagement, and achievement: A 3-year longitudinal study. *Journal of Educational Psychology, 100*, 1–14.

Hurtz, G. M., & Donovan, J. J. (2000). Personality and job performance: The Big Five revisited. *Journal of Applied Psychology, 85*, 869–879.

Jennings, P. A., & Greenberg, M. T. (2009). The prosocial classroom: Teacher social and emotional competence in relation to student and classroom outcomes. *Review of Educational Research, 79*, 491–525.

John, O. P., Donahue, E. M., & Kentle, R. L. (1991). *The Big Five Inventory—Versions 4a and 54.* Berkeley: University of California, Berkeley, Institute of Personality and Social Research.

Jones, B. D., Bryant, L. H., Snyder, J. D., & Malone, D. (2012). Preservice and inservice teachers' implicit theories of intelligence. *Teacher Education Quarterly, 39*, 87–101.

Judson, E. (2006). How teachers integrate technology and their beliefs about learning: Is there a connection? *Journal of Technology and Teacher Education, 14*, 581–597.

Kagan, D. M. (1992). Implication of research on teacher belief. *Educational Psychologist, 27*, 65–90.

Klassen, R. M., & Chiu, M. M. (2010). Effects on teachers' self-efficacy and job satisfaction: Teacher gender, years of experience, and job stress. *Journal of Educational Psychology, 102*, 741–756.

Klassen, R. M., Tze, V. M. C., Betts, S. M., & Gordon, K. A. (2011). Teacher efficacy research 1998-2009: Signs of progress or unfulfilled promise? *Educational Psychology Review, 23*, 21–43.

Kuklinski, M. R., & Weinstein, R. S. (2001). Classroom and developmental differences in a path model of teacher expectancy effects. *Child Development, 72*, 1554–1578.

Lee, M. (2010). Researching social capital in education: Some conceptual considerations relating to the contribution of network analysis. *British Journal of Sociology of Education, 31*, 779–792.

Leroy, N., Bressoux, P., Sarrazin, P., & Trouilloud, D. (2007). Impact of teachers' implicit theories and perceived pressures on the establishment of an autonomy supportive climate. *European Journal of Psychology of Education, 22*, 529–545.

Levine, T. H., & Marcus, A. S. (2007). Closing the achievement gap through teacher collaboration: Facilitating multiple trajectories of learning. *Journal of Advanced Academics, 19*, 116–138.

Levy, S. R., Stroessner, S. J., & Dweck, C. S. (1998). Stereotype formation and endorsement: The role of implicit theories. *Journal of Personality and Social Psychology, 74*, 1421–1436.

Madni, A., Griffin, N. C., & Delacruz, G. C. (2013, July). *Social and emotional learning in games.* Paper presented at the annual meeting of the American Psychological Association, Honolulu, HI.

Maldonado-Carreño, C., & Votruba-Drzal, E. (2011). Teacher–child relationships and the development of academic and behavioral skills during elementary school: A within-and between-child analysis. *Child Development, 82*, 601–616.

Malmberg, L.-E., Wanner, B., Nordmyr, A.-M., & Little, T. D. (2004). *The Teachers' Control, Agency, and Means-ends Belief Questionnaire (TCAM): Reliability and validity* (Publication No. 7). Vasa, Finland: Åbo Akademi University.

Mayer, J. D., Salovey, P., & Caruso, D. R. (2002). *Mayer–Salovey–Caruso Emotional Intelligence Test (MSCEIT) user's manual.* Toronto, Ontario, Canada: Multi-Health Systems.

Mayer, J. D., Salovey, P., Caruso, D. R., & Sitarenios, G. (2001). Emotional intelligence as a standard intelligence. *Emotion, 1,* 232–242. doi:10.1037/1528-3542.1.3.232

McKown, C., & Weinstein, R. S. (2008). Teacher expectations, classroom context, and the achievement gap. *Journal of School Psychology, 46,* 235–261.

Messick, S. (1995). Standards of validity and the validity of standards in performance assessment. *Educational Measurement: Issues and Practice, 14*(4), 5–8.

The MET Project. (2012, September). Asking students about teaching: Student perception surveys and their implementation (Policy and practice brief). Retrieved from http://www.metproject.org/downloads/Asking_Students_Practitioner_Brief.pdf

Midgley, C., Feldlaufer, H., & Eccles, J. S. (1989). Change in teacher efficacy and student self- and task-related beliefs in mathematics during the transition to junior high school. *Journal of Educational Psychology, 81,* 247–258.

Midgley, C., Maehr, M. L., Hruda, L. Z., Anderman, E. M., Anderman, L., Freeman, K. E., . . . Urdan, T. (2000). *PALS—Manual for the patterns of adaptive learning scales.* Retrieved from http://www.umich.edu/~pals/PALS%202000_V13Word97.pdf

Minke, K. M., Sheridan, S. M., Kim, E. M., Ryoo, J. H., & Koziol, N. A. (2014). Congruence in parent-teacher relationships: The role of shared perceptions. *Elementary School Journal, 114,* 527–546.

Miretzky, D. (2004). The communication requirements of democratic schools: Parent-teacher perspectives on their relationships. *Teachers College Record, 106,* 814–851.

Molden, D. C., & Dweck, C. S. (2000). Meaning and motivation. In J. M. Harackiewicz & C. Sansone (Eds.), *Intrinsic and extrinsic motivation: The search for optimal motivation and performance* (pp. 131–159). San Diego, CA: Academic.

Moolenaar, N. M. (2012). A social network perspective on teacher collaboration in schools: Theory, methodology, and applications. *American Journal of Education, 119,* 7–39.

Moolenaar, N. M., Daly, A. J., & Sleegers, P. J. (2011). Ties with potential: Social network structure and innovative climate in Dutch schools. *Teachers College Record, 113,* 1983–2017.

Moolenaar, N. M., Sleegers, P. J., & Daly, A. J. (2012). Teaming up: Linking collaboration networks, collective efficacy, and student achievement. *Teaching and Teacher Education, 28,* 251–262.

Mueller, C. M., & Dweck, C. S. (1998). Praise for intelligence can undermine children's motivation and performance. *Journal of Personality and Social Psychology, 75,* 33–52.

Murray, C. (2009). Parent and teacher relationships as predictors of school engagement and functioning among low-income urban youth. *Journal of Early Adolescence, 29,* 376–404.

Nzinga-Johnson, S., Baker, J. A., & Aupperlee, J. (2009). Teacher-parent relationships and school involvement among racially and educationally diverse parents of kindergartners. *Elementary School Journal, 110,* 81–91.

Olver, J. M., & Mooradian, T. A. (2003). Personality traits and personal values: A conceptual and empirical integration. *Personality and Individual Differences, 35,* 109–125.

O'Neil, H. F., Perez, R. S., & Baker, E. L. (Eds.). (2014). *Teaching and measuring cognitive readiness.* New York, NY: Springer.

Ormrod, J. E. (2011). *Educational psychology: Developing learners* (7th ed.). Boston, MA: Allyn & Bacon.

Pajares, M. F. (1992). Teachers' beliefs and educational research: Cleaning up a messy construct. *Review of Educational Research, 62,* 307–332.

Penrose, A., Perry, C., & Ball, I. (2007). Emotional intelligence and teacher self-efficacy: The contribution of teacher status and length of experience. *Issues in Educational Research, 17,* 107–126.

Pettus, A. M., & Allain, V. A. (1999). Using a questionnaire to assess prospective teachers' attitudes toward multicultural education issues. *Education, 119,* 651–657.

Pianta, R. C. (1999). *Enhancing relationships between children and teachers.* Washington, DC: American Psychological Association.

Pianta, R. C., & Steinberg, M. (1992). Teacher-child relationships and the process of adjusting to school. *New Directions for Child and Adolescent Development, 1992*(57), 61–80.

Pitts, V. M., & Spillane, J. P. (2009). Using social network methods to study school leadership. *International Journal of Research & Method in Education, 32*, 185–207.

Podsakoff, P. M., & Organ, D. W. (1986). Self-reports in organizational research: Problems and prospects. *Journal of Management, 12*, 531–544.

Pohan, C. A., & Aguilar, T. E. (2001). Measuring educators' beliefs about diversity in personal and professional contexts. *American Educational Research Journal, 38*, 159–182.

Popham, W. J. (2013). *Evaluating America's teachers: Mission possible?* Thousand Oaks, CA: Corwin.

Pretzlik, U., Olsson, J., Nabuco, M. E., & Cruz, I. (2003). Teachers' implicit view of intelligence predict pupils' self-perception as learners. *Cognitive Development, 18*, 579–599.

Quigley, D. D. (2000). *Parents and teachers working together to support third-grade achievement: Parents as Learning Partners (PLP) findings* (CRESST Report No. 530). Los Angeles: University of California, National Center for Research on Evaluation, Standards, and Student Testing.

Rattan, A., Good, C., & Dweck, C. S. (2012). "It's ok—Not everyone can be good at math": Instructors with an entity theory comfort (and demotivate) students. *Journal of Experimental Social Psychology, 48*, 731–737.

Retelsdorf, J., Butler, R., Streblow, L., & Schiefele, U. (2010). Teachers' goal orientations for teaching: Associations with instructional practices, interest in teaching, and burnout. *Learning and Instruction, 20*, 30–46.

Reyna, C. (2000). Lazy, dumb, or industrious: When stereotypes convey attribution information in the classroom. *Educational Psychology Review, 12*, 85–110.

Rizzo, A., John, B., Newman, B., Williams, J., Hartholt, A., Lethin, C., & Buckwalter, G. J. (2013). Virtual reality as a tool for delivering PTSD exposure therapy and stress resilience training. *Military Behavioral Health, 1*, 48–54.

Rose, J. S., & Medway, F. J. (1981). Measurement of teachers' beliefs in their control over student outcome. *Journal of Educational Research, 74*, 185–190.

Rosenthal, R. (1991). Teacher expectancy effects: A brief update 25 years after the Pygmalion experiment. *Journal of Research in Education, 1*, 3–12.

Rosenthal, R., & Jacobson, L. F. (1968). Pygmalion in the classroom. *Urban Review, 3*, 16–20.

Rubie-Davis, C. M. (2006). Teacher expectations and self-perceptions: Exploring relationships. *Psychology in the Schools, 43*, 537–552.

Rubie-Davis, C. M. (2010). Teacher expectations and perceptions of student attributes: Is there a relationship? *British Journal of Educational Psychology, 80*, 121–135.

Rueda, R., Lin, H. J., O'Neil, H. F., Griffin, N., Bockman, S., & Sirotnik, B. (2010). Ethnic differences on students' approaches to learning: Self-regulatory cognitive and motivational predictors of academic achievement for Latino/a and White college students. In M. S. Khine & I. M. Saleh (Eds.), *New science of learning* (pp. 133–161). New York, NY: Springer Science+Business Media.

Schutte, N. S., Malouff, J. M., Hall, L. E., Haggerty, D. J., Cooper, J. T., Golden, C. J., & Dornheim, L. (1998). Development and validation of a measure of emotional intelligence. *Personality and Individual Differences, 25*, 167–177.

Skaalvik, E. M., & Skaalvik, S. (2007). Dimensions of teacher self-efficacy and relations with strain factors, perceived collective teacher efficacy, and teacher burnout. *Journal of Educational Psychology, 99*, 611–625.

St. George, A. (1983). Teacher expectations and perceptions of Polynesian and Pakeha pupils and the relationship to classroom behaviour and school achievement. *British Journal of Educational Psychology, 53*, 48–59.

Stripling, R. (2012, February). *Detection and computational analysis of psychological signals (DCAPS): CRESST evaluation plan.* Paper presented at the Medicine Meets Virtual Reality (MMVR) annual meeting, Newport Beach, CA.

Stripling, R., Lee, J., & Cohn, J. V. (2014). *Guidelines for validating 21st century assessment tools. in using games and simulations for teaching and assessment: Key issues* (H. F. O'Neil, E. L. Baker, & R. S. Perez, Eds.). New York, NY: Routledge/Taylor & Francis.

Tenenbaum, H. R., & Ruck, M. D. (2007). Are teachers' expectations different for racial minority than for European American students? A meta-analysis. *Journal of Educational Psychology, 99*, 253–273.

Tschannen-Moran, M., & Barr, M. (2004). Fostering student learning: The relationship of collective teacher efficacy and student achievement. *Leadership and Policy in Schools, 3*, 189–209.

Tschannen-Moran, M., & Hoy, A. W. (2001). Teacher efficacy: Capturing and elusive construct. *Teaching and Teacher Education, 17*, 783–805.

Tschannen-Moran, M., Hoy, A. W., & Hoy, W. K. (1998). Teacher efficacy: Its meaning and measure. *Review of Educational Research, 68*, 202–248.

Vickers, H. S., & Minke, K. M. (1995). Exploring parent-teacher relationships: Joining and communication to others. *School Psychology Quarterly, 10*, 133–150.

Watanabe, M. (2006). "Some people think this school is tracked and some people don't": Using inquiry groups to unpack teachers' perspectives on detracking. *Theory Into Practice, 45*, 24–31.

Webb, N. L. (2007). Issues related to judging the alignment of curriculum standards and assessments. *Applied Measurement in Education, 20*, 1–25.

Weiner, B. (1985). An attributional theory of achievement motivation and emotion. *Psychological Review, 92*, 548–573.

Weiner, B. (1986). *An attributional theory of motivation and emotion.* New York, NY: Springer-Verlag

Weiner, B. (2004). Attribution theory revisited: Transforming cultural plurality into theoretical unity. In D. M. McInerney & S. Van Etten (Eds.), *Big theories revisited* (pp. 13–29). Grenwich, Ct.: Information Age.

Weiner, B. (2005). Motivation from an attribution perspective and the social psychology of perceived competence. In A. J. Elliot & C. S. Dweck (Eds.), *Handbook of competence and motivation* (pp. 73–84). New York, NY: Guilford.

Weiner, B. (2010). The development of an attribution-based theory of motivation: A history of ideas. *Educational Psychologist, 45*, 28–36.

Weinstein, R., Marshall, H., Sharp, L., & Botkin, M. (1987). Pygmalion and the student: Age and classroom differences in children's awareness of teacher expectations. *Child Development, 58*, 1079–1093.

Wigfield, A., & Eccles, J. S. (2000). Expectancy-value theory of achievement motivation. *Contemporary Educational Psychology, 25*, 68–81.

Woolfolk-Hoy, A., Davis, H., & Pape, S. J. (2006). Teacher knowledge and beliefs. In P. A. Alexander & P. H. Winne (Eds.), *Handbook of educational psychology* (2nd ed., pp. 715–737). Mahwah, NJ: Lawrence Erlbaum.

Woolfson, L., Grant, E., & Campbell, L. (2007). A comparison of special, general and support teachers' controllability and stability attributions for children's difficulties in learning. *Educational Psychology, 27*, 295–306.

Zhou, J., & Urhahne, D. (2013). Teacher judgment, student motivation, and the mediating effect of attributions. *European Journal of Psychology Education, 28*, 275–295.

Zimmerman, B. J. (2008). Investigating self-regulation and motivation: Historical background, methodological developments, and future prospects. *American Educational Research Journal, 45*, 166–183.

Zins, J. E., Bloodworth, M. R., Weissberg, R. P., & Walberg, H. J. (2007). The scientific base linking social and emotional learning to school success. *Journal of Educational and Psychological Consultation, 17*, 191–210.

Chapter 3

Developing Teachers' Knowledge and Skills at the Intersection of English Language Learners and Language Assessment

Kip Téllez
Eduardo Mosqueda
University of California, Santa Cruz

The growth of teachers'[1] professional knowledge and skills has been the topic of policy, research, and even philosophy for many decades. The assessment of English Learners (ELs), a more specific concern, has become an interest of the educational community in just the past 40 years (e.g., Harris, 1969). Our task in this chapter is to combine these two topics and consider their relations from empirical, practical, and historical perspectives (listed here in what we consider to be the rank order of importance).

At the intersection of any pedagogical practices, we are drawn into the complicated mix of generalized and specialized knowledge required for expert teaching. And although the theory/practice split might be a false dualism, we agree with Salvatori's (2003) characterization of the discipline:

> That historically pedagogy has been alternately and repeatedly "elevated" to *theory* or "reduced" to *practice* . . . can be construed as an implicit but dramatic demonstration of its fundamental complexity. Indeed, I would suggest that the reasons for pedagogy's various simplifications and reductions might be found in pedagogy's complexity, rather than in its inadequacy as a discipline. (p. 67)

It will be up to others to decide whether knowledge of the proper assessment of English learners is more complex than other interrelated constructs teachers must understand; nevertheless, we are confident that oversimplifying EL assessment will diminish achievement for students already at-risk. Because this chapter, like all those in the volume, is putatively designed to offer readers a comprehensive review of the available research and theory on the issue we have identified, we begin by

Review of Research in Education
March 2015, Vol. 39, pp. 87–121
DOI: 10.3102/0091732X14554552
© 2015 AERA. http://rre.aera.net

circumscribing our task: The scant existing research on this topic probably does not warrant a full chapter,[2] but we argue that (a) the dramatic growth of the EL population in the United States and worldwide, (b) the chronic underachievement among ELs, (c) the lack of confidence and preparation in teaching English as a new language reported by many teachers and teacher candidates, (d) the limited generalized assessment knowledge and skills among teachers, and (e) the consequences of the admixture of each of these conspire to reproduce the dismal EL academic achievement patterns and negative experiences. When teachers of ELs fail to understand the nuances of general language assessment and the intersection of language and content assessment (Abedi, 2004), the specialized assessment strategies required for ELs, and the assessment of bi- or multilingual learners (Duran, 2008; Klingner & Solano-Flores, 2007; Solano-Flores & Trumbull, 2003), classroom misplacement (Artiles & Ortiz, 2002), lowered expectations (Flores, 2007), inappropriate curriculum (Gándara & Rumberger, 2009; Rumberger & Gándara, 2004), and deleterious tracking (Mosqueda, 2010; Mosqueda & Maldonado, 2013), to name just a few, interact to diminish the academic performance of ELs. With these consequences in mind, we review the existing literature on the topic but also add our own accounts of teacher knowledge and skills as they relate to EL assessment, and devote a portion of the chapter to a discussion of policy changes and future research directions that promote increased educational achievement of ELs.[3] This is our overarching goal.

The chapter is organized into seven sections. In this section, we provide an overview of critical challenges in assessing ELs in their nondominant language. In the second section, we review state-of-the-art approaches for assessing the academic achievement of ELs. In the section "A Review of the Research on Preparing 'General Education' Teachers," we review research and policy on the preparation of teachers with respect to the assessment of ELs. In the section "Assessment Standards for Teachers of EL," we examine the development of disciplinary standards and the challenges of implementing such standards. In the section "An Overview of the Research on Effective Policies and Practices," we focus on the lack of teacher preparation for assessing ELs and provide recommendations for future research. In the sixth section, we examine the implications for policy and practice regarding the preparation of teachers for EL assessment. The final section concludes with a discussion of the consequences of our findings for future research and practice.

Our chapter expands on Duran's (2008) review of the literature delineating the challenges in assessing ELs in their nondominant language, which also provides a new direction for linking assessment and instructional practices to improve the educational experiences and outcomes of these students. In this chapter, however, we primarily review the issues relevant to teaching ELs in the U.S. context while recognizing that it is likely that a substantial proportion of English teachers worldwide now work outside of the United States, although this is a supposition on our part (the data are not clear). However, the *growth* in English teaching is almost certainly rising faster in countries outside the United States (Hu, 2003); we therefore include a few relevant international studies that mirror issues in the U.S. context. Teachers of native

Spanish-speaking ELs are the subjects in the vast majority of the research we review and proposals we advance. We admit to this bias but would point out that over 85% of ELs in the United States speak Spanish as their native language, and although limited, the majority of studies on ELs focus on Spanish-speaking students; therefore, their teachers are also far more numerous (see Téllez, 2010, for an overview). However, we want to acknowledge the diversity of languages (e.g., Mixteco, Zapoteco, Triqui, and Maya) spoken by an increasing number of immigrant students from Mexico and Central America, especially in our region of California. Last, native Spanish-speaking ELs are generally those whose academic achievement is of greatest concern and therefore the focus of teacher knowledge and skills. But before moving on to addressing these specific issues, we need to determine who is included in the definition of EL. We presently have no common national criteria for what determines EL status. Duran (2008) and others (Abedi, 2004; Celedón-Pattichis, 2004; Mahoney & MacSwan, 2005) point out that the classification of ELs is vague due to the lack of consistency and agreement for identifying such students among districts and states. Duran (2008) describes the problem:

ELLs participating in state large-scale assessments are in effect a policy construction, a category of students established by individual states to satisfy their education laws to deal with a growing group of students from non-English backgrounds who show some evidence of limited familiarity with English, patterns of low school achievement, low assessment scores in English, and propensity to drop out of school. (p. 300)

In short, ELs are in urgent need of a reformed school experience and improved opportunities to learn, but how can we create such enhancements when we do not even know who they are? Solving this problem begins with accurate and agreed-on assessment tools and systems.

As the research literature (Rivkin, Hanushek, & Kain, 2005) and popular press (Brooks, 2012) draw attention to the critical role of the teacher in academic achievement, the education community finds itself in a search for the right mix of teacher knowledge, skills, and attributes that, together, contribute to increased student achievement. At root, some teachers are more effective than others. No thoughtful educator, researcher, or policymaker would disagree on this point. The pervasive measuring and comparing of teachers (both preservice and in-service) as well as the designing of methods to improve the teaching profession through professional development offer evidence that we believe that good teachers can be made (or at least selected) and that even good teachers can significantly improve their instruction.

In fact, it is becoming increasingly clear that there are but two fundamental ways for schools to help students who are not meeting grade-level standards (a category that includes many ELs) to "catch up." The first way, which is growing in popularity, is simply to add to the time that students spend with teachers learning school objectives. In this model, teachers simply work more. For instance, schools that demand students spend 8 hours per day or more in school and attend on weekends will obviously have differential and mostly positive academic outcomes simply because they put more teacher time to meeting educational objectives (Gándara & Rumberger,

2009; Tuttle, Teh, Nichols-Barrer, Gill, & Gleason, 2010). Adding time in the form of an extended school day, after-school programs, or weekend classes is not new, and its "dimensions" are varied and complex, as Gándara (2000) and authors in her book point out (Anderson, 2000; Minicucci, 2000). We want to underscore this strategy because it appears that an increasing number of Latino learners (who comprise the largest group of ELs) are attending such schools. In these contexts, teachers' experience, knowledge, and skills appear to be irrelevant. In fact, some schools in this category specifically point out their teachers' inexperience and suggest that the school's purported success is owed primarily to the extra time given to teaching (Angrist, Dynarski, Kane, Pathak, & Walters, 2010).

The other way to "teach more" is make the time students spend with teachers more efficient, that is, use strategies that help students learn more in the same amount of time. This is the goal of teacher professional development—to expand the capacity of teachers to improve their instructional skills and, in turn, raise achievement. The relationship between time and efficiency can be expressed in the following equation: $E/T = L$, where E is efficiency, T is time, and L is learning (or what an economist would call productivity). If you lack efficiency, you must add time to learning. If you have a fixed amount of time, you need to be more efficient in order to gain the same amount of learning.

We believe this equation is particularly relevant to our topic. For instance, teachers who lack sufficient knowledge of EL assessment (i.e., efficiency) are likely to have their EL students doing work that is either too difficult or too easy and thus inefficient. On the other hand, a teacher who holds expert knowledge and skills with respect to EL assessment will know students' language levels and have them work at their instructional capacity,[4] which results in efficient teaching and learning.

We argue that both increased time and instructional efficiency are needed to enhance the academic success of ELs. But adding instructional time is a matter of policy decision making and resource commitment, and it is by far the easier lever to pull, although we would point out that time, in the end, is clearly fixed and limited.

Our task is to consider how we can improve the assessment of ELs, by enhancing the skills of teachers, and thus improve academic achievement for one of our most vulnerable populations. We are addressing an admittedly narrow slice of a much larger teacher development project that will be required to improve the education experiences of ELs, but for those of us who are deeply concerned about the education of our nation's roughly 7 million ELs, this topic is crucial. Imagine an EL student whose teacher does not know her/his native language *and* who lacks skills in EL assessment. Such a teacher has no reliable way of knowing what an EL student knows or does not know in either her/his native language or in English. The work assigned to ELs may be entirely inappropriate, but ELs cannot object because they often lack the language capacity or the social capital[5] (or both) to say so. This predicament, corroborated in research by Celedón-Pattichis (2004) and others (e.g., Rodriguez, 2009), is the fate of too many ELs, who consequently become disengaged and marginalized from healthy, productive school experiences.

For many of us in language education in the United States, the protests and eventual takeover of Crystal City, Texas, schools (Trujillo, 1998, 2005; Valenzuela, 2000) remain a watershed event, equal to Little Rock in importance.[6] But the heroic effort of the students and citizens in this remote Texas town, who initiated La Raza Unida Party, needs wider recognition for their insistence that students' native language be respected and that the teaching of new languages be compassionate. Their legacy, as well as other communities who protested cruel language teaching practices (e.g., San Miguel, 2004), motivates our work, and we are thankful that the editors of this volume share our urgency and invited us to write this chapter.[7]

As we begin the sections that form our review, it might be useful to share some of the questions that teachers of ELs should be asking based on our review of the available research on EL assessment:

- How much English do ELs know?
- Do ELs have relative strengths within their English capacities (i.e., are they better at reading and writing than speaking and listening)?
- Can ELs read in their native language? If so, how well?
- How much content knowledge do ELs have and understand in their native language?
- How is their growing knowledge of English influencing ELs' learning of content?
- Are ELs making "average" growth in learning English? If not, is it a result of a generalized language learning challenge or a challenge in learning *English specifically*?
- If I don't know the answers to these and other questions, how can I find out?

These questions will guide the content of the sections below. As mentioned, our task is to review the relevant literature, but we are also hoping to provide a few examples of pedagogical strategies, from both the literature and our own experiences. A final caveat: Although we need to consider what the field considers strong EL assessment, our task in this work is not to conduct an exhaustive review of appropriate assessment for EL, and refer readers to other sources (e.g., Abedi, 2004; Abedi & Lord, 2001; Duran, 2008; Solano-Flores, 2011; Solano-Flores & Trumbull, 2003; Téllez, Moschkovich, & Civil, 2011). We address only the specific assessment issues that intersect with our task of considering how teachers can better gain the necessary knowledge and skills required for sound assessment of ELs.

THE STATE-OF-THE-ART IN ASSESSING THE ACADEMIC ACHIEVEMENT AND ACADEMIC GROWTH OF ELS

All ELs are better described as emerging (Téllez, 1998) or emergent (O. García, Kleifgen, & Falchi, 2008) bilinguals, whose language and/or content capacities cannot be fully assessed in any single language.[8] As Valdes and Figueroa (1994) pointed out nearly 20 years ago, assessing bilingual learners presents distinct challenges, and ignoring the unique constellation of language skills in any EL may result in systematic bias in the interpretation of score results. The lack of proper assessment can have serious consequences on the academic preparation of ELs, particularly for those who are misdiagnosed and placed in special education. Such practices often result in the disproportionate placement of ELs in special education when it is unclear if ELs struggle to learn because of a disability or because of language acquisition issues (Artiles & Klingner, 2006; Artiles, Rueda, Salazar, & Higareda, 2005).

Although it may not be obvious to monolingual speakers, it is quite logical that EL students may know a word in their native language that they have yet to learn in English. For instance, a native Spanish-speaking student may know the word *harina* (flour in English) as a result of family cooking experiences but have no knowledge of its English counterpart. This example points out that knowledge of terms or linguistic structures in a student's native language can exist independent of target language knowledge, especially when such knowledge is separated by the terms and structures one might learn in school versus those more commonly learned at home. The ongoing debate on the "balance" of languages in the mind is beyond our goals for this chapter (see Grosjean, 1989), but the knowledge of this concept and its implications for assessment are crucial knowledge for the teacher of ELs.

Teachers and candidates must have some knowledge of what a student knows in the native versus target language. By way of exploring this knowledge and what EL professionals might be asked to understand, we review the efforts to assess bilingual verbal capacities and highlight the work of Muñoz-Sandoval, Cummins, Alvarado, and Ruef (1998), whose Bilingual Verbal Ability Test (BVAT), can be used to determine the linguistic capacity or linguistic aptitude of bilinguals. Briefly described, the test relies on the general structure of the Woodcock–Johnson test of linguistic aptitude (Woodcock, McGrew, & Mather, 2001). Students first take the English version and then retake the missed items in a parallel test given in their native language. The scores are combined using a correction factor and a composite linguistic capacity score is computed. The score is an estimate of a bilingual's linguistic capacity, regardless of the language in which it is "housed." Before going further, we want to suggest that the interest in measuring a student's linguistic aptitude has been unfairly cast as an attempt to, for instance, label students as learning disabled or to track them into low-level classes. Although one can cite many cases, mostly historical, in which aptitude tests have been used to further subjugate an already disempowered minority group (Gould, 1996; Hilliard, 2000), we argue that teachers of ELs must understand the difference and usage between tests of linguistic achievement and linguistic aptitude, especially when considering the constellation of a bilingual student's capacities. We would also point out that the BVAT has been used to identify gifted ELs when a linguistic capacity test in English and nonverbal assessments failed to recognize EL students' extraordinary intellectual capacity (Breedlove, 2007).

We are not necessarily arguing that all teachers gain the skills needed to administer a test such as the BVAT (although they would learn much from the training), but they must understand the concept behind the test. Simply put, how can a teacher understand proper assessment of ELs without also understanding the knowledge that a student has in the native language and the balance of the target and native languages? The BVAT results offer clear evidence that both a student's native language and English play a role in all assessment processes (Páez, 2008). We are also not recommending that schools take on the role of administering the BVAT to all its ELs. This effort would be prohibitively expensive and unnecessary. Rather, we are suggesting that an understanding of the purpose and practice of the BVAT will assist educators in knowing whether struggling ELs are challenged in learning English or learning language itself. This is a crucial distinction for educators: Mistakes can result in ELs failing to receive adequate special education services or, worse, in incorrect assumptions being made about a learner's effort and/or content knowledge understanding.

Although the BVAT and similar tests that claim to measure something called linguistic aptitude have been rightly questioned for their bias toward the experiences of middle-class children and youth (Valencia & Suzuki, 2000), the recent attacks on testing bias have come largely from critics of single language achievement tests when used to assess ELs. In a wide-ranging review of the issues connecting ELs to general academic assessment, Solórzano (2008) highlights the long-standing concerns regarding validity when students take a test in a language they are learning. Solórzano also reminds us that ELs are mandated to be included in the accountability scheme under No Child Left Behind (NCLB) and that most states, including California, make almost no allowance or modifications for ELs.[9] A host of researchers have argued that the rules of NCLB are unfair or should not apply to schools with high concentrations of ELs (Abedi, 2004; Harper, de Jong, & Platt, 2008; McCarty, 2009; Menken, 2008), but such calls have been mostly ignored. Solórzano (2008) also emphasizes a point made by Gándara (2002; as cited in Solórzano, 2008): that even when the manufacturers of the standardized assessments suggest that their products are not valid measures of EL academic achievement, legislators and policymakers tend to ignore these warnings and require ELs take them anyway, and then insist that their scores be used to rank and sort schools and school systems. Disciplinary standards (American Educational Research Association, American Psychological Association, & National Council on Measurement in Education, 1999) are just as easily ignored. Requiring emergent ELs, for instance, to take an achievement test in English (and only in English) is illogical, but this decision, at least in the case of NCLB, is enforced by policy, not by testing experts or even test development companies. Too often we find teachers, candidates, and other educators blaming the test itself when the rightful culprits are the policymakers (i.e., politicians) who should answer to the public, which includes a good many educators. Identifying who is at fault for irresponsible testing policies should be a primary goal of EL advocates, but teachers are often frustratingly apolitical and unwilling to confront officials (Bartolome, 2004). The test is what ELs struggle with—and what teachers see most clearly—but it is a poor metonymic device for misguided accountability schemes created by politicians motivated by the call for "higher standards," regardless of the manifest psychometric concerns.

The fact that so many ELs are now forced to take tests in English when it is clearly inappropriate has, paradoxically, encouraged a host of studies and proposals exploring the ways by which the language bias in such tests can be reduced. The question is essentially this: How can we estimate an EL's true knowledge of content (e.g., math, science) in a language they are learning? Or put more simply, is English a barrier for ELs who know the construct but cannot "find" the correct answer because they cannot understand the language of the question itself? The answer is certainly yes, but the degree of bias has been the subject of several key studies in the past decade. For instance, Martiniello (2009), using differential item functioning methods, found four types of construct-irrelevant text that diminished EL performance on mathematics tests:

- Syntactic: multi-clausal complex structures with embedded adverbial and relative clauses; long phrases with embedded noun and prepositional phrases; lack of clear relationships between the syntactic units.
- Lexical: unfamiliar vocabulary, high-frequency words usually learned at home and not in school; polysemous or multiple-meaning words.
- References to mainstream American culture.
- Test or text layout. Lack of one-to-one correspondence between the syntactic boundaries of clauses and the lay out of the text in the printed test. (p. 176)

However, the results indicated that the bias resulting from syntactic and lexical complexity was reduced if the item was presented with a schematic representation of the test taker's task. The implication of this research for teacher knowledge is that graphic organizers, a long-standing, successful instructional strategy for second language learners (Tang, 1992), are as useful in assessment as in instructional contexts. Recent studies (e.g., Haag, Heppt, Stanat, Kuhl, & Pant, 2013; Wolf & Leon, 2009) have corroborated Martiniello's (2009) findings.

Given that content area assessments make demands of EL language capacities, and that these demands can influence performance, we should be directing attention to exactly these concerns using common criteria. To this end, Shaw, Bunch, and Geaney (2010) provide a useful taxonomy and analytic frame for understanding the language demands on performance assessments in science. This tool can be useful for exploring assessments that will help educators gain a clear understanding of language in assessment.

In an article designed to reconsider the paradigm of testing for ELs, Solano-Flores and Trumbull (2003) suggest that testing for ELs must be reframed to include fundamental shifts in test development, test review, and the treatment of language as an added source of measurement error. This final point, that the language of a test should be considered error, represents a new and compelling argument in psychometrics. Educators working with ELs would do well to understand their assertion, but they must first understand the basic tenet of assessment theory—that is, when we measure any human quality, we are approximating some unknown true score. Whatever score or mark we ascribe to an individual is composed of two components, an observed score and measurement error. Although there are various techniques for estimating error, many of which lie beyond the needs of most educators, the simple calculation required to compute the standard error of measurement seems a reasonable expectation (McMillan, 2000; Popham, 2011).

The important point that Solano-Flores and Trumbull (2003) make is that ELs are, in fact, bilingual test takers and that each has a "unique set of weaknesses and strengths in English and a unique set of weaknesses and strengths in his or her native language" (p. 8). The error we find in the scores of EL is partly due to the distribution of knowledge across languages, a point we underscored in our discussion of the BVAT.

Thus far in this section we have addressed the shortcomings of what might be termed *summative tests* (i.e., manifold end-of-year achievement tests designed to assess a year's worth or more of learning), but researchers and school leaders have identified formative assessment as perhaps the more crucial knowledge for teachers due to their potential to inform and enhance instructional practice. Although the distinction between formative and summative assessments is not always clear (see Scriven, 1991, for a review), we recognize the need for teachers to understand and use those types of assessments, whatever their terms, that both guide ELs to the proper instructional level and offer teachers a valid and reliable way to know what students know and do not know in "real time."

In general, formative assessments involve a systematic process to continuously gather evidence and provide feedback about learning while instruction is underway (Heritage, 2007; Heritage, Kim, Vendlinski, & Herman, 2009), all the while making student thinking transparent to teachers and using such evidence to help teachers adapt their instructional strategies to help meet the desired learning goals (Ruiz–Primo, Furtak, Ayala, Yin, & Shavelson, 2010). Shepard (2006) has argued for a model of formative assessment where in addition to providing information that teachers can use to improve instruction, the information garnered should also guide student learning. Thus, formative assessments can include the following goals for students: identifying students' strengths and weaknesses; aiding students in guiding their own learning, revising their work, and gaining self-evaluation skills; and fostering increased autonomy and responsibility for learning on the part of the student (Cizek, 2010). Research has shown that well-designed, formative assessments can increase student achievement (Black, Harrison, Lee, Marshall, & Wiliam, 2004).

Formative assessments vary widely depending on their purpose (Ruiz-Primo et al., 2010), but most educators agree that formative assessments must be embedded within an instructional unit and the results should be used to inform the learning goals of a particular lesson (Ayala et al., 2008; Cizek, 2010; Ruiz-Primo et al., 2010). To realize the potential of formative assessment to help support and enhance instruction and student learning, the implementation process of formative assessments must address at least three dimensions that are encapsulated in three questions posed by Ramprasad (1983, as cited in Ruiz-Primo et al., 2010): Where are we going? Where are we now? How will we get there? As Ruiz-Primo et al. explain, the "Where are we going?" question focuses on the teacher "setting and clarifying learning goals" and identifying "evidence [for] achieving those learning goals," whereas the "Where are we now?" question refers to "specific practices in which teachers seek to understand students' current and prior knowledge" (p. 139). The third question, "How will we get there?" centers on how the teachers will modify their instruction to meet the needs of students (Ruiz-Primo et al., 2010). Moreover, another critical feature of formative assessments is the provision of effective feedback to students based on the assessments results (Sadler, 1989).

Despite the potential of formative assessments to improve teacher practice, their effective implementation requires a high degree of assessment and pedagogical knowledge. Heritage (2010) has found that teachers need to master four basic elements of teacher knowledge in order to implement formative assessments successfully: (a) domain knowledge, (b) pedagogical content knowledge, (c) knowledge of students' previous learning, and (d) knowledge of assessment. As previously discussed, researchers have raised concerns about the lack of useful assessment training in preservice teacher preparation programs and professional development opportunities available to practicing teachers to help develop their assessment literacy; thus, the complex nature of effectively implementing formative assessments is often taken for granted.

The literature focused on formative assessment of ELs is scant (Duran, 2008; Llosa, 2011). What does it mean to have a linguistically and culturally responsive assessment? Do formative assessments have the potential to be sensitive to linguistic and cultural learning needs of ELs? The works of Solano-Flores (2006) and Solano-Flores and Trumbull (2003), which examine the linguistic and cultural sources of measurement error on summative assessments, provide a useful framework for evaluating formative assessments. The accurate assessment of ELs' content knowledge mastery is a complex undertaking given the psychometric limitations not limited to construct-irrelevant variance, or the underestimation of subject matter understanding of ELs resulting from their low degrees of English language proficiency (Abedi, 2004; Duran, 2008; Heubert & Hauser, 1999).

A REVIEW OF THE RESEARCH ON PREPARING "GENERAL EDUCATION" TEACHERS FOR QUALITY ASSESSMENT PRACTICES

Before exploring the research and policy surrounding what teachers know and can do with respect to the assessment of ELs, we are obligated to understand what they know about general assessments of native English-speaking children in disciplinary content areas such as literacy and mathematics. It is our view that the assessment of ELs (or any second language learner for that matter) is a special and more complex case than that of native speakers. Monolingual, native speakers of English can be assessed in English, without regard for the distribution of language capacities in bi- or multilingual learners.

As we reviewed the literature on teachers' knowledge of assessment, an area that has come to be known as "assessment literacy" (Mertler & Campbell, 2005; Stiggins,

1991), we find almost unanimous disappointment from the research and policy communities. Popham (2011) defines assessment literacy as "an individual's *understandings* of the *fundamental assessment concepts and procedures* deemed *likely to influence educational decisions*" (p. 267). The malaise is summed up neatly in the titles of two articles by the assessment specialists Stiggins and Popham: "The Unfulfilled Promise of Classroom Assessment" (Stiggins, 2001) and "Seeking Redemption for Our Psychometric Sins" (Popham, 2003).

Stiggins's (2001) admonition is particularly strident, arguing that current conditions can be explained only by presenting a fictional scenario: "It is as if someone somewhere in the distant past decided that teachers would teach, and they would need to know nothing about accurate assessment" (p. 5). Popham (2006, 2011), as previously mentioned, has made the same case, and he is joined by a host of other researchers and policymakers (Cizek, Fitzgerald, & Rachor, 1995; Daniel & King, 1998; McMillan, 2003; Randall & Engelhard, 2010) whose empirical work confirms the general sentiment.

If teachers lack assessment knowledge, are there specific areas of this shortcoming? Plake, Impara, and Fager (1993) measured teachers' competencies on the seven basic assessment areas identified in the Standards for Teacher competence in Educational Assessment of Students. Overall, the results show that teachers were most knowledgeable in the areas of administering, scoring, and interpreting test results. The poorest performance came from those items measuring the teachers' knowledge about communicating test results. Although the authors report that the teachers' knowledge of assessment was deemed quite inadequate, the study offers some hope: It found that teachers who had training in measurement scored significantly higher than those who had not. This finding indicates that a general knowledge of assessment is not out of teachers' reach, perhaps only that professional development has not been widespread enough.

With such an identifiable shortcoming exposed, it is reasonable to ask if candidates are ever introduced to classroom assessment in their preservice professional programs. Indeed, teacher education is often blamed for the shortcomings we find in the general teacher population, whether the teachers we reproach are in their first or 30th year. In our view, it is folly to argue that professional school programs should equip teachers with all the knowledge the wider educational community wishes they had, not to mention prepare them for their work 10 years into their profession. We admit to some bias in this regard, if for no other reason than that we work primarily in preservice teacher education. However, preservice licensing programs have always had a marginal influence, which has only been diminished in recent years as states limited the number of credits professional programs could require for a license (Cochran-Smith, 2001). In short, the lack of assessment literacy preparation of beginning teachers is clear. Veenman's (1984) widely read review on the perceived problems of beginning teachers finds that "assessing students' work" tied for fourth on a list of 24 shortcomings found in the research literature. A range of recent studies has shown that beginning teachers enter the profession with scant knowledge of assessment (Maclellan, 2004) and that even after a course in assessment, candidates fail to enact their new knowledge (Campbell & Evans, 2000), suggesting that creating and using strong assessment practices could be developmental in nature. On the other hand, Weinstein (1989) found that candidates neither understand assessment nor regard it as important knowledge, so perhaps the lack of assessment literacy is more a matter of attitude than programmatic omission (see also Volante & Fazio, 2007).

The news on assessment literacy is not all bad. A recent study by Mertler (2009) demonstrated that even a 9-day course of study in assessment practices addressing general introductory topics (e.g., conducting an item analysis, developing valid grading procedures, developing a performance assessment and a scoring rubric) resulted in teachers who were more confident and who improved their assessment practices. It appears, then, that teachers and candidates may benefit from professional education on assessment practices but that current efforts are either nonexistent or underresourced.

ASSESSMENT STANDARDS FOR TEACHERS OF EL

The past 20 years have seen teacher licensing and professional growth turn to the development of comprehensive standards for the profession. Several major reports calling for the professionalization of teaching argued that teachers must take hold of professional standard setting if we are to establish confidence for our work among policymakers and the general public (e.g., The Holmes Group, 1986). The argument was that professionals must define high standards for those entering and continuing in the profession, set rigorous expectations, and then hold peers to these standards and expectations. Roth (1996) expertly documented—in some ways predicted—the early efforts of this movement, and we recommend that interested teacher educators recall his efforts to warn us of the consequences (Téllez, 2003). Darling-Hammond (1999) also offers a circumspect view of the development of disciplinary standards; she further suggests that the proliferation in standards is our own doing and that standards might not work as teacher educators envisioned. Even if a profession agrees to standards, it usually does not take long for policymakers to use the standards for political advantage (Cizek, 2000; Darling-Hammond, 2006; Téllez, in press).

More recently, and more forcefully, Taubman (2009) argues that standards in teacher education have had nothing but a corrosive influence on teaching, serving only to deprofessionalize the field. We also want to recognize our own bias against the pervasive use of standards in education and agree entirely with writers such as Faltis (1990), Pennycook (1999), Johnston (2002), and Kumaravadivelu (2005), who point out the reflexive and moral consequences when teaching ELs, both of which standards can obliterate.

A full discussion of costs and benefits of standards is beyond our task in this chapter, but with the widespread development of standards, we wanted to explore a select set of standards for those that specifically address assessment of ELs. If no government or professional entity required knowledge of EL assessment, then it would be less likely that candidates would gain such knowledge.

We begin by noting Bachman's (2000) call for increasing the training of language testing professionals and, predictably, for the development of standards of practice and mechanisms for ensuring their implementation. With the recognition the standards cannot alone bring about excellence, Bachman points out the dismal circumstances:

> Most professional programs, including certificate courses, master's and doctor's degree courses in language teaching or applied linguistics still require no coursework or guided practice specifically in language testing, so that the majority of practitioners who develop and use language tests, both in language classrooms and as part of applied linguistics research, still do so with little or no professional training. (pp. 19–20)

In the decade following Bachman's (2000) admonition, it appears that the assessment of ELs has made its way into standards for initial licensing, university- or college-based professional programs, and organizations designed to recognize the work of advanced professionals. We will explore an example taken from each of these categories, by first exploring California's Teaching Performance Expectations (required for licensure) and a performance assessment designed to assess the Expectations. We next examine the Teacher of English to Speakers of Other Languages (TESOL) and the U.S.-based National Council for Accreditation of Teacher Education (NCATE) standards for professional programs, and we end this section with an analysis of the National Board for Professional Teaching Standards.

California's Teaching Performance Expectations

California's recent restructuring of teacher education included new standards for licensure. As a consequence of the now-infamous Senate Bill 2042 legislation, the state developed the Teaching Performance Expectations (TPEs; California Commission on Teacher Credentialing [CCTC], 2013). As the state with the most English learners (1.4 million English learners, representing 23% of the entire school-age population; California Department of Education, 2011), educators and policy-makers were set on making certain that all new teachers were certified to teach ELs. Consequently, all state programs must ensure that candidates meet TPE 7: *Teaching English Learners*. Specific to our concern, this standard requires, among a longer list of competencies, that candidates "draw upon information about students' back-grounds and prior learning, including students' assessed levels of literacy in English and their first languages, as well as their proficiency in English, to provide instruction differentiated to students' language abilities."[10] In TPE 3: *Assessing Student Learning*, the standards specifically mention EL: "Candidates interpret assessment data to identify the level of proficiency of English language learners in English as well as in the students' primary language."

These standards represent challenging tasks for the preservice teacher candidate. Indeed, we are most struck by the emphasis on the knowledge and interpretation of assessments in both English and the students' native languages and wonder how many programs can make such knowledge mandatory among its candidates. We recall our earlier discussion regarding the BVAT and the range of knowledge required to understand the balance of languages.

For better or worse, policymakers in California wrote into Senate Bill 2040 law that all new teachers must be evaluated on the TPEs in a performance context. Teacher preparation programs in California can select the standardized Teaching Performance Assessment (TPA) system developed by the California Commission on Teacher Credentialing (CCTC), in partnership with the Educational Testing Service, or an alternative assessment that meets with the CCTC's assessment quality standards. After reviewing the TPA developed by the state, a group of universities and professional programs[11] developed an alternative performance assessment, known as the Performance Assessment for California Teachers (PACT; see www.pacttpa.org for a description and other information). We do not intend to provide an exhaustive review of the PACT and direct readers to other sources (e.g., Bunch, Aguirre, & Téllez, 2009; Porter, 2010; Sandholtz & Shea, 2012), but we would like to note aspects of the PACT that encourage—but not guarantee—a deep knowledge of EL assessment. First, the PACT is divided among four tasks (Planning, Instruction, Assessment, and Reflection) and built around a 2- to 3-day instructional segment. The Assessment task requires that candidates identify three student work samples (one must be an EL) that represent "class trends" in what students did and did not understand. Candidates must also provide a commentary that examines the standards/objectives of the lesson segment, analyzes the learning of individual students represented in the work samples, outlines feedback to students, and identifies next steps in instruction.

The PACT is distinguished primarily by a rubric assessing the candidate's knowledge of and instruction in academic language. It is on this point that the PACT is innovative with regard to EL assessment. For instance, to pass the PACT, candidates must demonstrate that they have used "scaffolding or other supports to address identified gaps between students' current language abilities and the language demands of the learning tasks and assessments, including selected genres and key linguistic features" (PACT, n.d.). Scoring at higher levels requires candidates to point out the role of the textual resources of the specific tasks/materials and how they are related to students' varied levels of academic language proficiency. It is when candidates aim for scores beyond passing that they often approach the comprehensive knowledge outlined in the TPEs (see Bunch et al., 2009).

The TESOL/NCATE Standards

Over a decade ago, the international organization TESOL and the U.S.-based NCATE jointly developed standards for programs preparing teachers for ELs. It is important to note that even though these standards are written with the candidate as the subject in most sentences in the document, these standards evaluate *programs*. And unlike California's TPEs, the standards require no direct assessment of candidates; rather, evidence gathered from program documents offers supporting evidence.

With respect to assessment knowledge and skills for teachers of ELs,[12] the domain is divided into three standards: Issues of Assessment for ELs, Language Proficiency Assessment, and Classroom-Based Assessment for ELs. We have included the citation for the entire standards document and do not have enough space to review these standards thoroughly, but we do wish to point out the text from the third standard: "Candidates can assess learners' content-area achievement independently from their language ability and should be able to adapt classroom tests and tasks for ELs at varying stages of English language and literacy development" (TESOL International Association, 2003, p. 64). Once again, we find that standards for teachers of ELs are demanding that teachers understand the relation between a general linguistic capacity and academic knowledge.

Overall, the TESOL/NCATE standards are comprehensive and lengthy. Although we do not have data on how many programs worldwide are approved using the standards, accredited institutions are likely graduating candidates better prepared for assessment of ELs than those not reviewed. We nevertheless agree with Newman and Hanauer (2005) who offer a thoughtful critique of the standards. They point out the overlapping and confusing nature of the assessment standards, in particular, and wonder how one can meaningfully separate the domain into three mutually exclusive areas of knowledge and skills. They also critique the breadth of the standards, noting that one standard requires candidates to understand the strengths and weaknesses of norm-referenced assessments. We agree that this skill is well beyond what should be expected of a beginning educator.

The National Board for Professional Teaching Standards

This well-known effort is designed to recognize exemplary, experienced teachers. Teachers produce a wide-ranging portfolio of their work, and if the criteria are met, they are given the distinction of Board-Certified teacher. In some states, teachers are given bonus pay for board certification (see http://www.k12.wa.us/certification/nbpts/teacherbonus.aspx for an example). The two categories of certification germane to our discussion are the Teaching English-as-a-New-Language portfolios for Early and Middle Childhood and Early Adolescence Through Young Adulthood (National Board for Professional Teaching Standards, 2012a, 2012b). The assessment sections of the standards are extraordinarily thorough, comprising the eight sections listed below (we have included sample text from three of the standards, pp. 77–85):

1. Variety in Assessment Techniques: "[Teachers] create their own tools for assessment that might incorporate students' daily class work, artwork, or exhibits."
2. Initial Placement Assessment
3. Assessment to Guide instructional or formative assessment
4. Assessment in the five language domains
5. English Language Proficiency Assessment

Accomplished teachers understand the purpose of proficiency assessments with regard to current local, state, and federal guidelines for monitoring the progress of students' English language development. Teachers collect and analyze data from formal sources. They know how to examine such assessment instruments critically and understand their uses and limitations in the practice of informed teaching. Teachers are knowledgeable about the psychometric properties of standardized tests when administered to ELs; academic language proficiency assessments; reading placement tests; and formative instructional assessments.

6. Standardized Content Assessment

Accomplished teachers work collaboratively with school staff to confirm the eligibility of English language learners to participate in content-area assessments and ascertain that students are assessed fairly. Teachers understand test validity and reliability and are able to explain to colleagues how these concepts relate to the unique features of evaluating English language learners.

7. Assessment for special purposes, in particular identifying gifted ELs
8. Substantive Assessment information for families and others

Naturally, these standards far exceed most of the requirements for initial licensure (cf. California's TPEs). The range and depth of knowledge is impressive, but we would draw attention to Standard 6, which requires that teachers understand and make certain that ELs are assessed fairly in the content areas. We also are intrigued by the fact that the Teaching English-as-a-New-Language portfolios are evaluated using a rubric that assesses a teacher's knowledge and instruction of academic language. As a relatively new concept for assessing teachers' knowledge at the intersection of language and content, teacher knowledge of academic language eliminates the false distinction that language can be learned without learning about anything (Bunch, Abram, Lotan, & Valdes, 2001; Laplante, 2000; Téllez, 2010).

AN OVERVIEW OF THE RESEARCH ON EFFECTIVE POLICIES AND PRACTICES IN PREPARING TEACHERS FOR PROPER ASSESSMENT OF EL AND RECOMMENDATIONS BASED ON THIS RESEARCH

The notion that teachers of EL need specialized preparation at all is a surprisingly recent development. We point to E. García's (1990) key chapter that illustrated the pitiful state of teacher quality for ELs. Citing the results from the available research and several national reports, he found that linguistic minority education programs were staffed by professionals not directly trained for such programs and who lacked adequate knowledge of second language teaching and learning.[13] What they learned, they learned "on the job." Teacher education researchers have discovered that a great many teachers of ELs, unprepared for conditions working with a linguistically diverse student population, fail to acquire much expertise at all (Gándara & Maxwell-Jolly, 2006; Gándara, Rumberger, Maxwell-Jolly, & Callahan, 2003). Instead, they grope for quick fix strategies, often becoming stressed at their limited options and lack of success. In a review of effective teacher professional growth practices, Knight and

Wiseman (2006) suggest that teachers of ELs need professional development focused on understanding language development that distinguishes between ELs' capacities for listening, speaking, reading, and writing. In fact, the early research conducted by Cummins (1982), who has more recently become a foremost international advocate for bilingual education, addressed this very concern; he demonstrated that when educators fail to recognize that ELs' proficiency in spoken English does not necessarily indicate full proficiency, ELs can be mislabeled as learning disabled, with disastrous consequences for the future learning opportunities of such students.

Self-reported data from teachers corroborate these findings, suggesting that teachers are confused and unsure about their capacities for effective teaching of ELs (Alexander, Heaviside, Farris, & Burns, 1998; Gándara & Maxwell-Jolly, 2006), although a recent study finds that teachers have greater confidence in their collective efficacy to provide strong EL instruction (Téllez & Manthey, in press).

E. García's (1990) admonition and other factors, such as a lack of teacher confidence as well as the growth in the EL population and their unacceptable academic performance, have motivated teacher educators and policymakers to initiate improvements in the quality of EL instruction. The decade of the 1990s saw a host of new policies and programs for the preparation of teachers of ELs. Many universities began specialized preparation for EL students, although some needed state legislation to initiate such improvements. Today we find a range of scholars and policymakers advocating for the importance of specialized preparation for teachers of ELs. Indeed, given the historical lack of attention to ELs, this burst of interest comes as somewhat of a surprise to those of us who have been working with ELs for decades (Theoharis & O'Toole, 2011).

As we consider the research that may point to effective strategies for preparing teachers of EL for better assessment strategies, we first consider what the research literature says about those competencies needed for quality EL teaching.[14] A long list of competencies and stances is quite impractical to the professional school teacher educator, who has but a year or two, perhaps three, to "prepare" teachers for their first year, or for the school professional development coordinator who must squeeze teacher learning regarding ELs into calendars already crowded with professional development. One recent research-based guide for competencies comes from Lucas and Villegas (2010), whose "Framework for the Preparation of Linguistically Responsive Teachers" includes the following elements: (a) sociolinguistic consciousness; (b) value for linguistic diversity; (c) inclination to advocate for EL students; (d) learning about EL students' language backgrounds, experiences, and proficiencies; (e) identifying the language demands of classroom discourse and tasks; (f) knowing and applying key principles of second language learning; and (g) scaffolding instruction to promote EL students' learning. Lucas and Villegas are careful to point out that these elements are not mutually exclusive and that the framework is neither intended as a formula and nor does it include every single knowledge and skill required for teaching ELs; however, assessment is notably missing from the list. Other works outlining what EL teachers should know and be able to do focus less on specific competencies and more on teacher socialization as a form of professional growth (e.g., Freeman, 1991; Freeman & Johnson, 1998), but knowledge of assessment is not specifically mentioned.

Again, we want to point out the value of these works and suggest that teacher educators would do well to heed their recommendations, but what might be the consequences of omitting assessment? Our discussion thus far has indicated that assessment may not make the top of the lists and that the research on professional development is quite sparse, offering scant guidance; nevertheless, the literature offers several excellent examples of EL teacher growth in assessment practices.

In a descriptive study that invited practicing bilingual teachers to develop concurrent tests of mathematics, one in Spanish, one in English, Solano-Flores, Trumbull, and Nelson-Barber (2002) found that teachers focused first on what might be called surface-level translation concerns. For instance, they wondered if the test should use metric values because these are the terms that native Spanish-speaking children, most Mexican American, would hear from their parents. As the teachers continued their translation work, they began to attend to what the authors termed the *deeper* concerns regarding the varying structures of the two languages. The teachers recognized that no two tests could ever be made entirely equal if they are written in different languages. The primary conclusion of the study revealed not that the teachers somehow got the translation correct and created equivalent forms, a complex task and arguably impossible feat, but rather that their collaborative work greatly enhanced their understanding of assessment. The study's authors conclude that teachers working in collaborative teams on assessment grow in their sophistication and that the collaboration was the key feature. We will find that the collaborative nature of teaching learning works in assessment literacy just as it does in other arenas of teacher development.

Our attention to the previous study, one focused on bilingual teachers and learners (in contrast to general English learners), raises an important question: Is bilingualism in educators a predictor of enhanced knowledge of language assessment? In other words, do we want all educators responsible for testing EL be bilingual themselves? If so, would we wish for them to be proficient in the native language of the students? The answer on both counts is, of course, yes. In fact, we always want people to speak more than one language. Who among us would not prefer to be multilingual if given the opportunity? But our question is more specific. Do bilingual educators have an advantage in assessment literacy? It would seem so, but we do not have any direct evidence. However, Zepeda, Castro, and Cronin (2011) argue convincingly that specialized assessment knowledge is crucial for teachers working in bilingual and dual language programs.

Artiles, Barreto, Pena, and McClafferty's (1998) longitudinal study found that two bilingual teachers' confidence in their teaching practice was related to the complexity of the bilingual programs in which they taught. In a study that calls to mind our earlier discussion of the assessment of bilingual verbal abilities, Ortiz et al. (2011) argue that bilingual education teachers should receive specific professional development on the assessment used to identify learning disabilities. Their role in the education of bilingual special learners should help other educators understand the "influence of language, culture, and other background characteristics on student performance" (p. 330).

A final example of teacher learning describes a professional development model designed to assist teachers understand more about the language demands of fourth- and fifth-grade mathematics with special attention to formative assessment practices (Thompson, 2008). The program was part of a larger funded project that sought to improve EL teaching practices across a statewide geographic range.[15] Therefore, bringing teachers together for multiple sessions was beyond the resources of the grant. As it turned out, this challenge turned into an opportunity. Ten teachers were invited to video record a mathematics lesson that they believed requires intensive instruction in mathematical language. The project sent a videographer to each teacher's classroom to assist in creating a quality video; the audio was especially important to capture. Each teacher's video was sent to another teacher in the project, one who taught the same grade. In nearly all cases, the teachers did not know each other prior to the project. Teachers were asked to watch their own video and their partner's and to make notes regarding specific academic language and formative assessment strategies they found. The teachers then came together for two face-to-face all-day meetings. The initial meeting was devoted almost entirely to a description of their classroom and school context, the establishment of common goals for the project, and the creation of trust among the group (Frederiksen & White, 1997; Halter 2006; Sherin & Han, 2004). The results of the study indicate that all of the teachers valued the ideas that emerged from teacher discussions; in particular, they suggested that contextualizing their teaching was an important part of the discussions. At the end of the project, they arrived at several key points that make mathematical language more comprehensible to ELs, as well as noting the importance of formative assessment in helping ELs reach new understandings.

The international context provides a few examples of studies on EL teacher assessment knowledge. For instance, Jones-Mackenzie's (2005) study of EL teacher knowledge of assessment among secondary English learners in Jamaica[16] addresses the following questions: (a) What sort of Knowledge About Language (KAL) do teachers report having? (b) Do teachers with KAL apply this information to the testing procedures employed? (c) Which aspects of testing show KAL use? (d) What factors inhibit the use of KAL in the testing process? First, although all the teachers reported some background in applied linguistics, only 2 of the 30 had taken a course specifically about testing. This finding corroborates the general lack of assessment preparation in professional schools. Specifically, Jones-Mackenzie found that KAL and language learning were insufficient: The teachers were aware of the importance of using KAL in testing, but they were not sure how to do so.

In a narrative study of Chinese English language teachers, Xu and Liu (2009) found that the teaching context influences educators' sense of security, which, in turn, influences the effectiveness of their assessment. If teachers are unsure and lack confidence in their pedagogy, they are less capable of making difficult evaluation decisions. They conclude that teachers' voices must be included in any reform policies, as well as repeating a common refrain of our review: the urgent need for professional development regarding quality assessment practices.

Given the general lack of assessment literacy among teachers of ELs, is teacher education (i.e., professional school preparation) to blame for failing to adequately prepare ELs' teachers? As we mentioned earlier, it makes little sense to expect that professional programs can be wholly responsible for everything we want teachers to know. But with respect to knowledge of EL assessment, we could not locate any research exploring candidate knowledge of EL assessment. Of course, this does not mean that professional school programs are not introducing candidates to the important concepts and practices. Some of the common texts used in EL methods courses address appropriate assessment (Diaz-Rico & Weed, 2009), but the research community has not studied the topic.

If the research on general knowledge of assessment is any guide, we can be confident that candidates lack an understanding of the nuances of EL assessment. Lacking research examples, we have decided to share a few of the practices used in our own program and invite readers to decide whether our methods might be useful.

Our own preservice teacher education program, for example, does not have a stand-alone course on assessment but rather addresses measurement concerns in each of several content-based methods courses. In particular, our program's course in English language development for elementary-level candidates requires assessment knowledge of reading by focusing on the released items from the California English Language Development Test (CELDT). (Note: the newly adopted California English Language Development Standards [California State Department of Education, 2012] will require the CELDT to be rewritten, a task not yet completed during the writing of this chapter.)

The general stance of our elementary EL preparation program is based largely on Halliday's (1969) language functions and tasks. Although not strictly a program or course of study based on Systemic Functional Linguistics, attention is drawn to the particular uses of language, and EL teachers must take care to develop each.

- Instrumental Language: For the work of life, to satisfy needs and wants
- Regulatory Language: For social control
- Interactional Language: For the establishment of social relationships
- Personal Language: To create a "self-text"
- Imaginative Language: To express and fantasize
- Heuristic Language: As a tool for learning about the world
- Informative Language: For the conveyance of information

Each of the functions could be assessed in some form, and we invite candidates to consider how they might evaluate their students' language skills in each function.

This task is open-ended and results in a wide-ranging discussion that often reaches into our candidates' general theories about teaching and learning. In contrast to this discussion, the hard realities of testing EL are presented in the form of released test items from the CELDT. We invite candidates to discuss why the items claim to assess reading, writing, and listening skills, as well as asking them to consider how the items might be biased against EL. Their general reaction is that language tests such as the CELDT are accurate but also tend to trivialize students' language capacities.

In addition, we ask students to learn more about receptive and expressive English usage by having them administer what we call a quick, informal language assessment.[17] Using Carmen Lomas Garza's painting "Tamalada," taken from her book *Cuadros de Familia* (1990), as a tool, candidates work with an individual EL, assessing the student's oral language by asking, for example, "Point to all the people sitting in chairs in the picture." As part of the expressive section, they ask an EL student to point to the stove hood and ask, "What is this? What is it for?" We also invite candidates to administer an oral story retell task (Blank & Frank, 1971), which offers them the opportunity to focus on the meaning of the story that ELs gain from the narrative. Finally, we invite them to present a few verbal analogies representing common forms (synonymic, antonymic, functional, linearly ordered, and categorical membership) to the student, based on their chronological age instead of their language level. Our candidates are routinely surprised by their EL's capacity to understand complex connections between individual words even when they assess beginning speakers, many of whom are still struggling to create complete, grammatically accurate sentences in English. The general reaction of our candidates is genuine surprise at how much English their ELs do know, as well as a deeper appreciation that teachers must create the conditions in which they can assess ELs' language capacities in individual settings.

If we can discern any common characteristics from the studies and cases described above, it is that teachers must collaborate to make genuine professional growth. In the context of EL teaching, this requirement seems only to grow in importance. In addition, they need to work within their own classroom walls. After reviewing all the literature on effective professional development, we find that the list of effective teacher learning compiled by Darling-Hammond and McLaughlin (1995) nearly 20 years ago remains relevant today. They recommend that effective professional development will adhere to the following principles:

- It must engage teachers in concrete tasks of teaching, *assessment* [italics added], observation, and reflection to enrich the learning and development processes.
- It must be based in inquiry, reflection, and experimentation that are participant-driven.
- It must be collaborative, involving a shared understanding among educators and a focus on teachers' communities of practice rather than on individual teachers.
- It must be connected to and derived from teachers' work with their students.
- It must be sustained, ongoing, intensive, and supported by modeling, coaching, and the collective solving of specific problems of practice.
- It must be connected to other aspects of school change. (p. 598)

The first casualty of this list is the so-called expert consultant who flies many miles to the school or district (after all, who can be a prophet in his own land?), deposits "expertise," and leaves. The big check is written and off goes our expert. No one is accountable—not the expert, not the administration. The only winner—beside the consultant's bank account—in this routine charade is the school leader, who can report that a professional development opportunity was presented to teachers. The note to the district office justifying the expense reads: "I had the expert tell the teachers how they should teach. If they don't do it, it's not my fault." Sometimes the consultant comes with a canned curriculum, also for sale, which promises to raise student achievement. Claims that the curriculum is research-based are never questioned, but purchases are made regardless. It is fascinating—and a bit disappointing—to find that this expert model survives in spite of decades of evidence documenting its failure (e.g., Datta, 1981).

Contrast this dismal scenario with a teacher learning group who *reads* what theorists and researchers have to say about language learning and assessment. Expert knowledge is not ignored or disparaged but rather filtered through the teachers' everyday experiences in their school, with their students, by reading and discussing what they have written. Teachers are compensated for their extra work; they are allowed to bill the district for the time they spend reading and learning. They test new ideas, new practices, in an environment that allows for experimentation and credible evaluation. The school system provides them with good data to make sound decisions, and given the right knowledge about the effectiveness of a program or strategy, teachers make the rational and pragmatic choice. Too many school leaders and politicians ignore the fact that teachers are nothing if not practical. If they have evidence that an instructional strategy does not help their students, they move on to what does. And if their trusted colleagues are those providing the evidence, a fortiori.

In this model, curriculum is built from the ground up, by teachers working together. It is difficult work and very time-consuming and sometimes more expensive than the consultant and the canned curriculum, but it has invested resources in enhancing teacher knowledge, which results in more efficient practices, which in turn raises student achievement.

We argue that if a school or school system is interested in enhancing the assessment knowledge of teachers of ELs, the principles outlined by Darling-Hammond and McLaughlin (1995) are even more relevant, with one important modification. When considering assessment practices, many of which are technical in nature (e.g., computing difficulty values), it makes sense to develop the expertise of a teacher (or teachers) who is (are) willing and able to understand these basic concepts and make them comprehensible to other educators at the school. The local teacher becomes the expert.

The most important point for school leaders to remember is that developing teacher knowledge takes time. The temptation to hire the expert, implement the off-the-shelf curriculum—to do it fast—must be restrained. Instead, schools leaders must focus on providing resources to schools emphasizing professional development that support teachers' instructional capacity and assessment literacy that informs instructional improvement; all the while focusing on how such teacher supports can be sustained over time.

The foregoing discussion has emphasized the importance of the school context in the proper assessment of ELs. Given the existing literature's focus on "curricular validity" and inequities regarding opportunities to learn, Abedi and Herman (2010), citing Herman, Klein, and Abedi, (2000) remind us of the potential barrier to EL student academic success resulting from the "lack of effective opportunity to learn (OTL)—students' access to and engagement in the academic content they need to perform well on tests and achieve standards" (p. 726).

For ELs, course-taking *opportunities* are often determined by linguistic measures, such as the degree of English language proficiency of students. Research has shown that ELs are likely to be placed in low-level courses according to their English proficiency (Callahan, 2005; Mosqueda, 2010; Mosqueda & Maldonado, 2013). Such placement practices are often made without an accurate assessment of students' English proficiency (Duran, 2008; Martiniello, 2008; Ruiz-de-Velasco & Fix, 2000). As a consequence, students' English proficiency can severely limit access to rigorous content courses, which might explain why they are disproportionly underenrolled in college preparatory coursework (Callahan, 2005). Furthermore, even when ELs are reclassified as English language proficient, they may still be denied access to rigorous courses (Valenzuela, 2010).

We end this section with an unfortunate contradiction. As Pandya (2011) found, educators seem to be particularly interested in testing their ELs but often rarely understand the results well enough to make good decisions based on the results. This misunderstanding often leads to additional and superfulous testing. To the extent that testing reduces instructional time, the burden of testing contributes to students' falling further behind in their content area opportunities to learn and their opportunities to develop English skills. If we continue to overtest students, we compromise opportunity to learn, particularly when such tests are not used to inform instruction.

CONTEMPORARY AND FUTURE CONCERNS REGARDING THE PREPARATION OF TEACHERS FOR THE SOUND ASSESSMENT OF EL

One does not learn (or teach) language in a way that resembles instruction in other aspects of human knowledge. Chomsky (1986), for example, was clear enough on this point. We can try to control it, atomize it, objectify it, but it will do what it wants, and always in relation to what its speaker intends. As we consider where assessment of ELs is leading, we find that Bunch's (2013) newly developed theoretical model of EL teacher knowledge has important applications to knowledge of assessment. Building on Shulman's (1987) well-known taxonomy of teacher knowledge, Bunch (2013) argues that what teachers need is pedagogical *language* knowledge that must be conceived of differently from either the pedagogical content knowledge about language needed by teachers specializing in second language teaching or the pedagogical content knowledge mainstream teachers need in the core subject matters. (p. 304)

Although these comments are directed at mainstream content teachers who teach ELs, we believe that his claim applies to all teachers of ELs, with particular implications for assessment. In his view, language is more than an object, more than a "tool" for learning about content. Bunch (2013) suggests that teachers must consider language learning as linked to students' ever-enlarging and shifting content knowledge. He maintains that teachers' knowledge of assessment must include the dimensions of time and context: a recognition that a student's growth in language will have inflection points and apexes, depending on his or her knowledge of the content. That is, what you know about the world depends on how much English you know, and vice versa. Thus, teachers of ELs must reconsider ways of assessing language and content as though the two were indistinguishable.

This view of assessment is, coincidentally, and perhaps by design, the cornerstone of the Common Core State Standards (CCSS) and the concomitant effort of the Smarter Balanced Assessment Consortium (SBAC; see http://www.smarterbalanced.org/).[18] The CCSS emphasizes "language use for communication and learning" in the content areas such as science and mathematics classrooms (Lee, Quinn, & Valdés, 2013, p. 223). Consequently, in the United States, we are entering a new era in the evaluation of K–12 learners. As schools and school systems begin to square their curriculum to the CCSS as well as addressing the daunting technical aspects of the SBAC plan, which will require all students to take the examinations in an online format, researchers and policymakers are considering how SBAC will be modified or otherwise adapted for ELs. A specific concern is whether low-income students from nondominant backgrounds will continue to be underserved in school. The CCSS's website home page includes a disclaimer that reads as follows:

The Standards set grade-specific standards but do not define the intervention methods or materials necessary to support students who are well below or well above grade-level expectations. It is also beyond the scope of the Standards to define the full range of supports appropriate for English language learners and for students with special needs. At the same time, all students must have the opportunity to learn and meet the same high standards if they are to access the knowledge and skills necessary in their post-school lives. (http://www.schoolimprovement.com/what-is-not-covered-by-the-standards/)

This acknowledged lack of attention to instructional and curricular supports for students who traditionally underachieve in schools can lead to a new set of national standards that merely replicates the long-standing disparities in academic achievement, unless strategies are put in place to help improve the educational outcomes of low-income students of color, particularly ELs.

The CCSS (2010) supports states that develop and implement common, high-quality assessments, including formative assessments that help inform classroom practice. At a minimum, such high-quality assessments are expected to measure the subject areas of reading/language arts and mathematics and provide information for each student annually in Grades 3 through 8.

Changes in assessment requirements under CCSS will offer useful information to middle school teachers and students, particularly ELs. Although policymakers will still use assessment results as summative indicators of learning, practitioners will also incorporate formative assessments of students' learning. Considering that such formative national assessments will include constructed-response items and measure speaking and listening skills, how such assessments affect the teaching and learning of ELs is an important educational policy and practice issue to follow.

With respect to teachers' knowledge of CCSS and ELs, though not specifically addressing the assessment of ELs in a CCSS world, Santos, Darling-Hammond, and Cheuk (2012) outline the shift in EL teacher knowledge by suggesting four primary points that will guide EL instruction under CCSS: (a) language progressions: how students learn language, both in terms of general language acquisition and in terms of the acquisition of discipline-specific academic language, (b) language demands: what kinds of linguistic expectations are embedded within specific texts and tasks with which students are being asked to engage, (c) language scaffolds: how specific representations and instructional strategies can be used to help students gain access to the concepts as well as to the language they need to learn, and (d) language supports: how classrooms and schools can be organized to support students in continually building a deep understanding of language and content.

Although they do not specifically mention a renewed knowledge of assessment strategies, such knowledge is embedded in these changes from previous goals for EL. In particular, if teachers of EL are to know deeply the language demands of academic tasks, they will have to be able to assess with good accuracy the *level* of language demands being placed on ELs (Celedón-Pattichis & Musanti, 2013; Lee et al., 2013). This is a question of sound assessment, of both the content (e.g., readability) and the learners (i.e., Are my students ready for the language demands they'll need to understand the lesson?).

CONCLUDING THOUGHTS

The linguistic turn in contemporary philosophy, which resulted in the discipline we now call poststructuralism, has emphasized that language itself, not our direct experience in the world and certainly not some externally wrought truth discovered independent of experience, is what structures our consciousness (Sarup, 1993). We are our language. It is the distinctiveness of our linguistic histories that makes us unique. And the linguistic histories of our ELs are far richer than most educators imagine.

We have tried to honor this complexity and nuance in our chapter while also recognizing the practical steps we can take to ensure that teachers are prepared and willing to assess their ELs expertly. Pedagogy cannot be made routine, and like the Salvatori (2003) quotation in the beginning of our chapter, we should be proud of the complicated messiness of our discipline. But the complexity often drives us to find prescriptions instead of compelling questions. Even the most comprehensive so-called solutions for addressing the proper assessment of ELs will fail when applied to individual students, who represent a linguistic and cultural profile that defies categorization.

The best educational assessments are mirrors, reflections of the larger achievement patterns found as a consequence of our priorities. It therefore makes little sense to expect that we can tinker with test content and design and eliminate score differences between ELs and their non-EL counterparts. After all, most ELs attend underfunded schools, cope with abject poverty (in spite of parents and other family members who work several jobs), and sometimes face harsh racism inside and outside the school. We should not expect any test to erase the effects of an inequitable and perhaps unjust society. We establish our priorities, and the measures of academic achievement reflect them. But we can and should be doing much more to help teachers, candidates, and other educators to know more about what makes for reliable and valid assessment for ELs. Assessments quickly turn into evaluations and therefore must be fair to all. This is the ideal we seek.

NOTES

[1]We use *teachers* to refer to in-service teachers, *candidates* to refer to preservice teachers earning the teaching license or certificate, and *students* for general elementary- and secondary-age learners.

[2]The happy advantage of the limited research is that we can devote significant attention to those papers that do address the topic.

[3]Our task was to complete a review of the available literature. Whereas less structured than a formal meta-analysis of the literature, we nevertheless held certain criteria for inclusion. In general, we tried to limit our review to peer-reviewed papers but we also included dissertations that we deemed to be of high quality. Search terms such as "bilingual" and "assessment" yielded works for the foundation of our review. Other terms used included "assessment literacy," which led us to the work we review in the section "The State-of-the-Art." In general, we relied on all the contemporary search techniques available and used indexing tools such as Google Scholar, which allows researchers to find similar articles, citations of key works, and works cited. We had access to all publications available in the University of California system, which holds one of the largest collections in the world

[4]Here we might recall Krashen's (1985) "i + 1" as a parallel concept to instructional level.

[5]By social capital, we mean the access to support via networks of institutional agents (school personnel) within schools that can potentially be activated by students to advocate on their behalf for more appropriate instructional learning opportunities (Stanton-Salazar, 2001).

[6]Crystal City is the small town in south Texas where, in 1969, Mexican American high school students staged a walkout in protest of harsh discrimination at the hands of an all-White school administration. After decades of discrimination and marginalization, Mexican Americans in Crystal City organized and were elected to the school board and other important political positions in the surrounding county. They soon implemented high school courses on the history of Mexican Americans, the first such course in the United States. They also inaugurated a maintenance bilingual education program, also a first. Scholars such as Angela Valenzuela (2000) have argued that the heroic efforts by the students and community in Crystal City helped to create civil rights era language education programs and ushered in the federal program known as the Office of Bilingual Education and Minority Language Affairs.

Sadly, these reforms have not lasted: During the George W. Bush administration (approximately 2002) the Office of Bilingual Education and Minority Language Affairs had its name changed to the Office of English Language Acquisition and, more or less, stopped funding bilingual education. The Obama administration has not changed this course. And our readers are no doubt aware of state legislation curtailing or outlawing native language instruction in places such as California and Arizona.

[7]Volumes by San Miguel (2004) and others (e.g., Cline, Necochea, & Rios, 2004) have documented the political struggles to retain quality language education in the United States. We recognize the importance of this topic but also know that a treatment of the political debates on language education would take many, many pages. For our purposes, ELs require sound language assessment across languages, regardless of the program in which they participate. Our view on the role of teachers in language policy is reflected in a recent article (Téllez & Varghese, 2013).

[8]Our preferred term would likely be *emerging bilinguals* or *multilinguals*, but we have decided to follow convention in this chapter and use *English Learner*.

[9]But if ELs were excluded from the testing regimes, would we not be concerned that schools would focus their attention on non-ELs, allowing ELs to languish because they were not part of the accountability scheme? If alternative tests were developed for ELs that reduced the language load and, subsequently, the cognitive and content complexity, would we not be concerned that such assessments would encourage lower expectations for ELs. On this point, we should not deceive ourselves: A test that "accommodates" a learner's developing knowledge of English will almost certainly diminish the complexity of the content to be measured. Our discipline's recent attention to the development of academic language is a clear admission of this fact.

[10]See http://www.ctc.ca.gov/educator-prep/standards/adopted-TPEs-2013.pdf, for the text of the California Teaching Expectations.

[11]Initially, in 2001, the Consortium consisted of 12 professional teacher preparation programs in eight University of California campuses, two California State Universities, Stanford University, and Mills College.

[12]The other domains are (a) Language; (b) Culture; (c) Planning, Implementing, and Managing Instruction; and (d) Professionalism.

[13]Although professional schools and school systems have been slow to develop specialized programs for teachers of EL, we recognize the long history of linguistics (often directed at adult "English as a second language" teachers) and foreign language programs devoted to teacher development.

[14]We recognize the overlap with the discussion of standards in the previous section, but what research recommends and what makes it into standards are not always the same.

[15]Both authors worked to develop this professional development experience.

[16]Jones-Mackenzie (2005) points out that the majority of the population in Jamaica, though often considered to be an English-speaking nation, speaks a creole as the first language. The schools teach English as new language.

[17]In advance of the assignment, we are very careful to tell candidates that the assessment is a class requirement only and that students' names will not be used in the discussion. Furthermore, we insist that they point out that this is an informal assessment designed only to help them learn more about oral language assessment. Even with these qualifications in place, a few of the schools call us concerned about how the results of the "tests" will be used. Such is the heightened scrutiny borne of harsh, punitive accountability schemes (i.e., NCLB).

[18]The SBAC is one of two efforts working to create assessments for the CCSS. The other is known as the Partnership for the Assessment of Readiness for College and Careers. We address only the SBAC strategy for several reasons. One is the fact that SBAC will be using a computer adaptive strategy, rather than the effort of the Partnership for the Assessment of Readiness for

College and Careers, which will be computer administered but not adaptive. Understanding computer adaptive testing is a more difficult concept for educators to grasp. Second, our own state of California, which has the largest number of ELs, has selected SBAC as its governing consortia. Texas, the state with the second most ELs, is not yet participating in CCSS.

REFERENCES

Abedi, J. (2004). The No Child Left Behind Act and English language learners: Assessment and accountability issues. *Educational Researcher, 33*(1), 4–14.

Abedi, J., & Herman, J. (2010). Assessing English language learners' opportunity to learn mathematics: Issues and limitations. *Teachers College Record, 112*, 723–746.

Abedi, J., & Lord, C. (2001). The language factor in mathematics tests. *Applied Measurement in Education, 14*, 219–234.

Alexander, D., Heaviside, S., Farris, E., & Burns, S. (1998). *Status of education reform in public elementary and secondary schools: Teachers' perspectives* (NCES No. 1999-045). Washington, DC: U.S. Department of Education, Office of Educational Research and Improvement.

American Educational Research Association, American Psychological Association, & National Council on Measurement in Education. (1999). *Standards for educational and psychological testing.* Washington, DC: American Psychological Association.

Anderson, L. W. (2000). Time, learning, and school reform: A conceptual framework. In P. C. Gandara. (Ed.), *The dimensions of time and the challenge of school reform* (pp. 13–29). Albany: SUNY Press.

Angrist, J. D., Dynarski, S. M., Kane, T. J., Pathak, P. A., & Walters, C. R. (2010). Inputs and impacts in charter schools: KIPP Lynn. *American Economic Review, 100*, 239–243.

Artiles, A. J., Barreto, R. M., Pena, L., & McClafferty, K. (1998). Pathways to teacher learning in multicultural contexts: A longitudinal case study of two novice bilingual teachers in urban schools. *Remedial and Special Education, 19*, 70–90.

Artiles, A. J., & Klingner, J. K. (2006). Forging a knowledge base on English language learners with special needs: Theoretical, population, and technical issues. *Teachers College Record, 108*, 2187–2194.

Artiles, A. J., & Ortiz, A. (Eds.). (2002). *English language learners with special needs: Identification, placement, and instruction.* Washington. DC: Center for Applied Linguistics.

Artiles, A. J., Rueda, R., Salazar, J. J., & Higareda, I. (2005). Within-group diversity in minority disproportionate representation: English language learners in urban school districts. *Exceptional Children, 71*, 283–300.

Ayala, C. C., Shavelson, R. J., Ruiz-Primo, M. A., Brandon, P. R., Yin, Y., Furtak, E. M., & Young, D. B. (2008). From formal embedded assessments to reflective lessons: The development of formative assessment studies. *Applied Measurement in Education, 21*, 315–334.

Bachman, L. F. (2000). Modern language testing at the turn of the century: Assuring that what we count counts. *Language Testing, 17*, 1–42.

Bartolome, L. I. (2004). Critical pedagogy and teacher education. *Teacher Education Quarterly, 31*, 97–122.

Black, P., Harrison, C., Lee, C., Marshall, B., & Wiliam, D. (2004). *Assessment for learning: Putting it into practice.* New York, NY: McGraw-Hill.

Blank, M., & Frank, S. M. (1971). Story recall in kindergarten children: Effect of method of presentation on psycholinguistic performance. *Child Development, 42*, 299–312.

Breedlove, L. (2007). Identifying linguistically diverse students as gifted and talented: A qualitative study of adding a new measure (Unpublished doctoral dissertation). Texas A&M University, College Station.

Brooks, D. (2012, March 22). The relationship school. *New York Times.* Retrieved from http://www.nytimes.com/2012/03/23/opinion/brooks-the-relationship-school.html?_r=0

Bunch, G. C. (2013). Pedagogical language knowledge: Preparing mainstream teachers for English learners in the new standards era. *Review of Research in Education, 37,* 298–341. doi:10.3102/0091732X12461772

Bunch, G. C., Abram, P. L., Lotan, R. A., & Valdes, G. (2001). Beyond sheltered instruction: Rethinking conditions for academic language development. *TESOL Journal, 10*(2), 2–3.

Bunch, G. C., Aguirre, J. M., & Téllez, K. (2009). Beyond the scores: Using candidate responses on a high stakes performance assessment to inform teacher preparation for English learners. *Issues in Teacher Education, 18*(1), 26.

California Commission on Teacher Credentialing. (2013). *California teaching performance expectations.* Retrieved from http://www.ctc.ca.gov/educator-prep/TPA-files/TPEs-Full-Version.pdf

California State Department of Education. (2012). *English Language Development Standards.* Retrieved from http://www.cde.ca.gov/sp/el/er/eldstandards.asp

Callahan, R. M. (2005). Tracking and high school English learners: Limiting opportunity to learn. *American Educational Research Journal, 42,* 305–328.

Campbell, C., & Evans, J. A. (2000). Investigation of preservice teachers' classroom assessment practices during student teaching. *Journal of Educational Research, 93,* 350–355.

Celedón-Pattichis, S. (2004). Rethinking policies and procedures for placing English language learners in mathematics. *NABE Journal of Research and Practice, 2,* 176–192.

Celedón-Pattichis, S., & Musanti, S. (2013). "Let's suppose that . . .": Developing base-ten thinking. In M. Gottlieb & G. Ernst-Slavit (Eds.), *Academic language demands for language learners: From text to context* (pp. 87–128). Thousand Oaks, CA: Corwin Press.

Chomsky, N. (1986). *Knowledge of language: Its nature, origin, and use.* New York, NY: Praeger.

Cizek, G. J. (2000). Pockets of resistance in the assessment revolution. *Educational Measurement: Issues and Practices, 19*(2), 16–23.

Cizek, G. J. (2010). An introduction to formative assessment: History, characteristics, and challenges. In H. Andrade & G. Cizek (Eds.). *Handbook of formative assessment* (pp. 3–18). New York, NY: Routledge.

Cizek, G. J., Fitzgerald, S. M., & Rachor, R. A. (1995). Teachers' assessment practices: Preparation, isolation, and the kitchen sink. *Educational Assessment, 3,* 159–179.

Cline, Z., Necochea, J., & Rios, F. (2004). The tyranny of democracy: Deconstructing the passage of racist propositions. *Journal of Latinos and Education, 3*(2), 67–85.

Cochran-Smith, M. (2001). The outcomes question in teacher education. *Teaching and Teacher Education, 17,* 527–546.

Common Core State Standards Initiative. (2010). *Common Core State Standards for English language arts & literacy in history/social studies, science, and technical subjects.* Washington, DC: CCSSO & National Governors Association.

Cummins, J. (1982). Tests, achievement, and bilingual students. *Focus, 9,* 1–8.

Daniel, L. G., & King, D. A. (1998). Knowledge and use of testing and measurement literacy of elementary and secondary teachers. *Journal of Educational Research, 91,* 331–344.

Darling-Hammond, L. (1999). *Reshaping teaching policy, preparation, and practice. Influences of the National Board for Professional Teaching Standards.* Washington, DC: American Association of Colleges for Teacher Education.

Darling-Hammond, L. (2006). Constructing 21st-century teacher education. *Journal of Teacher Education, 57,* 1–15.

Darling-Hammond, L., & McLaughlin, M. W. (1995). Policies that support professional development in an era of reform. *Phi Delta Kappan, 76,* 597–604.

Datta, L.-E. (1981). Damn the experts and full speed ahead: An examination of the study of Federal programs supporting educational change as evidence against directed development and for local problem-solving. *Evaluation Review, 5,* 5–32.

Diaz-Rico, L. T., & Weed, K. Z. (2009). *The crosscultural, language, and academic development handbook: A complete K-12 reference guide.* Boston, MA: Allyn & Bacon.

Duran, R. P. (2008). Assessing English-Language Learners' achievement. *Review of Research in Education, 32*(1), 292–327.

Faltis, C. (1990). Spanish for native speakers: Freirian and Vygotskian perspectives. *Foreign Language Annals, 23,* 117–125.

Flores, A. (2007). Examining disparities in mathematics education: Achievement gap or opportunity gap? *High School Journal, 91,* 29–42.

Frederiksen, J. R., & White, B. J. (1997). *Reflective assessment of students' research within an inquiry-based middle school science curriculum.* Paper presented at the annual meeting of the AERA, Chicago, IL.

Freeman, D. (1991). To make the tacit explicit: Teacher education, emerging discourse, and conceptions of teaching. *Teaching and Teacher Education, 7,* 439–454.

Freeman, D., & Johnson, K. E. (1998). Reconceptualizing the knowledge base of language teacher education. *TESOL Quarterly, 32,* 397–417.

Gándara, P. C. (2000). *The dimensions of time and the challenge of school reform.* Albany: SUNY Press.

Gándara, P. C., & Maxwell-Jolly, J. (2006). Critical issues in developing a teacher corps for English learners. In K. Téllez & H. C. Waxman (Eds.). *Preparing quality educators for English language learners: Research, policies, and practices* (pp. 99–120). Mahwah, NJ: Erlbaum.

Gándara, P., & Rumberger, R. (2009). Immigration, language, and education: How does language policy structure opportunity? *Teachers College Record, 111,* 750–782.

Gándara, P., Rumberger, R. W., Maxwell-Jolly, J., & Callahan, R. (2003). English language learners in California schools: Unequal resources, unequal chances. *Education Policy Analysis Archives, 11*(36). Retrieved from http://www.usc.edu/dept/education/CMMR/FullText/ELLs_in_California_Schools.pdf

García, E. (1990). Educating teachers for language minority students. In W. R. Houston (Ed.), *Handbook of research on teacher education* (pp. 717–729). New York, NY: Macmillan.

García, O., Kleifgen, J. A., & Falchi, L. (2008). *From English language learners to emergent bilinguals.* New York, NY: Teachers College.

Garza, C. L. (1990). *Family pictures/Cuadros de familia.* San Francisco, CA: Children's Book Press.

Gould, S. J. (1996). *The mismeasure of man* (Rev. ed.). New York, NY: W. W. Norton.

Grosjean, F. (1989). Neurolinguists, beware! The bilingual is not two monolinguals in one person. *Brain & Language, 36,* 3–15.

Haag, N., Heppt, B., Stanat, P., Kuhl, P., & Pant, H. A. (2013). Second language learners' performance in mathematics: Disentangling the effects of academic language features. *Learning and Instruction, 28,* 24–34.

Halliday, M. A. (1969). Relevant models of language. *Educational Review, 22*(1), 26–37.

Halter, C. P. (2006). The reflective lens: The effects of video analysis on preservice teacher development (Unpublished doctoral dissertation). University of California at San Diego.

Harper, C. A., de Jong, E. J., & Platt, E. J. (2008). Marginalizing English as a second language teacher expertise: The exclusionary consequence of No Child Left Behind. *Language Policy, 7,* 267–284.

Harris, D. P. (1969). *Testing English as a second language.* New York, NY: McGraw-Hill.

Heritage, M. (2007). What do teachers need to know and do? *Phi Delta Kappan, 89,* 140–145.

Heritage, M. (2010). *Formative assessment and next-generation assessment systems: Are we losing an opportunity?* Washington, DC: Council of Chief State School Officers.

Heritage, M. K., Kim, J., Vendlinski, T. P., & Herman, J. L. (2009). From evidence to action: A seamless process in formative assessment? *Educational Measurement: Issues and Practice, 28*(3), 24–31.

Heubert, J. P., & Hauser, R. M. (Eds.). (1999). *High stakes: Testing for tracking, promotion, and graduation.* Washington, DC: National Academies Press.

Hilliard, A. G. (2000). Excellence in education versus high-stakes standardized testing. *Journal of Teacher Education, 51,* 293–304.

Holmes Group. (1986). *Tomorrow's teachers: A report of the Holmes Group.* New York, NY: Author.

Hu, G. (2003). English language teaching in China: Regional differences and contributing factors. *Journal of Multilingual and Multicultural Development, 24,* 290–318.

Johnston, B. (2002). *Values in English language teaching.* Mahwah, NJ: Erlbaum.

Jones-Mackenzie, C. (2005). Knowledge about language and testing. In N. Bartels (Ed.), *Applied linguistics and language teacher education* (Vol. 4, pp. 313–324). New York, NY: Springer.

Klingner, J. K., & Solano-Flores, G. (2007). Cultural responsiveness in response-to-intervention models. In C. C. Laitusis & L. L. Cook (Eds.), *Large-scale assessment and accommodations: What works?* (pp. 229–241). Arlington, VA: Council for Exceptional Children.

Knight, S. L., & Wiseman, D. L. (2006). Lessons learned from a research synthesis on the effects of teachers' professional development on culturally diverse students. In K. Téllez & H. C. Waxman (Eds.), *Preparing quality educators for English language learners: Research, policy, and practice* (pp. 71–98. Mahwah, NJ: Erlbaum.

Krashen, S. D. (1985). *The input hypothesis: Issues and implications.* London, England: Longman.

Kumaravadivelu, B. (2005). *Understanding language teaching: From method to postmethod.* New York, NY: Routledge.

Laplante, B. (2000). Learning science is learning to "speak science": Students in immersion classes talk to us about chemical reactions. *Canadian Modern Language Review-Revue Canadienne Des Langues Vivantes, 57,* 245–271.

Lee, O., Quinn, H., & Valdés, G. (2013). Science and language for English language learners in relation to next generation Science Standards and with implications for Common Core State Standards for English Language Arts and mathematics. *Educational Researcher, 42,* 223–233.

Llosa, L. (2011). Standards-based classroom assessments of English proficiency: A review of issues, current developments, and future directions for research. *Language Testing, 28,* 367–382.

Lucas, T., & Villegas, A. M. (2010). The missing piece in teacher education: The preparation of linguistically responsive teachers. *National Society for the Study of Education, 109,* 297–318.

Maclellan, E. (2004). Initial knowledge states about assessment: Novice teachers' conceptualisations. *Teaching and Teacher Education, 20,* 523–535.

Mahoney, K. S., & MacSwan, J. (2005). Reexamining identification and reclassification of English language learners: A critical discussion of select state practices. *Bilingual Research Journal, 29,* 31–42.

Martiniello, M. (2008). Language and the performance of English-language learners in math word problems. *Harvard Educational Review, 78,* 333–368.

Martiniello, M. (2009). Linguistic complexity, schematic representations, and differential item functioning for English language learners in math tests. *Educational Assessment, 14,* 160–179.

McCarty, T. L. (2009). The impact of high-stakes accountability policies on Native American learners: Evidence from research. *Teaching Education, 20,* 7–29.

McMillan, J. H. (2000). Fundamental assessment principles for teachers and school administrators. *Practical Assessment, Research & Evaluation, 7*(8). Retrieved from http://pareonline.net/getvn.asp?v=7&n=8

McMillan, J. H. (2003). Understanding and improving teachers' classroom assessment decision making: Implications for theory and practice. *Educational Measurement: Issues and Practice, 22*(4), 34–43.

Menken, K. (2008). *English learners left behind: Standardized testing as language policy* (Vol. 65). Bristol, England: Multilingual matters.

Mertler, C. A. (2009). Teachers' assessment knowledge and their perceptions of the impact of classroom assessment professional development. *Improving Schools, 12,* 101–113.

Mertler, C. A., & Campbell, C. (2005, April). *Measuring teachers' knowledge and application of classroom assessment concepts: Development of the Assessment Literacy Inventory.* Paper presented at the annual meeting of the American Educational Research Association, Montreal, Quebec, Canada.

Minicucci, C. (2000). Effective use of time in the education of English language learners. In P. C. Gandara. (Ed.). *The dimensions of time and the challenge of school reform* (pp. 49–58). Albany: SUNY Press.

Mosqueda, E. (2010). Compounding inequalities: English proficiency and tracking and their relation to mathematics performance among Latina/o secondary school youth. *Journal of Urban Mathematics Education, 3,* 57–81.

Mosqueda, E., & Maldonado, S. I. (2013). The effects of English language proficiency and curricular pathways: Latina/os' mathematics achievement in secondary schools. *Equity & Excellence in Education, 46,* 202–219.

Muñoz-Sandoval, A. F., Cummins, J., Alvarado, C. G., & Ruef, M. L. (1998). *Bilingual verbal ability tests* (Comprehensive manual). Itasca, IL: Riverside.

National Board for Professional Teaching Standards. (2012a). *Early and middle childhood/English as a new language: Portfolio instructions.* Retrieved from http://www.nbpts.org/art-emc

National Board for Professional Teaching Standards. (2012b). *Early adolescence through young adulthood/English as a new language: Portfolio instructions.* Retrieved from http://www.nbpts.org/art-eaya

Newman, M., & Hanauer, D. (2005). The NCATE/TESOL teacher education standards: A critical review. *TESOL Quarterly, 39,* 753–764.

Ortiz, A. A., Robertson, P. M., Wilkinson, C. Y., Liu, Y.-J., McGhee, B. D., & Kushner, M. I. (2011). The role of bilingual education teachers in preventing inappropriate referrals of ELLs to special education: Implications for response to intervention. *Bilingual Research Journal, 34,* 316–333.

Páez, M. M. (2008). English language proficiency and bilingual verbal ability among Chinese, Dominican, and Haitian immigrant students. *Equity & Excellence in Education, 41,* 311–324.

Pandya, J. Z. (2011). *Overtested: How high-stakes accountability fails English language learners.* New York, NY: Teachers College Press.

Pennycook, A. (1999). Introduction: Critical approaches to TESOL. *TESOL Quarterly, 33,* 329–348.

Performance Assessment for California Teachers. (n.d.). *Frequently asked questions.* Retrieved from http://www.pacttpa.org/_main/hub.php?pageName=FAQ

Plake, B. S., Impara, J. C., & Fager, J. J. (1993). Assessment competencies of teachers: A national survey. *Educational Measurement: Issues and Practice, 12*(4), 10–12.

Popham, W. J. (2003). Seeking redemption for our psychometric sins. *Educational Measurement: Issues and Practice, 22*(1), 45–48.

Popham, W. J. (2006). Needed: A dose of assessment literacy. *Educational Leadership, 63*(6), 84–85.

Popham, W. J. (2011). Assessment literacy overlooked: A teacher educator's confession. *The Teacher Educator, 46,* 265–273.

Porter, J. M. (2010). *Performance Assessment for California Teachers (PACT): An evaluation of inter-rater reliability* (Unpublished doctoral dissertation). University of California, Davis.

Randall, J., & Engelhard, G. (2010). Examining the grading practices of teachers. *Teaching and Teacher Education, 26,* 1372–1380.

Rivkin, S. G., Hanushek, E. A., & Kain, J. F. (2005). Teachers, schools, and academic achievement. *Econometrica, 73,* 417–458.

Rodriguez, D. (2009). Meeting the needs of English language learners with disabilities in urban settings. *Urban Education, 44,* 452–464.

Roth, R. A. (1996). Standards for certification, licensure, and accreditation. In J. Sikula (Ed.), *Handbook of research on teacher education* (pp. 242–278). New York, NY: Macmillan.

Ruiz-de-Velasco, J., & Fix, M. (2000). *Overlooked and underserved: Immigrant students in U.S. secondary schools.* Washington, DC: Urban Institute.

Ruiz-Primo, M. A., Furtak, E. M., Ayala, C., Yin, Y., & Shavelson, R. J. (2010). Formative assessment, motivation, and science learning. In H. Andrade & G. Cizek (Eds.), *Handbook of formative assessment* (pp. 139–158). New York, NY: Routledge.

Rumberger, R., & Gándara, P. (2004). Seeking equity in the education of California's English learners. *Teachers College Record, 106,* 2031–2055.

Sadler, D. R. (1989). Formative assessment and the design of instructional systems. *Instructional Science, 18,* 119–144.

Salvatori, M. R. (2003). *Pedagogy: Disturbing history, 1819-1929.* Pittsburgh, PA: University of Pittsburgh Press.

Sandholtz, J. H., & Shea, L. M. (2012). Predicting performance: A comparison of university supervisors' predictions and teacher candidates' scores on a Teaching Performance Assessment. *Journal of Teacher Education, 63,* 39–50.

San Miguel, G. (2004). *Contested policy: The rise and fall of federal bilingual education in the United States, 1960-2001.* Denton: University of North Texas Press.

Santos, M., Darling-Hammond, L., & Cheuk, T. (2012). *Teacher development to support English language learners in the context of common core state standards.* Palo Alto, CA: Stanford University.

Sarup, M. (1993). *An introductory guide to post-structuralism and postmodernism.* Athens: University of Georgia Press.

Scriven, M. (1991). Beyond formative and summative evaluation. In M. W. McLaughlin & D. C. Phillips (Eds.), *Evaluation and education: At quarter century, 90th yearbook of the National Society for the Study of Education* (pp. 18–64). Chicago, IL: University of Chicago Press.

Shaw, J. M., Bunch, G. C., & Geaney, E. R. (2010). Analyzing language demands facing English learners on science performance assessments: The SALD framework. *Journal of Research in Science Teaching, 47,* 909–928.

Shepard, L. A. (2006). Classroom assessment. In R. Brenan (Ed.), *Educational Measurement* (4th ed., pp. 624–646). Westport, CT: Praeger.

Sherin, M. G., & Han, S. Y. (2004). Teacher learning in the context of a video club. *Teaching and Teacher Education, 20,* 163–183.

Shulman, L. S. (1987). Knowledge and teaching: Foundations of the new reform. *Harvard Educational Review, 57,* 1–22.

Solano-Flores, G. (2006). Language, dialect, and register: Sociolinguistics and the estimation of measurement error in the testing of English language learners. *The Teachers College Record, 108,* 2354–2379.

Solano-Flores, G. (2011). Language issues in mathematics and the assessment of English language learners. In K. Téllez, J. Moschkovich, & M. Civil (Eds.), *Latinos/as and mathematics education: Research on learning and teaching in classrooms and communities* (pp. 283–314). Charlotte, NC: Information Age.

Solano-Flores, G., & Trumbull, E. (2003). Examining language in context: The need for new research and practice paradigms in the testing of English-language learners. *Educational Researcher, 32*(2), 3–13.

Solano-Flores, G., Trumbull, E., & Nelson-Barber, S. (2002). Concurrent development of dual language assessments: An alternative to translating tests for linguistic minorities. *International Journal of Testing, 2,* 107–129.

Solórzano, R. W. (2008). High stakes testing: Issues, implications, and remedies for English language learners. *Review of Educational Research, 78,* 260–329.

Stanton-Salazar, R. D. (2001). Empowering relations of support between students and school personnel. In *Manufacturing hope and despair: The school and kin support networks of U.S.-Mexican youth.* New York, NY: Teachers College Press.

Stiggins, R. J. (1991). Assessment Literacy. *Phi Delta Kappan, 72,* 534–539.

Stiggins, R. J. (2001). The unfulfilled promise of classroom assessment. *Educational Measurement: Issues and Practice, 20*(3), 5–15.

Tang, G. (1992). The effect of graphic representation of knowledge structures on ESL reading comprehension. *Studies in Second Language Acquisition, 14,* 177–195.

Taubman, P. M. (2009). *Teaching by numbers: Deconstructing the discourse of standards and accountability in education.* New York, NY: Routledge.

Téllez, K. (1998). Class placement of elementary school emerging bilingual students. *Bilingual Research Journal, 22,* 279–295.

Téllez, K. (2003). Three themes on standards in teacher education: Legislative expediency, the role of external review, and test bias in the assessment of pedagogical knowledge. *Teacher Education Quarterly, 30,* 9–18.

Téllez, K. (2010). *Teaching English language learners: Fostering language and the democratic experience.* Boulder, CO: Paradigm.

Téllez, K. (in press). An analysis of the structure and assessment of standards for teacher candidates and programs. In H. C. Waxman, B. L. Alford, D. Brown, & K. Rollins (Eds.), *Preparing teachers to implement college and career readiness standards: Integrating research, policy, and practice.* Rotterdam, Netherlands: Sense.

Téllez, K., & Manthey, G. (in press). Teachers' perceptions of collective efficacy of school-wide programs and strategies for English language learners. *Learning Environments Research.*

Téllez, K., Moschkovich, J., & Civil, M. (Eds.). (2011). *Latinos/as and mathematics education: Research on learning and teaching in classrooms and communities.* Charlotte, NC: Information Age.

Téllez, K., & Varghese, M. (2013). Teachers as intellectuals and advocates: Professional development for bilingual education teachers. *Theory Into Practice, 52,* 128–135.

TESOL International Association. (2003). *Standards for the accreditation of initial programs in P–12 ESL teacher education.* Alexandria, VA: Author. Retrieved from http://www.tesol.org/docs/books/the-revised-tesol-ncate-standards-for-the-recognition-of-initial-tesol-programs-in-p-12-esl-teacher-education-(2010-pdf).pdf?sfvrsn=2

Theoharis, G., & O'Toole, J. (2011). Leading inclusive ELL social justice leadership for English Language learners. *Educational Administration Quarterly, 47,* 646–688.

Thompson, A. (2008, December). *Using video technology to provide a professional development forum for reflection on the use of academic language for mathematics in elementary school teachers.* Paper presented at conference of the California Mathematics Council North, Asilomar, CA.

Trujillo, A. L. (1998). *Chicano empowerment and bilingual education: Movimiento politics in Crystal City, Texas.* New York, NY: Taylor & Francis.

Trujillo, A. L. (2005). Politics, school philosophy, and language policy: The case of Crystal City schools. *Educational Policy, 19,* 621–654.

Tuttle, C. C., Teh, B.-R., Nichols-Barrer, I., Gill, B. P., & Gleason, P. (2010). *Student characteristics and achievement in 22 KIPP middle schools.* Washington, DC: Mathematica Policy Research.

Valdes, G., & Figueroa, R. A. (1994). *Bilingualism and testing: A special issue of bias.* Norwood, NJ: Abex.

Valencia, R. R., & Suzuki, L. A. (2000). *Intelligence testing and minority students: Foundations, performance factors, and assessment issues* (Vol. 3). Thousand Oaks, CA: Sage.

Valenzuela, A. (2000). Chicano empowerment and bilingual education: Movimiento politics in Crystal City, Texas by A. Trujillo. *Bilingual Research Journal, 24,* 207–212.

Valenzuela, A. (2010). *Subtractive schooling: US-Mexican youth and the politics of caring.* Albany: SUNY Press.

Veenman, S. (1984). Perceived problems of beginning teachers. *Review of Educational Research, 54,* 143–178.

Volante, L., & Fazio, X. (2007). Exploring teacher candidates' assessment literary: Implications for teacher education reform and professional development. *Canadian Journal of Education, 30,* 749–770.

Weinstein, C. S. (1989). Teacher education students' preconceptions of teaching. *Journal of Teacher Education, 40*(2), 53–60.

Wolf, M. K., & Leon, S. (2009). An investigation of the language demands in content assessments for English language learners. *Educational Assessment, 14,* 139–159.

Woodcock, R. W., McGrew, K., & Mather, N. (2001). *Woodcock-Johnson tests of achievement.* Itasca, IL: Riverside.

Xu, Y., & Liu, Y. (2009). Teacher assessment knowledge and practice: A narrative inquiry of a Chinese college EFL teacher's experience. *TESOL Quarterly, 43,* 492–513.

Zepeda, M., Castro, D. C., & Cronin, S. (2011). Preparing early childhood teachers to work with young dual language learners. *Child Development Perspectives, 5,* 10–14.

Chapter 4

Transformation in K–12 English Language Proficiency Assessment: Changing Contexts, Changing Constructs

Timothy Boals
University of Wisconsin-Madison

Dorry M. Kenyon
Center for Applied Linguistics

Alissa Blair
M. Elizabeth Cranley
Carsten Wilmes
University of Wisconsin-Madison

Laura J. Wright
Center for Applied Linguistics

INTRODUCTION

The educational rights of students learning English as an additional language have been federally protected for over 40 years. Since the landmark case of *Lau v. Nichols* (1974), language has been acknowledged as playing a central role in ensuring that English language learners (ELLs)[1] have equal access to academic content (Hakuta, 2011). These same years have seen numerous shifts in educational policy that have dramatically changed the ways in which ELLs are assessed for progress in learning English and core content areas. The reauthorization of the Elementary and Secondary Education Act (ESEA) under No Child Left Behind (NCLB) created heightened accountability provisions for ELLs (Abedi, 2004), and more recently, the College and Career Readiness (CCR) standards have elevated and made more explicit the language demands of content learning for all students, with particular consequences for ELLs (G. C. Bunch, Kibler, & Pimentel, 2012; Moschkovich, 2012; Quinn, Lee, & Valdés, 2012). New emphasis has also been placed on the need for measuring English language proficiency (ELP) and on clarifying what decisions can be reasonably made from ELP assessments (Abedi & Levine, 2013). From identification, classification,

Review of Research in Education
March 2015, Vol. 39, pp. 122–164
DOI: 10.3102/0091732X14556072
© 2015 AERA. http://rre.aera.net

placement, and instruction, to exiting from ELL status, the need for information about ELLs' language proficiency is critical for informing a vast range of decisions that affect their educational opportunities and outcomes.

Over the past decade and a half of educational reforms, the contexts and constructs informing ELP assessments have changed markedly. In turn, what ELP assessments measure has shifted (Wolf et al., 2008). The field of ELP testing has moved from lower stakes outcomes to higher stakes outcomes with respect to measuring language development (Abedi, 2004), and from assessments largely based on everyday language to assessments based on the notion of the academic uses of language or "academic language" (Bailey, 2007; Coleman & Goldenberg, 2012).

In the newest wave of standards-based reform, scholars have begun to explore the implications of CCR standards (e.g., Common Core State Standards [CCSS]) and Next-Generation Science Standards [NGSS]) for the instruction and assessment of ELLs, particularly where content testing and comprehensive assessment systems are concerned (see Abedi & Linquanti, 2012; Linquanti, 2011). However, a less systematic treatment has been conducted specific to ELP assessments.[2] Closer examination of ELP testing is timely and necessary given (a) the unprecedented level of language demands implicit in the CCR standards (Linquanti & Hakuta, 2012) and (b) the continued performance gap between ELL students and non-ELL students on standardized measures of academic achievement, notwithstanding data confirming that a "revolving door effect" makes the gap appear even worse as reclassified, former ELLs typically are not accounted for (Abedi & Gándara, 2006; Hopkins, Thompson, Linquanti, Hakuta, & August, 2013).

As professionals currently working with a particular English language development (ELD) standards and assessment consortium—the WIDA Consortium—we want to make known our stance toward assessment: Within a national policy context that previously ignored ELLs, we recognize the role of accountability in successfully focusing much needed attention on ELLs' academic development to ensure that federal civil rights mandates to provide equitable educational opportunities are upheld. Although we cannot ignore the well-documented consequences of high-stakes testing that have limited programming and curricula for ELLs (Menken, 2008, 2010), we proceed from the view that depending on how they are designed, implemented, and acted on, assessments can help ensure equitable educational opportunities for ELLs. We argue that ELP assessments provide a valuable source of information for promoting equitable opportunities for ELLs to learn and succeed in meeting CCR standards. Specifically, standardized ELP assessments help (a) clarify important school-based language expectations, (b) inform the educational community about how students are progressing in English language development, and (c) provide the information needed to ensure accountability to federal civil rights mandates so that ELL students receive the educational support services they need and are entitled to receive. As our discussion of assessment is mainly focused on large-scale, summative ELP tests for accountability purposes, this chapter will primarily be of interest to scholars interested in policy and to test developers and publishers, although users and practitioners will also benefit from the background and context on ELP assessment that this chapter provides.

In conducting this review, we examine literature that explores the merits and shortcomings of ELP test design and testing as they have evolved over time through the current era of CCR standards. In the first section, we situate the role of language testing in its broader historical and policy context. In the second section, we examine the evolving construct and operationalization of academic language. Here we provide an extended worked example of how the conceptualization of academic language is operationalized in the design, development, administration and use of a large-scale ELP assessment using what we are most familiar with, ACCESS for ELLs. We do not claim that this is the best or only approach; rather, it is a very concrete illustration applying state-of-the-art test design and construction. Within this context we examine issues of validity and accommodations in ELP testing. In the third section we explore expanded conceptualizations of assessment in the CCR era, in particular the purposes and uses of interim and formative assessments as part of a systems-wide approach. Finally, we offer a set of questions as a heuristic for test developers and educational professionals to continue to think critically about the role of ELP assessments in supporting the educational opportunities of ELLs in local contexts.

HISTORICAL BACKGROUND AND POLICY CONTEXT

The current state of ELP assessment in the United States both originates in and adds to the standards-based movement that has gained momentum over the past 30 years. In this review, changes in the evolving design of ELP assessments can be mapped over three major periods: the beginning of the Civil Rights era (1964–1980), the accountability era (1994–present), and the era of CCR (present and beyond).

The Beginning of the Civil Rights Era: Early ELP Testing

Early legislation affecting language minority students had more to do with extending equal access to meaningful instruction than with testing and accountability. The Civil Rights Act (1964) set the stage for federal involvement in dismantling segregation in education. As part of President Johnson's Great Society's Program, ESEA (1965) drew attention to disparities in achievement by certain social and economic groups (Halperin, 1975) but not language minorities. Three years later, Title VII, the Bilingual Education Act (1968), specifically addressed the instructional needs of linguistically diverse students by providing local funding to support educational programs in students' native languages (Hakuta, 2011). The class action suit, *Lau v. Nichols* (1974), resulted in legal protection for language minority students. Citing Title VI of the Civil Rights Act, the U.S. Supreme Court ruled that language discrimination amounted to discrimination of national origin (Gándara, Moran, & García, 2004). This decision created a need to identify and place students referred to as "limited English-proficient" (LEP) for bilingual or English as a second language (ESL) services (Wiese & García, 1998). The Equal Educational Opportunities Act of

1974 (Pub. L. No. 93-380) further required states to ensure that an education agency "take[s] appropriate action to overcome language barriers that impede equal participation by its students in its instructional programs" (20 U.S.C. Sec. 1703(f)). *Castañeda v. Pickard*, a 5th Circuit ruling (1981), interpreting the Equal Educational Opportunities Act, extended the notion that ELLs must receive appropriate educational services and that those services should be provided with defensible methodologies leading students to overcome the barrier to learning that emergent English proficiency presented (Salomone, 2012). Following this, many states created laws and administrative codes directing schools to identify and create programs for ELLs.

From the 1970s through the 1990s, then, ELP assessments existed in the form of commercially available tests that assisted local decision making in program implementation and monitoring of ELLs in a low-stakes environment. In this era, federal- and state-initiated but locally conceived and monitored ESL and bilingual services prevailed (Council of Chief State School Officers, 1991). Programs were typically envisioned as "transitional" in nature, meaning the goal was to provide students with enough support to "exit" the special program and succeed in the broader school environment. Schools often used the same English proficiency instruments, many times the same test form, to document entry and exit from special support services (Antunez, 2003). Assessment scores were coupled with anecdotal information about how students were performing in mainstream classes. Commercial ELP assessments such as the Language Assessment Scales and the Idea Proficiency Test gained popularity as they added consistency to the process, at least within a particular school or district where the same assessment was used. However, tests focused on what might be deemed "social" language and assessments were not systematically designed to measure progress of language attainment (Antunez, 2003; Wolf et al., 2008). Without statewide English language proficiency standards, commercial tests were usually based on unexamined assumptions of what English language proficiency meant. It was an inexact science, arguably one that resulted in a wide range of inconsistent decisions from one district to the next.

The Accountability Era: Toward Inclusion and Standardized Testing

The standards era as it exists today, with its emphasis on high standards for all students, was foreshadowed in the 1980s with *A Nation at Risk* (Gardner, 1983) and began implementation in earnest under the Improving America's Schools Act (IASA) of 1994. Public schooling came under scrutiny based on the presumption that the nation as a whole was "at risk" of not keeping up with international competition (Gardner, 1983) and that gaps in achievement persisted among certain groups of students (Kaufman, 1992). IASA was considered one of the key reauthorizations of ESEA as it emphasized outcomes (evidence of progress) over inputs (stipulations about how progress would be achieved; Riley, 1995). New, more challenging standards were required to be written under IASA that replaced minimum standards to hold all students accountable (Riddle, 2002).

One of the biggest changes under IASA was the mandate to ensure inclusion of all students in states' academic accountability systems, including ELLs (Billig, 1997). Congress agreed that states needed time to revamp their assessment systems so that they could provide valid and reliable assessment of these special populations that had previously been largely excluded. After the initial passage of IASA, most states did not require local districts to include ELLs in academic content testing based on the assumption that the current tests were not valid for them (Vincent, Hafner, & LaCelle-Peterson, 1997). In the newly emerging accountability era, however, it was painfully obvious that districts had only disincentives to include ELLs in testing as academic test scores averaged at the school level would likely be negatively affected by their participation. Typically with no time limits on exemption from testing and no consistent way to measure when an ELL met a reasonable threshold of English proficiency for valid testing of academic progress, students developing English as an additional language were in many cases never tested for academic progress, and schools and districts were not held accountable for ELLs' English language development or academic achievement (Lacelle-Peterson & Rivera, 1994). Thus, there was no system in place by which to determine whether or not federal mandates to ensure equitable education of ELLs were, in fact, upheld (Shaul & Ganson, 2005).

Not long after IASA's inclusion mandate took full effect in July 2000, the reauthorization of ESEA under NCLB (2001) effectively put in place an accountability system to reinforce the standards-based focus initiated by IASA (Hakuta, 2011). Four major changes under NCLB affected assessment of ELLs in particular: the definition of LEP students, the new requirement for ELP/D[3] standards (on which ELP assessments were based) to be tied to content standards, stipulations as to what ELP assessments measured and how, and accountability measures for tracking ELLs' linguistic and academic progress, known as Annual Measurable Achievement Objectives (AMAOs).

Consistent with earlier authorizations of ESEA, NCLB defines "limited English proficient" as a K–12 student whose difficulties in speaking, reading, writing, or understanding the English language may be sufficient to deny him or her the ability to (a) successfully achieve in classrooms where the language of instruction is English or (b) the opportunity to participate fully in society, and furthermore adds (c) the ability to meet the state's proficient level of achievement on state assessments (see Title IX, Part A § 9101 (25)(D)). One of the key indicators, then, of having sufficiently addressed the linguistic needs of ELLs is their ability to successfully participate in state content assessments (Cook, Linquanti, Chinen, & Jung, 2012).

For the first time, the reauthorized law called for ELP/D standards to correspond to academic content standards and for the ELP tests to be aligned to the revised ELP/D standards.[4] Thus, the previous generation of ELP instruments, which were never standards-based, became inadequate. Under the new accountability framework, previously developed ELP assessments were limited due to their inability to accurately measure language proficiency attainment over time validly and reliably and their lack of correspondence to state content and therefore the language of schooling associated with academic success (Parker, Louie, & O'Dwyer, 2009; Wolf et al., 2008). Although the NCLB definition of LEP links language proficiency to academic content proficiency as measured by state content tests, the processes and tools for identifying, classifying, and exiting ELLs were not uniform across states and districts.

With respect to improved assessment of ELLs, progress toward fulfilling the new mandates was slow, in particular because states faced challenges with capacity and finances to meet these new accountability provisions (Linquanti, 2011; Shaul & Ganson, 2005). States had and still have limited technical capacity and resources for serving ELLs and little experience developing ELP/D standards (Cook et al., 2012). Local ELP/D standards (where they existed), inadequately corresponded to language demands inherent in content standards and tended to emphasize form (i.e., English grammar) over function (i.e., communicative skills), serving more to focus on basic English development rather than helping teachers and students focus on the specific school-based and more complex language needed for school success (Antunez, 2003). Most states lacked the empirical data with which to consider progress criteria and performance targets, so they had little idea how to set appropriate goals to measure language growth, which in many cases were unrealistic (Cook et al., 2012).

To address some of the shortcomings of existing ELP assessments, the U.S. Department of Education sponsored an Enhanced Assessment Grants (EAGs) competition to develop new ELP assessments that would meet NCLB requirements. Up until that point, only a few states (e.g., California) had ELP/D standards in place or a standards-based ELP assessment. The EAGs awarded in March 2003 constituted a watershed moment when the federal government encouraged participating states to develop a new generation of ELP instruments more fully aligned and linked to the appropriate standards and capable of validly and reliably measuring progress over time. Recognizing that the technical requirements in Sections 3121 and 3122 of Title III depended on the availability of adequate funding, Title VI of NCLB (Section 6112) provided for an Enhanced Assessment Instrument competition that offered a total of $17,000,000 to support "alternatives for assessing students with disabilities and limited English proficient students" (Fed. Reg. 67/No. 99, May 22, 2002, p. 35979). Under this grant competition, a total of nine awards were made to consortia headed by state education agencies, four of which led to the creation of ELP assessment consortia. These four consortia were brought into being through the grants awarded to Pennsylvania, Nevada, Utah, and Wisconsin. The movement toward shared, consortia-based assessment systems had now begun as a means to alleviate a lack of resources within individual states to meet the new requirements of NCLB.

These newly created ELP assessments have been essential tools for monitoring two of the three AMAOs outlined by Title III: (a) progressing in English language acquisition and (b) reaching English language proficiency. The third AMAO, adequate progress for the ELL subgroup (under Title I) in meeting grade-level academic achievement standards in Reading/Language Arts and Mathematics, is monitored through state content assessments. The first two AMAOs require states to use standardized ELP assessments to monitor ELLs' language development and districts in order to ensure that ELLs were making progress at agreed-on rates toward a goal of reclassification as "proficient" with respect to English. However, there have been numerous critiques of how AMAOs are calculated, and benchmarking progress is complex. According to NCLB, all students are required to make the same rates of progress, but several research studies indicate that students at higher levels of proficiency make progress more slowly in comparison with the more rapid growth rates of students at lower levels of proficiency (Cook, Boals, & Lundberg, 2011; Hakuta, Butler, & Witt, 2000). In dealing with these issues in California, Linquanti and George (2007) used extant ELP assessment data to model options and support state policymakers in setting student progress expectations and district-level progress targets.

The third AMAO, concerned with adequate progress in meeting grade-level academic achievement standards, was a direct import of Title I Adequate Yearly Progress for the ELL subgroup now required to be disaggregated from the total student population in the 2001 legislation (Shaul & Ganson, 2005). Adequate Yearly Progress already required schools receiving Title I funding to make annual improvements in standardized test scores (Linn, Baker, & Betebenner, 2002). This is problematic for ELLs given that only reaching "proficient" academic status counts, yet the subgroup cycles in new students at lower English proficiency levels for whom demonstrating academic proficiency is challenging, and cycles out former ELLs after 2 years thus limiting the "credit" districts receive for their successes with this subgroup (Hopkins et al., 2013). Although the effects of NCLB accountability requirements for ELLs have been critiqued by many (Harper, Jong, & Platt, 2008; Menken, 2008, 2010; Sólorzano, 2008; Valenzuela, Prieto, & Hamilton, 2007), they have been seen as having one positive effect: NCLB has required disaggregation of data on ELLs and highlighted the need to better support these students (Lyons, 2013).

ELP Testing in the Era of College and Career Readiness

The most recent and highly anticipated wave of standards-based accountability has been driven by CCR standards, specifically, CCSS, and NGSS. As of this writing, 43 states and the District of Columbia have adopted the CCSS standards[5] and 13 states have adopted the NGSS. In comparison with previous content standards, the new standards place more explicit emphasis on language uses in content learning and performance for all students (Council of Chief State School Officers, 2012; Quinn et al., 2012). The CCSS explicitly describe language and literacy skills across history/social studies, science, and technology as an integral part of 6–12 English Language Arts standards, whereas the CCSS mathematics and NGSS standards describe much more explicitly than previous standards the uses of language needed to carry out key practices in these disciplines. Language test developers can benefit from all of these target expectations to create more consistent ELP measures (Bailey & Wolf, 2012). As a result, consortia and stand-alone states have either updated or largely reconceived ELP/D standards in light of the adoption of CCR standards (Cook et al., 2012).

The most recent shift in ELP assessment is currently underway. The U.S. Department of Education through its EAG program funded two ELP assessment consortia to develop technology enhanced ELP assessments aligned to CCR standards. The Assessment Services Supporting ELLs Through Technology Systems (ASSETS) Consortium, established in September 2011 by the WIDA Consortium, is developing a technology-enhanced assessment system to assess the development of ELLs' academic English language needed for college and career success. The comprehensive assessment system will be (a) technology-based, incorporating several major technological enhancements; (b) anchored in the established WIDA ELD[6] Standards, which are aligned with the CCR standards; (c) informed by ongoing research; and (d) supported by comprehensive professional development and outreach. Additionally, the English Language Proficiency for the 21st-Century Consortium (ELPA21) was funded in 2012 to develop ELP/D standards and a technology-enhanced summative ELP assessment. ELPA21's standards were released in 2013, and as of this writing item development is underway. Currently, 45 states are involved in these two ELP consortia, suggesting that in the future, there will be greater commonality in assessment practices for ELLs across the United States.

The current status of ELP assessments within the CCR context continues the importance of ELP testing under NCLB. Not only is growth in developing ELP required to be accurately measured, Local Education Agencies are also judged on demonstrating such growth in their ELLs. The CCR context also supports the NCLB requirements that ELP/D standards be aligned to ELP assessments and correspond to content standards. For as much as the CCSS and NGSS standards explicitly outline language demands associated with content performance, and much more so than previous standards, researchers have contended that these CCR standards also presuppose language skills that are not overtly acknowledged (Bailey & Wolf, 2012; Council of Chief State School Officers, 2012). Therefore, identifying the linguistic knowledge and skills associated with the standards is a pressing task to ensure that assessments are properly aligned to the standards. To support this work the CCSSO produced a document known as the *Framework for English Language Proficiency Development Standards Corresponding to the Common Core State Standards and the Next Generation Science Standards* to aid states in developing and organizing their ELP/D standards in relation to the CCR standards (Council of Chief State School Officers, 2012). Tools such as this can help ensure greater comparability and fairness in making judgments for accountability purposes since different states and consortia have different ELP/D standards (Linquanti, 2011). Thus, even as the content standards change, there continues to be a pressing need to understand the relationships between and among these multiple types of standards and their related assessments.

LARGE-SCALE ELP ASSESSMENTS

Closely examining current large-scale ELP assessments, especially as they contrast with pre-NCLB language measures, brings to light the advancements in language proficiency testing for ELLs. The relationship between language and content is certainly intertwined but still contested, both as a construct and in its operationalization for testing purposes (Bailey & Huang, 2011; Gutiérrez, 1995; Valdés, 2004). And although improvements in ELP testing have been made in recent years to better reflect the language students use to learn in academic contexts, much debate centers on the notion of academic language as a construct that can be assessed. In this section we examine the evolving understanding of the construct of academic language, its operationalization on ELP tests, and persistent validity issues in assessing ELLs.

Conceptual Developments: Understanding Academic Language[7]

One of the most significant changes in ELP testing in the past 10 years has been the emphasis on assessing the language needed for academic success commonly referred to as "academic language." Prior to NCLB, the conceptual frameworks and consequently the outcomes measured by ELP tests revolved around the types of language typically used in everyday contexts (Bailey, 2007). This focus contrasts sharply with the NCLB era ELP assessments, which center on the language needed to access academic content (Abedi, 2007). In addition, many of the early commercially produced assessment tools were built on a discrete view of language knowledge rather than on second language acquisition theory (Abedi, 2007; Wolf et al., 2008). For example, the Language Assessment Scales and Idea Proficiency Test were commonly used to identify ELLs to meet Civil Rights requirements rather than to measure language proficiency attainment. English language arts content assessments such as the Stanford 9 were developed to test grade-level knowledge and skills of English language arts rather than academic language proficiency across content areas (Antunez, 2003). Abedi (2007) and Wolf et al. (2008) assert that the constructs on which these assessments were built were based on a different perspective of language. That is to say, the tasks reflected the kinds of language needed for interaction in everyday social contexts rather than the language needed in academic contexts.

The advent of NCLB brought a need to demonstrate a relationship between proficiency as measured by ELP assessments and the language needed to achieve state academic content standards. A great deal of theory, research, and practice have supported the current wave of ELP assessments by specifying, through the ELP/D standards on which they are based, the nature of the language and language abilities to be assessed. Research on bilingualism and second language learning during the 1980s and 1990s began to lay a foundation for this. Work by Cummins (1981), for example, began to create an awareness of academic language, and work by Mohan (1986) sought to explain the relationship between language and content learning. These lines of research transformed pedagogical approaches that emphasized the role of language in learning academic content. The Sheltered Instruction Observation Protocol (Echevarría, Short, & Powers, 1999), Cognitive Academic Language Learning Approach (Chamot & O'Malley, 1994), and Specially Designed Academic Instruction in English (Jiménez, 1992) promoted teaching methodologies to provide

ELLs access to content in mainstream content classes, and focused on academic language development. Thus, a shift in research and practice had already begun to anticipate the linguistic needs of ELL students—namely, the need for academic language. However, from early on, controversies surrounded the notion of academic language (Rivera, 1984; Valdés, 2004; Wolf et al., 2008) and continue today.

For over three decades, views of academic language have emerged and diverged without widespread agreement as to how to define it. Regardless, because NCLB requires ELP/D standards to correspond to content standards, current ELP/D standards have had to operationalize academic language (either implicitly or explicitly). In this section, we review prominent theories of academic language, including cognitively, socioculturally, and linguistically oriented perspectives.

One of the earliest perspectives on academic language, put forth by Jim Cummins more than 30 years ago, is based on cognitive science theory (Cummins, 1981, 2000). Cummins introduced the terms *basic interpersonal communication skills* (BICS) and *cognitive academic language proficiency* (CALP) to describe the types of mastery students have over language use in different settings. Cummins (2013) noted that the distinction between BICS and CALP is intended to draw attention to the different time periods of language acquisition typical for immigrant students. Specifically, BICS refers to the language-related skills needed to communicate in everyday life. According to Cummins's theory, BICS are acquired within 1 to 2 years and may give a student the appearance of proficiency. On the other hand, CALP refers to language-related skills needed to communicate in academic contexts and reflects a language learner's "access to and command of specialized vocabulary, functions, and registers of language that are characteristic of the social institution of schooling" (Cummins, 2013, p. 10). Cummins proposes that CALP takes longer to acquire, as long as 4 to 7 years (Cummins, 1984, 1986). Central to Cummins's notion of BICS and CALP are theories about the role of cognition and context vis-à-vis language. Cummins views language, cognition, and context as all being related, proposing that social language poses less cognitive burden on students because it is contextually embedded and therefore easier to acquire.

Cummins's approach has been widely criticized over the years, most notably by sociocultural researchers and linguists, because it posits that there is a difference between social and academic language and that this difference has cognitive consequences (e.g., Edelsky, 1990; Romaine, 1989; Troike, 1984; Wiley, 2005). In contrast to Cummins, sociocultural researchers have emphasized the role of socialization in academic language development, attributing differences in linguistic ability to students' access to registers or styles of language use. For example, both Gee (1990, 2008) and Rymes (2010) propose that understanding students' development of academic language is related to their home language. Central to Gee's (1990) perspective is the notion of *discourse* referring to "ways of being in the world or forms of life which integrate words, acts, values, beliefs, attitudes, social identities, as well as gestures, glances, body positions, and clothes" (Gee, 1990, p. 142). According to Gee, discourses are "identity kits" because they are ways of identifying with various social groups. Building on this, Gee proposes the notions of *primary discourses* and *secondary discourses* to describe contexts in which language is learned and used. Primary discourses are those learned at home, and secondary discourses are those learned outside of the home. For some students, academic language is a primary discourse because it mirrors the way language is used at home. For others, it is a secondary discourse because it does not mirror the way language is used at home and must be learned at school. Rymes's (2010) approach also reflects the importance of language socialization, using the term *repertoires* to describe the ways in which students learn to use language in different contexts. Because some children are socialized to academic language practices at home (Heath, 1983), academic language is more familiar, and because some children first encounter academic language practices at school, they are less familiar. This, in turn, makes using academic language more or less comfortable for certain students. Socioculturally oriented perspectives tend to place an emphasis on teaching socially powerful forms and conventions explicitly to uncover hidden expectations about language use. Gee (2008) states,

Failing to teach all learners new ways with words privileges those whose conversational styles already incorporate aspects of academic language. It places at a disadvantage those students whose early language socialization has not incorporated aspects of academic language that are valued and recognized in school because they are left without the tools necessary for academic success. (pp. 68–69)

Sociocultural perspectives are useful pedagogically and may provide a cautionary tale for interpretations of assessment results in that students' linguistic abilities, as demonstrated on assessments, may be as much a reflection of their socialization to language practices as their cognitive abilities.

In addition to cognitive and sociocultural perspectives on academic language, linguistic perspectives are prevalent. These approaches tend to be descriptive, identifying an array of linguistic features associated with academic uses of language. One linguistic approach, Systemic Functional Linguistics (SFL), was originally developed in Australia and has gained popularity in the United States (Halliday, 1978; Schleppegrell, 2004). SFL describes academic language as a register associated with certain lexicogrammatical features. SFL studies have illustrated the unique characteristics of discipline-specific language, such as the language of science (e.g., Halliday & Martin, 1993; Lemke, 1990). For example, studies on scientific language have often discussed *nominalization* (e.g., transforming verbs into nouns by using derivational suffixes).[8] Research by Christie and Derewianka (2008), Halliday and Martin (1993), Gibbons (2003), Lemke (1990), O'Halloran (2004), Schleppegrell (2001, 2004, 2007), Veel (1999), and Unsworth (1999), among others, has sought to identify how language is used in different school content areas such as English language arts, science, mathematics, and history. These studies provide useful examples of how language is used to make meaning within different academic content areas, and how language use across content areas is slightly different.

Scarcella (2003) also takes a linguistic approach to describing academic language, identifying several linguistic dimensions including: phonological, lexical, grammatical, sociolinguistic, and discourse, as well as their associated features of language.

Scarcella proposes that academic language is a "variety or register of English used in professional books and characterized by the specific linguistic features associated with academic disciplines" (2003, p. 19). Because of its focus on professional books, this perspective places greater emphasis on the types of language used in written texts, rather than oral discourse.

Another linguistically oriented perspective offered by Snow and Uccelli (2009) also inventories characteristic linguistic features of academic language identified in previous research. Although they suggest that the inventory has some utility, they argue that describing features of language is not enough. They assert that a description of academic language must also explain *why* certain features are salient in particular contexts of language use. They propose a pragmatic approach that emphasizes that students must understand not only what they need to communicate but also to what end, and how to communicate it. Their perspective illustrates how the choice of linguistic forms is nested within sociocultural frames such as knowing one's audience.

From the perspective of operationalization for assessment purposes, linguistic approaches offer test developers useful tools to envision the types of language characteristically used in academic settings. However, the inventory of features identified by existing linguistic studies is not comprehensive enough to use as is. Studies have not relied on the same types of linguistic data—for example, spoken or written language—nor have they examined enough aspects of language across grades or curricula. Although linguistic approaches are useful, there is a need for further research to produce a comprehensive description addressing modalities of language use, age of students, and contexts of use.

The foregoing approaches theorize about academic language from cognitive, sociocultural, and linguistic perspectives and show the wide range of views prevalent in the field of language and education. The descriptions suggest how different understandings of academic language might affect how the construct is identified and defined for an ELP assessment. Wolf et al. (2008) assert that different approaches to academic language are likely to yield different items at the test construction level. This is important given the implementation of CCR standards, which are known for more rigorous language and literacy demands embedded in the standards across content areas (G. C. Bunch et al., 2012; Quinn et al., 2012). An alternative to the theoretical perspectives mentioned above is a practically oriented perspective (Wolf et al., 2008). Rather than theorizing about language development or language use, a practical orientation to academic language focuses on identifying what language demands are posed by content standards, textbooks, assessments, and so on (Bailey, 2007; Bailey, Butler, LaFramenta, & Ong, 2004). This approach has used linguistics as a way to describe these language demands but stops short of theorizing about language use or language development per se.

As new assessments are developed, articulating how academic language is approached is an important part of assessment design. It is clear that continued research is necessary to further understand and operationalize the construct of academic language (Wolf et al., 2008), especially since different ELP assessments, because of their varying approaches to defining and operationalizing academic language, may generate issues of comparability (Wolf et al., 2008). However, now more than in earlier generations of ELP tests for ELLs, federal requirements have required thought about the alignment between ELP/D standards and ELP assessments, and the correspondence between state content standards and ELP/D standards. This, in turn, may help ELP assessments offer a more accurate picture of what ELLs can do with the language needed for success in the context of U.S. schools (Bailey, 2007). Furthermore, current ELP assessments may be more internally coherent than previous assessments insofar as they (a) demonstrate alignment to ELP/D standards based on an understanding of academic language and (b) are related or correspond to state and consortia academic content standards, and thus operationalize the construct of academic language in ways that inform language instruction meant to facilitate mastery of academic content.

Operationalization of an Understanding of Academic Language Proficiency in a Large-Scale ELP Assessment

The translation of a conceptual and theoretical understanding of academic language proficiency into an operational ELP assessment is a complex matter. Although understandings and descriptions of academic language vary, it is essential that an ELP assessment successfully operationalize the descriptions and definitions of the construct chosen to underlie that specific assessment. In the current context, states are required to have ELP/D standards and to demonstrate that their ELP assessments are aligned with their standards. Whether more or less explicitly and coherently, each set of ELP/D standards embodies a definition, an understanding and descriptions of what academic language proficiency is and how it develops.

It is difficult, if not impossible, to discuss operationalizing an understanding of academic language proficiency into an assessment in abstract terms. Thus, to illustrate what is involved, we combine two frameworks to help make it more concrete: Evidence-Centered Design (ECD) as a powerful framework to systematically think through the complex issues involved in this endeavor and the WIDA ELD Standards as one understanding of academic English language proficiency. In choosing these two frameworks for the illustration, we neither claim that ECD is the best or only approach to test development nor that the WIDA ELD Standards and their accompanying assessments are in any way exemplary. Rather, what follows is intended as a very concrete illustration using one state-of-the-art approach to test design and construction as applied to operationalize a particularly complex construct—that of academic ELP—into an assessment with which the authors are directly involved, the WIDA ACCESS for ELLs, an annual summative ELP assessment.

Overview of Evidence-Centered Design

ECD (Mislevy, Steinberg, & Almond, 1999; Mislevy & Riconscente, 2006; Mislevy & Haertel, 2006) is a powerful tool used in the development of most

FIGURE 1
Evidence-Centered Design

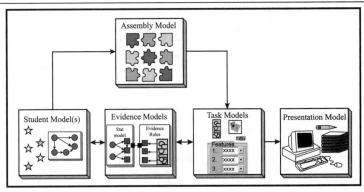

Delivery Model

modern testing programs, such as PARCC (Partnership for Assessment of Readiness for College and Careers) and Smarter Balanced (Herman & Linn, 2014).[9] ECD does not provide answers; instead, the ECD framework helps test developers systematically think through complex issues in test design. Since its original development in the late 1990s at the Educational Testing Service (Mislevy et al., 1999), it has been applied to the development of assessments in many different educational and operational fields (Mislevy et al., 1999; Mislevy & Yin, 2012; Mislevy, Steinberg, & Almond, 2002).

ECD organizes in one framework many streams of thought that test developers have been aware of for many years, yet centers them all on an evidence-built argument as the foundation for the validity of the assessment. The ECD framework posits five interconnected layers of activities, processes and elements: (a) Domain Analysis, (b) Domain Modeling, (c) the Conceptual Assessment Framework, (d) Assessment Assembly, and (e) Assessment Delivery. The Conceptual Assessment Framework itself details the interrelation of critical factors in assessment design through three interrelated models as shown in Figure 1: the student model, the evidence model, and the task model.

In test development, ECD serves as a tool enabling interdisciplinary teams to work together in order to address all the salient aspects of assessment design in a systematic manner. We now examine the layers and models of ECD and illustrate how they operate in concert to operationalize an understanding of academic English language into a large-scale annual language assessment.

Domain Analysis

This layer of the ECD framework concerns the process of collecting, understanding, and synthesizing all relevant information about what it is that will be assessed. This information concerns the domain's content, concepts, terminology, tools, and

FIGURE 2
WIDA English Language Development Standards

Standard		Abbreviation
English Language Development Standard 1	English language learners **communicate** for **Social** and **Instructional** purposes within the school setting	Social and Instructional language
English Language Development Standard 2	English language learners **communicate** information, ideas and concepts necessary for academic success in the content area of **Language Arts**	The language of Language Arts
English Language Development Standard 3	English language learners **communicate** information, ideas and concepts necessary for academic success in the content area of **Mathematics**	The language of Mathematics
English Language Development Standard 4	English language learners **communicate** information, ideas and concepts necessary for academic success in the content area of **Science**	The language of Science
English Language Development Standard 5	English language learners **communicate** information, ideas and concepts necessary for academic success in the content area of **Social Studies**	The language of Social Studies

Source. WIDA Consortium (2012). © Board of Regents of the University of Wisconsin System, on behalf of the WIDA Consortium. Reprinted with permission. All rights reserved.

representational forms; the nature and type of knowledge, skills, and abilities comprising the domain (e.g., listening, speaking, reading, writing); and the context or environment in which those knowledge, skills, and abilities are both gained and demonstrated.

As discussed earlier, in the context of ELP testing under NCLB, ELP assessments are required to be based on ELP/D standards. Because such standards are often the tools that communicate essential features of the domain of academic English that is to be both taught and assessed, in their core they contain a synthesis or summary of a domain analysis, describing an approach to how academic English may be conceptualized and described. Standards may be thought of as containing an initial and foundational domain analysis for the construction of an assessment.

As an illustration, the WIDA ELD Standards (WIDA Consortium, 2004, 2007, 2012) describe five areas of academic English language use, stating that ELLs communicate in English for social and instructional purposes in the school setting and communicate information, ideas, and concepts necessary for academic success in the content areas of Language Arts, Math, Science, and Social Studies (Figure 2). In this initial step, the WIDA ELD Standards begin to delineate an understanding of the domain of academic English language.

FIGURE 3
WIDA Features of Academic Language

The Features of Academic Language operate within sociocultural contexts for language use.

	Performance Criteria	Features
Discourse Level	**Linguistic Complexity** *(Quantity and variety of oral and written text)*	Amount of speech/written text Structure of speech/written text Density of speech/written text Organization and cohesion of ideas Variety of sentence types
Sentence Level	**Language Forms and Conventions** *(Types, array, and use of language structures)*	Types and variety of grammatical structures Conventions, mechanics, and fluency Match of language forms to purpose/perspective
Word/Phrase Level	**Vocabulary Usage** *(Specificity of word or phrase choice)*	General, specific, and technical language Multiple meanings of words and phrases Formulaic and idiomatic expressions Nuances and shades of meaning Collocations

The sociocultural contexts for language use involve the interaction between the student and the language environment, encompassing the…

- Register
- Genre/Text type
- Topic
- Task/Situation
- Participants' identities and social roles

The WIDA ELD Standards continue their summary of a type of domain analysis by providing further descriptions of a conceptualization of the domain of academic language proficiency. These additional descriptions include the following:

1. Descriptions of connections between academic language and academic content standards (e.g., the CCSS)
2. Examples of educational contexts for language use, contextualizing academic language use, and separating language complexity from cognitive complexity

FIGURE 4
WIDA Performance Definitions

WIDA Performance Definitions Listening and Reading Grades K-12

At each grade, toward the end of a given level of English language proficiency, and with instructional support, English language learners will process…

	Discourse Level	Sentence Level	Word/Phrase Level
	Linguistic Complexity	**Language Forms and Conventions**	**Vocabulary Usage**
	Level 6 – Reaching Language that meets all criteria through Level 5, Bridging		
Level 5 Bridging	• Rich descriptive discourse with complex sentences • Cohesive and organized related ideas	• Compound, complex grammatical constructions (e.g., multiple phrases and clauses) • A broad range of sentence patterns characteristic of particular content areas	• Technical and abstract content-area language • Words and expressions with shades of meaning for each content area
Level 4 Expanding	• Connected discourse with a variety of sentences • Expanded related ideas	• A variety of complex grammatical constructions • Sentence patterns characteristic of particular content areas	• Specific and some technical content-area language • Words and expressions with multiple meanings or collocations and idioms for each content area
Level 3 Developing	• Discourse with a series of extended sentences • Related ideas	• Compound and some complex (e.g., noun phrase, verb phrase, prepositional phrase) grammatical constructions • Sentence patterns across content areas	• Specific content words and expressions • Words or expressions related to content area with common collocations and idioms across content areas
Level 2 Emerging	• Multiple related simple sentences • An idea with details	• Compound grammatical constructions • Repetitive phrasal and sentence patterns across content areas	• General and some specific content words and expressions (including cognates) • Social and instructional words and expressions across content areas
Level 1 Entering	• Single statements or questions • An idea within words, phrases, or chunks of language	• Simple grammatical constructions (e.g., commands, Wh- questions, declaratives) • Common social and instructional forms and patterns	• General content-related words • Everyday social and instructional words and expressions

…within sociocultural contexts for language use.

WIDA Performance Definitions Speaking and Writing Grades K-12

At each grade, toward the end of a given level of English language proficiency, and with instructional support, English language learners will produce…

	Discourse Level	Sentence Level	Word/Phrase Level
	Linguistic Complexity	**Language Forms and Conventions**	**Vocabulary Usage**
	Level 6 – Reaching Language that meets all criteria through Level 5, Bridging		
Level 5 Bridging	• Multiple, complex sentences • Organized, cohesive, and coherent expression of ideas	• A variety of grammatical structures matched to purpose and nearly consistent use of conventions, including for effect • A broad range of sentence patterns characteristic of particular content areas	• Technical and abstract content-area language • Words and expressions with precise meaning related to content area topics
Level 4 Expanding	• Short, expanded, and some complex sentences • Organized expression of ideas with emerging cohesion	• A variety of grammatical structures and generally consistent use of conventions • Sentence patterns characteristic of particular content areas	• Specific and some technical content-area language • Words and expressions with multiple meanings or common collocations and idioms across content areas
Level 3 Developing	• Short and some expanded sentences with emerging complexity • Expanded expression of one idea or emerging expression of multiple related ideas	• Repetitive grammatical structures with occasional variation and emerging use of conventions • Sentence patterns across content areas	• Specific content words and expressions (including content-specific cognates) • Words or expressions related to content areas
Level 2 Emerging	• Phrases or short sentences • Emerging expression of ideas	• Formulaic grammatical structures and variable use of conventions • Repetitive phrasal and sentence patterns across content areas	• General content words and expressions (including common cognates) • Social and instructional words and expressions across content areas
Level 1 Entering	• Words, phrases, or chunks of language • Single words used to represent ideas	• Simple grammatical constructions (e.g., commands, Wh- questions, declaratives) • Phrasal patterns associated with common social and instructional situations	• General content-related words • Everyday social and instructional words and familiar expressions

…within sociocultural contexts for language use.

FIGURE 5
Sample Strand of Model Performance Indicators

	Level 1 Entering	Level 2 Emerging	Level 3 Developing	Level 4 Expanding	Level 5 Bridging	
SPEAKING	State how energy transfers using visual supports (e.g., "heat," "light," "sound")	Give examples of how energy transfers using sentence frames and graphic supports	Describe how energy transfers using sentence frames and graphic supports	Compare and contrast how energy transfers using graphic supports	Discuss how energy transfers using graphic supports	Level 6 – Reaching

Source. WIDA Consortium (2012). © Board of Regents of the University of Wisconsin System, on behalf of the WIDA Consortium. Reprinted with permission. All rights reserved.

3. Descriptions of features of academic language (see Figure 3), which address the "what" aspects of developing academic English language
4. Definitions of five levels of performance (see Figure 4), one addressing the receptive language domains of listening and reading and another addressing the productive language domains of speaking and writing; these performance definitions explicate the "how well" aspects of developing academic English

In addition, the WIDA ELD Standards provide illustrative Model Performance Indicators (MPIs) that provide examples for each language domain (listening, speaking, reading, writing) of how language is processed or produced within particular academic language use contexts. The MPIs reside at the intersection of the standard, ELD performance level, grade, and language domain. Each MPI contains three elements: a language function, an example academic content topic, and a description of appropriate linguistic support for each performance level.

MPIs are organized into strands across the five performance levels described in the WIDA ELD Standards. Figure 5 presents a sample strand of MPIs for Grade 8 in the language domain of speaking and for the standard of the language of science for the academic content of energy transfer (WIDA Consortium, 2012; WIDA ELD Standards, p. 97).

In operationalizing any understanding of the construct of academic ELP into an assessment, standards can provide general direction and initial starting points for the domain analysis layer of ECD. (Indeed, for standards to support the integration of curriculum, assessment, and instruction, performances on the assessment must be able to be interpreted in terms of the standards.) Yet standards by their very nature are broad. Further information needs to be collected in order to create specifications for an ELP assessment. For example, exactly what does an eighth-grade ELL at Performance Level 3 actually sound like when "describing how energy transfers?" What are the *linguistic characteristics* of an eighth-grade ELL's speech at Performance Level 5 when "discussing how energy transfers?" Thus, although in our example the descriptions and definitions from the WIDA ELD Standards and their illustrative MPIs provide a starting point for the domain analysis, additional information must be collected through literature reviews or conducting research in order to be able to provide a more complete understanding of the domain. Standards alone are not sufficient to describe the domain thoroughly enough to construct the most appropriate assessment tasks to each target language domain covered in an ELP assessment.

Domain Modeling

In general terms, this layer of ECD is concerned with how to articulate the argument, founded on the domain analysis, between the evidence collected from students in the assessment to inferences that may be made about them regarding their language use outside of the testing situation in the target language use domain—that is, the classroom. Mislevy and other authors find Toulmin's (1958) general argument structure a very useful and powerful tool to connect observations of student performance on assessments to inferential claims about them through the warrants and backing established on the basis of the domain analysis. Toulmin's model also reminds those constructing such arguments of the necessity to address potential alternative explanations with data or evidence to rebut them (or if they cannot be rebutted, to rethink the entire argument).

This layer of ECD requires designers of ELP assessments to clarify their thinking about how to design assessment tasks in order to make the connections between the evidence collected about a student's language in the assessment to claims about his or her language use in the target language use domain of the classroom. In the case of the WIDA ELD Standards and the WIDA ACCESS for ELLs, the domain model needs to ensure that performances on the ACCESS for ELLs provide evidence that ELLs are meeting the WIDA ELD Standards, and that ELLs' language proficiency can be categorized within one of five levels of performance based on the features of academic language as defined in the standards.

Because of this need, each assessment item or task on the ACCESS for ELLs is related to an associated MPI[10] (describing the contextual "what") and to a level described by the performance level definitions (describing the "how well" in terms of language use). Item and rubric development and review center on the question: If the ELL answers this question correctly or performs at this level on this constructed response task, has he or she provided evidence of meeting the associated MPI at the targeted performance level (for the given standard, domain, and grade level cluster)? Among other benefits, such domain modeling allows (a) assessment tasks to always be reviewed consistently vis-à-vis demonstration of evidence of meeting the MPI at the targeted performance level, (b) content reviews to annually check the match between assessment items and tasks and MPIs, and (c) psychometric analyses to provide evidence in support of the match between performance on items and tasks and the WIDA performance levels. Such domain modeling helps make transparent the alignment between ELP assessment tasks and the understanding of academic ELP embodied in the ELP/D standards.

Conceptual Assessment Framework

In ECD, the Conceptual Assessment Framework overlays three interrelated models: the student model, the evidence model, and the task model. This layer also addresses how the nuts and bolts of the operational assessment are connected. In illustrating how an understanding of academic English language can be operationalized into an assessment, we will look at each model in turn.

Student model. The student model describes and defines what it is (in terms of knowledge, skills, or other attributes) that the student or examinee possesses that is going to be assessed. In other words, it clarifies assessment claims about the observations of examinee performance on assessment tasks in terms of student variables that are the object of the assessment, answering the question: What do performances on the assessment tell us about the student?

In operationalizing the construct of academic ELP and the student model, competing claims may be made on the basis of differing perspectives of what it is the student has. For example, Mislevy and Yin (2012) summarize three main approaches to claims about students on language tests: a trait perspective, a behaviorist perspective, and an interactionist perspective. The authors stress that which perspective is chosen depends on the ultimate intent of the assessment: that is, the claims to be made about the student.

In our illustration of operationalizing the construct of academic English into an assessment, the performance definitions of the WIDA ELD Standards define what ELLs will "process" (listening and reading) or "produce" (speaking and writing) at a given grade and toward the end of a proficiency level, always within social-cultural contexts for language use, in terms of language features at the discourse, sentence and word/phrase level. Primary attention in the WIDA ELD Standards is, prima facie, on linguistic characteristics. The WIDA ELD Standards also acknowledge that communication takes place in a sociocultural context for language use that involves the interaction between the student and the language environment, encompassing the register, genre/text type, topic, task/situation, and the participants' identities and social roles. Thus, the basic student model derived from the WIDA ELD Standards is arguably interactionist. However, in keeping with the language focus of the WIDA ELD Standards, assessment tasks on the ACCESS for ELLs tend to focus on the varying linguistic features "processed" or "produced" by students across the five standards and at the five levels of performance.

Evidence model. In ECD, the evidence model consists of two parts. First, it describes and defines how "what the student has" will be assessed in terms of actual observations of student behavior (e.g., selected response choices scored right or wrong, or rubric-scored performances on a multipoint scale). Second, it describes how that observational data will be aggregated across assessment tasks and converted into numerical scores through a mathematical measurement or statistical model.

The evidence model must be optimized for the purposes of the assessment, to strengthen the use of evidence to support the claims being made. Pertinent observations of student behavior must be evaluated. Aggregations of observational data through appropriate mathematical modeling likewise provide strength to the evidence of the claims. The evidence model thus plays a major role in operationalizing the construct in the test design.

In terms of operationalizing the understanding of academic English embodied in the WIDA ELD Standards, as with any large-scale assessment, certain logistical constraints limit the types and amount of observational data that can be elicited in the assessment. Logistical constraints in terms of available assessment time and assessment delivery options pose many challenges. In the case of the ACCESS for ELLs, a priori decisions made by the WIDA member states' policy-setting body during the initial development stage predicated that listening and reading would be machine scored, so only dichotomous machine-scoreable selected response tasks would be used to assess those two domains. In other words, the observable behavior in these two domains would be limited to answering test items. The productive skills of writing and speaking would be assessed through performance-based tasks, though efficiency in terms of time would need to be optimized. A face-to-face approach was selected for assessing speaking; thus, the speaking portion of the assessment would need to be short as possible. To this end, rubrics for the scoring of writing and speaking were developed from the performance definitions of the WIDA ELD Standards to gather evidence for the presence of the features of language described in the Standards in the language produced by examinees.

In terms of a measurement model for converting observations of student behavior on test items and tasks to numerical measures, the Rasch model[11] was chosen for the ACCESS for ELLs. The properties of the Rasch model allow for a careful analysis that student performances on the assessment items and tasks conform to fundamental measurement principles.

Task model. The task model describes and defines the characteristics and features of the assessment items, tasks, and situations that will elicit the targeted student behaviors that provide the evidence for the assessment claims. In the operationalization of any understanding of academic English chosen to underlie the assessment, it is imperative that the tasks are optimally designed to elicit from examinees clear behavioral evidence supporting the examinees' possession (or lack) of what it is that is to be assessed.

For assessing listening and reading, because the WIDA ELD Standards emphasize the linguistic features of academic language that students need to process, assessment tasks are designed with great care to assess student ability to process listening passages and reading texts that are drawn from the appropriate academic contexts across the five WIDA ELD Standards and whose linguistic features characterize WIDA's five performance levels. In addition, each assessment item illustrates the function, topic, and level of support contained in the associated MPI. Thus, each combination of listening passage or reading text, together with its assessment item, targets a specific MPI at one of the five WIDA performance levels.

Similarly, specifications for speaking and writing tasks are designed to lead to the creation of tasks that optimize the opportunity for students to produce language characterized by the features described in the WIDA performance definitions. Again, the specific tasks are drawn from the academic contexts contained in the associated MPIs. Raters use a rubric, likewise derived from the performance definitions, to evaluate the evidence of expected linguistic features in the language produced by the students.

Using detailed specifications, items and tasks are thus developed for the operational assessment that allow students to produce observable data, whether answers to selected response items for listening and reading or spoken and written performances scored through the lens of a rubric operationalizing the WIDA performance definitions. In this way the construct of academic language contained in the WIDA ELD Standards is operationalized through the task model.

Assembly model. The assembly model layer of ECD defines and describes how the student, evidence, and task models work together to provide assessment evidence. Significant assessment questions addressed in this layer include how much of the observed student behavior is needed in order to accurately measure what we intend to measure. Accuracy needs to be understood both in psychometric (measurement) terms and in terms of the necessity of capturing evidence that reflects the breadth and diversity of the domain as aligned to the purpose of the assessment.

Constructing the assembly model is often an issue of optimizing real-world logistics and constraints. For example, assessments that are too long may tire examinees, introducing a variable into student behavior that confounds the student's production of observable evidence. Assessment length may also be associated with increased costs. The assembly model must support the collection of evidence from the student yet recognize real-world limitations.

In operationalizing the conception of academic English contained in the WIDA ELD Standards into the ACCESS for ELLs, several design decisions were made to optimize the interplay of student, evidence, and task models. There are five WIDA ELD Standards that needed to be reflected in the assessment of each of the four domains (Listening, Speaking, Reading, and Writing). To address this challenge, a "thematic folder" approach to the organization of items and tasks was adopted to maximize coverage of the standards yet minimize the possibility of examinees experiencing cognitive disjointedness. For example, sets of listening and reading items are presented within a thematically related unit (e.g., on energy transfer). Each item is independent, yet the context in which they are presented unifies their presentation in a cognitive whole. Because performance-based tasks are longer, tasks for speaking and writing are presented in thematic folders that integrate either academic language use in language arts and social studies or academic language use in math and science. Social and Instructional Language in these domains has its own thematic folder.

A second approach to optimization within the assembly model in the ACCESS for ELLs is the use of a "tiered" approach to assessing listening, reading and writing in the paper-and-pencil forms of the test. Since items and tasks are targeted to eliciting evidence related to the five performance levels defined in the standards, in order to minimize testing time and maximize assessment information across the five standards, test specifications delineate three overlapping tiers of the assessment. Tier A is targeted to collect evidence from students currently functioning in the lowest levels in the performance definitions (1 and 2) and contains items and tasks targeting Levels 1 through 3. Tier B targets students functioning at levels from high 2 to low 4 and contains items and tasks targeting Levels 2 through 4. Finally, Tier C targets students currently functioning in the highest levels and contains items and tasks targeting Levels 3 through 5.

A third approach to optimizing constraints is the use of a tailored approach to assess speaking. The speaking assessment contains three thematic folders. Within each are tasks that target each proficiency level defined in the WIDA ELD Standards. Students are presented with tasks in ascending order. After responding to the tasks at one level, the test administrator decides whether the student presented evidence of the expected characteristics of the task's targeted performance level or not. If yes, the administrator proceeds to the next, more challenging task. If not, the administrator ceases presenting tasks from that thematic folder and moves to the next, again beginning with easier tasks. In this way, lower proficiency students are presented with a shorter testing time.

A fourth approach to optimizing constraints within the assembly model deals with the relationship between test specifications and the weighting of the four domains in calculating the overall composite score. The WIDA member states' policy-setting body decided in advance that, because of its focus on academic English language use, the weighting of the domains in the overall composite score would emphasize the Reading and Writing domains, as follows: Listening 15%, Speaking 15%, Reading 35%, and Writing 35%. Because of this, more time (and more items or task-based scores on the rubric) were given to the Reading and Writing portions of the assessment, as follows: Listening (15%): 20 to 25 minutes; Speaking (15%): up to 15 minutes, administrator scored; Reading (35%): 35 to 40 minutes; and Writing (35%): up to 1 hour, rater scored centrally.

Assessment Implementation

Whereas the other layers of ECD focus on foundational design elements and are more conceptual in nature (and perhaps more critical in the operationalizing of the construct into an assessment), this layer of ECD focuses on the activities, processes, and procedures needed to actually implement an assessment. These activities include developing and refining assessment items and tasks, fine-tuning scoring rubrics and procedures (including rater training and quality control), and finalizing all aspects of converting observations into scores through the measurement model.

In our example, assessment implementation plays a role in the operationalizing of the construct embodied in the WIDA ELD Standards in at least one critical way. The initial drafts of all assessment items and tasks come from an annual item writing course offered to qualified teachers from throughout the states of the WIDA Consortium. Optimally, teachers work in pairs through the course. Each pair consists of one ESL specialist and one content area teacher. Teachers in the credit-bearing course have required readings that provide them the foundations to understanding the WIDA ELD Standards as well as the meaning of the features of academic language described in the Standards. Working with item and task specifications, the teacher pairs draw from teaching materials and curriculum-based tasks to draft reading texts and items, listening passages and items, writing tasks, and speaking tasks appropriate to their grade or grade-level cluster. Although these are later refined by test development specialists, involving ELL classroom educators helps both link the assessment to the classroom and disseminate understanding of how academic English is conceptualized in the WIDA ELD Standards.

Assessment Delivery

This layer of ECD concerns things such as the logistics of producing the assessment, distributing it to examinees, scoring the operational assessment, and reporting scores to test users. Although these mundane steps may be overlooked in considering how a construct is operationalized in an assessment, they actually play a critical role in supporting evidence-based argumentation for the validity of the assessment. Visual and textual information displayed in test booklets or on computer screens must be clear and mistake-proof to ensure that no construct relevant errors are introduced. The secure distribution of assessments is critical to ensuring the appropriateness of assessment evidence. Error-free machine scoring algorithms and highly reliable scoring of performance-based tasks are also necessary to support the strength of an evidence-centered approach to assessment. Finally, the clarity and interpretability of score reports are increasingly recognized as a critical step in the realization of an evidence-centered approach to assessment. If test score users are confused about the meaning of scores, they may make inappropriate inferences about examinees or take unsupported actions regarding test takers, no matter how well every other aspect of the assessment program functions. The operationalization of the construct in the testing program ends with a clear user-friendly score report fully aligned with all other parts of an assessment program designed following ECD principles.

In the case of the ACCESS for ELLs, there are layers of oversight committees of test stakeholders that review and sign off on the assessment at different stages of its development and operationalization to ensure that the error-free processes of producing assessments, scoring the assessments, and reporting scores are in place.

In this section, we illustrated how an understanding of the construct of academic ELP can be operationalized into an academic ELP assessment. ECD was used as the framework to present systematically how this complex process takes

place in the test design, development, and delivery process. The operationalization process was illustrated with examples drawn from the WIDA ELD Standards
as a conceptualization of academic English language and the ACCESS for ELLs
as the operational assessment. Clearly, as there are a variety of ways of conceptualizing and describing academic ELP, there are also a variety of ways to operationalize any given conceptualization of academic English language. What we have
described here is for illustrative purposes only. Ultimately the users of an assessment system will need to evaluate the appropriateness and adequacy of the steps
taken to translate a conceptualization of academic ELP into an operational assessment. ECD provides an approach to systematically present the decisions made
along the way.

Validity

Since Messick's (1989) seminal definition of validity, current conceptualizations
of validity have become much more nuanced, clarifying that validity is not a property
inherent in an assessment but is ultimately related to the use of assessment scores in
making inferences or taking actions related to students. For language testing, these
nuances have been most clearly articulated in the Assessment Use Argument, originally described by Bachman (2003) and further articulated in Bachman and Palmer
(2010). Although validity was previously viewed as evidence that a test was measuring what it was designed to measure, current conceptualizations of validity additionally attend to building a case for valid test use. For example, Bachman and Palmer's
Assessment Use Argument outlines five steps each building on the one below it. In
ascending order, the steps consider the following: (a) issues related to student performances on the assessment; (b) the qualities of the scores of the assessment, such as
reliability of test scores and fair and unbiased scoring; (c) empirically and theoretically based justifications for interpretations of the test scores in light of the construct
claimed to be measured by the assessment; (d) the nature of the decisions made about
students on the bases of their scores and supported interpretations; and (e) the consequences of such decisions for individuals and society (Bachman & Palmer, 2010).
ECD lays a solid foundation for designing a test with an argument-based approach
(e.g., Assessment Use Argument) with validity in mind. Indeed, that is the primary
goal of the domain modeling layer.

Issues related to modern conceptualizations of validity, illustrated in terms of
ELLs and high-stakes testing, are discussed by Mahon (2006) and Sólozano (2008)
and in terms of ELLs and ELP testing, by Wolf et al. (2008). Based on this view, the
burden of validity in the use of test scores, in some part, is to be shared by all stakeholders involved in the assessment, not only the developers of ELP tests but also
those who use those tests, namely, those who interpret test scores and make decisions
about ELLs based on their test scores. Currently, primary uses for large-scale standardized ELP testing is one piece of information in the initial identification of who
is an ELL, as an annual measure used to demonstrate progress in the acquisition of

academic English by ELLs from year to year for accountability purposes, and as a piece of information in the reclassification of ELLs out of ELL status.

The question of "who is an ELL" well illustrates the intricacies between tests and their uses as the current situation poses significant implications for testing and reporting as well as the educational trajectories of individual students (Abedi, 2008a; Solano-Flores, 2008; Wolf et al., 2008). The goal of classifying a student as an ELL ultimately has to do with ensuring adequate and fair learning conditions for that student, and then gathering evidence of progress along multiple points in his or her linguistic and academic development, until such time as that student may be reclassified as no longer an ELL in need of language support services. According to the 2012 Title III Implementation Report (Tanenbaum et al., 2012), states varied in how they identified and reclassified ELLs, a process that usually begins with a home language survey and then goes through additional screening processes. During the 2009–2010 academic year, eight states adopted statewide criteria for identification and exit procedures, while 42 states allowed the use of district discretion to make these decisions (Tanenbaum et al., 2012). Regardless of any qualities of an ELP assessment, opaque identification and exiting policies and procedures, including the use of test scores, create an issue of comparability of who is an ELL over time and across districts, which may, thus, confound any notion of a validity argument for the use of the assessment, since students are being treated differentially based on where they live. Although recently reclassified students are not included in some states' definitions of ELLs, which poses some problems for state-to-state comparability (Wolf et al., 2008), all states and the District of Columbia complied with the NCLB stipulation to track former ELLs for 2 years following reclassification (Tanenbaum et al., 2012), which is an indication that some consistency across states may be achieved.

To address these issues in differential approaches to identification and reclassification as part of testing in the era of CCR standards, a coordinated, multiyear effort has been launched to establish a common ELL definition (Linquanti & Cook, 2013). It is hoped that this effort will lend some consistency to the policy and technical issues surrounding the identification and reclassification of ELLs. Thus, whether an assessment is used to identify students, to track annual progress, to inform local programming decisions, or to reclassify students, the implications for studying the validity of the use of an ELP assessment are consequential (Wolf et al., 2008), yet nuanced and complex.

While a student is an ELL, ELP assessment data are used not only for accountability purposes to demonstrate growth in academic ELP but also as one piece of information to help satisfy wide-ranging needs for understanding ELLs' academic progress. Again according to the 2012 Title III implementation survey (Tanenbaum et al., 2012), Title III districts used ELP test data to inform professional development and technical assistance to make school and district improvements as well as to measure ELLs' progress in acquiring ELP. As discussed earlier, NCLB stipulations refrain from mandating specific instructional policies, programs, and practices, opting instead for an outcome-driven approach that leaves instructional decisions to local jurisdictions.

M. B. Bunch (2011), however, points out that although data from large-scale, standardized ELP assessments appropriately comply with federal reporting requirements, what students and teachers need most are assessments that can directly inform instruction. When combined with other sources of information as part of a comprehensive system of assessments, ELP measures may be used to inform decisions about eligibility for services and instruction in addition to accountability (Albers, Kenyon, & Boals, 2008). Albers et al. (2008) found that ELP assessments based on a conceptual framework of academic language were more useful in educational interventions for ELLs than pre-NCLB measures, and are therefore more useful in enhancing classroom instruction. The LADDER project at the Wisconsin Center for Educational Research has also illustrated how local districts and schools can use ELP test data to inform and enhance programming for ELLs (Spalter, 2011). Until such time as there are ELP assessments that can more directly inform instruction, efforts like these to maximize the use of information from data from ELP assessments to meet local district and school needs should be continued. Nonetheless, the need for ELP assessments that can more directly inform instruction remains.

It is clear that in the lives of ELLs, the consequences of ELP testing are salient, and some would argue too consequential, within a high-stakes accountability framework (Sólorzano, 2008). Despite the potential to provide useful information to states, schools and districts, ELP testing outcomes can have a washback effect on programs and possibly sanctions for schools, district, and states (Wolf et al., 2008). For any particular assessment, as building an Assessment Use Argument makes clear, the validation process is quite involved, taking into account, among other things, the construct to be measured, the interpretations to be drawn from the test, the purpose of a test, and the consequences of test use (Wolf et al., 2008). So although the use of a given test is subject to a rigorous validation process, including conducting critical validation studies, the need for information is vast.

Many issues related to validity are particular to assessing the ELP of ELLs. One critical issue is the relationship between language proficiency and academic proficiency. Although the goal of ELP assessments is assessing school-based English language, the intertwined relationship between language proficiency and content knowledge presents unique issues when evaluating the validity of ELP assessments and the inferences that can be drawn from them (Francis & Rivera, 2007). Given the complex nature of language development, some scholars worry about confounding language ability with academic aptitude (Solano-Flores & Trumbull, 2003). What is the expected relationship between ELP and academic achievement? Can academic achievement be used as the criterion for ELP?

To a certain point, there is an expected relationship between higher levels of ELP and higher levels of academic achievement demonstrated in English. Studies have shown such relationships (Parker et al., 2009). However, there are variations in academic achievement demonstrated by non-ELLs that putatively are not related to language. One approach to conceptualizing this complex issue is proposed by Cook, Boals, Wilmes, and Santos (2008). In this approach it is argued that a correlation between increases in performances on an annual assessment of ELP and increases on performances on annual assessments of content knowledge indicate that for the ELL, language, as well as content, is being assessed by the content assessments. The point on the continuum of developing ELP where there is no longer such a relationship is the point at which ELP no longer is playing a significant role in performances on content knowledge assessments. It may be at this point on the ELD continuum that specialized English language support is no longer needed.

In addition to academic achievement, are there other expected relationships between ELP assessments and external criteria that may lend support to the interpretation of the new assessments as measuring ELP? One early line of argument was to investigate the correlation between a new assessment of a construct and an older, established assessment of that same construct. A high degree of correlation can provide some evidence that performances on the new measure may be interpreted as measures of the construct measured by the established measure. Although this approach has some merit, there is no accepted golden standard among current ELP assessments. In comparison to pre-NCLB measures, current ELP assessments are much more focused on academic English than their long-used predecessors. Another issue is that the demands of the current assessments of what constitutes English proficient may be much higher. A technical report on a large study for WIDA ACCESS for ELLs used to bridge performances on ACCESS to four commonly used pre-NCLB assessments illustrates this (Gottlieb & Kenyon, 2006). Students were double-tested on ACCESS for ELLs and one of four earlier assessments. Whereas there were moderate to high correlations between ACCESS for ELLs and the older assessments, the level of performance required to be reclassified was much higher on ACCESS.

Because of these complexities, when building an argument for the valid use of an assessment through conducting validity studies, test developers and researchers must pay careful attention to all possible factors that could be a source of construct-irrelevant variance. It takes time to become proficient in school-based language (Cook et al., 2011; Hakuta et al., 2000) as it involves both language and academic growth. Although the new generation of ELP assessments have a higher assessment quality in comparison with the previous generation of tests (Abedi, 2008b), more work must be done if ELP measures are to inform assessment of ELLs that takes language development and academic growth into account appropriately.

A second issue of particular concern to ELP assessments (though applicable to all testing) is the cultural sensitivity of the assessments. ELP testing requires great sensitivity to the diverse educational, language, and cultural backgrounds of ELLs. As part of building an Assessment Use Argument for the ELP test, evidence must be provided that every student has the same opportunity to give his or her best performance and that those performances are scored the same way, regardless of the student's background. It is known that many factors contribute to variation in language ability (and academic content knowledge), including language and educational background and the quality and conditions of schooling (Wolf et al., 2008). According to

Solano-Flores and Trumbull (2003), understandings of nonmainstream language and culture are necessary to guide the entire assessment process and not only to complete bias and sensitivity reviews. ELP assessments that do not take into account consideration of students' first language proficiency, the range of English abilities within a proficiency level (Solano-Flores, 2008), and access to appropriate content instruction (Bailey & Butler, 2007) may be less able to produce valid measures of ELLs' language (as well as their academic knowledge). To improve the cultural sensitivity of assessments, Solano-Flores and Trumbull (2003) recommend (a) conducting item microanalysis through reviews during the test development process using a sociocultural perspective to reduce cultural bias and (b) incorporating local educators in the process of test development through a coordinated effort to review, pilot, and adapt items. To aid in this effort, ongoing research on performances of ELLs from a wide variety of linguistic, cultural, and educational backgrounds on standardized ELP assessments should be conducted to ensure not only that differences in performances are not due to issues of bias in favor of or against any particular ELL subgroup, but also that all ELLs have equal opportunity to give their best demonstration of their current level of proficiency in English. Related to the issue of giving one's best demonstration in testing is the practice of testing accommodations.

Accommodations in ELP testing

Accommodations are "practices and procedures in the areas of presentation, response, setting, and timing/scheduling that provide equitable access during instruction and assessments for students with disabilities" (Thompson, Morse, Sharpe, & Hall, 2005, p. 14). Assessment accommodations serve the important purpose of allowing students with disabilities the opportunity to participate in state accountability assessments and demonstrate what they know (Butler & Stevens, 2001, p. 413). Furthermore, federal law (IDEA, ESEA) requires that students with disabilities be provided with an opportunity to participate in state accountability assessments through appropriate accommodations (Rivera & Collum, 2006). This requirement puts significant pressure on schools and school districts to include in assessment activities "subgroups of students whose performance has lagged behind for many years" (Abedi, 2004, p. 5). Although a given accommodation may be appropriate for instructional use it does not necessarily follow that its use would be appropriate on a standardized assessment and could result in lowering or invalidating a student's score (Thompson et al., 2005).

The goal of providing eligible ELLs accommodations on ELP assessments is to increase the validity of test scores for ELLs with disabilities, yet the interpretation of accommodated results with ELLs in general on any assessment has proven challenging and controversial (Abedi & Levine, 2013). Participation in state assessments alone is not meaningful unless scores generated lead to valid inferences about students' achievement (Kieffer, Lesaux, Rivera, & Francis, 2009). Assessment accommodations must not alter the construct being assessed or lower learning expectations

(Elliott, Kratochwill, & Schulte, 1998; Koenig & Bachman, 2004). Furthermore, appropriate use of accommodations needs to follow the requirements detailed in the *Standards for Educational and Psychological Testing* (American Educational Research Association, American Psychological Association, National Council on Measurement in Education, Joint Committee on Standards for Educational & Psychological Testing, 2014).

The use of accommodations has been especially challenging in the case of ELLs as the concept of accommodations is not "well defined and is often misused, misdirected, and misinterpreted" (Abedi & Levine, 2013, p. 27). ELLs are a particularly heterogeneous subgroup and are often lumped together with students with disabilities, another heterogeneous population with their own unique needs (Liu & Anderson, 2008). Furthermore, for content and language testing, the more abundant research on students with disabilities has been drawn from to form state assessment policies when specifying accommodations for ELLs (Rivera, Acosta, & Willner, 2008; Rivera, Collum, Willner, & Sia, 2006). Consequently, there is a unique challenge in balancing required participation opportunities through accommodations and ensuring that test scores ultimately remain meaningful for their intended purposes.

Although the use of accommodations on content assessments has its challenges, a stronger case can be made that they provide an opportunity for students with disabilities to access content without affecting the construct being assessed. Many of the accommodations for ELLs on content assessments involve reducing unnecessary linguistic complexity, particularly construct relevant on language arts or reading assessments (Abedi, Hofstetter, & Lord, 2004; Rivera & Collum, 2006). Equally or more difficult are ELP assessments where the very purpose of the assessment is to measure proficiency in the medium of communication that is used to access content, and not the content itself, and it is here that the use of some accommodations that are routinely used on content assessments may be inappropriate. For example, the use of American Sign Language on an ELP listening subtest or braille or translations on an ELP reading subtest may be inappropriate accommodations as the meaningfulness of inferences based on test scores can no longer be guaranteed. Instead, the development of alternate items or assessments may have to be explored in order to enable students' participation (Albus & Thurlow, 2008).

In recent years, the use of principles of universal design has led to the creation of new assessments that are "designed and developed from the beginning to allow participation of the widest possible range of students, in a way that results in valid inferences about performance for all students who participate in the assessment" (Thompson, Johnston, & Thurlow, 2002, p. 2). In the case of current ELP assessments, this includes the use of graphic supports and color to provide accessibility for ELLs. Together with tailored accommodations (e.g., more time, more breaks, larger print, etc.), assessments can provide maximum accessibility for all students. Recent advances in technology-based test delivery, such as the Accessible Portable Item Protocol, provide new avenues to present students with customized test content that allows them to demonstrate their proficiency. The next-generation ELP assessments that are scheduled to be released for the 2015–2016 school year will be some of the first assessments to use these new possibilities.

While a shift to computer-based testing, built on the principles of ECD, within the next few years holds promises for all ELL students, including those with disabilities, the past 10 years have seen remarkable shifts in large-scale ELP testing, particularly in the nature of the language being measured as compared to pre-CCR era assessments. However, within this shift, there are multiple approaches to describing academic language (cognitive, sociocultural, linguistic), each with varying degrees of specificity or emphasis with regard to the descriptiveness of language. Operationalizing an understanding of academic language for testing purposes on a large-scale ELP assessment requires making explicit the theoretical approach to its operationalization of academic language. CCR era assessments share certain characteristics given federal requirements about the correspondence between ELP/D standards, ELP assessments, and state content standards. Nonetheless, the different approaches to understanding and describing academic language must be made explicit. The worked example using ECD and the WIDA ELD Standards illustrates the complexity of translating a conceptual and theoretical understanding of academic language into an operational ELP assessment. It is necessary to have an understanding of what is being measured and how it is being measured as well as what inferences can be made about students based on test results that explicitly link to the construct. Through ECD design, development and use of appropriate accommodations, and validity testing, the measurement criteria move from implicit to explicit—that is, these and similar practices clarify for the test maker and test consumer what is being testing and for what purposes.

ACCOUNTABILITY AND BEYOND

A close look at the innovations and persistent challenges of large-scale assessment over the last decade points to the larger question of how to fairly incorporate ELLs into the current standards-based accountability framework. In spite of the drawbacks of NCLB that continue to be grappled with in testing ELLs (Deville & Chalhoub-Deville, 2011), it is not likely standardized testing and accountability will disappear anytime soon. Within this paradigm, we propose that it is important to focus on the unique strengths of ELLs in order to ensure that the nature and uses of information generated by ELP assessments expand their opportunities for learning. In the section that follows, we examine ELP testing within the context of a system-wide approach to assessment, including large-scale tests and other forms of assessments, in order to highlight how assessments can be a tool to better support ELLs educationally.

System-Wide Approach

A system-wide approach to standards and assessment integrates formative, interim (aka benchmark), and summative assessment and has the potential to better meet educators' instructional needs as well as to communicate information about ELLs' progress to a wider variety of stakeholders. Assessment data needs vary by audience (policymaker, district and school leaders, teachers, parents, students) who are interested in different levels of detail (Forster, 2001). For example, teachers need fine-grained information to inform instruction (Duran, 2008; García & Pearson, 1994; Herman, 2013), schools and district leaders need information to make programmatic decisions, and policymakers need aggregate information to assess ELL programs and policies. A system-wide approach that allows for the coordination of multiple assessments and educator resources to meet the distinct information needs of various stakeholders at state, district, school, and classroom levels may prove to be a way to support ELLs at multiple levels.

Within a system-wide approach to assessment for ELLs, large-scale ELP assessments are one of several measures for tracking linguistic and academic progress at local and national levels, and fulfill federal mandates for accountability reporting. Other types of assessments, such as interim assessments and formative assessments, function differently and provide data at a different grain size, complementing that which is provided by summative assessments. Interim assessments are called "interim" because they are typically given one or more times between administration of summative assessments. That is to say, they occur in the "interim" between annual summative assessments. Interim assessments are typically designed to be measures of student achievement at the conclusion of units of instruction smaller than an entire academic year and generally serve the purpose of showing how well students did on smaller instructional components. Historically, interim assessments have been known by other names such as benchmark assessment or interim benchmark assessments, though there are distinctions between the purposes of each. Interim assessments are particularly useful at the school and district levels to evaluate progress of groups of students. Formative assessment, often referred to as *assessment for learning*, is the most "instructionally relevant" (Linquanti, 2011, p. 18) form of assessment because it is used to gauge students' progress and growth as they learn (M. B. Bunch, 2011; Gottlieb & Nguyen, 2007; Heritage, 2010). The information that teachers gain through formative assessment, in turn, helps guide their instructional decisions. Thus, formative assessments are particularly useful at the classroom level and can inform both teachers and students.

A system-wide approach that incorporates these types of assessments is becoming a common assessment practice in content and language testing. The Smarter Balanced Assessment Consortium, one of the two testing consortia recently funded under Race to the Top (http://www2.ed.gov/programs/racetothetop/index.html), provides an example of this approach. They are currently developing interim content assessments, formative tools, and a digital resource library for ongoing educator professional development and support (see http://www.smarterbalanced.org). WIDA has taken this approach as well with the development of educator resources and professional development to guide curriculum planning and formative assessment, and ELPA21 is actively collaborating with the Understanding Language Initiative at Stanford University, which provides resources and professional development for teachers to "heighten educator awareness of the critical role that language plays in the new

Common Core State Standards and Next Generation Science Standards" (http://ell. stanford.edu). A system-wide approach hinges on the need for understanding and using assessments as they are intended and validated, and has the potential to allow for more nuanced interpretations of data, as well as to inform instruction (Nelson, McGhee, Meno, & Slater, 2007). To achieve this, it is argued that ongoing and thoughtful attention to all types of assessment (formative, interim, summative) is needed to ensure that opportunities for assessment and instruction are realized with greater responsiveness to the unique strengths and needs of ELLs (Heritage, 2010; Linquanti, 2011).

The benefit of a systems approach is to better coordinate assessments, which, consortia led or state developed, can provide multiple measures of language and content knowledge and can also explicitly tie these assessments to the same language and content standards and communicate information about ELLs in a unified, systematic way. Linquanti and Hakuta (2012) contend that within a tightly linked standards and accountability system, the focus on language in content instruction must be explicit and consistent across standards, assessments, professional development, and teacher preparation. Enhancing teachers' understanding of the role of language in content standards is no small feat, yet encouraging educators to create language rich classrooms has the potential to expand ELLs' opportunities to learn through meaningful access to complex content and literacy development opportunities across academic contents (G. C. Bunch, 2013). A system-wide approach to standards and assessment, then, has the potential to inform policy and programmatic decisions, better meet educators' instructional needs, and communicate information about ELLs' progress to a wider variety of stakeholders.

CONCLUSION

In this chapter, we have described trends in assessing the English proficiency of ELLs within the United States with an eye toward understanding how these trends have been influenced by the standards and accountability movement and how they may ultimately change assessment and instruction for ELLs. These trends are unfolding with steps toward the following:

- A systems approach with ELP/D standards that are aligned to ELP assessments and that correspond to relevant content standards (e.g., CCSS and NGSS)
- Balanced and multiple assessments and hence
- Less emphasis on summative assessments (while acknowledging that current assessment policy places much greater emphasis on summative assessment within our current accountability models)
- More attention to the language used in and across core content areas
- More accurate measures and more complex approaches to validation
- More resources and long-term, coherent professional learning aimed at guiding and informing educators with respect to language development within school contexts

Given the changing contexts and constructs of ELP testing up through the newest wave of CCR standards and assessments, now is an opportune moment to reflect on the role of assessment in promoting equitable education for ELLs. Although there are no easy answers, the following set of questions is offered to test developers and educational professionals to think critically about the role of ELP assessments in fostering the educational opportunities of ELLs in local contexts.

1. *How can we better understand our ELL population?* Numerous calls for sensitivity to the heterogeneity of ELL populations have been made to improve assessment design, validity studies, and the appropriate use of accommodations (Abedi & Linquanti, 2012; Kopriva, Emick, Hipolito-Delgado, & Cameron, 2007; Linquanti, 2011). This requires knowledge of the population to be affected by testing. Taking into account this heterogeneity in assessment design requires careful consideration of the ways ELLs may differ. Differences that may have consequences for their learning and assessment include, for example, proficiency across different modalities in English and home language, language of instruction, and schooling conditions as well as developmental factors including age and the presence of disabilities (Gándara, Rumberger, Maxwell-Jolly, & Callahan, 2003; Solano-Flores, 2008). In attempting to get to know a particular ELL population, decisions need to be made about what information is collected, shared, and used. Even if these decisions are uniform across states, the information that is acted on is particular to a specific state or district and should reflect awareness of the local population.

2. *What assessment or combination of assessments is most appropriate to meet our needs for information about the language development of ELLs?* From summative to interim and formative assessment tools, clarity about assessment type and purpose is crucial. The proliferation of commercial, consortia, and state-based assessments can lead to confusion for states and districts when making decisions about how to organize a system-wide approach (Perie, Marion, & Gong, 2009). Therefore, at local levels of decision making, thoughtful evaluation of assessment options is needed to ensure the best fit of tests and related professional resources for the affected student and teacher populations.

3. *How can we train various stakeholders to understand and act on assessment data?* Results of standardized assessments require a high level of data literacy to accurately interpret them (Bailey & Wolf, 2012). As discussed earlier, the informational needs of a teacher working with individual students vary greatly from those of a program or curriculum coordinator making decisions about programming and curricula, which in turn varies significantly from those of the state educational leader or policymaker making evaluative judgments or funding decisions. Analyzing assessment data requires training as appropriate to the assessment, stakeholder, and informational needs so that reliable conclusions can be drawn.

4. *How can we ensure that all teachers are prepared to work with ELLs to help them become career and college ready?* One of the most obvious implications of the adoption of CCR standards in educating ELLs is the need for professional development. There have been many calls for all teachers to be prepared to teach and provide students opportunities to develop discipline-specific uses of language (G. C. Bunch et al., 2012; Santos, Darling-Hammond, & Cheuk, 2012; Walqui & Heritage, 2012). Linquanti (2011) and Linquanti and Hakuta (2012) contend that academic language skills should be more explicitly defined, practiced, and assessed, which require sufficiently delineating the sophisticated language competencies entailed in the CCR standards and corresponding ELP/D standards. What such professional learning looks like, how it is facilitated, and who takes responsibility for ensuring adequate professional training at each level of administration (state, district, school) are significant challenges that must be addressed.

5. *How can we ensure adequate technological infrastructure and prepare children for online test-taking?* As discussed earlier, computer-based formats offer important possibilities for developing and testing new accommodations. In the decision to incorporate technology and how, Bachman (2000) cautions that the formats possible because of computer-based testing "raise all the familiar validity issues, and may require us to redefine the very construct we believe we are assessing" (p. 9). Although computer-based testing is not yet standard for large-scale assessments, Chapelle (2003) recommends educational professionals to consider the negative and positive effects of technology in computer-aided testing of language. Children come to school with varying levels of experience with technology, which could conceivably disadvantage some test takers. With the expansion of computer-based testing it will be necessary to ensure that schools keep technology up-to-date and help children become more computer-literate (Chapelle, 2003), without reducing computer literacy to test taking.

Moving forward, the state of ELP testing in the United States hinges on the question of how ELLs are to be fairly included. Within the changing constructs and contexts of accountability, we advocate putting learners at the forefront of test design and assessment practices to embrace ELLs' language abilities as assets. From an opportunity-to-learn perspective, language and content assessment can serve as both the "means and the measure" of ensuring ELLs' opportunities for learning (Moss, Pullin, Gee, Haertel, & Young, 2008, p. 2). This means broadening the uses of assessment to support instruction and providing professional development that will enable educators to use assessment information appropriately and effectively. We see exciting possibilities for change that can help fulfill this call for strengthening and broadening the uses of assessment evidence, possibilities that continue with the evolving construct and operationalization of academic language, connections to instruction, integration of technology, and greater responsiveness to the diversity of ELL populations.

ACKNOWLEDGMENTS

We would like to thank our reviewers for their helpful comments on earlier drafts of this chapter, with a special thanks to Robert Linquanti for his particularly detailed and insightful feedback. Any omissions are our sole responsibility.

NOTES

[1]In this chapter we use the term *English language learner*, which is consistent with nomenclature in the literature to refer to children learning English as an additional language, although *limited English proficient* is still used in federal legislation.

[2]For an exception, see Bailey and Wolf (2012).

[3]We use ELP/D (English Language Proficiency/Development) to encompass the names for English language standards used by different states.

[4]Correspondence is used to refer to the relationship between differing standards or assessments, whereas alignment refers to the relationship between a set of standards and a test that is developed to assess those standards (see CCSSO, 2012).

[5]http://www.corestandards.org

[6]WIDA prefers *English Language Development Standards* to *Proficiency Standards* in order to note the fluid and ongoing nature of language development.

[7]Throughout this document, we refer to *Academic English language* as *academic language*. We recognize that languages other than English may also have academic varieties.

[8]*Nominalization* is a type of grammatical metaphor that allows language users to represent relationships between objects and events that are not necessarily congruent with everyday experience of the world. For example, through grammatical metaphor, actions and events can be nouns (nominalizations), and logical relationships can be construed as verbs.

[9]As an example of how fundamental ECD is to these programs, all proposals for recent Enhanced Assessment Grants for test and item development required applicants to explain in their proposals how they were using ECD to guide the development of their assessments; see for example, the *REQUEST FOR PROPOSAL (RFP) PARCC Speaking and Listening* from October 3, 2013, where one required deliverable is a "PARCC approved demonstrated documentation that EDC was used in the development of the Speaking and Listening Assessment" (http://blogs.edweek.org/edweek/marketplacek12/PARCCIncSpeakingandListeningRFP.pdf; p. 45)

[10]Although the three editions of the WIDA ELD Standards (WIDA Consortium, 2004, 2007, 2012) contain hundreds of MPIs, they are meant to be illustrative. The standards provide guidance on how MPIs may be modified or transformed. In actual test development, transformed MPIs are developed to serve as the foundation of the specifications for new items and tasks.

[11]The Rasch model is a mathematical model developed by the Danish mathematician Georg Rasch that, on the bases of performances of persons on tasks, posits that a probabilistic mathematical relationship between the ability of persons and the difficulty of items exists when fundamental measurement criteria are met (cf. Wright & Stone, 1979).

REFERENCES

Abedi, J. (2004). The No Child Left Behind Act and English language learners: Assessment and accountability issues. *Educational Researcher, 33*(1), 4–14. doi:10.3102/00131 89X033001004

Abedi, J. (2007). English language proficiency assessment and accountability under NCLB Title III: An overview. In J. Abedi (Ed.), *English language proficiency assessment in the nation: Current status and future practice* (pp. 3–10). Davis: University of California, Davis, School of Education.

Abedi, J. (2008a). Classification system for English language learners: Issues and recommendations. *Educational Measurement: Issues and Practice, 27*(3), 17–31. doi:10.1111/j.1745-3992.2008.00125.x

Abedi, J. (2008b). Measuring students' level of English proficiency: Educational significance and assessment requirements. *Educational Assessment, 13,* 193–214. doi:10.1080/10627190802394404

Abedi, J., & Gándara, P. (2006). Performance of English Language Learners as a subgroup in large-scale assessment: Interaction of research and policy. *Educational Measurement: Issues and Practice, 25*(4), 36–46. doi:10.1111/j.1745-3992.2006.00077.x

Abedi, J., Hofstetter, C. H., & Lord, C. (2004). Assessment accommodations for English language learners: Implications for policy-based empirical research. *Review of Educational Research, 74*(1), 1–28. doi:10.3102/00346543074001001

Abedi, J., & Levine, H. G. (2013). Fairness in assessment of English learners. *Leadership, 42*(3), 26–38.

Abedi, J., & Linquanti, R. (2012, January). *Issues and opportunities in improving the quality of large scale assessment systems for English language learners.* Paper presented at the Understanding Language Conference, Stanford University, Stanford, CA. Retrieved from http://ell.stanford.edu/sites/default/files/pdf/academic-papers/07-Abedi%20Linquanti%20Issues%20and%20Opportunities%20FINAL.pdf

Albers, C. A., Kenyon, D. M., & Boals, T. J. (2008). Measures for determining English language proficiency and the resulting implications for instructional provision and intervention. *Assessment for Effective Intervention, 34,* 74–85. doi:10.1177/1534508408314175

Albus, D., & Thurlow, M. L. (2008). Accommodating students with disabilities on state English language proficiency assessments. *Assessment for Effective Intervention, 33,* 156–166. doi:10.1177/1534508407313241

American Educational Research Association, American Psychological Association, & National Council on Measurement in Education, Joint Committee on Standards for Educational & Psychological Testing. (2014). *Standards for educational and psychological testing.* Washington, DC: American Educational Research Association.

Antunez, B. (2003). *Assessing English language learners in America's Great City Schools.* Washington, DC: Council of the Great City Schools. Retrieved from http://www.cgcs.org

Bachman, L. F. (2000). Modern language testing at the turn of the century: Assuring that what we count counts. *Language Testing, 17,* 1–42. doi:10.1177/026553220001700101

Bachman, L. F. (2003). Building and supporting a case for test use. *Language Assessment Quarterly, 2,* 1-34.

Bachman, L. F., & Palmer, A. (2010). *Language assessment in practice.* Oxford, England: Oxford University Press.

Bailey, A. L. (2007). *The language demands of school: Putting academic English to the test.* New Haven, CT: Yale University Press.

Bailey, A. L., & Butler, F. A. (2007). A conceptual framework of academic English language for broad application to education. In A. L. Bailey (Ed.), *The language demands of school: Putting academic English to the test* (pp. 68–102). New Haven, CT: Yale University Press.

Bailey, A. L., Butler, F., LaFramenta, C., & Ong, C. (2004). *Towards the characterization of academic language in upper elementary science classrooms* (CSE Report No. 621). Los Angeles, CA: CRESST. Retrieved from http://www.cse.ucla.edu/products/reports/R621.pdf

Bailey, A. L., & Huang, B. H. (2011). Do current English language development/proficiency standards reflect the English needed for success in school? *Language Testing, 28,* 343–365. doi:10.1177/0265532211404187

Bailey, A. L., & Wolf, M. K. (2012). *The challenge of assessing language proficiency aligned to the Common Core State Standards and some possible solutions.* Paper presented at the Understanding Language Conference, Stanford University, CA. Retrieved from http://ell.stanford.edu/sites/default/files/pdf/academic-papers/08-Bailey%20Wolf%20Challenges%20of%20Assessment%20Language%20Proficiency%20FINAL_0.pdf

Billig, H. S. (1997). Title I of the Improving America's Schools Act: What it looks like in practice. *Journal of Education for Students Placed at Risk, 2*, 329–343. doi:10.1207/s15327671espr0204_3

Bunch, G. C. (2013). Pedagogical language knowledge: Preparing mainstream teachers for English learners in the new standards era. *Review of Research in Education, 37*, 298–341. doi:10.3102/0091732X12461772

Bunch, G. C., Kibler, A., & Pimentel, S. (2012, January). *Realizing opportunities for English learners in the common core English language arts and disciplinary literacy standards.* Paper presented at the Understanding Language Conference, Stanford University, Stanford, CA. Retrieved from http://ell.stanford.edu/sites/default/files/pdf/academic-papers/01_Bunch_Kibler_Pimentel_RealizingOppinELA_FINAL_0.pdf

Bunch, M. B. (2011). Testing English language learners under No Child Left Behind. *Language Testing, 28*, 323–341. doi:10.1177/0265532211404186

Butler, F. A., & Stevens, R. (2001). Standardized assessment of the content knowledge of English language learners K-12: Current trends and old dilemmas. *Language Testing, 18*, 409–427. doi:10.1177/026553220101800406

Chamot, A. U., & O'Malley, J. M. (1994). *The CALLA handbook: Implementing the cognitive academic language learning approach.* Reading, MA: Addison-Wesley.

Chapelle, C. (2003). *English language learning and technology: Lectures on applied linguistics in the age of information and communication technology.* Philadelphia, PA: John Benjamins.

Christie, F., & Derewianka, B. (2008). *School discourse: Learning to write across the years of schooling.* London, England: Continuum.

Coleman, R., & Goldenberg, C. (2012). The common core challenge for ELLs. *Principal Leadership, 12*(5), 46–51.

Cook, H. G., Boals, T., & Lundberg, L. (2011). Developing informed expectations for the academic achievement of English learners: What can we reasonably expect? *Phi Delta Kappan, 93*(3), 66–69.

Cook, H. G., Boals, T., Wilmes, C., & Santos, M. (2008). *Issues in the development of Annual Measurable Achievement Objectives (AMAOs) for WIDA consortium states.* Madison, WI: WIDA Consortium.

Cook, H. G., Linquanti, R., Chinen, M., & Jung, H. (2012). *National evaluation of Title III implementation supplemental report: Exploring approaches to setting English language proficiency performance criteria and monitoring English learner progress.* Washington, DC: Office of Planning, Evaluation and Policy Development, U.S. Department of Education.

Council of Chief State School Officers. (1991). *Summary of state practices concerning the assessment of and the data collection about limited English proficient.* Washington, DC: Author.

Council of Chief State School Officers. (2012). *Framework for English language proficiency development standards corresponding to the Common Core State Standards and the Next Generation Science Standards.* Washington, DC: Author.

Cummins, J. (1981). The role of primary language development in promoting educational success for language minority students. In *Schooling and language minority students: A theoretical framework* (pp. 3–49). Los Angeles: Evaluation, Dissemination, and Assessment Center, California State University.

Cummins, J. (1984). *Bilingualism and special education: Issues in assessment and pedagogy.* Clevedon, England: Multilingual Matters.

Cummins, J. (1986). Empowering minority students: A framework for intervention. *Harvard Educational Review, 56*, 18–36.

Cummins, J. (2000). *Language, power, and pedagogy: Bilingual children in the crossfire.* Tonawanda, NY: Multilingual Matters.

Cummins, J. (2013). BICS and CALP: Empirical support, theoretical status and policy implications of a controversial distinction. In M. R. Hawkins (Ed.), *Framing languages and literacies* (pp. 10–23). New York, NY: Routledge.

Deville, C., & Chalhoub-Deville, M. (2011). Accountability-assessment under No Child Left Behind: Agenda, practice, and future. *Language Testing, 28*, 307–321.

Duran, R. P. (2008). Assessing English language learners' achievement. *Review of Research in Education, 32*, 292–327. doi:10.3102/0091732X07309372

Echevarría, J., Short, D., & Powers, K. (2006). School reform and standards-based education: A model for English-language learners. *Journal of Educational Research, 99*, 195–211. doi:10.3200/JOER.99.4.195-211

Edelsky, C. (1990). *With literacy and justice for all: Rethinking the social in language and education.* London, England: Falmer Press.

Elliott, S. N., Kratochwill, T. R., & Schulte, A. G. (1998). The assessment accommodation checklist: Who, what, where, when, why, and how? *Teaching Exceptional Children, 31*(2), 10–14.

Forster, M. (2001). *A policy maker's guide to systemwide assessment programs.* Camberwell, Victoria, Australia: ACER Press.

Francis, D. J., & Rivera, M. O. (2007). Chapter 2: Principles underlying English language proficiency tests and academic accountability for ELLs. In *English language proficiency assessment in the nation: Current status and future practice* (pp. 13–32). Davis: University of California, Davis, School of Education.

Gándara, P., Moran, R., & García, E. (2004). Legacy of Brown: Lau and language policy in the United States. *Review of Research in Education, 28*(1), 27–46. doi:10.3102/00917 32X028001027

Gándara, P., Rumberger, R., Maxwell-Jolly, J., & Callahan, R. (2003). English learners in California schools: Unequal resources, unequal outcomes. *Education Policy Analysis Archives, 11*(36), 1–54.

García, G. E., & Pearson, P. D. (1994). Chapter 8: Assessment and diversity. *Review of Research in Education, 20*, 337–391. doi:10.3102/0091732X020001337

Gardner, D. P. (1983). *A nation at risk: The imperative for educational reform.* Washington, DC: National Commission on Excellence in Education.

Gee, J. P. (1990). *Social linguistics and literacies: Ideology in discourses.* London, England: Falmer Press.

Gee, J. P. (2008). What is academic language? In A. S. Rosebery & B. Warren (Eds.), *Teaching science to English language learners: Building on students' strengths* (pp. 57–70). Arlington, VA: National Science Teachers Association.

Gibbons, P. (2003). Mediating language learning: Teacher interactions with ESL students in a content-based classroom. *TESOL Quarterly, 37*, 247–273. doi:10.2307/3588504

Gottlieb, M., & Kenyon, D. M. (2006). *The Bridge Study between tests of English language proficiency and ACCESS for ELLs®. Part I: Background and overview* (WIDA Consortium Technical Report No. 2). Retrieved from http://www.wida.us/assessment/ACCESS/TechReports/

Gottlieb, M., & Nguyen, D. (2007). *Assessment and accountability in language education programs.* Philadelphia, PA: Caslon.

Gutiérrez, K. D. (1995). Unpackaging academic discourse. *Discourse Processes, 19*, 21–37. doi:10.1080/01638539109544903

Hakuta, K. (2011). Educating language minority students and affirming their equal rights: Research and practical perspectives. *Educational Researcher, 40,* 163–174. doi:10.3102/0013189X11404943

Hakuta, K., Butler, Y. G., & Witt, D. (2000). *How long does it take English learners to attain proficiency.* Berkeley: University of California Linguistic Minority Research Institute.

Halliday, M. A. K. (1978). *Language as social semiotic.* Baltimore, MD: University Park Press.

Halliday, M. A. K., & Martin, J. R. (1993). *Writing science: Literacy and discursive power.* Pittsburgh, PA: University of Pittsburgh Press.

Halperin, S. (1975). ESEA ten years later. *Educational Researcher, 4*(8), 5–9.

Harper, C. A., Jong, E. J., & Platt, E. J. (2008). Marginalizing English as a second language teacher expertise: The exclusionary consequence of No Child Left Behind. *Language Policy, 7,* 267–284. doi:10.1007/s10993-008-9102-y

Heath, S. B. (1983). *Ways with words: Language, life and work in communities and classrooms.* New York, NY: Cambridge University Press.

Heritage, M. (2010). *Formative assessment and next-generation assessment systems: Are we losing an opportunity?* Washington, DC: Council of Chief State School Officers.

Herman, J. (2013). *Formative assessment for Next Generation Science Standards: A proposed model.* Washington, DC: K-12 Center. Retrieved from http://www.k12center.org/rsc/pdf/herman.pdf

Herman, J., & Linn, R. (2014). New assessments, new rigor. *Educational Leadership, 71*(6), 34–37.

Hopkins, M., Thompson, K. D., Linquanti, R., Hakuta, K., & August, D. (2013). Fully accounting for English learner performance: A key issue in ESEA reauthorization. *Educational Researcher, 42,* 101–108. doi:10.3102/0013189X12471426

Jiménez, L. (1992). *Raising the achievement level of English language learners through SDAIE.* Upper Saddle River, NJ: Pearson Education. Retrieved from http://www.foshaylc.org/ourpages/auto/2011/4/4/42519949/Raising%20the%20Achievement%20SDAIE.pdf

Kaufman, P. (1992). *Characteristics of at-risk students in NELS: 88. Contractor report.* Washington, DC: National Center for Education Statistics.

Kieffer, M. J., Lesaux, N. K., Rivera, M., & Francis, D. J. (2009). Accommodations for English language learners taking large-scale assessments: A meta-analysis on effectiveness and validity. *Review of Educational Research, 79,* 1168–1201. doi:10.3102/0034654309332490

Koenig, J. A., & Bachman, L. F. (2004). *Keeping score for all: The effects of inclusion and accommodation policies on large-scale educational assessment: Executive summary.* Washington, DC: National Academies Press.

Kopriva, R. J., Emick, J. E., Hipolito-Delgado, C. P., & Cameron, C. A. (2007). Measuring students' level of English proficiency: Educational significance and assessment requirements. *Educational Measurement: Issues and Practice, 26*(3), 11–20. doi:10.1111/j.1745-3992.2007.00097.x

Lacelle-Peterson, M. W., & Rivera, C. (1994). Is it real for all kids? A framework for equitable assessment policies for English language learners. *Harvard Educational Review, 64,* 55–76.

Lemke, J. (1990). *Talking science: Language, learning, and values.* Norwood, NJ: Ablex.

Linn, R. L., Baker, E. L., & Betebenner, D. W. (2002). Accountability systems: Implications of requirements of the No Child Left Behind Act of 2001. *Educational Researcher, 31*(6), 3–16. doi:10.3102/0013189X031006003

Linquanti, R. (2011). Strengthening assessment for English learner success: How can the promise of the common core state standards and innovative assessment systems be realized? In D. Plank & J. Norton (Eds.), *The road ahead for state assessments* (pp. 13–25). Palo Alto: Policy Analysis for California Education.

Linquanti, R., & Cook, H. G. (2013). *Toward a "common definition of English learner": A brief defining policy and technical issues and opportunities for state assessment consortia.* Washington, DC: Council of Chief State School Officers.

Linquanti, R., & George, C. (2007). Chapter 8: Establishing and utilizing an NCLB Title III accountability system: California's approach and findings to date. In J. Abedi (Ed.), *English language proficiency assessment in the nation: Current status and future practice* (pp. 105–118). Davis: University of California, Davis, School of Education.

Linquanti, R., & Hakuta, K. (2012). *How next-generation standards and assessments can foster success for California's English learners* (PACE Policy Brief No. 12-1). Palo Alto: Policy Analysis for California Education.

Liu, K. K., & Anderson, M. (2008). Universal design considerations for improving student achievement on English language proficiency tests. *Assessment for Effective Intervention, 33,* 167–176. doi:10.1177/1534508407313242

Mahon, E. A. (2006). High-stakes testing and English language learners: Questions of validity. *Bilingual Research Journal, 30,* 479–497. doi:10.1080/15235882.2006.10162886

Menken, K. (2008). *English learners left behind: Standardized testing as language policy.* Tonawanda, NY: Multilingual Matters.

Menken, K. (2010). NCLB and English language learners: Challenges and consequences. *Theory Into Practice, 49,* 121–128. doi:10.1080/00405841003626619

Messick, S. (1989). Validity. In R. L. Linn (Ed.), *Educational measurement* (3rd ed., pp. 13–103). New York, NY: Macmillan.

Mislevy, R. J., & Haertel, G. D. (2006). Implications of evidence-centered design for educational testing. *Educational Measurement: Issues and Practice, 25*(4), 6–20. doi:10.1111/j.1745-3992.2006.00075.x

Mislevy, R. J., & Riconscente, M. (2006). Evidence-centered assessment design. In S. M. Downing & T. M. Haladyna (Ed.), *Handbook of test development* (pp. 61–90). Mahwah, NJ: Lawrence Erlbaum.

Mislevy, R. J., Steinberg, L. S., & Almond, R. G. (1999). *On the roles of task model variables in assessment design* (CSE Report No. 500). Los Angeles, CA: CRESST.

Mislevy, R. J., Steinberg, L. S., & Almond, R. G. (2002). Design and analysis in task-based language assessment. *Language Testing, 19,* 477–496. doi:10.1191/0265532202lt241oa

Mislevy, R. J., & Yin, C. (2012). Evidence-centered design in language testing. In G. Fulcher & F. Davidson (Eds.), *The Routledge handbook of language testing* (pp. 208–222). New York, NY: Routledge.

Mohan, B. A. (1986). *Language and content.* Boston, MA: Addison-Wesley.

Moschkovich, J. (2012, January). *Mathematics, the Common Core, and language: Recommendations for mathematics instruction for ELLs aligned with the Common Core.* Paper presented at the Understanding Language Conference, Stanford University, Stanford, CA. Retrieved from http://ell.stanford.edu/publication/mathematics-common-core-and-language

Moss, P. A., Pullin, D. C., Gee, J. P., Haertel, E. H., & Young, L. J. (Eds.). (2008). *Assessment, equity, and opportunity to learn.* New York, NY: Cambridge University Press.

Nelson, S. W., McGhee, M. W., Meno, L. R., & Slater, C. L. (2007). Fulfilling the promise of educational accountability. *Phi Delta Kappan, 88,* 702–709.

O'Halloran, K. L. (2004). *Multimodal discourse analysis: Systemic functional perspectives.* London, England: Continuum.

Parker, C. E., Louie, J., & O'Dwyer, L. (2009). *New measures of English language proficiency and their relationship to performance on large-scale content assessments* (Issues & Answers Report, REL 2009–No. 066). Washington, DC: Institute of Education Sciences.

Perie, M., Marion, S., & Gong, B. (2009). Moving toward a comprehensive assessment system: A framework for considering interim assessments. *Educational Measurement: Issues and Practice, 28*(3), 5–13. doi:10.1111/j.1745-3992.2009.00149.x

Quinn, H., Lee, O., & Valdés, G. (2012, January). *Language demands and opportunities in relation to Next Generation Science Standards for English language learners: What teachers need to know.* Paper presented at the Understanding Language Conference, Stanford University, CA. Retrieved from http://ell.stanford.edu/publication/language-demands-and-opportunities-relation-next-generation-science-standards-ells

Riddle, W. (2002). *Education for the disadvantaged: ESEA Title 1 reauthorization issues* (Congressional Research Service issue brief). Washington, DC: Library of Congress.

Riley, R. W. (1995). Improving America's Schools Act and elementary and secondary education reform. *Journal of Law & Education, 24,* 513–566.

Rivera, C. (Ed.). (1984). *Language proficiency and academic achievement.* Tonawanda, NY: Multilingual Matters.

Rivera, C., Acosta, B. D., & Willner, L. S. (2008). *Guide for refining state assessment policies for accommodating English language learners.* Washington, DC: George Washington University Center for Equity and Excellence in Education. Retrieved from http://eric.ed.gov/?id=ED539746

Rivera, C., & Collum, E. (2006). *An analysis of state assessment policies addressing the accommodation of English language learners.* Washington, DC: National Assessment Governing Board.

Rivera, C., Collum, E., Willner, L. S., & Sia, J. K., Jr. (2006). An analysis of state assessment policies addressing the accommodation of English language learners. In C. Rivera & E. Collum (Eds.), *A national review of state assessment policy and practice for English language learners* (pp. 1–173). Mahwah, NJ: Lawrence Erlbaum.

Romaine, S. (1989). *Bilingualism.* Oxon, England: Blackwell.

Rymes, B. R. (2010). Classroom discourse analysis: A focus on communicative repertoires. In N. Hornberger & S. McKay (Eds.), *Sociolinguistics and language education* (pp. 528–548). Tonawanda, NY: Multilingual Matters.

Salomone, R. C. (2012). Equality of opportunity: Educating English learners: Reconciling bilingualism and accountability. *Harvard Law & Policy Review, 6,* 115–459.

Santos, M., Darling-Hammond, L., & Cheuk, T. (2012). *Teacher development appropriate to support English language learners.* Stanford, CA: Stanford University Press.

Scarcella, R. (2003b). *Academic English: A conceptual framework* (Technical Report No. 2003-1). Irvine: University of California Linguistic Minority Research Institute.

Schleppegrell, M. (2001). Linguistic features of the language of schooling. *Linguistics and Education, 12,* 431–459.

Schleppegrell, M. (2004). *The language of schooling: A functional linguistics perspective.* Mahwah, NJ: Lawrence Erlbaum.

Schleppegrell, M. (2007). The linguistic challenges of mathematics teaching and learning: A research review. *Reading & Writing Quarterly, 23,* 139–159. doi:10.1080/10573560601158461

Shaul, M. S., & Ganson, H. C. (2005). The No Child Left Behind Act of 2001: The federal government's role in strengthening accountability for student performance. *Review of Research in Education, 29,* 151–165.

Snow, C. E., & Uccelli, P. (2009). The challenge of academic language. In D. R. Olson & N. Torrance (Eds.), *The Cambridge handbook of literacy* (pp. 112–133). New York, NY: Cambridge University Press.

Solano-Flores, G. (2008). Who is given tests in what language by whom, when, and where? The need for probabilistic views of language in the testing of English language learners. *Educational Researcher, 37,* 189–199. doi:10.3102/0013189X08319569

Solano-Flores, G., & Trumbull, E. (2003). Examining language in context: The need for new research and practice paradigms in the testing of English-language learners. *Educational Researcher, 32*(2), 3–13. doi:10.3102/0013189X032002003

Sólorzano, R. W. (2008). High stakes testing: Issues, implications, and remedies for English language learners. *Review of Educational Research, 78,* 260–329. doi:10.3102/0034654308317845

Spalter, A. N. (2011). *Data-based decision making and team leadership for English language learners* (Unpublished doctoral dissertation). University of Wisconsin-Madison.

Tanenbaum, C., Boyle, A., Soga, K., Le Floch, K. C., Golden, L., Petroccia, M., . . . O'Day, J. (2012). *National evaluation of Title III implementation: Report on state and local implementation.* Washington, DC: American Institutes for Research.

Thompson, S. J., Morse, A. B., Sharpe, M., & Hall, S. (2005). *Accommodations manual: How to select, administer and evaluate use of accommodations and assessment for students with disabilities.* Washington, DC: Council of Chief State School Officers.

Thompson, S., Johnston, C. J., & Thurlow, M. L. (2002). *Universal design applied to large scale assessments* (Synthesis Report No. 44). Minneapolis: University of Minnesota, National Center on Educational Outcomes.

Toulmin, S. (1958). *The uses of argument.* New York, NY: Cambridge University Press.

Troike, R. (1984). Proficiency, social and cultural aspects of language. In C. Rivera (Ed.), *Language proficiency and academic achievement* (pp. 44–54). Avon, England: Multilingual Matters.

Unsworth, L. (1999). Developing critical understanding of the specialised language of school science and history texts: A functional grammatical perspective. *Journal of Adolescent & Adult Literacy, 42,* 508–521.

Valdés, G. (2004). Between support and marginalisation: The development of academic language in linguistic minority children. *International Journal of Bilingual Education and Bilingualism, 7,* 102–132. doi:10.1080/13670050408667804

Valenzuela, A., Prieto, L., & Hamilton, M. P. (2007). Introduction to the special issue: No Child Left Behind (NCLB) and minority youth: What the qualitative evidence suggests. *Anthropology & Education Quarterly, 38*(1), 1–8. doi:10.1525/aeq.2007.38.1.1

Veel, R. (1999). Language, knowledge and authority in school mathematics. In F. Christie (Ed.), *Pedagogy and the shaping of consciousness: Linguistic and social processes* (pp. 185–216). London, England: Cassell.

Vincent, C., Hafner, A., & LaCelle-Peterson, M. (1997). Statewide assessment programs: Policies and practices for the inclusion of limited English proficient students. *Practical Assessment, Research & Evaluation, 5*(13). Retrieved from http://pareonline.net/getvn.asp?v=5&n=13

Walqui, A., & Heritage, M. (2012, January). *Instruction for diverse groups of English language learners.* Paper presented at the Understanding Language Conference, Stanford University, Stanford, CA. Retrieved from http://ell.stanford.edu/sites/default/files/pdf/academic-papers/09-Walqui%20Heritage%20Instruction%20for%20Diverse%20Groups%20FINAL_0.pdf

WIDA Consortium. (2004). *English language proficiency standards, 2004 Edition, kindergarten through grade 12.* Madison, WI: Author.

WIDA Consortium. (2007). *English language proficiency standards and resource guide, 2007 Edition, kindergarten through grade 12.* Madison, WI: Author.

WIDA Consortium. (2012). *2012 Amplification of the English language development standards and resource guide, kindergarten-grade 12.* Madison, WI: Author.

Wiese, A. M., & García, E. E. (1998). The Bilingual Education Act: Language minority students and equal educational opportunity. *Bilingual Research Journal, 22,* 1–18. doi:10.1080/15235882.1998.10668670

Wiley, T. G. (2005). *Literacy and language diversity in the United States* (2nd ed.). Washington, DC: Center for Applied Linguistics.

Wolf, M. K., Kao, J. C., Herman, J., Bachman, L. F., Bailey, A. L., Bachman, P. L., . . . Chang, S. M. (2008). Issues in assessing English language learners: English language proficiency measures and accommodation uses: Literature review (CRESST Report No. 731). Los Angeles, CA: CRESST.

Wright, B. D., & Stone, M. H. (1979). *Best test design.* Chicago, IL: MESA Press.

Chapter 5

Psychometric Challenges in Assessing English Language Learners and Students With Disabilities

SUZANNE LANE
BRIAN LEVENTHAL
University of Pittsburgh

This chapter addresses the psychometric challenges in assessing English language learners (ELLs) and students with disabilities (SWDs). The first section addresses some general considerations in the assessment of ELLs and SWDs, including the prevalence of ELLs and SWDs in the student population, federal and state legislation that requires the inclusion of all students in large-scale assessments, validity considerations in the assessment of ELLs and SWDs, importance of test accommodations in their assessment, and an introduction to the psychometric challenges, which are intricately interwoven with validity and fairness considerations, in assessing ELLs and SWDs. The second section discusses the efficacy of test accommodations and modifications for SWDs and ELLs. The third section addresses the need for invariant measurement for ELLs and SWDs. In the assessment of a diverse student population it is important to examine the extent to which the psychometric properties of a test are invariant across groups of students. This necessitates obtaining evidence of reliability and score precision, internal structure evidence, external structure evidence, and evidence of equating invariance for ELLs and SWDs. The establishment of measurement invariance for ELLs and SWDs is required to make valid and fair score interpretations for these students and for group comparisons. Under the No Child Left Behind Act (NCLB) of 2002, growth measures have been implemented to help determine Annual Yearly Progress (U.S. Department of Education, 2005); however, the research on the efficacy of models for monitoring change for ELLs and SWDs has been scarce. Such research is crucial given that the federal Race to the Top initiative calls for multiple measures in educator evaluation systems, including measures that

Review of Research in Education
March 2015, Vol. 39, pp. 165–214
DOI: 10.3102/0091732X14556073
© 2015 AERA. http://rre.aera.net

assess student progress (U.S. Department of Education, 2010). The last section addresses issues related to including SWDs and ELLs in measures of "growth" and of educator effectiveness.

English Language Learners and Students With Disabilities

English language learners are the fastest growing group of the nation's student population, and it is projected that 25% of the students nationally will be ELLs by 2025 (National Clearinghouse for English Language Acquisition & Language Instruction Educational Programs, 2007). The definition of an ELL provided by Title IX of the Elementary and Secondary Education Act indicates that an ELL is a student between the ages of 3 and 21 years whose

difficulties in speaking, listening, reading, writing or understanding the English language may be sufficient to deny the individual the ability to meet the State's proficient level of achievement . . ., the ability to successfully achieve in classrooms where the language of instruction is English . . ." (English Learners Office, E. J. McClendon Educational Center, 2002)

To better understand the challenges in classifying students as ELLs, the reader is referred to Abedi (2008) who addresses the nuances in defining ELLs and provides recommendations for improving the validity of classifying students as ELLs. ELLs develop English language proficiency at different paces, with meaningful differences in their learning trajectories, and new ELLs enter schools each year. As a consequence, these students are variable in terms of both their English proficiency and their academic proficiency. It is important to recognize that ELLs differ from non-ELLs in terms of not only English language proficiency but also cultural and educational backgrounds (Abedi, 2004; Solano-Flores & Trumbull, 2003). There is ample evidence that there is a large performance gap between ELLs and non-ELLs in all content areas, particularly in those with heavy English language demands (Abedi, 2006; Abedi & Gandara, 2006; Solano-Flores & Trumbull, 2003). As described by Abedi and his colleagues (Abedi, 2004; Abedi & Gandara, 2006), there are many factors that contribute to the performance gap, including parent education level and poverty, challenges in second language (L2) acquisition, inequitable opportunities to learn (OTLs), and tests that are not well suited to assessing their knowledge and skills. Based on a three-state study, J. Kim and Herman (2009) suggested that both linguistic barriers and long-term ELL designation may contribute to achievement gaps for ELLs.

There are 6.6 million SWDs who receive special education, making up 13% of public school enrollment. They are disproportionally poor, minority, and identified as ELLs ("ESEA Reauthorization," 2010). The majority of SWDs, about 80% to 85%, are students without intellectual impairments; they are "students who with specially designated instruction, appropriate access, supports, and accommodations, as required by IDEA, can meet the same achievement standards as other students" ("ESEA Reauthorization, 2010, p. 39). The classification of students as SWDs and ELLs is not necessarily disjoint. ELLs who are at the lower end of the achievement scale tend to be overidentified as SWDs. Based on data from the 1998–1999 academic year in eleven urban school districts in California, Artiles, Rueda, Salazar and Higareda (2005) found that ELLs with minimal proficiency were at a greater risk of being identified as learning disabled and being placed in special education programs than any other group of students of similar achievement. Artiles and colleagues (2005) proposed several reasons why ELLs are overidentified as learning disabled, including problems with the screening process, invalid assessment instruments, the belief that language differences constitute a disability, and accountability pressures.

As implied above, SWDs and ELLs are not homogeneous groups, in that there is diversity within each of these groups of students. This diversity within SWDs and ELLs poses many validity and psychometric challenges in their assessment.

Federal and State Legislation for ELLs and SWDs

Federal (NCLB of 2002) and state legislation requires the inclusion of all students, including ELLs and SWDs, in large-scale assessments, holding districts and states accountable to the same standards for all students. To accomplish this, NCLB requires states to disaggregate their test data and report the performance of student subgroups, including SWDs and ELLs. Assessments therefore need to measure the targeted construct equally well for all examinees, regardless of group membership (Thompson, Blount, & Thurlow, 2002). The two assessment consortia, Partnership for Assessment of Readiness for College and Career (PARCC) and Smarter Balanced Assessment Consortium (Smarter Balanced; SBAC), will continue to provide disaggregated test data for student subgroups and have committed to ensuring comparability of test scores across students. The goals of the Smarter Balanced assessment system are to provide

accurate measures of achievement and growth for students with disabilities and English language learners. The assessments will address visual, auditory, and physical access barriers—as well as the unique needs of English language learners—allowing virtually all students to demonstrate what they know and can do. (http://www.smarterbalanced.org/parents-students/support-for-under-represented-students)

Similarly, a major goal of PARCC is to provide "all students, including but not limited to, students with disabilities, English learners, and underserved populations with equitable access to high-quality, 21st century PARCC assessments" (http://parcconline.org/parcc-accessibility-accommodations-and-fairness). PARCC and SBAC intend to promote student access through Universal Design principles, technology-enhanced accessibility features, and test accommodations. As an example, PARCC's specific design features that are intended to enhance student access are:

- Apply principles of **universal design** for accessible assessments throughout every stage of developing assessment components, items, and performance tasks;
- Minimize/eliminate features of the assessment that are irrelevant to what is being measured, so that all students can more **accurately demonstrate their knowledge and skills**
- Measure the **full range** of complexity of the standards

- Leverage technology for delivering assessment components as widely accessible as possible
- Build accessibility throughout the test itself with **no trade-off between accessibility and validity**
- Use a combination of **"accessible" authoring and accessible technologies** from the inception of items and tasks
- Establish **Committees on Accessibility, Accommodations, and Fairness** comprised of knowledgeable testing officials from member states and national experts

A major goal of such design principles for both PARCC and SBAC is to ensure the comparability of scores across students and subgroups of students, leading to equitable and valid score inferences and uses of test results.

Argument-Based Approach to Validity of Score Inferences

In the assessment of all students it is necessary to consider the evidence that is needed to support the validity of the score inferences and uses of the test results. This requires the specification of the inferences and uses, evaluation of the proposed inferences and their supporting assumptions using evidence, and consideration of plausible alternative interpretations. The argument-based approach to validity, which entails an interpretative and use (IU) argument and a validity argument, provides the foundation for test development and evaluation considerations (Kane, 2006, 2013). An IU argument explicitly links the inferences from performance to conclusions and decisions, including the actions resulting from the decisions. A validity argument provides a structure for evaluating the merits of the IU arguments; it requires the accumulation of theoretical and empirical support for the appropriateness of the claims (Kane, 2006). Each inference in the validity argument is based on a proposition or claim that requires support. The validity argument entails an overall evaluation of the plausibility of the proposed interpretations and uses of test scores by providing a coherent analysis of the evidence for and against the proposed interpretations and uses (American Educational Research Association [AERA], American Psychological Association [APA], & National Council on Measurement in Education [NCME], 2014; Cronbach, 1988, Kane, 1992; Messick, 1989).

Two sources of potential threat to the validity of score inferences are construct underrepresentation and construct-irrelevant variance (Messick, 1989). Construct underrepresentation occurs when an assessment does not fully capture the targeted construct, jeopardizing the generalizability of the score inferences to the larger domain. An example of when construct underrepresentation may occur is when ELLs are not assessed in their dominant language, which limits their access to the construct tested, resulting in test scores that do not represent their proficiency on the tested construct. This implies that test developers need to ensure that the knowledge and skills being assessed by the items and scoring rubrics represent the targeted knowledge and skills and that students have access to the content tested. Construct-irrelevant variance occurs when one or more constructs are being assessed, along with the intended construct, and systematically lowers or raises scores for subgroups of students. As an example, SWDs often have barriers that will have an impact on their performance on achievement tests. Potential sources of construct-irrelevant variance for SWDs and ELLs include, but are not limited to, linguistic demands of items, context and format of items, response mode, and rater's or computer's attention to irrelevant features of responses.

Test Accommodations for ELLs and SWDs

Test accommodations have an important role in discussions of fairness and accessibility, with direct implications for the validity of score interpretations for SWDs and ELLs. Test accommodations are typically provided to address both construct-irrelevant variance and construct underrepresentation. The purpose of accommodations is to ensure that SWDs and ELLs have full access to the construct the test is measuring and respond in a way that represents the students' knowledge, skills, and abilities on the intended construct, and to promote valid score interpretations and uses (Tindal & Fuchs, 1999). Accommodations are intended to increase the validity of score interpretations and uses by minimizing the impact of student attributes that are irrelevant to the construct being measured, and therefore allowing access to the construct the test is measuring. This allows for scores for accommodated students to be meaningfully compared to students for whom testing accommodations are not needed. Providing students with appropriate accommodations is considered a way to level the playing field for SWDs and ELLs. Consequently, it is necessary to examine how the accommodations provided to students affect the measurement of the targeted construct, that is, the extent to which the accommodations give SWDs and ELLs a fair and equal opportunity to demonstrate what they know and can do (see Thurlow & Kopriva, 2015, this volume, for a discussion on how accommodations can help ensure that all ELLs and SWDs have access to the content of the assessments).

Psychometric Challenges in the Assessment of ELLs and SWDs

The validity of score interpretations for subgroups at one occasion and across occasions requires equity and comparability of test scores, which implies the need for measurement invariance across subgroups. Underlying the measurement of students is a critical assumption that the test score scale is measuring the same construct with the same precision for all subgroups of students. If that assumption holds, analyses and comparisons of the scores for different subgroups are appropriate and can provide meaningful interpretations. But if that assumption does not hold, such analyses and comparisons are compromised.

The educational testing of SWDs and ELLs as well as other student subgroups poses a number of psychometric challenges. A major concern is the extent to which there is measurement invariance across tested subgroups. Measurement invariance implies that the internal structure (e.g., factorial structure) of the test is similar across subgroups and the items are functioning similarly across subgroups, providing support that the test is measuring the same construct(s) across the subgroups. Measurement invariance also implies that the score scale is comparable across subgroups and that the construct is being measured equally precisely for the subgroups, and consequently an evaluation of the reliability and score precision for the subgroups is needed. When forms of tests are equated, measurement invariance also requires that equating functions derived from different subgroups produce the same results if scores are to be equitable. Last, there are psychometric issues related to including SWDs and ELLs in the measurement of "growth" and educator effectiveness. Growth models have been used in NCLB accountability to monitor states' progress in closing achievement gaps and to set high expectations for annual improvement for all students. There has been little research however on the efficacy of these models for tracking and monitoring change for ELLs and SWDs. Furthermore, the Race to the Top initiative calls for multiple measures of educator evaluation systems, including measures of student growth (U.S. Department of Education, 2010).

A number of psychometric challenges arise when examining measurement invariance across subgroups. Many of these psychometric issues in testing SWDs and ELLs, including reliability, score precision, comparability, and equating, have been discussed in the literature (e.g., Abedi, 2002; Geisinger, 1994; Sireci, 2009; Sireci, Han, & Wells, 2008). Typically, the subgroups of interest tend to perform poorer than the general population, and it is likely that the test data may be more multidimensional for students performing at the lower end of the score scale because these students have acquired knowledge in some areas but not others (Abedi, 2002). Consequently, lack of measurement invariance may be a result of overall proficiency on the construct than ELL or SWD status. This implies that measurement invariance should be evaluated using not only the general population as a comparison group but also students who are scoring within the same score range as the subgroup of interest. A related concern is that indices that are used to examine measurement invariance are affected by restriction of score range. Examining measurement invariance with groups of students within similar score ranges will help alleviate some of these concerns. Furthermore, each of the groups, SWDs and ELLs, are heterogeneous, so when sample size permits, invariance in the reported scores should be evaluated with relevant subgroups of SWDs and ELLs, such as student groups defined by use of particular test accommodations and by language dialect (Sireci, 2009; Solano-Flores, 2006). The precision of the scores also need to be evaluated for different subgroups of students.

EFFICACY OF TEST ACCOMMODATIONS AND MODIFICATIONS FOR ELLS AND SWDS

To help alleviate construct-irrelevant barriers to the assessment and construct underrepresentation, test accommodations and test modifications are provided for SWDs and ELLs. Accommodations are changes to test materials and procedures that are assumed not to alter the construct tested, whereas modifications include changes in items (e.g., reducing length of reading passages) or test procedures for which it is not clear whether these modifications affect only access or also affect the construct being measured and, consequently, the score inferences that are drawn (Kettler, Elliott, & Beddow, 2009). As a result, modifications may affect the comparability of test scores for students who received the modification versus those who do not receive the modification. If there is no available evidence that scores remain comparable to the intended construct measured, changes to items or the test are commonly called modifications (S. E. Phillips & Camara, 2006). The *Standards for Educational and Psychological Testing* (AERA, APA, & NCME, 2014) indicates that test accommodations result in comparable measures that maintain the intended construct, whereas test modifications most likely will result in noncomparable measures that change the intended construct. The *Standards for Educational and Psychological Testing* (AERA, APA, & NCME, 1999) state that the purpose of an accommodation is to "minimize the impact of test taker attributes that are not relevant to the construct that is the primary focus of the assessment" (p. 101). Test accommodations can be categorized into five areas: timing (alternative test schedules), response (alternative ways to respond to the test), setting (changes to test setting); equipment and materials (use of additional references or devices); and presentation (alternative ways to present test materials) (Thurlow, Lazarus, & Christensen, 2013). For a more thorough description of the types of test accommodations, see Thurlow and Kopriva (2015, this volume).

The efficacy of test accommodations has been examined by comparing the mean performance level of either ELLs or SWDs on an accommodated test with the level on a nonaccommodated test. This approach has been criticized because improved performance on the accommodated test may indicate that the accommodated version was simply easier. Because of this, researchers have examined the improvement in average scores for the subgroup as compared to the general population. If accommodations have a positive effect for the subgroup but not the general population, it is assumed that construct-irrelevant variance (e.g., due to limited English proficiency for ELLs) was reduced, which has been termed the *interaction hypothesis*. Based on a review of studies examining the interaction hypothesis for SWDs, Sireci, Scarpati, and Li (2005) suggested that the interaction hypothesis needs to be refined, that is, gains may be observed for the general population on the accommodated version but the gains are significantly larger for the accommodated SWD group. This phenomenon is referred to as *differential boost*. The differential boost or disability group-by-accommodation interaction hypothesis refers to an accommodation improving performance of SWDs (or ELLs) more than it improves performance of students without disabilities (SWoDs; or non-ELLs; Fuchs & Fuchs, 2001).

Experimental studies in which accommodations are given to randomly assigned groups of students, SWDs and SWoDs or ELLs and non-ELLs, allow for more valid inferences regarding the effects of accommodations than inferences based on correlations. However, there are a number of challenges in conducting experimental studies, including small sample sizes and less representative samples. When interpreting the results of such studies, these issues should be considered. Some researchers have examined the effects of accommodations using large-scale assessment data as described below (e.g., Engelhard, Fincher, & Domaleski, 2011), which allows for a large representative sample of students in these subgroups.

Efficacy of Test Accommodations for SWDs

Some early studies examined the effects of accommodations for just SWDs, and did not compare them with SWoDs. As an example, the effects of extended time on the Reasoning section of the SAT were examined on scores of students with learning disabilities when they were first tested under standard conditions and then tested with extended time (Camara, Copeland, & Rosthschild, 1998). Score gains were 3 times larger for students with learning disabilities who had extended time as compared to SWoDs.

Sireci et al. (2005) provided a review of experimental research studies examining the effects of test accommodations for SWDs as compared to SWoDs. The most common accommodations were extended time and oral presentation, with many of the studies focusing on students with learning disabilities. For most of the studies testing the interaction hypothesis, all students—SWDs and SWoDs—performed better under the accommodated testing condition. Moreover, SWDs had greater score gains than SWoDs when provided with accommodations, giving support for the differential boost hypothesis (Fuchs & Fuchs, 2001). As an example, a study on the impact of accommodations on performance of elementary school SWDs and SWoDs found that students with learning disabilities had a differential boost from the read-aloud accommodation on a reading comprehension test but not from extended time or provision of large-print text (Fuchs, Fuchs, Eaton, Hamlett, & Karns, 2000). Kosciolek and Ysseldyke (2000) used a counterbalanced design to examine the effects of the oral accommodation on reading performance for a commercially produced test. Based on a repeated-measures analysis of variance (ANOVA), they found that SWDs had much larger gains under the oral administration of the test as compared to SWoDs (effect size =.56). Other research on extra time as an accommodation indicates that SWDs benefit differentially when compared with SWoDs and that extra time does not appear to alter the constructs tested by most state achievement tests (Sireci, Li, & Scarpati, 2003). In an experimental study using a mathematics state test, Johnson (2000) reported that SWDs gained considerably more than SWoDs when tested under standard conditions and then retested with an oral accommodation of the test.

In the 2010 National Center for Educational Outcomes report, Cormier, Altman, Shyyan, and Thurlow reviewed studies published in 2007 and 2008 for read-aloud accommodations for SWDs. Three studies indicated differential boost and three indicated no differential boost for SWDs. Subsequently, the National Center for Educational Outcomes examined studies published in 2009 and 2010 and reported that there was a differential boost in three read-aloud studies for SWDs and parallel boosts in two other studies (Rogers, Christian, & Thurlow, 2012).

For the purpose of this chapter, published studies in peer-reviewed journals evaluating the differential boost hypothesis for SWDs were examined from 2004 to 2013.[1] This time period was chosen because Sireci et al. (2005) reviewed studies examining the effects of test accommodations through the 2003 year. Our review indicated that evidence for differential boost was not independent of type of research design being implemented, age of the students, type of accommodation, construct being measured, and sample size. For the review, individual studies were subgrouped by grade level, accommodation, and construct measured; a study with two accommodations each at two grade levels is described as four separate studies. Of the 11 studies that used an experimental design, 4 showed evidence of a differential boost. Evidence of differential boost was found in 29% (2 of 7) of studies that examined fewer than 500 students (SWDs and general population) and 44% (4 of 9) of studies with more than 500 students. Studies based on large-scale assessments showed evidence of the interaction hypothesis in 4 out of 8 cases. Evidence of differential boost was found in 50% (3 of 6) of the studies that examined elementary school students and 30% (3 of 10) of the studies that examined middle school and high school students. When reading was the measured construct, 4 out of 10 (2 elementary and 2 secondary) studies showed evidence of differential boost compared to 2 out of 6 (1 elementary and 1 secondary) studies when mathematics was the construct measured.

Elbaum (2007) conducted a counterbalanced randomized experimental design to test 327 (n_{SWD} = 187) middle school and 316 (n_{SWD} = 204) high school students on two equivalent alternative forms of a mathematics test designed to mimic a statewide test. By testing all students in both the standard test taking condition and with the aid of an oral accommodation, data were analyzed using repeated-measures ANOVA. Test condition was statistically significant, $p < .001$, as was the main effect of disability status, $p < .001$. The interaction effect of disability by test condition was also significant, $p < .001$, and partial $\eta^2 = .02$, indicating that SWoDs benefited more from the read-aloud accommodation than SWDs. Even though SWoDs benefitted more from the accommodation, when the two groups were subcategorized into the upper and lower 50% scoring students (under the accommodation), the differences of the subcategory effect sizes within disability status were similar. In other words, the top 50% scoring SWDs and SWoDs had a much larger, and relatively equivalent, effect from the accommodation than those in the lower 50% of their respective group. Elbaum (2007) noted that regardless of disability status, the effect of the accommodation depended on the students' prior mathematics skill set.

Randall and Engelhard (2010a) examined the differential boost hypothesis for a third- to fourth-grade band and a sixth- to seventh-grade band of students on a state reading test when an oral accommodation or resource guides were provided. Students were nested within schools that were randomly assigned to one of the three conditions. The read-aloud accommodation group included 945 students (n_{SWD} = 459) in third grade whereas the resource guide group included 995 (n_{SWD} = 428) students in sixth grade. Students were pretested at the end of third grade and sixth grade under the standard administration of the state test and then retested in the fourth and seventh grades under their assigned condition. Using repeated measures ANOVA, the effect size for performance gains for Grade 4 SWDs when oral administrations were provided was .22, whereas it was .02 for SWoDs, indicating that Grade 4 SWDs benefitted more from the oral administration as compared to SWoDs. Grade 4 SWDs who had the use of a resource guide test were negatively afected by this accommodation (effect size = –.12), suggesting that the use of a resource guide can hinder performance. For Grade 7 students, SWDs and SWoDs had a similar boost in mean test scores when they had an oral accommodation (effect size = .17 and .20, respectively). These results provide support for the differential boost hypothesis for elementary-grade students when they receive an oral accommodation on a reading test but not for the middle-grade students. As suggested by the authors, the construct may be altered when providing read-aloud accommodations for elementary students. Earlier studies that have examined the effects of a read-aloud accommodation for reading tests have indicated no significant gains for SWDs and SWoDs (McKevitt & Elliott, 2003) or similar gains for both students with learning disabilities and students without learning disabilities on reading, science, and math commercially published tests (Meloy, Deville, & Frisbie, 2000). However, these studies had relatively small sample sizes. In addition, differences in item types, tested content, and grade levels as well as the composition of the SWD samples may account for differences in the results.

Other studies have tried to control for student background variables when examining the effect of oral administration accommodations using relatively large sample sizes. Using regression procedures, Huynh, Meyer, and Gallant (2004) examined the effect of oral administration accommodation on student performance on a Grade 10 state mathematics test and reported that after controlling for student background variables, including gender, ethnicity, and Grade 8 mathematics and reading test performance, SWDs under oral administration performed better than SWDs under the standard administration (effect size = .21) and that both of these groups performed poorer than SWoDs. As they indicated, this effect size would be considered small by Cohen's criteria; however, if a 50% proficient rate is assumed for all students, the effect size of .21 represents a proficient rate of 58%, indicating an 8% improvement for these students.

In an effort to target students who would most likely benefit most from an oral administration, Laitusis (2010) examined the differential boost hypothesis for students with reading-based learning disabilities (SRLDs). Using an experimental design with repeated measures, Laitusis (2010) found that 1,181 fourth-grade and 847 eighth-grade SRLDs benefited differentially from read-aloud accommodations on a commercially published reading comprehension test after controlling for reading fluency and ceiling effects, with the differential performance boost greater in Grade 4 than Grade 8. For Grade 4, the effect size for SRLDs was .57 and for non-SRLDs it was .14. For Grade 8, the effect size was .32 for SRLDs and .06 for non-SRLDs. This pattern was also observed when controlling for reading fluency. The oral administration studies have generally found a greater effect for elementary school students than middle and high school students.

Lewandowski, Lovett, and Rogers (2008) explored the effect of the extended time accommodation for SRLDs. Sixty-four students, 32 with disabilities, in Grades 10 to 12 were provided a subtest of the Nelson-Denny Reading Test (Brown, Fishco, & Hanna, 1993) in which they were told to change the pen color at the 13-minute mark and asked to drop their pens after 19.5 minutes. This change was to determine differences under the standard condition (13 minutes) and an extended accommodation (additional 6.5 minutes) in which the number of items correct, number of items attempted, and percentage correct were marked at each time point. Using three 2 × 2 mixed-model ANOVA procedures, no evidence of a differential boost was established when comparing SWoD to students with reading disabilities for items correct (d = 2.68 standard time, d = 3.39 extended time), items attempted (d = 2.39 standard time, d = 3.13 extended time), nor percentage correct (no significant interaction of disability × accommodation), indicating that extended time on a reading test did not affect students with reading disabilities differently than SWoD.

Additionally, H. Li (2013) used hierarchical linear modeling (HLM) to examine the effects of read-aloud accommodations for SWDs and SWoDs through a meta-analysis of 27 studies, published and unpublished. HLM is a valuable statistical method for meta-analyses because it provides a means to explain variations in effect sizes. The majority of the SWDs in these studies had learning disabilities. The variation of the 128 effect sizes across the studies was captured in the Level 1 model and the Level 2 model allowed for the identification of potential sources of this variation, including disability status, construct measured, delivery method, grade level, and extra time. The results indicated that the effect of read-aloud accommodations for SWDs was significantly stronger than the effect for SWoDs (differential boost due to disability status SDs ranged from 0.161 to 1.75). The accommodation effect was also significantly stronger when the subject area was reading and when the test was read by human proctors than when video/audio players or computers were used. Furthermore, the effect of read-aloud accommodations was significantly stronger for elementary school students than middle school students.

Efficacy of Test Modifications for SWDs

Federal legislation allowed states to use modified versions of their general assessment for up to 2% of the total student population to be counted as proficient (U.S. Department of Education, 2007). These were assessments based on modified academic achievement standards for SWDs who had an individualized education program and were unlikely to reach proficient on the general state test. These tests were intended to provide universal access and reduce cognitive load while providing valid score inferences regarding the same constructs measured on the general test. Elliott and others (2010) and Kettler and others (2011) examined the impact of item and test modifications on performance and score precision for SWDs and SWoDs. Three groups of eighth-grade students (n = 755) defined by eligibility and disability from four states were administered original and modified versions of reading and mathematics tests. There were approximately equal numbers of SWDs who were eligible for the modified test, SWDs who were not eligible, and SWoDs. The most common item modifications were removal of a distractor, simplification of language, addition of graphic support, and reorganization of layout. An experimental design was used with students experiencing each of three conditions (original, modified, and modified with reading support) but receiving each item in only one of the three conditions. Using a meta-analytic approach to estimate coefficient alpha, they reported minimal changes in score reliability across groups and conditions (between .88 and .94 for reading and between .85 and .90 for math). A differential boost was also reported when controlling for ability level using item response theory (IRT), that is, there were larger reductions in item difficulty for SWDs who would be eligible to take the modified test than students who would not be eligible. In addition, the results provided evidence for the modification of shortening the length of the item stem and evidence for the modification of using visuals for mathematics items. Additional guidelines on how to modify items to improve accessibility is provided by Kettler (2011).

Efficacy of Test Accommodations for ELLs

Research in the early 2000s has shown that the achievement gap between ELLs and non-ELLs is greater on tests that are linguistically complex, that is, tests that have a greater English language demand (Abedi, 2003; Abedi & Lord, 2001). Items with unnecessary linguistic complexity in tests such as mathematics and science are a source of construct-irrelevant variance, introducing unintended multidimensionality, and have fairness implications when assessing ELLs (Abedi, Leon, & Mirocha, 2000; Abedi, 2004). Examinees' limited proficiency in the language in which tests are administered is a threat to the validity of score interpretations when language is not the construct being measured (AERA, APA, & NCME, 2014). The validity of score inferences can be threatened also by the linguistic skills of individuals who write or adapt items, and it has been proposed that language-based accommodations are needed for those administering tests to ELLs and those who are scoring their written responses (Solano-Flores, 2008).

Linguistic modification as a form of accommodation makes the test more accessible to ELLs. Abedi and his colleagues examined the impact of linguistic modification on ELL performance (Abedi, 2009; Abedi et al., 2000). As an example, an early study by Abedi et al. (2000) examined the performance of Grade 8 students with different accommodations, including modified linguistic structures, extra time, and provision of a glossary, and found that only the linguistic accommodation narrowed the performance gap between ELLs and non-ELLs significantly.

Similar to the section on the efficacy of accommodations for SWDs, published studies in peer-reviewed journals evaluating the differential boost hypothesis for ELLs were examined from 2004 to 2013.[2] Twelve of 16 (75%) studies that implemented an experimental design found evidence of a differential boost. Studies with a sample size less than 500 showed evidence of a differential boost 10 out of 19 (53%)

times whereas the 2 studies that used a sample size greater than 500 did not show evidence of differential boost. Results of studies based on large-scale assessments showed evidence of a differential boost in all 8 of the cases. Seven of the 11 studies using elementary students demonstrated differential boost whereas 4 of the 11 studies using secondary-level students showed evidence of differential boost. Seventy-eight percent of the studies using science tests demonstrated differential boost (6 of 7 elementary, 1 of 2 secondary) whereas those using a mathematics test showed differential boost in 40% (5 of 11 elementary, 3 of 9 secondary) of the cases.

Abedi (2009) examined the accessibility and validity of computer-based testing for ELLs and non-ELLs. He examined several accommodations used in an administration of mathematics tests administered to ELLs in Grades 4 and 8, including a computer administration with a pop-up glossary, a customized English dictionary, and extended time (Grade 4 only). The math test included public released items from the National Assessment of Educational Progress (NAEP) and the Trends in International Mathematics and Science Study. Items were rated in terms of their linguistic complexity on a scale from 0 to 4. A latent composite of multiple measures of students' English proficiency was used as a covariate and a proportional random sampling method was used to assign both ELLs and non-ELLs to each of the accommodation conditions and a nonaccommodation condition. For both Grades 4 and 8, ELL student performance was highest in the computer condition. For Grade 4, adjusting for initial differences in the level of English proficiency among the ELL groups, a 0.5 SD difference between the means for the computer condition and the nonaccommodated condition was reported. The obtained coefficient of determination, $\eta^2 = .03$, indicated that the computer as an accommodation explains 3% of the test score variance for ELLs. The other statistically significant difference was for the comparison of extended time and the nonaccommodated condition, with a $\eta^2 = .024$. For Grade 8, adjusting for differences in the level of English proficiency among the ELL groups, the adjusted mean of 10.66 for the computer condition was significantly higher than the adjusted mean of 9.11 for the nonaccommodated condition. As a comparison, there were no statistically significant differences between the means of the accommodated conditions with the nonaccommodated condition for non-ELLs in both Grades 4 and 8, providing some evidence for the effectiveness of the computer accommodation for ELLs.

The effects of the accommodations for two levels of linguistic complexity of the items were also examined. Using a multivariate analysis of covariance model, for Grade 4 ELLs all three accommodations made a significant difference on performance on the more linguistically complex items, and two of the accommodations (computer and extra time) made a significant difference on the performance on the less linguistically complex items. For Grade 8 ELLs, the computer accommodation produced significant differences on the more linguistically complex items, and there were no significant differences on the less linguistically complex items. Grade 8 ELLs spent nearly 3 times as much time glossing as compared to non-ELLs, providing additional support for the computer accommodation (Abedi, 2009).

Studies have examined the effects of academic language versus linguistic complexity on ELL performance. Solano-Flores, Barnett-Clarke, and Kachchaf (2013) compared ELL and non-ELL performance on Grades 4 and 5 mathematics content knowledge and academic language tests consisting of multiple-choice items. Pretests were administered prior to instruction, followed by posttests after instruction. The content knowledge items focused on computation and problem solving, and the academic language items focused on terms used to refer to mathematical concepts (e.g., mixed number). The study included 579 (ELLs = 338) and 564 (ELLs = 333) students in Grade 4 and 464 (ELLs = 231) and 484 (ELLs = 254) in Grade 5 for the content knowledge and academic language assessments, respectively. For both ELLs and non-ELLs, the percentage of items correct was higher for the academic language tests than the content knowledge tests and higher for the posttest than the pretest. The authors argued that because the academic language items have a greater number of words, on average, the performance differences can be attributed, in part, to the emphasis on academic language in instruction and not due to the linguistic complexity of the items. Repeated-measures ANOVAs indicated that non-ELLs had significantly higher gain scores than ELLs for both tests and in both grades (partial η^2 = .029–.176). The gain score differences for the ELL group as compared to non-ELL group tended to be greater for the academic language test than the content knowledge test. In summary, both groups performed better on the academic language test than the content test, but non-ELLs outperformed ELLs on both tests. In terms of score gains, smaller gains were found for the academic language tests, in particular for ELLs. Based on these results, the authors argued that ELLs may not have developed a meaning-making system prior to instruction to meet the different sets of interpretative demands of the two types of items, and suggested that caution is needed in including ELL students in large-scale testing before they have developed academic language proficiency. They also argued that academic language should be taken into consideration during test development and that the analysis of the semiotic structure of items can help ensure that the language demands of items are consistent with the targeted construct.

Several studies that conducted a meta-analysis to examine differential boost for ELLs were not included in the review described previously. Kieffer, Lesaux, Rivera and Francis (2009) examined accommodations for ELLs on large scale assessments. A meta-analysis was performed using 11 studies with 23,999 participants, n_{ELL} = 6,554, to examine the effects of seven different types of accommodations: simplified English, English dictionaries or glossaries, bilingual dictionaries or glossaries, tests in the native language, dual language test booklets, dual-language questions for English passages, and extra time. Only English dictionaries and glossaries had a positive and statistically significant average effect size. Separating out the 4 studies that involved quasi experiments and only including those from randomized experiments, the average effect size was still found to be statistically significant, $g^u = .12, p = .021$. The authors used HLM to examine the effects of moderator variables on this mean effect. Extra time, provision of a dictionary for the computerized format, grade level of the student, and domain of the test did not explain significant variation in effect sizes. However, the use of English dictionaries and glossaries had a 24% reduction in the science achievement gap and a 20% reduction in the mathematics achievement gap for ELLs. The older students experienced less of an effect as there was only an 11% reduction for eighth-grade students in math and 9% reduction for eighth-grade students in science.

In 2012 Kieffer, Rivera, and Francis expanded the 2009 meta-analysis to include more recent studies. Their results indicated that the achievement gap between ELLs and non-ELLs was between 9% and 19% when given simplified language. When given English dictionaries there was an 11% to 21% reduction in the performance gap, and when provided extra time or an untimed assessment the performance gap was reduced between 15% and 31% in ELLs and non-ELLs on large scale assessments. However, when the language of the test was matched to the language of instruction there was no reduction of performance gap.

Pennock-Roman and Rivera (2011) performed a meta-analysis using 14 studies that either randomly assigned ELLs to test accommodation versus control conditions or used repeated measures in counterbalanced order. In their analysis, they accounted for language proficiency, test format, and time constraints, which allowed them to examine the factors that led to effective accommodations. When students were provided with sufficient time, most accommodations did improve performance of ELLs. When given enough time, the most effective accommodations were dual language, the bilingual glossary, and the English glossary conditions (Glass's d effect size values were .299, .247, and .229, respectively). The pop-up English glossary was the most effective accommodation under restricted time conditions (Glass's d was .285). The most effective accommodation for ELLs with low English language proficiency and/or who were receiving instruction in Spanish, their native language, was a Spanish test version as compared to an English test version (Glass's d effect size values of .95 and 1.45 for the Spanish version as opposed to .13 and .40 for the English version). Whereas the Spanish version accommodation was not effective for ELLs with intermediate levels of English language proficiency, students receiving individualized education programs, and students with a home language background other than Spanish. These results suggest that construct-irrelevant variance due to English proficiency was reduced for some accommodations and were dependent on level of English proficiency, time constraints, and test format, indicating the need for accounting for test format, language proficiency, and test time when examining the effects of test accommodations for ELLs.

Using HLM, a meta-analysis was conducted to investigate the effects of accommodations on the performance of ELLs (H. Li & Suen, 2012). This analysis included data from 19 studies with 85 effect sizes, including journal articles, reports, theses, and conference papers. It also included a wide range of tested subjects. The Level 1 model in HLM examined the variation of effect sizes of the accommodations across studies and the Level 2 model attempted to explain the potential sources of this variation. The variables considered to account for variation of effects of accommodations were ethnicity, grade level, test subject, English proficiency, and accommodation type. The results indicated that, on average, the accommodated ELLs scored 0.157 *SD*s above the nonaccommodated ELLs, suggesting that accommodations improved their test performance, and the estimated variance of the effect sizes was significant. Of the Level 2 variables examined, only a low level of English proficiency had a significant effect, indicating that those with low levels of English proficiency had higher accommodation effects. The other four variables did not help explain the variability in effect sizes. For example, there were no significant differences between math/science and other subjects in terms of accommodation effects. Furthermore, accommodation type (linguistic simplification, dual-language booklet, Spanish version, dictionary and glossary, extra time) was not statistically significant. The final model indicated that accommodated ELLs who did not have low English proficiency scored, on average, 0.079 *SD* units above the nonaccommodated groups, whereas accommodated low English proficiency ELLs scored up to 0.569 *SD* units above their nonaccommodated groups, providing some evidence of the benefits of accommodations for ELLs, especially for those with low English proficiency. Also, approximately 38% of the variability in the effect sizes was explained by the students' English proficiency in the final model. It should be noted, however, that the studies used in these analyses did not include non-ELLs as a control group, and thus further research on the appropriateness of accommodations is warranted.

Efficacy for Test Modifications for ELLs

Shaftel, Belton-Kocher, Glasnapp, and Poggio (2003) examined the effects of item modifications on student performance for ELLs and non-ELLs using a state mathematics test for Grades 5, 8, and 11. Sample sizes ranged from 177 (ELL) to 1,030 (non-ELL) across the three grades. Using a counterbalanced design for a modified version of the state test (simplified language) with an unmodified version, the non-ELL group showed no significant differences. To analyze differences within the ELL group, data were evaluated from ELLs who took the original version of the test in spring 2000 with matched items from the modified version on the spring 2001 assessment. Using a common item anchor block equating design and an analysis of covariance with items as the covariate, it was found that at Grade 7, ELLs taking the original items tended to perform better than the ELLs taking the modified version of the test. At Grade 4, ELLs taking the modified version had a significantly higher adjusted mean score of 0.49 points whereas students in Grade 10 had a significant difference of 0.91 compared to the nonmodified version. The researchers also used IRT procedures to obtain estimates for student ability and item parameters for the modified and unmodified versions of the tests for ELLs. In Grade 4, item discrimination and difficulty estimates were nearly identical using the two versions of the test. For Grade 7 there were differences in the mean item difficulty estimates with the modified version being more difficult but no differences were obtained in ability or discrimination estimates. Finally for Grade 10, the mean ability estimate for the modified version was

.303 whereas the original version yielded a mean ability estimate of .003. Even with significant differences using analysis of covariance, the differences were very small with large sample sizes. Taking this into account with minimal differences in the IRT estimates, the authors concluded that there is no evidence that the modified version yielded differences compared to the unmodified version.

MEASUREMENT INVARIANCE

Although the observance of a differential boost can support the use of accommodations for SWDs and ELLs, it can be challenged because better performance of SWDs and ELLs is not equivalent to assessments that provide valid score inferences (Sireci et al., 2005). It is necessary to examine the extent to which the psychometric properties of a test are invariant across groups of students and test administration formats. The establishment of measurement invariance across ELLs and SWDs is required to make valid score interpretations for individual students and for group comparisons. If accommodations function as intended, item and test measurement properties should be similar when the test is administered to ELLs (or SWDs) who require accommodations and receive them and ELLs (or SWDs) who do not require accommodations. Similarly, these item and test measurement properties should be similar to those for non-ELLs and SWoDs. A measure can be considered invariant when members of different subpopulations who have the same standing on the construct being assessed obtain the same score on the test with the same precision.

Measurement invariance studies directly examine the item and test measurement characteristics for ELLs and SWDs. Invariance of the internal structure of the test across subgroups, or factorial invariance, is needed to ensure comparable and valid score interpretations. However, it is important to recognize that factorial invariance alone is insufficient evidence to ensure valid score interpretations and uses. Other aspects of comparability need to be examined across subgroups of students, including the precision of scores and accuracy of classification rates, the relationship between test scores and other measures (i.e., external structure evidence), cognitive processes evoked by the test items, and consequences of test score inferences (AERA, APA, & NCME, 2014).

This section addresses reliability and score precision for ELLs and SWDs, computer-adaptive testing to improve measurement accuracy and precision, language of testing and rater language background as a source of measurement error for ELLs, internal structure evidence for ELLs and SWDs using factor analysis and differential item functioning (DIF), external structure evidence for ELLs and SWDs, and equating invariance for ELLs and SWDs.

Reliability, Measurement Error, and Score Precision

A relatively large percentage of ELLs and SWDs demonstrate lower performance on large-scale assessments (Abedi, Leon, & Kao, 2007; Thurlow, Bremer, & Albus, 2011). This raises concerns in assessing ELLs and SWDs because test scores tend to be less precise at the ends of the score scale, resulting in less reliable scores for many ELLs and SWDs. This was demonstrated for SWDs using data from a fourth- and eighth-grade mathematics test and English language test from one state (Laitusis, Buzick, Cook, & Stone, 2011). The results indicated that SWDs scoring at chance level ranged from 12% to 22%, whereas only 1% to 3% of SWoDs scored at chance level, resulting in less precise scores for many SWDs. Internal consistency indices, such as coefficient alpha, are commonly used as measures of test score reliability. These indices are affected by restricted ranges of performance, which is common in the assessment of SWDs and ELLs. Furthermore, using these indices when some items measure an irrelevant construct in addition to the intended construct for subgroups will produce more measurement error and lower reliability estimates.

Reliability and Score Precision for ELLs

Abedi (2002, 2003) examined the precision of measurement across examinee groups and reported that internal consistency reliabilities (coefficient alphas) for scores from commercially developed tests were consistently lower for ELLs than non-ELLs in Grades 2 and 9 in reading, mathematics, language, science (Grade 9 only), and social science (Grade 9 only). For Grade 2 the differences in the reliability coefficients for ELLs and non-ELLs ranged from .013 to .062 and for Grade 9 they ranged from .096 to .120. As indicated by the authors, the increase in reliability differences from the lower to upper grades may be due to more complex language structures in tests in the upper grades. For 10th- and 11th-grade students Abedi (2003) reported that on reading, science, and math commercially published tests the coefficient alphas were higher for non-ELLs than for both nonaccommodated ELLs and accommodated ELLs with one exception (coefficient alphas were higher for both ELL groups than the non-ELL group for the Grade 10 math test). As indicated by Abedi (2003) a number of factors, including language background, restriction of range, socioeconomic status (SES), and OTL, may contribute to the observed differences in reliabilities.

Young et al. (2008) reported coefficient alphas for Grade 5 and Grade 8 students taking mathematics and science state tests for NCLB accountability. The coefficients were higher for non-ELLs (.878–.939) than for both accommodated ELLs (.603–.911) and nonaccommodated ELLs (.750–.912), with sample sizes ranging from 183 to 1,246 for the accommodated ELL groups. The accommodations included translated directions and access to glossaries. For the science tests, the reliabilities were higher for the nonaccommodated ELLs than for the accommodated ELLs, whereas this pattern did not hold for the mathematics tests.

Generalizability theory has also been used to examine the precision of ELL scores on large-scale assessments. Generalizability theory (Brennan, 2001; Cronbach, Gleser, Nanda, & Rajaratnam, 1972) allows for examining the contribution of various sources of measurement error to the generalizability of test scores to the large construct domain. D. Li and Brennan (2007) examined differential precision of a commercially published reading comprehension test using univariate and multivariate person × item and person × (item: passage/process) generalizability studies. There were eight reading passages, and the items associated with the reading passages were categorized into three process areas: factual understanding, inference and interpretation, and analysis and generalization. Using these designs they were able to examine three sources of error: reading passages, processes, and items nested within the cross-classification of passages and cognitive processes. The data were from 500 ELL and 500 non-ELL students. The results indicated that reading passages had a larger variance for ELLs than for non-ELLs, which was primarily due to the larger variability of one of the cognitive process areas—generalization. The generalizability coefficients from the multivariate design were consistently lower for the ELLs than the non-ELLs; the greatest difference (.18) was for the generalization area. The generalizability coefficients for the three process areas ranged from .754 to .769 for non-ELLs and .579 and .672 for ELLs. The generalizability coefficient for the composite was .898 for non-ELLs and .831 for ELLs, suggesting differences in the validity of the score interpretations for ELLs and non-ELLs.

Lakin and Lai (2012) examined differential reliability of a commercially published ability test with measures for verbal, quantitative, and nonverbal/figural reasoning across 144 ELLs and 236 non-ELLs in Grades 3 and 4. Such tests are used in conjunction with other information to provide differential instruction to students, typically in the elementary grades. The non-ELL group performed significantly better than the ELL group on the verbal, quantitative, and nonverbal tests (Cohen's *d* indices 1.13, .78, and .68, respectively). It is important to note that the standard deviation for the verbal test was nearly twice as large for the non-ELL group than the ELL group, 14.37 and 7.67, respectively, and over half as large for the quantitative test, 12.75 and 9.09, respectively, whereas the standard deviations for the nonverbal test were more similar. Using univariate and multivariate person × item generalizability studies, they observed that verbal and quantitative reasoning skills were measured less precisely for ELLs (generalizability coefficients of .838 and .883, respectively) than they were for non-ELLs (generalizability coefficients of .961 and .953, respectively), which is partly a function of the restricted range of scores for ELLs. From their analysis, they estimated that ELLs would need to respond to more than twice as many quantitative items and more than 3 times as many verbal items in order to obtain comparable precision as non-ELLs. The composite score across the three areas had relatively high generalizability estimates for both ELLs (.95) and non-ELLs (.98). As the authors indicated, although the reliability of the composite scores are high and similar across the two groups, the use of student performance profiles across the three reasoning tests to inform instructional decisions at the student level should be done cautiously for ELLs.

Reliability and Score Precision for SWDs

The reliability of test scores for SWDs in Grade 8 when reading comprehension passages were segmented (with relevant items) was examined by Abedi et al. (2010).

Most of the SWDs had specific learning disabilities (107 out of 117). For the original version of the reading test, the researchers reported a .52 coefficient alpha for SWDs and .78 for SWoDs. Similar to the other studies, there was greater variability in the scores for SWoDs (SD = 4.58, n = 302) than for SWDs (SD = and 3.32 and n = 52). SWDs performed better on the segmented version of the test and had more variability in their scores (SD = 4.20 and n = 58), resulting in a higher coefficient alpha, .69, as compared to the original version. Test statistics for SWoDs were similar across versions, with a coefficient alpha of .79 for the segmented version (SD = 4.67 and n = 294).

With larger sample sizes, Huynh and Barton (2006) reported coefficient alphas of .875, .892, and .895 for SWDs who received an oral accommodation on a state Grade 10 reading test, SWDs who did not receive an accommodation, and SWoDs, respectively. Although the two SWD group means were lower than the mean for the SWoDs, the standard deviations were not as disparate as in the previously discussed studies (accommodated SWDs SD = 76.3, nonaccommodated SWDs SD = 89.3, and SWoDs SD = 89.6). Huynh et al. (2004) reported similar coefficient alphas for the state's Grade 10 mathematics test for SWDs who received an oral accommodation (.878), nonaccommodated SWDs (.881), and SWoDs (.895).

For Grade 4 students, Randall and Engelhard (2010b) obtained coefficient alphas of .940 for SWDs who received an oral accommodation on a reading state test and .916 for SWDs who did not receive an accommodation. The coefficient alphas were .976 for SWoDs who received an oral accommodation on the reading test and .960 for nonaccommodated SWoDs. This pattern did not hold for Grade 7 students. For Grade 7 students, the coefficient alphas were .903 for oral accommodated SWDs and .918 for nonaccommodated SWDs; and .898 for oral accommodated SWoDs and .954 for nonaccommodated SWoDs. These results may suggest that oral accommodations lead to increased precision for SWDs at lower grade levels but not for students at upper grade levels.

Computer-Adaptive Testing to Increase Measurement Accuracy and Precision

Stone and Davey (2011) discuss some of the advantages of using computer adaptive testing (CAT) with SWDs, including more precise measurement of SWDs and ELLs (G. Phillips, 2009), capability of tracking which accommodations are being used and when they are employed by students (Thurlow, Lazarus, Albus, & Hodgson, 2010), and allowing for a wider array of accommodations for SWDs (Thurlow et al., 2010). The latter two are advantages for any computer-based test. Computer-based testing, whether it is adaptive or not, can allow for more flexibility in tailoring the access tools (e.g., magnification, color contrast) and supplemental accessibility information (audio, braille, tactile versions of item content, simplified vocabulary) to the individual student so as to help ensure students have access to the targeted test construct (Russell, 2011). Consequently, these accessibility tools and supplemental information can enhance the validity of the test score inferences for students. As indicated by Russell, depending on a student's access needs, flexible tailoring may require an adaptation to the presentation of item content [e.g., magnifying], the interaction with that content [e.g., masking content to decrease distractions], the response mode [e.g., assistive communication device to produce a response], or the representational form in which content is communicated [e.g., audio or alternate language]. (p. 9)

It is imperative to explicitly specify the knowledge and skills assessed by the item. This will allow for evaluating whether the use of the accessibility tools and information promotes valid score interpretations about student achievement of the targeted construct or whether such use alters the intended construct (see Russell, 2011, for additional challenges to accessible test design).

The tailoring of items to the ability level of the students is attractive in the assessment of SWDs and ELLs because current tests tend to target students in the middle of the score range, resulting in less precise measurement of SWDs and ELLs who tend to perform at the lower end of the score scale. Another attractive feature of CAT is the potential for the administration of fewer items to reach sufficient measurement precision. Smarter Balanced assessment has adopted a CAT system and PARCC will use computer-delivered assessments.

There are also some challenges in using CAT for SWDs because these students have divergent learning profiles and may find items that are typically more challenging easier than some typically less challenging items. As indicated by Thurlow in an ESEA report ("ESEA Reauthorization," 2010), computer adaptive practices

must be transparent enough to detect when a student is inaccurately measured because of splinter skills common for some students with disabilities, for example, with poor basic skills in areas like computation and decoding, but with good higher level skills, such as problem solving, built with appropriate accommodations to address the barriers of poor basic skills. (p. 43)

Stone and Davey (2011) discussed some of these challenges. Item response functions may differ for SWDs due to, for example, accommodation status, divergent learning profiles, less access to computers, and less familiarity with keyboarding. Similar concerns arise when assessing ELLs because of their divergent learning profiles. Consequently, SWDs and ELLs should be included in the calibration sample for the item bank, and if not, subgroup analyses are needed to examine the appropriateness of the item parameters for the different groups. Divergent learning profiles may also lead to less stable and less accurate estimation of SWDs' standing on the latent construct. Stone and Davey (2011) reiterated the need for the detection of discrepant response patterns for SWDs. As they indicated, if SWDs respond incorrectly to the first few easy items due to divergent learning profiles, they may not be administered more challenging items that are within their proficiency range. Others have argued that the use of CAT will allow for spanning of grade-level content on the assessments designed based on the Common Core State Standards, resulting in more precise measurement of students at the extreme levels, including SWDs and ELLs, although others oppose practices that may resemble off-grade–level testing (Way et al., 2010).

Language of Testing as a Source of Measurement Error for ELLs

In an early study examining the effects of testing ELLs in their native, first language (L1) as opposed to being tested in English, their L2, Solano-Flores, Lara, Sexton, and Navarrete (2001) found that native speakers of Spanish, Haitian-Creole, and Mandarin Chinese did not necessarily benefit when math and science items were administered in their native language as compared to English. They conducted a student × rater × item × language of administration generalizability study and found that the largest variance component across the three linguistic groups was the student × item × language, indicating that some students performed on some items better when administered in L1, whereas other students performed better on some items when administered in L2.

In an effort to disentangle the measurement error when testing ELLs and to demonstrate the linguistic heterogeneity of ELLs, Solano-Flores and Li (2006, 2009, 2013) examined language and dialect as sources of measurement error using generalizability theory. In the Solano-Flores and Li (2006) generalizability study, native speakers of two dialects of Haitian-Creole in Grades 4 and 5 were given a set of NAEP math items either in the standard dialects of L1 and L2 or their local dialect and the standard dialects of L1. They found that the student × item × language accounted for the largest amount of variation in test scores for students tested across languages (39%; English and standard dialect) and the student × item × dialect accounted for the largest amount of test score variation for students tested across dialects (33% for site A and 38% for site B; standard dialect and local dialect). These results indicate that students perform better in dialect A over dialect B for some items but perform better in dialect B over dialect A for other items. As indicated by the authors, the interaction of dialect with student and item is as important a source of measurement error as the interaction of language with student. Furthermore, they demonstrated that the number of items needed to obtain dependable measures of achievement may vary for students speaking different dialects of Spanish, implying the need for dialect-level analyses in the testing of ELLs. To further investigate dialect as a source of measurement error, native Spanish speaker ELLs in Grades 4 and 5 were given the same set of NAEP math items in both their L1 and L2 (Solano-Flores & Li, 2009). Using a student × item × rater × language and student × item × rater × dialect generalizability study for each site, they found that the student × item × language interaction accounted for the largest amount of total score variation (45% and 48%) and the student × item × dialect interaction accounted for the largest amount of total score variation (41% to 48%), respectively. For both of these studies the sample of items chosen did not include any schematic representations (e.g., graphs, tables, illustrations). It would be of value to conduct a study that includes items that have accompanying schematic representations to evaluate whether these results generalize to test items with schematic representations. As Martiniello (2009) suggested, the impact of the linguistic complexity is attenuated when items have schematic representations that may help ELLs make meaning of text. The author suggests that including them may help diminish the negative effect of linguistic complexity on ELL performance.

Rater Language Background as a Source for Measurement Error for ELLs

In addition to limited proficiency in language in which tests are administered, the raters' language background can be a source of construct-irrelevant variance and contribute to measurement error. Researchers have examined how rater language background has an influence in their scoring of ELL responses to constructed-response items (Kachchaf & Solano-Flores, 2012). Typically, these researchers examine mean differences of scores given by raters of different language backgrounds and conduct generalizability studies that examine different sources of error contributing to the scores, including error due to the language background of raters. In a study conducted by Kachchaf and Solano-Flores, four native English-speaking and four native Spanish-speaking certified bilingual teachers, who had experience in teaching ELLs, scored responses to mathematics constructed-response items for fourth- and fifth-grade Spanish-speaking ELLs. Students were administered the items in Spanish and English on different testing occasions, with the sequence of items administered randomly determined. There was no significant difference in mean scores due to language of testing or the interaction of language of testing and rater language background. The results of the student × language of testing × item × (rater: language background) revealed that the largest amounts of variance was due to the interaction of student and item (36%) and the interaction of student, language of testing, and item (22%), which is consistent with previous studies (Solano-Flores, 2006, 2008). The error variances due to rater language background and the rater nested within rater language background were negligible. The results of this study are consistent with previous findings that suggest experienced educators, who teach the population of interest (in this case, bilingual teachers of ELLs), can reliably score student responses to mathematics constructed-response items provided that they receive well-developed training materials and procedures (Lane & Stone, 2006).

Internal Structure Evidence Using Factor Analysis and Differential Item Functioning

Evaluation of the internal structure of the test can be examined through exploratory or confirmatory factor analyses (CFAs), including multigroup analyses and IRT analyses. Using exploratory factor analyses, the data are evaluated separately for each group to identify the number of factors underlying test performance. This can be followed by a multigroup CFA to determine whether the same factors are underlying test performance across groups (Cook, Eignor, Steinberg, Sawaki, & Cline, 2009). Nested CFA models allow for testing whether specific features of the internal structure of the test are invariant across groups, including the number of factors, factor loadings and errors in their estimation, factor intercorrelations, item intercept, and item uniqueness.

DIF, differential bundle functioning (DBF), and differential distractor functioning (DDF) allow for examining the equivalence of subgroup performance at the item level (or at the level of a coherent subset of items). DIF occurs when examinees of equal standing on the measured construct but from different subgroups differ in their probability of responding correctly to an item (Holland & Thayer, 1988). When DIF occurs, it indicates that the item measures some additional construct for one of the subgroups, which negatively affects the validity and comparability of test score interpretations and uses. DIF can be conceptualized as multidimensionality in the test data. DIF can be considered a shift in the distribution of ability along a secondary construct that influences the probability of a correct response (Camilli, 1992). For example, one group may be more able on a secondary construct, such as English reading skills, on a mathematics test.

There are a number of factors that can have an impact on the validity of the results of invariance analyses, including small sample sizes, nonoverlapping proficiency distributions, and lack of measurement precision (Sireci, 2009). The use of large-scale test data and the evaluation of effect sizes help minimize the impact of sample size in interpreting the results. Nonoverlapping proficiency distributions arise because the SWD or ELL groups have distributions that are centered lower on the score scale than the general population. The poorer performance of SWDs and ELLs may be due, in part, to lack of access to the construct being measured. Consequently, these subgroups typically have a restricted range of scores. Differences in distributions affect the results of invariance studies in predictable ways such as easy items flagged for DIF in favor of the focal group (SWDs or ELLs) and the first factor identified in a factor analysis is not as strong for the reference group (general population; Sireci, 2009). In addition, restriction of range can account for lower reliability estimates and poorer predictive validity evidence for these subgroups. To minimize the effect of differential restriction of range across the groups, the reference group (general population) can be selected to have the same distribution as the SWD or ELL group.

Lack of measurement precision can arise from a number of factors, including restriction of range for the SWD and ELL groups, more guessing within these groups when the test is less accessible to them, and the use of individual items instead of item sets or parcels for DIF and factor analyses. A concern with using individual items as the unit of analysis in DIF studies and studies examining the factorial structure of a test is the lack of precision and noise at the item level. Conducting these analyses with meaningful item parcels instead of individual items has been recommended to alleviate this concern (Cattell & Burdsal, 1975). However, as Sireci (2009) has indicated, item parceling may mitigate any effects if the item level data is multidimensional. Using both item level and item parceling help alleviate this concern. Furthermore, results may differ when the analyses are conducted on raw scores versus IRT-scaled scores, because scale transformations are most affected at the lower end of the score distribution and ELLs and SWDs tend to score at the lower end.

Differential Item Functioning

As previously indicated, DIF occurs when examinees of equal standing on the measured construct but from different subgroups differ in their probability of answering an item correctly. If DIF occurs, it indicates that the item measures some additional construct for one of the subgroups, which affects the validity and comparability of the score interpretations. For those students who need accommodations or modifications and are provided them, if the accommodations or modifications are effective it is more likely that DIF will not be detected. It should be noted, however, that DIF may still occur due to reasons not associated with the accommodations. Accommodations are intended to allow for a "level playing field," providing support for the comparability and fairness of the assessment without giving undue advantage to the subgroup receiving the accommodation or modification.

Clauser and Mazor (1998) outlined the steps in examining DIF, including specifying the comparison groups, selecting a matching criterion, choosing a statistical approach, and interpreting and making decisions regarding items that are flagged as DIF. As discussed by Buzick and Stone (2011), to ensure valid inferences, scores on the criterion measure need to be reliable, valid, and free of statistical bias (Clauser & Mazor, 1998); standardized conditions are needed for the administration of the criterion measure for the focal and reference groups (Dorans & Holland, 1993); sample sizes need to be sufficient for the reference and focal groups (Zieky, 1993); and focal and reference groups need similar ability distributions, especially when IRT methods are not used (Mazor, Clauser, & Hambleton, 1992).

DIF studies for SWDs and ELLs typically use an internal matching criterion—total test score—and the test is administered to the focal and reference groups under standardized conditions. When an internal matching criterion is used, there is little impact on the validity and reliability of the matching criterion, particularly when purification of the matching criterion is done (i.e., when the total test score excludes the DIF items). However, as previously mentioned, reliability and validity differ for SWDs and ELLs as compared to SWoDs and non-ELLs. Threats to the validity of DIF results are primarily due to the heterogeneity of the samples, sample size, and differences in the ability distributions for the groups.

Differential Bundle Functioning

Standard DIF detection and review procedures have not been very useful in explaining why DIF occurs in the flagged items (AERA, APA, & NCME, 2014). To address this problem, Roussos and Stout (1996) developed an approach to test DIF hypotheses that are generated from theory and substantive item analyses. They argue that the DIF analysis approach has suffered from both lack of power primarily due to exploratory analysis of single items and inflation of Type I errors (over identification of DIF) due to inappropriate matching criteria for matching examinees. They proposed DBF in which sets of items are bundled according to some organizing principle. An organizing principle for examining DBF for ELLs may be the level of English language demands. DBF examines whether two groups with equal ability have the same probability of answering a bundle of items correctly. DBF is considered to be a confirmatory approach to examining DIF in that hypotheses are stated regarding one group being assessed on the second dimension to a greater extent than its matched group (Douglas, Roussos, & Stout, 1996). The advantages of DBF as compared to DIF analyses are potentially better control of Type I errors and greater statistical power. Moreover, bundles for items are grouped based on a substantive hypothesis about differential performance on the bundle of items for the reference and focal group. An organizing principle for bundling items for ELL students (i.e., the measurement of a secondary construct) may be the amount and/or complexity of reading or writing required by items. The categorization of items into bundles can be accomplished by expert opinion alone or dimensionality analysis augmented by expert opinion. One approach is to group items according to different levels of reading complexity and conduct DBF analyses. DBF allows for examining trends across items that differ in content, cognitive skill, reading complexity, or other item characteristics. Researchers have also conducted analyses on the cognitive skills evoked by different subgroups to help explain potential sources of DIF (e.g., Ercikan et al., 2010; Lane, Wang, & Magone, 1996).

Differential Item Functioning for SWDs

Studies have examined DIF for SWoDs compared to SWDs (e.g., Barton & Finch, 2004; Cohen, Gregg, & Deng, 2005) as well as for students with different categories of disability (e.g., Kato, Moen, & Thurlow, 2009; Stone, Cook, Laitusis, & Cline, 2010). Examining DIF across different categories of disability acknowledges the heterogeneity of SWDs and has the potential to provide more meaningful results.

Barton and Finch (2004) examined DIF for accommodated SWDs and SWoDs on both a mathematics and reading test. Their results indicated that some items favored the accommodated SWD group and others favored the SWoD group. Several of the items that favored the accommodated SWD group had heavier reading loads than other items. One of the most common accommodations was reading the items aloud, indicating that having the items read to the accommodated SWDs may have provided them better access to the tested construct of comprehension. DIF was examined for 1,250 accommodated SWDs and 1,250 SWoDs on a mathematics test with extended time as the only accommodation using a mixture Rasch model (Cohen et al., 2005). The results suggested that DIF was not related to the accommodation – extended time, but was related to differences in difficulty with types of mathematics content (e.g., word problems, intuitive geometry and measurement, and plane geometry and algebraic or symbolic manipulation), indicating the multidimensionality of test data. This study recognized the need to consider item difficulty and student proficiency level in accommodation validity research, suggesting that students' accommodation status is not adequate in explaining the occurrence of DIF.

Further, none of the group differences were due to reading proficiency. This study was unique in that it examined SWDs with only one accommodation, extended time, which is the most common accommodation.

Finch, Barton, and Meyer (2009) examined DIF for accommodated SWDs and SWoDs in Grades 3 to 8 on mathematics and reading tests using a two-stage analysis. They first used SIBTEST to identify an initial pool of items detected as DIF. Next, a total score was obtained for those items that did not exhibit DIF, and this total score was used for matching in logistic regression analyses of DIF that allowed for the detection of both uniform and nonuniform DIF. Uniform DIF occurs if the item favors one subgroup across the ability scale, whereas nonuniform DIF occurs if the item favors one subgroup on a region of the ability scale but favors the other subgroup on another region of the ability scale. The logistic regression analysis was also conducted for the four most common types of accommodations: Questions Read Aloud, Directions Read Aloud, Alternate Testing Setting, and Extended Time. Overall for the language test items that displayed uniform DIF, SWDs not receiving accommodations were favored. The items that displayed nonuniform DIF at the lower grade levels favored nonaccommodated SWDs at the lower levels of proficiency and favored accommodated SWDs at the higher levels of proficiency. The authors suggested that younger accommodated SWDs may not be able to take advantage of the accommodations to the same extent as older accommodated SWDs. In particular, younger SWDs with lower proficiency levels who receive read-aloud accommodations were at a disadvantage on items that required a heavy navigational load (i.e., integration of text with tables and indices), which was consistent with findings from Barton and Huynh (2003). The mathematics items typically displayed uniform DIF, with 7 of the 11 DIF items favoring nonaccommodated SWDs. The results suggested that accommodations associated with oral administration, extra time, and alternate test settings were associated with mathematics DIF items favoring nonaccommodated SWDs.

Cho, Lee, and Kingston (2012) expanded on these studies by also examining the effects of item characteristics. Using IRT methods, they examined potential causes of DIF for SWoDs and accommodated SWDs, including item difficulty, item discrimination, item type, and item features, as well as accommodation status and ability on a mathematics test for Grade 3 to Grade 8 students. Moreover, for examining DIF for these two groups they used matched samples, with demographic variables and mathematics test scores serving as the matching variables. Overall, they found that mathematics item types (story, explanation, straightforward) and features were significantly related to item difficulty but not to DIF. Story items were not always more difficult than explanation and straightforward items. They found no significant differences among story items, explanation items, and straightforward items for most of the grades, challenging the belief that story items are more challenging because of the required reading (Cho et al., 2012). There were significant differences among item type for two of the six grades: Story items were significantly more difficult than explanation items in Grade 3 (partial η^2 = .13), and explanation items were easier than story and straightforward items (partial η^2 =.12) in Grade 5. Across the grades, 73 out of the 470 items had significantly different IRT b-parameter estimates, indicating DIF, and 34% of these 73 items favored the nonaccommodated SWDs and 76% favored the nonaccommodated SWoDs. Item type was not related to DIF, that is, DIF was observed similarly among items of different item types.

Using an IRT model, they found that there was no consistent interaction between accommodation status and student ability with respect to DIF. For only Grades 3 and 5 was this interaction significant. For these grades not all students in the accommodated SWD and nonaccommodated SWoD groups were consistently advantaged or disadvantaged by the DIF items. As suggested by the authors, additional studies are needed to examine this interaction given that the results in four of the six grades do not support Scarpati, Wells, Lewis, and Jirka's (2009) conclusion that accommodated SWDs with high performance levels may be better able than those at lower performance levels to make effective use of their accommodation needs.

To examine context effects of DIF on a mathematics test for SWDs in one state, Randall, Cheong, and Engelhard (2011) used a hierarchical generalized linear model (HGLM)—an explanatory model—that incorporated item response models into hierarchical models in multilevel settings. They also used the many-faceted Rasch model (MFRM)—a descriptive IRT model. They argued for the use of MFRM since it provides fit statistics for all facets (e.g., item, student, disability group, and test condition) so that model fit issues can be addressed before examining DIF. As a fixed effects model, MFRM treats schools as a fixed facet. Whereas, as a random effects model, a hierarchical generalized linear model can use both student- and school-level variance in the outcome measure to predict the impact of DIF. The authors randomly assigned students with a wide range of disabilities and SWoDs from 74 schools to one of three conditions (resource guide modification, calculation use modification, or standard test administration). Their results suggest that some problem-solving items may not be invariant across disability status and test condition, with some items under the calculator use condition favoring SWDs and others favoring SWoDs.

Kato et al. (2009) examined DIF as well as DDF using a multistep multinomial logistic regression analysis for students with specific categories of disabilities (speech/language impairments, learning disabilities, and emotional behavior disorders) on third- and fifth-grade state reading tests. Although a relatively large number of items displayed statistically significant DIF and DDF, they found that only a small number of items displayed substantive DIF and DDF, and they were for students with learning disabilities. As indicated by the authors, this finding emphasizes the importance of treating SWDs as a heterogeneous group, and when sample size permits studies should be conducted on students within specific categories of disabilities. Their results were in contrast to previous DIF analyses with undifferentiated SWDs (Abedi et al., 2007) in that DIF did not increase for items toward the end of the test. The authors suggested that DIF may be due to specific characteristics of items.

Differential Item Functioning for ELLs

The linguistic complexity of tests as a source of construct-irrelevant variance may threaten the validity and fairness of the assessment of all students. Although ELLs may have the content knowledge in areas of mathematics and science, they may not have language skills that allow access to the content of the test items. Consequently, similar to SWDs, DIF may occur for ELL students because of lack of access to the construct being measured.

Abedi and his colleagues (Abedi & Lord, 2001; Abedi, Lord, & Plummer, 1997, Abedi, Lord, & Hofstetter, 1998) have reported a relationship between linguistic features and the difficulty level of content knowledge items, such as mathematics, science, and history, for ELLs; however, the performance of ELLs on these types of items varied across tests and across grades. Of the features studied, only item length has shown consistent negative effects on item difficulty for ELLs. Item length has shown greater difficulty value differences for ELLs and non-ELLs in the eighth-grade NAEP mathematics test (Abedi et al., 1997). The effects of other linguistic features on the difficulty of mathematics items for ELLs have been relatively inconsistent across tests and grades (Shaftel et al., 2006), suggesting that the grade level, academic content, and other factors may contribute to DIF for ELLs. Abedi, Courtney, Leon, Keo, and Azzam (2006), however, have shown that aggregating linguistic features, including both syntactic and lexical features, to form a composite linguistic complexity score resulted in a significant effect for ELLs. A linguistic complexity score based on familiarity of nonmathematical vocabulary, presence of syntactically complex sentences, relative clauses, and abstract format of the item statement significantly predicted the difference between the item difficulty value for ELLs and non-ELLs in the NAEP Grade 8 national test data. This study examined the impact of linguistic features on item difficulty values for ELLs without conditioning on ability level as done in DIF analyses.

Using a meta-analytic DIF procedure, Koo, Becker, and Kim (2014) examined DIF trends in ELLs and non-ELLs on a state reading test for the 3rd and 10th grades. This approach allowed for examining variation in DIF indices that are related to item content features. Their results indicated that reading items requiring knowledge of words and phrases in context favored non-ELLs in Grade 3 but not in Grade 10. The items requiring knowledge of words and phrases in context were overall more difficult for ELL third graders than non-ELLs, suggesting that ELLs at lower grade levels may have not acquired sufficient strategies to learn vocabulary (Koo et al., 2014). Items requiring evaluation skills favored ELLs in Grade 10 but not Grade 3. DIF was not observed for main idea items or cause-effect items for ELLs.

Martiniello (2009) examined whether the relative difficulty of mathematics word problems in a fourth-grade state test for ELLs is associated with construct-irrelevant linguistic complexity and the use of nonlinguistic (schematic) representations using IRT DIF methods. Linguistic complexity and schematic representation correlated significantly with DIF statistics ($r = .58$ and $r = -.55$, respectively). Items with greater linguistic complexity tended to favor non-ELLs over ELLs, whereas items with schematic representations tended to favor ELLs over non-ELLs. Using ordinary least squares (OLS) multiple regression, the results indicated that linguistic complexity and its interaction with schematic representation accounted for 66% of the variation of DIF statistics across the two groups. The author hypothesized that the impact of linguistic complexity is attenuated when items have schematic representations that may help ELLs make meaning of text. The author suggests that including them may help diminish the negative effect of linguistic complexity on ELL performance.

Wolf and Leon (2009) examined whether the language demands of items on several states' mathematics and science tests were associated with the degree of DIF for ELLs. A total of 542 items from 11 tests at Grades 4, 5, 7, and 8 from three states were rated for the linguistic complexity. They found a stronger association between the linguistic rating and DIF statistics for ELLs for easier items but not for the more difficult items. General academic vocabulary and the amount of language in an item had the strongest relationship with DIF values, particularly for ELLs with low English proficiency levels. The items were grouped into four bundles to examine more closely the relationship between language demands and ELL student performance. DBF results indicated that as language demands increased more DBF was obtained.

Sinharay, Dorans, and Liang (2011) demonstrated how methods can be used to evaluate whether the inclusion or exclusion of students for whom English is not their first language (NEFL) has an impact on the results of DIF analyses. They conducted DIF analyses on the mathematics section of the PSAT (Preliminary SAT) using Whites as the reference group with various focal groups such as Hispanic and Asian, and using English as the first language (EFL) as a proxy for English language proficiency. DIF analyses were conducted for samples consisting of those examinees that indicated EFL as well as a combined sample (EFL and NEFL). The correlations of the Mantel-Haenszel DIF statistics between the EFL group and combined group were above .987, indicating that the ordering of items with respect to DIF is the same across the groups. The same DIF analyses were conducted after simulating higher proportions of NEFLs in the combined sample, ranging from .1 to .9 in increments of .1. Although the DIF results were very similar across subgroups for the proportion of NEFLs in the actual test data (approximately 9.5%), as the proportion of NEFL examinees increased (above .4) the DIF statistics for the EFL and combined groups differed for the ethnic/cultural groups, especially for the Hispanic group. As indicated by the authors, it is of no consequence if DIF analysis is performed on the EFL group or on the combined group under present conditions; however, as the proportion of NEFL examinees increases over the years it is expected to have an effect on the DIF results.

Factorial Invariance

To have a common test scale for various groups of examinees, there is a need to establish measurement invariance of the construct being tested. Multigroup CFA and IRT models can be used to establish the invariance of the construct being measured across groups. Measurement invariance is typically tested across groups at a set of hierarchical structured levels: factor loadings, intercepts of measured variables and factors, and residual variances of observed variables. Multigroup CFA examines the change in the goodness-of-fit index (GFI) when cross-group constraints are imposed on a measurement model. Standardized root mean square residual, comparative fit index, and root mean square error of approximation are typically examined to evaluate the results.

Factorial Invariance for ELLs

Using CFA to examine the internal structure of Grade 9 data from commercially published tests of reading, math, and science, Abedi (2002) reported that correlations of item bundles with the latent factors were consistently lower for ELLs than non-ELLs. For reading, the correlations ranged from .719 to .779 for ELLs and from .832 to .858 for non-ELLs, and for math, the correlations ranged from .657 to .789 for ELLs and from .796 to .862 for non-ELLs. As indicated by Abedi (2003), a number of factors, including language background, restriction of score range, SES, and OTL, may contribute to the observed differences.

In another study examining the internal structure of tests, Abedi, Courtney, and Leon (2003) observed a single factor with 83% of the variance of the item performance explained by the first factor for non-ELLs, whereas only 45% of the variance was explained by the first factor for ELLs. This implies that the test is primarily unidimensional for the non-ELL group, whereas the test is multidimensional for the ELL group, suggesting that more than one construct is being measured for the ELL group.

Factorial Invariance for SWDs

In an early study examining the internal structure using CFA, Rock, Bennett, and Kaplan (1987) reported that the SAT-Verbal and SAT-Mathematical factors were similar for SWDs and SWoDs, but the correlation between the two factors identified in the analyses was slightly lower in some of the SWD groups than in SWoD group. Rock, Bennett, Kaplan, and Jirele (1988) replicated the Rock et al. (1987) study with GRE data and reported that the fit of the three-factor solution (Verbal, Quantitative, and Analytic) was acceptable for most subgroups. For those receiving the nonstandard administration (i.e., cassette-recorded version of administration), however, a four-factor model was preferred, in which the Analytic factor represented two components, logical reasoning and analytical reasoning, especially for students with physical disabilities and those needing the large-type version. A study comparing the internal structure on the Maryland School Performance Assessment Program for accommodated SWDs and nonaccommodated SWDs reported similar factor structures (Tippets & Michaels, 1997).

Using maximum likelihood factor analysis, Huynh et al. (2004) examined the internal structure of a state Grade 10 math test for SWDs who were tested under standard conditions, SWDs who were given an oral accommodation and SWoDs who were tested under standard conditions. The preliminary principal component analysis and maximum likelihood factor analysis indicated that the internal structure of the test data was similar across groups, especially between the two disability groups.

For the two disability groups, the first eigenvalue accounted for 61% of the variation in the test data and for the SWoD group it accounted for 66% of the variation. The second eigenvalue accounted for approximately 13% of the total variation for the two SWD groups and 11% for the SWoDs. In another study, Huynh and Barton (2006) examined the internal structure of a state Grade 10 reading test for SWoDs who were tested under standard conditions, SWDs who were tested under standard conditions, and SWDs who were given an oral accommodation. Using CFA, the root mean square error of approximation, standardized root mean square residual, and GFI indices supported the hypothesis that a common factorial model could be used to represent the test data for all three groups of students. The factor analysis that was performed for descriptive purposes generally supported the hypothesis; however, there were some moderate differences of .158 and .101 in factor loadings for two of the subtests, details and main idea, across the groups.

Using factor analysis, Cook et al. (2009) demonstrated that the reading comprehension construct assessed by a commercially published test was invariant when a read-aloud accommodation (audio CD) was provided for Grade 4 and Grade 8 students with reading-based disabilities and SWoDs. In another study, Cook, Eignor, Sawaki, Steinberg, and Cline (2010) examined whether a state standards–based Grade 4 English Language Arts (ELA) assessment measured the same construct for SWoDs, SWDs who took the test under standard conditions, and SWDs who took the test with accommodations as specified in their individualized education program or 504 plan, and SWDs who took the test with a read-aloud accommodation. Using multigroup CFAs with item bundle scores, the RMSEA, comparative fit index, and GFI indices indicated that the factor structures across the four groups were similar, providing support for measurement invariance across the groups.

D. Kim and Huynh (2010) examined the comparability of scores from a ninth-grade online and paper-and-pencil administration of a state end-of-course English test for SWoDs and SWDs, specifically students with learning disabilities. Computer-based testing can include features that make tests more assessable for all students, including greater flexibility in administration to accommodate different learning styles, standardization of accommodated administration for SWDs, built-in accommodation (e.g., text-to-speech support, video), and built-in tutorials and practice tests (Thompson, Thurlow, Quenemoen, & Lehr, 2002). D. Kim and Huynh (2010) examined four levels of nested hierarchy factorial invariance: (a) all parameters were freely estimated, (b) factor loadings were constrained to be equal across groups (weak invariance), (c) factor loadings and intercept constrained to be equal across groups (strong invariance), and (d) factor loadings, intercept, and residual variances constrained to be equal across groups. The results of testing the hierarchical models indicated that the factor structure, factor ladings, intercepts, and error variances were invariant between the online and paper-and-pencil for both SWoDs and students with learning disabilities, that is, the highest level of measurement invariance was confirmed. They concluded that intergroup differences between the means of observed items reflect differences in means of the construct. Other researchers have used both CFA and the Rasch model to assess measurement invariance in high stakes tests (Randall & Engelhard, 2010b).

External Structure Evidence

The external structure of a test refers to the relationship between test scores to other variables, including relationships to measures of the same construct (convergent validity evidence), to future performance (predictive validity evidence), and to measures of different constructs (discriminant validity evidence; AERA, APA, & NCME, 2014). These relationships are expected to be invariant across subgroups within the population and evaluations of the invariance of the relationship between the measures across groups are warranted, including a comparison of the correlations and the linear relationships across the groups (Linn, 1978).

Using simulated data and real data sets, Kane and Mroch (2010) demonstrate the impact of regression toward the mean, which tends to introduce bias, in differential validity studies that examine convergent and discriminant validity evidence. They demonstrate that although measures can have the same correlation between groups, when both measures contain measurement error, the slopes and intercepts can differ across groups using OLS regression models. This concern is relevant when comparing group-specific regression lines for ELLs and SWDs with those from the general population because even if the true-score relationship between the variables for the subgroup of interest and the general population is the same, the regression lines for the groups will differ due to regression toward the mean. This occurs because the subgroups tend to have lower means on the two measures. This will lead to inaccurate interpretations regarding the relationship between the variables for the student groups. The orthogonal regression approach within principal component analysis for estimating true-score relationships is not subject to regression toward the mean and can more accurately estimate true-score relationships between the two variables as demonstrated by Kane and Mroch (2010).

Using structural equation modeling to examine the external structure of Grade 9 data from commercially published tests of reading, mathematics, and science, Abedi (2002) reported higher correlations for latent factors underlying test performance for ELLs than non-ELLs. The correlation between latent factors for math and reading for non-ELLs was .782 as compared to .645 for ELLs and for reading and science for non-ELLs it was .837 and for ELLs it was .806. Koretz and Hamilton (2000) provided evidence for a format effect for accommodated SWDs on state tests composed of constructed-response items and multiple-choice items. The correlations for constructed-response items in different subjects were larger than the correlations between constructed-response and multiple-choice items in the same subject for accommodated SWDs but not for other students, in particular, at the lower grades. They provide an example for Grade 7 in which the correlations between the constructed-responses in different subjects was .63 for accommodated SWDs and the correlations between constructed-responses and multiple-choice responses in the same subjects were .55 and .57.

Predictive validity studies have examined college performance of accommodated and nonaccommodated SWDs in comparison with accommodated and non-accommodated SWoDs. Cahalan, Mandinach, and Camara (2002) investigated the predictive validity of the SAT I Reasoning Test for examinees with learning disabilities and extended time accommodations. The use of the SAT I test scores alone to predict freshman GPA tended to overpredict for accommodated male students and accurately predict for accommodated female students. Using OLS regression, a more recent study examined the differential validity of the SAT for students whose best language is not English (Mattern, Patterson, Shaw, Kobrin, & Barbuti, 2008). They reported that the SAT accurately predicts freshman GPA for students whose best language is English, the critical reading and writing SAT sections underpredict for students whose best language is not English (mean standardized residual of .40 and .37, respectively), and the mathematics section provides accurate predictions for students whose best language is not English. For students who indicated that their best language is English and another language, the SAT tends to slightly overpredict freshman GPA (standardized residuals ranging from −.09 to −.02).

For K–12 large-scale assessment, the absence of criterion measures has resulted in more emphasis on examining the internal psychometric properties of tests administered to subgroups of students (Koretz & Hamilton, 2006). However, states are currently examining the extent to which their state test scores, especially at the high school level, are related to criterion measures such as SAT and ACT scores as an attempt to provide evidence that the scores are related to college and career readiness. Some states are also using test scores in the middle school grades to predict performance at the high school level.

Equating Invariance

The invariance in reported scores across groups of students defined by subgroup or test accommodations is necessary for the validity of the score interpretations and comparisons across groups. Population invariance requires that the equating functions derived from different subpopulations produce the same results across forms if they are to be equitable. Score equity assessment (SEA; Dorans, 2004) is a psychometric approach for examining fairness and equity in reported test scores by evaluating equating invariance across different groups. The analysis is conducted at the group level. This approach provides information on whether student subgroups can be considered from the same population when equating. If groups of examinees are from different populations, there is a lack of equity in the reported scores. This implies that there is a lack of score comparability, and the validity of score interpretations is hindered.

Equating is a psychometric procedure used to adjust scores for differences in difficulty across two or more forms of a test (Kolen & Brennan, 2004). Raw scores on each form are equated to the same scale before they are reported to help ensure equity. The property of equating invariance is met when subpopulations within the overall population have the same equating relationship from raw to reported scores.

Group-level score equity and comparability across groups are achieved when an equating is invariant (Dorans & Holland, 2000; Kolen & Brennan, 2004). Raw scores for tests that exhibit invariant factor structures and item response functions across groups are expected to have equating invariance in SEA analysis. This implies that the construct is being assessed in the same way, and the precision of scores is the same across groups. SEA compares each group in a population to the overall population of examinees.

Sinharay et al. (2011) showed how methods can be used to evaluate whether the inclusion or exclusion of students for whom English is not their first language (NEFL) has an impact on equating results. Equating procedures ensure that test scores on different forms are interchangeable. The authors conducted the equating of the PSAT to the SAT on three examinee samples: students for whom English is their first language (EFL), NEFL, and Total (EFL and NEFL group). As the authors indicated, their equating procedures are similar to a score equity evaluation that examines the invariance of equating across subpopulations, addressing fairness at the test score level. Using the unsmoothed chained equipercentile equating method, they reported that the results were similar across the groups. The results were also similar for the simulated subsamples for which the proportion of NEFL examinees increased considerably above the actual proportion of approximately 9.5%. Based on these results, it appears that there is little consequence if equating of the PSAT to the SAT is conducted on the EFL sample or the Total sample (EFL and NEFL) now or in the future when the proportion of ELLs will be greater in the population of students in this country.

The effect of language on the invariance of equating functions with different test formats has also been examined. The population invariance of equating for a teacher certification paper-and-pencil and computer-based tests was examined when equating results were obtained from subgroups defined by English as Secondary Language (ESL) status (Cid & Spitalny, 2013). The results from this study indicated differences between equating conversions of the total and ESL groups at score levels near the cut scores on the scale for both modes of testing, whereas there were no differences between the total group and the group of students whose primary language was English. Because the differences between equating conversions for the total and ESL group comparisons were similar in each mode of testing, the authors indicated that the mode of testing does not differentially affect the degree to which the equating functions of the subgroups were invariant.

Using the SEA approach, equating invariance was examined for a fifth-grade state science test for groups of students defined by SWD status, ELL status, and use of accommodations (Huggins & Elbaum, 2013). Measurement comparability and reported score equity was confirmed for SWDs and ELLs who used accommodations across all score ranges; however, it was not confirmed for SWDs and ELLs who did not use accommodations. The researchers also examined invariance at the high-stakes cut score by comparing the classification profiles across a student's equated scores; one score was based on the equating of the overall population and the other based on the equating for the student's subgroup. The equating for SWD and ELL groups with accommodations had a higher classification consistency rate as compared to the equating for SWD and ELL groups without accommodations. In both analyses the differences were small, and as indicated by the authors, these differences may be due to small subgroup sizes, lack of measurement invariance, or both. As an example, for students in the SWD and/or ELL group with accommodations, there was a 96.38% agreement rate between the two proficiency classifications, whereas in the SWD and/or ELL group without accommodations there was a 95.13% agreement rate. With larger samples, PARCC and SBAC will be able to conduct such analyses for students with specific disabilities and ELLs from different language and cultural backgrounds.

ISSUES RELATED TO INCLUDING SWDS AND ELLS IN MEASURES OF "GROWTH" AND AF EDUCATOR EFFECTIVENESS

States have used "growth" models for educational accountability purposes since the Growth Model Pilot Project was initiated in 2005 (U.S. Department of Education, 2005). These models are used in NCLB accountability to monitor states' progress in closing achievement gaps and to set high expectations for annual improvement for all students, including SWDs and ELLs. As growth measures have been implemented to help determine annual yearly progress (U.S. Department of Education, 2005), it has become apparent that low- and high-performing students are not being measured as precisely even though they can be accurately classified in a performance level. There has been little research on the efficacy of growth models for tracking change for ELLs and SWDs. Such research is crucial given that the federal Race to the Top initiative calls for multiple measures in educator evaluation systems, including measures of student growth (U.S. Department of Education, 2010). It should be noted that the term *growth* is used in this chapter because of current practice, but it has been argued that it is inappropriate to use the term in association with these models because they do not actually estimate performance over time (Castellano & Ho, 2013).

While arguing for the need for educator evaluation systems to fairly account for the inclusion of SWDs and ELLs in mainstream classrooms, Jones, Buzick, and Turkan (2013) discussed a number of challenges in including these subgroups, including challenges when estimating growth models used for accountability purposes. They discussed issues associated with value-added scores that are obtained from statistical models that attempt to explain the contribution of individual teachers to student achievement, by accounting for prior student achievement and in some cases student and school characteristics. They described a number of measurement challenges that need to be considered in including SWDs and ELLs when estimating growth models and including them in the evaluation of educator effectiveness. First, there is an inconsistent use of testing accommodations over time, which can increase measurement error and have an impact on change in student test scores (Abedi, Hofstetter, & Lord, 2004; Sireci et al., 2005). Careful attention needs to be paid to identifying students who need accommodations and ensuring that there is consistency for students over time in providing accommodations. Second, a relatively large percentage of ELLs and SWDs demonstrate low performance on state assessments (Abedi et al., 2007; Thurlow et al., 2011), threatening the validity of student changes in achievement as a measure of teacher effectiveness. Because scores at either end of the score scale are not as precise as those in the middle of the score scale, measures of effectiveness for teachers with large numbers of ELLs and SWDs, who tend to score at the lower end of the score scale, will be adversely affected due to the lack of score precision. Students scoring at the lower end of the scale are likely to guess more when responding to items. This was demonstrated using data from a fourth- and eighth-grade math and ELA test from one state by Laitusis et al. (2011). They found that SWDs scoring at chance level ranged from 12% to 22%, whereas only 1% to 3% of SWoDs scored at chance level. It should be noted that a goal of the two consortia, PARCC and SBAC, is to more precisely measure students who are at the lower end of the score scale. Third, SWDs and ELLs are both heterogeneous groups, varying in terms of student characteristics, special services, OTL, and accessibility. For example, some ELLs may enter school late in the year, making it difficult to isolate teacher effects. Fourth, it is difficult to attribute student progress to individual teachers. As an example, mainstream teachers share responsibility of instruction with special education teachers and ESL teachers.

Other researchers have discussed these challenges as well as additional concerns when including ELLs and SWDs in the measurement of growth and teacher effectiveness (Lakin & Young, 2013; Stevens, Zvoch, & Biancarosa, 2012). There is a potential for more missing data because of high mobility rates, resulting in exclusion of students from accountability indices using growth data. Changes in the use of accommodations from year to year for ELLs and SWDs may have several unintended outcomes such as masking real academic progress or indicating spurious progress, producing differential trajectories of progress for ELLs and SWDs as compared to non-ELLs/SWDs, and leading to differences in proficiency classification and classification accuracy across the growth models for ELLs and SWDs.

Jones et al. (2013) provided suggestions in response to these challenges. First, they proposed that practitioners use a roster validation system, with both the special education and general education teachers being 100% responsible for their shared students. Second, they argued for precision across the score scale so as to reduce the amount of measurement error in low-performing students as well as high-performing students, which is a goal of the two assessment consortia—PARCC and SBAC. A system that accurately assigns, records, and monitors the use of test accommodations should be a priority so that this information can be used when interpreting measures of growth in the evaluation of teachers. Third, they called for more studies examining the validity of value-added modeling and investigating the variables that account for heterogeneity of subgroups and their effects on valued added scores.

A recent study examined variations among three "growth" models, value tables (change in student proficiency categories over time), projection models, and student growth percentiles (SGPs; change in a student's normative position in an achievement distribution over time), in terms of their sensitivity to ELL status with respect to the number of on-track classifications and the predictive accuracy of those classifications for ELLs (Lakin & Young, 2013). They used state mathematics and ELA test data from a large California school district for students in the 2012–2015 high school graduating classes. Data from the 2012 year were used as the calibration year for the projection and SPG models. The year at which all students needed to meet the status proficiency goal was set at Grade 7 and students in Grades 4 to 6 were evaluated for growth targets. For the ELA data, the value table model identified the largest number of ELL students on track (42% to 52% dependent on grade level), followed by the SGP model (12% to 15%), and the smallest number was identified by the projection model (1% to 4%). This pattern held for non-ELLs; however, the percentage identified for the value table model and the projection model for non-ELLs differed from the ELL classification rate (38% to 52% and 2% to 6%, respectively). Across both ELA and math test data, the value table model had the largest number of differences in on-track classification rates, indicating that more ELL students than non-ELLs were on track.

They also examined the accuracy of the models in predicting the 23% of ELL and 25% of non-ELL students who were not proficient in Grade 3 but were proficient by Grade 7. Although the value table model identified more ELLs as on-track, those identified were less likely to be proficient at Grade 7. The projection model was the most accurate of the three models, but it identified the fewest number of students as on-track. A regression residual analysis showed that ELA and mathematics scores were more likely to be underestimated for ELLs as compared to non-ELLs, indicating that ELLs were being underestimated in the early grades for their future success by the projection model. The SGP model had slightly lower accuracy than the projection model and had similar accuracy for ELLs and non-ELLs. Lakin and Young (2013) suggested that the projection model "may unfairly penalize schools with large numbers of ELL students because it fails to identify accurately all of the ELL students who will later be successful" (p. 22). This result also has implications for using these models for evaluating educators with a relatively large number of ELLs in their classes. It is important to note that their sample comprised nearly 50% ELLs. If these models are applied to samples consisting of a relatively small percentage of ELLs, the rate of errors produced by these models will be greater.

In summary, there are a number of challenges in including ELLs and SWDs in models evaluating educator effectiveness: the number of ELLs and SWDs in classrooms, the inconsistent use of accommodations across years, the mobility of ELLs and SWDs and the subsequent omission of their test scores in these models, and the imprecision in measuring students who perform at the lower end of the score scale. The assessment consortia are addressing some of these concerns, by attempting to design tests with better access for these students and more precision across the scale and by designing systems for assigning and monitoring accommodations used by students.

CONCLUSION

There are a number of research design and psychometric issues that affect the validity and fairness of assessing SWDs and ELLs. One design issue is related to identifying students who are classified within each of these subgroups and the various classification schemes across districts and states. In discussing the nuances in defining ELLs, Abedi (2008) addressed concerns with various procedures used by states to classify students as ELLs. Depending on who is included in the samples will affect the results of studies examining the validity and fairness of assessing ELLs and SWDs. A clear delineation of the sample is needed to ensure that the results can be interpreted in a meaningful way.

A related issue is the heterogeneity of students within both ELL and SWD subgroups. Heterogeneity needs to be addressed when examining the efficacy of accommodation for SWDs and ELLs as well as when examining the psychometric characteristics of the item and test scores for these subgroups. The experiences of students during the assessment, and consequently their performances, are affected by a complex interaction of test characteristics (e.g., academic content, test language, item type, scoring) and cultural, language, economic, and educational histories of the students (Abedi, 2006; Abedi & Gandara, 2006; Solano-Flores, 2008; Solano-Flores & Trumbull, 2003). English is acquired at different paces by ELLs, and new ELLs enter schools each year, resulting in this group of students being variable in terms of both their English proficiency and academic proficiency. More research on the assessment of ELLs is needed on disaggregated groups. Additional research is also needed on disaggregated groups of SWDs (Sireci, 2009). Combining students with very different disabilities in one group to obtain sample sizes that allow for sufficient statistical power when evaluating SWDs and SWoDs may hide true effects. Although there have been some studies examining the efficacy of test accommodations on performance and measurement invariance within each SWD and ELL group, sample sizes tend to be small. With larger sample sizes for subgroups within ELLs and SWDs, PARCC and SBAC will be in a position to examine test and item properties for student groups with specific disabilities and ELL groups from different cultural and linguistic backgrounds.

In an attempt to address heterogeneity of ELLs when examining DIF, Ercikan, Roth, Simon, Sandilands, and Lyons-Thomas (2014) examined whether students who spoke French at home may contribute to diversity among linguistic minority groups in Canada. Using the PISA (Program for International Student Assessment) data for reading, science, and math, they found that the consistency of DIF identification ranged between 7% and 10% in separate DIF analyses for the students who speak French at home and those who do not speak French at home, whereas the consistency of DIF identification ranged from 24% to 54% for the combined group. As Ercikan et al. state, "This highlights the methodological problems with investigating measurement comparability for groups with great degrees of population heterogeneity . . ." (p. 283). They also stressed the need to identify the sources of DIF. Their review of the items used in the study suggested that the linguistic load of the item, the vocabulary, and the complexity of sentence structure may be factors that disadvantaged the students. These results are in support of the work of Abedi and his colleagues.

Test accommodations are provided to SWDs and ELLs to address both construct-irrelevant variance and construct underrepresentation. Accommodations help ensure that SWDs and ELLs have full access to the construct the test is measuring and respond in a way that represents their knowledge, skills, and abilities on the intended construct (Tindal & Fuchs, 1999). When studying the efficacy of accommodations, however, the presence of multiple and different accommodations for SWDs and ELLs confounds the results, making it difficult to determine the effects of a particular accommodation (Sireci et al., 2003). Although some recent studies that have examined the efficacy of accommodations included SWDs and ELLs who received only one accommodation, additional studies are needed to examine the effects of accommodations for groups receiving just one accommodation so that the effects can be attributed to a given accommodation. The assessment consortia, PARCC and SBAC, will have computer administration of their tests, requiring additional research on the efficacy of online strategies and accommodations on ELL and SWD performance.

Although the observance of a differential boost can support the use of accommodations for SWDs and ELLs, it can be challenged because better performance of SWDs and ELLs is not equivalent to assessments that provide valid score inferences. Evidence is needed for measurement invariance across ELLs and SWDs so as to make valid score interpretations for individual students as well as for group comparisons. Measurement invariance studies examine the stability of item and test measurement characteristics across groups. An evaluation of the stability of the estimated item parameters across groups is an important initial step for examining measurement invariance. Factorial invariance and other test and item characteristics that help ensure comparability, including the precision of scores, accuracy of classification rates, and the relationship between test scores and other measures, have been examined for SWDs and ELLs.

Because test scores tend to be less precise at the lower end of the score scale and many ELLs and SWDs demonstrate relatively low performance on large-scale assessments (Abedi et al., 2007; Thurlow et al., 2011), studies have obtained lower reliability estimates for ELLs and SWDs. Internal consistency indices, such as coefficient alpha, are commonly used as measures of test score reliability. These indices are affected by restricted ranges in performance. Furthermore, using these indices when some items measure an irrelevant construct in addition to the intended construct for subgroups will lead to lower reliability estimates. A number of factors, including language background, restriction of range, SES, and OTL, may contribute to the observed differences in reliabilities for ELLs (Abedi, 2003).

The evaluation of the comparability of the internal structure of the test has been examined through exploratory factor analyses and CFAs, including multigroup analyses and IRT analyses. DIF and DBF have been used to examine the equivalence of subgroup performance at the item level and at the level of a coherent subset of items. When DIF occurs, it indicates that the item measures some additional construct for one of the subgroups, which negatively affects the validity and comparability of test score interpretations and uses. As indicated by Camilli (1992), DIF can be considered a shift in the distribution of ability along a secondary construct that influences the probability of a correct response. One group may be less able on a secondary construct, such as English reading skills on a science test for ELLs. The use of technology-enhanced items by PARCC and SBAC will require studies examining the extent to which these novel items are measuring the same construct for ELLs and SWDs as compared to the general student population.

There are a number of factors that can have an impact of the validity of the results of invariance analyses, including heterogeneity of samples, small and differing sample sizes, differential guessing rates, nonoverlapping proficiency distributions, and lack of measurement precision. The use of large-scale test data and the evaluation of effect sizes help minimize the impact of sample size in interpreting the results. As previously indicated, nonoverlapping proficiency distributions arise because the SWD or ELL groups have distributions that are centered lower on the score scale than the general population. Consequently, these groups typically have a restricted range in scores. Differences in distributions affect the results of invariance studies in predictable ways such as easy items flagged for DIF in favor of the focal group (SWDs or ELLs; Sireci, 2009). In addition, restriction of range can also account for lower reliability estimates and poorer predictive validity evidence for these groups as well as differences in factorial structure. To minimize the effect of differential restriction of range across the groups, the reference group (general population) can be selected to have the same distribution as the SWD or ELL group.

The finding by some research (e.g., Kato et al., 2009) that results differ by disability category "underscores the importance of recognizing the limitations of treating all students with disabilities as a single homogenous group and suggests that the behavior of students with different kinds of disabilities needs to be examined separately whenever possible" (p. 38). The sample sizes for the focal groups (SWDs and ELLs) tend to be much smaller than the reference group and this may affect the statistical values. As an example, when examining DIF and calculating the difference in R^2 to compare models, the values are based on the entire sample and may be smaller than when group sizes are approximately equal (Kato et al., 2009).

When forms of tests are equated, measurement invariance also requires that equating functions derived from different subgroups produce the same results if scores are to be equitable. Therefore, when sample size permits, the equating functions for different subgroups should be examined when establishing measurement invariance. If vertical scales are developed to measure student progress, the validity of the vertical scales need be examined for ELL and SWD groups. Differences in learning profiles and trajectories for these students suggest that the vertical scale developed for the general population may not be appropriate for these students.

The tailoring of items to the ability level of the students is attractive in the assessment of SWDs and ELLs because current paper-and-pencil tests tend to target students at the middle of the score scale range, resulting in less precise measurement of SWDs and ELLs who tend to perform at the lower end of the score scale. Another attractive feature of CAT is the potential for the administration of fewer items to reach sufficient measurement precision. SBAC has adopted a CAT system and PARCC will use computer-delivered assessments. Stone and Davey (2011) discussed some of the advantages of using CAT with SWDs, including more precise measurement of SWDs. They also addressed some of the challenges of using CAT, including item response functions differing for SWDs due to accommodation status, divergent learning profiles, less access to computers, and less familiarity with keyboarding. Consequently, SWDs and other subgroups, such as ELLs, should be included in the calibration sample for the item bank, and if not, subgroup analyses are needed to examine the appropriateness of the item parameters for the different groups. Divergent learning profiles may also lead to less precise estimation of SWDs' and ELLs' standing on the latent construct. Stone and Davey reiterated the need for the detection of discrepant response patterns for subgroups.

Research on the efficacy of models for monitoring change for ELLs and SWDs is needed. Such research is crucial given that the federal Race to the Top initiative calls for measures that assess student progress (U.S. Department of Education, 2010). A number of challenges in including ELLs and SWDs in models evaluating educator effectiveness have been identified, including the number of ELLs and SWDs in classrooms, the inconsistent use of accommodations across years, the mobility of ELLs and SWDs, and the imprecision in measuring students who perform at the lower end of the score scale. The assessment consortiums are attempting to address some of these concerns, by designing tests that are more accessible for these students in the attempt to achieve more comparable scores as well as designing systems for assigning and monitoring accommodations used by students. Empirical evidence will be warranted to establish the extent to which the consortia have achieved their goals in providing a more valid assessment of ELL and SWD groups.

NOTES

[1]Studies included are denoted with single asterisk (*) in the references. It should be noted that articles may have been inadvertently missed.

[2]Studies included are denoted with double asterisks (**) in the references. It should be noted that some articles may have been inadvertently missed.

REFERENCES

Abedi, J. (2002). Standardized achievement tests and English Language Learners: Psychometric issues. *Educational Assessment, 8,* 231–257.

Abedi, J. (2003). *Impact of student language background on content-based performance: Analyses of extant data* (CSE Report No. 603). Los Angeles: University of California, National Center for Research on Evaluation, Standards, and Student Testing.

Abedi, J. (2004). The No Child Left Behind Act and English language learners: Assessment and accountability issues. *Educational Researcher, 33*(1), 4–14.

Abedi, J. (2006). Language issues in item development. In S. M. Downing & T. M. Haladyna (Eds.), *Handbook of test development* (pp. 377–399). Mahwah, NJ: Lawrence Erlbaum.

Abedi, J. (2008). Classification system for English language learners: Issues and recommendations. *Educational Measurement: Issues and Practice, 27*(3), 17–31.

**Abedi, J. (2009). Computer testing as a form of accommodation for English language learners. *Educational Assessment, 13,* 195–211.

Abedi, J., Courtney, M., & Leon, S. (2003). *Effectiveness and validity of accommodations for English language learners in large-scale assessment.* (CSE Tech. Rep. No. 608). Los Angeles: University of California: Center for the Study of Evaluation/National Center for Research on Evaluation, Standards, and Student Testing.

**Abedi, J., Courtney, M., Leon, S., Keo, J., & Azzam, T. (2006). *English language learners and math achievement: A study of opportunity to learn and language accommodation* (CSE Report). Los Angeles: University of California, National Center for Research on Evaluation, Standards, and Student Testing.

**Abedi, J., Courtney, M., Mirocha, J., Leon, S., & Goldberg, J. (2005). *Language accommodations for English language learners in large-scale assessments: Bilingual dictionaries and linguistic modification* (CSE Report 666). Los Angeles: University of California, National Center for Research on Evaluation, Standards, and Student Testing.

Abedi, J., & Gandara, P. (2006). Performance of English Language Learners as a subgroup in large-scale assessment: Interaction of research and policy. *Educational Measurement: Issues and Practice, 25*(4), 36–46.

Abedi, J., Hofstetter, C., & Lord, C. (2004). Assessment accommodations for English language learners: Implications for policy-based empirical research. *Review of Educational Research, 74*(1), 1–28.

Abedi, J., Kao, J. C., Leon, S., Mastergeorge, A. M., Sullivan, L., Herman, J., & Pope, R. (2010). Accessibility of segmented reading comprehension passages for students with disabilities. *Applied Measurement in Education, 23*, 168–186.

Abedi, J., Leon, S., & Kao, J. (2007). *Examining differential item functioning in reading assessments for students with disabilities.* Minneapolis: University of Minnesota, Partnership for Accessible Reading Assessment. Retrieved from http://www.readingassessment.info/resources

Abedi, J., Leon, S., & Mirocha, J. (2000). *Examining ELL and non-ELL student performance differences and their relationship to background factors: Continued analysis of extant data.* Los Angeles: University of California, National Center for Research on Evaluation, Standards, and Student Testing.

Abedi, J., & Lord, C. (2001). The language factor in mathematics. *Applied Measurement in Education, 14*, 219–234.

Abedi, J., Lord, C., & Hofstetter, C. (1998). *Impact of selected background variables on students' NAEP math performance* (CSE Technical Report No. 478). Los Angeles. University of California, National Center for Research on Evaluation, Standards, and Student Testing.

Abedi, J., Lord, C., & Plummer, J. R. (1997). *Final report of language background as a variable in NAEP mathematics performance* (CSE Technical Report No. 429). Los Angeles. University of California, National Center for Research on Evaluation, Standards, and Student Testing.

American Educational Research Association, American Psychological Association, & National Council on Measurement in Education. (1999). *Standards for educational and psychological testing.* Washington, DC: American Educational Research Association.

American Educational Research Association, American Psychological Association, & National Council on Measurement in Education. (2014). *Standards for educational and psychological testing.* Washington, DC: American Educational Research Association.

Artiles, A. J., Rueda, R., Salazar, J., & Higareda, I. (2005). Within-group diversity in minority disproportionate representation: English language learners in urban school districts. *Exceptional Children, 71*, 283–300.

Barton, K., & Finch, W. H. (2004, April). *Using DIF analyses to examine bias and assumptions of unidimensionality across students with and without disabilities and students with accommodations.* Paper presented at the annual meeting of the National Council on Measurement in Education, San Diego, CA.

Barton, K., & Huynh, H. (2003). Patterns of errors made by students with disabilities on a reading test with oral reading administration. *Educational and Psychological Measurement, 63*, 602–614.

Brennan, R. L. (2001). *Generalizability theory*. New York, NY: Springer-Verlag.

Brown, J. I., Fishco, V. V., & Hanna, G. (1993). *Nelson–Denny Reading Test, Form H*. Itasca, IL: Riverside.

Buzick, H., & Stone, E. (2011). *Recommendations for conducting differential item functioning (DIF) analyses for students with disabilities based on previous DIF studies* (ETS RR-11-34). Princeton, NJ: Educational Testing Service.

Cahalan, C., Mandinach, E. B., & Camara, W. J. (2002). *Predictive validity of SAT I: Reasoning test for test-takers with learning disabilities and extended time accommodations* (College Bard Research Report 2002-05). New York, NY: The College Board.

Camara, W. J., Copeland, T., & Rosthschild, B. (1998). *Effects of extended time on the SAT I: Reasoning test score growth for students with learning disabilities* (Research Report No. 1998-7). New York, NY: College Entrance Exam Board.

Camilli, G. (1992). A conceptual analysis of differential item function in terms of a multidimensional item response model. *Applied Psychological Measurement, 16*, 129–147.

Castellano, K. E., & Ho, A. D. (2013). Contrasting OLS and quantile regression approaches to student "growth" percentiles. *Journal of Educational and Behavioral Statistics, 38*, 190–214.

Cattell, R. B., & Burdsal, C. A. (1975). The radial parcel double factoring design: A solution to the item-vs.-parcel controversy. *Multivariate Behavioral Research, 10*, 165–179.

Cho, H., Lee, J., & Kingston, N. (2012). Examining the effectiveness of test accommodation using DIF and a mixture IRT model. *Applied Measurement in Education, 25*, 281–304.

Cid, J., & Spitalny, I. (2013, April). *Investigating the effect of language on the invariance of equating functions in paper-and-pencil and computer-based tests*. Paper presented at the annual meeting of the National Council on Measurement in Education, San Francisco, CA.

Clauser, B. E., & Mazor, K. M. (1998). Using statistical procedures to identify differentially functioning test items. *Educational Measurement: Issues and Practice, 17*(1), 31–44.

Cohen, A. S., Gregg, N., & Deng, M. (2005). The role of extended time and item content on a high-stakes mathematics test. *Learning Disabilities Research & Practice, 20*, 225–233.

Cook, L., Eignor, D., Steinberg, J., Sawaki, Y., & Cline, F. (2009). Using factor analysis to investigate the impact of accommodations on the scores of students with disabilities on a reading comprehension assessment. *Journal of Applied Testing, 10*(2). Retrieved from http://atpu.memberclicks.net/assets/documents/Special%20issue%20article%203.pdf

Cook, L., Eignor, D., Sawaki, Y., Steinberg, J., & Cline, F. (2010). Using factor analysis to investigate accommodations used by students with disabilities on an English-language arts assessment. *Applied Measurement in Education, 23*, 187–208.

Cormier, D. C., Altman, J. R., Shyyan, V., & Thurlow, M. L. (2010). *A summary of the research on the effects of test accommodations: 2007-2008* (Technical Report No. 56). Minneapolis: University of Minnesota, National Center on Educational Outcomes.

Cronbach, L. J. (1988). Five perspectives on validity argument. In H. Wainer & H. Braun (Eds.), *Test validity* (pp. 3–17), Hillsdale, NJ: Erlbaum.

Cronbach, L. J., Gleser, G. C., Nanda, H., & Rajaratnam, N. (1972). *The dependability of behavioral measurements: Theory of generalizability of scores and profiles*. New York, NY: John Wiley.

Dorans, N. J. (2004). Using subpopulation invariance to assess test score equity. *Journal of Educational Measurement, 37*(4), 43–68.

Dorans, N. J., & Holland, P. W. (1993). DIF detection and description: Mantel-Haenszel and standardization. In P. W. Holland & H. Wainer (Eds.), *Differential item functioning* (pp. 35–66). Hillsdale, NJ: Erlbaum.

Dorans, N. J., & Holland, P. W. (2000). Population invariance and the equitability of tests: Basic theory and the linear case. *Journal of Educational Measurement, 41*, 43–68.

Douglas, J. A., Roussos, L. A., & Stout, W. (1996). Item-bundle DIF hypothesis testing: Identifying suspect bundles and assessing their differential functioning. *Journal of Educational Measurement, 33*(4), 465–484.

*Elbaum, B. (2007). Effects of an oral testing accommodation on the mathematics performance of secondary students with and without learning disabilities. *Journal of Special Education, 40*, 218–229.

*Elbaum, B., Arguelles, M. E., Campbell, Y., & Saleh, M. B. (2004). Effects of a student-reads-aloud accommodation on the performance of students with and without learning disabilities on a test of reading comprehension. *Exceptionality: A Special Education Journal, 12*(2), 71–87.

Elliott, S. N.,Kettler, R. J., Beddow, P. A., Kurz, A., Compton, E. ... & Roach, A. T. (2010). Effects of using modified items to test students with persistent academic difficulties. *Exceptional Children, 76*, 475–495.

Engelhard, G., Fincher, M., & Domaleski, C. S. (2011). Mathematics performance of students with and without disabilities under accommodated conditions using resource guides and calculators on high stakes tests. *Applied Measurement in Education, 37*, 281–306.

English Learners Office, E. J. McClendon Educational Center. (2002). *Federal definition of an English Language Learner (ELL)*. Retrieved from http://ell.pccs.k12.mi.us/sites/ell.pccs.k12.mi.us/files/shared/2011-2012/Federal%20Definition%20of%20ELL.pdf

Ercikan, K., Arim, R. G., Law, D. M., Lacroix, S., Gagnon, F., & Domene, J. F. (2010). Application of think-aloud protocols in examining sources of differential item functioning. *Educational Measurement: Issues and Practice, 29*(2), 24–35.

Ercikan, K., Roth, W.-M., Simon, M., Sandilands, D., & Lyons-Thomas, J. (2014). Inconsistencies in DIF detection for sub-groups in heterogeneous language groups. *Applied Measurement in Education, 27*, 273–285.

ESEA reauthorization: Standards and assessments: Hearings before the Health, Education, Labor, and Pensions Committee, United States Senate, 111th Cong., 2nd Sess. (2010). (Testimony of Martha Thurlow). Retrieved from http://www.gpo.gov/fdsys/pkg/CHRG-111shrg56288/pdf/CHRG-111shrg56288.pdf

*Feldman, E., Kim, J. S., & Elliott, S. N. (2011). The effects of accommodations on adolescents' self-efficacy and test performance. *Journal of Special Education, 45*(2), 77–88.

Finch, H., Barton, K., & Meyer, P. (2009). Differential item functioning analysis for accommodated versus non-accommodated students. *Educational Assessment, 14*, 38–56.

Fuchs, L. S., & Fuchs, D. (2001). Helping teachers formulate sound accommodation decisions for students with learning disabilities. *Learning Disabilities Research & Practice, 16*, 174–181.

Fuchs, L. S., Fuchs, D., Eaton, S., Hamlett, C. L., & Karns, K. (2000). Supplementing teachers' judgments of mathematics test accommodations with objective data sources. *School Psychology Review, 29*, 65–85.

Geisinger, K. F. (1994). Psychometric issues in testing students with disabilities. *Applied Measurement in Education, 7*, 121–140.

Holland, P. W., & Thayer, D. T. (1988). Differential item performance and the Mantel Haenszel procedure. In H. Wainer & H. I. Braun (Eds.), *Test validity* (pp. 129–145). Hillsdale, NJ: Erlbaum.

Huggins, A. C., & Elbaum, B. (2013). Test accommodations and equating invariance on a fifth-grade science exam. *Educational Assessment, 18*, 49–72.

Huynh, H., & Barton, K. (2006). Performance of students with disabilities under regular and oral administrations for a high-stakes reading examination. *Applied Measurement in Education, 19*, 21–39.

Huynh, H., Meyer, P., & Gallant, D. J. (2004). Comparability of student performance between regular and oral administrations for a high-stakes mathematics test. *Applied Measurement in Education, 17*, 39–57.

**Johnson, E., & Monroe, B. (2004). Simplified language as an accommodation on math tests. *Assessment for Effective Intervention, 29*(3), 35–45.

Johnson, E. S. (2000). The effects of accommodations on performance assessments. *Remedial and Special Education, 21,* 261–268.

Jones, N. D., Buzick, H. M., & Turkan, S. (2013). Including students with disabilities and English learners in measures of educator effectiveness. *Educational Researcher, 42,* 234–241.

Kachchaf, R., & Solano-Flores, G. (2012). Rater language background as a source of measurement error in testing of English Language Learners. *Applied Measurement in Education, 25,* 162–177.

Kane, M. T. (1992). An argument-based approach to validity. *Psychological Bulletin, 112,* 527–535.

Kane, M. T. (2006). Validation. In R. L. Brennan (Ed.), *Educational measurement* (4th ed., pp. 17–64). Washington, DC: American Council on Education/Praeger.

Kane, M. T. (2013). Validating the interpretations and uses of test scores. *Journal of Educational Measurement, 50,* 1–73.

Kane, M. T., & Mroch, A. A. (2010). Modeling group differences in OLS and orthogonal regression: Implications for differential validity studies. *Applied Measurement in Education, 23,* 215–241.

Kato, K., Moen, R. E., & Thurlow, M. L. (2009). Differential of a state reading assessment: Item functioning, distractor functioning and omission frequency for disability categories. *Educational Measurement: Issues and Practice, 28*(2), 28–40.

*Ketterlin-Geller, L. R., Yovanoff, P., & Tindal, G. (2007). Developing a new paradigm for conducting research on accommodations in mathematics testing. *Exceptional Children, 73,* 331–347.

Kettler, R. J. (2011). Effect of packages of modifications to improve test and item accessibility: Less is more. In S. N. Elliott, R. J. Kettler, P. A., Beddow, & A. Kurz (Eds.), *Handbook of accessible achievement tests for all students: Bridging the gaps between research practice, and policy* (pp. 231–242). New York, NY: Springer.

Kettler, R. J., Elliott, S. N., & Beddow, P. A. (2009). Modifying achievement test items: A theory-guided and data-based approach for better measurement of what SWDs know. *Peabody Journal of Education, 84,* 529–551.

*Kettler, R. J., Rodriguez, M. R., Bolt, D. M., Elliott, S. N., Bedow, P. A., & Kruz, A. (2011). Modified multiple-choice items for alternate assessments: Reliability, difficulty, and differential boost. *Applied Measurement in Education, 24,* 210–234.

Kieffer, M. J., Lesaux, N. K., Rivera, M., & Francis, D. J. (2009). Accommodations for English Language Learners taking large-scale assessments: A meta-analysis on effectiveness and validity. *Review of Educational Research, 79,* 1168–1201.

Kieffer, M. J., Rivera, M., & Francis, D. J. (2012). *Practical guidelines for the education of English language learners: Research-based recommendations for the use of accommodations in large-scale assessments. 2012 update.* Portsmouth, NH: RMC Research Corporation, Center of Instruction.

Kim, J., & Herman, J. L. (2009). A three-state study of English learner progress. *Educational Assessment, 13,* 212–231.

Kim, D., & Huynh, H. (2010). Equivalence of paper-and-pencil and online administration modes of the statewide English test for students with and without disabilities. *Educational Assessment, 15,* 107–212.

Kolen, M. J., & Brennan, R. L. (2004). *Test equating, scaling, and linking* (2nd ed.). New York, NY: Springer.

Koo, J. K., Becker, B. J., & Kim, Y. (2014). Examining differential item functioning trends for English language learners in a reading test: A meta-analytic approach. *Language Testing,*

31, 89–109. Retrieved from http://ltj.sagepub.com/content/early/2013/07/25/0265532 213496097

Koretz, D., & Hamilton, L. (2000). Assessment of students with disabilities in Kentucky: Inclusion, student performance and validity. *Educational Evaluation and Policy Analysis*, *22*, 255–272.

Koretz, D., & Hamilton, L. (2006). Testing for accountability in K-12. In B. Brennan (Ed.), *Educational measurement* (pp. 579–623). New York, NY: Praeger.

Kosciolek, S., & Ysseldyke, J. E. (2000). *Effects of a reading accommodation on the validity of a reading test* (NCEO Technical Report No. 28). Minneapolis: University of Minnesota, National Center on Educational Outcomes.

*Laitusis, C. C. (2010). Examining the impact of audio presentation on tests of reading comprehension. *Applied Measurement in Education*, *23*, 153–167.

Laitusis, C. C., Buzick, H. M., Cook, L. L., & Stone, E. (2011). Adaptive testing options for accountability assessments. In M. Russell (Ed.), *Assessing students in the margins: Challenges, strategies, and techniques* (pp. 291–310). Charlotte, NC: Information Age.

Lakin, J. M., & Lai, E. R. (2012). Multigroup generalizability analysis of verbal, quantitative, and nonverbal ability tests for culturally and linguistically diverse students. *Educational and Psychological Measurement*, *72*, 139–158.

Lakin, J. M., & Young, J. W. (2013). Evaluating growth for ELL students: Implications for accountability policies. *Educational Measurement: Issues and Practice*, *32*(3), 11–26.

Lane, S., & Stone, C. A. (2006). Performance assessments. In B. Brennan (Ed.), *Educational measurement* (pp. 387–432). New York, NY: Praeger.

Lane, S., Wang, N., & Magone, M. (1996). Gender related differential item functioning on a middle school mathematics performance assessment. *Educational Measurement: Issues and Practice*, *15*(4), 21–27.

*Lewandowski, L. J., Lovett, B. J., & Rogers, C. L. (2008). Extended time as a testing accommodation for students with reading disabilities: Does a rising tide lift all ships? *Journal of Psychoeducational Assessment*, *26*, 315–324.

*Lewandowski, L. J., Lovett, B. J., Parolin, R., Gordon, M., & Codding, R. S. (2007). Extended time accommodations and the mathematics performance of students with and without ADHD. *Journal of Psychoeducational Assessment*, *25*, 17–28.

Li, D., & Brennan, R. L. (2007). *A multi-group generalizability analysis of a large-scale reading comprehension test* (CASMA Research Report No. 25). Iowa City, IA: Center for Advanced Studies in Measurement and Assessment.

Li, H. (2013, April). *The effects of read-aloud accommodations for students with and without disabilities: A meta-analysis*. Presentation at the annual meeting of the National Council on Measurement in Education, San Francisco, CA.

Li, H., & Suen, H. K. (2012). The effects of test accommodations for English Language Learners: A meta-analysis. *Applied Measurement in Education*, *25*, 327–346.

Linn, R. L. (1978). Single-group validity, differential validity, and differential prediction. *Journal of Applied Psychology*, *63*, 507–512.

Martiniello, M. (2009). Linguistic complexity, schematic representations, and differential item functioning for English Language Learners in math tests. *Educational Assessment*, *14*, 160–179.

Mattern, K. D., Patterson, B. F., Shaw, E., Kobrin, J. L., & Barbuti (2008). *Differential validity and prediction of the SAT* (Research Report No. 2008-4). New York, NY: College Board.

Mazor, K. M., Clauser, B. E., & Hambleton, R. K. (1992). The effect of sample size on the functioning of the Mantel-Haenszel statistic. *Educational and Psychological Measurement*, *52*, 443–451.

McKevitt, B. C., & Elliott, S. N. (2003). Effects and perceived consequences of using read aloud and teacher-recommended testing accommodations on a reading achievement test. *School Psychology Review, 32*, 583–600.

Meloy, L., Deville, C., & Frisbie, D. (2000, April). *The effects of a reading accommodation on standardized test scores of learning disabled and non learning disabled students.* Paper presented at the annual meeting of the National Council on Measurement in Education, New Orleans, LA

Messick, S. (1989). Validity. In R. L. Linn (Ed.), *Educational measurement* (3rd ed., pp. 13–104). New York, NY: American Council on Education and Macmillan.

National Clearinghouse for English Language Acquisition & Language Instruction Educational Programs. (2007). Retrieved from http://sbo.nn.k12.va.us/esl/documents/ncela_fast_faqs.pdf

Pennock-Roman, M., & Rivera, C. (2011). Mean effects of test accommodations for ELLs and non-ELLs: A meta-analysis of experimental studies. *Educational Measurement: Issues and Practice, 30*(3), 10–28.

Phillips, G. (2009, December). *Race to the Top Assessment Program: A new generation of comparable state assessments.* Presentation at the U.S. Department of Education Public Hearings, Denver, CO.

Phillips, S. E., & Camara, W. J. (2006). Legal and ethical issues. In R. Brennan (Ed.), *Educational measurement* (4th ed., pp. 734–755). Westport, CT: Praeger.

*Randall, J., & Engelhard, G. (2010a). Performance of students with and without disabilities under modified conditions: Using resource guides and read-aloud test modifications on a high-stakes reading test. *Journal of Special Education, 44*, 79–93.

Randall, J., & Engelhard, G. (2010b). Using confirmatory factor analysis and the Rasch model to assess measurement invariance in a high stakes reading assessment. *Applied Measurement in Education, 23*, 286–306.

Randall, J., Cheong, Y. F., & Engelhard, G. (2011). Using explanatory item response theory modeling to investigate context effects of differential item functioning for students with disabilities. *Educational and Psychological Measurement, 17*, 129–147.

**Rivera, C., & Stansfield, C. W. (2004). The effect of linguistic simplification of science test items on score comparability. *Educational Assessment, 9*(3), 79–105.

Rock, D. A., Bennett, R. E., & Kaplan, B. A. (1987). Internal construct validity of a college admissions test across handicapped and non-handicapped groups. *Educational and Psychological Measurement, 47*, 193–205.

Rock, D. A., Bennett, R. E., Kaplan, B. A., & Jirele, T. (1988). Factor structure of the Graduate Record examinations' general test in handicapped and nonhandicapped groups. *Journal of Applied Psychology, 73*, 382–392.

Rogers, C. M., Christian, E. M., & Thurlow, M. L. (2012). *A summary of the research on the effects of test accommodations: 2009-2010* (Technical Report No. 65). Minneapolis: University of Minnesota, National Center on Educational Outcomes.

Roussos, L., & Stout, W. (1996). A multidimensionality-based DIF analysis paradigm. *Applied Psychological Measurement, 20*, 355–371.

Russell, M. (2011). *Digital test delivery: Empowering accessible test design to increase test validity for all students.* Bill & Melinda Gates Foundation. Retrieved from https://www.measuredprogress.org/documents/10157/18439/Michael_Russell-Digital_Test_Delivery.pdf

Scarpati, S. E., Wells, C. S., Lewis, C., & Jirka, S. (2009). Accommodations and item-level analyses using mixture differential item functioning models. *Journal of Special Education, 45*, 54–62.

Shaftel, J., Belton-Kocher, E., Glasnapp, D. R., & Poggio, J. P. (2003). *The differential impact of accommodations in statewide assessment: Research summary.* Minneapolis: University of Minnesota, National Center on Educational Outcomes. Retrieved from http://www.cehd.umn.edu/nceo/topicareas/accommodations/Kansas.htm

Shaftel, J., Belton-Kocher, E., Glasnapp, D., & Poggio, J. (2006). The impact of language characteristics in mathematics test items on the performance of English language learners and students with disabilities. *Educational Assessment, 11*, 105–126.

Sinharay, S., Dorans, N. J., & Liang, L. (2011). First language of test takers and fairness assessment procedures. *Educational Measurement: Issues and Practice, 30*(2), 25–35.

Sireci, S. G. (2009). No more excuses: New research on assessing students with disabilities. *Journal of Applied Testing, 10*(2). Retrieved fromhttp://www.testpublishers.org/assets/documents/Special%20Issue%20Article%201.%20pdf

Sireci, S. G., Han, K. T., & Wells, C. (2008). Methods for evaluating the validity of test scores for English language learners. *Educational Assessment, 13*, 108–131.

Sireci, S. G., Li, S., & Scarpati, S. E. (2003). *The effects of test accommodations on test performance: A review of the literature. Commissioned paper by the National Academy of Sciences/National Research Council's Board on Testing and Assessment.* Washington, DC: National Research Council.

Sireci, S. G., Scarpati, S. E., & Li, S. (2005). Test accommodations for SWDs: An analysis of the interaction hypothesis. *Review of Educational Research, 75*, 457–490.

Solano-Flores, G. (2006). Language, dialect, and register: Sociolinguistics and the estimation of measurement error in the testing of English-language learners. *Teachers College Record, 108*, 2354–2379.

Solano-Flores, G. (2008). Who is given tests in what language by whom, when and where? The need for probabilistic views of language in the testing of English Language Learners. *Educational Researcher, 37*, 189–199.

**Solano-Flores, G., Barnett-Clarke, C., & Kachchaf, R. R. (2013). Semiotic structure and meaning making: The performance of English language learners on mathematics tests. *Educational Assessment, 18*, 147–161.

Solano-Flores, G., Lara, E. J., Sexton, U., & Navarrete, C. (2001). *Testing English language learners: A sampler of student responses to science and mathematics test items.* Washington, DC: Council of Chief State School Officers.

Solano-Flores, G., & Li, M. (2006). The use of generalizability (G) theory in the testing of linguistic minorities. *Educational Measurement: Issues and Practice, 25*, 13–22.

Solano-Flores, G., & Li, M. (2009). Language variation and score variation in the testing of English Language Learners, native Spanish speakers (2009). *Educational Assessment, 14*, 180–194.

Solano-Flores, G., & Li, M. (2013). Generalizability theory and the fair and valid assessment of linguistic minorities. *Educational Research and Evaluation: An International Journal on Theory and Practice, 19*, 245–263.

Solano-Flores, G., & Trumbull, E. (2003). Examining language in context: The need for new research and practice paradigms in the testing of English-language learners. *Educational Researcher, 32*(2), 3–13.

Stevens, J., Zvoch, K., & Biancarosa, G. (2012, April). *Technical issues in the use and interpretation of growth models for students with and without disabilities.* Paper presented at the annual meeting of the National Council on Measurement in Education, Vancouver, British Columbia, Canada.

Stone, E., Cook, L., Laitusis, C. C., & Cline, F. (2010). Using differential item functioning to investigate the impact of testing accommodations on an English-language arts assessment for students who are blind or visually impaired. *Applied Measurement in Education, 23*, 132–152.

Stone, E., & Davey, T. (2011, August). *Computer-adaptive testing for students with disabilities: A review of the literature* (ETS Research Report No. RR-11-32). Princeton, NJ: ETS.

Thompson, S. J., Blount, A., & Thurlow, M. L. (2002). *A summary of research on effects of test accommodations-1999 through 2001.* Minneapolis: University of Minnesota, National Center on Educational Outcomes.

Thompson, S. J., Thurlow, M. L., Quenemoen, R. F., & Lehr, C. A. (2002). *Access to computer-based testing for students with disabilities* (Synthesis Report 45). Minneapolis: University of Minnesota, National Center on Educational Outcomes. Retrieved from http://www.cehd.umn.edu/NCEO/onlinepubs/synthesis45.html

Thurlow, M., Lazarus, S. S., Albus, D., & Hodgson, J. (2010). *Computer-based testing: Practices and considerations* (Synthesis Report No. 78). Minneapolis: University of Minnesota, National Center on Educational Outcomes.

Thurlow, M. L., Bremer, C., & Albus, D. (2011). *2008-09 publicly reported assessment results for students with disabilities and ELLs with disabilities* (Technical Report No. 59). Minneapolis: University of Minnesota, National Center on Educational Outcomes.

Thurlow, M. L., & Kopriva, R. J. (2015). Advancing accessibility and accommodations in content assessments for students with disabilities and English learners. *Review of Research in Education, 39*, 331–369.

Thurlow, M. L., Lazarus, S. S.,& Christensen, L. L. (2013).Accommodations for assessment (pp. 94–110). In Lloyd, J. W., Landrum, T. J., Cook, B. G., & Tankersley, M. (Eds.), *Research-based practices in assessment*. Upper Saddle River, NJ: Pearson Education, Inc.

Tindal, G., & Fuchs, L. (1999). *A summary of research on test changes: An empirical basis for defining accommodations*. Lexington, KY: Mid-South Regional Resource Center.

Tippets, E., & Michaels, H. (1997, April). *Factor structure invariance of accommodated and non-accommodated performance assessments*. Paper presented at the annual meeting of the National Council on Measurement in Education, Chicago, IL.

U.S. Department of Education. (2005). *Secretary Spellings announces Growth Model Pilot, addresses Chief State School Officers' annual policy forum in Richmond*. Retrieved from https://www2.ed.gov/news/pressreleases/2005/11/11182005.html

U.S. Department of Education. (2007). *Standards and assessments peer review guidance*. Washington, DC: Author.

U.S. Department of Education. (2010). *Race to the Top*. Retrieved from https://www2.ed.gov/programs/racetothetop/executive-summary.pdf

Way, W. D., Twing, J. S., Camara, W., Sweeney, K., Lazer, S., & Mazzeo, J. (2010). *Some considerations related to the use of adaptive testing for the common core assessments*. Princeton, NJ: Educational Testing Service.

**Wolf, M. K., Kim, J., & Kao, J. (2012). The effects of glossary and read-aloud accommodations on English Language Learners' performance on a mathematics assessment. *Applied Measurement in Education, 25*, 347–374.

Wolf, M. K., & Leon, S. (2009). An investigation of the language demands in content assessments for English Language Learners. *Educational Assessment, 14*, 139–159.

Young, J. W., Cho, Y., Ling, G., Cline, F., Steinberg, J., & Stone, E. (2008). Validity and fairness of state standards-based assessments for English language learners. *Educational Assessment, 13*, 170–192.

Zieky, M. (1993). Practical questions in the use of DIF statistics in test development. In P. W. Holland & H. Wainer (Eds.), *Differential item functioning* (pp. 337–347). Hillsdale, NJ: Erlbaum.

Chapter 6

Promoting Validity in the Assessment of English Learners

STEPHEN G. SIRECI
MOLLY FAULKNER-BOND
University of Massachusetts Amherst

A cross the globe, educational tests are being used at a rapidly increasing rate. Traditional uses of educational assessments include measuring students' achievement with respect to subject matter taught during a particular period in time, gauging students' academic strengths and weaknesses, and providing information to admissions officers and others who make decisions about admissions, scholarships, or eligibility to special programs. More recently, educational tests are being used to inform educational policy and for holding educators accountable for student learning. In fact, achievement testing for accountability purposes is one of the defining characteristics of 21st-century educational assessments.

One reason educational assessments are used for these important purposes is that they are considered to provide reliable and objective information regarding students' achievement. The fact that these tests are *standardized*, meaning the content, test administration conditions, and scoring are uniform (consistent) across all test takers, supports this perception of objectivity. However, no test is perfectly suited for all students and so educational tests typically do the best they can for the majority of the population tested (Geisinger, 2000). For this reason, it is important to consider identifiable *subgroups* of the examinee population when considering the fairness and appropriateness of educational tests.

In the United States, one important subgroup that presents particularly difficult challenges to valid measurement is *English learners*. In this article, we define ELs and the difficult challenges inherent in assessing their academic knowledge, skills, and abilities. We also discuss key validity issues, such as actions that can be taken to promote valid interpretations for these students or to evaluate the degree to which a

Review of Research in Education
March 2015, Vol. 39, pp. 215–252
DOI: 10.3102/0091732X14557003
© 2015 AERA. http://rre.aera.net

particular assessment may be appropriate for them. In particular, we discuss providing accommodations for ELs, and various steps test developers and users can take to ensure that ELs in the United States can demonstrate their academic knowledge and skills in ways that are fair, valid, and reliable.

We begin our discussion with a description of ELs in the United States and their representation in current educational assessments. However, it is important to note that the issue of valid assessment of *linguistic minorities* generalizes beyond the United States, and applies with equal force to linguistic minorities in other countries. As the *Standards for Educational and Psychological Testing* (American Educational Research Association [AERA], American Psychological Association, & National Council on Measurement in Education, 1999) pointed out,

For all test takers, any test that employs language is, in part, a measure of their language skills. This is of particular concern for test takers whose first language is not the language of the test. Test use with individuals who have not sufficiently acquired the language of the test may introduce construct-irrelevant components to the testing process. In such instances, test results may not reflect accurately the qualities and competencies intended to be measured. (p. 91)

A key point in this statement is the interaction between language and content for examinees who are not fully proficient in the language in which the test is administered. English proficiency is not always *construct-irrelevant* (a term we describe later) in educational testing; however, the ways in which (or the extent to which) language is relevant can vary considerably from context to context and must be articulated and considered carefully. In discussing valid assessment of ELs, we must distinguish between assessments designed to measure proficiency in the English language and assessments designed to measure other academic proficiencies. For English language proficiency (ELP) assessments, ELP is the target of measurement; in fact, it is the *construct* the test attempts to measure. As the academic construct targeted by a test departs from ELP, proficiency in English changes along a continuum from *relevant* to *irrelevant*, and can be a potential source of bias. For this reason, we distinguish validity issues related to ELP assessments and those related to assessment of ELs' knowledge and skills in other academic areas.

ENGLISH LEARNERS IN THE UNITED STATES

ELs, referred to as limited English proficient (LEP) students in the *No Child Left Behind* Act of 2001 (NCLB), are defined by a cluster of criteria as students who lack the English proficiency necessary to meaningfully participate in or benefit from educational instruction delivered in English. In the 2009–2010 school year, the U.S. Department of Education reported an EL population of approximately 4.7 million students, or 9.5% of the overall student population[1] (National Center for Education Statistics, n.d.). Over three quarters of these students (77%) are Spanish speakers (U.S. Department of Education, 2011), and are more likely to come from a low-socioeconomic status (SES) background relative to the general population (Lakin &

Young, 2013; Swanson, 2009). ELs reside in all 50 states and the District of Columbia, although they tend to be concentrated in pockets within and across states. For example, nationwide, nearly two third of all ELs (62%) reside in the 5 states with the largest EL populations—California, Texas, Florida, New York, and Illinois (U.S. Department of Education, 2011). Or, as an example of linguistic concentration, Arabic speakers represent only 1% of the EL population nationwide but 23% of the EL population in Michigan (U.S. Department of Education, 2011).

Ultimately, regardless of the size, diversity, or distribution of its EL population, every state is compelled by various laws to identify these students and provide them with language instruction to help them learn English and grade-level appropriate academics. To ensure states are fulfilling this responsibility, NCLB introduced a number of new assessment and accountability requirements designed to draw attention to the progress and performance of ELs in meeting the goals of English proficiency and academic content proficiency.

Assessment Requirements for ELs in the United States

Under NCLB, ELs in public schools may be required to participate in as many as four summative assessments each year, depending on their grade level. These include content assessments of English language arts (ELA) and mathematics (in Grades 3 through 8 and once in high school), content assessments of science (once each in Grade 3 through 5, 6 through 8, and high school), and ELP assessments (for ELs in all public schools, K–12). States and districts are held accountable for EL inclusion and performance benchmarks for these assessments each year, and must submit annual consolidated state performance reports to the U.S. Department of Education detailing their progress in meeting these and other goals of NCLB. Each of these assessments serves specific purposes under the law and their scores are used in a variety of ways that may affect ELs at both the general and individual levels. In Table 1 we list the different ways in which these assessments are currently used.

EL performance on academic content assessments is used to identify schools and districts where ELs are failing to meet achievement benchmarks set for all students. The goal is to require these agencies to improve their programming for ELs and, hence, improve their achievement.[2] Thus, for ELA and math programming, scores from subject area assessments may be used in decisions about funding, program design, and professional development foci. ELP assessment scores are used similarly—for program evaluation, resource allocations, and general accountability for student performance—in the slightly narrower realm of language instruction.

In addition to these more familiar uses for test scores, another use specific to ELs is to support reclassification decisions. *Reclassification*, or redesignation, is the process by which ELs are judged to have mastered the (English) language skills necessary for school, and are ready to be reclassified as no longer needing special linguistic support or instruction. By law, reclassified students must be monitored for 2 school years following their exit before they are fully dissociated from the EL subgroup for reporting purposes. As Forte, Faulkner-Bond, Waring, Kuti, and Fenner (2010) pointed out,

TABLE 1

Group- and Individual-Level Uses for EL Assessment Scores

	Score Type	
Score Use	Content	Language (ELP)
Evaluate instructional programs in math and reading	✓	
Identify schools and districts where ELs are meeting academic standards	✓	
Evaluate language instruction programs		✓
Identify schools and school districts where ELs are attaining proficiency in English		✓
Identify ELs who are ready to be reclassified as former ELs	✓	✓

Note. EL = English learner; ELP = English language proficient.

this situation constitutes the sole instance under NCLB in which assessment scores are used to make a high-stakes decision—that is, of continued identification as an EL or not—that directly affects individual children (see also Bailey & Carroll, 2015, this volume).

At present, states[3] are free to set their own criteria for reclassification decisions, and most use multiple measures, including scores from both ELP and content assessments (Grissom, 2004; Linquanti, 2001; Ragan & Lesaux, 2006). However, it is unclear whether and how these two types of scores can or should be appropriately used to determine when an EL has demonstrated sufficient mastery of language to be classified as a former EL (Grissom, 2004; Kim & Herman, 2009; Robinson, 2011; U.S. Department of Education, 2012). Important issues for research in this area include the effects different criteria may have on opportunity to learn (OTL), achievement gaps, and score interpretation.

Ultimately, assessing ELs' proficiencies, whether mandated by NCLB or otherwise, is intended to improve their education. The extent to which this goal is realized is dependent on (a) the degree to which the assessments accurately measure ELs' true knowledge and skills and (b) the degree to which the assessment results are appropriate indicators for the purpose at hand. For these reasons, a Working Group on EL Policy (2010), comprising language, assessment, and policy experts, recommended that test makers and users be required to "certify that the validity of the tests to be used for the assessment of ELLs' academic achievement are consistent with the APA/AERA/NCME Standards."

Understanding the Complexities Within the EL Population

Although ELs share a designation based on their proficiency with English, they are a diverse subgroup of students who may vary greatly from one another—both within and across states—on variables such as home language, age, SES, immigration status, migrant status, and literacy or education in their native language. As Abedi and Linquanti (2012) noted, "While assessment and accountability systems usually treat the ELL category as binary (a student is ELL or not), ELLs are very diverse and exhibit a wide range of language and academic competencies, both in English and their primary language" (p. 1).

Although the prototypical EL in the United States is a Spanish-speaking student from a low-SES background living in a state with a large EL population, hundreds of thousands of ELs across the country do not match this prototype. Among ELs, the most visible and salient source of variance may be native language itself. There is considerable linguistic diversity in the 77% of population that speak dialects of Spanish, as these students come from a number of different countries and backgrounds, many of which use markedly different forms of Spanish (e.g., Puerto Rican Spanish differs in key ways from the Spanish spoken in some South American countries like Colombia). For the remaining 23% non–Spanish-speaking EL population, the linguistic diversity is staggering. Estimates of the number of home languages represented in the EL population range from about 50 on the low end (U.S. Department of Education, 2011), to well over 100 (Swanson, 2009), with some states reporting more than 180 languages within their state populations alone (O'Conner, Abedi, & Tung, 2012a, 2012b)! Thus, in considering validity issues in the assessment of ELs, it is important to keep in mind we are discussing a very diverse group of examinees.

VALIDITY ISSUES IN ASSESSING ELS

According to the AERA, American Psychological Association, and National Council on Measurement in Education (2014) *Standards for Educational and Psychological Testing* (hereafter referred to as the *Standards*), validity is "the degree to which evidence and theory support the interpretations of test scores for proposed uses of tests" (p. 11). This definition underscores the importance of understanding the intended purposes and uses of test scores, because what needs to be validated is not the test itself but the use of a test for a particular purpose. In Table 1, we listed seven potential uses of test results that affect ELs. Some validity questions that are associated with these uses include the following:

1. Do these assessments measure the knowledge and skills they purport to measure?
2. For the content assessments that are not measures of English proficiency, does English proficiency interfere with proper measurement of the knowledge and skills tested?
3. Are ELs' scores on these assessments reliable?
4. Do the scores provide useful information that will improve instruction for ELs?
5. When ELs' scores are aggregated for accountability purposes, are those aggregates useful for evaluating effective instruction for ELs?

6. When accommodations are provided for ELs do they result in more accurate measurement of their knowledge and skills?

These questions are just a sample of the types of validity issues that are important to consider when assessing the proficiencies of ELs. It is important to note that different questions may be more or less relevant for assessments of language proficiency than for assessments of content knowledge. The choice of validity questions to investigate should be informed by the particular type of score and score use. For example, an evaluation of the validity of mathematics assessments scores for program evaluation purposes may focus on very different questions than an evaluation of the validity of ELP assessment scores for the purpose of redesignation.

In considering a framework for determining the most important validity issues and questions to address with respect to the assessment of ELs, we suggest using a validation framework based on the AERA et al. (2014) *Standards*. However, before introducing this framework, we first discuss two important concepts in validity theory: *construct underrepresentation* and *construct-irrelevant variance*, which are important in evaluating the validity of interpretations of test scores, as well as understanding potential threats to validity.

Construct Underrepresentation and Construct-Irrelevant Variance

Valid assessment of ELs' knowledge, skills, and abilities centers on the degree to which the assessments adequately measure the "constructs" they are designed to measure. By the term *construct*, we mean the hypothesized attribute measured by a test, such as English proficiency, mathematics achievement, science proficiency, quantitative reasoning, and so forth. In describing the *threats* to valid assessment, Messick (1989) stated, "Tests are imperfect measures of constructs because they either leave out something that should be included . . . or else include something that should be left out, or both" (p. 34). When a test is incomplete in its measurement of a construct, the term *construct underrepresentation* is used. For example, if the construct of English proficiency is defined as comprising the skills of listening, reading, speaking, and writing; but the test measures only reading and writing, the test would be seen as "underrepresenting" the construct. In this situation, it would be invalid to interpret students' test scores as measures of English proficiency as defined by the four-component definition of the construct.

Another source of invalidity in educational assessment is when a test measures "something that should be left out." Messick (1989) described this situation as a test containing "construct-irrelevant variance" (p. 34). He further defined *construct-irrelevant easiness* as when the extraneous variable measured invalidly inflates test scores (e.g., some examinees have seen the items before the test begins) and *construct-irrelevant difficulty* as when the extraneous variable interferes with successful test performance (e.g., an unfamiliar and confusing item format is used). For non-ELP assessments (i.e., when the construct measured is *not* English proficiency), English proficiency can be a major source of construct-irrelevant variance that impacts their test performance (AERA et al., 2014). Martiniello (2008) described this situation in the context of a mathematics assessment:

> The use of testing in education presupposes that a student's test score is an accurate reflection of her mastery of a particular content area. However, if the student is an [EL] and the math test includes questions the student might have trouble understanding, it is unknown whether the low score is due to the student's lack of mastery of the math content, limited English proficiency, or both. (p. 334)

Studies can be conducted to assess construct underrepresentation and the presence of construct-irrelevant variance as threats to valid assessment of ELs. In the next section, we explain how the AERA et al. (2014) *Standards* can be used as a research (validation) framework for evaluating the degree to which interpretations of ELs' performance on educational tests are valid for their intended purposes.

The *Standards* as a Validation Framework

The AERA et al. (2014) *Standards* describe test validation as a process of gathering and evaluating evidence that would support or refute the use of a test for a particular purpose. Kane (1992, 2006, 2013) described the validation process as developing a *validity argument*. This term is used in the *Standards* to emphasize the need to use both theory and research to defend the use of a test for a particular purpose. As described in the *Standards*, "A sound validity argument integrates various strands of evidence into a coherent account of the degree to which existing evidence and theory support the intended interpretation of test scores for specific uses (p. 21).

This excerpt illustrates that for test scores to be valid for their intended purposes, there should be a sound theory underlying test construction, quality control procedures should be followed throughout the test development process, and empirical studies should be conducted to support each test use and evaluate potential weaknesses or limitations of test scores for each use. To guide such research, the *Standards* classify validity evidence into five sources "that might be used in evaluating a proposed interpretation of test scores for a particular use" (AERA et al., 2014, p. 13). The sources are validity evidence based on (a) test content, (b) response processes, (c) internal structure, (d) relations to other variables, and (e) consequences of testing. Although the particular mix of evidence used to construct a validity argument will change depending on the particular testing purpose, all sources are relevant to our discussion of validating ELP and other academic assessments of ELs. Brief descriptions of each source are provided next.

Validity Evidence Based on Test Content

Validity evidence based on *test content* is particularly important for educational tests because the scores from these tests are typically interpreted with reference to a carefully defined domain of content (e.g., statewide mathematics curriculum). Validity evidence in this category includes "traditional" content validity studies and alignment studies that require independent subject matter experts (SMEs) to review and rate test items according to their content relevance, representativeness, or alignment to curricular objectives (Crocker, Miller, & Franks, 1989; Martone & Sireci, 2009), as well as practice (job) analyses in the case of employment, licensure, or certification tests. In assessing ELP, for example, evidence would be needed that the assessment adequately represents the type of linguistic knowledge and skills ELs need to navigate school contexts such as classroom instruction and discussion, assessments, homework, and other types of academic communication. For both content and ELP assessments, SMEs should confirm that the test adequately represents the targeted constructs.

Validity Evidence Based on Response Processes

Validity evidence based on *response processes* refers to "evidence concerning the fit between the construct and the detailed nature of performance or response actually engaged in by examinees" (AERA et al., 2014, p. 15). Such evidence includes interviewing students about their responses to the test items, statistical analysis of item response time data, and evaluation of the reasoning processes examinees use when completing the simulation (Messick, 1989).

Examples of validity studies focusing on response processes are studies that ask ELs to "think aloud" as they respond to test items flagged for being potentially biased against ELs (e.g., Martiniello, 2008). Another example involves an analysis of scoring ELs' responses to open-ended test items. For example, Kachchaf and Solano-Flores (2012) investigated whether scorers rated ELs' responses differently, based on the ethnic background and native language of the *scorers*. They found that certified bilingual teachers reliably scored ELs' responses to test items regardless of their native language (i.e., English as a native or second language). Thus, this study illustrates an example of evaluating the cognitive processes of the *scorers*.

Validity Evidence Based on Internal Structure

Validity evidence based on *internal structure* refers to statistical analysis of item and subscore data to investigate the primary and secondary (if any) dimensions measured by an assessment. Reliability estimation could also be categorized here, and would require evidence that the "scores" assigned to students are relatively consistent over samples of test items, and any classifications based on these scores (e.g., "pass" or "fail") are also consistent. Examples of studies in this area include evaluating whether the dimensionality of an assessment is consistent across ELs and non-ELs, and the degree to which classification decisions are equally reliable (consistent) across ELs and non-ELs. Analysis of "differential item functioning" (DIF), which is a statistical analysis to assess potential item bias, also falls under the internal structure category.

Validity studies focusing on internal structure evidence often focus on the number of statistical dimensions that are needed to characterize examinees' responses to items on an assessment, and how well those dimensions represent the dimensions hypothesized by the test developers. These types of studies have been applied to ELP assessments to determine whether the construct measured is a single dimension of language proficiency, or whether there are separate dimensions for each component of language. For example, Luecht and Ackerman (2007) found that a single dimension based on item response theory (IRT) was sufficient for calibrating students' responses to reading, writing, speaking, and listening items onto a single scale for the Oregon English Language Proficiency Assessment. However, other researchers looking at other ELP exams concluded that multidimensional, bifactor, or higher order models specifying different language components are more appropriate. For example, Sawaki, Stricker, and Oranje, (2009) found that a higher order model (with the four domains subsumed under general language ability) best fit the TOEFL iBT, and In'nami and Koizumi (2012) made the same conclusion for the TOEIC. Kuriakose (2011) found evidence to support a bifactor model for the English Language Development Assessment, which is a K–12 ELP assessment currently used in six U.S. states. In all three studies, these bifactor models were found to offer superior fit to a single-factor model using only general language proficiency.

Thus, validity evidence based on response processes can be used to investigate not just "Is this language assessment unidimensional?" but rather "What dimensional structure best fits this assessment?" These types of dimensionality studies are important for content assessments, too. Some validity studies on content assessments have evaluated the degree to which these assessments have the same dimensionality across subgroups of EL and non-EL students (e.g., Abedi, Lord, Hofstetter, & Baker, 2000).

Validity Evidence Based on Relations to Other Variables

Validity evidence based on *relations to other variables* refers to traditional forms of criterion-related validity evidence such as concurrent and predictive validity studies, as well as more comprehensive investigations of the relationships among test scores and other variables (e.g., Campbell & Fiske's, 1959, multitrait-multimethod studies). For example, some studies have looked at the relationship between ELs' scores on ELP assessments and on content area assessments (e.g., Parker, Louie, & O'Dwyer, 2009). Evidence in this category may also include analysis of group differences in test performance that are considered related to the construct measured (e.g., groups that differ with respect to the instruction received).

Several have used validity evidence based on relations to other variables to estimate the degree to which English proficiency accounts for variation in ELs' test performance on non-English proficiency tests. Pennock-Roman (2002), for example, used regression analysis to look at the degree to which English proficiency was related to performance on postgraduate admissions tests for a sample of 451 native Spanish-speaking students who had taken (a) English proficiency tests; (b) the Prueba de Admisio´n Para Estudios Graduados, a graduate school admissions test (administered in Spanish) that is used in Puerto Rico; and (c) the Graduate Records Exam (GRE) general test and subject tests in biology and psychology. Although she found the largest proportion of test score variance accounted for by English proficiency was for the GRE Verbal subtest (34%), and this variance might be considered construct-relevant, she also found that English proficiency accounted for 18% of the variance in these students' Psychology test scores, 17% of the variance in their Biology test scores, and 16% of the variance in their Analytical Reasoning test scores. The magnitude of this source of construct-irrelevant variance is similar to the proportion of variance accounted for in postgraduate GPA for these students and so represents a significant issue in interpreting the GRE scores for these students.

Another example of a validity study based on relations to other variables is by Zwick and Schlemer (2004), who evaluated the predictive validity of SAT scores for Latinos and Asian Americans at the University of Santa Barbara. Although not strictly a study of ELs, they acknowledged a "substantial number of Latino and Asian-American test takers are not native English speakers" (p. 6). In general, they found some ELs had freshman GPAs that were *over*predicted, but when adding SAT scores to the prediction equation, the overprediction was greatly reduced. They concluded SAT scores "played an important role in predicting the freshman grades of language minority students" (p. 14), thus supporting the validity of SAT scores for these students.

Validity Evidence Based on Consequences of Testing

The fifth source of validity evidence stipulated in the AERA et al. (2014) *Standards*, evidence based on *consequences of testing*, refers to evaluation of the intended and unintended consequences associated with an assessment. Examples include investigations of adverse impact, evaluation of the effects of testing on employee productivity, and evaluation of the effects of testing on issues such as employee motivation and satisfaction (Lane, 2014). A key issue for ELs in this category is the degree to which reclassification decisions based on EL proficiency assessments lead to better educational outcomes for ELs.

As a student population generally at risk for failure, ELs deserve an ongoing commitment from the research field to identify and evaluate any negative consequences, intended or unintended, that may stem from the design or use of content or language assessments. Valuable research has been conducted on aspects of assessment design that may have differential consequences for ELs on both language and content assessment including item format (Currie & Chiramanee, 2010; In'nami & Koizumi, 2009), subscore calculation (De la Torre, Song, & Hong, 2011), language structure and dimensionality (In'nami & Koizumi, 2012; Kuriakose, 2011; Römhild, Kenyon, & MacGregor, 2011; Sawaki et al. 2009), and different measurement models (McNamara & Knoch, 2012; Wilson & Moore, 2011; Zhang, 2010).

In addition, the unique high-stakes context of redesignation for ELs, including its potential to affect instruction and OTL, is particularly important to evaluate in terms of its consequences for these students. For example, if ELs who have been redesignated continue to lag behind peers who have never been ELs (a common finding in the literature; e.g., Kim & Herman, 2012), does this mean that ELs are exiting prematurely or that their continued lag is due to a lack of access to challenging, high-quality content instruction during the time they spend as ELs? We are not aware of any studies that empirically explored this question.

Carroll and Bailey (2014) demonstrated that different types of classification models (e.g., compensatory, conjunctive, or some combination of the two) can have profound effects on which students exit versus remain classified as ELs. Furthermore, they also found that certain classification criteria for redesignation may identify even native speakers with high scores on ELA and math assessments as ELs who are not ready to exit! Given the impact remaining an EL may have on students' access to challenging courses, such findings are concerning, and indicate the potential negative consequences of (lack of) redesignation that should be routinely investigated. Whether the redesignation decision is made using ELP assessment scores only, or in combination with content assessment scores, it is important to collect evidence that students who remain ELs *and* students who are redesignated as former ELs do not face adverse impact from such decisions.

Proposing and Evaluating a Validity Argument

In the previous section, we described the AERA et al.'s (2014) five sources of validity evidence and provided some examples of validity studies related to the assessment of ELs that have been conducted using these different types of evidence. From our discussion of validity thus far, the following principles should be clear:

1. Validity refers to the use of a test for a particular purpose. Thus, what needs to be validated is the *use* or *interpretations* of test scores, not the test itself.
2. The process of validation can be organized using the *Standards'* five sources of validity evidence.
3. In addition to gathering and analyzing evidence to support test use, potential test *misuse*, or unintended negative consequences, should be investigated.

Drawing from these principles, in this section, we describe the importance of going beyond a single validity study to develop a comprehensive body of research that could be used to support the use of a test for ELs for a particular purpose. This synthesis of validity information can be called a "validity argument."

Kane (2013) proposed developing an "interpretation and use argument" to (a) clearly delineate how test scores are to be interpreted and used and (b) identify and prioritize the validity studies needed to support it. Sireci (2013) suggested using the purposes of a testing program explicitly stated by the testing agency as the interpretation and use argument, and also suggested using the *Standards'* five sources of validity evidence as the organizing structure for validation. Regardless of the form the validity argument takes, the key principles for validation are to (a) focus the validation on how test scores are used and (b) gather evidence to evaluate the appropriateness of such use. To support the use of a test for a particular purpose, evidence in the argument should clearly indicate the test is realizing its goals, is producing the intended outcomes, and does not result in unintended negative consequences. In the next section, we pick a specific use of an educational test and show how the five sources of validity evidence can be combined into a validity argument.

An Example of a Validation Framework for an ELP Assessment

As mentioned earlier, under NCLB, states must assess the English proficiency of ELs to determine when they have the English skills necessary to succeed in school. This testing purpose might be described as follows: "to determine whether ELs have mastered the English knowledge and skills necessary to fully participate in classrooms where English is the medium of instruction." Given a clear testing purpose, we can establish a framework for developing the validity argument to support the use of this test for that purpose.

Using the AERA et al. (2014) *Standards'* five sources of validity evidence as our validation framework, we determined the following sources of validity evidence are required: validity evidence based on (a) test content, to ensure the relevant language knowledge and skills were appropriately represented on the test; (b) internal structure, to ensure that the dimensionality of the data (i.e., students' responses to the test items) is consistent with the construct as defined for the purpose of the test *and* that the scores and classification decisions were reliable; (c) relations to other variables, to ensure the test scores were related to other measures of English proficiency, (d) testing consequences, to ensure that students who were classified as proficient in English by the test were actually prepared for instruction in English-only classrooms (and vice versa); and (e) response processes, to ensure students understand what is required of them on constructed-response items. Evidence based on test content, internal structure, and relations to other variables, together with evidence based on response processes, could also be used to identify potential sources of construct-irrelevant variance (e.g., inappropriate linguistic complexity).

Validity Evidence Based on Test Content

What validity studies based on test content could be conducted to support the use of the ELP test for reclassification decisions? The first evidence needed is to confirm that the construct, or domain to be tested, is appropriately defined. For an ELP test, this would amount to defining "English language proficiency" in a way that is appropriate to support decisions about a student's preparedness to participate in classrooms where English is the language of instruction. One way to provide such evidence is to have external SMEs review and discuss the definition proposed by the test developers and reach consensus regarding its appropriateness, given the testing purpose.

Additional validity evidence based on test content for this ELP assessment would be needed to confirm the test represents the domain definition. To collect such evidence, English language SMEs could be recruited to participate in an alignment study. These SMEs would be asked to review (a) the ELP standards developed by the state or consortium of states (sometimes also referred to as English language development [ELD] standards), (b) the test specifications for the ELP assessment, and (c) the items comprising the assessment.

Although there are options for conducting such studies, a typical study in this area might proceed as follows. First, the SMEs could be asked how well the test specifications capture the linguistic knowledge and skills stipulated in the ELP/ELD standards. Separate ratings could be gathered for subdomains (e.g., expressive language, the language of mathematics, writing), along with open-ended comments regarding their impressions of how well the test specifications are congruent with the ELP/ELD standards. Next, the SMEs would be asked to review test items and rate the degree to which each item adequately measures its intended proficiency benchmark. There are many different methods for structuring this task, such as alignment-based methods (e.g., Bhola, Impara, & Buckendahl, 2003; Martone & Sireci, 2009) or those based on more traditional content validity studies (e.g., Crocker et al., 1989; Sireci, 1998). The data from these ratings can be aggregated across items to evaluate the degree to which language proficiency, as defined by the ELP/ELD standards, is adequately represented on the assessment.

Validity evidence based on test content can also be used to evaluate the appropriateness of the cut scores that are used to classify students as being sufficiently proficient in English. "Item mapping" studies that would illustrate how well students who are "just above" the cut score perform on items near the cut score fall into this category. By reviewing the knowledge and skills needed to succeed on these items vis-à-vis the performance-level descriptions of English proficiency, SMEs can help evaluate the degree to which the cut score is reflecting the intended level of performance on the test.

Validity Evidence Based on Internal Structure

What types of validity evidence based on internal structure would be needed to support use of this ELP assessment for reclassification decisions? We believe two types of studies are critical. The first type refers to the reliability of the (re)classification decision. The second type of study refers to the dimensionality of the assessment.

With respect to reliability, we note that traditional estimates of the reliability of a test scores are insufficient whenever classification decisions are made. That is, rather than asking whether a student would receive a similar *score* on the test, we must ask whether a student would receive the same English proficiency *classification*. Thus, rather than an internal consistency reliability estimate, studies are needed to estimate *decision consistency*.

A concept similar to decision consistency is decision accuracy, which is the extent to which students' classifications based on their observed test scores are congruent with their *true* classifications, with true classifications based on simulation studies or a split-half estimate. Most statewide testing programs provide estimates of decision accuracy and consistency based on classical methods (e.g., Livingston & Lewis, 1995) or IRT methods (Lee, 2008; Rudner, 2001, 2004). Estimates of .80 or above, for example, would indicate that most students would receive the same classification on retesting, which would support use of the test for such decision making.

With respect to dimensionality studies, evidence is needed that the hypothesized dimensionality of the ELP assessment is supported by analysis of students' responses to the test items. For example, if separate scores are computed for the listening, reading, writing, and speaking domains, one would expect separate dimensions or factors to emerge in factor analysis (or multidimensional scaling analysis) of the data. On the other hand, if items measuring these different domains are calibrated onto a single scale, and only one score is reported, then one would expect a strong, dominant factor to underlie students' responses to the items.

Validity Evidence Based on Relations to Other Variables

For the ELP assessment in our example to be seen as valid for reclassifying ELs, evidence that scores from the assessment were positively correlated with other measures of English proficiency would be helpful. Although it is difficult to find "perfect" external measures of English proficiency, there are several options such as grades assigned by teachers, scores from other English proficiency assessments, scores from "can-do" statements completed by students or teachers, and independent observations or interviews of ELs conducted by language experts. It is important to note, however, that although it may seem natural to use ELA performance as an external variable for comparison, the ELA domain is distinct from ELP and the two should not be treated interchangeably. For instance, a student's inability to define the word "metaphor" or restate an author's argument would be grounds for judging the student to be nonproficient in ELA, but it would not necessarily suggest that the student is not proficient in English.

Given that the ELP test in our example has a cut score that signifies English proficiency, evidence that students who meet this proficiency standard actually have the skills implied by the standard is needed. Kane (1994) described this type of evidence as "external" validity evidence for standard setting. To gather this type of evidence, the student classifications based on the ELP assessment would need to be related to other measures of English proficiency by (a) testing for group differences (e.g., do proficient and below-proficient students differ significantly on the external measure), (b) cross-tabulating proficiency classifications based on the ELP test with classifications based on other measures and testing for congruence, or (c) both approaches.

One way of evaluating cut scores for ELP assessments is to evaluate the performance of ELs before and after redesignation. This kind of study can determine whether students who are meeting the "proficiency" cut score are performing in such a way that supports the conclusion that English no longer impedes their academic performance. Robinson (2011) argued that the sign of an appropriately set redesignation threshold is one that shows neither a bump nor a drop in content performance for ELs before and after they transition. A drop in content performance would suggest that the redesignation threshold may be too low, and a bump would suggest that students should have been reclassified sooner. To this point, both Robinson (2011) and Grissom (2004) found evidence of what Grissom referred to as "an overprotected group of EL students" (p. 30) in the California school system, who were meeting the state criteria for redesignation on the content assessment but were not meeting ELP performance standards and therefore were not transitioning. Such a finding suggests the cut score for the ELP system should be reevaluated.

As another approach to setting and evaluating cut scores, the U.S. Department of Education (2012) recently proposed three quantitative methods that states could use in concert to identify and triangulate an appropriate redesignation criteria for ELs, using both content and language assessments. All three methods focus on identifying the point at which language performance ceases to predict or correlate with content performance beyond the level of chance. This approach is based on the premise that language may always play *some* role in ELs content performance but that redesignation should occur at the point where knowing a student's language score is no longer sufficient to predict the student's content performance. In other words, when language does not predict content performance beyond the level of chance, we have reason to believe that the content performance score reflects something different from linguistic proficiency.

The first method is to use decision consistency analysis to identify the ELP score that maximizes "consistent" EL classifications, which are defined as scoring either proficient or above on both assessments, or below proficient on both assessments. Thus, this method seeks to minimize the number of students who score proficient on either the ELP or content assessment but not both. The second method proposes logistic regression to set performance standards, where past language performance is used to predict a performance threshold above which ELs have at least a 50% chance of scoring proficient on the content assessment. The third model is a descriptive box plot analysis to identify the ELP level at which 50% or more of ELs earn proficient content scores. For all three methods—which, to reiterate, the authors recommend using in concert, rather than picking only one—the focus is on examining the language-content relationship across the performance continuum to pinpoint the threshold at which the relationship has been reduced enough so that content performance for an EL can support the same quality of interpretations that it has for native speakers.

Validity Evidence Based on Testing Consequences

ELP tests are designed to help ELs by ensuring that they have the English skills necessary to succeed in English-only instruction. This laudable goal assumes that without the test, many ELs would be placed in classrooms where they would be unable to keep pace with the instruction due to their lack of English proficiency. It also assumes students who reach the proficiency classification on the ELP test will be able to handle instruction in English-only classrooms. Gathering validity evidence based on testing consequences involves evaluating these assumptions, and others. For example, are the ELs who are classified as proficient able to follow instruction in English? Are those who did not pass the test being denied a quality education? Would they benefit from instruction in English if they were not required to pass the ELP test? Do teachers in English-only classrooms feel more confident teaching ELs who demonstrated proficiency on the assessment? Answers to these questions could be gathered by surveying teachers, observing students in classrooms, surveying parents, and tracking classroom performance and dropout rates of ELs with different levels of performance on the assessment.

For ELs, questions about OTL are particularly important to explore. Several studies have found what may ultimately hold some ELs back from transitioning is not their language performance but their content performance (Grissom, 2004; Robinson, 2011). Other studies have found that ELs in higher grades may have a harder time transitioning out of EL status or meeting academic content standards once they do (American Institutes for Research, 2013; Massachusetts Department of Elementary and Secondary Education, 2012; Robinson, 2011). Validity studies based on testing consequences would explore causes for these findings. For example, these findings may stem from inadequate language instruction for older ELs (e.g., they are not being taught language that is rigorous enough to help them meet the demands of academic content in higher grade levels), or perhaps they are due to scheduling restrictions or teacher capacity that prevent ELs from enrolling in challenging content courses. Whatever the cause, such findings warrant further research, as their overall effect is to create achievement gaps between ELs and non-ELs.

Validity Evidence Based on Response Processes

When test items are developed, test developers assume students use specific cognitive skills when responding to the items. Validity studies focusing on examinees' response processes evaluate this assumption. Think-aloud protocols are sometimes used where students explain what they are thinking when responding to test items. Cognitive interviews, where specific questions are asked of students based on their responses to test their understanding of the task (Padilla & Benitez, 2014) are also used. In addition, analysis of omit rates, particularly on constructed-response items, can be conducted. Some recent research has shown that many ELs tend to omit constructed-response items (Sireci, Wells, & Hu, 2014), which suggests they are not comprehending what is being asked, or have some other cognitive difficulty with such items.

Summary of Validation Example

To demonstrate how a validation framework could be developed for a test used for ELs, we selected an English proficiency test with a specific purpose. We used the AERA et al. (2014) *Standards'* five sources of validity evidence to illustrate the framework and the types of studies that could be conducted to develop a validity argument to support the use of the test for that purpose. The framework and studies are illustrated in Table 2. Of course, the elements in Table 2 would change as the purpose of the assessment changed, and so the entries are only examples.

It is important to note that we only provided an example based on an ELP assessment. A validity argument for an academic content assessment would involve different studies focusing on the different purposes those assessments serve. With respect to the appropriateness of academic content assessments for ELs, the validity research should include evaluating the appropriateness of the content and scoring procedures

TABLE 2
Validity Framework and Validity Studies for Hypothetical ELP Test

Testing Purpose: *Determine whether students have sufficient skills in English . . .*

Source of Validity Evidence	Sample Validity Studies
Test content	(a) Subject matter experts review curriculum frameworks, test specifications, and test items; rate items for congruence or alignment; (b) item mapping studies to evaluate cut scores
Internal structure	(a) estimates of decision consistency and decision accuracy, (b) dimensionality assessment
Relations to other variables	(a) correlations of ELP test scores with other measures of English proficiency, (b) congruence of ELP classifications with those based on other measures, (c) Differences across students grouped by English proficiency on other measures
Testing consequences	(a) surveys of teachers, (b) classroom observations, (c) analysis of ELs' performance over time
(Response processes)	(Optional. Not considered required for *this* purpose, but could supplement other studies.)

Note. EL = English learner; ELP = English language proficient.

for ELs, as well as the invariance of the dimensionality across EL and non-EL populations (among other studies).

VALIDITY ISSUES IN TEST CONSTRUCTION

Up to this point, we have discussed validity issues inherent in testing ELs, described a validation framework for evaluating the validity of interpretations of ELs' test scores for specific purposes, and summarized some of the validity research in this area. In this section, we focus on what can be done to facilitate validity in the assessment of ELs *before* the test is administered, rather than evaluate the validity after the fact. Specifically, we focus on steps test developers can take to design tests with the needs and unique characteristics of ELs in mind. These steps involve (a) understanding the complexities within the EL population of students to be tested, (b) incorporating the principles of universal test design (UTD), (c) considering linguistic complexity and diversity in item development, and (d) performing qualitative and statistical analyses of test items to identify any problems before the operational tests are assembled. The steps described here should be relevant for any type of assessment—language assessment or content assessment—but they are particularly important for academic content assessments. This is because ELP assessments are essentially designed for ELs (only), whereas content assessments are designed for the general student population, within which ELs are a small subgroup with special circumstances.

In addition to the AERA et al. (2014) *Standards*, there are many guidelines for considering ELs throughout the test development process, many of which are documents prepared by conscientious testing programs. Examples include the *Guidelines for the Assessment of English Learners* (Educational Testing Service, 2009) and the *Guidelines for Accessibility of English Language Learners* (Young, Pitoniak, King, & Ayad, 2012). Many of the issues we discuss in this section and the guidelines we recommend are consistent with these and other internal documents developed by test developers to promote universal design and fairness for their assessments.

Understanding Diversity Within EL Populations

Earlier, we stressed the importance of understanding the cultural, linguistic, and socioeconomic differences that exist within EL populations. In addition, it is important for test developers to ascertain ELs' literacy in their native languages. For ELs with low or no literacy in their native language, test accommodations such as translated booklets or bilingual dictionaries are not likely to be helpful. Another variable of interest is acculturation. ELs who are relatively new to the United States, or who live within isolated communities, may be unfamiliar with the stakes associated with educational tests and the item formats used in the United States

For these reasons, we recommend that practice tests be developed and targeted to students who are unfamiliar with taking standardized assessments, particularly tests that involve multiple-choice items, use of the computer, or other administration conditions with which they may be unfamiliar. For ELs, practice tests that include directions in multiple languages may be helpful. By taking these practice tests, ELs will better understand the testing experience and how they are expected to respond to test items. Therefore, it may be advisable to require all students to be thoroughly familiar with the practice tests before taking the operational assessments.

Incorporating the Principles of Universal Test Design

UTD refers to the development of tests that are more attuned to the differing needs of subgroups of examinees (Thompson, Blount, & Thurlow, 2002). Essentially, UTD calls for test construction practices focused on eliminating construct-irrelevant variance and more flexible test administration conditions that would make the provision of test accommodations for ELs and students with disabilities unnecessary. For example, "pop-up" glossaries, definitions of key words, screen-reading software, and other accessibility features could be provided to all test takers. Many accommodations designed for ELs (discussed later) could benefit *all* students taking a test, just as closed-captioned TV, which was initially designed for deaf/hard-of-hearing individuals, is now commonly used by the general public.

UTD in test development also refers to identifying and eliminating sources of construct-irrelevant variance. Actions test developers can take include qualitative analyses such as sensitivity review, and quantitative analyses such as DIF analyses, which are discussed in the next section.

Performing Qualitative and Statistical Reviews of Items

Qualitative analysis of items and other test material can go a long way toward identifying potential sources of construct-irrelevant variance that may impede valid assessment of ELs. This type of analysis is typically called *sensitivity review*, which refers to the process of having a diverse group of professionals review tests to flag material that may be problematic for some test takers such as ELs (Ramsey, 1993; Sireci & Mullane, 1994). Sensitivity reviewers should review preliminary test items, stimuli, and directions for material that may (a) be construed as offensive to ELs, (b) portray ELs unfavorably (e.g., in stereotypical fashion), (c) be unnecessarily advantageous or disadvantageous to ELs, or (d) be unfamiliar to ELs.

Another issue pertinent to sensitivity review is the *inclusion* of the types of texts and contexts ELs are likely to experience outside the classroom. Many math and reading tests use stimuli such as tables, figures, graphs, and reading passages. These passages should include information and text that would be familiar to students of different backgrounds, such as ELs. When people's names are used in items and passages, including culturally diverse names, such as Juana and Ahmed, may go a long way in illustrating consideration of diversity within the population of test takers.

Although not related to qualitative review of items, another way test developers can illustrate they are aware of the linguistic diversity within the EL population is to include item writers who are not native speakers of English in the pool of item writers from which test items are drawn. Nonnative speakers of English could also be included in item review studies such as content review and alignment studies. Of course, these item writers and reviewers would need to be proficient in English and qualify as SMEs for the academic areas measured.

With respect to statistical analyses, DIF analyses can promote the validity of assessments for ELs by identifying items that might be biased against them (Hauger & Sireci, 2008; Lane & Leventhal, 2015, this volume). The goal of a DIF analysis is to identify items that "function differentially" for different groups of students such as ELs and non-ELs. To understand DIF, three related concepts must be distinguished: item impact, DIF, and item bias. Item impact refers to a significant group difference on an item, for example, when a higher proportion of non-ELs correctly answers an item compared to ELs. Item impact may stem from true differences in academic performance between ELs and non-ELs, or may be due to item bias. DIF is a statistical observation that involves *matching* test takers from different groups on the proficiency measured and then looking for performance differences on an item. Test takers of equal proficiency who belong to different groups should respond similarly to a given test item. If they do not, the item is said to function differently across groups and is classified as a DIF item (Holland & Wainer, 1993). Item bias is present when an item has been statistically flagged for DIF *and the reason for the DIF is traced to a factor irrelevant to the construct the test is intended to measure.*

For a DIF item to be considered biased against ELs, a characteristic of the item that is unfair to ELs would need to be identified. Thus, a determination of item bias requires a subjective judgment that the statistical observation (i.e., DIF) is due to some aspect of an item that is irrelevant to the construct measured. We believe DIF analyses for ELs should be part of standard test development procedures for educational tests involving ELs and items flagged for DIF should be reviewed to see if they should be revised or eliminated. As Martiniello (2008) and Padilla and Benitez (2014) illustrated, think-aloud protocols and cognitive interviews can be conducted to help understand whether items flagged for DIF may be biased against ELs.

It is important to note, however, that to do quantitative analyses such as DIF requires adequate sample sizes of ELs. Therefore, whenever possible, test developers should strive to include representative samples of ELs in pilot studies that form the statistical foundation from which operational tests are created.

VALIDITY ISSUES IN TEST ACCOMMODATIONS FOR ELS

In the previous section, we focused on test development considerations for facilitating the validity of interpretations of test scores for ELs. However, conscientious test development is not likely to lead to assessments that are valid for all ELs and so other methods for facilitating validity should be considered. One method is the provision of test accommodations, which is particularly applicable to academic content assessments (e.g., to mitigate the role of language on assessments where this is not the focus).

One method for addressing the problem of English proficiency introducing construct-irrelevant variance in students' test performance is to provide adjustments to the testing situation that might reduce the linguistic barrier. These adjustments are called *accommodations* and represent changes to the test content or test administration conditions that deviate from standard testing conditions. Test accommodations, such as providing extra time or a large-print copy of a test booklet, have long been proposed for students with disabilities. However, given the difficult problems in assessing ELs' academic performance, they have also been used to facilitate valid assessment of ELs. The fact that both the Smarter Balanced and Partnership for the Assessment of Readiness for College and Career (PARCC) assessment consortia have developed accommodations guidelines suggests this practice is likely to persevere for the foreseeable future (PARCC, 2013; Smarter Balanced Assessment Consortium, 2013).

Different types of test accommodations are typically classified into one of four categories: *presentation, setting, timing,* or *response.* Rivera, Collum, Willner, and Sia (2006) and Pennock-Roman and Rivera (2011) classified accommodations for ELs into two categories—direct linguistic support and indirect linguistic support. Direct linguistic support accommodations typically fall under the "presentation" category and represent changes to the test content, such as translation of test components (e.g., directions, items, both) and simplification of text. These types of accommodations are more likely to be granted to ELs on academic content assessments but not on ELP assessments. Indirect linguistic support involves accommodations to test administration conditions refer to setting (e.g., separate testing location) and timing (e.g., extended time) accommodations. Indirect linguistic support accommodations are considered appropriate for both ELP assessments and academic content assessments because they do not interfere with the measurement of English proficiency by providing direct linguistic support. Other accommodations include allowing ELs to provide their responses to items in a nonstandard way, such as responding in their native language. Depending on the construct measured (e.g., "Is writing in English part of the construct measured?"), such accommodations may not be allowed on ELP or other assessments.

In a review of state assessment accommodation policies for ELs, Willner, Rivera, and Acosta (2008) counted 104 different types of accommodations offered to ELs. Of these, the direct linguistic supports included simplified English, provision of various types of dictionaries (e.g., commercial, customized, bilingual) and various forms of reading test material aloud, translation of test material (e.g., items, directions, entire test, dual-language booklets), and responding in the student's native language. They found the most common accommodations given were (a) extended time, (b) provision of commercial dictionaries, and (c) read-aloud of test items. However, it is important to note that their review, and others on test accommodations for ELs, focused on accommodations for academic content assessments, not ELP assessments.

The provision of accommodations to standardized testing conditions is seen as one way of promoting access to a test for examinees for whom standard testing conditions may impede their performance. Shepard, Taylor, and Betebenner (1998), for example, found that when test accommodations were provided to ELs on a math test, the participation rate for ELs was about 11% higher than on a comparable test offered in the same state without accommodations.

Although accommodations might improve access for ELs, whenever standard test administration conditions are altered, there is a chance the construct measured is also altered. Thus, where feasible, the AERA et al. (2014) *Standards* encourage researchers to gather evidence to evaluate whether the construct measured is changed by the accommodations, and whether such alterations affect score interpretations.

Several studies have been conducted to evaluate the degree to which accommodations for ELs improve their performance on standardized tests, and whether they may have altered the construct measured. Before reviewing these studies, we first describe some direct linguistic support test accommodations that have been designed to improve measurement of ELs' academic proficiencies. Understanding what these accommodations are is necessary for understanding the literature in this area.

Test Translation/Adaption

The most substantial accommodation for ELs that represents direct linguistic support is translating (adapting)[4] the test from one language to other languages. Such translation may involve adapting an existing test from one language into another or simultaneous development of the test in two or more languages (Solano-Flores, Trumbull, & Nelson-Barber, 2002). In some cases, "dual-language" test booklets may be created where test material is presented in two languages in the same booklet (often side-by-side; see Duncan et al., 2005). The logic behind test translation is this: If language proficiency is not part of the construct measured, we can best assess the construct by using the students' most dominant language. Therefore, translation is permitted only on academic content assessments that are not designed to measure an aspect of English proficiency.

Stansfield (2003) pointed out that NCLB required states to assess ELs using "assessments in the language and form most likely to yield accurate data on what such students know and can do in academic content areas, until such students have achieved English language proficiency" (NCLB, 2002, cited in Stansfield, 2003, p. 203). Currently, about 14 states allow some form of translation of their NCLB assessments (Sireci, Rios, & Powers, in press), but only in math and science, because translation of ELA tests would represent a change in the construct the test is measuring.

In reviewing the literature on test translation as an accommodation for ELs, Abedi, Hofstetter, and Lord (2004) and Pennock-Roman and Rivera (2011) concluded that native language versions of tests should only be used with ELs of low English proficiency who are *instructed* in their native language. This conclusion is similar to a common guideline for providing accommodations to students with disabilities—that is, accommodations provided on tests should match the accommodations provided for instruction. However, Solano-Flores and Li (2009) cautioned that translation may actually introduce construct-irrelevant variance due to differences in dialects and other variations within the language into which the test was translated.

Solano-Flores (2012) developed a test translation framework for the Smarter Balanced Assessment Consortium, designed to provide guidance for the process of translating their math assessments into Spanish. His framework emphasized the importance of approaching translation as part of the test development process, and incorporating the judgments of experts from multiple areas in making translation decisions to maximize the validity and comparability of translated forms and items. He identified four acceptable types of translation as accommodations for ELs on mathematics tests: Test Version in the Native Language, Side-by-Side Bilingual Version of the Test, Directions Translated Into Native Language, and Bilingual Glossary. He concluded the use of carefully constructed bilingual glossaries, used in the pop-up format, was the most promising translation accommodation currently available. However, he emphasized that the utility of this accommodation hinges on the quality of the translations provided in the glossary.

Linguistic Simplification

Another method suggested for providing direct linguistic support accommodations for ELs is linguistic simplification (also called linguistic modification or simplified English), which involves reducing the language load of items and other test materials in order to reduce the degree to which proficiency in the language of the test will influence test performance. Although there is some support for this practice (e.g.,

Pennock-Roman & Rivera, 2011), we note that standard item writing guidelines (e.g., Haladyna & Rodriguez, 2014) call for minimizing verbosity and matching the language load of items to the characteristics of the examinee population. Thus, we believe linguistic simplification should be part of the standard test development process, rather than being thought of as an accommodation, and items that go beyond a reasonable language load should be flagged and corrected via sensitivity review. As Abedi (2001) stated, "Modifying test questions to reduce unnecessary language complexity should be a priority in the development and improvement of all large-scale assessment programs" (p. 106). It is possible that through better test development processes, linguistic simplification will disappear as an accommodation for ELs.

Dictionaries and Glossaries

Another direct linguistic accommodation provided to ELs is the provision of dictionaries or glossaries to explain key terms on the test. Sometimes commercial dictionaries are provided in English and other times bilingual dictionaries are used. A more tailored version of this accommodation is a customized dictionary or glossary created for the testing situation that includes only key terms within the test that are targeted for translation or definition. "Glosses" represent a 21st-century version of this accommodation. Glosses are underlined or highlighted words or phrases on a computer screen over which an examinee can slide his or her their cursor to have a "pop-up" definition, translation, or visual cue in order to understand what the word or phrase means. UTD could be used to make glosses available to all examinees, thereby reducing the need to provide special accommodations for ELs.

EVALUATING TEST ACCOMMODATIONS FOR ELS

In the previous section, we discussed the types of accommodations that have been provided or suggested for ELs. There is an emerging literature evaluating the effectiveness and validity of these accommodations. In this section, we describe some of this literature, as well as some recent guidelines for providing test accommodations for ELs that are based on this research.

Research on Test Accommodations for ELs

The accommodation classifications made by Abedi and Ewers (2013) were based in part on reviews of empirical studies evaluating the effectiveness and validity of accommodations. In addition to their work, there have been at least four literature reviews on the effectiveness of test accommodations for ELs (see also Lane & Leventhal, 2015, this volume). In chronological order they are Sireci, Li, and Scarpati (2003), Kieffer, Lesaux, Rivera, and Francis (2009), Pennock-Roman and Rivera (2011), and Li and Suen (2012). The three latter reviews included meta-analysis of the reviewed studies. All reviews pertained to accommodations on academic content assessments, not ELP assessments. In this section, we describe these meta-analyses and some more recent studies that investigated the validity of accommodations for ELs.

Sireci et al. (2003) reviewed 12 studies on test accommodations for ELs focusing on the *interaction hypothesis*, which states that test accommodations will lead to improved test scores for students who need the accommodation but not for students who do not need the accommodation (Malouf, 2001, cited in Koenig & Bachman, 2004; Shepard et al., 1998). The accommodations investigated across the 12 studies were linguistic modification, bilingual dictionaries, customized dictionaries, test translation, extra time, and read-aloud. Seven of the 12 studies used an experimental design that randomly assigned accommodations to ELs and non-ELs, and 11 of the studies evaluated the interaction hypothesis. The results from only 4 of the studies supported the interaction hypothesis. Sireci et al. (2003) concluded that although the results across all studies were equivocal, "some accommodations, such as linguistic modification and provision of a dictionary or glossary, show promise" (p. 59).

The Kieffer et al. (2009) meta-analysis also supported the promise of dictionary and glossary accommodations. Their meta-analysis focused on 11 studies and seven accommodations—simplified English, English dictionary or glossary, bilingual dictionary or glossary, extra time, Spanish version, dual-language items, and dual-language booklet. They investigated the "effectiveness" and "validity" of each accommodation, with effectiveness defined as ELs exhibiting higher test scores on the accommodated assessment, and validity defined as the accommodation providing no improvement for non-ELs. They concluded that all seven accommodations passed the "validity" criterion, but only English dictionary or glossary demonstrated nonnegligible effectiveness.

Pennock-Roman and Rivera (2011) conducted a subsequent meta-analysis, where they reviewed 14 studies, including many of those reviewed by Kieffer et al. (2009). In their meta-analysis, they distinguished between low–English-proficient ELs and moderate–English-proficient ELs, where possible. They found that four of five direct linguistic accommodations—"pop-up" glossaries, dual-language test booklet, English dictionary/glossary coupled with extended time, and bilingual glossary coupled with extended time—were effective in improving the performance of ELs. They noted that extended time was needed to realize the effectiveness of any paper-based dictionaries or glossaries, and they hypothesized this extra time was needed to navigate the extra paper materials. As they described, "Most accommodations did improve the test performance of ELLs beyond a trivial level *when students were allowed sufficient time to work with the extra printed materials provided*" (Pennock-Roman & Rivera, 2011, pp. 21–22).

Pennock-Roman and Rivera (2011) also noted the lack of effectiveness for simplified English in general, but they found some evidence of its effectiveness for ELs of moderate English proficiency. They recommended that future studies evaluate accommodations for ELs who have different levels of English proficiency. They also noted a lack of effectiveness for the "read-aloud" accommodation, even though it was used in 40 states at the time of their study. With respect to translating a test into Spanish, they concluded,

This accommodation shows promise and the highest effect sizes of all, but only when assigned appropriately—for students with literacy skills in their native language, who have had instruction on the subject matter in their native language, and who have low English proficiency. (p. 21)

Li and Suen (2012) analyzed the results from 19 studies (involving 85 effect sizes) to evaluate the effectiveness of accommodations for ELs, using hierarchical linear modeling to test whether other variables mediated the effects of the accommodation. Level 1 in their model gathered information on the variability of effect sizes across studies, and Level 2 used characteristics of the studies to explain the variation. Overall, they found a small, positive effect size for accommodations (about .16 standard deviations). The only study characteristic that accounted for significant variation was ELP, with a larger effect of accommodations for ELs of lower English proficiency (about .6 standard deviations).

In addition to these literature reviews and meta-analyses, there have also been additional studies on the use and effectiveness of specific accommodations for ELs. For example, Wolf, Kim, and Kao (2012) evaluated the effects of read-aloud and glossary accommodations on math tests in two states. They used an experimental design where the accommodation conditions were randomly assigned to ELs and non-ELs. In one state, the accommodations did not have any effect for either group. In the other state, the read-aloud accommodation led to improved performance for the ELs, with an overall effect size (Cohen's *d*) of .65. Using think-aloud protocols on a subset of students they found that 50% to 60% of the students did not even use the glossaries that were provided. Therefore, accommodation *use* appears to be an important variable to study to better understand the effectiveness of accommodations.

Crotts and Sireci (2014) reached a similar conclusion in evaluating accommodation use in a statewide experiment on accommodations for ELs on history and math tests. Although they found many ELs did not use available accommodations, ELs' accommodation use was statistically significantly greater than non-ELs. They also noted that use of the computer-based accommodations they studied (pop-up glossaries and sticker paraphrasing tools) required more testing time. They concluded that when direct linguistic accommodations are provided to ELs but are not used by them, interpreting their scores may be problematic.

Research-Based Guidelines on Test Accommodations for ELs

In a commissioned study by the Smarter Balanced Assessment Consortium, Abedi and Ewers (2013) convened a panel of five experts on accommodations for both students with disabilities and ELs to conduct a systematic review of accommodations research and provide recommendations regarding the appropriateness and validity of different types of accommodations. Based on a review of the literature and their expertise, each panelist rated accommodations on two dimensions: (a) whether the accommodation would alter the construct measured by the test and (b) whether the accommodation would make the test more accessible for the students who would need it. They also determined whether each accommodation might improve the performance of *all* students (not just ELs) in a way that would not affect the construct. If so, they listed the accommodation as "access" and concluded that the accommodation improved access for all students by reducing construct-irrelevant variance.

In Table 3, we present a summary of Abedi and Ewers's (2013) classifications of the accommodations they recommended be considered for ELs. They identified 19 potential accommodations and classified them according to "risk" (the degree to which the accommodation might change the construct measured) and "access." Although Abedi and Ewers classified the 19 accommodations in Table 3 as appropriate to use for ELs, they noted that some were at risk of altering the construct measured, and therefore, based on a review of the literature and the opinion of the panel of experts, they classified them according to such risk (indicated in the second column of Table 3). Of these 19 accommodations, 8 were considered to have no risk, 7 were considered to have minor risk, 2 were considered to have moderate risk, and 2 were considered high risk. Nine of the 19 accommodations were seen as providing access (i.e., reduce construct-irrelevant variance) for both ELs and non-ELs.

Assigning Accommodations to ELs

The research reviewed in the previous section indicates that in many situations accommodations can make assessment scores more valid representations of what ELs know and can do. The literature reviews, meta-analyses, and classifications of Abedi and Ewers (2013) help us understand the types of accommodations that are most likely to be effective for removing linguistic barriers on an assessment while staying true to the construct measured. However, more important than making accommodations available is the assignment of particular accommodations to specific students. Kopriva, Emick, Hipolito-Delgado, and Cameron (2007) pointed out that teachers and school administrators do not often understand the accommodations that would be best for a particular student and often use the "blanket method" (p. 12), where they provide all allowable accommodations without understanding how they might help or hurt a particular student's performance on a particular test.

To address this problem, a computerized system designed to help teachers make more appropriate accommodation assignments for ELs, called STELLA, was created (Kopriva & Hedgspeth, 2005). The STELLA system involves inputting information about a student along seven dimensions such as language proficiency, time in the United States, performance in school, and testing experience. To evaluate the degree to which appropriately matching accommodations to ELs, Kopriva et al. (2007) conducted an experiment where third-grade and fourth-grade ELs were randomly assigned to standardized or accommodated administrations of a computerized mathematics test. The accommodation conditions were a picture dictionary, a bilingual glossary, oral reading of test items in English, or combinations of two or three of these accommodations. After testing was completed, the researchers compared the accommodations given to each student with the accommodations that would be optimal based on information typically input into STELLA. They found statistically significant

TABLE 3
Summary of Recommended Accommodations for English Learners From Abedi and Ewers (2013)

Accommodation	Risk	Access
Traditional glossary with Spanish translations (content-related terms removed)		
Traditional glossary with Spanish translations and extra time (content-related terms removed)		
Customized dictionary/glossary in English (content-related terms removed)		Yes
Customized dictionary in English (content-related terms removed) and extra time		Yes
Computer-based test		Yes
Pop-up glossary (computer-based test; content-related terms excluded)		Yes
Modified (simplified English)		Yes
Extra time within the testing day (not combined with another accommodation)		Yes
Read-aloud of test directions in student's native language	Minor	
Picture dictionary (alone; combined with oral reading of test items in English; and combined with bilingual glossary)	Minor	
Bilingual dictionary	Minor	
Test break	Minor	Yes
Test in a familiar environment with other English language learners	Minor	
Small group setting	Minor	Yes
Read-aloud of test questions (math, science, history/social science) to student by teacher or electronic media	Minor	Yes
Spanish translation of test	Moderate	
Dual-language translation of test	Moderate	
Read-aloud of test questions (English language arts) to student by teacher or electronic media	High	
Commercial dictionary/glossary in English	High	

differences between the group of students that had the appropriate accommodations and those who had nonoptimal accommodations or no accommodations. Thus, their research underscores the importance of not just providing accommodations to ELs but also ensuring that they are provided with the accommodations they need (and only the accommodations they need).

FUTURE ASSESSMENT OF ELS

In this article, we reviewed validity issues for ELs, summarized validity research in this area, and discussed strategies test developers can use to promote validity in the assessment of ELs. In this section we discuss emerging trends relevant to EL assessment and provide some suggestions for future research and test development activities in this area.

Emerging Trends in EL Assessments

The current trends we envision in assessment of ELs include changes in how the domain of English proficiency is operationally defined for ELP assessments, and a better understanding of the relationships between English proficiency and proficiency in other academic subject areas. Both of these trends are already visible in new standards for ELD/ELP that have been released in the era of the Common Core State Standards (CCSS; California Department of Education, 2012; Council of Chief State School Officers, 2013; WIDA Consortium, 2012), which tend to define language modalities in terms of use and communication (e.g., expressive and receptive language and the ability to communicate ideas and participate in linguistic exchanges, rather than discrete tests of linguistic skills in separate domains), with specific linkages to academic content standards (most notably, the CCSS).

These new ELD/P standards, as well as the new assessments that will be built on them, should provide different and more valid information about whether ELs have mastered the specific linguistic skills and knowledge they need to receive and produce information pertaining to academic content areas. We also envision design implications for ELP assessments based on concerns and research on how language proficiency develops over time and interacts with growth in proficiency in other academic areas. Finally, we see increased interest in evaluating the appropriateness of educational tests for ELs.

Academic Language, ELP Assessment, and Content Assessments

With respect to ELP assessment, the specialized ways in which language is used in school settings are receiving more attention (Anstrom, DiCerbo, Katz, Millet, & Rivera, 2010; Bailey & Butler, 2007; Bailey & Huang, 2011; Schleppegrell & O'Hallaron, 2011; Wolf & Leon, 2009), as is determining whether and how ELs should be taught or held accountable for academic language (AL). ELs are now being required to develop strong mastery of not only general English but also academic English language, so they may participate in and contribute to academic discourse at the same level expected of native English-speaking peers. All current and next-generation ELP assessments claim at least some emphasis on AL (Abedi, 2007; Wolf, Wang, & Holtzman, 2011), though most are designed, scored, and reported based primarily on linguistic domains such as reading, writing, and speaking (Abedi, 2007; Bunch, 2011).

At the same time, however, there are concerns about when or whether an emphasis on AL blurs the line between language and content and ultimately holds ELs to unfair standards or penalizes their content performance for language skills that may not be construct-relevant. These concerns have been amplified in the era of the

CCSS, which, according to Abedi and Linquanti (2012), "specify to an unprecedented degree the kinds of academic language competencies that students need in order to perform content area tasks and demonstrate subject matter mastery" (p. 2). Abedi and Linquanti caution that "assessment developers still need to carefully distinguish what language is content-related (construct-relevant) in order to ensure that language that is unrelated to the focal construct (construct-irrelevant) is not confounded with the content being measured" (p. 2).

These concerns suggest that an important area for research in the coming years will be the relationship (both intended and observed) between language and content performance, and the extent to which this relationship should be interpreted, scored, reported, and used to make decisions about students and programs. To the extent that language plays a more central role in the CCSS relative to previously used content standards, it may be important to provide feedback on the linguistic performance of *all* students who are held to these standards, not just ELs.

Related questions are whether and how language and content performance can or should be evaluated simultaneously, both for the general population and for ELs. If the Race to the Top assessments are as language-rich as the standards they are designed to represent, it will be important to monitor the extent to which such assessments adhere to the unidimensionality assumption of IRT and whether the presence of a language dimension should be considered construct-relevant. If a language dimension were present and deemed important, this could in turn raise the question of whether a single assessment could or should be used to evaluate students on both content and AL as part of a single assessment, rather than as two separate assessments. Such a development could reduce testing time for EL and limit their segregation from the general population for instruction, though research would be needed on how to design, model, score, and interpret the results from such an assessment.

Language Learning Progressions and Dimensionality

Another area for future research is better mapping of the language development process for assessment development and use. In the area of content assessment, there is currently a great deal of interest in (a) articulating the common cognitive trajectories (often referred to as learning progressions or learning trajectories) that students tend to follow as they develop mastery in a content area (see, Mosher, 2011, for a summary of this trend) and (b) developing both formative and summative assessments whose outcomes provide instructionally relevant diagnostic information about where students stand on such trajectories (Bennett, 2010). Although current consensus holds that ELs likely need 4 to 5 years of instruction to reach AL proficiency (Working Group on ELL Policy, 2010), less conversation has occurred between linguistic researchers and test developers to provide detail about what typically goes on within this period in terms of learning and development, or how such learning could appropriately be modeled.

To the extent that learning progressions are useful for assessment design and score use, knowledge about language learning progressions could be useful for improving the validity of EL assessments in several ways. First, information about the second language development process (e.g., the relative pace and ordering at which different domains like writing and speaking develop, variations in the pace or order of ELD across speakers of different languages, etc.) could be invaluable to support decisions about subscore weights, cut scores, and vertical scaling.

For instance, it is somewhat common on ELP assessments for many students to do well on oral language subtests (e.g., speaking and listening) but for fewer students to do well on ELP writing assessments. This may be due to the fact that oral language skills often develop first for second language learners (and ultimately play an important catalytic role in the development of written language; Saunders & Goldenberg, 2010). This fact, however, may render oral language subtest scores less discriminating, since students with a wide range of actual ELP all earn high scores; writing scores, on the other hand, might be highly discriminating in that they do the best job of separating "truly" proficient students from those who need more time to develop.

In such an instance, the classification model used to determine overall proficiency and redesignation, as well as the relative weights assigned to the different domains, might benefit from putting this type of knowledge to use (if, of course, it is supported by quantitative analyses of the data). Similarly, the importance of oral language skills, writing skills, or reading skills may vary for younger versus older students depending on the demands of their classroom environments—thus, using different domain weights for students in different grade levels, and scaling the overall proficiency score accordingly, might produce more valid scores and decisions.

Second, information about learning progressions could be used to interpret performance and set realistic standards for ELs in content areas like ELA and mathematics, particularly for standards within the CCSS that are more language-centric. Multiple experts have recommended setting differential content performance standards for ELs based on their level of ELP, relative to an expected time frame to attain proficiency (Abedi & Linquanti, 2012; Cook, Wilmes, Boals, & Santos, 2008; Working Group on ELL Policy, 2010). Obviously, such systems would rely on (or at least benefit from) the availability of a research-based map of what goes within such a time frame, to ensure that the differential performance standards are appropriate and challenging given students' projected knowledge or skills at various points along the way.

Currently, the Dynamic Language Learning Progressions project (UCLA, n.d.) is working to develop these types of trajectories, based on collaborations and observations with teachers and students in California. The Dynamic Language Learning Progressions developed through this project may be a rich resource for evaluation, assessment design, and policymaking for ELs in years to come, and may help improve the validity of score uses and interpretations for these students.

Validation Research for ELs

At this juncture, sufficient statistical procedures and research methodologies are in place to comprehensively evaluate tests used for ELs. In addition, there is greater attention to the need to evaluate the validity of assessments for ELs. For example the *Standards and Assessments Peer Review Guidelines* associated with NCLB assessments (U.S. Department of Education, Office of Elementary and Secondary Education, 2009) encourages research to support the validity of assessments for ELs, and the new "fairness" chapter in the AERA et al. (2014) *Standards* contains several examples of validity issues of concern to ELs. Therefore, we predict validity studies to evaluate appropriate test use and interpretation with respect to ELs will continue, and we hope these studies include validity evidence based on the consequences for ELs who take educational assessments. Clearly, more research is needed on the benefits and potential negative consequences associated with the decisions that are made on the basis of test scores for the millions of ELs who take educational assessments.

SUMMARY AND CONCLUSIONS

In this article, we reviewed validity issues inherent in the assessment of ELs, discussed validation strategies for interpreting ELs test scores, reviewed studies in the areas of test accommodations for ELs, and discussed ways in which test developers can promote more valid assessment of ELs. Although it remains difficult to validly measure complex constructs such as English language acquisition and to measure academic constructs like math and science proficiency in a manner that is independent of ELP, much progress has been made.

There are several areas in which progress is noted. First, testing agencies are more aware of linguistic diversity within student populations, which should help make academic content assessments more accessible for ELs. Better data are being gathered to help test developers understand EL populations, and so we hope that they will be explicitly included (and maybe even oversampled) in pilot testing and other statistical evaluations that are part of the test development process. Second, also with respect to academic content assessments, we have learned a great deal about the types of accommodations that may benefit ELs and how to assign them. Third, as our discussion of several validation studies illustrated, there are many statistical techniques that can be used to (a) evaluate the invariance of test properties across EL and non-EL populations (e.g., confirmatory factor analysis), (b) evaluate item functioning (DIF), and (c) evaluate the presence of construct-irrelevant factors that may impede EL's performance (e.g., multiple regression).

In addition, the language testing community has taken steps to define and assess ELP in more careful and specific ways that are relevant and important to ELs' success in academic settings. Moreover, test developers and users are attending more carefully to the relationships—both intended and unintended—between language and content for ELs, to ensure that scores from both ELP and content assessments are being used and interpreted in ways that validly support ELs' best interests in school (see also Bailey & Carroll, 2015, this volume). We are seeing an integration of information across these types of assessments, rather than interpreting them in isolation. It appears that the K–12 education community is much more aware of the important role AL plays in the learning and performance of all students, not just ELs.

In conclusion, although threats to valid assessment of ELs remain, we know how to study these threats, and we continue to make progress in improving test development processes in order to make educational assessments as fair as possible for ELs. Hopefully, what is possible will continue to grow, so that interpretations of ELs' test performance will be on par with those of *all* other test takers.

NOTES

Correspondence concerning this article should be addressed to Stephen G. Sireci, Center for Educational Assessment, University of Massachusetts, Amherst, MA 01003; e-mail: sireci@acad.umass.edu.

[1]Exact counts of the LEP/EL population vary depending on their source; although NCLB provides a definition for LEP students, the ways in which different instruments identify and count ELs vary, as do state definitions and practices. For a deeper discussion on this issue, see *Allocating Federal Funds for State Programs for English Language Learners* (National Research Council, 2011).

[2]For critiques of this logic model see Cook et al. (2008), Forte (2010), U.S. Department of Education (2012), and Working Group on ELL Policy (2010).

[3]Some states allow districts to set performance standards for exit decisions, thus criteria may also vary within states.

[4]In the cross-lingual assessment community the term *adaptation* is more common than translation because it does not imply a literal word-for-word translation. Adaptation specifies translating the intended meaning of test material across languages without the constraints of a literal translation (International Test Commission, 2010).

REFERENCES

Abedi, J. (2001, December). *Language accommodation for large-scale assessment in science: Assessing English language learners* (Final Deliverable, Project 2.4 Accommodation). Los Angeles: National Center for Research on Evaluation, Standards, and Student Testing, University of California Los Angeles.

Abedi, J. (Ed.). (2007). *English language proficiency assessment in the nation: Current status and future practice.* Davis: University of California, Davis, School of Education.

Abedi, J., & Ewers, N. (2013). *Accommodations for English learners and students with disabilities: A research based decision algorithm.* Retrieved from http://www.smarterbalanced.org/wordpress/wp-content/uploads/2012/08/Accomodations-for-under-represented-students.pdf

Abedi, J., & Linquanti, R. (2012, January). *Issues and opportunities in improving the quality of large scale assessment systems for ELLs.* Paper presented the Understanding Language conference, Palo Alto, CA. Retrieved from http://ell.stanford.edu/publication/issues-and-opportunities-improving-quality-large-scale-assessment-systems-ells

Abedi, J., Lord, C., Hofstetter, C., & Baker, E. (2000). Impact of accommodation strategies on English language learners' test performance. *Educational Measurement: Issues and Practice, 19*(3), 16–26.

Abedi, J., Hofstetter, C. H., & Lord, C. (2004). Assessment accommodations for English language learners: Implications for policy-based empirical research. *Review of Educational Research, 74*, 1–28.

American Educational Research Association, American Psychological Association, & National Council on Measurement in Education. (1999). *Standards for educational and psychological testing.* Washington, DC: American Educational Research Association.

American Educational Research Association, American Psychological Association, & National Council on Measurement in Education. (2014). *Standards for educational and psychological testing.* Washington, DC: American Educational Research Association.

American Institutes for Research. (2013). *ELPA-to-ELPA Look Back.* Washington DC. Retrieved from http://www.ode.state.or.us/teachlearn/standards/contentperformance/elpa-to-elpa_look-back_report_02052013.pdf

Anstrom, K., DiCerbo, P., Katz, A., Millet, J., & Rivera, C. (2010). *A review of the literature on academic English: Implications for K-12 English language learners.* Arlington, VA: The George Washington University Center for Equity and Excellence in Education.

Bailey, A. L., & Butler, F. (2007). A conceptual framework for academic English language for broad application to education. In A. L. Bailey (Ed.), *The language demands of school: Putting academic English to the test* (pp. 68–102). New Haven, CT: Yale University Press.

Bailey, A. L., & Carroll, P. E. (2015). Assessment of English language learners in the era of new academic content standards. *Review of Research in Education, 39*, 253–294.

Bailey, A. L., & Huang, B. H. (2011). Do current English language development/proficiency standards reflect the English needed for success in school? *Language Testing, 28*, 343–365.

Bennett, R. E. (2010). Cognitively based assessment of, for, and as learning (CBAL): A preliminary theory of action for summative and formative assessment. *Measurement: Interdisciplinary Research and Perspectives, 8*, 70–91.

Bhola, D. S., Impara, J. C., & Buckendahl, C. W. (2003). Aligning tests with states' content standards: Methods and issues. *Educational Measurement: Issues and Practice, 22*(3), 21–29.

Bunch, M. B. (2011). Testing English language learners under No Child Left Behind. *Language Testing, 28*, 323–341. doi:10.1177/026553221140418.

California Department of Education. (2012, November). *Overview of the California English language development standards and proficiency level descriptors.* Retrieved from http://www.cde.ca.gov/sp/el/er/documents/sbeoverviewpld.pdf

Campbell, D. T., & Fiske, D. W. (1959). Convergent and discriminant validation by the multitrait-multimethod matrix. *Psychological Bulletin, 56*, 81–105.

Carroll, P., & Bailey, A. (2014, April). *Classification models and English learner redesignation: High performing students left behind?* Paper presented at the annual meeting of the National Council on Measurement in Education, Philadelphia, PA.

Cook, H. G., Wilmes, C., Boals, T., & Santos, M. (2008). *Issues in the development of annual measurable achievement objectives for WIDA Consortium states* (WCER Working Paper No. 2008-2). Madison: Wisconsin Center for Education Research.

Council of Chief State School Officers. (2013). *English language proficiency (ELP) standards with correspondences to K-12 English language arts (ELA), mathematics, and science practices, K-12 ELA standards, and 6-12 literacy standards.* Washington, DC: Author.

Crocker, L. M., Miller, D., & Franks, E. A. (1989). Quantitative methods for assessing the fit between test and curriculum. *Applied Measurement in Education, 2*, 179–194.

Crotts, K., & Sireci, S. G. (2014, April). *Evaluating computer-based test accommodations for English learners.* Paper presented at the annual meeting of the National Council on Measurement in Education, Philadelphia, PA.

Currie, M., & Chiramanee, T. (2010). The effect of the multiple-choice item format on the measurement of knowledge of language structure. *Language Testing, 27*, 471–491. doi:10.1177/0265532209356790

De la Torre, J., Song, H., & Hong, Y. (2011). A comparison of four methods of IRT subscoring. *Applied Psychological Measurement, 35*, 296–316. doi:10.1177/0146621610378653

Duncan, G. D., del Rio Parant, L., Chen, W.-H., Ferrara, S., Johnson, E., Oppler, S., & Shieh, Y.-Y. (2005). Study of a dual-language test booklet in eighth-grade mathematics. *Applied Measurement in Education, 18*, 129–161.

Educational Testing Service. (2009). *Guidelines for the assessment of English learners*. Princeton, NJ: Author.

Forte, E. (2010). Examining the assumptions underlying the NCLB federal accountability policy on School Improvement. *Educational Psychologist, 45*, 76–88.

Forte, E., Faulkner-Bond, M., Waring, S., Kuti, L., & Fenner, D. S. (2010). *The administrator's guide to federal programs for English learners*. Washington, DC: Thompson.

Geisinger, K. F. (2000). Psychological testing at the end of the millennium: A brief historical review. *Professional Psychology: Research and Practice, 31*, 117–118.

Grissom, J. B. (2004). Reclassification of English Learners. *Education Policy Analysis Archives, 12*(36). Retrieved from http://isla.tamucc.edu/files/esl_reclassificationenglishlearners.pdf

Haladyna, T. M., & Rodriguez, M. C. (2014). *Developing and validating test items*. New York, NY: Routledge.

Hauger, J. B., & Sireci, S. G. (2008). Detecting differential item functioning across examinees tested in their dominant language and examinees tested in a second language. *International Journal of Testing, 8*, 237–250.

Holland, P. W., & Wainer, H. (Eds.). (1993). *Differential item functioning*. Hillsdale, NJ: Lawrence Erlbaum.

In'nami, Y., & Koizumi, R. (2009). A meta-analysis of test format effects on reading and listening test performance: Focus on multiple-choice and open-ended formats. *Language Testing, 26*, 219–244. doi:10.1177/0265532208101006

In'nami, Y., & Koizumi, R. (2012). Factor structure of the Revised TOEIC[R] Test: A multiple-sample analysis. *Language Testing, 29*, 131–152.

International Test Commission (2010). *Guidelines for translating and adapting tests*. Retrieved from http://www.intestcom.org. Accessed October 12, 2014.

Kachchaf, R., & Solano-Flores, G. (2012). Rater language background as a source of measurement error in the testing of English language learners. *Applied Measurement in Education, 25*, 162–177.

Kane, M. (1994). Validating the performance standards associated with passing scores. *Review of Educational Research, 64*, 425–461.

Kane, M. (2006). Validation. In R. L. Brennan (Ed.), *Educational measurement* (4th ed., pp. 17–64). Washington, DC: American Council on Education/Praeger.

Kane, M. (2013). Validating the interpretations and uses of test scores. *Journal of Educational Measurement, 50*, 1–73.

Kane, M. T. (1992). An argument-based approach to validity. *Psychological Bulletin, 112*, 527–535.

Kieffer, M. J., Lesaux, N. K., Rivera, M., & Francis, D. J. (2009). Accommodations for English language learners taking large-scale assessments: A meta-analysis on effectiveness and validity. *Review of Educational Research, 79*, 1168–1201.

Kim, J., & Herman, J. L. (2009). A three-state study of English learner progress. *Educational Assessment, 14*, 212–231. doi:10.1080/10627190903422831

Kim, J., & Herman, J. L. (2012). *Understanding patterns and precursors of ELL success subsequent to reclassification* (CRESST Report No. 818). Los Angeles, CA: National Center for Research on Evaluation, Standards, and Student Testing.

Koenig, J. A., & Bachman, L. F. (2004). *Keeping score for all: The effects of inclusion and accommodation policies on large-scale educational assessments*. Washington, DC: National Academies Press.

Kopriva, R. J., & Hedgspeth, C. (2005). *Technical manual, selection taxonomy for English language learner accommodation (STELLA) decision-making systems*. College Park: University of Maryland, C-SAVE.

Kopriva, R. J., Emick, J. E., Hipolito-Delgado, C. P., & Cameron, C. A. (2007). Do proper accommodation assignments make a difference? Examining the impact of improved decision making on scores of English language learners. *Educational Measurement: Issues and Practice, 26*(3), 11–20.

Kuriakose, A. (2011, January 1). *The factor structure of the English language development assessment: A confirmatory factor analysis* (Doctoral dissertation). Available from ProQuest Dissertations and Theses database. (ED535975)

Lakin, J. M., & Young, J. W. (2013). Evaluating growth for ELL students: Implications for accountability policies. *Educational Measurement: Issues and Practice, 32*(3), 11–26. doi:10.1111/emip.12012

Lane, S. (2014). Validity evidence based on testing consequences. *Psicothema, 26,* 127–135. doi:10.7334/psicothema2013.258

Lane, S., & Leventhal, B (2015). Psychometric challenges in assessing English language learners and students with disabilities. *Review of Research in Education, 39,* 165–214.

Lee, W. (2008). *Classification consistency and accuracy for complex assessments using item response theory* (CASMA Research Report No. 27). Iowa City: University of Iowa.

Li, H., & Suen, H. K. (2012). The effects of test accommodations for English learners: A meta-analysis. *Applied Measurement in Education, 25,* 327–346.

Linquanti, R. (2001). *The redesignation dilemma: Challenges and choices in fostering meaningful accountability for English learners* (Policy Report No. 2001-1). Santa Barbara: University of California Linguistic Minority Research Institute.

Livingston, S. A., & Lewis, C. (1995). Estimating the consistency and accuracy of classifications based on test scores. *Journal of Educational Measurement, 32,* 179–197.

Luecht, R. M., & Ackerman, T. (2007). *Oregon English Language Proficiency Examination (EPLA) dimensionality analysis for blended-domain locator blocks.* Greensboro, NC: Center for Assessment Research and Technology.

Martiniello, M. (2008). Language and the performance of English-language learners in math word problems. *Harvard Educational Review, 78,* 333–368.

Martone, A., & Sireci, S. G. (2009). Evaluating alignment between curriculum, assessments, and instruction. *Review of Educational Research, 4,* 1332–1361.

Massachusetts Department of Elementary and Secondary Education. (2012). *Transitioning English language learners in Massachusetts: An exploratory data review.* Malden, MA: Author. Retrieved from http://www.nciea.org/publication_PDFs/Transitioning%20ELL_CD12.pdf

McNamara, T., & Knoch, U. (2012). The Rasch wars: The emergence of Rasch measurement in language testing. *Language Testing, 29,* 555–576. doi:10.1177/0265532211430367

Messick, S. (1989). Validity. In R. Linn (Ed.), *Educational measurement* (3rd ed., pp. 13–100). Washington, DC: American Council on Education.

Mosher, F. A. (2011). *The role of learning progressions in standards-based education reform* (Policy Brief No. RB-52). Philadelphia, PA: Consortium for Policy Research in Education.

National Center for Education Statistics. (n.d.). *Common core of data* (CCD). Retrieved from http://nces.ed.gov/ccd/index.asp

National Research Council. (2011). *Allocating federal funds for state programs for English language learners.* Washington, DC: National Academies Press. Retrieved from http://www.nap.edu/openbook.php?record_id=13090

O'Conner, R., Abedi, J., & Tung, S. (2012a). A descriptive analysis of enrollment and achievement among English language learner students in Pennsylvania: Summary (Issues & Answers, REL 2012-No. *127).* Retrieved from http://files.eric.ed.gov/fulltext/ED531429.pdf

O'Conner, R., Abedi, J., & Tung, S. (2012b). A descriptive analysis of enrollment and achievement among limited English proficient students in New Jersey (Issues & Answers, REL 2012-No. *108).* Retrieved from http://files.eric.ed.gov/fulltext/ED531432.pdf

Padilla, J.-L., & Benitez, I. (2014). Validity evidence based on response processes. *Psicothema, 26,* 110–117.

Parker, C., Louie, J., & O'Dwyer, L. (2009). *New measures of English language proficiency and their relationship to performance on large-scale content assessments* (Issues & Answers, REL 2009 No. 066). Washington, DC: U.S. Department of Education, Institute of Education Sciences, National Center for Education Evaluation and Regional Assistance, Regional Educational Laboratory Northeast and Islands. Retrieved from http://ies.ed.gov/ncee/edlabs

Partnership for the Assessment of Readiness for College and Career. (2013). *Accessibility features and accommodations manual.* Washington, DC: Author.

Pennock-Roman, M. (2002). Relative effects of English proficiency on general admissions tests versus subject tests. *Research in Higher Education, 43,* 601–623.

Pennock-Roman, M., & Rivera, C. (2011). Mean effects of test accommodations for ELLs and non-ELLs: A meta-analysis of experimental studies. *Educational Measurement: Issues and Practice, 30*(3), 10–28.

Ragan, A., & Lesaux, N. (2006). Federal, state, and district level English language learner program entry and exit requirements: Effects on the education of language minority learners. *Education Policy Analysis Archives, 14*(20), 1–32.

Ramsey, P. A. (1993). Sensitivity review: The ETS experience as a case study. In P. W. Holland, & H. Wainer (Eds.), *Differential item functioning* (pp. 367–388). Hillsdale, NJ: Erlbaum.

Rivera, C., Collum, E., Willner, L. S., & Sia, J. K., Jr. (2006). An analysis of state assessment policies addressing the accommodation of English language learners. In C. Rivera, & E. Collum (Eds.), *A national review of state assessment policy and practice for English language learners* (pp. 1–173). Mahwah, NJ: Lawrence Erlbaum.

Robinson, J. P. (2011). Evaluating criteria for English learner reclassification: A causal-effects approach using a binding-score regression discontinuity design with instrumental variables. *Educational Evaluation and Policy Analysis, 33,* 267–292. doi:10.3102/0162373711407912

Römhild, A., Kenyon, D., & MacGregor, D. (2011). Exploring domain-general and domain-specific linguistic knowledge in the assessment of academic English language proficiency. *Language Assessment Quarterly, 8,* 213–228. doi:10.1080/15434303.2011.558146

Rudner, L. M. (2001). Computing the expected proportions of misclassified examinees. *Practical Assessment, Research & Evaluation, 7*(14).

Rudner, L. M. (2004, April). *Expected classification accuracy.* Paper presented at the annual meeting of the National Council on Measurement in Education, San Diego, CA.

Saunders, W. M., & Goldenberg, C. (2010). Research to guide English language development instruction. In *Improving education for English learners: Research-based approaches* (pp. 20–81). Sacramento: California Department of Education.

Sawaki, Y., Stricker, L. J., & Oranje, A. H. (2009). Factor structure of the TOEFL Internet-based test. *Language Testing, 26,* 5–30.

Schleppegrell, M. J., & O'Hallaron, C. L. (2011). Teaching academic language in L2 secondary settings. *Annual Review of Applied Linguistics, 31,* 3–18. doi:10.1017/S0267190511000067

Shepard, L., Taylor, G., & Betebenner, D. (1998). *Inclusion of limited-English-proficient students in Rhode Island's grade 4 mathematics performance assessment.* Los Angeles: University of California, Center for the Study of Evaluation/National Center for Research on Evaluation, Standards, and Student Testing.

Sireci, S. G. (1998). Gathering and analyzing content validity data. *Educational Assessment, 5,* 299–321.

Sireci, S. G. (2013). Agreeing on validity arguments. *Journal of Educational Measurement, 50,* 99–104.

Sireci, S. G., Li, S., & Scarpati, S. (2003). *The effects of tests accommodations on test performance: A review of the literature.* Commissioned paper by the National Academy of Sciences/

National Research Council's Board on Testing and Assessment. Washington, DC: National Research Council.

Sireci, S. G., & Mullane, L. A. (1994). Evaluating test fairness in licensure testing: The sensitivity review process. *CLEAR Exam Review, 5*(2), 22–28.

Sireci, S. G., Rios, J. A., & Powers, S. (in press). Comparing test scores from tests administered in different languages. In N. Dorans, & L. Cook (Eds.) *Fairness.* New York, NY: Routledge.

Sireci, S. G., Wells, C., & Hu, H. (2014, April). *Using internal structure validity evidence to evaluate test accommodations.* Paper presented at the annual meeting of the National Council on Measurement in Education, Philadelphia, PA.

Smarter Balanced Assessment Consortium. (2013). *Usability, accessibility, and accommodations guidelines.* San Francisco, CA: WestEd.

Solano-Flores, G. (2012). *Translation accommodations framework for testing English language learners in mathematics.* Retrieved from http://www.smarterbalanced.org/wordpress/wp-content/uploads/2012/09/Translation-Accommodations-Framework-for-Testing-ELL-Math.pdf

Solano-Flores, G., & Li, M. (2009). Language variation and score variation in the testing of English language learners, native Spanish speakers. *Educational Assessment, 14,* 180–194.

Solano-Flores, G., Trumbull, E., & Nelson-Barber, S. (2002). Concurrent development of dual language assessments: An alternative to translating tests for linguistic minorities. *International Journal of Testing, 2,* 107–129.

Stansfield, C. W. (2003). Test translation and adaptation in public education in the USA. *Language Testing, 20,* 188–206.

Swanson, C. B. (2009). *Perspectives on a population: English-language learners in American Schools.* Bethesda, MD: Editorial Projects in Education Research Center.

Thompson, S., Blount, A., & Thurlow, M. (2002). *A summary of research on the effects of test accommodations: 1999 through 2001* (Technical Report No. 34). Minneapolis: University of Minnesota, National Center on Educational Outcomes. Retrieved from http://education.umn.edu/NCEO/OnlinePubs/Technical34.htm

UCLA. (n.d.). *Dynamic Language Learning Progression Project: Resources on learning progressions.* Retrieved from http://www.dllp.org/index.php/resources/

U.S. Department of Education. (2011). *Consolidated state performance reports: Parts I and II school years 2009-2010.* Washington, DC: Office of Elementary and Secondary Education. Retrieved from http://www2.ed.gov/admins/lead/account/consolidated/index.html#sy09-10

U.S. Department of Education. (2012). *National evaluation of Title III implementation supplemental report: Exploring approaches to setting English language proficiency performance criteria and monitoring English learner progress.* Washington, DC: Author.

U.S. Department of Education, Office of Elementary and Secondary Education. (2009). *Standards and assessments peer review guidance: Information and examples for meeting the requirements of the No Child Left Behind Act of 2001* (Third revision). Washington, DC: Author.

WIDA Consortium. (2012). *2012 Amplification of the English language development standards, Kindergarten-Grade 12.* Madison: Board of Regents of the University of Wisconsin System.

Willner, L., Rivera, C., & Acosta, B. (2008). *Descriptive study of state assessment policies for accommodating English language learners.* Arlington, VA: George Washington University Center for Equity and Excellence in Education.

Wilson, M., & Moore, S. (2011). Building out a measurement model to incorporate complexities of testing in the language domain. *Language Testing, 28,* 441–462. doi:10.1177/0265532210394142

Wolf, M. K., Kim, J., & Kao, J. (2012). The effects of glossary and read-aloud accommodations on English language learners' performance on a mathematics assessment. *Applied Measurement in Education, 25,* 347–374.

Wolf, M. K., & Leon, S. (2009). An investigation of the language demands in content assessments for English language learners. *Educational Assessment, 14*, 139–159. doi:10.1080/10627190903425883

Wolf, M. K., Wang, Y., & Holtzman, S. (2011, April). *Investigating the constructs of English language proficiency assessments and ELLs' performance on the assessments.* Paper presented at the annual meeting of the American Educational Research Association, New Orleans, LA.

Working Group on ELL Policy. (2010). *Improving educational outcomes for English language learners: Recommendations for the reauthorization of the Elementary and Secondary Education Act.* Retrieved from http://ellpolicy.org/wp-content/uploads/ESEAFinal.pdf

Young, J. W., Pitoniak, M. J., King, T. C., & Ayad, E. (2012). Guidelines for accessibility for English language learners. Retrieved from http://www.smarterbalanced.org/wordpress/wp-content/uploads/2012/05/TaskItemSpecifications/Guidelines/AccessibilityandAccommodations/GuidelinesforAccessibilityforELL.pdf

Zhang, B. (2010). Assessing the accuracy and consistency of language proficiency classification under competing measurement models. *Language Testing, 27*, 119–140.

Zwick, R., & Schlemer, L. (2004). SAT validity for linguistic minorities at the University of California, Santa Barbara. *Educational Measurement: Issues and Practice, 23*, 6–16.

Chapter 7

Assessment of English Language Learners in the Era of New Academic Content Standards

ALISON L. BAILEY
University of California, Los Angeles

PATRICIA E. CARROLL
University of California, Los Angeles
California State University, Los Angeles

INTRODUCTION

The intended ultimate effect of the mandated assessment of English language learner (ELL) students is their successful academic achievement in U.S. public schools. Information yielded by assessments is used to inform state and federal agencies about the efficacy of states' efforts to support this achievement and, at the individual student level, is used to inform educators how best to respond to the instructional needs (both linguistic and academic) of their students.[1] Absent any official language planning policy in the United States, currently assessment decisions affecting ELL students operate as de facto language policies in the way that they predominantly privilege English proficiency over the maintenance of minority languages for content learning (Menken, 2008). Specifically, "The language policies currently being created in U.S. schools as a byproduct of testing policy occur in an ad hoc way, without careful language planning" (p. 5). We might go so far as to argue that additionally there is no coordinated testing policy; rather, there exists a collection of somewhat disconnected mandated federal and widely varying state-level regulations along with optional initiatives and recommendations offered to school districts for them to implement. Assessment of ELL students therefore involves many components, with different aspects having different purposes directed from different loci of control (federal, state, local) and based on different sources of funding (National Research Council [NRC], 2011).[2] Consequently, we are reluctant to call the suite of ELL assessments a full-fledged system until greater scrutiny of it has been conducted and a defensible argument made in its favor.

Review of Research in Education
March 2015, Vol. 39, pp. 253–294
DOI: 10.3102/0091732X14556074
© 2015 AERA. http://rre.aera.net

However, with many components interacting with one another, a systems view is still needed to both effectively document progression of ELL student language and content learning and coordinate efforts to support and monitor this learning in more strategic and tactical ways. Indeed, many aspects of ELL assessment in the United States need to be considered equally from federal, state, and local perspectives so that meaningful and comparable practices might be implemented with ELL students wherever they reside in the nation. The current lack of systematicity is particularly pernicious because of the high-stakes nature of ELL testing policies and practices, not just for states, districts, and schools in terms of funding but also at the individual student level in terms of student placement, access to core content, and eligibility for gifted and other advanced programs. We add these concerns to other aspects of ELL assessment that have already been called out for greater capacity building by federal, state, and local authorities in the areas of monitoring current and redesignated ELL students, establishing realistic time lines for language proficiency attainment, and expectations for ELL student academic achievement (Hopkins, Thompson, Linquanti, Hakuta, & August, 2013).

The purpose of this chapter is twofold: (1) to provide a detailed review of current language assessment policies and practices with ELL students under the federal requirements of the No Child Left Behind Act (NCLB; 2001) and relevant research in order to evaluate their technical quality and validity, and (2) to examine the intersection of language assessment and academic content assessment in terms of their purposeful interpretation and use by educators in decision making.

We outline a theory of action suggested by the established policies and practices of the putative ELL assessment system and critique the interpretive claims, uses, and asserted outcomes based on the available evidence.[3] Recommendations are offered for further research that focuses on aligning and improving the disparate parts and purposes of the ELL assessment system to affect positive outcomes in ELL education. The four main components of the system function to discriminate between those students who should and those who should not receive services under Title III of NCLB with its focus on ELL language support. The system begins with the ubiquitous yet nonmandated and widely varying practice of administering a home language survey (HLS) to families to identify students as potential ELL students (see Figure 1). The next component in the system is the screening tool and or placement test used to confirm ELL status and instructional placement for Title III services (e.g., any language programming, such as Structured English Immersion or bilingual education, collectively known as Language Instruction Educational Programs [LIEPs]; see Faulkner-Bond et al., 2012). This is followed by the required annual monitoring of student English language growth and proficiency using a standards-based English language proficiency assessment (ELPA). Here we also include the desirable but professional development–dependent use of formative assessment techniques for instructional decision making in the areas of both language learning and academic content instruction with ELL students. The fourth and final component of the system comprises the reclassification of students as English-proficient and their exit from ELL

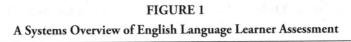

FIGURE 1

A Systems Overview of English Language Learner Assessment

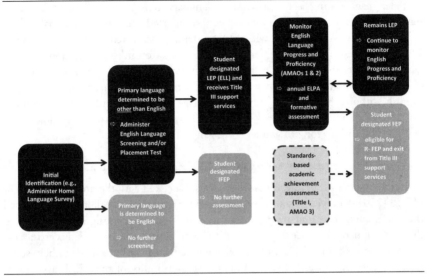

programming based on state and local district formula with 2-year monitoring post exit. The entire *system* as such needs to be evaluated, not just a single component or even several components evaluated independently.

In addition to English language assessment, ELL students are included in academic content assessment on an annual basis under the provisions of the Elementary and Secondary Education Act (ESEA) through its reauthorization in the form of NCLB, and there is no reason not to expect this mandate to continue with the reauthorization of ESEA in the near future. NCLB "challenged states to develop an integrated system of ELP standards, assessments, and objectives that are linked to states' academic content and student achievement standards set in accordance with other parts of ESEA" (NRC, 2011, p. 6). Specifically,

States now must annually assess ELL students' progress in becoming English language proficient, and they must include these students in annual assessments in all content areas. The states are being held accountable for demonstrating that ELL students are making progress in learning academic subjects. (NRC, 2011, p. 6)

States must expect that all educators will hold ELL students to high academic content standards. However, when students are being assessed for content knowledge in a language they are still learning, fair and valid (i.e., meaningful) interpretations depend on clear measurement of the construct (e.g., avoiding irrelevant construct variance caused by measuring language abilities rather than the intended mathematics or science knowledge) and appropriately implementing testing accommodations.

DESCRIBING ELL ASSESSMENT NEEDS: ENGLISH LANGUAGE AND CONTENT LEARNING

If language testing is tantamount to language policy in the United States, it behooves us to clearly state here how we have inferred the educational goals of the collection of assessments used with ELL students. The current suite of assessments ELL students encounter for the most part are geared toward the educational goal of having students enter or remain in ELL programming when deemed necessary and exiting ELL programming when ready to learn grade-level academic content in English without that support.[4] English language proficiency and academic content assessments should be considered concurrently by those who make educational programming decisions for ELL students (Ragan & Lesaux, 2006).

Theory of Action for an ELL Assessment System

In the past decade of rewards and sanctions associated with the implementation of NCLB (2001), individual states and consortia have developed, validated, and refined their assessment instruments piece by piece. It is only a working assumption that these components interact to produce the overall desired outcome of successful academic achievement for ELL students, although efforts have been made to help states foster a "common interpretive argument" for the validity of their ELL assessment systems. This common interpretative argument is representative of the mutual interpretative claims and assumptions inherent in the theories of action or logic models underlying the specified purposes and goals of the states' respective ELPA and the broader ELL assessment systems into which they fit (Perie & Forte, 2011). According to Forte, Perie, and Paek (2012), the fundamental validity question is "whether a student who is deemed proficient by an ELPA can successfully function without language supports in academic classes taught in English" (p. 8). By combining a theory of inputs, outputs, and eventual outcomes (Bennett, 2010) with an interpretation/use argument (Kane, 2013), the theory of action we infer from established ELL assessment policies and practices includes a level of specificity for each assessment use (i.e., how data and test scores are used at the federal/state and individual student levels) and outlines the serial connections between the components of an overarching ELL assessment system.

The theory of action represented in Table 1 shows the four main components, each with an output serving as prerequisite for the next component. Cycling through these components culminates in the global assertion that language minority students as a protected class of individuals under federal law (those with home language influences other than or additional to English) can be accurately identified and their English language measured at various junctures to receive (or continue to receive) support services to ensure successful completion of K–12 education under Title III of NCLB. To wit, the ELL assessment system should be designed to identify all potential ELL students, identify who will receive Title III services (either Initial Fluent English Proficient [IFEP], i.e., not eligible for Title III services; or Limited English

TABLE 1

Theory of Action With Embedded Interpretive Claims and Uses of the ELL Assessment System

Component	Purpose	Interpretive Claims and Uses	Action Mechanisms and Prerequisites for Subsequent Components (in bold)	Intended Ultimate Effects
1. Initial Identification	**Title III Eligibility** Survey all families to identify language minority students	**Home Language Survey (HLS)** identifies the "right" pool of students by differentiating between students with and without "primary home language other than English" **Federal/State-level Use:** Initial step in accurate identification of students eligible for Title III.[a] **Student-level Use:** Pre-determine that ELL placement test results are due to home language influence other than English.	• If HLS determines English is the primary language, student is not eligible for Title III. Student will not be further screened • If HLS determines primary language other than English, student may need Title III services. Student must be given the *initial English screening and/or placement test*	Ensures all eligible students will have access to Title III services
2. Initial Screening and/ or Placement	**Title III Allocation** Identify who needs/ does not need Title III services Designate students as LEP (need Title III services) or IFEP	**English Language Screener and/or Placement Test** differentiates between students who need and do not need Title III. Test performance determines level placement into Title III program and designates "ELL" status **Federal/State-level Use:** Confirms accurate count of students eligible for Title III to allocate state funding and provide baseline to measure progress toward proficiency **Student-level Use:** ELL placement test results presume performance is due to primary home language other than English	• If test performance is "proficient", student is designated IFEP and not given Title III services • If test performance is "not proficient", student designated LEP (ELL) and is eligible for Title III services that include *monitoring English Language Progress and Proficiency.*	Ensures all eligible students will have access to Title III services

(continued)

TABLE 1 (CONTINUED)

Component	Purpose	Interpretive Claims and Uses	Action Mechanisms and Prerequisites for Subsequent Components (in bold)	Intended Ultimate Effects
3. Monitoring English Language Progress and Proficiency	**3a. Assessment for Language Instruction** Target student language learning needs	**English Language Proficiency Assessment (annual)** differentiates between students who need and do not need Title III. Students who do no are not eligible for reclassification review. Students who still need Title III are placed into instruction by scores/levels.	• If test performance is "not proficient", student remains LEP (ELL) and in Title III. • If test performance is "proficient", student is **designated FEP & eligible for reclassification review to exit Title III.**	Ensures progress and proficiency of students in Title III services
	3b. Annual Progress Monitoring Measure student progress within Title III programs Measure student attainment of English language proficiency	**Federal/State-level Use:** Accurate designations (LEP/FEP) and counts of students receiving Title III services in order to allocate funding and measure state-wide progress towards proficiency **Student-Level Use:** Results accurately reflect growth in language proficiency and allow for LEP/FEP determination.		
	3c. On-going Proficiency Status and Placement Identify student readiness for reclassification Identify student readiness to exit Title III services	**Formative Assessment of English language progress** provides teachers with evidence of student language learning in specific areas and informs next-steps instruction **Federal/State-level Use:** No mandate for formative assessment of Title III **Student-Level Use:** tailors instruction to student language learning needs		

(continued)

TABLE 1 (CONTINUED)

Component	Purpose	Interpretive Claims and Uses	Action Mechanisms and Prerequisites for Subsequent Components (in bold)	Intended Ultimate Effects
4. Reclassification	**Title III Exit (or Continuation)** Identify eligibility for reclassification (R-FEP) Identify eligibility to exit Title III services	**English Language Proficiency Assessment minimally, or aggregate of several sources of evidence** including ELP assessments, state standards-based academic achievement assessments (Title I), and possibly other measures used to identify student eligibility to exit Title III (varies by state/district) **Federal/State-level Use:** Accurate designations (LEP/R-FEP) and counts to allocate funding **Student-Level Use:** Measures indicating "eligible for FEP" presume that language abilities displayed in content areas indicate readiness for classes without Title III	• If decision rule indicates "ineligible", student remains LEP (ELL) and in Title III. • If decision rule indicates "eligible", *student is reclassified-FEP (R-FEP), exits Title III* and receives 2 years of monitoring [b]	Ensures the standard for Title III exit (or continuation) and facilitates student success in K-12 education

Note. ELL = English language learner; IFEP = Initial Fluent English Proficient; LEP = Limited English Proficient; R-FEP = Reclassified Fluent English Proficient; FEP= Fluent English Proficient; ELP = English language proficiency; R-FEP = Reclassified Fluent English Proficient.

[a]According to the NRC (2011), the federal government currently allocates Title III funding to states based on the U.S. Census Bureau's American Community Survey data rather than on counts of students found eligible via ELP screening.

[b]These actions are prerequisite to a two-year R-FEP monitoring system, but we limit our review of the ELL assessment system to students' reaching this phase.

Proficient [LEP], the terminology of the federal law for those eligible for Title III services), measure progress attained within Title III services (for both accountability as well as instructional purposes), monitor progress in content areas under Title I,[5] measure attainment of proficiency and exit from Title III services, and monitor maintenance of proficiency for exited (former ELL) students.

For *federal NCLB reporting*, states report totals and percentages for Title III accountability, and these results are used to determine allocation of funding. Thus, the theory of action for *federal NCLB reporting* is that the ELL assessment system facilitates fair and appropriate allocation of Title III funding, which will in turn enable schools to provide adequate Title III services to all identifiable ELL students with the goal of successful K–12 completion for all.[6] Such allocation of funding may be evaluated in comparison with other states, thus standardization and comparability are key.

For *student-level data use*, states report scale scores and levels to schools, and schools use these data to determine Title III placement, continuation, and exit for individual students. Thus, the theory of action for *student-level data use* is that the ELL assessment system facilitates fair and appropriate allocation of Title III services to all identifiable ELL students with the goal of successful K–12 completion for all. Such allocation of funding may be evaluated in comparison to curricular pathways and outcomes for comparable students, and thus accuracy at the individual level is key. The ELL assessment system stands unique in its reliance on large-scale standardized test data for use in individual educational programming, despite the common agreement that multiple sources of evidence are preferred for high-stakes decision making.[7]

A student designated LEP (more widely referred to as ELL) is expected to make progress and subsequently reach a point where other language influences are not impeding English progress, at which point the student is considered ready for redesignation (i.e., reclassified as FEP or commonly R-FEP) and exit from Title III services. It is expected that this exit point is calibrated to ensure students' placement in English-only classes is successful. Whether it be IFEP, LEP, or FEP, the resultant educational programming is intended to ensure that all students successfully complete their K–12 education. Notably absent from this description of a theory of action, yet integral to student success, are measures of instructional quality and opportunity to learn. This is indicative of a system built piecemeal around a specific funded mandate (Title III) and should be considered when further managing or evaluating the ELL assessment system.[8]

It is important to note that the ELL assessments as a whole differ from the assessment systems being developed to measure proficiency on the new content standards (e.g., Common Core State Standards Initiative [CCSS Initiative], 2010a, 2010b; the Next Generation Science Standards [NGSS] Lead States, 2013) in that the data generated by ELL assessments are used to create designations (IFEP, LEP, FEP) that affect educational programming at the individual student level. These designations are used to determine a language minority student's placement into and out of Title III programming as well as the level (e.g., Level 2 "Advanced Beginner") and intensity (i.e., frequency and duration) of services given in that instructional program. Thus, by design there are cause-effect relationships among data-generating mechanisms, decision-making routines, and instructional components in accordance with the designations of IFEP, LEP, and FEP, which can make data difficult to interpret. Importantly, data cannot act alone: In fact, data do not act at all. Decision makers who interpret these data, alongside other sources of evidence, are prone to biases and limitations, yet their observant use of data is essential to ongoing evaluation and betterment of the system as a whole. With this conceptual grounding, we turn now to the review of assessment practices more specifically, first for ELP followed by current content assessment practices with ELL students.

English Language Proficiency Assessment

Prior to NCLB, ELP assessments were used for educational programming only. The mandates accompanying NCLB mean that measures of ELP are now largely fashioned for accountability purposes. With the strong emphasis on students reaching proficient levels of competence on the content area standards, there has also been a shift in rhetoric from assessing the English language *development* of students to assessing students' English language *proficiency* for standardized testing purposes. This situation is reflected in some states and consortia adopting English language proficiency standards (e.g., WIDA Consortium, 2004, 2007). The most recent manifestation of an intentional difference in the use of the two terms is seen in the *Framework for English Language Proficiency Development Standards* (*ELPD Framework*; Council of Chief State School Officers [CCSSO], 2012). Unfortunately this adoption of both terms in one framework has the potential to add further confusion to the already quixotic nomenclature found in the field of education. We do surmise, however, from the use of both *proficiency* and *development* in the title of the framework that proficiency in English is prized but couched in a manner that also emphasizes proficiency developing incrementally over time. In this chapter we use the abbreviation ELD/P when referring to English language standards for students acquiring English as a second or an additional language because states continue with standards that are termed either *ELD* or *ELP*.[9]

Below we review assessment of ELL students organized by six identifiable assessment uses: (1) initially identifying students who may be potential ELL students; (2) confirming ELL status and eligibility for Title III services as well as placing students within programs; (3) periodic assessment that can be further divided into (a) the much-needed emphasis on classroom-level assessment (i.e., formative assessment) of ELD for ongoing instructional purposes at the point students are acquiring both English and new content area material, (b) the monitoring of annual progress on route to fluent or "full" English proficiency, (c) for on-going proficiency status placement, and (4) reclassifying students to FEP and their exit from Title III services (e.g., G. García, McKoon, & August, 2006; see also the schematic in NRC, 2011, p. 78).[10]

Initial Identification of Potential ELL Students

Much relies on the type and quality of instruments states and districts use to iden-tify the initial pool of students who, with further screening or assessment, may prove eligible for Title III services. To identify potential ELL students, the vast majority of states use some form of survey administered to parents or guardians of students at first enrollment in public education no matter their linguistic background (Bailey & Kelly, 2013; Kindler, 2002; NRC, 2011; Wolf et al., 2008). Such surveys may ask parents to identify which language they consider to be their child's dominant or pri-mary language, which language their child learned to speak first, and which language they, the parents, use with their child. However, as Bailey and Kelly (2013) point out,

The U.S. Department of Education Office for Civil Rights *December 3, 1985 Memorandum* and *1991 OCR Policy* address the requirement to have a program in place for adequately identifying students in need of services, but recognize that this may differ widely due to student demographics. . . . No wording in these memoranda obligates states to specifically enforce the use of an HLS in order to initially identify students. (p. 799)

Nevertheless, in their review, Bailey and Kelly (2013) identified all but 4 states rely-ing on an HLS to make the initial identification of which students should be in the pool for further English language screening or assessment. The majority (23 states and Washington, D.C.) has created a single HLS form and mandates its use in schools statewide. A further 17 states mandate use of an HLS and have created a sample HLS for districts to adopt or substitute with their own version, and 6 states mandate use of an HLS but have created neither a required nor sample HLS, allowing districts to create their own. The 4 states with no mandated HLS recommend options for dis-tricts to follow that include an HLS to identify students for further screening but may also list alternate practices such as the use of existing reading scores on state tests and observational scales.

The theory of action we have adopted allows us to clarify the intended purpose(s) of the initial identification instrument. Such an instrument has one apparent objec-tive: to focus in on the pool of students in the general K–12 population who, by dint of their language minority standing, are most likely in need of the language and academic support services to which they are entitled. This group of *potential* ELLs can then be screened or assessed further to determine actual need. Frequently it is as informative to state what use an instrument is not intended for as it is to state what it is intended for, and in the case of the HLS it bears emphasizing that it is not intended to measure English "proficiency." However, a secondary purpose may be to yield information on the students' language backgrounds that may aide schools and teachers programmatically (i.e., offering bilingual education programs in high-inci-dence languages) and instructionally (e.g., teaching students strategies for transfer-ring reading skills in a first language to their English reading development). As it stands, the HLS is a poor substitute for instruments that could accomplish these measurement tasks.

Even though HLS use is the most common practice in initial identification, it does not necessarily follow that it is a *best* practice. Other instruments such as interviews, observational protocols, preschool assessment results, and universal screening, although rarely used, have been proposed as alternatives to or for use in combination with HLS as multiple indictors of potential ELL status (Abedi, 2008; Bailey & Kelly, 2013). Moreover, HLS use is a practice based on little research of the quality of the data HLS yield (Bailey, 2010). In fact, there has been little attention by states and the research community to how tight the initial identification instrument or "net" must be in order to be sure of including all students who may be potential ELL students (Linquanti & Bailey, 2014). Consequently, we are hesitant to single out any given HLS to say it is the "best" HLS for the intended purpose of identifying potential ELL students. Students from a language minority background are an extremely heterogeneous group in terms of actual language proficiency; they may know a lot, a little, or no English and may speak a language other than English entirely, be fluently bilingual, or be English-only speaking (while nevertheless being exposed to a minority language by parents and other family members; Bailey & Kelly, 2013). It is likely that an HLS that incorporates this array of information will be most useful to schools and teachers in terms of program planning (e.g., see the tiered approach taken by the Home Language Identification Survey of the New York City Department of Education to elicit information for screening eligibility, instructional planning, and parent information), but it remains an empirical question, and one that could and should be tested, whether such extensive surveys are more effective at identifying the "right" pool of students for further screening and placement.

We do however get a sense of the type of information that is most relevant for determining which students should be considered for further screening or assessment in a rare natural experiment that presented itself in Arizona in 2009 and was subsequently capitalized on by Goldenberg and Quach (2010). For a short period of time, the state reduced a three-question HLS to ask for just the primary language of the student with parenthetical instructions to interpret *primary* as the language the student used most often. The focus on language dominance in terms of amount of language usage may lead to the underidentification of students who are potential ELL students because students may neither have received extensive exposure to English despite using it the most often nor have reached a level of proficiency sufficient for content learning in English. Indeed, Goldenberg and Quach were able to calculate *before and after* effects of the change in Arizona surveys because in two districts they worked with, families had completed both the original three-question survey and the replacement one-question survey. They found that among the students who were potential ELL students 11% of kindergarten students in one district and 18% of the K–5 students in a second district would have initially gone unidentified using the single primary language question. Of these students, the vast majority went on to be assessed and found to be eligible for English language services. Had the one-question HLS been the sole criterion, these students would have remained outside the ELL assessment and services systems indefinitely or until their need for language services became undeniable.

Bailey and Kelly (2013) have attempted to address issues of the technical quality of and practices with HLS by reviewing available empirical research and describing potentially relevant constructs to be included and validated with future HLS (e.g., current language dominance and current language exposure contexts, exposure histories, and degree of literacy in the first language that may signal academic readiness). In light of this review, and recent work by Palermo et al. (2013) at the preschool level that suggests exposure to English at home and with peers is associated with Spanish-speaking children's English receptive and expressive vocabulary skills, Linquanti and Bailey (2014, p. 3) have articulated constructs for future HLS development in terms of degree of relevance for a student's *current* language use:

a. *Essential constructs*: for example, student's current language(s) spoken, frequency of English language use (by student), frequency of English language exposure (provided by parents, peers, others)
b. *Associated constructs*: for example, languages spoken among adults to one another in the home, history of student's language environment such as first language spoken, use of other language(s); years in U.S. schooling, literacy skills in all language(s)
c. *Irrelevant constructs*: for example, country of origin, information that may have no bearing on a child's current language use

With the constructs delineated in such a salient fashion, the usefulness of the information solicited by any given HLS should be easier to evaluate, but the composition of HLS based on these constructs suggested in the literature awaits empirical testing. A further and equally important contextual factor addressed by Linquanti and Bailey (2014) is the potential for an inconsistently or unfairly administered HLS to also undermine the validity of HLS interpretation. The HLS and its purposes need to be thoroughly explained to parents. The HLS needs to be completed by parents (not by administrators' best guesses) receiving the survey in their native languages or given access to interpreters in cases where they may not be literate in their first language or English. Later we make specific recommendations calling for fundamental research focused on establishing the validity of HLS based on reasoned taxonomies of constructs and principled administrative procedures. Validity here is primarily concerned with devising an HLS that will not misidentify those students who if screened further would be found eligible for Title III services. Missing a screening opportunity may bring an even higher cost later on for those students who need services yet slip through the net; certainly there could be a time lag before classroom teachers refer students they observe struggling to appropriate ELL screening (see Bailey, 2011, for discussion of such a teacher safety net). The ELL assessment system needs to be set to avoid such issues. State and local administrators can err on the side of overidentifying students knowing that immediate further screening *should* remedy any misidentification of students who do not need services but safely include all those who do. We turn next to what happens to those students who rightly or wrongly are identified by the HLS as potential ELL students.

ELL Status Eligibility and Initial Placement

States have the option to choose one or more assessments or screeners to follow the initial identification stage to determine which students are indeed eligible for Title III services. According to the NRC (2011), some states currently administer the same ELPA used for annual testing (e.g., California and Connecticut) whereas most other states use something briefer, typically a placement test or a screener. These measures are meant to provide information about a student's level of English proficiency in four domains (speaking, listening, reading, and writing) and differ in test length, item types, and content alignment (see NRC, 2011, for a review). According to the NRC, a majority of states mandate the use of a single test, either a screener (27 states) or their own ELPA (4 states). The remaining states allow districts to choose between their ELPA and a screener (2 states) or to select their own screener (17 states) although a list is generally provided (NRC, 2011, p. 84). Standard-setting procedures applied to these assessments determine a twofold educational placement: Students who meet or exceed the standard are designated IFEP, and receive instruction with non-ELL students, and students who fail to meet the standard are considered eligible for Title III services, designated as LEP, and provided with that programming.

Standard-setting procedures and decision rules applied to one or more sources of data should take into account the implications of Type I and Type II error for both groups of students and conduct validation studies accordingly. These decision rules set into motion the trajectory of instruction provided to students. Perhaps as a consequence of the legal effort that proceeded the Title III mandate (Hakuta, 2011), assessments—and their cutoffs, or standards—have been created to place all eligible language minority students *in* Title III programming. Yet concern over the growing number of students spending extended time in Title III, called "long-term ELLs," has researchers asking how we place students *out* of Title III (Gándara, Rumberger, Maxwell-Jolly, & Callahan, 2003; Kim & Herman, 2010; Olsen, 2010; Robinson, 2011). Overdesignation of students in initial placement is a plausible, yet rarely mentioned, antecedent to long-term ELL schooling experience and its consequences, such as lower levels of school persistence and less access to college (Kim, 2011). Such incorrectly identified students may not quickly qualify for reclassification in subsequent assessment because reclassification is not automatically enacted at the district or school level for every grade K–12. For example, a study of reclassification in California found that

> nearly half or more of all districts report that they do not reclassify in the early grades (K–2): About 30 percent of districts report permitting reclassification in kindergarten, 47 percent in grade 1, and 54 percent in grade 2. (Hill, Weston, & Hayes, 2014, p. 28)

There is some evidence that districts who do not reclassify prior to third grade have lower overall rates of reclassification (Parrish et al., 2006), lending credence to concerns that ready-to-be reclassified students in early elementary grades may experience deleterious effects from remaining in Title III programming. Studies have found a relationship between protracted time designated as ELL and lack of school persistence, including dropping out of high school (e.g., Kim, 2011). However, the relationship between protracted ELL status, the type, the quantity and quality of instruction received, and academic outcomes is likely to vary at state, district, and school levels and would be best interpreted by mixed-method studies, an approach that is seldom used in this field. In reclassification at the higher grades, the exit criteria are far more extensive and challenging than the initial placement criterion, requiring a student to reach a threshold performance in ELA and in some instances additional content areas (see below). In the case of the inverse situation of underidentification, safeguards to protect against missing a student who should receive Title III services vary at state and local levels (e.g., teacher referral), and to date, no systematic review of such practices has been conducted to our knowledge.

Setting the IFEP standard depends on the state. According to available information (NRC, 2011), the classification as IFEP is based on one of the following: (1) a single score (e.g., screener), (2) a composite score (e.g., ELPA), or (3) an aggregated set of scores (e.g., ELPA and screener). Making a high-stakes decision based on one score is strongly discouraged (see Standard 12.10, American Educational Research Association [AERA], American Psychological Association, & National Council on Measurement in Education, 2014).[11] Just adding multiple sources of evidence, however, does not guarantee the benefit of enhanced overall validity. When one decision rule determines two educational trajectories (eligible for or exempt from Title III services), the management of Type I and Type II error rates (false positive and false negative, respectively) is more difficult. How multiple sources are prioritized and aggregated is equally important because decision accuracy can be severely attenuated by the number of measures (Mosier, 1943) and choice of decision rule (Abedi, 2004).

For criterion-referenced tests, standard-setting techniques are absolute (comparing to the standard) so the cut score is set to minimize either false negatives or false positives. In the context of ELL status eligibility, we consider "false negatives" as students wrongly identified as LEP when actually IFEP and as "false positives" as students wrongly identified IFEP when actually LEP. To minimize "false positives" and try to ensure Title III services for all eligible children, standards may be set at a high level to make the screener difficult to pass (e.g., using a response probability [RP] = .80 standard in the Bookmark method; Mitzel, Lewis, Patz, & Green, 2001). Casting this wide net, however, carries the risk of overidentifying English-proficient language minority students as ELLs. Federal law also requires that we minimize "false negatives" to protect children from inappropriate placement in LEP instruction, especially in cases where English is one of the child's native languages (NCLB, 2001; Title VII, ESEA of 1965; The Civil Rights Act of 1964).

To err on the side of minimizing false negatives, standards could be set to a "readiness" cutoff (e.g., RP = .67 in the Bookmark method). It is up to each state to negotiate the standard that balances these known risks, thus determining the state (or local) definition[12] of what constitutes eligibility for, or exemption from, Title III programming. This standard-setting choice is especially impactful in states where the majority of initial placements happen prior to third grade. Title III requires two sources of standardized testing data to determine "proficiency," an idea adopted by states to determine program exit. This means that students in some states have to wait for second-grade standardized testing data, often delivered to districts in the summer prior to third grade, as the second source of data. Thus, students placed in Title III services in kindergarten could be retained in services for 3 years until second-grade state standards-based test data are available for use in redesignation and reclassification. Discussion of time spent in programs designed for ELL students when students may be wrongly identified is not intended to imply that these programs are inferior in terms of access to academic content instruction; rather, it is meant to illustrate yet another example of how federal accountability has affected ELL testing and use of test data. Furthermore, it calls into question whether any placement test used at kindergarten is fit for the task of determining 3-year ELL placement, especially as some studies suggest the limited reliability of kindergarten ELP assessments for even a 1-year placement (e.g., the MI-ELP assessment in Michigan: Winke, 2011; the California English Language Development Test [CELDT] in California: García Bedolla & Rodriguez, 2011).

Language minority students are also subject to differing degrees of reliability in their designation and placement depending on their state, their grade at enrollment, the screener or placement test they are administered, and the cutoff standard used in that academic year. For example, a language minority student entering kindergarten in Illinois would be given the MODEL-K (WIDA Consortium, 2011), which is used for initial placement and consists of two subdomains naturally weighted: listening (50%) and speaking (50%). Illinois, like each state using the MODEL-K, sets its own cutoff score for IFEP placement, and this standard is subject to regular adjustments ("standards reconsideration"). That same language minority student entering kindergarten in Texas would be administered an Oral Language Proficiency Test measuring listening and speaking only but in California would be administered the CELDT, which includes reading and writing tests weighted as follows: listening (45%), speaking (45%), reading (5%), and writing (5%). The differing likelihoods of IFEP designation based on just these factors have yet to be documented. California statewide data suggest that the percentage of IFEP designations has decreased since the inclusion of reading and writing at the kindergarten level, but this trend is difficult to interpret without further evidence. In addition, the extent to which standard setting is affecting fair placement is as yet unknown.

The new content standards assessments are not likely to affect initial placement practices. However, if a student is transferring from one district or state to another, it is hoped that the new content standards assessments will in fact aid in appropriate ELL placement. With a common measure of achievement in English language arts, for example, it is hoped that the information a student brings to a new district will be more easily interpreted. Crossing state boundaries and encountering a different ELA assessment, however, continue to present challenges for equivalency in the placement of ELL students (Linquanti & Cook, 2013) and is a situation not likely to be completely remedied by establishing two new content assessment consortia to which different states can belong even with the intended linking efforts between the two consortia. Once placement is established, students will receive instruction (e.g., mainstream *plus* Title III services) and their English language progress will be measured in various ways and for various purposes as their language learning is assumed to progress.

Monitoring English Language Progress

We divide the use of ELL assessment for monitoring progress into three subsections: (a) assessment for ongoing language instruction, (b) monitoring annual progress, and (c) assessing for ongoing proficiency status and placement.

Assessment for language instruction. Once students are placed in Title III services, teachers are expected to be continually monitoring the progress of their students' English language and literacy development. Assessments operate at either a *macro level* or a *micro level* in terms of the length of the period covered and the level of the detail of learning obtained (Black, Wilson, & Yao, 2011). Although NCLB requires the annual assessment of English language proficiency based on ELD/P standards (see the next section), the inferences drawn from the results of these macro-level assessments may be inadequate for instructional purposes. The language content sampled in such large-scale, standardized assessments cannot provide sufficient information to teachers about any one specific language skill or knowledge of their students (Durán, 2008).

From an assessment use perspective, such assessments were not designed for, and hence cannot be reliably used for, such purposes. For understanding and appropriately responding to student learning in more incremental ways, teachers additionally need a continual flow of information about their students' language abilities at the micro level. This type of assessment is typically referred to as *formative assessment*, but this term covers a wide spectrum of approaches and may best be described as assessment used *for* learning rather than *of* learning (Black & Wiliam, 1998). Formative assessment has been used to describe the close monitoring that may take place during the act of instruction itself (e.g., Bailey & Heritage, 2008; Bailey, Heritage, & Butler, 2014; Durán, 2008; Heritage, 2010), or the more deliberate collection of information on student performances obtained after instruction has taken place (e.g., teacher-generated classroom assessments, Abedi, 2009, 2010; Llosa, 2008).

The former approach to formative assessment takes place from observing student-to-student talk, by regularly conferencing with or interviewing students about their learning, or by taking note of the ways in which students formulate their questions, for example, and allows teachers to most flexibly decide suitable next-steps instruction (Torrance & Pryor, 1998). Moreover, formative assessment in a moment-to-moment or "proximal" interactive manner (Erickson, 2007) provides teachers with a way to make contingent instructional responses to students' immediate learning needs (Heritage & Heritage, 2011; Heritage, Walqui, & Linquanti, 2013) and, we might argue, is perhaps the most challenging and skillful application of the formative approach to assessment. This application of formative assessment may be especially effective for addressing the learning and assessment needs of ELL students; research shows that the immediate feedback that formative assessment can offer is most effective with students with less background knowledge and lower academic performance profiles (McMillan, 2010). Coleman and Goldenberg (2010) in a review of effective practices with ELL students found that schools and districts that included regular assessment used to inform instruction (along with sustained and coherent leadership, learning goals, consistent curricula, professional development, and ongoing support and supervision) reported higher academic achievement in ELL students.

A key construct concern with assessment for instruction includes defining the necessary English language skills and knowledge that are predictably needed for academic achievement (Bailey, 2007). Features of language used in academic settings that include teacher talk, texts, tests, and standards documents have been analyzed, and commonalities and differences in vocabulary, sentence structures and language functions (e.g., explanations, descriptions) across different content areas (e.g., Bailey, Butler, Stevens, & Lord, 2007), and differences between language use in academic and conversational settings in terms of degree of contextualization and formality (e.g., Snow & Uccelli, 2009) have been noted. One recent approach has been to identify the "Key Practices and Disciplinary Core Ideas" in the new content standards and the receptive and productive language functions that likely will be required to carry out these practices (*ELPD Framework*, CCSSO, 2012). For example, in the area of CCSS English language arts/literacy, students are expected to engage in the following practices: "construct valid arguments from evidence" and "critique the reasoning of others," and the *ELPD Framework* postulates what language functions students may need in order to carry out these practices such as "Comprehend oral and written classroom discourse about argumentation" and "Providing explanation of an argument through the logical presentation of its steps" (pp. 14–15).

This approach includes high-level descriptions of language uses rather than attempting to specify discrete language structures that provide a foundation for language. Indeed, the following example that we have taken from Kindergarten Earth's System Standards (K-ESS) of the NGSS (2013) demonstrates the complexities of identifying the English language inherent in the new content standards.

K-ESS2-1. Construct an argument supported by evidence for how plants and animals (including humans) can change the environment to meet their needs.

To successfully meet this standard, kindergarteners are expected to engage in argument (presumably orally) using the language structures and related vocabulary that will allow them to construct an argument with evidence to support a specific scientific claim. To meet the demands of NGSS K-ESS2-1 linguistically, young students will need the discourse skills to first state a claim and provide evidence (descriptive statements) for or against the claim in order to make an argument that either supports the claim or refutes the claim. At a minimum, they will require knowledge of cause and effect vocabulary and sentence structures (e.g., *because, if . . . then*) and will likely need control of modal verbs to express their stance and the more subtle rela-tions between plants, animals, and the environment (e.g., Tree roots *could, should, would* be in search of water . . .).

Characterizing the inherent language demands (at the word, sentence, and dis-course levels) of the new academic content standards, although challenging, will be necessary to support instructional practices and align ELL assessments (both class-room and large-scale) to the new academic content standards (Bailey & Wolf, 2012). One such attempt has been to build language learning progressions, analogous to the content progressions developed for science and mathematics learning. The Dynamic Language Learning Progressions Project (Bailey & Heritage, 2014) has collected data on student oral and written language in grades K–6 to create empirically based trajec-tories of student language development in the contexts of explanations of personal routines and mathematical problem-solving tasks. With such progressions, teachers will have access to a features analysis of audio- and text-based samples that gives them the capability of formulating customizable learning progressions taking into account a wide array of information on the linguistic and personal background characteristics of students. To date, educators have had no such system to guide them in the forma-tive assessment of student language growth and next-steps instructional decision making.

Finally, it should also be stressed that many students who are acquiring two lan-guages simultaneously may also be receiving content instruction in both English and another language. To present an accurate profile of their language (first and second) and content learning, these dual-language learners will therefore require ongoing assessment both of and in their two languages (e.g., Valdés & Figueroa, 1995).

Annual progress monitoring. Under NCLB, Annual Measurable Achievement Objective (AMAO) 1 is intended to measure students' annual progress in learning English. States set targets for growth that are expected of ELL students in the domains of listening, speaking, reading, writing, and comprehension (typically a composite of the listening and reading comprehension subtests of the listening and reading domains of the state ELP assessment). Measuring this objective is a key intended purpose of the ELD/P standards-based assessment that each state is required to administer with ELL students on an annual basis under Title III. All but seven states belong to a consortium that currently has a test (the ACCESS for ELLS of the WIDA Consortium) or is developing an ELP assessment for annual assessment (the ELPA21 Consortium). The remaining states have developed their own (the CELDT in Cali-fornia, the New York State English as a Second Language Achievement Test in New York, the Texas English Language Proficiency Assessment System in Texas, the Idaho Language Proficiency Assessment in Idaho), have modified an existing commercial assessment (the Arizona English Language Learner Assessment in Arizona), or use a commercially available assessment (the LAS Links, Connecticut and Indiana).

Growth can be measured in increments of proficiency levels with students required to show an increase in at least one level per annum. Using baseline data from the earliest years of a state's AMAO ELP assessment cohort data, targets are set for the expected number of ELL students to meet the annual target in any given year. Myriad attendant issues are raised, such as knowing what increments of growth are reasonable to set and whether the target number of students meeting the desired rate of progress should be set higher as states become familiar with meeting the instructional needs of ELL students (see Mayer, 2007) and the psychometric considerations thereof (e.g., Cook, Boals, Wilmes, & Santos, 2008; Kenyon, MacGregor, Li, & Cook, 2011; see also Boals, Kenyon, Blair, Cranley, Wilmes, & Wright, 2015, this volume).

In the remainder of this section, we focus on two key issues affecting the measurement of language growth: (1) the alignment of ELP assessments to state ELD/P standards and relatedly the adequacy of ELD/P standards to capture the relevant language demands of the academic context, and (2) accurately understanding and measuring meaningful growth in English proficiency.

Starting with the premise that inasmuch as ELP assessments are well aligned with ELD/P standards and curricula, their utility in measuring the language necessary to succeed in academic content classes and on content tests is tied to how well the ELD/P standard themselves reflect the tasks, activities, and knowledge of the academic content areas. ELP assessments have undergone considerable revision in recent years to create test items that reflect the academic uses of language at the K–12 level; they were modified or newly created first to reflect the inherent language of academic content standards required under Title I of NCLB and then more recently to reflect the more overt emphasis on the communication of content knowledge found in the CCSS and the NGSS (see Frantz, Bailey, Starr, & Perea, in press, for a recent review of these developments). Alignment between new ELP assessments and new ELD/P standards should be made tenable with the existence of guiding frameworks such as the *ELPD Framework* developed by language test developers and educational linguists working in tandem (CCSSO, 2012). Earlier ELD/P standards were derived from either ELA standards or hypothetical tasks possibly encountered in content areas rather than from academic content standards (for review, see Bailey & Huang, 2011). In contrast, the *ELPD Framework* and the ELPA21 Consortium ELP standards informed by it, as well as the WIDA Consortium ELD standards and the independently-created standards of states (Arizona, California, Connecticut, New York, and Texas), have all included a focus on the academic *contexts* of the new content standards in which presumably English language develops for the majority of ELL students.

However, less attention has been given to the *language content* in the new ELD/P standards, namely, specific features of English (e.g., word-, sentence- and discourse-level features) and how they develop over time as a result of instruction and experience (Bailey & Heritage, 2014). To date, the education field does not have good descriptions of the trajectories of English language growth in both monolingual English-speaking students and students learning English as a second or additional language (Hoff, 2013). Developmental trajectories or learning progressions are important because they can provide the specificity necessary to guide the kinds of language learning that should occur on route to proficiency in English. Empirically derived language learning progressions based on authentic examples of the features of student language performance at different developmental points could change assessment design by complementing the standards in identifying key characteristics for interim and summative assessment. In the area of formative assessment, they can provide the interpretative framework by which teachers can learn to draw inferences about an ELL student's current language status during a variety of ongoing activity settings in the classroom (Bailey & Heritage, 2014).

Second, in terms of understanding and accurately measuring language growth, Bailey and Heritage (2014) have attempted to explicate the different ways in which language might be expected to progress in terms of amount, quality, rate, and order of development, and depth and breadth of repertoires, relative to the myriad instructional and experiential characteristics pertaining to students' backgrounds. Detailed studies of the growth of language in K–12 student populations taking account of different student dimensions are still necessary if such studies are to inform ELP assessment development. Indeed, a recent study of adolescent ELL students suggests that different rates of English language growth do occur as a function of student background characteristics. Specifically, foreign-born ELL students arriving at ninth grade in U.S. schools acquired English proficiency at faster rates than their U.S.-born peers to attain the same levels of English proficiency by the end of high school (Slama, 2012). The same study highlights how U.S.-born ELL students have been on an enormously delayed trajectory to proficiency having already received Title III services for more than 9 years by the start of the study.

Given that the ELP assessment is used to capture annual growth for accountability purposes, in addition to being the instrument for ascertaining English proficient status, and in some circumstances also the instrument of screening and placement (e.g., the CELDT as it is currently used in California, and optionally LAS Links in Connecticut), serious doubts have been raised as to whether one assessment can realistically be expected to fulfill all of these tasks adequately. However, if an assessment were aligned to an underlying learning progression for English language, then it arguably should be able to serve each of these different purposes. In the absence of such test design and development, multipurpose ELP assessments have been criticized. For example, Stokes-Guinan and Goldenberg (2010) examined the use of the CELDT for multiple purposes including monitoring growth and concluded that it is neither valid nor reliable for measuring individual student growth. This ELP assessment was not originally designed to measure individual student growth year on year. Even with the creation of a common scale to compensate for the lack of vertical scaling needed for reporting yearly growth across the different forms of the test for five different grade spans, the authors caution against its use for reporting the language proficiency growth of individual students, because proficiency level designations were as high as 60% inaccurate in any given year. At best it was considered likely sufficiently valid and reliable for interpreting the growth in English proficiency of *groups* of students.

Stokes-Guinan and Goldenberg (2010), among many others, advise that rather than rely on one assessment for multiple purposes, educators should be relying on multiple assessments for one purpose to counteract the adverse impact of any one poorly devised test. It bears noting that the consideration of multiple sources of evidence in an "all evidence pass" approach (conjunctive) could produce even greater inaccuracy as the decision is based on the least reliable component, as opposed to a "some evidence pass" compensatory approach. Thus the choice of decision rule when aggregating evidence is also crucial (Carroll & Bailey, 2013a, 2013b).

Ongoing proficiency status and placement. Use of a state ELP assessment is also mandated through NCLB in AMAO 2 to account for the number of students attaining a level of English that is deemed "proficient." The state ELP assessment is also used to indicate readiness to exit Title III services, but in this latter instance it is typically one among other measures depending on the state and district (see also the next section). It is also used to determine continuation in LIEPs, as well as to determine level of placement within those programs. The levels of proficiency determined by an ELP assessment can be the only source of data used to determine programming for students classified at Levels 1 to 5[13] who have not yet reached the cut point for English language "proficient." These levels should determine to what extent the programming a student receives will differ in intensity, frequency, and curriculum (see Estrada, 2014; Estrada & Wang, 2013, for an example of these *curricular streams*).

In terms of determining the cut point for English language "proficient" (signaling readiness to exit Title III services on this one indicator), each state determines the way the four subdomains (listening, speaking, reading, and writing) are combined and where the final standard is set. There are four general decision rules (Carroll, 2012; Chester, 2003; Wise, 2011):

a. Conjunctive: all indicator pass
b. Compensatory: some indicator pass
c. Complementary: either/or indicator pass
d. Mixed: combination of models, for example, conjunctive-compensatory

Choice of model depends on the type of error one wishes to avoid. Standards set close to cut points are at high risk for measurement error (AERA et al., 2014), so for ELP assessments, compensatory models can be used to increase the reliability of the overall classification. In a state using two or more sources of evidence in a conjunctive approach, the entire decision may hinge on the measurement precision of the least reliable evidence. It is then that opt-in and opt-out safeguards, such as parent's right to waive Title III services, protect the rights of individual students.

Although classification validity is routinely reported by test vendors in terms of decision accuracy or consistency, empirical evidence is rarely used to justify the use of a certain classification model or scheme. Empirical studies that have examined models applied to ELP assessments have found that conjunctive classification models can underidentify English language proficient cases (Carroll, 2012; Carroll & Bailey, 2013a, 2013b), yet are preferred to minimize false positives.[14] Evidence suggests that compensatory models are preferable for ELP assessments as subdomain tests (listening, speaking, reading, and writing) have few items, are highly correlated, and often have cut points set at or near the mean, increasing the likelihood of erroneous interpretation (Carroll & Bailey, 2013b). Compensatory models may allow undesirable "uneven" proficiency profiles where one subdomain score is dramatically lower than others. There are contexts where compensatory models have been avoided for this reason (see Abedi, 2004; Clauser, Clyman, Margolis, & Ross, 1996; Hambleton, Jaeger, Plake, & Mills, 2000; Hambleton & Pitoniak, 2006). The actual likelihood of uneven profiles in an ELP assessment context, however, has rarely been investigated. One study by Carroll and Bailey (2012) reanalyzed fifth-grade student ELP assessment performance data ($N = 875$) using conjunctive and compensatory models. The authors examined the prevalence of uneven profiles in comparison to false negatives (identification of proficient students as nonproficient) by model. The conjunctive model produced no uneven profiles yet a high number of potential false negatives ($n = 400$), whereas the compensatory model produced some uneven profiles ($n = 15$) yet far fewer potential false negatives ($n = 162$). This finding suggests the need for a well-reasoned model choice to mitigate overidentification and underidentification rather than avoidance of models that may yield uneven profiles.

Standard setting for overall performance standards (e.g., overall Levels 1–5) also determines the intensity and duration of educational programming (see Florez, 2012) and is subject to choice of standard-setting procedures (e.g., Bookmark method; Mitzel et al., 2001) and the alignment and/or vertical scaling techniques applied to test forms within the K–12 testing system (Kenyon et al., 2011). As ELP assessment forms are created in grade span clusters (e.g., K, 1–2, 3–5, 6–8, 9–12), standard-setting and alignment procedures are constrained within the assumptions of how students will perform within and between test forms (e.g., a test developer will set a cut point for the fourth-grade higher than the third-grade cut point but lower than the fifth-grade cut point). As ELL students are heterogeneous in many ways that may defy these assumptions (Durán, 2008), more evidence needs to be gathered, preferably from assessments other than ELP assessments, to verify these procedures.

Reclassification

The final component in the ELL assessment system is reclassification, which determines which students will exit from, or remain in, Title III services. Although effective classification is the goal, misclassification in either direction can be detrimental to student achievement. Instances of students being designated R-FEP and exiting Title III too soon have been the subject of federal oversight, and students reclassified during the early elementary grades have been found to experience academic difficulties later on, showing declining performances on standards-based assessments of mathematics and English language arts by fifth grade compared both to their earlier performances and to their non-ELL fifth-grade peers (Slama, 2014). Concern has also mounted for those who may exit too late—misclassification that leads to continuation in Title III services. Although such placements may not prevent access to grade-level content, students who do not need Title III services may spend some of their day receiving instruction below their linguistic capability, instruction that is often paired with additional remedial coursework, a phenomenon named by Estrada and Wang (2013) as an "additive remediation strategy" with "multiple interventions, each of which moves [ELLs] farther from access to the core and full curriculum and the mainstream" (p. 8). Kim (2011) has found that protracted time in ELL status was related to diminished school persistence. This "long-term ELL" epidemic (Gándara et al., 2003) is strongly linked to assessments and procedures associated with reclassification.

In terms of federal accountability, a change in Title III services is an accountability mandate and is subject to certain federal criteria (AMAOs 2 and 3). At the state (or local) level, this change in service affects educational programming and can be subject to additional local criteria, often grade-specific. The evidence used for reclassification (or Title III continuation) decisions includes ELP assessment classifications (overall "proficient" or "nonproficient"), state standards-based assessment of English/Language Arts (typically overall level of "Basic" or above), grades or GPA, teacher recommendation, and consultation with parents to obtain their opinions about a student's proficiency in English. Typically at the younger grades (K–3), curriculum-based measures of language development (e.g., literacy, reading) are used in addition to, or in lieu of, state standards-based ELA assessment data, which are not collected until the end of second grade. As reclassification criteria are at once double-edged, determining who will exit and who will remain in Title III services, misclassification is difficult to prevent. Effective classification depends on many factors, including the reliability and validity of each measure and criterion, the timeliness of data relative to decision making, and the decision rules used to aggregate the criteria.

The ELP assessment criteria for reclassification are an overall "proficient" classification, whereas "nonproficient" signifies continuation in Title III programs. While investigating the validity of inferences from ELP assessment classifications, studies have investigated the test development process (Davidson, Kim, Lee, Li, & López, 2007; E. E. Garcia, Lawton, & Diniz de Figueiredo, 2010), the impact of test formats and measurement models (Zhang, 2010), and the impact of cut scores (Florez, 2012; Wang, Niemi, & Wang, 2007). Standard-setting procedures, including those commonly used in ELP assessment development, have been subject to scrutiny (e.g., the Bookmark method; Hein & Skaggs, 2009; Karatonis & Sireci, 2006), yet these investigations alone are insufficient for assuring validity of procedures used for setting levels within subdomain tests in ELPAs. Classifications from ELPAs have been criticized for being too lenient in comparison to other sources of proficiency (e.g., Stanford English Language Proficiency Test [SELP]; Mahoney, Haladyna, & MacSwan, 2009) or inconsistent in comparison to other ELPAs (Del Vecchio & Guerrero, 1995, as cited in Estrada, 2010), yet analyses have rarely investigated the impact of an overall classification in terms of reliability, fairness, or ability to produce valid inferences for educational programming.

Although ELP assessment classifications are considered prima facie evidence for readiness to exit Title III, the use of multiple measures is preferred (Ragan & Lesaux, 2006). However, the prioritization and consideration of multiple sources of data depend entirely on the decision rules (e.g., conjunctive—all indicator pass; compensatory—some indicator pass). For example, when all reclassification criteria must be attained (i.e., conjunctive decision rule), a classification of "nonproficient" on the ELP assessment can be the single source of evidence used to retain a student in Title III. This is the case in many states, if not all, as illustrated in the commonly used augmented-classification model (Abedi, 2008). Under a compensatory approach, all evidence may be considered with the allowance of one criterion falling slightly below a cutoff, or within a predetermined zone of indecision (e.g., confidence interval). Although rigid cutoffs may be necessary for federal accountability purposes, compensatory approaches are more aligned with evidence-based data use for individual-level decisions as they allow for greater reliability of the overall aggregate classification. In addition, procedural safeguards such as opt-in and opt-out or parent waivers should accompany an intensified scrutiny of the reliability and validity of each inference, knowing that the least reliable indicator could unfortunately become the gatekeeper. For a more comprehensive review of reliability and validity information gathered on ELP measures, see NRC (2011) and Porter and Vega (2007).

The criterion of "English proficient" as measured by a state's standards-based assessment of English language arts is a matter of state (or local) control. Recommendations have been made for the optimal criterion, which range from "above the 35th to 40th percentile" (Gándara, 2000), yet it has been reported that states interpret age/grade appropriate levels "as scoring above the 50th percentile . . . or even at the 32nd percentile" (Abedi, 2008, p. 21), which illustrates the propensity for within and between state variation. In addition, state standards assessments have gone through many changes in the past decades, moving past the "minimum competency test" programs of the 1970s and 1980s to NCLB era assessments that embodied "much higher standards" (Heubert, 2004 p. 220) to the college- and career-ready standards of the current era.[15]

With ELL assessment consortia (i.e., ELPA21 and WIDA) and statewide data systems (e.g., California Longitudinal Pupil Achievement Data System in California), existing data that come with the student should be more easily interpreted between and within states. Even though states will have their own exit standards attached to these ELP assessments that can include performance on the new content assessments, the potential for more transparency and comparability across states is welcome. See also Linquanti and Cook (2013) and Cook and MacDonald (2014) for the role of reference performance-level descriptors (PLDs) for English proficiency levels in an attempt to create a "common definition of English learner" across states in this regard.

This raises the problem of (un)timely reclassification evidence. In their recent Title III report, Cook, Linquanti, Chinen, and Jung (2012) suggest that policymakers review the timing of the administration of assessments as well as the delivery of assessment data:

Where the ELP is administered several months before the academic achievement assessment, EL students' actual level of English language proficiency when they take the academic content assessment may be quite different from that indicated by their ELP assessment result. Furthermore, the direction of this difference may vary, in part, according to the exact time of year when each assessment is given, and the linguistic environment of the EL student population. (p. 27)

The timing of assessments, data delivery, and reclassification reporting deadlines are also issues of great importance at the local level (Estrada & Wang, 2013). The practical mechanism of decision making depends on timely, useful data, and this is the joint responsibility of policymakers and state departments of education. When assessments used for federal accountability are also used for local decision making, it is the child-level decisions that should take priority. Data delivery systems should be designed to first fulfill this purpose.

Overall, the determination of readiness for Title III program exit has been the focus of most validation studies investigating ELPAs and mostly with an eye on accountability: specifically, looking at the ability of English language "proficient" classifications to predict future academic success (Ragan & Lesaux, 2006). Such studies have examined the outcomes of reclassified students in comparison to English-only students (Crane, Barrat, & Huang, 2011), in comparison to other reclassified students with higher or lower eligibility levels for R-FEP (Kim & Herman, 2010) and in comparison to students who did not reclassify (Abedi, 2008; Grissom, 2004). Studies focused on policy have explored methods for setting reclassification standards (Robinson, 2011) and performance standards for accountability targets related to reclassification (Cook et al., 2008). Few studies have examined academic outcomes for students remaining in LIEPs despite high levels of reclassification readiness, with a notable exception being the current work of Estrada and Wang (2013). In the year-one findings of this reclassification study, researchers found ELL students at all grades, but especially third grade, who were prevented from reclassification due to ELP assessment evidence despite strong performances on all other criteria. These students were subsequently kept in educational programming below their abilities, limiting their chances to access pathways, or *curricular streams* (Estrada, 2014), that would more likely ensure college readiness.

The other indicators for Title III exit, such as grades, teacher report, and parent recommendation, are complex and difficult to interpret in their own ways. The shrinking role of these "nonstandardized" indicators is becoming evident as accountability mandates stipulate the exclusive use of standardized measures in federal reporting. However, their importance and usefulness at the individual level cannot be understated. What remains to be seen is to what extent a prolonged emphasis on standardized measures will change the regard of personal accounts in this process. In this current era of new academic content standards, the types of evidence that comprise the ELL assessment system will continue to be, in the words of Elmore (2004), "to say the least, works in progress" (as cited in Fuhrman & Elmore, 2004, p. 278).

Academic Content Assessment With ELL Students

In this section, we review research focused on two key threats to the valid inferences drawn from academic content assessment use with ELL students, namely, construct irrelevant variance and misuse of test accommodations and how both may be evolving in light of the changing language demands of the new content standards. Both validity concerns arise in the context of interpreting the meaningfulness of results obtained for AMAO 3 at the nexus of Title I and Title III under NCLB. This third and final mandated objective of ELL assessment focuses on the English language arts and mathematics achievement of ELL students as a subgroup of the general student population for federal accountability reporting purposes (see Lane & Leventhal, 2015, this volume; Sireci & Faulkner-Bond, 2015, this volume). Every ELL student who has been resident in the United States for longer than 12 months must participate in their state's annual testing program along with their English-speaking peers. However, where cultural and linguistic factors are paramount in ELL student testing (Durán, 2011; Solano-Flores, 2011), there are additional caveats necessary for the interpretation of scores on state standards-based content assessments as accurate indicators of ELL student content knowledge.

Changing Views on Construct Irrelevant Variance

The NRC (2011) warns,

> The sizable ELL population is a particular challenge because students are at varying levels of ELP and may not be sufficiently proficient in English to demonstrate proficiency in academic content areas. Because they have the task of learning English and academic content simultaneously, it is not surprising that, as a group, they do not meet the proficient level in academic subjects: the academic gap between the group and the non-ELL population is considerable. (p. 7)

It is also important to remember that the most proficient students in the ELL population are exited from ELL status, meaning that students in the ELL subgroup are necessarily and by definition those students not yet proficient in English.

However, Dutro (2006) has referred to the academic achievement gap between ELL and non-ELL students as the "linguistic gap" because of the language demands placed on ELL students that may eclipse their display of academic content knowledge. In fact, we may argue that we do not have sufficient details about the content knowledge of ELL students under existing testing conditions to validly interpret scores as demonstrating a gap in content knowledge between ELL and non-ELL students. Some proportion of the academic achievement gap may be due not to an ELL student's lack of content knowledge but to the content assessment's inability to accurately measure that knowledge when insufficient language proficiency stands in the way. This is the construct irrelevant variance that has previously been identified as a major threat to the validity and therefore potential usefulness of assessments of the content knowledge of ELL students (Abedi, 2002; Haladyna & Downing, 2004). If the language proficiency level of an ELL student is insufficient for the student to understand the language of a mathematics assessment, for example, then the assessment may, in part, be measuring the wrong construct (i.e., measuring language knowledge rather than mathematics knowledge).

In the past, researchers have documented differential item functioning with ELL students that was thought to be the result of construct-irrelevant variance. For example, in the study of ELL and non-ELL student performances on a state standards-based mathematics test, Martiniello (2009) found that greater lexical and syntactic complexity of math word problems favored the math outcomes of non-ELL students. Furthermore, she found that differential item functioning is attenuated when items included nonlinguistic schematic representations that ELL students could use to make meaning of the mathematics test items. However, the new content standards specify the teaching and assessment of the *communication* of content knowledge in addition to the content knowledge itself, and it may be pertinent to now consider how effectively students can communicate their mathematics content knowledge, for example, as an additional aspect of the mathematics construct to be assessed (Haladyna & Downing, 2004). In effect, language has become construct-*relevant* in the era of the new content standards. Furthermore, the four Cs, namely, *critical thinking, communication, collaboration, and creativity,* that have been articulated by the Partnership for 21st Century Skills are reflected in the new content standards (National Education Association, 2011). In the future, the onus will be on test developers to clearly articulate the content construct so that item writers can include or not include additional verbiage as appropriate to avoid construct-irrelevant linguistic complexity. Unfortunately, the distinction between communication and unnecessary linguistic complexity may have become less determinate with the new standards.

Henceforth students will need to be equipped with the linguistic acumen to take part in classroom interactions that support their deeper content learning. For example, when partnered with other students, they will need familiarity with language practices and routines to negotiate their involvement in activities, solve problems cooperatively, and discuss and support one another's ideas (CCSS Initiative, 2010a, 2010b). Studies will be needed to document the kinds of language that teachers report students need to participate in various tasks tied to their implementation of the new content standards. For example, one observation that the participating teachers in the Dynamic Language Learning Progressions Project have made has been around the development of a repertoire of modal verbs and of causal embedding in students' language that appear necessary for negotiating collaborative activities such as building representations of their content learning (e.g., I would like to build . . ., we should do this part first because . . ., If we do this part first then we could . . .; Bailey & Heritage, 2014).

The communication and collaboration emphases in the new content standards will have ramifications for the interpretation of academic content test scores for ELL students, as well as important implications for valid development of both academic content and ELP assessments. First, this change in emphasis in the academic content standards may mean that ELL students will find the new content assessments an even greater challenge than existing assessments in English language arts, mathematics, and science if ELD instruction is not commensurately redesigned and implemented to keep up with the new language demands of the new academic content standards.[16] Potentially, poor performances may be misinterpreted as lack of the deeper content knowledge called for in the new content standards but may be due to either a lack of opportunity to learn content as a result of the new linguistically and communicatively more demanding instructional environment (witness the complexity of the language of modals above) and/or the language demands of the new content assessments, which will act as a barrier to students being able to show what they know.

Second, this change in emphasis implies that the assessments of content knowledge may no longer be unidimensional; rather, they may have both a content knowledge construct and an interactive/communicative ability component that determines how well students can convey their academic content knowledge to others. Moreover, new curriculum-based assessments may need to be developed that also address dimensionality issues so that they are capable of measuring the range of linguistic abilities as well as new communicative competencies aligned with the realities of classrooms configured to teach the objectives of the new content standards.

Implementing Effective Testing Accommodations

Accommodations are provided to address concerns with accessibility of academic content assessments and meaningful interpretation of scores. These testing accommodations are made available to students who need them, including students with certain disabilities and students classified with limited English proficiency. However, fair and equitable accommodation practices differ for ELL students in meaningful ways that affect valid interpretation and use of scores. Furthermore, the use of scores from content area testing affects educational programming and Title III service designations for ELL students, which further magnifies the importance of effective accommodations.

Durán (2008) raises two main concerns in the case of accommodations for ELL students: (1) Does the accommodation adequately facilitate ELL students' ability to access the information required for problem-solving of content area items? (2) Does the accommodation confer an advantage that could alter the meaning of the underlying construct of the measure? Administrators selecting accommodations for ELLs taking state content assessments may be aware that accommodations are classified by whether they alter the underlying construct being tested (e.g., in the unlikely and extreme case that a dictionary were provided during a spelling test) or not, but this classification system is not currently based on research findings. Although there are ways to address the effectiveness of accommodations psychometrically (e.g., the interaction hypothesis, see Sireci, Li, & Scarpati, 2003) the broad heterogeneity of the ELL student population makes interpretation and generalizability of findings challenging. Kieffer, Rivera, and Francis (2012) have provided an updated compendium of the recommended uses of accommodations on large-scale assessments with

ELL students, including specific guidelines applicable to state-level decision makers. Abedi, Hofstetter, and Lord (2004) also raise the concern of feasibility for decision makers: "Is this accommodation strategy practical and affordable, even for large-scale assessments?" (p. 15). Lack of feasibility, or lack of funding to support accommodation practices, is an unfortunate reality for many schools striving to address the needs of ELL students. Furthermore, ELL students with disabilities are entitled to accommodations required by their Individual Education Plans to address their disability as well as accommodations to assist with their English language needs, which may lead to a complex set of choices for educators (see Abedi 2009, for discussion).

The promise of the new computer-adaptive content assessments is that accommodations will be built into the interactive platform of the tests, thus giving test vendors and state departments of education the opportunity to choose, implement, and monitor the effectiveness, validity, and impact of the accommodations. However, the efforts to create reference PLDs common across the states will also contribute to increasing the comparability of accommodations use at certain PLDs (Linquanti & Cook, 2013). Such issues of fair, valid, and interpretable inferences from scores resulting from accommodated testing are paramount and are further discussed by Thurlow and Kopriva (2015, this volume; see also Kieffer et al., 2012; Kieffer, Lesaux, Rivera, & Francis, 2009; Young et al., 2008, Young et al., 2010).

ELL ASSESSMENT COMPONENTS: ONE SYSTEM OR MANY PIECES?

If initial identification practices are sound, then one should expect few students to be identified as IFEP at the next stage of ELL assessment as this would signal that the questions on the HLS overidentified students as potential ELL students when they were not. In other words, HLS questions may have measured construct-irrelevant factors such as having been born outside the United States or even prevented parents from indicating that their child was fluent in both English and another language. The very use of the initial identification phase is to narrow down the population in order to avoid the unnecessary testing of students ineligible for Title III services, a cost both to the student and to the state, but without severely curtailing the chances of including those students who may need services. To date there is no guidance on what proportion of a state's students should reasonably be expected to test as IFEP and that would give an indication that the "right" students had been filtered through the initial identification stage and on to screening or assessment to determine ELL status eligibility.

Similarly in the routines of placement in, continuation in, and placement out of Title III services, our theory of action states that the intended ultimate effects of these components is the progress and eventual English language proficiency of ELL students. Yet measurement error abounds, not only within the assessments themselves but in the assignment of cutoffs and proficiency standards for each decision-making purpose. For the system, and each measure within it, to yield useful interpretations that are valid for each use of testing data (Kane, 2013), all stakeholders need access to information that allows interpretation of scores and error at the individual level. Particularly for state ELP assessments that are developed and validated in grade clusters (e.g., for Grades 3–5), progress monitoring relies heavily on the accuracy of cutoffs and proficiency standards.

Turning to the roles of language and academic content assessments within the system, federal reporting requirements integrated with Title I (i.e., AMAO 3) clearly provide a structure by which states and districts are held accountable for the academic progress of the ELL student subgroup. Furthermore, there is integration of the two assessment components through the service delivery model that NCLB supports, namely, Title III services for those identified as ELL are embedded within the wider Title I services (Figure 1, p. 631, Winke, 2011). Less clear, however, is how the *content* of the two assessment components (English language and academic content) might be connected in a cogent way. The *ELPD Framework* (CCSSO, 2012) has played the most visible role in this regard and is a device by which to consider the relationship between language and academic content, specifically adopting a view that the new content standards "articulate both disciplinary practices and embedded language practices" (p. 2). The *ELPD Framework* is predicated on the conceptualization adopted by the Understanding Language Initiative (e.g., van Lier & Walqui, 2012) that students learn language *and* content simultaneously in complex adaptive systems by responding to "affordances" emerging from dynamic communicative situations. As already mentioned, the purpose of the framework is to guide state ELD/P standards creation and evaluation. However, by its framing of key language practices corresponding with the new academic content standards, the framework may help forge stronger ties between ELD/P and academic content assessment. For example, its extension to assessment scenarios could provide closer connections between the language observed/monitored at the classroom level and the language students will need to display during interactions in content classrooms, or closer connections between the language tested on new ELP assessments and the language students need for their responses to test items on the new academic content assessments.

RECOMMENDATIONS FOR SYSTEM IMPROVEMENTS AND RESEARCH

The research reviewed here has revealed that all components of the system as well as the system in its entirety have flaws requiring changes and subsequent evaluation if the theory of action we initially laid out is to be fully realized. If language testing policies are functioning as de facto language planning policy, then the research and education communities must critically evaluate the assessment system, not just for the technical quality of the assessments but also for the larger purpose and consequences they have on the education of ELL students. First, in the area of initial identification, the HLS needs to be reinvented as a tool to help gauge the language environments a child is currently exposed to and thus the *likelihood* a child has acquired English prior to enrolling in a U.S. school. As part of the larger effort by

CCSSO to support the move toward a "common definition of English learner" across states (Linquanti & Cook, 2013), Linquanti and Bailey (2014) have proposed the development of new HLS informed by the construct-relevant taxonomy outlined in the section on initial identification. By following this proposal, although states may not develop a common HLS, they will have articulated the same set of underlying constructs and they will have reflectively chosen which constructs to include or exclude. It is anticipated that interpretation of HLS results will therefore be more effective because parent responses to HLS questions will more accurately identify the constructs of interest.[17] Moreover, to improve initial identification, we reiterate the recommendation made by Bailey and Kelly (2013) to states to conduct studies of redesigned HLS instruments with parent groups, administrators, and subsequent language proficiency data to determine if they are valid for the purposes to which they are put (see Standard 12.13 in AERA, 2014).

Second, to ensure fair and equitable allocation of Title III services, initial placement tools and the accompanying standards or cutoffs will require ongoing review. Although recent studies have suggested state placement test cutoffs would place many non-ELL students into Title III programs (e.g., 50% of first graders and 75% of kindergarteners in non-ELL sample; García Bedolla & Rodriguez, 2011), it seems that test developers and state departments of education alike are unable or unwilling to interpret these findings in their own Title III systems. There is little doubt that cutoff scores on initial placement tests affect the prevalence of misclassified students. What seems clear from the research reviewed here is that the solution to misclassification, whatever the extent, will not be psychometric. There is simply no way to achieve acceptable levels of misclassification risk for *both* false positives and false negatives, especially on grade cluster tests, which already suffer from borderline reliability at each grade level. State- and district-level Title III coordinators would do well to establish wraparound procedures for each system component in order to amend for the known risks of misclassification. Such procedures could include systematic double-check procedures for students whose scores fall within the confidence intervals of the cutoff and streamlined opt-in and opt-out procedures that include the input of teachers and parents so decisions are made as close to the child as possible. This may include an exploration of the role of bilingual assessment for intake and placement decisions as well.[18] Furthermore, the prevalence and characteristics of the students found ineligible for Title III services (i.e., designated as IFEP) is an area still in need of study along with more robust validation procedures to ensure standard setting and reconsideration are meeting established testing standards (AERA et al., 2014).

Third, to successfully assess the language and content learning of ELL students for instructional purposes, educational administrators need to provide the necessary supports and opportunities for professional development so teachers can learn how to design valid English language assessments for learning and effectively use the information they yield (Bailey & Heritage, 2008; Bailey, Heritage, & Butler, 2014; Briggs, Ruiz-Primo, Furtak, Shepard, & Yin, 2012; Heritage, 2010; Llosa, 2008). The expertise of ELD specialists (including ESL, ELD, and LIEP teachers) and content teachers will need to be combined and used in order to successfully implement class-room assessment of language *and* academic content knowledge during the course of instruction. The *ELPD Framework* (CCSSO, 2012), although laying out extensive connections between language and academic content, is not intended as an aide to teachers despite its importance to their work. Consequently, additional collaboration between researchers, policymakers, and teachers is needed to ensure that teachers are supported in their work.[19] For example, teachers could greatly benefit from exposure to authentic exemplars of language performances to which they could hold ELL students, as well as information about how language develops along situated learning progressions that they could scaffold for ELL students (Bailey et al., 2014; Bailey & Heritage, 2014). How teachers may be assisted to use progressions in on-going for-mative assessment and how well students learn from changes to teacher assessment knowledge and practices still need to be determined by research. Furthermore, lan-guage learning progressions could be used to form the underlying backbone or spine of a unified instructional and assessment system. Specifically, both instruction and assessment could be "aligned" via the same set of learning progressions articulating the incremental developments in student English language and offering far more specificity than aspirations or expectations found in standards. To date, much of the research on learning progressions has been confined to the fields of mathematics and science (e.g., Sztajn, Confrey, Wilson, & Edgington, 2012), but if the work were to be extended more concertedly to language learning contexts it could help improve both assessment and instruction and help states measure growth and proficiency using a desirable multiple-measures approach.

Fourth, we recommend more validity studies focused on the consequences of ELP assessment like Winke's (2011) study conducted to better understand how ELP assessment in Michigan played out at the local level in the hands of districts, princi-pals, and teachers. Such studies will help "ensure that large-scale testing programs like ELP assessment are accountable not only to the entities that mandated them, but also to those for whom the tests are intended to serve—students, educators, and the pub-lic at large" (p. 654). With an eye to the academic content assessments being devel-oped by Smarter Balanced and the Partnership for Assessment of Readiness for College and Careers, we especially need to consider innovative ways to assess aca-demic content with students who are acquiring English. This can include greater exploration of bilingual assessment of the content areas.

Use of language accommodations on the new content assessment will require evaluation for impact on underlying ELA and mathematics constructs. Not only would this information be necessary for states making accommodation selection decisions, but states would also benefit from additional research that can elaborate on the validity and effectiveness of the use of multiple accommodations in the case of ELL students with disabilities. Related to the use of accommodations is the opportu-nity for new kinds of assessment formats due to the electronic platforms of the new content assessments. An extension of Obtaining Necessary Parity Through Academic

Rigor (ONPAR) assessments from the realm of students with disabilities to ELL students, for example, is one attempt to help remedy language as a confound of content measurement (Kopriva & Albers, 2013; Kopriva, Gabel, & Cameron, 2011). ONPAR assessments are computer-based multisemiotic representations (i.e., visual simulations or animations) of knowledge and can minimize the oral and written language needed by students to display their learning. A combination of verbal and nonverbal methods can be used for ELLs to determine their content knowledge both with and without potential language barriers. Such combinations could address not only construct-irrelevant variance concerns at one level but also the need for the *communication* of content knowledge (cf. the new routines and activities requiring language and expected of the learning inherent in the new content standards) when language becomes construct-*essential* for displaying content knowledge. Both the inclusion of technology and the notion of communication of content knowledge take ELL assessment into new realms that will need to be carefully examined for both linguistic and cultural aspects of the validity argument. Admittedly these efforts could be cost-prohibitive if undertaken by individual states, although ELP consortia could leverage developments in the content assessment arena for use with the ELL assessment system. Minimally, states can conduct accessibility reviews of current test items to uncover threats to the interpretive claims of ELP assessments. Of course, even with embedded accommodations implemented during computer administration, professional development will still need to address the skills required of teachers and administrators for identifying accommodations that meet individual ELL student needs (including the complexities of accommodations used with students with disabilities).

Fifth, there are concerns that exit standards-setting procedures may be limiting qualified students from achieving FEP designation (Carroll, 2012, 2014). As with initial placement concerns dealt with in the second recommendation, opt-in and opt-out procedures, such as parent waiver, could help mitigate these inaccuracies and help ensure fair and appropriate continued educational services. Currently, each state (or local) system is left to determine, develop and validate its own opt-in or opt-out system. In the absence of such procedures, students who are underidentified (e.g., Arizona; see Goldenberg & Quach, 2010) or overidentified (e.g., California; see García Bedolla & Rodriguez, 2011) are likely to remain in a mismatched educational setting, perhaps indefinitely. We suggest a more careful, reasoned use of multiple measures and opt-in, opt-out systems, starting with each state or district outlining the decision rules, or proprietary formulas, used at any/all points in the ELL assessment system (see Standard 12.1, AERA et al., 2014). In addition, more careful documentation of multiple sources of validity (beyond coefficient alpha, which is of limited interpretive value in this context; Brown, 2014), including classification consistency, should accompany each state's ELP assessment for each interpretation and use of scores (Kane, 2013). Finally, we recommend systematic review of the academic performances and socioemotional outcomes of former ELL students who are monitored for 2 years after exiting Title III services. The information this yields can provide further evidence of whether educational programs as a whole are meeting the different needs of ELL students (e.g., Castro-Olivo, Preciado, Sanford, & Perry, 2011; Kim & Herman, 2010; Ragan & Lesaux, 2006).

CONCLUDING REMARKS

The validity argument for ELL student assessment is based on the premise that the collection of instruments measure what they claim to (e.g., levels of English that suggest students are eligible for Title III services and the relevant language proficiency needed for academic achievement) and are used in intended ways. The theory of action outlined here has framed the review of ELL assessment polices and related research, and it has assisted in evaluating the system as a whole. The system needs improvements at every level, and to be most effective, we make a final recommendation that the ELL assessment system also be improved on *as a whole*; different ELL assessment components need to relate to one another in a more cohesive manner so that ultimately the elicited data and score inferences are meaningful and useful to states in making certain that all students have received the education that the new academic content standards were created to ensure.[20]

NOTES

[1]Other uses of ELL assessments not explored here include their role in evaluating program effectiveness with consequences for the kinds of instruction students are offered and their subsequent access to learning.

[2]The focus is on federal and state policies and practices. We acknowledge that local implementation of these policies by districts and schools varies greatly and indeed may have the most impact on ELL students' experiences with assessment (see Carroll, 2014).

[3]We are guided throughout this review by Bennett (2010, p. 82), who has set forth five questions for evaluating the theory of action of educational assessment systems: (1) Is the theory of action logical, coherent, and scientifically defensible? (2) Was the assessment system implemented as designed? (3) Were the interpretive claims empirically supported? (4) Were the intended effects on individuals and institutions achieved, and did the postulated mechanisms appear to cause those effects? (5)What important unintended effects appear to have occurred?

[4]In states that still offer bilingual education, ELL students in maintenance dual-language programs are also assessed and can be reclassified as FEP but stay in the program (see Gándara & Merino, 1993, for discussion of pre–NCLB era practices with ELL students in bilingual education).

[5]In school year 2014–2015, for the majority of states, this will be one of the new Race to the Top Consortia assessments tied to the new content standards (i.e., Smarter Balanced or the Partnership for Assessment of Readiness for College and Careers [PARCC]).

[6]While all identified ELL students are entitled under the law to receive access to ELD and core content, some Local Education Agencies (LEAs) provide services without the financial supplement of Title III if they chose not to apply for funding (e.g., too few ELL students to apply without joining an LEA consortium, or if reapplying means entering corrective measures after not meeting AMAO targets). At the individual child level, families may turn down Title III services. Although we adopt achievement as the assumed purpose of education, we acknowledge the contested nature of the purpose of education (cf. Goodlad, Mantle-Bromley, & Goodlad, 2004).

[7] *Standards for Educational and Psychological Testing* (American Educational Research Association, American Psychological Association, & National Council on Measurement in Education, 2014).

[8] A wider systems view could incorporate these and other pertinent factors such as a broader range of stakeholders (e.g., the history teacher whose instructional approaches may need to be modified to successfully include ELL participation in classroom discussions).

[9] Indeed the WIDA Consortium adopted *ELD* for its 2012 standards (WIDA Consortium, 2012) after using *ELP* in two earlier editions (WIDA Consortium, 2004, 2007). Conversely, Oregon, the lead ELPA21 Consortium state, adopted ELP standards, October 2013, and New York State has recently adopted *New Language Arts* and *Home Language Arts Progressions*, introducing further terminology into the mix (EngageNY, 2013).

[10] We note the trend in the literature toward use of the term *former ELL* rather than reclassified-Fluent English proficient (R-FEP).

[11] Standard 12.10: "In educational settings, a decision or characterization that will have major impact on a student should take into consideration not just scores from a single test but other relevant information."

[12] "Uniform Classification" movements, such as Senate Bill 1108 in California and under discussion by CCSSO (Linquanti & Cook, 2013), are moving to limit interpretability of standards at the local level in an effort to make reclassification fairer across district and state lines. However, this type of policy could also affect initial classification (see Linquanti & Hakuta, 2012).

[13] We generally think of ELL students receiving Title III as being at Levels 1 to 3 or 1 to 4, but depending on decision rules, it is plausible—and even prevalent in some states—that students with LEP designation can be at Level 5. Depending on grade level and LIEP offerings, providing Title III services that are Level 4/Level 5 appropriate can be a challenge.

[14] This is especially in the case of initial placement tests as states want to ensure all students eligible for Title III services receive them.

[15] Because of disruptions in the transition to new assessments aligned with the college- and career-ready standards (i.e., 2013–2014 assessment is being used by Smarter Balanced and PARCC testing consortia for field testing only), some states and districts will be grappling with a lack of validated data for the English language arts criterion. Consequently, students in Title III programs will be subject to reclassification decisions based on alternative, and perhaps unproven, criteria.

[16] This concern extends even to non-ELL students, many of whom may also be unfamiliar with the language demands of the new academic content standards.

[17] In addition to revised HLS questions, the administrative rules (e.g., guidelines for use of interpreters and translations for parents) and the decision rules (e.g., guidance to specify how responses are used to make potential ELL determinations) accompanying the surveys also need to be devised and empirically tested for adequacy.

[18] For example, a child's proficiency in the first language is a significant predictor of later reading abilities in English (Miller et al., 2006). Furthermore, from a programming perspective, a child may be sufficiently bilingual in English and another language to be placed in a dual-language program rather than in Structured English Immersion, or if bilingual testing reveals a child is not proficient in the reported home language, a language delay or even disability may be suspected and not necessarily, or exclusively, limited English proficiency.

[19] The Smarter Balanced Digital Library is an example of a collaboration with teachers and higher education institutions. Professional development modules on formative assessment of academic content will include an emphasis on ELL students (see http://www.smarterbalanced.org). We recommend that such efforts also be evaluated for their effectiveness with ELL students.

[20] Overseeing and evaluating the ELL assessment system at its broadest level may best be attempted by entities such as state ELP peer review panels or those conducting validation studies for the state testing consortia.

REFERENCES

Abedi, J. (2002). Standardized achievement tests and English language learners: Psychometrics issues. *Educational Assessment, 8*, 231–257.

Abedi, J. (2004). The No Child Left Behind Act and English language learners: Assessment and accountability issues. *Educational Researcher, 33*(1), 4–14.

Abedi, J. (Ed.). (2007). *English language proficiency assessment in the nation: Current status and future practice.* Davis: UC Davis School of Education.

Abedi, J. (2008). Classification system for English language learners: Issues and recommendations. *Educational Measurement: Issues and Practice, 27*(3), 17–31.

Abedi, J. (2009). English Language Learners with disabilities: Classification, assessment, and accommodation issues. *Journal of Applied Testing Technology, 10*(2), 1–30.

Abedi, J. (2010). Research and recommendations for formative assessment with English language learners. In H. L. Andrade, & G. J. Cizek (Eds.), *Handbook of formative assessment* (pp. 37–66). New York, NY: Routledge.

Abedi, J., Hofstetter, C. H., & Lord, C. (2004). Assessment accommodations for English language learners: Implications for policy-based empirical research. *Review of Educational Research, 74*, 1–28.

American Educational Research Association, American Psychological Association, & National Council on Measurement in Education. (2014). *Standards for educational and psychological testing.* Washington, DC: American Educational Research Association.

Bailey, A. L. (Ed.). (2007). *The language demands of school: Putting academic language to the test.* New Haven, CT: Yale University Press.

Bailey, A. L. (2010). Implications for instruction and assessment. In M. Shatz, & L. Wilkinson (Eds.), *The education of English language learners* (pp. 222–247). New York, NY: Guilford Press.

Bailey, A. L. (2011). Lessons from AZ's EL identification struggle: How guidance could strengthen process. *NCLB Advisor, 6*(4), 5–8.

Bailey, A. L., Butler, F. A., Stevens, R., & Lord, C. (2007). Further specifying the language demands of School. In A. L. Bailey (Ed.), *The language demands of school: Putting academic language to the test* (pp. 103–156). New Haven, CT: Yale University Press.

Bailey, A. L., & Heritage, M. (2008). *Formative assessment for literacy, Grades K-6: Building reading and academic language skills across the curriculum.* Thousand Oaks, CA: Sage.

Bailey, A. L., & Heritage, M. (2014). The role of language learning progressions in improved instruction and assessment of English language learners. *TESOL Quarterly, 48*, 480–506.

Bailey, A. L., Heritage, M., & Butler, F. A. (2014). Developmental considerations and curricular contexts in the assessment of young language learners. In A. J. Kunnan (Ed.), *The companion to language assessment* (pp. 421–439). Hoboken, NJ: Wiley-Blackwell.

Bailey, A. L., & Huang, B. H. (2011). Do current English language development/proficiency standards reflect the English needed for success in school? *Language Testing, 28*, 343–365.

Bailey, A. L., & Kelly, K. R. (2013). Home language survey practices in the initial identification of English learners in the United States. *Educational Policy, 27*, 770–804.

Bailey, A. L., & Wolf, M. K. (2012). *The challenge of assessing language proficiency aligned to the Common Core State Standards and some possible solutions* (Understanding Language Initiative, commissioned paper). Stanford University, CA. Retrieved from http://ell.stanford.edu/publication/challenge-assessing-language-proficiency-aligned-common-core-state-standards-and-some

Bennett, R. E. (2010). Cognitively based assessment of, for, and as learning (CBAL): A preliminary theory of action for summative and formative assessment. *Measurement, 8*(2–3), 70–91.

Black, P., & Wiliam, D. (1998). *Inside the black box: Raising standards through classroom assessment.* London, England: Granada Learning Group.

Black, P. J., Wilson, M., & Yao, S.-Y. (2011). Road maps for learning: A guide to the navigation of learning progressions. *Measurement, 9*(2/3), 71–123.

Boals, T., Kenyon, D. M., Blair, A., Cranley, M. E., Wilmes, C., & Wright, L. J. (2015). Transformation in K–12 English language proficiency assessment: Changing contexts, changing constructs. *Review of Research in Education, 39*, 122–164.

Briggs, D. C., Ruiz-Primo, M. A., Furtak, E., Shepard, L., & Yin, Y. (2012). Meta-analytic methodology and inferences about the efficacy of formative assessment. *Educational Measurement: Issues and Practice, 31*(4), 13–17.

Brown, J. D. (2014). Score dependability and decision consistency. In A.J. Kunnan (Ed.), *The companion to language assessment* (pp. 1182–1206). Hoboken, NJ: Wiley-Blackwell.

Carroll, P. E. (2012). *Examining the validity of classifications from an English language proficiency assessment for English language learners and native English speakers in fifth grade* (Master's thesis). Available from ProQuest Dissertations and Theses database. (UMI No. 1516569)

Carroll, P. E. (2014, October). *Where policy meets practice: Data use in a Title III program.* Paper presented at the Northeastern Educational Research Association Annual Conference, Trumbull, CT.

Carroll, P. E., & Bailey, A. L. (2012, November). *Examining conjunctive and compensatory classification models for an English language proficiency assessment: A descriptive study of English learners and native English speakers.* Paper presented at the conference to honor Ronald Hambleton, University of Massachusetts, Amherst.

Carroll, P. E., & Bailey, A.L. (2013a, April). *Combining multiple indicators in classifications of English language proficiency: A descriptive study.* Paper presented at the annual meeting of the National Council on Measurement in Education, San Francisco, CA.

Carroll, P. E., & Bailey, A. L. (2013b, April). *Language-as-resource in English learner assessment systems: Evaluating the fit of classification models.* Paper presented at the annual meeting of the American Educational Research Association, San Francisco, CA.

Castro-Olivo, S. M., Preciado, J. A., Sanford, A. K., & Perry, V. (2011). The academic and social-emotional needs of secondary Latino English learners: Implications for screening, identification, and instructional planning. *Exceptionality, 19*, 160–174.

Council of Chief State School Officers. (2012, June). *Framework for English language proficiency/development standards corresponding to the Common Core State Standards and the Next Generation Science Standards.* Washington, DC: Author.

Chester, M. D. (2003). Multiple measures and high-stakes decisions: A framework for combining measures. *Educational Measurement: Issues in Practice, 22*(2), 32–41.

Clauser, B. E., Clyman, S. G., Margolis, M. J., & Ross, L. P. (1996). Are fully compensatory models appropriate for setting standards on performance assessments of clinical skills? *Academic Medicine, 71*(1 Suppl.), S90–S92.

Coleman, R., & Goldenberg, C. (2010). What does research say about effective practices for English learners? Part IV: Models for schools and districts. *Kappa Delta Pi Record, 46*, 156–163.

Common Core State Standards Initiative. (2010a). *Common core state standards for English language arts & literacy in history/social studies, science, and technical subjects.* Retrieved from http://www.corestandards.org/assets/CCSSI_ELA%20Standards.pdf

Common Core State Standards Initiative. (2010b). *Common core state standards for mathematics.* Retrieved from http://www.corestandards.org/assets/CCSSI_Math%20Standards.pdf

Cook, H. G., Boals, T., Wilmes, C., & Santos, M. (2008). *Issues in the development of annual measurable achievement objectives for WIDA consortium states* (WCER Working Paper No. 2008-2). Madison: University of Wisconsin-Madison, Wisconsin Center for Education Research. Retrieved from http://www.wcer.wisc.edu/publications/workingPapers/Working_Paper_No_2008_02.pdf

Cook, H. G., Linquanti, R., Chinen, M., & Jung, H. (2012). *National evaluation of Title III implementation supplemental report: Exploring approaches to setting English language proficiency performance criteria and monitoring English learner progress.* Washington, DC: U.S. Department of Education, Office of Planning, Evaluation, and Policy Development, Policy and Program Studies Service. Retrieved from http://www.ed.gov/about/offices/list/opepd/ppss/index.html

Cook, H. G., & MacDonald, R. (2014). *Reference performance level descriptors: Summary of a national working session on policies, practices, and tools for identifying potential English learners.* Washington, DC: Council of Chief State School Officers.

Crane, E. W., Barrat, V. X., & Huang, M. (2011). *The relationship between English proficiency and content knowledge for English language learner students in Grades 10 and 11 in Utah* (Issues & Answers report, REL 2011-No. 110). Washington, DC: Regional Educational Laboratory West.

Davidson, F., Kim, J. T., Lee, H., Li, J., & López, A. A. (2007). English language testing: Evidence from the evolution of test specifications. In A. L. Bailey (Ed.), *The language demands of school: Putting academic English to the test* (pp. 157–170). New Haven, CT: Yale University Press.

Durán, R. P. (2008). Assessing English-language learners' achievement. *Review of Research in Education, 32,* 292–327.

Durán, R. P. (2011). Ensuring valid educational assessments for ELL students: Scores, score interpretation, and assessment uses. In M. R. Basterra, E. Trumbull, & G. Solano-Flores (Eds.), *Cultural validity in assessment: Addressing linguistic and cultural diversity* (pp. 115–142). New York, NY: Routledge.

Dutro, S. (2006, January). *Providing language instruction. Aiming high/Aspirando a lo Mejor resource.* Santa Rosa, CA: Sonoma County Office of Education.

Elmore, R. F. (2004). Conclusion: The problem of stakes in performance-based accountability systems. In S. Fuhrman, & R. F. Elmore (Eds.), *Redesigning accountability systems for education* (Vol. 38, pp. 274–296). New York, NY: Teachers College Press.

EngageNY. (2013). *NYS Bilingual Common Core Initiative: Theoretical foundations.* Retrieved from https://www.engageny.org/resource/new-york-state-bilingual-common-core-initiative

Erickson, F. (2007). Some thoughts on "proximal" formative assessment of student learning. In P. Moss (Ed.), *Evidence in decision making: Yearbook of the National Society for the Study of Education* (Vol. 106, pp. 186–216). Malden, MA: Blackwell.

Estrada, P. (2010, May). *Expanding or eclipsing horizons for EL students: A cross-case analysis.* Paper presented at the American Educational Research Association, Denver, Colorado.

Estrada, P. (2014). English learner curricular streams in four middle schools: Triage in the trenches. *Urban Review.* Retrieved from http://link.springer.com/article/10.1007/s11256-014-0276-7

Estrada, P., & Wang, H. (2013, May). *Reclassifying and not reclassifying English learners to fluent English proficient, year 1 findings: Factors impeding and facilitating reclassification and access to the core.* Paper presented at the American Educational Research Association, San Francisco, California.

Faulkner-Bond, M., Waring, S., Forte, E., Crenshaw, R. L., Tindle, K., & Belkap, B. (2012). *Language instruction educational programs (LIEPs): A review of the foundational literature.* Washington, DC: U.S. Department of Education; Office of Planning, Evaluation and Policy Development; Policy and Program Studies Service. Retrieved from http://www2.ed.gov/rschstat/eval/title-iii/language-instruction-ed-programs-report.pdf

Florez, I. R. (2012). Examining the validity of the Arizona English Language Learners Assessment cut scores. *Language Policy, 11*(1), 33–45.

Forte, E., Perie, M., & Paek, P. (2012). *Exploring the relationship between English language proficiency and English language arts assessments.* Retrieved from http://www.eveaproject.com/doc/EVEA%20ELPA%20ELA%20paper_03-5-12.pdf

Frantz, R. S., Bailey, A. L., Starr, L., & Perea, L. (in press). Measuring academic language proficiency in school-age English language proficiency assessments under New College and Career Readiness Standards in the U.S. *Language Assessment Quarterly.*

Gándara, P. (2000). In the aftermath of the storm: English learners in the post-227 era. *Bilingual Research Journal, 24*(1&2), 1–13.

Gándara, P., Rumberger, R., Maxwell-Jolly, J., & Callahan, R. (2003, October 7). English learners in California schools: Unequal resources, unequal outcomes. *Education Policy Analysis Archives, 11*(36). Retrieved from http://epaa.asu.edu/epaa/v11n36/

Gándara, P., & Merino, B. (1993), Measuring the outcome of LEP programs: Test scores, exit rates, and other mythological data. *Educational Evaluation and Policy Analysis, 15*, 320–338.

Garcia, E. E., Lawton, K., Diniz de & Figueiredo, E. H. (2010). *Assessment of young English language learners in Arizona: Questioning the validity of the state measure of English proficiency.* Los Angeles: Civil Rights Project, University of California. Retrieved from http://civilrightsproject.ucla.edu/research

García, G., McKoon, G., & August, D. (2006). Language and literacy assessment of language-minority students. In D. August, & T. Shanahan (Eds.), *Developing literacy in second-language learners* (pp. 597–624). Mahwah, NJ: Lawrence Erlbaum.

García Bedolla, L. G., & Rodriguez, R. (2011). *Classifying California's English learners: Is the CELDT too blunt an instrument?* (Policy reports and research briefs). Berkeley: Center for Latino Policy Research, Institute for the Study of Societal Issues, UC Berkeley.

Goldenberg, G., & Quach, S. R. (2010). *The Arizona Home Language Survey and the identification of students For ELL services.* Los Angeles: Civil Rights Project/Proyecto Derechos Civiles, UCLA. Retrieved from http://civilrightsproject.ucla.edu/research/k-12-education/language-minority-students/the-arizona-home-language-survey-and-the-identification-of-students-for-ell-services/AZ-PHLOTEGO8-17-10revision.pdf

Goodlad, J. I., Mantle-Bromley, C., & Goodlad, S. J. (2004). *Education for everyone: Agenda for education in a democracy.* Indianapolis, IN: Jossey-Bass.

Grissom, J. B. (2004, July 30). Reclassification of English learners. *Education Policy Analysis Archives, 12*(36). Retrieved from http://epaa.asu.edu/ojs/article/view/191/317

Hakuta, K. (2011). Educating language minority students and affirming their equal rights: Research and practical perspectives. *Educational Researcher, 40*, 163–174.

Haladyna, T. M., & Downing, S. M. (2004). Construct-irrelevant variance in high-stakes testing. *Educational Measurement: Issues and Practice, 23*(1), 17–27.

Hambleton, R. K., Jaeger, R. M., Plake, B. S., & Mills, C. (2000). Setting performance standards on complex educational assessments. *Applied Psychological Measurement, 24*, 355–366.

Hambleton, R. K., & Pitoniak, M. J. (2006). Setting performance standards. In R. Brennan (Ed.), *Educational measurement* (4th ed., pp. 433–470). Portsmouth, NH: Praeger.

Hein, S. F., & Skaggs, G. E. (2009). A qualitative investigation of panelists' experiences of standard setting using two variations of the Bookmark method. *Applied Measurement in Education, 22*, 207–228.

Heritage, M. (2010). *Formative assessment and next-generation assessment systems: Are we losing an opportunity?* Washington, DC: Council of Chief State School Officers.

Heritage, M., & Heritage, J. (2011, April). *Teacher questioning: The epicenter of instruction and assessment.* Paper presented at the annual meeting of the American Educational Research Association, New Orleans, LA.

Heritage, M., Walqui, A., & Linquanti, R. T. (2013, April). *Formative assessment as contingent communication: Perspectives on assessment as and for language learning in the content areas.* Paper presented at the annual meeting of the American Educational Research Association, San Francisco, CA.

Heubert, J. P. (2004). High-stakes testing in a changing environment: Disparate impact, opportunity to learn, and current legal protections. In S. H. Fuhrman, & R. F. Elmore (Eds.), *Redesigning accountability systems for education* (Vol. 38, pp. 220–242). New York, NY: Teachers College Press.

Hill, L., Weston, M., & Hayes, J. (2014). *Reclassification of English-learner students in California.* San Francisco: Public Policy Institute of California.

Hoff, E. (2013). Interpreting the early language trajectories of children from low-SES and language minority homes: Implications for closing achievement gaps. *Developmental Psychology, 49*, 4–14.

Hopkins, M., Thompson, K. D., Linquanti, R., Hakuta, K., & August, D. (2013). Fully accounting for English learner performance: A key issue in ESEA reauthorization. *Educational Researcher, 42*, 101–108.

Kane, M. (2013). Validating the interpretations and uses of test scores. *Journal of Educational Measurement, 50*, 1–73.

Karatonis, A., & Sireci, S. G. (2006). The Bookmark standard-setting method: A literature review. *Educational Measurement: Issues and Practice, 25*(1), 4–12.

Kenyon, D. M., MacGregor, D., Li, D., & Cook, H. G. (2011). Issues in vertical scaling of a K-12 English language proficiency test. *Language Testing, 28*, 383–400.

Kieffer, M. J., Lesaux, N. K., Rivera, M., & Francis, D. J. (2009). Accommodations for English language learners taking large-scale assessments: A meta-analysis of effectiveness and validity. *Review of Educational Research, 79*, 1168–1201.

Kieffer, M. J., Rivera, M., & Francis, D. J. (2012). *Practical guidelines for the education of English language learners: Book 4. Research-based recommendations for the use of accommodations in large-scale assessments: 2012 Update.* Portsmouth, NH: Center on Instruction.

Kim, J. (2011). *Relationships among and between ELL status, demographic characteristics, enrollment history, and school persistence* (CRESST Report No. 810). Los Angeles: University of California, National Center for Research on Evaluation, Standards, and Student Testing.

Kim, J., & Herman, J. L. (2010). *When to exit ELL students: monitoring success and failure in mainstream classrooms after ELLs' reclassification* (CRESST Report No. 779). Los Angeles: University of California, National Center for Research on Evaluation, Standards, and Student Testing.

Kindler, A. (2002). *Survey of the states' limited English proficient students and available educational programs and services: 2000-2001 Summary report.* Washington, DC: National Clearinghouse for English Language Acquisition.

Kopriva, R., & Albers, C. A. (2013). Considerations for achievement testing of students with individual needs. In K. F. Geisinger (Ed.), *Handbook of testing and assessment in psychology* (pp. 370–390). Washington, DC: American Psychological Association.

Kopriva, R., Gabel, D., & Cameron, C. (2011). *Designing dynamic and interactive assessments for English learners that directly measure targeted science constructs.* Evanston, IL: Society for Research on Educational Effectiveness.

Lane, S., & Leventhal, B. (2015). Psychometric challenges in assessing English language learners and students with disabilites. *Review of Research in Education, 39*, 165–214.

Linquanti, R., & Bailey, A. L. (2014). *Reprising the Home Language Survey: Summary of a national working session on policies, practices, and tools for identifying potential English learners.* Washington, DC: Council of Chief State School Officers.

Linquanti, R., & Cook, H. G. (2013). *Toward a "common definition of English learner": Guidance for states and state assessment consortia in defining and addressing policy and technical issues and options.* Washington, DC: Council of Chief State School Officers.

Linquanti, R., & Hakuta, K. (2012). *How next-generation standards and assessments can foster success for California's English learners* (PACE Policy Brief No. 12-1). Stanford, CA: School of Education, Stanford University. Retrieved from http://www.edpolicyinca.org

Llosa, L. (2008). Building and supporting a validity argument for a standards-based classroom assessment of English proficiency based on teacher judgments. *Educational Measurement: Issues and Practice, 27*(3), 32–42.

Mahoney, K. S., Haladyna, T., & MacSwan, J. (2009). The need for multiple measures in reclassification decisions: A validity study of the Stanford English Language Proficiency Test. In T. G. Wiley, J. S. Lee, & R. W. Rumberger (Eds.), *The education of language minority immigrants in the United States* (pp. 240–262). Tonawanda, NY: Multilingual Matters.

Martiniello, M. (2009). Linguistic complexity, schematic representations, and differential item functioning for English language learners in math tests. *Educational Assessment, 14*, 160–179.

Mayer, J. (2007). Policy needs: What federal and state governments need from language research. In A. L. Bailey (Ed.), *The language demands of school: Putting academic language to the test*. New Haven, CT: Yale University Press.

McMillan, J. H. (2010). The practical implications of educational aims and contexts for formative assessment. In H. L. Andrade, & G. J. Cizek (Eds.), *Handbook of formative assessment* (pp. 41–58). New York, NY: Routledge.

Menken, K. (2008). *English learners left behind: Standardized testing as language policy* (Vol. 65). Cleveden, England: Multilingual Matters.

Miller, J. F., Heilmann, J., Nockerts, A., Iglesias, A., Fabiano, L., & Francis, D. J. (2006). Oral language and reading in bilingual children. *Learning Disabilities Research & Practice, 21*, 30–43.

Mitzel, H. C., Lewis, D. M., Patz, R. J., & Green, D. R. (2001). The bookmark procedure: Psychological perspectives. In G. J. Cizek (Ed.), *Setting performance standards: Concepts, methods, and perspectives* (pp. 249–281). Mahwah, NJ: Lawrence Erlbaum.

Mosier, C. I. (1943). On the reliability of a weighted composite. *Psychometrika, 8*, 161–168.

National Education Association. (2011). *Preparing 21st century students for a global society: An educator's guide to the "four Cs."* Retrieved from http://www.nea.org/assets/docs/A-Guide-to-Four-Cs.pdf

National Research Council. (2011). *Allocating federal funds for state programs for English language learners*. Washington, DC: National Academies Press.

NGSS Lead States. (2013). *Next Generation Science Standards. For states, by states*. Washington, DC: National Academies Press.

No Child Left Behind Act of 2001. *Conference report to accompany H.R., 1*, Rep. No. 107-334, House of Representatives, 107th Congress, 1st Session, December 13. Pub. L. No. 107-110, 115 Stat. 1425.

Olsen, L. (2010). *Reparable harm: Fulfilling the unkept promise of educational opportunity for long term English Learners*. Long Beach: Californians Together.

Palermo, F., Mikulski, A. M., Fabes, R. A., Hanish, L. D., Martin, C. L., & Stargel, L. E. (2013). English exposure in the home and classroom: Predictions to Spanish-speaking preschoolers' English vocabulary skills. *Applied Psycholinguistics, 35*, 1163–1187.

Parrish, T. B., Merickel, A., Perez, M., Linquanti, R., Socias, M., Spain, A., . . . & Delancey, D. (2006). Effects of the implementation of Proposition 227 on the education of English learners, K-12: Findings from a five-year evaluation. Palo Alto, CA: American Institutes for Research and WestEd.

Perie, M., & Forte, E. (2011). Developing a validity argument for assessments of students in the margins. In M. Russell (Ed.), *Assessing students in the margins: Challenges, strategies, and techniques* (pp. 335–378). Charlotte, NC: Information Age.

Porter, S. G., & Vega, J. (2007). Overview of existing English language proficiency tests. In J. Abedi (Ed.), *English language proficiency assessment in the nation: Current status and future practice* (pp. 93–104). Davis: UC Davis School of Education.

Ragan, A., & Lesaux, N. (2006). Federal, state, and district level English language learner program entry and exit requirements: Effects on the education of language minority learners. *Education Policy Analysis Archives, 14*, 1–29. Retrieved from http://epaa.asu.edu/ojs/article/view/91

Robinson, J. P. (2011). Evaluating criteria for English learner reclassification: A causal-effects approach using a binding-score regression discontinuity design with instrumental variables. *Educational Evaluation and Policy Analysis, 33*, 267–292.

Sireci, S. G., & Faulkner-Bond, M. (2015). Promoting validity in the assessment of English learners. *Review of Research in Education, 39*, 215–252.

Sireci, S. G., Li, S., & Scarpati, S. (2003). *The effects of test accommodation on test performance: A review of the literature* (Center for Educational Assessment Research Report No. 485). Retrieved from http://www.cehd.umn.edu/nceo/onlinepubs/testaccommlitreview.pdf

Slama, R. B. (2012). A longitudinal analysis of academic English proficiency outcomes for adolescent English language learners in the United States. *Journal of Educational Psychology, 104*, 265–285.

Slama, R. B. (2014). Investigating whether and when English learners are reclassified into mainstream classrooms in the United States A discrete-time survival analysis. *American Educational Research Journal, 51*, 220–252.

Snow, C. E., & Uccelli, P. (2009). The challenge of academic language. In D. R. Olson, & N. Torrance (Eds.), *The Cambridge handbook of literacy* (pp. 112–133). New York, NY: Cambridge University Press.

Solano-Flores, G. (2011). Assessing the cultural validity of assessment practices: An introduction. In M. R. Basterra, E. Trumbull, E., & G. Solano-Flores (Eds.), *Cultural validity in assessment: Addressing linguistic and cultural diversity* (pp. 3–21). New York, NY: Routledge.

Stokes-Guinan, K., & Goldenberg, C. (2010). Use with caution: What CELDT results can and cannot tell us. *CATESOL Journal, 22*, 189–202.

Sztajn, P., Confrey, J., Wilson, P. H., & Edgington, C. (2012). Learning trajectory based instruction: Toward a theory of teaching. *Educational Researcher, 41*, 147–156.

Thurlow, M. L., & Kopriva, R. J. (2015). Advancing accessibility and accommodations in content assessments for students with disabilities and English learners. *Review of Research in Education, 39*, 331–369.

Torrance, H., & Pryor, J. (1998). *Investigating formative assessment.* Philadelphia: Open University Press.

Valdés, G., & Figueroa, R. A. (1995). *Bilingualism and testing: A special case of bias.* Norwood, NJ: Ablex.

van Lier, L., & Walqui, A. (2012). Language and the common core standards. In K. Hakuta, & M. Santos (Eds.), *Understanding language: Commissioned papers on language and literacy issues in the Common Core State Standards and Next Generation Science Standards* (pp. 44–51). Palo Alto, CA: Stanford University

Wang, J., Niemi, D., & Wang, H. (2007). *Impact of different performance assessment cut scores on student promotion* (CSE Report No. 719). Retrieved from http://files.eric.ed.gov/fulltext/ED498443.pdf

WIDA Consortium. (2004). *English language proficiency standards for English language learners in pre-kindergarten through Grade 12.* Madison: Board of Regents of the University of Wisconsin System.

WIDA Consortium. (2007). *English language proficiency standards for English language learners in pre-kindergarten through Grade 12.* Madison: Board of Regents of the University of Wisconsin System.

WIDA Consortium. (2011). *MODEL-K.* Madison, WI: Board of Regents of the University of Wisconsin System.

WIDA Consortium. (2012). *Amplification of the English Language Development Standards.* Madison: Board of Regents of the University of Wisconsin System. Retrieved from http://www.wida.us/standards/eld.aspx

Winke, P. (2011). Evaluating the validity of a high-stakes ESL test: Why teachers' perceptions matter. *TESOL Quarterly, 45*, 628–660.

Wise, L. L. (2011). *Combining multiple indicators* (Paper for the PARCC technical advisory group). Retrieved from http://www.parcconline.org/sites/parcc/files/PARCCTACPaperCombiningMultipleIndicatorsRevised09-06-2011.pdf

Wolf, M. K., Kao, J. Griffin, N., Herman, J. L., Bachman, P. L., Chang, S., & Farnsworth, T. (2008). *Issues in assessing English language learners: English language proficiency measures and accommodation uses—Practice review* (CSE Tech. Rep. No. 732). Los Angeles: University of California, National Center for Research on Evaluation, Standards, and Student Testing.

Young, J. W., Cho, Y., Ling, G., Cline, F., Steinberg, J., & Stone, E. (2008). Validity and fairness of state standards-based assessments for English language learners. *Educational Assessment, 13*, 170–192.

Young, J. W., Steinberg, J., Cline, F., Stone, E., Martiniello, M., Ling, G., & Cho, Y. (2010). Examining the validity of standards-based assessments for initially fluent students and former English language learners. *Educational Assessment, 15*, 87–106.

Zhang, B. (2010). Assessing the accuracy and consistency of language proficiency classification under competing measurement models. *Language Testing, 27*, 119–140.

Chapter 8

Adaptations and Access to Assessment of Common Core Content

RYAN J. KETTLER

Rutgers, the State University of New Jersey

This chapter introduces theory that undergirds the role of testing adaptations in assessment, provides examples of item modifications and testing accommodations, reviews research relevant to each, and introduces a new paradigm that incorporates opportunity to learn (OTL), academic enablers, testing adaptations, and inferences that can be made from scores. The purpose is to document the substantial research that has been completed on testing adaptations, along with critical findings, and to push the field to reexamine the methods that we use to answer questions about the appropriateness of the evidence that has typically been collected. Now let's get started with Item 1.

You have 1 minute to solve Item 1. Do NOT use a calculator.

Solve.

1.

$$\begin{array}{r} 74 \\ \times\ 16 \\ \hline \end{array}$$

    a. 90
    b. 518
    c. 1184
    d. 4514

Review of Research in Education
March 2015, Vol. 39, pp. 295–330
DOI: 10.3102/0091732X14556075
© 2015 AERA. http://rre.aera.net

We have all been asked to solve items like Item 1 at some point in our lives; let us consider it. What is the content of Item 1? How difficult is it? For which students would it be appropriate? What is the construct that Item 1 is intended to measure?

According to the Common Core Standards for mathematics, at the fourth-grade level within the domain Number and Operations in Base 10 (NOB10), Standard B.5 states:

> Multiply a whole number of up to four digits by a one-digit whole number, and multiply two two-digit numbers, using strategies based on place value and the properties of operations. Illustrate and explain the calculation by using equations, rectangular arrays, and/or area models. (Common Core State Standards Initiative, 2013)

Item 1 could be one of many items included on a test of fourth-grade mathematics achievement, designed to address the narrow construct described in B.5, as well as the broader construct of NOB10. The item involves the multiplication of two, 2-digit numbers. The answer choices include (a) a distractor (i.e., incorrect answer choice) that would be attractive if addition were used instead of multiplication, (b) a distractor that would be attractive if a 0 was not inserted into the ones' place of the answer when multiplying 1×74, (c) the correct answer, and (d) a distractor that would be attractive if the 0 was erroneously used in the ones' place when multiplying 6×74, rather than when multiplying 1×74.

How good is Item 1? How accessible is it for a diverse population of test takers? In other words, can students from all groups show what they know and can do via Item 1, or might some groups do poorly on it for reasons unrelated to mathematics and NOB10? Can Item 1 be adapted in any way to increase accessibility, without otherwise compromising its effectiveness as an item? These questions illustrate the central issues that will be addressed in this chapter.

ACCESSIBILITY AND ADAPTATIONS

Confusion exists with regard to the meaning of access in assessment; the concept of providing access via a test or other form of assessment is complex. In a given situation, an administrator might view access as the opportunity for students to complete the test in an environment that is free of barriers that interfere with performance. A teacher might view access as the opportunity to engage with items whose content has been taught in class. A parent might view access as the opportunity to complete the test with the potential to obtain a high score. All of these conceptualizations address important aspects of access in assessment, but to fully understand the concept, one must consider the reason that we assess students. We assess students to gain a better understanding of what they know and can do on the tested or target construct. (What we do with that information may vary, as it may be used to direct future instruction in formative assessment or to make evaluative decisions in summative assessment, but for any of these steps to be successful the test score must reflect the target construct for the student.) In psychometric terms, access in education is maximized when the proportion of the variance in a set of scores that is attributable to the construct of interest is maximized. The best methods for evaluating such access are the same methods used to collect reliability and validity evidence for scores from tests in their original forms, administered under standardized conditions. When the reliability and validity evidence obtained for a subgroup of students under a special set of conditions is strong or very similar to the evidence obtained for the general population under standard conditions, we can conclude that access for this subgroup is acceptable under these conditions.

Content Versus Construct

The terms *content* and *construct* are too often confused in the discussion about testing adaptations. The content of an item or test includes its components that are observable. For a multiple-choice item, this often includes a passage, perhaps a visual, an item stem or question, and answer choices (one correct answer and multiple distractors). The content of an item can be conceptualized as the important parts that *can* be seen, and the construct of the item can be conceptualized as the important parts that *cannot* be seen. With all of these tests, we are using behaviors or permanent products that are observable and recordable (e.g., the answer to Item 1, whether it is correct, and perhaps the steps the examinee took to obtain the answer) to draw conclusions about constructs that are not observable (e.g., double-digit multiplication using strategies based on place value and the properties of operations, NOB10, mathematics). Every item or test has at least one underlying construct that it is designed to measure. In the case of a test that has subscale and composite scores, it is likely that a single item is designed to indicate two or more underlying constructs, with subscale scores representing narrower constructs (e.g., NOB10) and composite scores representing broader constructs (e.g., mathematics).

Testing adaptations should always be *intended* to improve the precision of measurement of the underlying construct by a test and its constituent item set. The most widely accepted distinction between testing accommodations and modifications is that accommodations (e.g., extra time, read-aloud) do not change the content of a test, whereas modifications (e.g., reducing the number of digits, removing one distractor) do change the content of the test. A common misperception is that modifications by their very nature change the underlying construct of an item or test. This is not accurate, at least by the conventional terminology as defined in the *Standards for Educational and Psychological Testing* (*Testing Standards*; American Educational Research Association [AERA], American Psychological Association, & National Council on Measurement in Education, 1999) and in *Educational Measurement* (Koretz & Hamilton, 2006; Phillips & Camara, 2006). Adapting an item or the method of interacting with the item to the point that the underlying construct being addressed is different, and subsequently attempting to draw inferences about the original construct, would be inappropriate; this is true regardless of whether the adaptation was an attempt at an accommodation or at a modification.

In addition to content and construct being similar-sounding words and sharing a nonorthogonal relationship, the two are further confused within the world of large-scale assessment because the underlying *construct* is defined in large part by the *content standards*. As typically written, content standards (e.g., including the aforementioned B.5) are not directly observable, but they provide guidelines for the content of the test and define both narrowly (at the standard level) and more broadly (at the domain level) the construct being measured by the test.

The issue of whether the content of an item has been changed (i.e., a modification has been made) via a test adaptation is a relatively easy distinction to make. Whether this change was appropriate for an item intended to measure an unchanged construct is a more complicated question that is best answered empirically. Consider the following example.

Case Study

Alison is a fourth-grade student who is struggling in mathematics, and particularly on tests. Her global intelligence is near the normative mean of her age peers, and her processing speed is about 1 standard deviation below the normative mean. Alison's academic fluency scores are nearly 2 standard deviations below the normative mean, so she clearly has difficulty with timed tasks. From a measurement standpoint, a primary concern in Alison's case is that a functional impairment (i.e., a deficit in a skill needed for access) in processing speed could keep her from showing what she knows and can do in NOB10. Put another way, her score from a timed test of NOB10 may be as reflective or more reflective of her processing speed as it is of her achievement in NOB10.

Two types of adaptations that may increase accessibility for Alison are accommodations and modifications. Since it is possible that either type of adaptation may also be classified as appropriate versus inappropriate, the 2 × 2 matrix depicted in Figure 1 represents four relevant scenarios (i.e., Item 1a: an appropriate accommodation, Item 1b: an appropriate modification, Item 1c: an inappropriate accommodation, and Item 1d: an inappropriate modification).

The content in Item 1a is identical to the aforementioned Item 1, addressing the narrow construct of double-digit multiplication using strategies based on place value and the properties of operations, as well as the broader construct of NOB10, and at the broadest level mathematics achievement. Alison is provided 50% extra time, so she has 90 seconds rather than 60 seconds. Given her functional impairment, the added time will theoretically allow Alison to respond on the item similarly to how students without such impairments perform in the standard 60 seconds. Gathering evidence that this accommodation is actually appropriate (i.e., the construct is unchanged) is more practical if using multiple similar items and multiple examinees with similar functional impairments. For the sake of this illustration, we will assume that Alison did everything exactly the same way that the typical student without a functional impairment would, except it took her 50% longer due to lower processing speed.

FIGURE 1
Appropriate and Inappropriate Accommodations and Modifications

	Adaptation	
	Accommodation	Modification
	(50% Extra Time)	(Simplified a digit)

Appropriate	**1a.**
	
	  7 4
	x 1 6
	
	a. 90
	b. 518
	c. 1184
	d. 4514
		1b.
		
		  7 4
		x 1 2
		
		a. 86
		b. 222
		c. 888
		d. 1554

	(Calculator)	(Changed 2-digit to 1-digit)

Inappropriate	**1c.**
	
	  7 4
	x 1 6
	
	a. 90
	b. 518
	c. 1184
	d. 4514
		1d.
		
		  7 4
		x 6
		
		a. 66
		b. 68
		c. 80
		d. 444

Note. For a student with a functional impairment in processing speed, both appropriate and inappropriate accommodations and modifications are available for a test of double-digit multiplication, Numbers & Operations in Base 10, and mathematics achievement.

The content of Item 1b is slightly different from Item 1. Changing the "6" in the original item to a "2" allowed Alison to complete the item with all the same steps but without having to carry the "2" in the 10s spot from multiplying 6 × 4. The answer choices were also modified to match the new correct answer and plausible distractors. Item 1b is easier than Item 1 but appears to still address the narrow construct of double-digit multiplication using strategies based on place value and the properties of operations, as well as the broader constructs of NOB10 and mathematics achievement.

The content of Item 1c is again identical to Item 1; however, Alison is allowed to use a calculator on 1c. The item still addresses double-digit multiplication, NOB10, and mathematics, but to a degree the construct seems changed based on many steps that would have been conducted mentally or on paper now being conducted using the calculator. Double-digit multiplication with a calculator does not require using strategies based on place value and the properties of operations but instead requires an understanding of how to use a calculator to multiply. The narrower the construct, the more it seems changed: double-digit multiplication without a calculator is different from double-digit calculation with a calculator, and whether Item 1c completed using a calculator represents double-digit multiplication as an unchanged construct is questionable. Allowing a calculator seems to only somewhat change the broader construct NOB10, and to an even lesser degree change the broad mathematics achievement construct. One final note on Item 1c: Due to the accommodation, distractors "b" and "d" are no longer plausible, because they do not connect to mistakes that an examinee would make while using a calculator. (The distractors could be changed to be more informative about examinees using calculators, but that would be a modification, based on the change in content.) The point is that in this example it is possible to conceive of a testing accommodation (i.e., the calculator for Item 1c) that is much more of a threat to the construct being measured than are some item modifications (e.g., the digit simplification for Item 1b).

To complete the 2 × 2 matrix, the content of Item 1d is modified in a way that clearly changes the construct from Item 1. Changing the "16" in the original item to "6" takes it out of alignment with double-digit multiplication. The answer choices were also modified to match the new correct answer and to make the answer choices plausible. Item 1d may still reflect the broader constructs being measured (NOB10 and mathematics achievement), but it likely does not reflect double-digit multiplication as well as Item 1, Item 1a, and Item 1b do.

Access Skills Versus Target Skills

In the preceding example, some hypotheses were made about accommodations and modifications that are appropriate (i.e., preserve the construct) versus inappropriate (i.e., change the construct). Specifically, I postulated that extra time is likely to be an appropriate accommodation for Alison on a test of double-digit calculation, and that a calculator is not likely to be an appropriate accommodation for her on such a test. This assertion is based on a three-step process of testing accommodation selection using questions about (a) access skills, (b) available accommodations, and (c) targeted skills or knowledge (Kettler, 2012). The access skills question involves whether the student has a functional impairment in a skill needed to access the test, and the targeted skills or knowledge question involves whether the adaptation selected to address that impairment changes the construct being measured by the test. (The available accommodations question is more one of practicality than psychometrics, and will be addressed in the next section.) Access skills are those skills that are not intended to be measured by a test but are necessary to show what one knows and can do on the test. They are the prerequisite skills that examinees are assumed to have obtained in order to take the test (Carrizales & Tindal, 2009). Alison's timed mathematics assessment was not designed to be a measure of processing speed or fluency but was designed for a group of examinees who are above a minimal threshold on that access skill. Targeted skills or knowledge, by contrast, are the target construct or constructs that are intended to be measured by the test. Sufficient levels of all access skills allow the score on the test to be most reflective of the target construct. The target constructs of Alison's test were double-digit multiplication, NOB10, and mathematics achievement.

When access skills are not sufficient for the student to show what she or he knows on the test, the score from the test reflects in part deficiencies in these areas, rather than in the construct being measured. In the case of Alison completing Item 1 without extra time, she may not have as good of a chance as her fellow examinees to be successful, even if she knows double-digit multiplication just as well. Over the course of an entire test form of items, administered under standard time conditions, Alison may get a lower score than other students who have similar abilities with double-digit multiplication but whose processing speeds are around the normative mean. Alison's subsequent low score on the test could be more reflective of her processing speed than of her double-digit multiplication, NOB10, or mathematics achievement. The impact of access skills deficits and other threats to the relationship between the target construct and the test score can be conceptualized using the framework described in the next section.

Construct-Relevant Variance and Error

In classic test theory, the variance in each array of scores can be conceptualized as partially construct relevant and partially construct irrelevant. The portion that is construct-irrelevant variance can be further subdivided into systematic error and random error. If the portion of the variance that is random error is lower, the scores are more reliable. The higher the proportion of the variance that is construct relevant, the more valid the inferences that can be drawn from the scores are. Access skills can affect both the proportion of variance in scores that is due to random error and the proportion that is due to systematic error. If the time limit on a test is such that the vast majority of students (i.e., those who do not have functional impairments in processing speed) finish without having to rush, processing speed affects the scores of only a select few students and is random error.

Conversely, if the time limit is such that nobody finishes and anybody taking the test would perform better if they could work more quickly or have extra time, the error from timing would be systematic. For example, on a test full of items like Item 1 with a time limit such that nobody would finish, scores would be influenced by construct-relevant variance (i.e., variance in double-digit multiplication ability) and systematic error variance (i.e., variance in processing speed). Please note that the distinction between construct-relevant variance and systematic error variance depends in part on the inferences to be drawn from the scores. If the target construct of the test is conceived as a hybrid between double-digit multiplication and processing speed (e.g., multiplication fluency), all of the aforementioned variance may be considered construct relevant.

Reliability

Reliability is the consistency of a set of scores, and it is estimated using various approaches that approximate situations in which scores should be highly consistent. Of the forms of estimates typically calculated, internal consistency is usually the highest. Internal consistency estimates the degree of cohesiveness among a set of items that are summed to yield the score of a test. The estimates have the advantage of being calculated on a single set of scores but the disadvantage of being based on correlations between subsets of the items summed for a score, rather than among correlations involving full scores. Historically split-half reliability has been a popular indicator of internal consistency. Split-half reliability involves subdividing all the items of a test into equal one-half–length forms, and calculating correlations between scores yielded by the two halves. Coefficient alpha is a more computationally intensive technique based on split-half reliability; it is the average of all possible split halves among a set of items (Cronbach, 1951). The item-level equivalent of internal consistency is the item-to-total biserial correlation, which indicates the shared variance between an individual item and the total score from the set of items. (Sometimes the item-to-total biserial is "corrected" by deleting the item in question from the total score.)

Other forms of reliability evidence pertinent to item adaptations include alternate form reliability and test-retest stability. For total scores typically reported on interval scales, both are calculated using the Pearson correlation. Test-retest stability is estimated by having the same group of examinees complete the same test at two different points in time and calculating the correlation between the scores at the two times. Alternate form reliability is estimated by having the same group of examinees take two different forms of a test concurrently, and by calculating the correlation between scores from the same form. Although both test-retest stability and alternate form reliability have the advantage of being calculated at the total score level, unlike internal consistency, they each have sensitivities that internal consistency does not have. Test-retest stability is sensitive to changes over time, such as growth. Alternate form reliability is sensitive to differences between the two forms. The item-level equivalent of test-retest stability and alternate form reliability is percentage agreement on each item between the two test sessions or forms.

Construct Validity

Construct validity is the degree to which inferences drawn from a score are supported by evidence that the score reflects the underlying construct. In other words, it is evident that variance in the scores is construct relevant, rather than construct irrelevant. The four types of construct validity evidence described in the *Testing Standards* (AERA et al., 1999) are based on (a) content, (b) response processes, (c) internal structure, and (d) relations to other variables.

Content validity evidence represents the degree to which the items and other content of a test reflect the construct that is being measured. It is typically established through expert review of the items to establish clarity and fit to the intended construct. Content validity is usually interpreted at the item level, with experts evaluating whether each item is (a) essential, (b) useful but not essential, or (c) nonnecessary to reflect the underlying construct.

Validity evidence based on response processes reflects the degree to which examinees interact with items and tests in the manner intended by the developer. It is most often established through cognitive labs, item analysis protocols, and surveys of examinees after taking the tests. Cognitive labs require test takers to speak aloud about their thought processes while completing items. Item analysis protocols prompt examinees to record their thoughts after each item, and surveys include overarching questions about the testing experience at the end of a section or test. Each of these methods provides evidence from the examinee perspective about the test-taking experience. Completion times and patterns of incorrect responses may also provide validity evidence based on response processes.

Validity evidence based on internal structure reflects the degree to which a test's constituent parts (e.g., items, subscales) fit together as predicted from the underlying theory of the measure. Pearson correlations among subscales and factor analysis are common forms of internal structure validity evidence. Factor analysis provides evidence at the item level, in the form of loadings on factors. Item response theory (IRT) also includes forms of internal structure validity evidence at the item level (e.g., item difficulty, discrimination).

Validity evidence based on relations to other variables includes the degree to which tests agree with measures of similar constructs (i.e., convergent validity), disagree with measures of dissimilar constructs (i.e., divergent validity), and are unrelated to measures of neutral constructs (i.e., discriminant validity). Common analytic techniques for evidence based on relations to other variables include Pearson correlations (between scores on interval scales), differential item functioning (DIF), and *t* tests or analyses of variance among known groups. Whereas a Pearson correlation may be computed between total scores from two measures of the same construct (e.g., mathematics on a state achievement test and on the Wechsler Individual Achievement Test–Third Edition; Wechsler, 2009), items can also be evaluated individually using point-biserial correlations with the criterion measure. DIF is based on IRT and is computed at the item level, addressing whether group status (e.g., students with functional impairments vs. students without functional impairments) can explain differences in the precision or accuracy of items. In the realm of testing adaptations, the most common paradigm of evidence based on relations to other variables is the differential boost, which is addressed next.

Differential Boost

Differential boost is validity evidence based on relations to other variables that requires both students with and without functional impairments, completing tests both with and without adaptations (Fuchs & Fuchs, 2001; Fuchs, Fuchs, Eaton, Hamlett, & Karns, 2000). The most powerful form of this evidence incorporates a within-groups design, such that the change in performance from original to adapted condition for students with functional impairments is compared to the change in performance for students without functional impairments. The expectation is that students with functional impairments will score lower in the original condition but that their scores will improve more from the adaptations than will the scores from students without functional impairments. Figure 2 depicts differential boost on an achievement test. Within an analysis of variance, the hypothesis of interest involves the interaction between group status (with functional impairments vs. without functional impairments) and condition (original vs. adapted). A stricter version of differential boost, known as the interaction hypothesis, posits that scores from students without functional impairments should not increase from testing adaptations (Sireci, Scarpati, & Li, 2005, p. 481).

Differential boost has been used extensively to design research studies on the effectiveness of accommodations and modifications for students with functional impairments (Fuchs, Fuchs, & Capizzi, 2005; Kettler, 2011a; Sireci et al., 2005). Differential boost has also been incorporated into tools such as the Dynamic Assessment of Testing Accommodations (Fuchs & Fuchs, 2001) and the Nelson-Denny Reading Test (Brown, Fishco, & Hanna, 1993) that provide equivalent forms and norms in both accommodated and unaccommodated conditions, such that an individual examinee's boost can be compared with the average boost experienced in the normative population. Lastly, differential boost has been used at the item level, substituting item difficulty (i.e., percentage correct) for mean total scores to determine which item modifications are most helpful for students with disabilities (Kettler et al., 2012).

Although differential boost has been the dominant paradigm for assessing the validity of testing adaptations over the past two decades, it is a limited one. The implication of adapting a test based on mean differences in performance between groups, with the intent of leveling that mean performance, is that the test is somehow biased against the group that scores lower. A test would be biased if a person from one group *who achieves equivalently* to a person from another group is likely to obtain a lower score based on group status. Although differences in mean performance are one sign of bias, such differences on their own are not enough to prove bias. In this case, there are a number of logical reasons that students with functional impairments could

FIGURE 2
Differential Boost on an Achievement Test

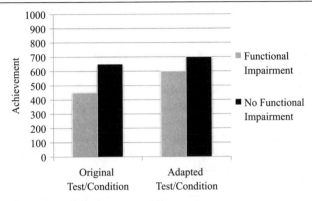

Note. Differential boost is evident when students with functional impairments gain more from adaptations than do students without functional impairments.

perform less well than students without functional impairments—regardless of test quality. Such reasons include that instructional adaptations may not be applied well in the classroom; that instruction for students with functional impairments may progress at a relatively slow pace, therefore covering less content; and that deficits measured by the tests overlap with those that are symptoms of the functional impairments. All of these explanations are consistent with lower scores on a test that is working well for students from both groups. In her extensive review *U.S. Legal Issues in Educational Testing of Special Populations*, Phillips (2011) concluded that adaptations made to narrow the gap in performance between students with and without functional impairments are more focused on *success* than they are on *access*. Although differential boost is one form of evidence that testing adaptations may be appropriate, it has the aforementioned limitations (i.e., focusing on success) and should be used in conjunction with a number of other approaches to draw informed conclusions.

Concluding Remarks on Adaptations and Accessibility

Accessibility in assessment is maximized when the greatest number of students is able to show what is known or can be done with regard to the target construct. The proper method for using a test to draw inferences is to determine whether it yields scores that are reliable and valid for the intended population, then to administer the test, and finally to interpret the score. The collection of reliability and validity indices discussed in this section are the best evidence of such accessibility, because barriers to access are likely to reduce reliability and validity by increasing the influence of construct-irrelevant variance. The initial symptom of inaccessible or difficult to access items and tests is lower test scores, and unfortunately, the attention of stakeholders in assessment often begins and ends with these scores. However, without examination of the psychometric properties of items and tests for students with functional impairments, it is impossible to distinguish between (a) imprecise measurement that creates the illusion of an achievement gap and (b) accurate measurement that indicates a true disparity. Since the Improving America's Schools Act in 1994, states have been required on their assessments to report the disaggregated results for students with disabilities. Disaggregated reliability and validity evidence should also have been required, and remains the best evidence for determining whether tests are equally accessible for students with and without functional impairments. Until we hold the assessment of students with functional impairments to the same standards that we hold the assessment of students without functional impairments, maximum access to the benefits of assessment will remain unrealized.

A FULL MENU OF TESTING ADAPTATION OPTIONS

The menu of testing adaptation options is virtually limitless, varying in appropriateness based on the interaction between examinee characteristics and test characteristics. The classic example of an appropriate testing accommodation—eyeglasses for a person with vision impairment to use on a driving test—is a situation that is much cleaner than is typically met in education. The testing adaptations discussed in this section may or may not be appropriate depending on the characteristics of the examinee and the test in question, but all have been considered in one situation or another to help an individual show what she or he knows or can do via a test.

Examples of Item Modifications

Kettler, Elliott, and Beddow (2009) described a process of item modification that was grounded in both theory and research. Theories that influenced their research on improving accessibility included Universal Design (Center for Universal Design [CUD], 1997) and cognitive load (Chandler & Sweller, 1991). Universal Design for Assessment borrows practices from architecture, intended to make buildings and rooms as accessible as possible for the broadest population of users, and applies these principles to testing and other forms of assessment. The seven primary aspects of Universal Design are (a) equitable use, (b) flexibility in use, (c) simple and intuitive use, (d) perceptible information, (e) tolerance for error, (f) low physical effort, and (g) size and space for approach and use (CUD, 1997). Collectively these aspects direct the test designer to a format and a platform that are broadly accessible to as many persons as possible, without the need for accommodations retrofitted to the testing situation.

Cognitive load theory disaggregates the cognitive demands of any task into intrinsic load, germane load, and extraneous load (Chandler & Sweller, 1991). When the sum of the three types of load exceeds a person's working memory capacity, the examinee is not able to be successful on the item. Intrinsic load is the essential cognitive demand that is necessary for the task, and is directly connected to the target construct (e.g., double-digit multiplication for Item 1). Extraneous load is nonessential load, and could be increased in many ways, such as including an unnecessary figure, using ineffective distractors, or spreading content across multiple pages. Germane load is relevant to the construct being tested but is nonessential. It could include a passage built around the aforementioned Item 1 to make it a story problem; such a passage would not be necessary to show achievement in double-digit multiplication, but being able to solve such a problem might demonstrate better fluency with that skill. Item modifications are intended to remove extraneous load, and possibly reduce germane load, without affecting intrinsic load necessary to complete an item.

Item modifications have also been inspired by research on item development. Based on multiple research studies, Haladyna, Downing, and Rodriguez (2002) wrote extensive guidelines for multiple-choice items. Recommendations included writing items of moderate specificity, avoiding items designed to trick the examinee, and keeping the vocabulary and reading load of items as simple as possible. Extending this line of work, Rodriguez (2005) reviewed 27 studies on the number of answer choices that are optimal for multiple-choice items. The researcher determined that the average item with three distractors is neither more reliable nor more discriminating than the average item with two distractors. This is because it is very rare for an item to have three distractors that are each selected by a large number of examinees. Rodriguez concluded that it is only helpful to include distractors that are plausible.

Kettler et al. (2009) divided common modifications, developed based on the aforementioned theories and research findings, into three categories. These categories and examples of such modifications are included in Table 1. Many modifications fit in the category Modifications to Reduce Unnecessary Language Load (e.g., Simplify sentence and text structure with an emphasis on clarity), and are intended to ensure that tests do not systematically measure language ability along with, or instead of, the target construct. A second category of modifications fit in the category Modifications to Answer Choices (e.g., Avoid cuing for a correct or incorrect answer), and are designed to make sure that the tests do not systematically measure test-taking skills such as choosing the answer choice that contains the central idea or has something in common with each of the other answer choices. A final category of Other General Modifications (e.g., Use bold text for important words) are all intended to help the examinee focus on the intrinsic content and to ultimately increase construct-relevant variance and reduce construct-irrelevant variance.

Examples of Testing Accommodations

Testing accommodations are usually classified within four categories, depending on whether they address (a) presentation format, (b) response format, (c) setting, or (d) timing/scheduling. Testing accommodations to the presentation format (e.g., read-aloud) are changes in the way the test is presented to students. Accommodations to the response format (e.g., calculator) change the method students use to provide answers. Accommodations to the setting (e.g., individual administration) affect the

TABLE 1
Examples of Modifications by Category

Modifications to Reduce Unnecessary Language Load
  Rewrite to replace pronouns with proper nouns
  Simplify sentence and text structure with an emphasis on clarity
  Reduce vocabulary load and nonconstruct subject area language
  Chunk and segment the text into manageable pieces
  Base the item on the construct it is written to measure by removing any trivial content
  Minimize the amount of reading necessary by reducing excess text
  Replace negatives (e.g., NOT or EXCEPT) with positive wording
  Edit the items for errors in grammar, punctuation, capitalization, and spelling
Modifications to Answer Choices
  Eliminate any implausible distractors until as few as three answer choices are possible
  Move a central idea that is in the item choices to the item stem
  Avoid cuing for a correct or incorrect answer
  Place answer choices in a logical order and make them structurally homogenous
Other General Modifications
  Make items more factual rather than opinion-based
  Add white space to make tracking easier
  Remove visuals that are not necessary or helpful
  Format items to be read vertically
  Use bold text for important words

Source. Kettler, Elliott, and Beddow (2009). Reprinted by permission of Taylor & Francis Ltd.

environment in which the test is administered. Accommodations to the timing/scheduling (e.g., extra time) add flexibility to the pace of a test. Table 2 contains examples of accommodations organized by the aforementioned categories.

Although no list of testing accommodations is exhaustive, a couple of helpful inventories should be considered when attempting to identify appropriate adaptations. The Assessment Accommodations Checklist (AAC; Elliott, Kratochwill, & Schulte, 1999) is a list of 67 adaptations designed to assist in selecting accommodations for use during testing. The AAC breaks accommodations into eight categories based on the aspects of testing that they address: (a) assistance prior to administering the test, (b) motivational accommodations, (c) scheduling accommodations, (d) setting accommodations, (e) assistance with test directions, (f) assistance during assessment, (g) equipment or assistive technology, and (h) test format accommodations.

In their *Guidelines for Using the Results of Standardized Tests Administered Under Nonstandard Conditions,* CTB/McGraw-Hill (2000) provided a list of accommodations (adapted from Thurlow, House, Boys, Scott, & Ysseldyke, 2000) categorized not by the areas addressed but by the likelihood of influencing the target construct. The classification system has three categories defined by the levels of caution that are

TABLE 2
Examples of Testing Accommodations by Category

Presentation format
    Computer administration (of a paper-and-pencil test)
    Magnification device
    Paper-and-pencil administration (of a computer test)
    Point to important information in items
    Read-aloud (by an adult or computer) test content
Response format
    Calculator
    Computer to record responses
    Record responses in a test booklet rather than on an answer sheet
    Transcriber records the student's responses
Setting
    Classroom, small group, or individual administration
    Distraction-free testing room
    Front (or other part) of the classroom seating
    Special education teacher or aid as proctor
    Special lighting
Timing/scheduling
    Additional breaks
    Change in order of tests
    Extra time
    Morning/afternoon testing
    Multiple day testing

necessary when implementing and interpreting testing accommodations. According to CTB/McGraw-Hill, Category 1 accommodations are not expected to affect the interpretation of scores, and are therefore expected to be appropriate. Category 2 accommodations may under some circumstances affect interpretation, and may therefore sometimes be inappropriate. Category 3 accommodations change the target construct, and interpretation of these scores without acknowledgement of such a change is inappropriate. Although a classification system such as this is extremely helpful in reminding users of the danger that testing accommodations can pose to the validity of inferences from test scores, the issue of whether an accommodation is appropriate is still contingent on the interaction between examinee needs and test characteristics, and the general appropriateness of accommodations remains an empirical issue.

One final issue regarding the aforementioned taxonomies of testing accommodations is that they were largely conceived prior to policy and research focusing on the impact of item modifications. As such, several of the adaptations that appear on these lists might more correctly be considered modifications, based on strict interpretation of the criterion of changes to the content of a test. Accommodations may affect the setting and method by which a test is delivered, or how responses are given, but not the item content. Both the AAC and the CTB-McGraw Hill *Guidelines* contain entries such as enlarged print, highlighting portions of the directions, and offering a computer presentation of a test that is not typically delivered by computer. Although there are many situations in which such adaptations would likely be appropriate because they do not change the target construct, all three of these examples change the appearance of a test by modifying the content. Examples such as these highlight the need to categorize testing adaptations by two separate continua: accommodation versus modification, and appropriate versus inappropriate. The next section is a review of research conducted on the appropriateness of each of these types of testing adaptations.

RESEARCH ON TESTING ADAPTATIONS

Inspired by changes in federal policy for special education (Individuals With Disabilities Education Act, 1997) and regular education (No Child Left Behind Act, 2001), a great deal of research on item modifications and testing accommodations has been published over the past two decades. The majority of this research has addressed whether the accommodations have provided success to students with functional impairments, and many studies have also addressed access to more precise assessment for this group. Although the question of whether a testing adaptation works is largely dependent on the examinee and the test in question, much of the research on modifications and accommodations has incorporated the differential boost framework to evaluate whether specific testing adaptations reduce or remove the gap in performance between these two groups. Although the majority of the experimental work on test modifications occurred later than the work on testing accommodations, conceptually the issue of whether a test should be modified precedes the issue of whether testing accommodations are needed to access it, so I will first address the body of research on item modifications.

Research on Item Modifications[1]

In 2007, the final regulations of the No Child Left Behind Act (U.S. Department of Education, 2007a, 2007b) provided for a new alternate assessment that would be appropriate for students who are taught grade-level content, and can make progress but whose disabling conditions make it highly unlikely that they will be found proficient. The new assessment was titled the *alternate assessment based on modified academic achievement standards* but was typically called the *modified assessment* or the AA-MAS. States were allowed to develop items that were less difficult than those on the general assessment, so long as those items still connected to grade-level content standards (e.g., consider Items 1 and 1b). A subset of states quickly took advantage of this option to create a new test on which up to 2% of their student population could demonstrate proficiency. Although the next wave of large-scale achievement assessment (Partnership for Assessment of Readiness for College and Careers [PARCC], 2013; Smarter Balanced Assessment Consortium [Smarter Balanced], 2013) has largely replaced the modified assessment, studies conducted by state departments of education and federally funded researchers have provided numerous lessons on item modifications and accessibility.

Following theory (Chandler & Sweller, 1991; CUD, 1997) and research (Haladyna et al., 2002; Rodriguez, 2005) as described in the previous section, researchers have typically used a "package" approach to studies of modifications. Individual modifications (e.g., removal of a distractor, increased white space) were not often studied in isolation; rather, the effect of using combinations or packages of modifications customized to each item was the focus. Both the package approach (Elliott et al., 2009; Elliott et al., 2010; Kettler et al., 2011; Kettler et al., 2012; Roach, Beddow, Kurz, Kettler, & Elliott, 2010) and isolated modifications (Russell & Famularo, 2009; Smith & Chard, 2007) are illustrated in this section by research findings from experimental studies and state technical manuals (Data Recognition Corporation & WestEd, 2008 [Louisiana]; Louisiana Department of Education, 2008a; North Dakota Department of Public Instruction, 2009; Poggio, Yang, Irwin, Glasnapp, & Poggio, 2006 [Kansas]; Texas Student Assessment Program, 2007). The findings are organized by the various types of reliability and validity evidence discussed earlier. Table 3 includes characteristics of five experimental studies and four state test technical manuals that address a range of modifications, content areas, and grade levels.

Reliability Evidence

The first large scale, experimental, within-subjects study on the impact of item modifications was funded by the U.S. Department of Education as part of the Consortium for Alternate Assessment Validity and Experimental Studies (CAAVES;[2] Elliott & Compton: 2006–2009) project. The researchers (Elliott et al., 2010; Kettler et al., 2011) administered short forms of achievement tests in reading and mathematics to eighth-grade students ($n = 755$) in four states. Each student was a member of one of three groups: students without disabilities (SWODs), students with disabilities who would *not* be eligible for a modified assessment (SWD-NEs), and students with disabilities who would be eligible for a modified assessment (SWD-Es). Each student completed parallel versions of the test forms in three conditions; one condition contained original items representative of a general assessment, and the other two conditions contained modified items. In one of the modified conditions, students read the items to themselves from a computer screen, and in the other modified condition, some parts of the items (i.e., directions, stem, answer choices) were read aloud to the students by voiceover technology. Items in the modified conditions contained 28% less words in reading and 26% less words in mathematics compared to the original condition. Because the forms were short and coefficient alpha is dependent on the length of a test, the researchers used the Spearman-Brown prophecy formula to estimate the reliability coefficients of tests with 39 items. All correlations across the three groups, three conditions, and two content areas were between .85

TABLE 3
Characteristics of Item Modification Studies

	Question Types	Examples of Modifications Studied	Grades		
			Reading/ English/ Language Arts	Math	Science
Experimental studies					
CAAVES	MC	Remove a response option, simplify language, add graphic, change layout	8	8	
CMA	MC	Remove a response option, read-aloud, simplify language, add graphic	2, 3, 5	2, 3, 5	5
CMAADI	MC	Remove a response option, embed questions in passages, simplify graphics	7	7	
NECAP	MC	Reduce context in passage, change layout, simplify numbers, reduce steps		8	
OAASIS	MC	Remove a response option, voiceover, simplify language, simplify graphics			9–12
Modified assessment technical manuals					
KAMM	MC	Remove a response option, select less items and less complex items	3–8, 11	3–8, 10	
LAA 2	MC, CR	Select items from general pool that are less cognitively complex	4–10	4–10	4, 8, 11
NDAA 2	MC, CR	Custom developed by teachers writing items, 3 response options	3–8, 11	3–8, 11	4, 8, 11
TAKS-M	MC, CR	Remove a response option, increase font, change layout, simplify text	3–8, 10	3–8, 10	5, 8, 10

Note. CAAVES = Consortium for Alternate Assessment Validity and Experimental Studies; CMA = California Modified Assessment; CMAADI = Consortium for Modified Alternate Assessment Development and Implementation; NECAP = New England Common Assessments Program; OAASIS = Operationalizing Alternate Assessment for Science Inquiry Standards; MC = multiple choice; CR = constructed response; KAMM = Kansas Assessment of Modified Measures; LAA 2 = Louisiana Educational Assessment Program Alternate Assessment, Level 2; NDAA 2 = North Dakota Alternate Assessment 2; TAKS-M = Texas Assessment of Knowledge and Skills–Modified.

and .94. In all conditions and content areas the tests were more reliable among SWODs than among SWD-NEs, and in all but one analysis the tests were more reliable among SWD-NEs than among SWD-Es. These differences in coefficient alpha were small and not significant. In other words, the modifications did not change the reliability of the tests (Kettler et al., 2011). This finding allows for the possibility that tests may be modified without the target construct being changed.

Researchers have conducted two replications of the CAAVES study (Elliott et al., 2009; Kettler et al., 2012). As part of the Consortium for Modified Alternate Assessment Development and Implementation (CMAADI)[3] project, Elliott et al. (2009) studied original and modified sets of items from the Arizona Instrument to Measure Standards (Arizona Department of Education, 2008). The participants (*n* = 152) in the CMAADI study included seventh-grade SWODs and SWD-Es. Each student completed two 20-item sets, which they read silently in both conditions, in either reading or mathematics. The modification process resulted in better measurement for SWD-Es. Estimated coefficient alpha for a 40-item set improved for reading through modification, and was nearly equal in mathematics. Mean item-to-total correlations increased by .11 in reading and by .01 in mathematics. These results were supportive of the modification process, indicating that modifications can improve the precision with which the target construct is measured.

The Operationalizing Alternate Assessment for Science Inquiry Skills (OAASIS)[4] project involved three groups of students (*n* = 400)—SWODs, SWD-NEs, and SWD-Es—from three states (Kettler et al., 2012). Each student completed two 20-item sets of online, high school biology, multiple-choice items. The items were read silently in the original condition but were read aloud using voiceover technology in the modified condition. Items in the modified condition contained, on average, 30% fewer words compared to the original condition. In the OAASIS study, the modification process yielded mixed results regarding measurement precision for SWD-Es. Coefficient alpha for the two sets of items differed greatly in the original condition, and alpha was reduced for one set whereas it was increased for the other set. These results indicated the difficulty in systematically improving the precision of all items using a single process. Items are unique and their precision can be sensitive to small changes; a modification that improves one item may negatively affect another.

Kettler (2011b) reviewed four technical manuals or reports from states that provided psychometric information for both the general assessment and the modified assessment: Kansas (Poggio et al., 2006), Louisiana (Data Recognition Corporation & Pacific Metrics Corporation, 2008a, 2008b; Louisiana Department of Education, 2008b, 2009), North Dakota (CTB McGraw-Hill, 2008), and Texas (Texas Education Agency, 2009). All of these reports included reliability estimates disaggregated by content area and grade level. The researcher compared coefficient alpha between the general and modified assessments under the premise that measurement of student abilities using the general assessment represents a "gold standard" for which modified assessment developers and users should strive.

The general trend was that coefficient alphas for modified assessments were often acceptable but were almost always exceeded by coefficient alphas for general assessments (Kettler, 2011b). For modified reading and English/language arts assessments, 21 of 34 coefficient alphas exceeded .80. In all 34 comparisons based on state and grade, the estimate for the general assessment equaled or exceeded the estimate for the modified assessment. The difference exceeded .10 in 12 of 34 cases. For modified mathematics assessments, 18 of 27 coefficient alphas exceeded .80. In 26 out of 27 comparisons, the estimate for the general assessment equaled or exceeded the estimate for the modified assessment. The difference exceeded .10 in 11 of 26 cases. For modified science assessments, 4 of 9 coefficient alphas exceeded .80. In all 9 comparisons, the estimate for the general assessment equaled or exceeded the estimate for the modified assessment. The difference exceeded .10 in 5 of the 9 cases.

Content Validity Evidence

General and modified technical manuals from all four states included information on content validation (Kettler, 2011b). Review committees composed of regular education teachers, special education teachers, and content specialists evaluated the items for match to content standards, complexity, format, consistency, and potential bias. Although all states used review committees as part of their development of modified assessments, some states also had committees review the items and tests at later stages or in their final forms. For example, when developing the Texas Assessment of Knowledge and Skills–Modified, review committees compared items in their original and modified forms, evaluating whether the modifications were sufficient, the construct was preserved, and the modification matched the method by which the construct was taught in the classroom (Texas Student Assessment Program, 2007).

Evidence Based on Response Processes

As part of the CAAVES Project, Roach et al. (2010) studied the effects of item modifications with a small sample ($n = 9$) of eighth-grade students in a cognitive lab. All students completed reading and mathematics items in original and modified conditions, speaking aloud about their cognitions during test completion. The researchers found that regardless of eligibility status, students spent less time, made fewer reading mistakes and required fewer prompts to keep speaking in the modified condition. These differences were particularly notable among SWD-Es. Students in all groups specifically endorsed added visuals and bolded key terms, and also endorsed the overall impact of the modifications used as a package.

Roach et al. (2010) also surveyed the students ($n = 709$) from the larger CAAVES experimental study and found that the majority of participants in all three groups perceived the items to be equally difficult across conditions. Students indicated that reading support made items easier, and were split on whether two other key modifications (i.e., bolding key terms, removing one distractor) made items easier or did not change the items; students did not indicate that the modifications made the items harder. Prompted by reviewing two reading items in both original and modified conditions, students were again split regarding whether the modified item was easier or equally difficult. Consistent with other findings, very few students indicated that the modified item was more difficult. Prompted by reviewing one mathematics item in both conditions, the large majority of students indicated that modifications made the item easier. The trends for the full sample and for SWD-Es were consistent with each other.

Validity Evidence Based on Internal Structure

Internal structure validity evidence was rarely collected in research on modified assessments. One exception was the North Dakota Alternate Assessment–2 *Technical Manual* (North Dakota Department of Public Instruction, 2009), which was exemplary with regard to the amount of evidence reported, and with regard to consistency with the technical manual for the general assessment (North Dakota State Assessments; CTB McGraw-Hill, 2008). Both technical manuals included evidence in the form of exploratory factor analyses, correlations among content areas, and DIF.

Validity Evidence Based on Relations to Other Variables

Working with the New England Common Assessment Program, Russell and Famularo (2009) used an online test with a large sample (*n* = 2,365) of eighth-grade students to study the effects of modifications on four complicated algebra items from various content strands. For each item, the authors created an equally complex "sibling" item, and then used modifications to create multiple "child" items that were simpler. Students were classified into three groups: students who met proficiency, Gap 1 students whose teachers believed they were proficient but who did not meet proficiency, and Gap 2 students who scored in the lowest achievement category. Across strands, gap students experienced more success on some of the child items than they did on the parent item (i.e., the original item). The effectiveness of specific modifications was different in different strands. The researchers concluded that removing the context of some items might close the performance gap, and that simplifying some items might help students in the gap solve them correctly. Russell and Famularo (2009) cautioned that simplification sometimes took items off grade level but indicated that an assessment with both parent and child items might meet the dual goals of measuring achievement against grade-level expectations and providing teachers information about their students and the target construct.

To prepare the California Modified Assessment, Smith and Chard (2007) pilot tested modified items in English/language arts, mathematics, and science among samples of second-, third-, and fifth-grade students. Modifications in each content area were systematically manipulated across items on each of several 40-item forms, so that the individual effect of modifications could be measured at each unique grade level and content area. Participants in the study included about 2,000 students per content area and grade level, with approximately 285 students completing each form. The main findings included that read-aloud for the passage and item stem increased the percentage correct, and that items with three answer choices tended to be easier than items with four answer choices, across the three content areas. In mathematics and science, stem and passage length were also modified, but no effect was observed. These findings were consistent across groups of students defined by proficiency level.

Researchers in the CAAVES, CMAADI, and OAASIS studies used the differential boost framework to interpret findings for students with and without disabilities completing tests in original and modified conditions. Elliott et al. (2010) found parallel boost from original condition to modified, and from modified to modified with reading support, for all three groups. Parallel boost means that scores from all three groups increased to a comparable degree. Kettler et al. (2011) reanalyzed data from the CAAVES study using an IRT framework to control for differences in ability when testing for differential boost. The researchers found a significant interaction between group status and condition, indicating that SWD-Es benefited more from the modifications than did SWODs or SWD-NEs. In the CMAADI study, Elliott et al. (2009) found differential boost in both reading and mathematics, reducing the gap in performance between SWODs and SWD-Es. The effect sizes based on modification were approximately twice as large for SWD-Es, compared to the effect sizes for SWODs. In the OAASIS study, parallel boost was found for SWODs and SWD-Es, increasing from original condition to modified with reading support.

Differential boost at the item level was used in the CAAVES and OAASIS studies to identify modifications that were particularly effective. In the CAAVES study, items that were well modified and poorly modified in this regard were identified within an IRT framework by comparing the decrease in difficulty from original to modified conditions, for SWODs versus for SWD-Es. In the OAASIS study, items that were well modified and poorly modified were defined within a classic test theory framework by comparing the change in difficulty and in point-biserial correlations, across groups and modification conditions. Individual modifications in both cases were coded as effective when they were represented more often among well modified items than among poorly modified items; ineffective modifications had the opposite profile. Results of both studies supported the modification of shortening the item stem. In the CAAVES study, adding visuals appeared to be a poor modification to reading items. In the OAASIS study, changing graphics and changing passages to bulleted notes both appeared to be poor modifications.

Lessons Learned From Item Modification Research

Collectively, the research on item modifications indicates that an approach based on theory and research can make items easier for all groups. In some cases, the approach will improve the precision of measurement for students with functional impairments, but such improvements are not yet consistently attainable. Modifications tend to reduce the content of an item by removing unnecessary text, visuals, and distractors, often while preserving the construct targeted by the item. This is particularly true on assessments of reading and language arts, and on assessments at the elementary grade band. Reliability of modified examinations tends to be lower at the middle and high school grade bands in mathematics and science (Kettler, 2011b).

TABLE 4
Validity Findings for Testing Accommodations Across Literature Reviews

Fuchs, Fuchs, and Capizzi (2005)	Sireci, Scarpati, and Li (2005)	National Center on Educational Outcomes
Read-aloud		
Results were mixed, but authors concluded that read-aloud may be valid for mathematics tests.	Differential boost was found in 5 of 10 studies. All 5 studies were in mathematics.	Differential boost was found in 7 of 12 studies that tested for it. Internal structure evidence was equal across conditions in 4 other studies.
Extra time		
Authors concluded that extra time increases scores across groups, but not differentially.	Differential boost was found in 5 studies, boost for both groups in 1 study, and no boosts in 2 studies.	Differential boost was found in 3 of 9 studies that tested for it. Internal structure evidence was equal across conditions in 3 other studies.
Packages of accommodations		
Authors considered studying packages prior to studying specific accommodations to be inefficient.	Differential boost was found in all 4 experimental studies that were reviewed.	Differential boost was found in 2 of 5 studies that tested for it.

When modifications are successfully completed, developers have the option to develop a shorter test (in terms of number of words) that can be completed more quickly, or to add items (while holding the number of words constant) in order to increase the reliability and validity for inferences drawn from the test score.

Research on Testing Accommodations[5]

Two extensive research reviews have used the differential boost framework to evaluate testing accommodations (Fuchs et al., 2005; Sireci et al., 2005). In 2005, both Sireci et al. and Fuchs et al. addressed the accommodations of reading a test aloud and of providing extra time, as well as packages of accommodations used together. Every 2 years since that time, the National Center on Education Outcomes (NCEO) has published a review of research on testing accommodations (Cormier, Altman, Shyyan, & Thurlow, 2010; Rogers, Christian, & Thurlow, 2012; Zenisky & Sireci, 2007). Table 4 provides a brief summary of the findings from the two reviews published in 2005 and aggregated results of NCEO-reviewed testing accommodations research since then.

I next provide a synthesis of findings across these three reviews.

Read-Aloud Accommodations

Having all or part of an examination read aloud to students who have functional impairments in reading is the most researched accommodation, likely because it has clear implications for the knowledge targeted by many tests of reading (Cormier et al., 2010). CTB/McGraw-Hill (2000) classifies read-aloud accommodations in Category 3 for tests measuring reading comprehension and in Category 2 for tests measuring anything else.

Research reviewed by Fuchs et al. (2005) was mixed with regard to the read-aloud accommodation and differential boost, but findings supporting this accommodation's appropriateness were much more likely in mathematics than in reading. Sireci et al. (2005) reviewed 10 studies of the read-aloud accommodation, including 7 that were experimental. The reviewers focused on the interaction hypothesis, which extends differential boost with the additional requirement that the scores of SWODs cannot be increased by appropriate testing accommodations. Even with this stricter criterion, Sireci et al. found that the read-aloud accommodation was appropriate in 5 of the studies, including 4 of the experimental studies. In each of these cases, the test was in mathematics, raising concerns about generalizing these findings to other content areas. Between 2005 and 2010, NCEO reviewed 12 studies that tested for differential boost based on the read-aloud accommodation: differential boost was found in 7 studies, whereas parallel boost was found in 2 studies, and no boost was found in 3 studies. In 4 other studies that did not address SWODs, the read-aloud accommodation was found to help SWDs perform better. NCEO also reviewed 4 studies focused on differences in internal structure validity evidence between the original condition and the read-aloud condition, and all 4 studies indicated that the underlying construct was unchanged (Rogers et al., 2012).

In one study that did not employ the differential boost framework, Randall and Engelhard (2010) used confirmatory factor analysis and the Rasch model to examine scores from a subscale of a state achievement test designed to measure reading comprehension. The study involved SWODs ($n = 569$) and SWDs ($n = 219$). Each student completed the test in one of three conditions: (a) standard condition, (b) with a resource guide, and (c) read-aloud. A one-factor model was supported across student groups and conditions. A test of invariance indicated complete factorial invariance across groups. Although the factor structure was not invariant across conditions, the differences were traced to two items, and the authors concluded that the majority of the items were invariant. Findings from the Rasch model indicated that only one item functioned differentially across groups, and that all items were invariant across conditions. Collectively these findings indicate that the accommodations may have marginally changed the construct (i.e., reading comprehension) being measured, but that the change could be isolated to a few items.

The existing body of research indicates that a read-aloud accommodation is likely to be appropriate on a test of mathematics but not on a test of reading. Application to other content areas should be considered on a case by case basis, with the intrinsic reading load of the target construct being a major factor in the decision.

Extra Time Accommodations

Extra time is the accommodation most frequently awarded to students (Fuchs & Fuchs, 2001). CTB/McGraw-Hill classifies extra time accommodations in Category 2.

Fuchs et al. (2005) found parallel boosts from extra time provided to SWDs and SWODs, and in one case the researchers found differential boost in the wrong direction (Fuchs et al., 2000), actually widening the gap in performance. In five studies, Sireci et al. (2005) found some support for the extra time accommodation based on the interaction hypothesis but did not find such support in three others. The researchers concluded that evidence was in the direction of the accommodation being more helpful for SWDs. Between 2005 and 2010, NCEO reviewed nine studies that tested for differential boost based on the extra time accommodation: Differential boost was found in three studies, whereas parallel boost was found in three studies, and no boost was found in three studies. In two other studies that did not address SWODs, the extra time accommodation was found to help SWDs perform better. NCEO also reviewed three studies focused on differences in internal structure validity evidence between the original condition and an extra time condition, and all three studies indicated that the underlying construct was unchanged (Cormier et al., 2010; Zenisky & Sireci, 2007).

In one of the studies reviewed by NCEO (Cormier et al., 2010), Lindstrom and Gregg (2007) used factor analysis to evaluate the Scholastic Aptitude Reasoning Test (SAT®; College Board, 2005) for SWODs ($n = 2,476$) in a standard time condition and for SWDs ($n = 2,476$) in an extra time condition. Students were tested in critical reading, mathematics, and writing. Reliability estimates were calculated for each of the six group-by-condition combinations (e.g., SWODs, critical reading) and were consistent, varying by less than .02 within any content area. One-factor models were supported for each content area and group combination. Tests of invariance yielded relative invariance across groups in all three content areas. Collectively, findings indicated that the items measuring critical thinking, mathematics, and reading on the SAT function similarly across the two groups.

The existing body of research indicates that an extra time accommodation is likely to increase the performance of SWDs and SWODs alike. Kettler (2012) noted that "while most tests in education are not speed tests, they do contain a time limit that requires students to demonstrate target skills with some degree of fluency" (p. 59). Extra time appears to be an appropriate accommodation only for students with impairments in processing speed or fluency to use when taking tests that are not intended to measure processing speed or fluency at all.

Accommodations in Packages

A great deal of research has also been conducted on the effects of packages of accommodations used together. Such research is pragmatic in that it simulates actual practice; accommodations are rarely recommended or used in isolation. Fuchs et al. (2005) did not review such research, indicating that it is inefficient to study accommodations in packages prior to knowing their isolated effects.

Sireci et al. (2005) reviewed seven studies on packages of accommodations, including four that were experimental. Differential boost was yielded in each of these four studies. Between 2005 and 2010, NCEO reviewed five studies that tested for differential boost based on packages of accommodations: differential boost was found in two studies, whereas parallel boost was found in two studies, and no boost was found in one study. In two other studies that did not address SWODs, packages of accommodations were found to help SWDs perform better.

In another study that did not employ the differential boost framework, Cook, Eignor, Sawaki, Steinberg, and Cline (2010) used factor analysis to evaluate a fourth-grade English/language arts assessment. The researchers examined factor structures for the test when taken by four separate group-by-condition combinations, each consisting of 500 students: (a) SWODs under standard conditions, (b) SWDs under standard conditions, (c) SWDs using accommodations (often in packages) from their Individualized Educational Programs (IEPs), and (d) SWDs using a read aloud accommodation. Based on confirmatory factor analysis, a two-factor model (i.e., reading and writing) was tested for all four groups. Most indices from the test of invariance supported factor invariance across the four groups, indicating that the same construct was being measured. This is evidence in support of packaged accommodations, as well as the read-aloud accommodation, for SWDs on ELA tests.

Collectively the reviewed research indicates that packages of accommodations have a greater positive impact for SWDs than for SWODs. However, interpreting research on packages of accommodations is more complicated because each student is provided a unique package, and because the interactions of accommodations within each package are largely unknown.

THE NEW FRONTIER FOR TESTING ADAPTATIONS

Changes in large-scale testing procedures, theory, and available tools make this an exciting time to conduct research on testing adaptations. Although previous reviews (Fuchs et al., 2005; Sireci et al., 2005) of testing accommodations have included sections on mode of response accommodations such as computer delivery, such research seems less relevant as we move into an era where computer delivery is the norm for all students, rather than the exception. Also, federal initiatives such as the Teacher Incentive Fund (U.S. Department of Education, 2012) competition recognize the need to move to more sophisticated systems for evaluating educator performance. Continued research is needed to guide educators and policymakers through this new frontier for testing adaptations.

Common Core Standards and the Impending Race to the Top Assessments

In 2010 the U.S. Department of Education funded two large consortia of states to develop assessment systems aligned to the common core state standards by the 2014–2015 school year. Both the PARCC (2013) and Smarter Balanced (2013) are developing tests to measure student achievement in English/language arts and mathematics that will be delivered using computer platforms, and both published guidelines addressing accessibility and testing adaptations in 2013 (i.e., the *PARCC Accessibility Features and Accommodations Manual* and the *Smarter Balanced Assessment Consortium: Usability, Accessibility, and Accommodations Guidelines*). Both consortia conceptualize steps taken toward accessibility along a continuum, starting with

Universal Design principles to make the tests and their platforms work for as diverse a population of test takers as possible, and both recognize the need for individualization beyond Universal Design in order to include all examinees.

PARCC uses a three-layered system that includes accessibility features for all students, accessibility features identified in advance, and accommodations. Accessibility features for all students (e.g., blank paper, flag items for review, highlight tool) are either incorporated through the computer platform or provided by an adult. Accessibility features identified in advance (e.g., ability to change font or background color, text-to-speech software for mathematics, ability to cover answer options) are documented on each student's Personal Needs Profile (PNP), which also includes demographic information and testing accommodations. For SWDs, the PNP is created by the IEP team. For SWODs, an informal team consisting of the student, a parent, and the primary educator in the content area create the PNP. Accommodations (e.g., tactile graphics, extra time, calculation device on the noncalculator sessions) are available on PARCC assessments for SWODs with approved IEP or 504 plans and for students who use the accommodation regularly during classroom instruction and on other assessments. Each accommodation is accompanied by administration guidelines to help ensure the consistency of application and the validity of ensuing inferences. PARCC also describes an accommodations decision-making process that appropriately incorporates both student characteristics and test characteristics.

Smarter Balanced uses a similar three-layered accessibility system that includes universal tools, designated supports, and accommodations. Universal tools (e.g., breaks, expandable passages, keyboard navigation) are available to all students to select based on preference. Designated supports (e.g., color contrast, masking, translated test directions for mathematics items) are available for any student if the need has been indicated by an educator or by a team of similar makeup to PARCC's PNP team. Accommodations (e.g., braille, abacus, speech-to-text) are available for SWODs as designated by their IEPs or 504 plans. Each designated support and accommodation is accompanied by recommendations for use to help ensure the consistency of application and validity of ensuing inferences.

Both PARCC and Smarter Balanced address the three critical questions for appropriateness of accommodations (i.e., the access skills question, the available accommodations question, and the targeted skills or knowledge question), although in some cases the questions are addressed by redirecting to resources beyond the accommodations guidelines. Whether the examinee has a functional impairment in an access skill needed for the examination is largely left in the hands of IEP and 504 teams. The available accommodations question is addressed by long lists of options in both PARCC's manual and Smarter Balanced's guidelines. Test characteristics are also presented in these resources, as well as in greater depth on the consortia's websites (www.parcconline.org, www.smarterbalanced.org). Both assessment systems have the potential to fit well in a new paradigm for practice and research on the interpretation of achievement scores, the focus of the next section.

FIGURE 3
Interpretation of Achievement Test Scores Paradigm for Practice and Research

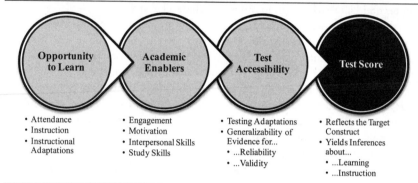

Note. The Interpretation of Achievement Test Scores Paradigm for practice and research takes into consideration the critical steps and related constructs that substantially affect the inferences that can be drawn about teachers, classrooms, and schools.

A New Paradigm for Practice and Research

For over a decade educator effectiveness has been evaluated primarily based on student test scores in reading and mathematics. This practice is understandable from the standpoint that the ultimate goal of our teachers and schools is to increase student learning. One criticism of this approach is that instruction is not learning, so it is unfair to draw inferences about teaching based solely on student achievement, even if that achievement is measured based on growth rather than status. Instruction and learning are related variables, but there is simply too much happening in a student's life—both within the classroom and outside of it—that affects learning for even the best measures of student achievement outcomes to be used as proxies for teacher instructional processes. The requirement to include large-scale testing in reading and mathematics at many grade levels was a positive step, and the logical next step is to use a model and a diverse suite of measures that allow more sophisticated inferences to be drawn from the resulting scores. Figure 3 depicts such a model, the focus of this section.

This Interpretation of Achievement Test Scores (IATS) Paradigm focuses on the within-classroom variables that are involved in the educational process, beginning with a student entering a classroom for the OTL and ending with inferences being drawn about the teacher's instruction based on the student's test score. In between the OTL and the test score, two other broad classes of variables—academic enablers and test accessibility—must be considered to draw many valid inferences. As I discuss each of these sets of variables, I will share a contemporary measure that could be used to collect data to aid in the interpretation of the test score. Researchers should consider using these or similar measures to enrich the lessons learned when evaluating the effectiveness of assessment for a diverse population of examinees.

Opportunity to Learn

Herman, Klein, and Abedi (2000) defined OTL as "the opportunities which schools provide students to learn what is expected of them" (p. 16). Given this definition, a lengthy list of subfactors could be generated to document all of the different methods that schools use to help students learn. The IATS Paradigm includes three basic factors that affect each student's OTL. Although attendance is not necessarily the most salient variable in the model, it is a starting point for assessing educator performance, from the standpoint that it is illogical to hold teachers responsible for opportunities lost when the student is absent from class. The quality of instruction is included because it certainly affects student test scores. In fact, instruction on grade-level content standards is the central variable about which we are often trying to draw inferences from achievement test scores. Kurz (2011) identified time, content, and quality of instruct as the key strands that should be addressed when considering OTL. Instructional adaptations are used by effective educators to complement instruction by differentiating for learners with a diverse set of needs (Ketterlin-Geller & Jamgochian, 2011). Like testing adaptations, instructional adaptations should be selected to address functional impairments, in this case to be certain that barriers (e.g., excess working memory load, unclear directions, environmental distractions) do not keep the target construct from being learned.

One convenient and sophisticated system for measuring OTL is the Instructional Learning Opportunities Guidance System (MyiLOGS; Kurz, Elliott, & Shrago, 2009). MyiLOGS is an online teacher-rating measure based on content standards that can emanate from the common core or be specific to the state or teacher completing the measure. Teachers log their practices daily, including time spent on each (a) content standard, (b) cognitive process, (c) instructional practice, and (d) grouping format. Indices are then reported on instructional time and content coverage, as well as the percentage of time spent on higher order thinking skills, empirically supported practices, and individual or small group formats. Research findings on MyiLOGS are documented at the measure's website (www.myilogs.com).

Academic Enablers

Academic enablers (e.g., motivation, study skills) are students' characteristics that facilitate access to instruction in schools. Unlike content-specific academic skills (e.g., reading, mathematics), enabling behaviors influence performance across a range of content areas. Academic enablers are included within the IATS Paradigm because they affect the degree to which instruction can be converted into learning of the target construct. Academic enablers facilitate student access to instruction, allowing students to individually capitalize on opportunities to learn in schools. DiPerna and Elliott (1999) proposed a model of academic competence that included academic skills and four academic enablers: interpersonal skills, academic motivation, participation, and study skills. The relationship between these enablers and academic achievement in reading and mathematics was later confirmed through structural equation modeling (DiPerna, Volpe, & Elliott, 2002, 2005).

DiPerna and Elliott (2000) included a measure of academic enablers on the Academic Competence Evaluation System (ACES), a teacher-rating scale designed to provide prereferral information on students' strengths and weaknesses in both academic skills and enabling behaviors. Academic Enablers subscales measured by the ACES include Interpersonal Skills, Engagement, Motivation, and Study Skills. Teachers completing the ACES evaluate the frequency for enablers on a 5-point scale (1 = *never*, 2 = *seldom*, 3 = *sometimes*, 4 = *often*, and 5 = *almost always*). Substantial evidence of the validity of both forms of the ACES is available in the *ACES Manual* (DiPerna & Elliott, 2000).

Test Accessibility

Access in assessment is the examinee's opportunity to demonstrate ability or achievement on the targeted construct of the test. Test accessibility is included within the IATS Paradigm because it has clear implications for the relationship between instruction and the test score; a student who cannot access a test cannot obtain an interpretable score. Kettler et al. (2009) indicated, "Access, therefore, must be understood as an interaction between individual test-taker characteristics and features of the test itself" (p. 530). The degree to which a test is accessible ultimately varies from examinee to examinee, but accessibility as a test characteristic can refer to the degree to which a test allows a broad range of examinees to show what they know and can do on the target construct. For example, a test that includes all necessary content for solving an item on one page rather than spread across several may be more accessible for examinees with limitations in working memory, and equally accessible for students who do not have such limitations.

The Test Accessibility and Modification Inventory (TAMI; Beddow, Kettler, & Elliott, 2008) is a tool that can be used for evaluating the accessibility of a measure prior to collecting reliability and validity evidence. The TAMI is an inventory of considerations across six different categories (e.g., item stem, visuals) for paper-and-pencil tests and 10 different categories (e.g., test layout, training) for computer-based tests designed to help test developers and users systematically evaluate the accessibility of their items. The inventory is applied to items and tests, rather than to examinees. The TAMI contains 57 considerations such as: (a) readability analyses indicate appropriate grade level, (b) visuals are relevant to essential item content, and (c) all answer choices are about equal in length. The TAMI can be an effective screen for the barriers to accessibility that keep students from showing what they know, and if used consistently can improve the overall process of item development.

Consistent with the conceptualization of accessibility as an interaction between the examinee and the test, testing adaptations are also included in the IATS Paradigm in the test accessibility section. The TAMI may be used to evaluate item and test accessibility and to subsequently inform which modifications and accommodations are necessary for individuals and groups of test takers. All item modifications and testing accommodations should be provided with the intent of increasing accessibility. In cases where adaptations are needed and not provided, test accessibility is depressed, and the degree to which desired inferences can be drawn from the test score is reduced.

Lastly, although the TAMI measures accessibility, any barriers to access will result in depressed reliability and validity indices across the various evidence categories described in this chapter. To the degree that a test is inaccessible, variance in the test scores reflects error, rather than the target construct. The best evidence for test accessibility is, therefore, high-quality reliability and validity research. In cases where the accessibility of tests for certain subgroups (e.g., students with functional impairments) is questioned, the evidence should be collected and analyzed with those subgroups, to determine whether the test meets psychometric standards. In cases where testing adaptations are used with certain subgroups, reliability and validity evidence should be collected on samples from those subgroups using those same item modifications and testing accommodations. Historically, too much of the research on testing adaptations has focused on *performance* among students with functional impairments, rather than on the *precision* of measurement for students with functional impairments. As a field, we need to prioritize establishing what a score represents, prior to interpreting its magnitude.

TEST SCORES, SUBSEQUENT INFERENCES, AND OTHER CONCLUSIONS

At the end of the IATS Paradigm there is a test score. Alison completed Item 1 correctly, earning an item score of 1, as part of a set of items she completed for a raw test score of 8. That raw score converted to a percentile rank of 10, indicating that Alison's score was equal to or exceeded only 10% of her statewide peers on the fourth-grade mathematics examination. We can draw the inference—within some confidence band dictated by the reliability of the test—Alison is equal to or better than about 1 in 10 of her statewide peers at the fourth-grade math test. And that is about all we can infer.

Some primary inferences that we would like to draw from Alison's performance (along with the performance of her classmates) include the quality of her classroom instruction, teacher, and school. However, we have not established that the test was accessible, reliable, and valid for drawing inferences about Alison, so we do not even know that the score reflected her achievement in mathematics, let alone the quality of mathematics instruction she received. For example, without the extra time accommodation, Alison's functional impairment in processing speed may have kept her from showing what she knew in mathematics.

Assuming that the test was accessible for Alison, so that it reliably and validly yielded scores about her mathematics achievement, we know that she is better than about 1 in 10 of her statewide peers at mathematics. Why has Alison not learned more in mathematics? Without accounting for academic enablers, we do not know that Alison's struggles are based on difficulty understanding the material; her struggles may be based on inability to be motivated and engaged in the material, to interact in the classroom in a positive way, or to study effectively. For example, a lack of engagement in the classroom could be a barrier that keeps Alison from accessing mathematics lessons.

Assuming that Alison has sufficient academic enablers, the most likely within-classroom explanation for her performance is based on OTL. Failure to attend and be exposed to grade-level content through a combination of high-quality instruction and any necessary instructional adaptations could have caused poor performance on the examination. It is also possible that OTL is high and that Alison's performance is attributable to factors outside the school or classroom. Recall that achievement is a primary outcome of effective instruction but that the two are only related variables; they are not one in the same. A situation in which a score is low whereas indicators of OTL (e.g., MyiLOGS), academic enablers (e.g., ACES), and test accessibility (e.g., TAMI) are high may be rare, but it does not necessarily imply that one of the indicators is wrong. It is a case where additional hypotheses and data collection are necessary to identify the barriers to learning and demonstrating proficiency.

We are all familiar with the phrase "Numbers don't lie," and as educators and researchers we are equally familiar with the danger in making that assumption. Just as it is necessary for educators to move beyond face value interpretation of test results, it is necessary for researchers to move beyond studies that focus solely on group performance in evaluating accessibility and testing adaptations. The performance gap between groups of students with and without functional impairments is problematic, and potentially reflects poorly on the quality of achievement tests. Findings of differential boosts that narrow this gap are positive in most cases, and should be considered. However, it is also critical for researchers to focus on other disparities that might disadvantage students with functional impairments, such as gaps in OTL, in academic enablers, and in test accessibility. Increased understanding of the complex relationships among these variables will provide invaluable guidance for users hoping to obtain more information from achievement test scores.

ACKNOWLEDGMENTS

The author wishes to express gratitude to Leah Dembitzer for her able research assistance in developing this chapter. Please direct all correspondence concerning this chapter to Ryan J. Kettler, 152 Frelinghuysen Road, Piscataway, NJ 08854, USA.

NOTES

[1]In 2011, I reviewed research on item modifications in a chapter titled "Holding Modified Assessments Accountable: Applying a Unified Reliability and Validity Framework to the Development and Evaluation of AA-MASs" (Kettler, 2011b). This section is an update of that chapter.

[2]CAAVES was a U.S. Department of Education Enhanced Assessment grant codirected by Elizabeth Compton and Stephen N. Elliott. Several studies on item modification were conducted within this multistate project during 2007–2009.

[3]CMAADI was a U.S. Department of Education General Supervision Enhancement grant codirected by Stephen N. Elliott, Michael C. Rodriguez, Andrew T. Roach, and Ryan J. Kettler. Several studies on item modification were conducted within this multistate project during 2007–2010.
[4]OAASIS was a U.S. Department of Education Enhanced Assessment grant directed by Courtney J. Foster. Several studies on item modification were conducted within this multistate project during 2008–2010.
[5]In 2012, I reviewed research on item modifications in an article titled "Testing Accommodations: Theory and Research to Inform Practice" (Kettler, 2012). This section is an update of that article.

REFERENCES

American Educational Research Association, American Psychological Association, & National Council on Measurement in Education. (1999). *Standards for educational and psychological testing.* Washington, DC: Author.

Arizona Department of Education (2008). *Arizona's Instrument to Measure Standards.* Retrieved from http://www.azed.gov/assessment/aims/

Beddow, P. A., Kettler, R. J., & Elliott, S. N. (2008). *Test Accessibility and Modification Inventory.* Nashville, TN: Vanderbilt University. Retrieved from http://peabody.vanderbilt.edu/research/pro/about_peabody_research/funded_projects/caaves_project_home/tami_project.php

Brown, J. I., Fishco, V. V., & Hanna, G. (1993). *Nelson-Denny Reading Test: Technical report forms G & H.* Chicago, IL: Riverside.

Carrizales, D., & Tindal, G. (2009). Test design and validation of inferences for the Oregon alternate assessment In R. Lissitz & W. Schafer (Eds.), *Assessments in educational reform* (pp. 240–275). Baltimore, MD: Paul H. Brookes.

Center for Universal Design. (1997). *The principles of universal design.* Retrieved from http://www.ncsu.edu/ncsu/design/cud/about_ud/udprinciples.htm

Chandler, P., & Sweller, J. (1991). Cognitive load theory and the format of instruction. *Cognition and Instruction, 8,* 293–332.

College Board. (2005). *The Scholastic Aptitude Test.* New York, NY: Author.

Common Core State Standards Initiative. (2013). *Grade 4: Number & operations in base 10.* Retrieved from http://www.corestandards.org/Math/Content/4/NBT

Cook, L., Eignor, D., Sawaki, Y., Steinberg, J., & Cline, F. (2010). Using factor analysis to investigate accommodations used by students with disabilities on an English-language arts assessment. *Applied Measurement in Education, 23,* 187–208.

Cormier, D. C., Altman, J. R., Shyyan, V., & Thurlow, M. L. (2010). *A summary of the research on the effects of test accommodations: 2007-2008* (Technical Report No. 56). Minneapolis: University of Minnesota, National Center on Educational Outcomes.

Cronbach, L. J. (1951). Coefficient alpha and the internal structure of tests. *Psychometrika, 16,* 297–334.

CTB/McGraw-Hill (2000). *Guidelines for using the results of standardized tests administered under nonstandard conditions.* Monterey, CA: Author.

CTB McGraw-Hill. (2008). *North Dakota State Assessments: Fall 2008 administration final technical report.* Monterey, CA: Author.

Data Recognition Corporation & WestEd. (2008). *LAA 2: 2008 Operational technical report.* Washington, DC: Author.

Data Recognition Corporation & Pacific Metric Corporation. (2008a). *iLEAP 2008: Operational technical report.* Washington, DC: Author.

Data Recognition Corporation & Pacific Metric Corporation. (2008b). *LEAP 2008: Operational technical report.* Washington, DC: Author.

DiPerna, J. C., & Elliott, S. N. (1999). Development and validation of the Academic Competence Evaluation Scales. *Journal of Psychoeducational Assessment, 17,* 207–255.

DiPerna, J. C., & Elliott, S. N. (2000). *Academic Competence Evaluation Scales manual K-12.* Washington, DC: Psychological Corporation.

DiPerna, J. C., Volpe, R. J., & Elliott, S. N. (2002). A model of academic enablers and elementary reading/language arts achievement. *School Psychology Review, 31,* 298–312.

DiPerna, J. C., Volpe, R. J., & Elliott, S. N. (2005). A model of academic enablers and mathematics achievement in the elementary grades. *Journal of School Psychology, 43,* 379–392.

Elliott, S. N., Kettler, R. J., Beddow, P. A., Kurz, A., Compton, E., McGrath, D., . . . Roach, A. T. (2010). Effects of using modified items to test students with persistent academic difficulties. *Exceptional Children, 76,* 475–495.

Elliott, S. N., Kratochwill, T. R., & Schulte, A. (1999). *The Assessment Accommodation Checklist.* Monterey, CA: CTB/McGraw-Hill.

Elliott, S. N., Rodriguez, M. C., Roach, A. T., Kettler, R. J., Beddow, P. A., & Kurz, A. (2009). *AIMS EA 2009 pilot study.* Nashville, TN: Learning Sciences Institute, Vanderbilt University.

Fuchs, L. S., & Fuchs, D. (2001). Helping teachers formulate sound test accommodation decisions for students with learning disabilities. *Learning Disabilities Research & Practice, 16,* 174–181.

Fuchs, L. S., Fuchs, D., Eaton, S. B., Hamlett, C., & Karns, K. (2000). Supplementing teacher judgments of test accommodations with objective data sources. *School Psychology Review, 29,* 65–85.

Fuchs, L. S., Fuchs, D., & Capizzi, A. M. (2005). Identifying appropriate test accommodations for students with learning disabilities. *Focus on Exceptional Children, 37*(6), 1–8.

Haladyna, T. M., Downing, S. M., & Rodriguez, M. C. (2002). A review of multiple-choice item-writing guidelines for classroom assessment. *Applied Measurement in Education, 15,* 309–344.

Herman, J. L., Klein, D. C., & Abedi, J. (2000). Assessing students' opportunity to learn: Teacher and student perspectives. *Educational Measurement: Issues and Practice, 19*(4), 16–24.

Improving America's Schools Act of 1994. Pub. L. 103-382, 108 Stat. 3518.

Individuals With Disabilities Education Act of 1997. Pub. L. 101-476, 104 Stat. 1142.

Ketterlin-Geller, L. R., & Jamgochian, E. M. (2011). Instructional adaptations: Accommodations and modifications that support accessible instruction. In S. N. Elliott, R. J. Kettler, P. A. Beddow, & A. Kurz (Eds.), *Handbook of accessible achievement tests for all students: Bridging the gaps between research, practice, and policy* (pp. 131–146). New York, NY: Springer.

Kettler, R. J. (2011a). Effects of packages of modifications to improve test and item accessibility: Less is more. In S. N. Elliott, R. J. Kettler, P. A. Beddow, & A. Kurz (Eds.), *Handbook of accessible achievement tests for all students: Bridging the gaps between research, practice, and policy* (pp. 231–242). New York, NY: Springer. doi:10.1007/978-1-4419-9356-4_13

Kettler, R. J. (2011b). Holding modified assessments accountable: Applying a unified reliability and validity framework to the development and evaluation of AA-MASs. In M. Russell (Ed.), *Assessing students in the margins: Challenges, strategies, and techniques* (pp. 311–334). Charlotte, NC: Information Age Publishing.

Kettler, R. J. (2012). Testing accommodations: Theory and research to inform practice. *International Journal of Disability, Development and Education, 5,* 53–66. doi:10.1080/1034912X.2012.654952

Kettler, R. J., Dickenson, T. S., Bennett, H. L., Morgan, G. B., Gilmore, J. A., Beddow, P. A., . . . Palmer, P. W. (2012). Enhancing the accessibility of high school science tests: A multi-state experiment. *Exceptional Children, 79,* 91–106.

Kettler, R. J., Elliott, S. N., & Beddow, P. A. (2009). Modifying achievement test items: A theory-guided and data-based approach for better measurement of what students with disabilities know. *Peabody Journal of Education, 84*, 529–551. doi:10.1080/01619560903240996

Kettler, R. J., Rodriguez, M. R., Bolt, D. M., Elliott, S. N., Beddow, P. A., & Kurz, A. (2011). Modified multiple-choice items for alternate assessments: Reliability, difficulty, and differential boost. *Applied Measurement in Education, 24*, 210–234. doi:10.1080/0895734 7.2011.580620

Koretz, D. M., & Hamilton, L. S. (2006). Testing for accountability in K-12. In R. L. Brennan (Ed.), *Educational measurement* (4th ed., pp. 531–578). Washington, DC: American Council on Education.

Kurz, A. (2011). Access to what should be taught and will be tested: Students' opportunity to learn the intended curriculum. In S. N. Elliott, R. J. Kettler, P. A. Beddow, & A. Kurz (Eds.), *Handbook of accessible achievement tests for all students: Bridging the gaps between research, practice, and policy* (pp. 99–129). New York, NY: Springer.

Kurz, A., Elliott, S. N., & Shrago, J. S. (2009). *MyiLOGS: My instructional learning opportunities guidance system*. Nashville, TN: Vanderbilt University.

Lindstrom, J. H., & Gregg, N. (2007). The role of extended time on the SAT for students with learning disabilities and/or attention-deficit/hyperactivity disorder. *Learning Disabilities Research & Practice, 22*, 85–95.

Louisiana Department of Education. (2008a). *2008 LAA 2 technical summary*. Baton Rouge, LA: Author.

Louisiana Department of Education. (2008b). *LEAP GEE 2008 technical summary*. Baton Rouge, LA: Author.

Louisiana Department of Education. (2009). *iLEAP 2009 technical summary*. Baton Rouge, LA: Author.

No Child Left Behind Act of 2001, Pub. L. No. 107-110, § 115, Stat. 1425 (2002).

North Dakota Department of Public Instruction. (2009). *North Dakota Alternate Assessment-2: Technical manual final report*. Bismarck, ND: Author.

Partnership for Assessment of Readiness for College and Careers. (2013, July 25). *PARCC Accessibility features and accommodations manual, guidance for districts and decision-making teams to ensure that PARCC mid-year, performance-based, and end-of-year assessments produce valid results for all students*. Author.

Phillips, S. (2011). U.S. legal issues in educational testing of special populations. In S. N. Elliott, R. J. Kettler, P. A. Beddow, & A. Kurz (Eds.), *Handbook of accessible achievement tests for all students: Bridging the gaps between research, practice, and policy* (pp. 231–242). New York, NY: Springer.

Phillips, S. E., & Camara, W. J. (2006). Legal and ethical issues. In R. L. Brennan (Ed.), *Educational measurement* (4th ed., 733–757). Washington, DC: American Council on Education.

Poggio, A. J., Yang, X., Irwin, P. M., Glasnapp, D. R., & Poggio, J. P. (2006). *Kansas Assessments in Reading and Mathematics: Technical manual*. Lawrence: University of Kansas, Center for Educational Testing and Evaluation. Retrieved from https://cete.ku.edu/sites/cete. drupal.ku.edu/files/docs/Technical_Reports/2007/irwin2007_KAMM.pdf

Randall, J., & Engelhard, G. (2010). Using confirmatory factor analysis and the Rasch model to assess measurement invariance in a high stakes reading assessment. *Applied Measurement in Education, 23*, 286–306.

Roach, A. T., Beddow, P. A., Kurz, A., Kettler, R. J., & Elliott, S. N. (2010). Incorporating student input in developing alternate assessments based on modified academic achievement standards. *Exceptional Children, 77*, 61–80.

Rodriguez, M. C. (2005). Three options are optimal for multiple-choice items: A meta-analysis of 80 years of research. *Educational Measurement: Issues and Practice, 24*(2), 3–13.

Rogers, C. M., Christian, E. M., & Thurlow, M. L. (2012). *A summary of the research on the effects of test accommodations: 2009-2010* (Technical Report No. 65). Minneapolis: University of Minnesota, National Center on Educational Outcomes.

Russell, M., & Famularo, L. (2009). Testing what students in the gap can do. *Journal of Applied Testing Technology, 9*(4), 1–28.

Sireci, S. G., Scarpati, S. E., & Li, S. (2005). Test accommodations for students with disabilities: An analysis of the interaction hypothesis. *Review of Educational Research, 75,* 457–490.

Smarter Balanced Assessment Consortium. (2013). *Smarter Balanced Assessment Consortium: Usability, accessibility, and accommodations guidelines.* Retrieved from http://www.smarterbalanced.org/wordpress/wp-content/uploads/2014/03/SmarterBalanced_Guidelines_091113.pdf

Smith, R. L., & Chard, L. (2007). *A study of item format and delivery mode from the California Modified Assessment (CMA) pilot test.* Princeton, NJ: Educational Testing Service.

Texas Education Agency. (2009, May 7). *Technical digest 2007-2008.* Austin, TX: Author. Retrieved from http://www.tea.state.tx.us

Texas Student Assessment Program. (2007). *Texas Assessment of Knowledge and Skills-Modified: Technical report.* Austin, TX: Author. Retrieved from http://www.tea.state.tx.us

Thurlow, A., House, C., Boys, D., Scott, J., & Ysseldyke, J. E. (2000). *State participation and accommodation policies for students with disabilities: 1999 Update* (Synthesis Report No. 33). Minneapolis: National Center on Educational Outcomes.

U.S. Department of Education. (2007a). *Modified academic achievement standards: Non-regulatory guidance.* Washington, DC: Author.

U.S. Department of Education. (2007b). *Standards and assessments peer review guidance.* Washington, DC: Author.

U.S. Department of Education. (2012). *Teacher Incentive Fund.* Retrieved from www2.ed.gov/programs/teacherincentive

Wechsler, D. (2009). *Wechsler Individual Achievement Test: 3rd edition* (WIAT-III). San Antonio, TX: Psychological Corporation.

Zenisky, A. L., & Sireci, S. G. (2007). *A summary of the research on the effects of test accommodations: 2005-2006* (Technical Report No. 47). Minneapolis: University of Minnesota, National Center on Educational Outcomes.

Chapter 9

Advancing Accessibility and Accommodations in Content Assessments for Students With Disabilities and English Learners

Martha L. Thurlow
University of Minnesota

Rebecca J. Kopriva
University of Wisconsin

Accessibility and accommodations in assessments now are seen as critical elements of an appropriately designed and implemented assessment of student achievement. The inclusion of all students in assessment systems designed to measure student knowledge and skills in various content areas has generated considerable and sometimes frenzied activity during the past two decades. This activity has taken place primarily at the state and national levels. With the funding of large consortia of states developing common assessments designed to measure college and career readiness, attention to accessibility and accommodations is being considered as well.

The purpose of this chapter is to review what has happened, and what is likely to happen, as accessibility and accommodations research and practice for content assessments are advanced to ensure the appropriate inclusion and validity of assessment results for English learners (ELs) and students with disabilities. A description of accommodations and research specific to access for these two populations is beyond the scope and can be found in other chapters. Although we focus primarily on large-scale content assessments used at the state, consortia, and national levels, much of what has happened in these assessments has direct implications for district content assessments and classroom-based assessments (e.g., online embedded tasks, publisher quizzes, teacher-developed quizzes, observational tools, performance tasks, etc.). Thus, we highlight some of those implications as well.

Toward this end, we start by defining the many terms that have emerged around the topics of accessibility and accommodations. We address how these concepts have

Review of Research in Education
March 2015, Vol. 39, pp. 331–369
DOI: 10.3102/0091732X14556076
© 2014 AERA. http://rre.aera.net

changed in revisions of the *Standards for Educational and Psychological Testing* during the past 40 years, as well as how they have been included in other documents that guide the work of assessment developers. Following this, we provide a brief history of the push for assessment accessibility and accommodations, including reminders of the numbers and characteristics of students with disabilities, ELs, and ELs with disabilities; the dramatic shifts that have occurred in the participation of ELs and students with disabilities in national and state assessments; and the legal basis for many of the changes in inclusion, accessibility, and accommodations. We address in some depth accessibility and accommodations considerations for students with disabilities, starting from foundational assumptions, then moving to research findings and needs, and concluding with implications for district and classroom assessments. Following this, we address these same topics for ELs, and then for ELs with disabilities.

TERMINOLOGY

A number of terms surround the concepts of accessibility and accommodations. The definitions of many of these terms have changed over time, reflecting a refinement process based on increased knowledge about their application to assessments. In the assessment arena, terminology is related to the ideal of controlling for sources of construct-irrelevant variance (Haladyna & Downing, 2004) so that assessments measure what students know and can do, rather than measuring variance due to language and cultural differences or disability barriers. Continued evolution in terminology is occurring as consortia of states work together on common approaches to their assessments (e.g., note new terms such as *universal tools, accessibility features*, and *designated supports*).

Despite the new terminology, the following are the primary terms that have influenced the field during the increased attention to including ELs and students with disabilities in assessments: *accessibility, universal design, accommodations*, and *modifications*. Each of these is described in brief here.

Accessibility

Access in academic testing is a multifaceted concept, meaning that many design, development, implementation, scoring, and analytic components need to be included in order to successfully provide students appropriate access to the item requirements *and* to the capability to tell those receiving the results what the students know. Access to the former without meaningful entrée to the latter is not an accessible assessment. The issue of test access and accessibility for all students, including both ELs and students with disabilities, is explained in detail in Kopriva (2008c), and can be applied to both standardized and informal classroom assessments. Kopriva also documents the salient topics relevant for EL access on content tests and the research that has been conducted to date toward that end. Thurlow et al. (2009) described accessible reading assessments for students with disabilities in the following way:

Accessible assessments move beyond merely providing a way for students to participate in assessments. They provide a means for determining whether the knowledge and skills of each student meet standards-based criteria. . . . Accessibility does not entail measuring different knowledge and skills for students with disabilities from what would be measured for peers without disabilities. (p. 2)

Others have defined the characteristics of assessment systems that are inclusive of all students (Thurlow, Quenemoen, et al., 2008).

Universal Design

The first push for improving assessments came through the topic of universal design. This was a broad concept that covered everything from the definition of the population to be included in the assessment to specific descriptions of legible text (Johnstone, Altman, & Thurlow, 2006; Kopriva, 2000; Thompson, Thurlow, & Malouf, 2004). The concept broadened further with the recognition of universal design for learning, which emphasized multiple means of presentation, multiple means of expression, and multiple means of engagement (Rose & Meyer, 2002). The purpose and application of universal design concepts to assessment led to greater clarity about the targeted skills of an assessment and other access skills that might inadvertently be assessed (Ketterlin-Geller, 2008; Kettler, 2012; Kopriva, 2008a, 2008d). Evidence of the application of universal design is now routinely found in states' requests for proposals to develop items and tests (Altman et al., 2008; Rieke, Lazarus, Thurlow, & Dominguez, 2013).

Although there certainly are similarities between needs of students with disabilities and ELs, a thoughtful understanding of some distinctive features is important as well. Both common and unique aspects of universal design for these diverse populations need to be taken into consideration.

Accommodations

Accommodations are changes to materials or procedures that provide students access to instruction and assessments and improve the validity of assessment results for students who need them. Considerable care has been taken to clarify what assessment accommodations are, in contrast to assessment modifications. Appropriate assessment accommodations, as now defined, are changes in test materials or procedures that *do not* alter the construct being measured (Lazarus, Thurlow, Lail, & Christensen, 2009; Thurlow, 2012). Accommodations for students with disabilities typically were grouped into categories, such as presentation, response, setting, timing/scheduling, and others (Thurlow, Ysseldyke, & Silverstein, 1995).

With increased attention to including ELs, categories focused on the linguistic characteristics of the accommodations, with a distinction made between linguistic and non-linguistic accommodations (Rivera, Collum, Willner, & Sia, 2006). For ELs, the focus on linguistic elements of the test forms themselves has brought to the fore the importance of using accessible communication strategies. Historically, this has meant translations of forms, but this unitary approach has been found to be largely insufficient.

Simplified language and visuals have been shown to have promise for ELs (see Abedi & Lord, 2001; Abedi, Lord, Hofstetter, & Baker, 2000), most often when more basic knowledge and skills are being measured (Carr, 2008; Emick & Kopriva, 2007). When measuring more challenging concepts and skills, researchers are trying to unravel how to best communicate what the items and tests are asking ELs to do, without changing the underlying constructs measured on the general test. Because more complex content typically involves a heavier and more dense language load, communication includes considering how questions and contexts are presented beyond just text, and affording accessible response opportunities so ELs can tell us what they know (Kopriva, Triscari, & Carr, 2014; Kopriva, Winter, Triscari, Carr, Cameron, & Gabel, 2013; Sireci & Wells, 2010). As with all accommodations, care must be taken to ensure that communication strategies are well conceived and effectively implemented so they do not change the essential parameters of item adaptations across populations (Cawthon, Leppo, Carr, & Kopriva, 2013). Interactions of communication strategies with the constructs in English Language Arts also need to be considered.

Modifications

Assessment modifications are defined as changes in test materials or procedures that *do alter* the content being measured. Instructional accommodations and modifications generally have been less carefully defined, allowing occasionally for the use of changes (e.g., scaffolding and similar supports) that may alter the concepts being taught in some way (Elliott & Thurlow, 2006). As understanding of the distinction between accommodations and modifications evolved, supported by changes in federal policy (only scores from accommodations that produced valid assessment results counted), modifications were more clearly defined and avoided in large-scale assessments. Typically, modifications in large-scale assessments are not allowed for ELs. Rather, it is expected that appropriate accommodations will be made to offset their language and literacy challenges.

ACCESSIBILITY AND ACCOMMODATIONS IN TESTING STANDARDS

Professional associations regularly develop standards to guide best practice in testing. Perhaps the best known set of standards is the *Standards for Educational and Psychological Testing*, developed jointly by the American Educational Research Association (AERA), the American Psychological Association (APA), and the National Council on Measurement in Education (NCME). Other relevant standards include the recently released *Operational Best Practices for Statewide Large-Scale Assessment Programs* (Council of Chief State School Officers & Association of Test Publishers, 2010) and the recommended practices in the *Testing and Data Integrity in the Administration of Statewide Student Assessment Programs* (NCME, 2012). Each of these sets of standards and practices addresses accessibility and accommodations.

The joint *Standards* (AERA, APA, & NCME, 2014) are generally viewed as the gold standard for assessments. In the 2014 version, fairness is presented as one of the three critical features of an assessment (along with validity and reliability). Discussion of the diversity of students in the population (including those who are ELs and those who have disabilities) is threaded throughout the *Standards*. The distinction between accommodations and modifications is clearly stated. In addition, accessibility and universal design are not just concepts for individuals with disabilities or limited English proficiency but rather are relevant for all individuals.

Other standards documents similarly now address ELs and individuals with disabilities. For example, the *Operational Best Practices* (Council of Chief State School Officers & Association of Test Publishers, 2010) includes the concepts of universal design and accessibility. NCME's (2012) *Testing and Data Integrity in the Administration of Statewide Student Assessment Programs* mentions accommodations, both via the recognition that some students need them (see Recommended Practice 4) and via the concern about their overuse (see Appendix A, "Some Threats to Test Integrity," p. 7) during testing.

In 2005, the National Assessment Governing Board (NAGB) added a substantial amount of language to Chapter 4, the item writing specifications of the National Assessment of Educational Progress (NAEP) Assessment Framework in Mathematics that outlined specific guidelines for writing accessible test items. This language has remained in the item writing specifications chapter of all subsequent NAEP frameworks to date. As discussed later in the chapter, NAGB has also been sensitive to broadening its inclusion and accommodation policies to involve a greater range of ELs and students with disabilities in NAEP test administrations.

BRIEF HISTORY OF THE PUSH FOR ASSESSMENT ACCESSIBILITY AND ACCOMMODATIONS

Much has changed in perceptions, practices, and policies related to assessment accessibility and accommodations for ELs, students with disabilities, and ELs with disabilities during the past 25 years. To portray the shifts, we highlight four topics: (a) the numbers and characteristics of students with disabilities, ELs, and ELs with disabilities; (b) the pushes for inclusion of these students in assessment systems; (c) the evolution of thinking about validity and implications for accessibility; and (d) the legal basis for inclusion, accessibility, and accommodations.

Who Are the Students?

Understanding the numbers and characteristics of students is an important part of any validity argument for an assessment. Assessment developers must be able to document that they have considered all the students who will take part in an assessment during the development process, field testing, and implementation.

Students With Disabilities

Students with disabilities who receive special education services as required by the Individuals With Disabilities Education Act (IDEA) currently make up 13% of public school enrollment, with percentages in states varying from 10% to 19%. Disability category can serve as a proxy for understanding that only a small percentage of special education students has a disability that may require different achievement standards (see Thurlow, Quenemoen, & Lazarus, 2011). This small group would include some, but not all, students with intellectual impairments, autism, or multiple disabilities and a small number of students with other disability category labels. These students, who participate in assessments based on alternate achievement standards, are not the focus of this chapter, although attention to their assessment needs is very important (Kearns, Towles-Reeves, Kleinert, Kleinert, & Kleine-Kracht, 2011; Towles-Reeves, Kearns, Kleinert, & Kleinert, 2009).

Although categories may serve as a proxy for characteristics, there are many challenges associated with assigning a disability category to a student. McDonnell, McLaughlin, and Morison (1997) noted the unreliability of the diagnosis of a disability. Not only are there overlapping characteristics across disability category labels, but classification criteria also vary within and among states.

For accessibility and accommodations considerations, educators and Individualized Education Program (IEP) decision makers must identify each student's needs and characteristics and determine from those the most appropriate assessment accommodations. This is a difficult task, one with which the field continues to struggle (Ketterlin-Geller, Alonzo, Braun-Monegan, & Tindal, 2007; Thurlow, Lazarus, & Christensen, 2008). It also creates challenges for conducting research on the effects of accommodations. All too often, researchers have relied on disability category as the basis for comparing the effects of accommodations.

English Learners

ELs are a diverse group of students, only some of whom receive services to help them learn English. Across the 50 states in the United States, approximately 9% of public school students receive EL services (National Center on Educational Outcomes, 2011b). Still, the range across states is very large, from less than 1% to almost 25% of the school-age population in 2008–2009. Although the language spoken most frequently by ELs across states is Spanish, the top five languages differ dramatically, with Vietnamese being the second-most frequent language in the top five, followed by Arabic.

English learners differ quite substantially in a number of ways (Kopriva, 2008b). Beyond different home languages, the effects of various cultures, including cultural mores and perspectives, and how these interact with their experiences in this country and with experiences of native-born speakers of English and their home or first language (L1), can substantially affect learning and test taking for these students. Furthermore, the individualized, dynamic interplay of progressively learning a new language and how meaning-making fluctuates as this learning takes place heightens the profound heterogeneity identified by background characteristics experienced within and across countries of origin. Upward of 40% of ELs are actually born in the United States, and their experiences to some extent dynamically mimic both the characteristics of their relatives' countries of origin, as well as the U.S. culture as they experience it to date. Overall, these factors affect how they experience test expectations, understand item shorthand, and understand what the test items are asking them to do and how test items allow ELs to respond.

For ELs, most decisions about accommodations for individual students are left to one of the teachers, most often the teacher in charge of the students' English language development and sometimes in consultation with content teachers. Even with guidance from states, this informal policy has led to wildly different accommodations for students with similar needs (Kopriva & Koran, 2008). The testing consortia are interested in improving how ELs are assigned accommodations, but suitable changes will likely not be available for some time.

ELs With Disabilities

Students who are both ELs and have a disability represent a group of students that is often ignored in policy and practice. These students, as might be expected, are increasing in number as the number of ELs increases. Across the United States, the percentage of ELs with disabilities is almost 8% of all public school students with disabilities (National Center on Educational Outcomes, 2011b), ranging from close to 0% to over 28% of students receiving special education services in a state. To date, little work has been accumulated about how to reliably identify and teach these students, much less how to accommodate them properly on content assessments. In a recent funding submission, Abedi and Bayley (2014) are hoping to improve the classification markers for ELs, students with learning disabilities, and those who have challenges in both domains. The WIDA (World-Class Instructional Design and Assessment) consortium, whose *Access* test measures English language proficiency for ELs, has been allowing accommodations for students with identified disabilities for some time; however, plans to track need, use, and effectiveness are just now being considered (Lynn Shafer Willner, personal communication, August 2014).

The Push for Inclusion in Assessments

A multitude of pushes from policy and practice led to concerns about the inclusion of ELs and students with disabilities in assessment systems, as well as about the accessibility of those assessments. These pushes are summarized here in terms of (a) the series of historical events that pushed for greater inclusion; (b) policy analyses that promoted the inclusion of ELs and students with disabilities in assessments; (c) documented shifts in the participation of ELs and students with disabilities in assessments; (d) inclusion, accessibility, and accommodations approaches of consortia of states developing new assessment systems; and (e) the evolution in thinking about assessment validity and its relation to inclusion.

Historical Events

Initial concerns about access to assessment systems started to take the public stage in the early 1990s. Before that, attention to the inclusion of students with disabilities and ELs was minimal, although there was attention to the right to education in early civil rights laws. It was the entry of standards-based education that provided one of the primary incentives for the right of ELs and students with disabilities to the same standards-based reform to which other students had access. Standards-based reform grew out of the work of governors in the mid-1980s (National Governors' Association, 1986), and continues to be the major reform in place today (Shepard, Hannaway, & Baker, 2009). Standards-based reforms shifted the focus from sorting students to measuring outcomes and focusing on the success of schools and school districts (Goertz, 2007) with their students.

Early studies of the inclusion of students with disabilities and ELs in state and national assessment systems revealed considerable exclusion of these students. For example, early investigations of national data bases indicated that students with disabilities either were not included or were not identified if they were included (McGrew, Algozzine, Ysseldyke, Thurlow, & Spiegel, 1995; McGrew, Thurlow, & Spiegel, 1993). An early summary of research on the inclusion of students with disabilities in large-scale assessments found minimal research had been conducted (Thurlow, Ysseldyke, et al., 1995; Thurlow, Ysseldyke, & Silverstein, 1993). Similarly, all but the most proficient English learners were routinely waived from state and national content assessments until the late 1990s (Kopriva & Lara, 2009; Lara & August, 1996).

Policy Analyses

Early policy analyses focused on assessment participation and accommodation policies for students with disabilities. In the early 1990s, researchers found that only about half of all states had explicit policies about the participation of students with disabilities in assessments and their use of accommodations during those assessments (Thurlow et al., 1993; Thurlow, Ysseldyke, et al., 1995). Continued analyses of participation and accommodations policies have documented an increase to 38 states in 1995 (Thurlow, Scott, & Ysseldyke, 1995), 39 in 1997 (Thurlow, Seyfarth, Scott, & Ysseldyke, 1997), 48 in 1999 (Thurlow, House, Boys, Scott, & Ysseldyke, 2000), and finally 50 states in 2001 (Thurlow, Lazarus, Thompson, & Robey, 2002). Since that time, every state and many of the U.S. territories have been found to have written policies on participation and accommodations for students with disabilities in assessments (Thurlow, 2013). Similarly, numbers of states with participation and accommodation policies grew for ELs over time, although specific policies for ELs tended to lag behind those for students with disabilities (Rivera & Collum, 2004; Rivera et al., 2006; Rivera & Stansfield, 2000).

Policies that indicate which accommodations are allowed or prohibited for state assessments have become increasingly complex over time, and vary depending on the accommodation and the state. Policies also define which changes in test materials or procedures will result in lower scores if used and which scores will not be added to other scores for school accountability. A clear change in the policy language has occurred across time, with the distinction between "accommodations" and "modifications" now reflected in nearly all state policies and guidelines (Christensen, Braam, Scullin, & Thurlow, 2011).

For students with disabilities, among the most controversial accommodations historically have been those that require a human to provide the accommodations. Readers, sign language interpreters, and scribes are among these controversial accommodations. The controversy lies, in part, in the concern that the human will divulge the answers to questions or provide other hints about answers, even if unintended. There also have been concerns about the security of items when humans have access to the tests before the administration of the test. Increasingly, states are providing guidelines about the specific ways to provide accommodations that involve humans (Christensen et al., 2011; Clapper, Morse, Thompson, & Thurlow, 2005). Continued concern about these types of accommodations (see Hodgson, Lazarus, Price, Altman, & Thurlow, 2012) has led many to believe that the answer lies in incorporating accommodations within computer-based delivery systems, thereby eliminating the human element.

Many of the arguments being made about the needs for students with disabilities applied to ELs as well. These included arguments to participate in large-scale assessments and to have access to accommodations that allow them to understand what items are asking, and proper response access to be able to show their knowledge, skills, and abilities (Abedi et al., 2000; Abedi & Ewers, 2013; Koenig & Bachman, 2004). Still, early state and national accommodation policies for ELs tended to reflect almost a wholesale replication of those for students with disabilities (Lara & August, 1996). Over time, appropriate accommodations for ELs began to be identified, with Rivera and Collum's (2006) identification of relevant accommodations and the grouping of these accommodations as having primarily either a direct or an indirect linguistic impact. More recently, researchers such as Solano-Flores (2014) and others (e.g., Ercikan, Roth, Simon, Sandilands, & Lyons-Thomas, in press) have also called for a more nuanced set of accommodations depending on the dynamic interplay of L1 and English language development and other cultural and background factors that affect students' access to academic language in English in tests and test items.

As increasing numbers of states and districts adopt online and computer-based assessments (Thurlow, Lazarus, Albus, & Hodgson, 2010), it has become apparent that technology platforms not only will transform the efficiency of testing (Madaus, Russell, & Higgins, 2009) but also will open up the possibility that more accommodations can be presented via the technology platform rather than via a human (Russell, 2011). In fact, researchers and test developers argue that more accommodations can be part of the assessment itself—embedded features of the assessment (National Center on Educational Outcomes, 2011a)—rather than external changes in materials or procedures (Meyen, Poggio, Seok, & Smith, 2006; Russell, Hoffman, & Higgins, 2009a; Thompson, Quenemoen, & Thurlow, 2006). One drawback for ELs, however, is that by requiring students to type in open-ended responses, the students lose the ability to use drawing and other auxiliary methods to convey their answers. The policies developed by the consortia of states developing common technology-based assessments seem to confirm this.

Shifts in Participation of ELs and Students With Disabilities

Dramatic shifts in the participation rates of both students with disabilities and ELs are now evident. This is the case for both state assessments and for the NAEP. For example, in 1996 Lara and August reported that few ELs were included in statewide tests anywhere in the country. Similarly, Heubert and Hauser (1999) found that 41 states and the District of Columbia permitted most ELs to be exempted from state-wide content assessments, usually on the basis of amount of time in the United States or length of time in the school program where they learned English. Now, more than 95% are participating in state assessments. For students with disabilities, rates have gone from having most states with fewer than 10% of their students with disabilities in state assessments (Shriner & Thurlow, 1993) to nearly all states having more than 95% of their students with disabilities in state assessments (Vang & Thurlow, 2013).

Similar dramatic increases have been noted in the rates of participation in the NAEP. The NAGB, which oversees the NAEP assessments, has attempted to make NAEP participation representative of the population enrolled in the nation's public schools while maintaining the ability to defensibly make comparisons across states. A major challenge for NAEP has been including ELs and students with disabilities in the assessment so that their participation is consistently representative of the state or district participating in NAEP. One focus has been on "who to include" so that results can be compared defensibly across jurisdictions. Another focus for NAEP has been on "how to include." This latter lens addresses how students with disabilities and ELs can meaningfully and validly access the test through the use of accommodations that are properly selected, administered, and monitored.

Despite the challenges that NAEP faced in reaching agreement about how to have consistent policies across states, the 2013 report on NAEP (National Center for Education Statistics, 2013) noted that it has made considerable progress reducing the exclusion of special populations from its assessments. For example, in its eighth-grade reading assessment, the exclusion rate for students with disabilities decreased from 31% in 1998 to 15% in 2013. For ELs, the exclusion rate decreased from 29% in 1998 to 10% in 2013. Still, there is considerable variability among states in exclusion rates, something that is generally attributed to differences in accommodations policies (Gerwertz, 2013).

This variability in participation is related to the *quality* of inclusion and how ELs and students with disabilities are allowed to take the assessments so that their scores reflect adequately their knowledge and skills. The challenge is in improving how the connections between student and proper accommodations are made, and in increasing oversight associated with local accommodation decisions and implementation.

As noted above, since the development of the 2005 NAEP mathematics framework, guidelines for writing items in all NAEP subject areas have included a large chapter section devoted to principles and methods for writing more accessible items (NAGB, 2005). Starting in 2002, a small number of accommodations were allowed in NAEP, most of which were primarily applicable for students with disabilities. This number has steadily increased, and, as of 2009, decision trees used by NAEP identified approximately 20 accommodations offered to students with disabilities in at least some content areas, and about 12 offered to ELs (Kopriva & Lara, 2009). Over the past few years, NAEP also has increased its training of coordinators and has made improvements in test administration materials to address accommodations and testing students with disabilities and ELs.

Assessment Consortia Approaches to Inclusion, Accessibility, and Accommodations

Consortia of states developing general assessments of reading and mathematics aligned to college and career ready standards have introduced new cross-state approaches to the inclusion of all ELs (except for inclusion of ELs in the reading tests for those in their first year in U.S. schools) and students with disabilities (except those participating in the alternate assessment based on alternate achievement standards).

Both of the consortia of states developing general assessments—the Partnership for Assessment of Readiness for College and Careers (PARCC), and the Smarter Balanced Assessment Consortium (Smarter Balanced)—have established a three-level approach to accessibility. PARCC includes (a) Accessibility Features for all students, (b) Accessibility Features identified in advance, and (c) Accommodations. Smarter Balanced includes (a) Universal Tools for all students, (b) Designated Supports for students with documented needs, and (c) Accommodations. Although similar in structure, the approaches used by PARCC and Smarter Balanced differ in their approaches to ELs and students with disabilities.

A notable difference between the two consortia is that Smarter Balanced allows accommodations only for students with disabilities (those with IEPs and those with 504 accommodation plans), moving features such as translations into designated supports; PARCC identifies several accommodations for ELs. In developing online assessments, both PARCC and Smarter Balanced have identified a number of changes in materials or procedures as accessibility features or universal design tools that will be built into the assessment setup and administration. This differs from most state policies that were typically developed to handle paper-and-pencil assessments when adaptations to the test forms themselves were often limited. In this situation (whether the state tests were delivered in hard copy or online), accommodations were usually added over and above the general administration.

In building in some adaptive features into test and item designs themselves, the consortia have reduced the lists of accommodations as traditionally conceptualized. Furthermore, some documentation from the consortia highlights additional steps they are considering to further adapt the items or administration of the assessments once the new online tests are underway. This is especially the case for ELs, where now, in many cases, ELs face a heavy text load even with the adaptive features. Furthermore, constructed response items currently require students to type in responses, which leaves many ELs at a distinct disadvantage because this is often the most difficult language domain for many of these students to use effectively. Several researchers and experts are urging the field and the consortia to broaden the ways ELs can demonstrate and express what they know and can do on open-ended items in ways that retain the integrity of challenging test items and not reduce their cognitive complexity (Gee, 2007, 2008; Kopriva et al., 2014; Willner, in press).

Evolution in Thinking About Measurement Validity and Implications for Access

One of the most dramatic changes that occurred as the inclusion of students with disabilities and ELs came to the forefront of policy was an evolution in thinking about what a valid assessment was. No longer driven primarily by the concept of a single approach to standardization as the basis of validity across students, thinking evolved considerably from what it was five decades ago.

In 1950, Gulliksen's *Theory of Mental Tests* focused primarily on reliability and essentially viewed validity as the correlation between the target test and an external criterion, such as a parallel form. Cronbach and Meehl (1955) transformed the concept of measurement validation, reformulating it as analogous to theory validation as the philosophy of science understands it occurring in scientific fields. This perspective greatly expanded the array of evidence useful in establishing validity. Textbooks from the mid-1970s defined validity as the degree to which a test or an evaluation tool serves the purposes for which it is intended (e.g., Ahmann & Glock, 1975). Three types of validity were generally described: content validity, criterion-related validity, and construct validity, and practitioners were advised to collect data to support the type of validity consistent with the intended use of the test results.

Messick (1989) expanded the kinds of evidence that could be used in validation, advancing the view of validity as a unitary concept that requires consideration of content, criterion, construct, and consequences, with construct as the unifying force. With that, Messick emphasized the distinction between construct-relevant and construct-irrelevant variance, laying the groundwork for considering how variables other than the content of interest can and do affect the validity of testing. Although Messick did not spend much time arguing that these variables can be tied to student factors, one of the implications of his work in this area led to differential considerations of construct-irrelevant variance for different students, such as students with disabilities and ELs. He contended,

Just because a process is never-ending does not mean that it should not have a beginning. And a good beginning, at the least, is to attempt to discount plausible rival hypotheses about construct-irrelevant variance in the test. For example, a plausible rival hypothesis for a subject-matter achievement test is that it might, by virtue of its vocabulary level, be in part a reading comprehension test in disguise . . . A variety of correlational, experimental, or logical approaches could be taken to render such rival hypotheses much less plausible. (p. 41)

Mislevy (1994) argued that the traditional argument for common inferences of student achievement had traditionally been on procedural grounds, which is what led to requiring common products and testing conditions. In practice, test development procedures, including control of content coverage through the item and test specifications, internal review procedures during development, and the use of standardized administration procedures for all students, were traditionally considered to be sufficient to ensure that the test was measuring what was intended and that the same inferences could be made with confidence about all students tested.

But it is the common inferences test developers were interested in holding constant, not the procedures per se. Mislevy (1994) and others (e.g., Kopriva, 1999; Popham, 1994; Rigney & Pettit, 1995; Shepard, 2001; Wiley & Haertel, 1995) argued that a priori validation arguments, rather than procedures, should form the basis of evaluation of scores purportedly collected to support the inferences. They called for more explicit links between what constructs and objectives the items are targeting; the processes that are used to develop, implement, and produce the scores on the assessments; and the evidence needed to demonstrate whether the items and tests were functioning as intended. In 2003, Mislevy, Steinberg, and Almond explained the concept of Evidence-Centered Design, saying that this conceptual argument should be built on providing adequate evidence about the knowledge and skills of interest, necessary observations, the properties of tasks or items designed to elicit the observations, and the assessment situations where students interact with assessment requests. This approach suggests that data may be collected under alternate conditions, as long as there is proper documentation and evidence that it is measuring what was intended for particular groups of students. If implemented correctly, linking the validation argument with evidence collected under standard differential conditions that can be defended as minimizing barriers to the questions and how students with different needs can respond back has paved the way for increased access in mainstream large-scale content tests for ELs and students with disabilities. Using the Evidence-Centered Design approach, researchers (Koenig & Bachman, 2004; Kopriva, 2008c) have explained in detail when and how alternative arguments or claims can be made for students with disabilities and ELs, respectively, and have suggested the kinds of evidence that might be collected to defend these claims.

Legal Basis for Inclusion, Accessibility, and Accommodations

There are several requirements (federal laws and regulations) as well as court cases that have provided a legal basis for attention to inclusion, accessibility, and accommodations in assessments.

ESEA 1994 (Improving America's Schools Act)

The Improving America's Schools Act (IASA) was the first federal education law to rely on standards to define the target of education for disadvantaged students, and to require that a consistent measure be used across students within a state to determine whether students were benefitting from Title I services. This law required that all students within a state be held to the same standards, and that the state have an assessment to measure performance on those standards. Although not widely recognized, ESEA 1994 specifically required that states include students with disabilities and ELs in the assessments, and that they report on the performance of these groups.

IDEA 1997

Public Law 94-142, the Education of All Handicapped Children Act, was passed in 1975 to ensure that students with disabilities receive a free, appropriate public education. This law and its successor in 1990, the IDEA, did not address the topic of large-scale assessments of academic achievement, but accommodations were mentioned in relation to instruction and the IEP. It was the reauthorization of IDEA in 1997 that introduced, for the first time, the notion of access to state- and district-wide assessments and referenced accommodations as an aspect of participation in assessments. Although ESEA 1994, the IASA, had previously required the participation of students with disabilities in state standards-based assessment, most states recognized the requirement when it came out in special education law. IDEA 1997 required that the state assessment results of students with disabilities be reported in the same way and with the same frequency as results were reported for other students. IDEA 1997 also introduced the requirement that each state develop an alternate assessment for those students unable to participate in the general assessment. These requirements for the participation of all students with disabilities in state assessments was a sea change for most states, one that was reinforced in subsequent reauthorizations of ESEA (Elementary and Secondary Education Act) and IDEA.

ESEA 2001

The reauthorization of the Elementary and Secondary Education Act in 2001, widely known as the No Child Left Behind Act, introduced strong accountability requirements for states (e.g., adequate yearly progress, with 100% of students to be proficient by 2013–2014). Strong statements indicated that the participation, assessment, and accountability requirements in the law applied to all students, including subgroups of students (students with disabilities, English language learners, economically disadvantaged, ethnic groups, etc.). ESEA also recognized the need for accommodations for ELs. States determined who could and who could not receive accommodations in their assessments (Thurlow, 2013).

ESEA 2001 has had several regulations associated with it that have addressed accountability (e.g., allowing for proficient performance on the alternate assessment to be counted toward the overall proficiency rate). In one of these regulations (April 2007), the U.S. Department of Education indicated that students taking assessments with accommodations that produced invalid results (i.e., modifications) would not count as participants in the assessment toward the 95% minimum participation rate. This reauthorization and its regulations galvanized many of the states to drastically increase the participation rates of ELs and students with disabilities and update their accommodation policies.

IDEA 2004

IDEA was reauthorized in 2004, and added a requirement that states report on the number of students receiving accommodations for state assessments. The 2004 reauthorization also referenced the same goals, standards, and accountability requirements that applied to all students under ESEA. Although the focus in IDEA is generally on individual accountability and the focus in ESEA generally is on systems accountability, the reauthorization of IDEA in 2004 confirmed that the laws systematically work together with the goal of raising academic achievement through high expectations and high-quality education programs (Cortiella, 2006).

Related Laws

In addition to IDEA and ESEA, two other federal laws specifically address the provision of accommodations to individuals with disabilities: Section 504 of the Rehabilitation Act of 1973 and the Americans With Disabilities Act (ADA). Section 504 states that any institution receiving federal funds has to ensure that admissions tests are selected and administered so as best to ensure that when a test is administered to an applicant who has a handicap that impairs sensory, manual, or speaking skills, the test results accurately reflect the applicant's aptitude or achievement level or whatever other factor the test purports to measure, rather than reflecting the applicant's impaired sensory, manual, or speaking skills (except where those skills are the factors that the test purports to measure)—Section 84.42(b)(3).

This was the first indication that it was considered discriminatory for a test to reflect an individual's disability rather than his or her knowledge and skills. Section 504 allows for the provision of accommodations to individuals with disabilities, including those of school age regardless of their eligibility for special education services. Students who receive accommodations but are not receiving special education services are considered to be "504 students" who have 504 accommodation plans.

ADA was enacted in 1990, and included requirements for accommodations and adaptations to be made by businesses and agencies receiving federal funds:

(A) making existing facilities used by employees readily accessible to and usable by individuals with disabilities; and (B) . . . acquisition or modification of equipment or devices, appropriate adjustment or modifications of examinations, training materials or policies, the provision of qualified readers or interpreters, and other similar accommodations for individuals with disabilities. (42 U.S.C. 12/11, Section 101[9])

ADA was reauthorized in 2008, and added clarifications of the definition of a "disability," which was defined in 1990 as an individual with a physical or mental impairment that substantially limits one or more major life activities, who has a record of such an impairment, or who is regarded as having an impairment. The clarifications included, for example, expanding the "illustrative" list of "major life activities" to include as examples concentrating, thinking, and communicating. Cortiella and Kaloi (2009) suggested that ADA 2008 had implications for Section 504 and how that law may affect "children with disabilities, including learning disabilities, as well as other conditions such as Attention-Deficit/Hyperactivity Disorder (AD/HD), Aspergers Syndrome, diabetes, asthma, and life-threatening food allergies" (p. 1).

Relevant Court Cases

There have been numerous court cases that have reinforced access to the curriculum and accommodations for students with disabilities and ELs. Our purpose here is not to list and describe all of these court cases. Instead we highlight a few that have played significant roles in the assessment of ELs and students with disabilities.

For students with disabilities, most legal cases have focused on accommodations policies for assessments that have implications for high school graduation, college entrance, or certification. Highlighted here are just a few of the "game-changing" cases. These include a case in Oregon that was settled out of court after a Blue Ribbon panel of experts recommended a new approach in which accommodations could be accepted as valid unless shown to be otherwise (Disability Rights Advocates, 2001). Another significant case involved the flagging of scores from graduate school entrance exams (Breimhorst vs. ETS, 2001), again settled out of court with the resolution that scores from accommodated assessments (other than those resulting in the removal of an entire test section) would no longer be flagged; ETS, ACT, and College Board adopted this policy.

For ELs the argument for inclusion and access to fair testing practices came vis-á-vis cases legislating their right to timely, ongoing, and equitable content instruction and holding public agencies accountable for their content learning. The two most often cited court cases for ELs were *Lau v. Nichols* (1974) and *Castañeda v. Pickard* (1981). In the Supreme Court case of *Lau v. Nichols*, the judges ruled that schools must provide English language instruction for ELs in a timely and effective manner such that ELs can learn English and thus have access to the content instruction programs. Both *Lau v. Nichols* and *Castañeda v. Pickard* also specified that ELs have the right to receive an education in academic content, just as native English speakers do. Further, the ruling in *Castañeda v. Pickard* clarified that it was not sufficient to wait until students were proficient in English before teaching content. Rather, ELs should *not* be put in a position where instruction in the English language would necessitate them being behind their native English-speaking peers in learning academic content. In 2000 a resource guide issued from the U.S. Office for Civil Rights extended the interpretation of equal access in academic classrooms for ELs to the right of access in large-scale assessments measuring academic content. This document connected legal precedence to the considerations of access and fairness as inextricable aspects of the concept of measurement validity articulated in the 1999 revision of the AERA/APA/NCME (1999) Testing Standards.

ACCESSIBILITY AND ACCOMMODATIONS CONSIDERATIONS FOR ELS

Many aspects of accessibility and accommodations considerations for ELs are unique in their bases and the research that has been conducted; selected aspects share some commonalities with some students with disabilities. Considerations of unique issues facing ELs include examining the following: (a) foundational assumptions, (b) research findings, (c) policy analyses, and (d) implications for district and classroom assessments.

Foundational Assumptions/Considerations

Until the passage of IASA, almost all but the most English-proficient ELs were routinely waived from large-scale content-testing programs, because it was argued that they could not handle the language load of the assessments. What policy researchers noted was that there was a direct relationship between these students taking part in standardized exams assessing K–12 content knowledge and skills, and the resources expended by the schools, districts, and states to teach them academic content in addition to teaching them English (Lara & August, 1996). With its emphasis on inclusion, the federal legislation became a wake-up call for public agencies to consider how to teach ELs academic subjects such as mathematics, and how to include the nonliteracy components of the grade-level ELA curriculum into their programs of study. Since that time, several foundational challenges and issues associated with properly assessing the academic knowledge and skills of ELs at different levels of English proficiency have been summarized. Of these, two are briefly mentioned here.

First, it needs to be remembered that not only are ELs learning English literacy skills, they are also learning the language of English at the same time. Furthermore, the nature of learning English for ELs is dynamic and ever-changing. At its essence, English language development involves different particular learning trajectories for different students consonant with various cultural, background, and situational factors, and the fact is that these factors differentially affect their relationships to content learning and testing (Solano-Flores, 2014). This vibrant interplay of variables and conditions means that ELs are a widely heterogeneous group between *and* within students at different points in time, beyond just the identification of literacy in the home language and their English language proficiency. This means that as ELs progress in their academic content schooling and English, their needs and how to accommodate them in content assessments change. What works well for students with certain common characteristics or for one student at one point may be quite different for others or at other times. Far more attention needs to be paid to how to prioritize the most salient variables associated with needs of ELs based on both common characteristics and English maturity (Kopriva, Emick, Hipolito-Delgado, & Cameron, 2007). This necessitates a far more nuanced profile of students beyond overly gross indicators such as EL status or not, level of English language proficiency, or time in the United States. Some work has been done to begin to untangle these issues, for instance, Carr and Kopriva (2009), Solano-Flores and Li (2009), and Ercikan et al. (in press). To date, the testing community has been very slow to embrace this more fine-grained approach to identifying needs of ELs in testing. Although the consortia are interested in establishing EL profiles to assign accommodations, the effort to improve on current approaches has lagged.

Commensurate with this challenge is the knotty problem of ensuring that the full range of content, including more challenging subject matter, is taught to ELs beginning when they first enter school (Kopriva, Gabel, & Cameron, 2009; Willner, in press). Addressing this issue is essential because once ELs have been identified as not learning content to par, often because of low expectations, or because language-heavy instructional materials and tests have been used, they are tracked into lower groups and remedial classes from which they cannot catch up (Callahan & Gándara, 2004). It is true that more sophisticated English language structures and discourse methods are directly related to more complex content.

In practice, many educators restrict the type of content they teach ELs to the level they have mastery of English, resulting in a focus on more basic content for students with fewer English skills. This occurs even though linguistics and EL experts argue that these students are learning more challenging content if given the opportunity (albeit using unconventional methods rather than relying so heavily on English text and oral approaches to convey meaning; e.g., Gee, 2007; Grice, 1975; Schleppegrell, 2004). They explain that although ELs with less maturity in English lack facility in comprehending and producing distinctive academic language, they can and do use alternate communication channels and multisemiotic methods to learn more difficult knowledge and skills. Two action points arise from this problem: First, as Schleppergrell notes, more content teachers need to be instructed explicitly about how to teach challenging content to students who have not yet mastered the higher levels of English. Second, Gee (2007) and Kopriva, Winter, et al. (2013) argue that content assessments also need to use methods beyond just language to give a wide number of ELs opportunity to demonstrate their knowledge, skills, and abilities in more complex subject matter. Most lower English ELs certainly need this assistance, and recent research has found higher English-proficient ELs also seem to benefit from using multisemiotic methods to teach and assess rigorous content in older grades (Kopriva, Winter, et al., 2013). This includes enhancing not only how the topics and problems are presented to ELs but also how the students are allowed to respond and show or explain what they know.

Research Findings

In the early years of accommodations use in large-scale summative testing, ELs were mostly offered accommodations that had been designated for students with disabilities (Rivera & Collum, 2004; Rivera & Stansfield, 2000). Early research for ELs focused mostly on simplified English, and then a selection of other accommodations like reading aloud of the directions and extra time (e.g., Abedi et al., 2000; Abedi & Lord, 2001). In 2003 Sireci, Li, and Scarpati published a meta-analysis of research to date where they noted that use of experimental research designs were largely wanting, and results of particular accommodations seemed generally inconclusive. Since that time, progress has been made in identifying the types of accommodations that are likely to address the linguistic needs of ELs (e.g., bilingual dictionaries, glossaries, translations). Rivera and Collum (2006) grouped relevant accommodations for ELs by direct and indirect accommodation supports.

Over time the number of published studies continued to grow with more quasi-experimental and experimental research. In two meta-analyses, Kieffer, Lesaux, Rivera, and Francis (2009) and Pennock-Roman and Rivera (2011) noted that some direct linguistic supports appeared to be significantly more effective for ELs, although there was still a lot of "noise" in the results overall. Furthermore, researchers paid increasing attention to differential boost of accommodations for ELs versus native English speakers (see Sireci et al., 2003, for an explanation of differential boost). Most studies still did not tend to group ELs by need or even English proficiency level, however, and only occasionally would investigations that separated ELs by need or proficiency also make use of EL control groups where ELs who needed certain accommodations did and did not receive them (Abedi, 2012; Kopriva, 2008c). These two shortcomings meant that results still tend to be blunted because it is difficult to know whether an accommodation is truly effective for ELs who need it, versus a heterogeneous group of ELs generally.

Emick and Kopriva (2007) found in a study of elementary mathematics that it was mostly higher English proficient ELs (vs. lower English ELs) and native English speakers that benefited more by plain (or simplified) language and visuals. In a random assignment of forms, Carr (2008) found that lower ELs scored significantly higher on universally designed (UD) versions of items versus the traditional items than did their higher EL and native English-speaking peers. But closer inspection indicated that these gains occurred primarily in mathematics, science, and social studies items measuring basic skills. Most of the gains were lost for low ELs in items measuring more challenging content.

Lately, a number of other studies have been concerned with broadening how accommodations might be presented to ELs and how they are able to respond. Sireci and Wells (2010) studied the structural integrity of tests for native English speakers and ELs of Spanish or Arabic background when they were presented the traditional state mathematics test in English versus when they not only were provided the traditional test but also watched a video that pointed to the questions in the English text while students listened to the questions in Spanish or Arabic. Overall they found that the oral L1 approach led to higher scores for ELs, and that the structural equivalence of this type of dual-language approach was consistent with the integrity of the tests for native speakers over grades and language groups.

Kopriva et al. (2014), Kopriva et al. (2013), and Kopriva et al. (2009) developed technology-interactive science items, called ONPAR, using performance-based multimodal techniques, including language, at elementary, middle, and high school that were designed to measure the same constructs as challenging items using traditional item types. After controlling for science ability and randomly assigning the traditional and ONPAR forms to ELs of different levels of proficiency and native English speakers, they found overall that the differential boosts between and within treatments was significantly higher for lower English ELs in the lower grades than for their native English-speaking peers, and favored ONPAR over the traditional forms. Similar findings were noted for more proficient ELs relative to native speakers, and ONPAR versus traditional forms, in high school biology (Kopriva et al., 2013). Additionally, science and cognition experts indicated that ONPAR's performance methodology showed promise for more deeply measuring challenging constructs for all students, including but not limited to vulnerable ELs. In over 250 cognitive labs that investigated the viability of various techniques used in ONPAR, Wright and colleagues (Wright & Kopriva, 2009; Wright & Logan-Terry, 2014; Wright, Staehr-Fenner, Moxley, Kopriva, & Carr, 2013) pinpointed how the nontext multisemiotic elements could be effectively used in substantially conveying meaning to and from students. This is in contrast to the traditional uses of multimedia in items, which typically act as secondary or tertiary supports to language in conveying meaning in items.

Solano-Flores and colleagues (Solano-Flores, 2006, in press; Solano-Flores & Gustafson, 2012; Solano-Flores & Li, 2009) have investigated how item features, different background characteristics, and different language characteristics interact with English and L1 text in items for ELs, helping researchers understand the dynamic interplay leading to more or less access to items. Ercikan et al. (in press) investigated the impact of immediate and dominant culture environments for different language groups, and a number of studies have been completed by them (e.g., Ercikan et al., in press; Oliveri, Ercikan, & Zumbo, 2014; Roth, Oliveri, Sandilands, Lyons-Thomas, & Ercikan, 2013) that demonstrate how differential item functioning (DIF) results differ significantly by methods for ELs and differentially interact across groups of language minority students, kinds of environmental influences, and English language proficiency levels. Roth et al. posited that at least some of the dissimilar DIF patterns may reflect different forms of reasoning.

Similar to concerns about dependable accommodation assignments raised repeatedly by policy researchers associated with the NAEP tests (e.g., Fields, 2008; Kitmitto & Bandeira de Mello, 2008), Kopriva and Koran (2008) reviewed findings from past and current methods that practitioners and academic test programs use to assign accommodations to students in large-scale content assessment settings. They concluded that relevant and consistent assignment continues to be a major problem for ELs. After a series of focus groups, Douglas (2004) suggested that teachers of ELs (including EL specialists and content teachers) have a hard time identifying particular accommodations for ELs with different needs, and Koran, Kopriva, Emick, Monroe, and Garavaglia (2006) found that teachers were not able to recommend accommodations any more effectively than when a random set of accommodations were generated for individual students even when explicit assignment criteria were delineated. Kopriva et al. (2007) reported that when ELs were provided accommodations specifically identified for them to match their needs, they scored significantly higher on a mathematics test as opposed to when they received only some of the accommodations or no accommodations. Troubling was that there was no difference in test scores between those receiving an incomplete accommodation set and no accommodations whatsoever, suggesting that this is an important and often overlooked aspect of access for ELs.

Implications for District and Classroom Assessments

In the past 15 years there has been more concerted, systematic attention and research paid to considering how content learning and formative assessment in general can be improved for ELs. Most of this work has focused on considering and improving the language of content as an integral part of instruction in content classrooms. For instance, Janzen (2008) conducted a meta-analysis of approaches to teaching ELs in specific subjects and noted that the majority of the approaches he analyzed had not yet been subjected to rigorous evaluations. In a couple of experimental studies from that time, Lee, Maerten-Rivera, Penfield, LeRoy, and Secada (2008) found gains in science outcomes when mostly inquiry-based instructional methods, along with explicit attention to the ELs' language and literacy skills, were developed. Vaughn et al. (2009) found improvement in social studies scores for ELs when the teachers used both multicomponent linguistic support for ELs, with liberal ongoing utilization of nontext visual and interactive techniques.

Recently, Lee, Quinn, and Valdés (2013) identified key classroom disciplinary practices resulting from unpacking the English Language Proficiency/Development Framework associated within the Common Core and Next Generation Science Standards. Although most of the later work is still focused on improving how language is used in content classroom instruction, Solano-Flores and Gustafson (2012) urged teachers and content assessment developers and users at district and classroom, as well as at state levels, to not water down the application of the content standards to be commensurate with ELs' English language abilities. Furthermore, Heritage and Heritage (2013) explained how properly applied teacher questioning can become a powerful tool in the ongoing formative assessment of content for students, including ELs. Abedi, Heckman, and Herman (2010) have a 5-year project researching the state of formative assessment of mathematics throughout California, including the scope, prevalence, and use of strategies and tools in schools; how formative assessment is being supported at administrative levels; and identifying recommendations for useful formative assessment systems. Their work is focused on the needs and effective strategies in place in higher preforming schools with significant numbers of underrepresented students, including ELs. Kopriva (2014) was recently awarded an Institute of Education Sciences grant to investigate how to use multimedia capacities to assess challenging mathematics and science knowledge, skills, and abilities of ELs in classrooms. All of these initiatives suggest that formative assessment, at least at the classroom levels, is being actively considered for ELs.

ACCESSIBILITY AND ACCOMMODATIONS CONSIDERATIONS FOR STUDENTS WITH DISABILITIES

In the same way that there are unique considerations about accessibility and accommodations for ELs, there are unique considerations for students with disabilities. We review these considerations by examining (a) foundational assumptions, (b) research findings, (c) policy analyses, and (d) implications for district and classroom assessments.

Foundational Assumptions/Considerations

Many of the foundational assumptions underlying the need for participation in assessments, with appropriate accommodations, were documented in the landmark study by the National Research Council (McDonnell et al., 1997). That study confirmed the importance of the participation of students with disabilities in large-scale assessments, particularly state assessments, if students with disabilities were to benefit from standards-based education reforms. The National Research Council report also pointed to the importance of accommodations for providing students access to the general curriculum and for being able to show their knowledge and skills on assessments.

Initial accommodations policies indicated that the purpose of accommodations was to ensure that students could participate in assessments and to level the playing field for these students. Concerns frequently emerged about knowing what a "level playing field" is and how to be sure that changes that are provided in the name of accommodations do not actually create an "advantage" for the students who received them. The focus became on the *validity* of assessments when accommodations are used—do the users of assessment results receive the same information for those students who used accommodations as they do for those who did not? In other words, are the assessment results valid or did the accommodations alter in some fundamental way what the assessment was intended to measure and thus provide an unfair advantage to students (Koretz & Hamilton, 2000)?

Another set of considerations that undergirded approaches to accessibility and accommodations for students with disabilities focused on the ways in which students with disabilities were excluded during all phases of assessment development, from the initial conceptualization of who would participate in the assessments (e.g., only those taking it in the standard way), the expertise needed by those who developed or reviewed items (e.g., not those with an understanding of special education students), and who was included in pilot and field testing. Early assessment development focused on including only those students who would take an assessment in a "standard" way. These conditions led to assumptions about what needed to be in place to ensure that assessments were developed with all students in mind, including initial approaches to UD assessments (Thompson et al., 2004), and to suggestions about how the appropriateness of accommodations should be determined through research (Laitusis, 2007; Phillips, 1994).

With these considerations in mind, there remain at least three vexing challenges for accessibility and accommodations for students with disabilities. The first challenge is related to the assumption that category is not a good basis for determining accessibility and accommodation needs. Without this "easy" basis for determining needs, educators and researchers are left to determine the characteristics and needs of students that make sense for making decisions and for conducting research. A second challenge is related to the fact that students with disabilities rarely need only one accommodation. This means that targeted research is always confounded in one way or another by the provision (or lack of provision) of other accommodations. Finally, there are significant challenges related to the decision making and implementation of accommodations, which in turn confound research findings.

Research Findings

Most research that has been conducted has focused on the effects of specific accommodations or groups of accommodations. However, there have been some studies to investigate universal design and decision making/implementation. In this section, we briefly highlight research findings on (a) universal design, (b) accommodations research, and (c) decision making and implementation.

Universal Design

Researchers have addressed various ways to apply universal design approaches to the development of assessments in general (Johnstone, Thompson, Miller, & Thurlow, 2008; Ketterlin-Geller, 2005; Thurlow, Johnstone, & Ketterlin-Geller, 2008; Thurlow, Johnstone, Thompson, & Case, 2008) and specifically in relation to computer-based assessment (Dolan et al., 2009; Russell, 2011). They also have conducted studies to explore the applicability of universal design principles (Almond et al., 2010; Johnstone et al., 2008; Johnstone, Liu, Altman, & Thurlow, 2007). Generally, these articles and studies have supported the applicability of universal design, but with the caveat that too often students with disabilities are challenged by not having had access to the content, which in turn makes it difficult to accurately assess the effects of various universal design approaches.

Accommodations

Approaches to studying the effects of accommodations on the validity of assessment results have evolved over time. One of the earliest explications of the conditions that needed to be met to demonstrate the effectiveness of an accommodation for producing valid assessment results was proposed by Phillips (1994). She outlined three conditions that needed to be checked before allowing accommodations: (a) the accommodation should not alter what the test is measuring; (b) scores between students who received the accommodation and those who did not should be comparable; and (c) accommodations should benefit only students with disabilities, not those without disabilities. This latter condition has sometimes been referred to as an interaction hypothesis—it argued that an accommodation produces no change in scores for test takers, unless they have a disability. The interaction hypothesis has been a theoretical basis for much of the early research into the effects of accommodations (Sireci, Scarpati, & Li, 2005).

As noted previously, researchers documenting the effects of accommodations most recently have replaced the interaction hypothesis with the differential boost hypothesis (Fuchs & Fuchs, 1999; Laitusis, 2007; Sireci et al., 2005). This theoretical perspective argued that students without disabilities might benefit (i.e., show improved performance) with the use of accommodations but that the benefit obtained by students with disabilities would be differentially (and significantly) larger than that obtained by students without disabilities. The differential boost hypothesis recently has been the primary driving force in experimental and quasi-experimental studies on the effects of accommodations. Some research has focused on the effects of accommodations for single students using all of the accommodations that they would typically use. This single-subject research approach (e.g., McKevitt et al., 2000) has been used much less frequently than the group approaches to research. Others have focused, as recommended by Crawford (2007), on bundled accommodations (Fletcher et al., 2006; Fletcher et al., 2009).

Some studies of the effects of accommodations are based on extant data analyses. These studies typically examine the factor structure of the assessment when accommodations are used compared to when accommodations are not used (e.g., Cook, Eignor, Steinberg, Sawaki, & Cline, 2009; Kim, Schneider, & Siskind, 2009). The assumption is that an appropriate accommodation results in a test with the same factor structure as the test shows without accommodations being used. Some extant data analyses have used DIF to determine whether the use of accommodations alters the characteristics of items (e.g., Abedi, Leon, & Kao, 2008a; Bolt & Ysseldyke, 2006; Cahalan-Laitusis, Morgan, Bridgeman, Zanna, & Stone, 2007; Finch, Barton, & Meyer, 2009). More recently, researchers have also looked at differential distractor functioning, which examines whether the provision of accommodations alters the selection of incorrect responses by those who do not choose the right answer on a multiple-choice item (e.g., Abedi, Leon, & Kao, 2008b; Kato, Moen, & Thurlow, 2009).

Considerable research now has been conducted to examine the effects of accommodations on assessment results. The research has changed over time. Early research (e.g., Laing & Farmer, 1984; Mazzeo, Carlson, Voekl, & Lutkus, 2000; Willingham et al., 1988) was groundbreaking in many ways, yet it also suffered from many complexities that confounded results. Many hundreds of studies have been conducted since these early studies, and they have continued to portray the complexities of conducting research on accommodations and reaching strong conclusions based on the research (e.g., Thurlow, Lazarus, & Christensen, 2013).

According to summaries of the disability research on accommodations conducted by Tindal and Fuchs (2000), numerous investigators at the National Center on Educational Outcomes (Cormier, Altman, Shyyan, & Thurlow, 2010; Johnstone,

Altman, Thurlow, & Thompson, 2006; Rogers, Christian, & Thurlow, 2012; Thompson, Blount, & Thurlow, 2002; Zenisky & Sireci, 2007), and others (Laitusis, Buzick, Stone, Hansen, & Hakkinen, 2012; Pitoniak & Royer, 2001), the number of studies on assessment accommodations has increased dramatically over the years.

The primary design of most of the recent accommodations studies was quasi experimental, followed by those considered to be descriptive quantitative, descriptive qualitative, and correlational (Rogers et al., 2012). Few studies are considered to be experimental, meaning that they included random assignment of students to conditions. Most studies have involved students with learning disabilities, attention problems, emotional-behavioral disabilities, and visual impairments. Most studies examined presentation accommodations such as computer administration, braille, and sign language interpretation.

Several studies have specifically examined whether changes that were previously provided as external accommodations could be provided via the computer (Dolan, Hall, Banerjee, Chun, & Strangman, 2005; Erdogan, 2008; Kamei-Hannan, 2008; Russell, Hoffman, & Higgins, 2009b). Other studies have explored the comparability of computer-based and paper assessments, though not always specifically considering the accommodations aspect of comparability (Kingston, 2009; Russell, 1999). The pending incorporation of what were previously viewed as accommodations into technology platforms raises a host of possibilities for greater access (e.g., Madaus et al., 2009) as well as a number of new issues to be addressed (Thurlow et al., 2011; Thurlow, Lazarus, et al., 2010).

Despite the increase in the number of studies on the effects of accommodations, the results of the research remain inconclusive for the most part. Some researchers have concluded that only extended time has a clear research basis (Sireci et al., 2005). Although continued research is considered to be important for demonstrating the validity of accommodated assessment results, the research likely will need to target accommodations for specific tests and for students with specific characteristics and access needs.

Decision Making/Implementation

Several studies have examined issues surrounding the implementation of accommodations (DeStefano, Shriner, & Lloyd, 2001; Hodgson et al., 2012; Rhode Island Department of Education, 2003; Shriner & DeStefano, 2003) and inconsistencies in the decision-making process (Ketterlin-Geller et al., 2007). Logistical concerns were raised as well in response to concerns about the need to have test administrators or other school personnel to provide accommodations during testing (Bowen & Ferrell, 2003; Hodgson et al., 2012). On the whole, this research highlighted significant lapses and challenges in decision making and implementation. Recent training efforts have focused on these challenges (e.g., see www.nceo.info/OnlineAccommodationsTraining. html; www.ivared.info/training.html).

Implications for District and Classroom Assessments

Assessments used to measure students more frequently during the course of the year are an important part of a comprehensive assessment system. These assessments must be designed with the same attention to access as is now being used for state summative assessments. In addition to considering the design of these assessments and the use of accommodations, developers must address content issues. For example, the argument that formative assessments must be sensitive to the student's instructional level must be weighed in light of the need to focus the student's instruction on grade-level content (Quenemoen, Thurlow, Moen, Thompson, & Morse, 2003).

Although the use of accommodations during formative, interim, and summative assessments should be aligned, this is generally not the case. Some commonly accepted accommodations for instruction and summative assessments, such as providing a braille version for students who are blind, are treated as yielding invalid results by several formative assessments (Thurlow & Lazarus, 2009). Without thoughtful alignment across assessments, it is likely that there will be systematic exclusion of students with disabilities from the benefits of formative and interim measures.

ACCESSIBILITY AND ACCOMMODATIONS CONSIDERATIONS FOR ELS WITH DISABILITIES

It is relatively recently that ELs with disabilities have been considered in relation to assessment accessibility and accommodations. Only in the past couple of years has policy (e.g., Albus & Thurlow, 2007) and practice (e.g., Albus & Thurlow, 2013; Liu et al., 2013) been examined for these students, who too often in the past were simply exempted from testing. Research related to including these students in assessments is just beginning, and much of it is policy research (e.g., Christensen, Albus, Liu, Thurlow, & Kincaid, 2013; Thurlow, Liu, Ward, & Christensen, 2013). As the prevalence of ELs with disabilities increases across the United States, it is likely that attention to the inclusion of these students in accessibility and accommodations considerations for these assessments will increase.

IMPLICATIONS FOR THE FUTURE

As recently as the early 1990s the measurement field considered large-scale tests results to be invalid if almost any procedure was altered for any student (Rigney, Wiley, & Kopriva, 2008). Under pressure to allow some restricted accommodations for individuals with disabilities, scores from these students were flagged with caveats questioning the validity of their results and concerns about whether the conditions provided an advantage to those students using them (Koretz & Hamilton, 2000). Over the past two decades, the profound shift in including and adapting conditions for ELs and students with disabilities in general K–12 large-scale academic testing systems has been led most centrally by federal policy and legal directives, underpinned by strong advocate lobbies, and the evolution of the concept of measurement validity and what it means for these populations (Rigney et al., 2008). In time, the point of the discussion has focused on the disadvantage imposed on students who did not receive needed accommodations:

Accommodations are designed to decrease noise and maximize the strength of the inference based on a student's score. Without accommodations, many students are at a disadvantage in demonstrating what they actually know and can do. (Madaus et al., 2009, p. 182)

Although cost and feasibility are still considerable concerns, schools, testing programs, and accountability agencies now expect students with disabilities and ELs to be included in academic assessment programs, and there continues to be pressure for them to be included properly. As the field of measurement continues to consider how to do this effectively and defensibly, substantial movement has been made over the past 20 years to address this objective (Kopriva, 2008c; Thurlow et al., 2011). For instance, the academic testing consortia are planning features previously considered to be accommodations to instead be included in the general assessment platforms available for many more students. In addition, research continues about how to include many ELs and students with disabilities when these changes are not sufficient. Adaptations to the items themselves without changing the nature of the underlying constructs are an example where additional work is needed for some ELs (Kopriva et al., 2014).

For students with disabilities it will be important for researchers and assessment programs to reevaluate whether the theoretical perspective of differential boost makes sense for groups defined by disability or category of disability, and instead define it by student need (e.g., Laitusis, 2010). The same is true for ELs where defining ELs as a homogeneous status category or by English language proficiency only may be less effective than focusing on need (Kopriva, 2008c). This would be consistent with the finding that some ELs and students with disabilities, and some students who are native English speakers and without disabilities, show differential boost compared to students with disabilities and ELs who do not need the same accommodation (e.g., Thurlow, Moen, Lekwa, & Scullin, 2010). Second, moving ahead, calling for better research methods will help clarify effective and noneffective solutions. For instance, thoughtful experimental research should use control groups of students with the same needs, rather than distorting results by assuming that control groups can be made up of any other students who either are ELs or have a disability.

Third, shifting to online administrations allows test makers to use the myriad capacities of technology. This includes integrating accommodation aspects such as text to speech and pop-ups of text, graphic, or animated glossaries (Powers & Strain-Seymour, 2013), and it also includes broadening the opportunities for how students can show their skills or knowledge (Kopriva et al., 2014). In addition, it opens up how interchangeable versions might be conceived and implemented without changing the underlying constructs. For ELs and some students with disabilities, accessible versions need to consider using media in more central ways to help communicate essential meaning. Adding a window where deaf and hard-of-hearing students see the signing while also viewing the text and simulations of the base or "general item" is one example (Cawthon et al., 2013). Fourth, it will be important, as the conceptual basis for a wider range of text editing considerations, integrated access features, and broader set of response types take hold, that the item and test development processes include strong oversight procedures, staffed by content specialists and specialists adept in considering the needs for ELs, students with disabilities, and perhaps others.

Finally, there is a need to address inconsistencies between K–12 and postsecondary education and work settings. As students who have used accommodations move toward college and career, there should be a smooth transition. Although in many ways, postsecondary settings are more "accommodating" than are K–12 assessment environments (Gregg, 2009; Thurlow, Johnstone, & Ketterlin-Geller, 2008), entrance exams continue to place restrictions on which students may have access to accommodations, thereby possibly limiting the number of students who enter postsecondary education (U.S. Government Accountability Office, 2011). For instance, there are currently no accommodations allowed for ELs on post-secondary admissions tests, such as extra time or the use of bilingual glossaries. The same questions should emerge for post–K-12 assessments as for K–12 assessments. It may be that the work of the consortia of states, with their accommodations policies aligned to college and career readiness, will push this forward, or it may be the work of a new generation of policymakers and researchers to point the direction, study the trade-offs and implications, and posit some solutions that are feasible, reasonable, and effective.

REFERENCES

Abedi, J. (2012). Validity issues in designing accommodations. In G. Fulcher & F. Davidson (Eds.), *The Routledge handbook of language testing in a nutshell* (pp. 48–62). New York, NY: Routledge.

Abedi, J., & Bayley, R. (2014). *Improving language outcomes by distinguishing between low English proficiency and learning disabilities* [Funding proposal]. Washington, DC: Institute of Education Sciences.

Abedi, J., & Ewers, N. (2013). *Smarter Balanced Assessment Consortium: Accommodations for English language learners and students with disabilities: A research-based decision algorithm.* Retrieved from http://www.smarterbalanced.org/wordpress/wp-content/uploads/2012/08/Accommodations-for-under-represented-students.pdf

Abedi, J, Heckman, P., & Herman, J. (2010). *The Formative Assessment Project.* Arlington, VA: National Science Foundation.

Abedi, J., Leon, S., & Kao, J. (2008a). *Examining differential distractor functioning in reading assessments for students with disabilities* (CSE Report 743). Los Angeles: University of California, Center for the Study of Evaluation/National Center for Research on Evaluation, Standards, and Student Testing.

Abedi, J., Leon, S., & Kao, J. (2008b). *Examining differential item functioning in reading assessments for students with disabilities* (CSE Report 744). Los Angeles: University of California, Center for the Study of Evaluation/National Center for Research on Evaluation, Standards, and Student Testing.

Abedi, J., & Lord, C. (2001). The language factor in mathematics tests. *Applied Measurement in Education, 14,* 219–234.

Abedi, J., Lord, C., Hofstetter, C., & Baker, E. (2000). Impact of accommodation strategies on English language learners' test performance. *Educational Measurement: Issues and Practice, 19*(3), 16–26.

Ahmann, J. S., & Glock, M. D. (1975). *Measuring and evaluating educational achievement.* Boston, MA: Allyn & Bacon.

Albus, D., & Thurlow, M. (2013). *2010-11 publicly reported assessment results for students with disabilities and ELLs with disabilities* (Technical Report 68). Minneapolis: University of Minnesota, National Center on Educational Outcomes.

Albus, D. A., & Thurlow, M. L. (2007). *English language learners with disabilities in state English language proficiency assessments: A review of state accommodation policies* (Synthesis Report 66). Minneapolis: University of Minnesota, National Center on Educational Outcomes.

Almond, P., Winter, P., Cameto, R., Russell, M., Sato, E., Clarke-Midura, J., . . . Lazarus, S. (2010). Technology-enabled and universally designed assessment: Considering access in measuring the achievement of students with disabilities—a foundation for research. *Journal of Technology, Learning, and Assessment, 10*(5). Retrieved from http://ejournals.bc.edu/ojs/index.php/jtla/article/view/1605/1453

Altman, J. R., Lazarus, S. S., Thurlow, M. L., Quenemoen, R. F., Cuthbert, M., & Cormier, D. C. (2008). *2007 survey of states.* Minneapolis: University of Minnesota, National Center on Educational Outcomes.

American Educational Research Association, American Psychological Association, & National Council on Measurement in Education. (2014). *Standards for educational & psychological tests.* Washington, DC: American Psychological Association.

Bolt, S. E., & Ysseldyke, J. E. (2006). Comparing DIF across math and reading/language arts tests for students receiving a read-aloud accommodation. *Applied Measurement in Education, 19*, 329–355.

Bowen, S., & Ferrell, K. (2003). Assessment in low-incidence disabilities: The day-to-day realities. *Rural Special Education Quarterly, 22*(4), 10–19.

Breimhorst v. ETS (N.D. Cal, March 27, 2001). Chapman/Kidd v. California Department of Education. Prelim Injunction, C 01-01780 CRB, n.d. CA (2002).

Cahalan-Laitusis, C., Morgan, D., Bridgeman, B., Zanna, J., & Stone, E. (2007). *Examination of fatigue effects from extended time accommodations on the SAT Reasoning Test.* New York, NY: College Board.

Callahan, R., & Gándara, P. (2004). On nobody's agenda: Improving English-language learners' access to higher education. In M. Sadowski (Ed.), *Teaching immigrant and second-language students: Strategies for success* (pp. 107–127). Cambridge, MA: Harvard Education Press.

Carr, T. G. (2008, March). *Qualitative review of items that worked and didn't work.* Paper presented at the National Council of Measurement in Education annual meeting, New York, NY.

Carr, T. G., & Kopriva, R. J. (2009, April). *It's about time: Matching English Learners and the ways they take tests by using an online tool to properly address individual needs.* Paper presented at the National Council of Measurement in Education annual meeting, San Diego, CA.

Castañeda v. Pickard. 648 F. 2d 989 (5th Cir. 1981).

Cawthon, S., Leppo, R., Carr, T. G., & Kopriva, R. J. (2013). Towards accessible assessments: The promises and limitations of test item adaptations for students with disabilities and English language learners. *Educational Assessment, 18*, 73–98.

Christensen, L. L., Albus, D. A., Liu, K. K., Thurlow, M. L., & Kincaid, A. (2013). *Accommodations for students with disabilities on state English language proficiency assessments: A review of 2011 state policies.* Minneapolis: University of Minnesota,

Improving the Validity of Assessment Results for English Language Learners with Disabilities (IVARED).

Christensen, L. L., Braam, M., Scullin, S., & Thurlow, M. L. (2011). *2009 state policies on assessment participation and accommodations for students with disabilities* (Synthesis Report 83). Minneapolis: University of Minnesota, National Center on Educational Outcomes.

Clapper, A. T., Morse, A. B., Thompson, S. J., & Thurlow, M. L. (2005). *Access assistants for state assessments: A study of state guidelines for scribes, readers, and sign language interpreters* (Synthesis Report 58). Minneapolis: University of Minnesota, National Center on Educational Outcomes.

Cook, L., Eignor, D., Steinberg, J., Sawaki, Y., & Cline, F. (2009). Using factor analysis to investigate the impact of accommodations on the scores of students with disabilities on a reading comprehension assessment. *Journal of Applied Testing Technology, 10*(2). Retrieved from http://www.jattjournal.com/index.php/atp/issue/view/4186

Cormier, D. C., Altman, J. R., Shyyan, V., & Thurlow, M. L. (2010). *A summary of the research on the effects of test accommodations: 2007-2008* (Technical Report 56). Minneapolis: University of Minnesota, National Center on Educational Outcomes.

Cortiella, C. (2006). *NCLB and IDEA: What parents of students with disabilities need to know and do.* Minneapolis: University of Minnesota, National Center on Educational Outcomes.

Cortiella, C., & Kaloi, L. (2009). *Understanding the Americans With Disabilities Act amendments and Section 504 of the Rehabilitation Act.* New York, NY: National Center for Learning Disabilities.

Council of Chief State School Officers & Association of Test Publishers. (2010). *Operational best practices for statewide large-scale assessment programs.* Washington, DC: Author.

Crawford, L. (2007). *State testing accommodations: A look at their value and validity.* New York, NY: National Center for Learning Disabilities.

Cronbach, L. J., & Meehl, O. E. (1995). Construct validity in psychological tests. *Psychological Bulletin, 52*, 281–302.

DeStefano, L., Shriner, J. G., & Lloyd, C. A. (2001). Teacher decision making in participation of students with disabilities in large-scale assessment. *Exceptional Children, 68*(1), 7–22.

Disability Rights Advocates. (2001). *Do no harm—High stakes testing and students with learning disabilities.* Oakland, CA: Author.

Dolan, R. P., Burling, K. S., Harms, M., Beck, R., Hanna, E., Jude, J., . . . Way, W. (2009). *Universal design for computer-based testing guidelines.* Iowa City, IA: Pearson.

Dolan, R. P., Hall, T. E., Banerjee, M., Chun, E., & Strangman, N. (2005). Applying principles of universal design to test delivery: The effect of computer-based read-aloud on test performance of high school students with learning disabilities. *Journal of Technology, Learning, and Assessment, 3*(7), 1–31.

Douglas, K. (2004). *Teacher ideas on teaching and testing English language learners: Summary of focus group discussions* (Report No. 219). College Park: University of Maryland, Center for the Study of Assessment Validity and Evaluation.

Elliott, J. L., & Thurlow, M. L. (2006). *Improving test performance of students with disabilities on district and state assessments* (2nd ed.). Thousand Oaks, CA: Corwin.

Emick, J., & Kopriva, R. J. (2007, April). *The validity of large-scale assessment scores for ELLs under optimal testing conditions: Does validity vary by language proficiency?* Presentation at the American Educational Research Association annual meeting, Chicago, IL.

Ercikan, K., Roth, W. M., Simon, M., Sandilands, D., & Lyons-Thomas, J (in press). Tests fair for all linguistic minority students? Validity and fairness of measurements for diverse linguistic minority students. *Applied Measurement in Education.*

Erdogan, Y. (2008). Paper-based and computer-based concept mapping: The effects on computer achievement, computer anxiety and computer attitude. *British Journal of Educational Technology, 40,* 821–836.

Fields, R. (2008). *Inclusion of special populations in the national assessment: A review of relevant laws and regulations.* Washington, DC: National Assessment Governing Board.

Finch, H., Barton, K., & Meyer, P. (2009). Differential item functioning analysis for accommodated versus non-accommodated students. *Educational Assessment, 14*(1), 38–56.

Fletcher, J. M., Francis, D. J., Boudousquie, A., Copeland, K., Young, V., Kalinowski, S., & Vaughn, S. (2006). Effects of accommodations on high-stakes testing for students with reading disabilities. *Exceptional Children, 72,* 136–150.

Fletcher, J. M., Francis, D. J., O'Malley, K., Copeland, K., Mehta, P., Caldwell, C. J., . . . Vaughn, S. (2009). Effects of a bundled accommodations package on high-stakes testing for middle school students with reading disabilities. *Exceptional Children, 75,* 447–463.

Fuchs, L. S., & Fuchs, D. (1999). Fair and unfair testing accommodations. *School Administrator, 56*(10), 24–29.

Gee, J. P. (2007). *What video games have to teach us about learning and literacy* (2nd ed.). New York, NY: Palgrave Macmillan.

Gee, J. P. (2008). *Good video games + good learning: Collected essays on video games, learning, and literacy.* New York, NY: Peter Lang.

Gerwertz, C. (2013, November 7). U.S. math, reading achievement edges up, but gaps remain. *Education Week, 33*(12). Retrieved from http://www.edweek.org/ew/articles/2013/11/07/12naep.h33.html

Goertz, M. (2007, June). *Standards-based reform: Lessons from the past, directions for the future.* Paper presented at Clio at the Table: A Conference on the Uses of History to Inform and Improve Education Policy, Brown University, Providence, RI. Retrieved from http://www7.nationalacademies.org/cfe/Goertz%20Paper.pdf

Gregg, N. (2009). *Adolescents and adults with learning disabilities and ADHD: Assessment and accommodation.* New York, NY: Guilford.

Grice, H. P. (1975). Logic and conversation. In P. Cole & J. L. Morgan (Eds.), *Syntax and semantics: Vol. 3. Speech acts* (pp. 41–58). New York, NY: Academic Publishers.

Gulliksen, H. (1950). *Theory of mental tests.* New York, NY: Wiley.

Haladyna, R. M., & Downing, S. M. (2004). Construct-irrelevant variance in high-stakes testing. *Educational Measurement: Issues and Practice, 23*(1), 17–27.

Heritage, M., & Heritage, J. (2013). *Teacher questioning: The epicenter of instruction and assessment.* New York, NY: Routledge.

Heubert, J. P., & Hauser, R. M. (1999). *High stakes: Testing for tracking, promotion and graduation.* Washington, DC: National Academies Press.

Hodgson, J. R., Lazarus, S. S., Price, L., Altman, J. R., & Thurlow, M. L. (2012). *Test administrators' perspectives on the use of the read aloud accommodation on state tests for accountability* (Technical Report No. 66). Minneapolis: University of Minnesota, National Center on Educational Outcomes.

Janzen, J. (2008). Teaching English language learners in the content areas. *Review of Educational Research, 78,* 1010–1038.

Johnstone, C. J., Altman, J. R., & Thurlow, M. L. (2006). *A state guide to the development of universally designed assessments.* Minneapolis: University of Minnesota, National Center on Educational Outcomes.

Johnstone, C. J., Altman, J., Thurlow, M. L., & Thompson, S. J. (2006). *A summary of research on the effects of test accommodations: 2002 through 2004* (Technical Report No. 45). Minneapolis: University of Minnesota, National Center on Educational Outcomes.

Johnstone, C., Liu, K., Altman, J., & Thurlow, M. (2007). *Student think aloud reflections on comprehensible and readable assessment items: Perspectives on what does and does not make an item readable* (Technical Report No. 48). Minneapolis: National Center on Educational Outcomes.

Johnstone, C. J., Thompson, S. J., Miller, N. A., & Thurlow, M. L. (2008). Universal design and multi-method approaches to item review. *Educational Measurement: Issues and Practice, 27*(1), 25–36.

Kamei-Hannan, C. (2008). Examining the accessibility of a computerized adapted test using assistive technology. *Journal of Visual Impairment and Blindness, 102,* 261–271.

Kato, K., Moen, R., & Thurlow, M. (2009). Differentials of a state reading assessment: Item functioning, distractor functioning, and omission frequency for disability categories. *Educational Measurement: Issues and Practice, 28*(2), 28–40.

Kearns, J. F., Towles-Reeves, E., Kleinert, H. L., Kleinert, J. O., & Kleine-Kracht, M. (2011). Characteristics of and implications for students participating in alternate assessments based on alternate academic achievement standards. *Journal of Special Education, 45*(3), 3–14. doi:10.1177/0022466909344223.

Ketterlin-Geller, L. R. (2005). Knowing what all students know: Procedures for developing universal design for assessment. *Journal of Technology, Learning and Assessment, 4*(2), 1–23.

Ketterlin-Geller, L. R. (2008). Testing students with special needs: A model for understanding the interaction between assessment and student characteristics in a universally designed environment. *Educational Measurement: Issues and Practice, 27*(3), 3–16.

Ketterlin-Geller, L. R., Alonzo, J., Braun-Monegan, J., & Tindal, G. (2007). Recommendations for accommodations: Implications of (in)consistency. *Remedial and Special Education, 28,* 194–206.

Kettler, R. J. (2012). Testing accommodations: Theory and research to inform practice. *International Journal of Disability, Development and Education, 59*(1), 53–66.

Kieffer, M. J., Lesaux, N. K., Rivera, M., & Francis, D. J. (2009). Accommodations for English language learners taking large-scale assessments: A meta-analysis on effectiveness and validity. *Review of Educational Research, 79,* 1168–1201.

Kim, D. H., Schneider, C., & Siskind, T. (2009). Examining the underlying factor structure of a statewide science test under oral and standard administrations. *Journal of Psychoeducational Assessment, 27,* 323–333.

Kingston, N. M. (2009). Comparability of computer- and paper-administered multiple-choice tests for K-12 populations: A synthesis. *Applied Measurement in Education, 22*(1), 22–27.

Kitmitto, S., & Bandeira de Mello, V. (2008). *Measuring the status and change of NAEP state inclusion rates for students with disabilities* (NCES 2009-453). Washington, DC: National Center for Education Statistics, Institute of Education Sciences, U.S. Department of Education.

Koenig, J. A., & Bachman, L. F. (Eds.). (2004). *Keeping score for all: The effects of inclusion and accommodation policies on large-scale educational assessments.* Washington, DC: National Academies Press.

Kopriva, R.J. (1999). *Making state tests inclusive for special populations: Training guidelines for developing and implementing Inclusive Title 1 Assessments.* Washington, DC: Council of Chief State School Officers.

Kopriva, R.J. (2000). *Ensuring accuracy in testing for English language learners: A practical guide for assessment development.* Washington, DC: Council of Chief State School Officers.

Kopriva, R. J. (2008a). Access-based item development. In *Improving testing for English language learners* (pp. 279–318). New York, NY: Routledge.

Kopriva, R. J. (2008b). Changing demographics in a testing culture: Why this issue matters. In *Improving testing for English language learners: A comprehensive approach to designing, building, implementing, and interpreting better academic assessments* (pp. 13–36). New York, NY: Routledge.

Kopriva, R. J. (2008c). *Improving testing for English language learners: A comprehensive approach to designing, building, implementing, and interpreting better academic assessments.* New York, NY: Routledge.

Kopriva, R. J. (2008d). Providing the foundation of principled test construction: Maintaining the integrity of the item targets. In *Improving testing for English language learners* (pp. 279–318). New York, NY: Routledge.

Kopriva, R. J. (2014). *Technology-interactive classroom-embedded modules for measuring challenging math and science skills of ELs* [Research project]. Madison: University of Wisconsin.

Kopriva, R. J., Emick, J. E., Hipolito-Delgado, C. P., & Cameron, C. A. (2007). Do proper accommodation assignments make a difference? Examining the impact of improving decision making on scores for English Language Learners. *Educational Measurement: Issues and Practice, 26*(3), 11–20.

Kopriva, R. J., Gabel, D., & Cameron, C. (2009). *Overview of results from the ONPAR elementary and middle school science experimental study with ELs and non-ELs: A promising new approach for measuring complex content knowledge of English Learners with lower proficiency.* Retrieved from http://iiassessment.wceruw.org/research/researchPapers/Overview% 20Results%20ONPAR%20El%20and%20MS%20Science_7%2012c_13.pdf

Kopriva, R. J., & Koran, J. (2008). Proper assignment of accommodations to individual students. In *Improving testing for English language learners: A comprehensive approach to designing, building, implementing, and interpreting better academic assessments* (pp. 221–258). New York, NY: Routledge.

Kopriva, R. J., & Lara, J. (2009). *Looking back and looking forward: Inclusion of all students in NAEP, U.S.'s National Assessment of Educational Progress* (Commissioned paper). Washington, DC: National Assessment Governing Board.

Kopriva, R. J., Triscari, R., & Carr, T. G. (2014). *Exploring a technology-based, multi-semiotic methodology for measuring challenging content knowledge and skills of low English proficient students.* Manuscript submitted for publication.

Kopriva, R. J., Winter, P. C., Triscari, R., Carr, T. G., Cameron, C., & Gabel, D. (2013). *Assessing the knowledge, skills, and abilities of ELs, selected students with disabilities and controls on challenging high-school science content: Results from randomized trials of ONPAR and technology-enhanced traditional end-of-course biology and chemistry tests.* Retrieved from http:// iiassessment.wceruw.org/research/researchPapers/Assesing%20KSAs%20ONPAR% 20HS%20Exper%20Study%20Results%203%205%2013.pdf

Koran, J., Kopriva, R. J., Emick, J., Monroe, J. R., & Garavaglia, D. (2006, April). *Teacher and multi-source computerized approaches for making individualized test accommodation decisions for English language learners.* Paper presented at the annual meeting of the National Council of Measurement in Education, San Francisco, CA.

Koretz, D. M., & Hamilton, L. (2000). Assessing students with disabilities in Kentucky: Inclusion, student performance, and validity. *Educational Evaluation and Policy Analysis, 22*, 255–272.

Laing, J., & Farmer, M. (1984). *Use of the ACT assessment by examinees with disabilities* (Research Report No. 84). Iowa City, IA: American College Testing Program.

Laitusis, C. C. (2007). Research designs and analysis for studying accommodations on assessments. In C. C. Laitusis & L. L. Cook (Eds.), *Large-scale assessment and accommodations: What works?* (pp. 67–79). Arlington, VA: Council for Exceptional Children.

Laitusis, C. C. (2010). Examining the impact of audio presentation on tests of reading comprehension. *Applied Measurement in Education, 23*, 153–167.

Laitusis, C., Buzick, H., Stone, E., Hansen, E., & Hakkinen, M. (2012). *Smarter Balanced Assessment Consortium: Literature review of testing accommodations and accessibility tools for students with disabilities.* Retrieved from http://www.smarterbalanced.org/wordpress/

wp-content/uploads/2012/08/Smarter-Balanced-Students-with-Disabilities-Literature-Review.pdf

Lara, J., & August, D. (1996). *Systemic reform and limited English proficient students.* Washington, DC: Council of Chief State School Officers.

Lau v. Nichols. 414 U.S. 563 (1974).

Lazarus, S. S., Thurlow, M. L., Lail, K. E., & Christensen, L. (2009). A longitudinal analysis of state accommodations policies: Twelve years of change 1993-2005. *Journal of Special Education, 43*(2), 67–80.

Lee, O., Maerten-Rivera, J., Penfield, R. D., LeRoy, K., & Secada, W. G. (2008). Science achievement of English language learners in urban elementary schools: Results of a first-year professional development intervention. *Journal of Research in Science Teaching, 45*(1), 31–52.

Lee, O., Quinn, H., & Valdés, G. (2013). Science and language for English language learners in relation to Next Generation Science Standards and with implication for Common Core State Standards for English language arts and mathematics. *Educational Researcher, 42,* 223–233.

Liu, K. K., Goldstone, L. S., Thurlow, M. L., Ward, J. M., Hatten, J., & Christensen, L. L. (2013). *Voices from the field: Making state assessment decisions for English language learners with disabilities.* Minneapolis: University of Minnesota, Improving the Validity of Assessment Results for English Language Learners with Disabilities (IVARED).

Madaus, G., Russell, M., & Higgins, J. (2009). *The paradoxes of high stakes testing: How they affect students, their parents, teachers, principals, schools, and society.* Charlotte, NC: Information.

Mazzeo, J., Carlson, J. E., Voekl, K. E., & Lutkus, A. D. (2000). *Increasing the participation of special needs students in NAEP* (NCES 2000-473). Washington, DC: U.S. Department of Education, Office of Educational Research and Improvement.

McDonnell, L. M., McLaughlin, M. J., & Morison, P. (Eds.). (1997). *Educating one & all: Students with disabilities and standards-based reform.* Washington, DC: National Academies Press.

McGrew, K. S., Algozzine, B., Ysseldyke, J. E., Thurlow, M. L., & Spiegel, A. N. (1995). The identification of individuals with disabilities in national databases: Creating a failure to communicate. *Journal of Special Education, 28,* 472–487.

McGrew, K. S., Thurlow, M. L., & Spiegel, A. N. (1993). An investigation of the exclusion of students with disabilities in national data collection programs. *Educational Evaluation and Policy Analysis, 15,* 339–352.

McKevitt, B., Marquart, A., Mroch, A., Schulte, A. G., Elliott, S. N., & Kratochwill, T. R. (2000, March). *Understanding the effects of testing accommodations: A single case approach.* Paper presented at the annual meeting of the Council of Chief State School Officers, Snowbird, UT.

Messick, S. (1989). Validity. In R. L. Linn (Ed.), *Educational measurement* (3rd ed., pp. 13–103). Washington, DC: American Council on Education and National Council on Measurement in Education.

Meyen, E., Poggio, J., Seok, S., & Smith, S. (2006). Equity for students with high-incidence disabilities in statewide assessments: A technology-based solution. *Focus on Exceptional Children, 38*(7), 1–8.

Mislevy, R. J. (1994) Evidence and inference in educational assessment. *Psychometrika, 58,* 79–85.

Mislevy, R. J., Steinberg, L. S., & Almond, R. G. (2003). On the structure of educational assessments. *Measurements: Interdisciplinary Research and Perspectives, 1*(1), 3–62.

National Assessment Governing Board. (2005). *NAEP mathematics assessment and item specifications.* Washington, DC: Author.

National Center for Education Statistics. (2013). *A first look: 2013 mathematics and reading* (NCES 2014-451). Washington, DC: U.S. Department of Education, Institute of Education Sciences. Retrieved from http://nationsreportcard.gov/reading_math_2013

National Center on Educational Outcomes. (2011a). *Don't forget accommodations! Five questions to ask when moving to technology-based assessments* (NCEO Brief No. 1). Minneapolis: University of Minnesota, National Center on Educational Outcomes.

National Center on Educational Outcomes. (2011b). *Understanding subgroups in common state assessments: Special education students and ELLs* (NCEO Brief No. 4). Minneapolis: University of Minnesota, National Center on Educational Outcomes.

National Council on Measurement in Education. (2012). *Testing and data integrity in the administration of statewide student assessment programs.* Washington, DC: Author.

National Governors' Association. (1986). *Time for results: The governors' 1991 report.* Washington, DC: Author.

Office of Civil Rights. (2000). *The use of tests as part of high stakes decision-making for students: A resource guide for educators and policy makers.* Washington, DC: U.S. Department of Education.

Oliveri, M. E., Ercikan, K., & Zumbo, B. D. (2014). Effects of population heterogeneity on accuracy of DIF detection. *Applied Measurement in Education, 27,* 286–300.

Pennock-Roman, M., & Rivera, C. (2011). Mean effects of test accommodations for ELLs and non-ELLs: A meta-analysis of experimental studies. *Educational Measurement: Issues and Practice, 30,* 10–18.

Phillips, S. E. (1994). High-stakes testing accommodations: validity versus disabled rights. *Applied Measurement in Education, 7,* 93–120.

Pitoniak, M. J., & Royer, J. M. (2001). Testing accommodations for examinees with disabilities: A review of psychometric, legal, and social policy issues. *Review of Educational Research, 71,* 53–104.

Popham, W. J. (1994). The instructional consequences of criterion-referenced clarity. *Educational Measurement: Issues and Practice, 13,* 15–18.

Powers, S., & Strain-Seymour, E. (2013, April). *Integrating research paradigms to provide validity evidence for next-generation English language learner assessments.* Presentation at the American Education Research Association Annual Meeting, San Francisco, CA.

Quenemoen, R., Thurlow, M., Moen, R., Thompson, S., & Morse, A. B. (2003). *Progress monitoring in an inclusive standards-based assessment and accountability system* (Synthesis Report No. 53). Minneapolis: University of Minnesota, National Center on Educational Outcomes.

Rhode Island Department of Education. (2003). *Rhode Island assessment accommodation study: Research summary.* Minneapolis: University of Minnesota, National Center on Educational Outcomes.

Rieke, R., Lazarus, S. S., Thurlow, M. L., & Dominguez, L. M. (2013). *2012 Survey of states: Successes and challenges during a time of change.* Minneapolis: University of Minnesota, National Center on Educational Outcomes.

Rigney, S., & Pettit, M. (1995, April). *Criteria for producing equivalent scores on portfolio assessments: Vermont's approach.* Presented at the annual meeting of the American Educational Research Association, San Francisco, CA.

Rigney, S., Wiley, D. E., & Kopriva, R. J. (2008). The past as preparation: Measurement, public policy and implications for access. In R. J. Kopriva (Ed.), *Improving testing for English Language learners: A comprehensive approach to designing, building, implementing, and interpreting better academic assessments* (pp. 37–64). New York, NY: Routledge.

Rivera, C., & Collum, E. (2004). *An analysis of state assessment policies addressing the accommodation of English language learners* (Issue paper) Arlington, VA: National Assessment Governing Board, Center for Equity and Excellence in Education, The George Washington University.

Rivera, C., & Collum, E. (Eds.). (2006). *A national review of state assessment policy and practice for English language learners.* Mahwah, NJ: Erlbaum.

Rivera, C., Collum, E., Willner, L. S., & Sia, J. K., Jr. (2006). An analysis of state assessment policies addressing the accommodation of English language learners. In C. Rivera & E. Collum (Eds.), *A national review of state assessment policy and practice for English language learners* (pp. 1–173). Mahwah, NJ: Erlbaum.

Rivera, C., & Stansfield, C. (2000). *An analysis of state policies for the inclusion and accommodation of English language learners in state assessment programs during 1998–1999 (Executive summary).* Washington, DC: Center for Equity and Excellence in Education, The George Washington University.

Rogers, C. M., Christian, E. M., & Thurlow, M. L. (2012). *A summary of the research on the effects of test accommodations: 2009-2010* (Technical Report No. 65). Minneapolis: University of Minnesota, National Center on Educational Outcomes.

Rose, D., & Meyer, A. (2002). *Teaching every student in the digital age: Universal design for learning.* Alexandria, VA: ASCD.

Roth, W.-M., Oliveri, M. E., Sandilands, D., Lyons-Thomas, J., & Ercikan, K. (2013). Investigating sources of differential item functioning using expert think-aloud protocols. *International Journal of Science Education, 35,* 546–576.

Russell, M. (1999). Testing on computers: A follow-up study comparing performance on computer and on paper. *Education Policy Analysis Archives, 7*(20). Retrieved from http://www.bc.edu/research/intasc/PDF/TestCompFollowUp.pdf

Russell, M. (2011). *Digital test delivery: Empowering accessible test design to increase test validity for all students.* Washington, DC: Arabella Advisors.

Russell, M., Hoffman, R., & Higgins, J. (2009a). Meeting the needs of all students: A universal design approach to computer-based testing. *Innovate: Journal of Online Education, 5*(4).

Russell, M., Hoffman, R., & Higgins, J. (2009b). Nimble Tools: A universally designed test delivery system. *Teaching Exceptional Children, 42*(2), 6–12.

Schleppegrell, M. J. (2004). *The language of schooling: A functional linguistics perspective.* Mahwah, NJ: Erlbaum.

Shepard, L. A. (2001). The role of classroom assessment in teaching and learning. In V. Richardson (Ed.), *The handbook of research on teaching* (4th ed., pp. 1066–1101). Washington, DC: American Educational Research Association.

Shepard, L., Hannaway, J., & Baker, E. (Eds.). (2009). *Standards, assessments, and accountability* (Education Policy White Paper). Washington, DC: National Academy of Education. Retrieved from http://www.naeducation.org/cs/groups/naedsite/documents/webpage/naed_080866.pdf

Shriner, J. G., & DeStefano, L. (2003). Participation and accommodation in state assessment: The role of Individualized Education Programs. *Exceptional Children, 69,* 147–161.

Shriner, J. G., & Thurlow, M. L. (1993). *State special education outcomes 1992.* Minneapolis: University of Minnesota, National Center on Educational Outcomes.

Sireci, S. G., Li, S., & Scarpati, S. (2003). *The effects of test accommodations on test performance: A review of the literature* (Center for Educational Assessment Research Report No. 485) Amherst: School of Education, University of Massachusetts.

Sireci, S. G., Scarpati, S. E., & Li, S. (2005). Test accommodations for students with disabilities: An analysis of the interaction hypothesis. *Review of Educational Research, 75,* 457–490.

Sireci, S. G., & Wells, C. (2010). Evaluating the comparability of English and Spanish video accommodations for English language learners. In P. C. Winter (Ed.), *Evaluating the comparability of scores from educational achievement test variations* (pp. 33–68). Washington, DC: Council of Chief State School Officers.

Solano-Flores, G. (2006). Language, dialect, and register: Sociolinguistics and the estimation of measurement error in the testing of English-language learners. *Teachers College Record, 108*, 2354–2379.

Solano-Flores, G. (in press). Simultaneous test development. In C. R. Reynolds, R. W. Kamphaus, & C. DiStefano (Eds.), *Encyclopedia of psychological and educational testing: Clinical and psychoeducational applications.* New York, NY: Oxford University Press.

Solano-Flores, G. (2014). Probabilistic approaches to examining linguistic features of test items and their effect on the performance of English language learners. *Applied Measurement in Education, 27*, 236–247.

Solano-Flores, G., & Gustafson, M. (2012). Assessment of English language learners: A critical, probabilistic, systemic view. In M. Simon, K. Ercikan, & M. Rousseau (Eds.), *Improving large scale assessment in education: Theory, issues, and practice* (pp. 87–109). New York, NY: Routledge.

Solano-Flores, G., & Li, M. (2009). Language variation and score variation in the testing of English language learners, native Spanish speakers. *Educational Assessment, 14*, 1–15.

Thompson, S., Blount, A., & Thurlow, M. (2002). *A summary of research on the effects of test accommodations: 1999 through 2001* (Technical Report No. 34). Minneapolis: University of Minnesota, National Center on Educational Outcomes.

Thompson, S. J., Quenemoen, R., & Thurlow, M. L. (2006). Factors to consider in the design of inclusive online assessments. In M. Hricko (Ed.), *Online assessment and measurement: Foundations and challenges* (pp. 102–117). Hershey, PA: Information Science.

Thompson, S. J., Thurlow, M. L., & Malouf, D. (2004). Creating better tests for everyone through universally designed assessments. *Journal of Applied Testing Technology, 10*(2). Retrieved from http://www.jattjournal.com/index.php/atp/article/view/48341

Thurlow, M. L. (2012). Students with disabilities, testing accommodations. In J. A. Banks (Ed.), *Encyclopedia of diversity in education* (pp. 2090–2092). Thousand Oaks, CA: Sage.

Thurlow, M. L. (2013). Accommodation for challenge, diversity, and variance in human characteristics. Paper prepared for the Gordon Commission. Available at www.gordoncommission.org/rsc/pdf/thurlow_accommodation_challenge_diversity_variance.pdf

Thurlow, M. L., House, A., Boys, C., Scott, D., & Ysseldyke, J. (2000). *State participation and accommodations policies for students with disabilities: 1999 update* (Synthesis Report No. 33). Minneapolis: University of Minnesota, National Center on Educational Outcomes.

Thurlow, M. L., Johnstone, C., & Ketterlin-Geller, L. (2008). Universal design of assessment. In S. Burgstahler & R. Cory (Eds.), *Universal design in post-secondary education: From principles to practice* (pp. 73–81). Cambridge, MA: Harvard Education Press.

Thurlow, M. L., Johnstone, C., Thompson, S., & Case, B. (2008). Using universal design research and perspectives to increase the validity of scores on large-scale assessments. In R. C. Johnson & R. E. Mitchell (Eds.), *Testing deaf students in an age of accountability* (pp. 63–75). Washington, DC: Gallaudet University Press.

Thurlow, M. L., Laitusis, C. C., Dillon, D. R., Cook, L. L., Moen, R. E., Abedi, J., & O'Brien, D. G. (2009). *Accessibility principles for reading assessments.* Minneapolis, MN: National Accessible Reading Assessment Projects.

Thurlow, M. L., & Lazarus, S. (2009, April). *Accommodations for all testing: Curriculum based, formative, district, and state* (Presession Workshop No. 17). Council for Exceptional Children, Seattle, WA.

Thurlow, M. L., Lazarus, S. S., & Christensen, L. L. (2008). Role of assessment accommodations in accountability. *Perspectives, 45*(4), 17–20.

Thurlow, M., Lazarus, S. S., Albus, D., & Hodgson, J. (2010). *Computer-based testing: Practices and considerations* (Synthesis Report No. 78). Minneapolis: University of Minnesota, National Center on Educational Outcomes.

Thurlow, M. L., Lazarus, S. S., & Christensen, L. L. (2013). Accommodations and modifications for assessment. In B. Cook & M. Tankersley (Eds.), *Effective practices in special education* (pp. 311–327). Iowa City, IA: Pearson.

Thurlow, M. L., Lazarus, S., Thompson, S., & Robey, J. (2002). 2001 state policies on assessment participation and accommodations (Synthesis Report No. 46). Minneapolis: University of Minnesota, National Center on Educational Outcomes.

Thurlow, M. L., Liu, K., Ward, J., & Christensen, L. (2013). *Assessment principles and guidelines for ELLs with disabilities.* Minneapolis: University of Minnesota, Improving the Validity of Assessment Results for English Language Learners with Disabilities (IVARED).

Thurlow, M. L., Moen, R. E., Lekwa, A. J., & Scullin, S. B. (2010). *Examination of a reading pen as a partial auditory accommodation for reading assessment.* Minneapolis: University of Minnesota, Partnership for Accessible Reading Assessment.

Thurlow, M. L., Quenemoen, R. F., & Lazarus, S. S. (2011). *Meeting the needs of special education students: Recommendations for the Race to the Top consortia and states.* Washington, DC: Arabella Advisors.

Thurlow, M. L., Quenemoen, R. F., Lazarus, S. S., Moen, R. E., Johnstone, C. J., Liu, K. K., . . .Altman, J. (2008). *A principled approach to accountability assessments for students with disabilities* (Synthesis Report No. 70). Minneapolis: University of Minnesota, National Center on Educational Outcomes.

Thurlow, M. L., Scott, D., & Ysseldyke, J. E. (1995). *A compilation of states' guidelines for accommodations in assessment for students with disabilities* (Synthesis Report No. 18). Minneapolis: University of Minnesota, National Center on Educational Outcomes.

Thurlow, M. L., Seyfarth, A. L., Scott, D. L., & Ysseldyke, J. E. (1997). *State assessment policies on participation and accommodations for students with disabilities: 1997 update* (Synthesis Report No. 29). Minneapolis: University of Minnesota, National Center on Educational Outcomes.

Thurlow, M. L., Ysseldyke, J. E., & Silverstein, B. (1993). *Testing accommodations for students with disabilities: A review of the literature* (Synthesis Report No. 4). Minneapolis: University of Minnesota, National Center on Educational Outcomes.

Thurlow, M. L., Ysseldyke, J. E., & Silverstein, B. (1995). Testing accommodations for students with disabilities. *Remedial and Special Education, 16,* 260–270.

Tindal, G., & Fuchs, L. (2000). A summary of research on test changes: An empirical basis for defining accommodations. Lexington, KY: Mid-South Regional Resource Center. (ERIC Document Reproduction Service No. ED 442245)

Towles-Reeves, E., Kearns, J., Kleinert, H., & Kleinert, J. (2009). An analysis of the learning characteristics of students taking alternate assessments based on alternate achievement standards. *Journal of Special Education, 42,* 241–254.

U.S. Government Accountability Office. (2011). *Higher education and disability: Improved federal enforcement needed to better protect students' rights to testing accommodations* (GAO-12–40). Washington, DC: Author.

Vang, M., & Thurlow, M. (2013). *2010-2011 APR snapshot #4: State assessment participation and performance of students receiving special education services.* Minneapolis: University of Minnesota, National Center on Educational Outcomes.

Vaughn, S., Martinez, L. R., Linan-Thompson, S., Reutebach, C. K., Carlson, C. D., & Francis, D. J. (2009). Enhancing social studies vocabulary and comprehension for seventh-grade English language learners: Findings from two experimental studies. *Journal of Research on Educational Effectiveness, 2,* 297–324.

Wiley, D. E., & Haertel, E. (1995). Extended assessment tasks: Purposes, definition, scoring and accuracy. In R. Mitchell (Ed.), *Implementing performance assessment: Promises, problems and challenges* (pp. 61–90). Hillsdale, NJ: Lawrence Erlbaum.

Willingham, W. W., Ragosta, M., Bennett, R. E., Braun, H., Rock, D. A., & Powers, D. E. (Eds.). (1988). *Testing handicapped people.* Boston, MA: Allyn & Bacon.

Willner, L. S. (in press). *CSAI Brief: Increasing student access to the language of the more cognitively challenging college and career-ready standards.* San Francisco, CA: Center on Standards and Assessment Implementation.

Wright, L. J., & Kopriva, R. J. (2009). *Using cognitive labs to refine technology-enhanced assessment tasks and ensure their accessibility: Insights from data collected to inform ONPAR elementary and middle school science task development.* Retrieved from http://iiassessment. wceruw.org/research/researchPapers/Insights%20ONPAR%20El%20and%20MS%20 Science%20Cog%20Labs%2009b.pdf

Wright, L. J., & Logan-Terry, A. (2014). *Multimodality and measurement: A discourse analysis of English learners' interactions with traditional and multisemiotic test tasks.* Manuscript submitted for publication.

Wright, L. J., Staehr-Fenner, D., Moxley, K., Kopriva, R. J., & Carr, T. G. (2013). *Exploring how diverse learners interact with computerized, multi-semiotic representations of meaning: Highlights from cognitive labs conducted with ONPAR end-of-course biology and chemistry assessment tasks.* Retrieved from http://www.iiassessment.wceruw.org

Zenisky, A. L., & Sireci, S. G. (2007). *A summary of the research on the effects of test accommodations: 2005-2006* (Technical Report No. 47). Minneapolis: University of Minnesota, National Center on Educational Outcomes.

Chapter 10

The Changing Nature of Educational Assessment

RANDY ELLIOT BENNETT
Educational Testing Service

On the surface, this chapter concerns the evolution of educational assessment from a paper-based technology to an electronic one. On a deeper level, that evolution is more substantive. As has been noted, that evolution can be viewed in terms of developmental stages (Bennett, 1998, 2010b; Bunderson, Inouye, & Olsen, 1989). In the first section of this chapter, those stages are briefly described and used to place the new generation of assessments being created by the two comprehensive Common Core State Assessment (CCSA) consortia, the Partnership for the Assessment of Readiness for College and Careers (PARCC), and the Smarter Balanced Assessment Consortium (SBAC).[1] That placement is primarily employed to make the characteristics of each stage concrete, as well as to highlight key aspects of the consortia's emerging assessment designs. Next, some of the more substantive factors that differentiate the most advanced stage from the earlier ones are discussed, as well as the challenges in producing assessments fit for that most advanced stage. In that most advanced stage, such innovations are considered as the continuous testing made possible by electronic learning environments (e.g., games, simulations, e-books, massive open online courses). This section identifies, in passing, advanced features that the CCSA consortia are actively incorporating, as well as ones to which they might at some point aspire. Finally, a conclusion is offered, including suggestions for research.

THE EVOLUTION OF LARGE-SCALE, TECHNOLOGY-BASED EDUCATIONAL ASSESSMENT

The evolution of technology-based assessment in education can be conceptualized in terms of three stages or generations (Bennett, 1998, 2010b). First-generation technology-based testing is largely an infrastructure-building activity, laying the foundation for tests to be delivered in a new medium. To minimize the complexity and cost

Review of Research in Education
March 2015, Vol. 39, pp. 370–407
DOI: 10.3102/0091732X14554179

of that transition, first-generation measures closely resemble traditional tests. First-generation tests primarily function to serve institutional needs (e.g., school accountability); differ marginally in design and item format from their paper counterparts; are administered as an isolated, "onetime" event; and take limited advantage of technology.

The heart of this infrastructure building is the transition from the old development and delivery process into a new, considerably different one. For such end users as local schools, that transition may involve investing extensively in computer hardware (e.g., tablets, laptops, proxy servers) and networking equipment, training technology staff to set up and troubleshoot the test delivery software, and training teachers to administer and proctor online examinations, including how to deal with technology failure. For the development and delivery agency, item creation, item banking, test assembly, quality control, and security will require adopting new processes, licensing software, and retraining staff. As should be apparent, the extent of infrastructure development associated with shifting from paper to computer is decidedly nontrivial (Chandler, 2013; Dragsow, Luecht, & Bennett, 2006).

Whereas much about first-generation testing is traditional, one way in which this generation does capitalize on technology is that its measures may be given adaptively (i.e., the next item is selected based on the test's current best estimate of the student's competency level; Wainer, 2000). Adaptive testing allows for relatively equal measurement precision throughout the score scale (Weiss, 1982). For students whose skills are well above or below the proficiency standard typical for their grade placement, this capability makes it possible to estimate better where their skill levels might fall (which might be more helpful than simply knowing that a given student's level was *somewhere* above or below that standard). For all except students with the most severe disabilities, this technology places performance on the same score scale, making inclusion in the general assessment program more straightforward, at least from the perspective of expressing the scores of all students in a common metric (see, however, Stone & Davey, 2011, for a discussion of issues related to the adaptive assessment of students with disabilities).

In second-generation tests, qualitative (but incremental) change and efficiency improvement become the driving goals (Bennett, 1998, 2010b). In principle, second-generation tests use less traditional item formats (e.g., ones involving multimedia stimuli, short constructed response, static performance tasks like essays) and may make initial attempts to measure new constructs, beginning to change what is assessed. These tests also attempt to improve efficiency through means such as automatic item generation (Gierl & Haladyna, 2013; Irvine & Kyllonen, 2010), automated scoring (Shermis & Burstein, 2013), and the use of the Internet for a wide variety of internal processes (item review, standard setting, human online scoring), as well as for interactions with test users. Because of its novelty, the use of technology in this generation may sometimes take precedence over substantive considerations. That is, new item types may be incorporated as much because they are different from traditional multiple-choice questions, have visual appeal, or are otherwise "interesting" as because they target key competencies that could not otherwise be measured or modeled. Automated scoring may similarly be used because it predicts the scores that operational human raters assign, regardless of how it makes those predictions and of whether the substantive basis used by the modeled raters in making their judgments is understood (Bennett & Bejar, 1998; Bennett & Zhang, in press; Bridgeman, 2013).

The third generation of assessments is one of reinvention occurring on multiple fronts simultaneously (Bennett, 1998, 2010b). It is in this third generation that what was, at first, an evolution driven primarily by technology becomes driven by substance. For one, these assessments serve both institutional and individual-learning purposes. Second, they are designed from cognitive principles and theory-based domain models. Third, the assessments use complex simulations and other interactive performance tasks that replicate important features of real environments, allow more natural interaction with computers, and assess new skills in more sophisticated ways. Finally, the assessments are more integrated with instruction, sampling performance repeatedly over time.

The stage structure just described might be useful to the extent that it characterizes real testing programs and predicts the path of their evolution. In K–12 education, the Virginia Standards of Learning Tests appears to be following a path consistent with that structure. For well over a decade, the Virginia Department of Education and local school districts gradually made the needed infrastructure investments, allowing the program's volume to grow from a small pilot in 2000 to approximately 2.7 million tests delivered annually by 2013, or 94% of the total (Chandler, 2013). For the better part of this history, the program created assessments that were highly similar in form, content, and design to the paper measures they replaced. But once the infrastructure appeared to be reliably in place, the program began to incorporate technology-enhanced items and use the Internet for internal processes, evolving from its first-generation roots toward a second-generation operation (Virginia Department of Education, 2012). A similar claim can be made with respect to the Graduate Record Examinations (GRE) revised General Test, the Test of English as a Foreign Language Internet-Based Test (TOEFL iBT), and the Graduate Management Admission Test (GMAT), all of which began as computerized versions of paper tests and evolved over significant periods to employ at least some of the characteristics of second-generation assessments, including essay tasks with automated scoring (Attali, 2011; Ramineni, Trapani, Williamson, Davey, & Bridgeman, 2012; Rudner, Garcia, & Welch, 2006).

Where do the CCSAs fall? They might be characterized as late first-generation since for many schools, districts, and even states, their implementation is an infrastructure-building activity (Tan, 2014). That activity will be significant enough that both PARCC and Smarter Balanced are offering paper versions for at least the first administration year (PARCC, 2013e; SBAC, 2012a). As an infrastructure building activity, these tests cannot provide too much technological advancement because that advancement would only serve to increase infrastructure requirements, prolonging the need for paper versions. Consequently, the innovations to be introduced are likely to be important but relatively modest. Smarter Balanced will, for example, employ adaptive testing. The technology that is likely to be used, a derivation of item-level adaptive testing, has a long track record, having appeared among the very first computerized tests in the middle 1980s, including the military Computerized Adaptive Screening Test, the College Board's ACCUPLACER, ACT's COMPASS, and the Northwest Evaluation Association's Measures of Academic Progress (Kingsbury & Houser, 1999; Ward, 1988). In the 1990s, tests like the GRE General Test and the Graduate Management Admission Test also used this technology (Durso, Golub-Smith, Mills, Schaeffer, & Steffen, 1995; Rudner, 2010). The Oregon Assessment of Knowledge and Skills and its predecessor, the Technology Enhanced Student Assessment, have used it since the early 2000s.[2]

The fact that the CCSAs will need to have paper versions also necessarily limits near-term innovation because the paper and computer versions will need to produce comparable scores. Said another way, to the extent that the computer and paper versions differ materially in what they measure, their scores might not be equatable, raising fairness issues. In such an instance, some students would be measured on one set of CCSA competencies and other students would be measured on a substantively different set, with that difference entirely due to where those students happened to attend school.

With respect to comparability, the American Psychological Association's (1986) *Guidelines for Computer-Based Tests and Interpretations* offers a rudimentary definition. This document states that scores may be considered equivalent, or comparable, when the rank orders of individuals closely approximate one another and when the score distributions are approximately the same, or have been made approximately the same through rescaling (see Holland & Dorans, 2006, p. 194, for a more complete definition).

The scores from paper and computer versions of the same test can diverge for several reasons. Among the reasons are differences in (a) presentation characteristics such as the number of items on the screen versus the number on the printed page, or the size of text fonts, (b) response requirements (e.g., filling out the grid-in answer sheet vs. having to point, click, drag, drop, and scroll with the mouse; using a pencil vs. the keyboard to enter and edit text), and (c) general administration characteristics (as when the computer test is administered adaptively while the paper test contains the same items in the same order for all individuals; Drasgow et al., 2006).

To the extent that the CCSAs produce paper and computer forms that are substantially the same in their presentation characteristics, response requirements, and general administration characteristics, comparability may not be an issue. Several meta-analyses of studies conducted with K–12 tests have addressed this question (e.g., Kingston, 2008; Wang, Jiao, Young, Brooks, & Olson, 2007a, 2007b). Whereas these analyses have generally supported comparability, the studies they reviewed typically employed multiple-choice tests; used small, unrepresentative student samples;

and often considered only mean score differences, without attention to differences in rank ordering.

Perhaps the most comprehensive research to date was done through the National Assessment of Educational Progress (NAEP; Bennett et al., 2008; Horkay, Bennett, Allen, Kaplan, & Yan, 2006). That research used nationally representative samples taking tests that were parallel at the item level, and that were composed of multiple-choice, short constructed-response, technology-enhanced, and essay items. The studies employed within-group as well as between-group designs, thereby permitting consideration of both level and order differences. Studies in mathematics and in writing found that paper-based and computer scores were not comparable. Because student familiarity with computers is likely to have changed dramatically since these data were collected in 2001–2002, and because the CCSAs will have important differences from the instruments used in the NAEP studies (e.g., adaptive administration), the most relevant data will be those collected on the paper and computer versions of the CCSAs themselves.[3]

Although concerns for comparability of delivery modes may prevent the CCSAs from advancing into second-generation tests as quickly as might be desired, some CCSA features are already indicative of the qualitative (but incremental) change characteristic of this second stage. As one example, the CCSAs use so-called technology-enhanced items, which may call for response behaviors more similar to the ones students employ in carrying out academic tasks (e.g., highlighting text in reading passages). Additionally, because of the requirements of the Common Core State Standards (CCSS; Common Core State Standards Initiative, 2010), the PARCC and Smarter Balanced assessments will measure "writing from sources." This construct is considerably different from the one typically targeted on K–12 writing tests in that reading, summarizing, analysis, and synthesis of those sources are likely to come into play.

Perhaps the most interesting example of qualitative change is the embedding of accessibility features directly into test delivery. Smarter Balanced organizes these features into universal tools (available to all students), designated supports (available to any student for whom school officials have indicated the need), and accommodations (available to those students with documented need through either an Individualized Education Program or a 504 accommodation plan; SBAC, 2014). Universal tools include English glossary (i.e., pop-up definitions for selected construct-irrelevant words), highlighter, spell-check (for selected English language arts [ELA] items), and zoom. Designated tools include masking, color contrast, text-to-speech (for all items except reading passages), and glossary translation in 11 languages. Among the accommodations are American Sign Language video presentation (for listening and math items), braille, text-to-speech (for reading passages in Grades 6 and above), and closed-captioning (for listening items).[4]

The CCSAs also show signs of moving in small but important ways toward third-generation tests. Perhaps most fundamentally, they have replaced the "single-event" test. Both the PARCC and Smarter Balanced assessments will have two parts administered at separate times in each of math and ELA. In PARCC's case, the administrations will occur after 75% and 90% of the school year have been completed, with the parts aggregated to create a single proficiency estimate (PARCC, 2013d). A second advanced characteristic toward which the CCSAs appear to be working is the service of individual-learning, as well as more traditional institutional, purposes. To achieve those multiple purposes, the consortia will create *systems* of assessment.

As suggested, the CCSAs only begin to hint at the broader set of themes that distinguishes third-generation assessment. In the next section, five such themes, and the challenges associated with realizing them, are discussed. These themes concern a shift from serving only institutional purposes to serving institutional and individual-learning purposes, grounding assessment design in the learning sciences, using complex simulations and other performance tasks, increasing the frequency with which evidence of learning is gathered, and using automated methods for scoring complex performances validly.

AN ELABORATION OF THIRD-GENERATION ASSESSMENT THEMES

Serving Institutional *and* Individual-Learning Purposes

Over the past several decades, the most common use of educational tests has been for institutional purposes. Among those purposes have been federal and state school accountability, promotion and graduation, college and graduate admissions, and college developmental course placement. The magnitude of assessment conducted to serve those institutional purposes has been extensive, affecting individuals throughout the education system, and, partially because of that fact, highly controversial (Koretz & Hamilton, 2006; Lemann, 1999; Ravitch, 2013). Testing to serve these purposes is very likely to continue, if not increase, because those purposes are key to institutional, and arguably state and national, interests. For example, education policymakers need trustworthy information on which to base decisions about system effectiveness, including what system components—programs, school leaders, teachers, and students—to target for special attention (Bennett & Gitomer, 2009).

Whereas testing to serve institutional purposes may not diminish in absolute terms, there is reason to believe it will diminish in relative terms as assessment to serve individual-learning purposes becomes more frequent (Gordon Commission on the Future of Assessment in Education, 2013). The increasing prominence of assessment for this purpose is being driven by many factors, including the need to improve the achievement of U.S. students, the belief that assessment information can contribute directly to the teaching and learning process, the emergence of electronic learning environments, advances in our understanding of the structure of domains and the paths students are likely to take toward mastery of them, and advances in measurement and data science.

Building on the maxim that a single assessment cannot effectively serve multiple purposes, Bennett and Gitomer (2009), among others, proposed the notion of an integrated system of assessment and exemplified it through a demonstration

FIGURE 1
A Logic Diagram Summarizing the Theory of Action for a Model Assessment System

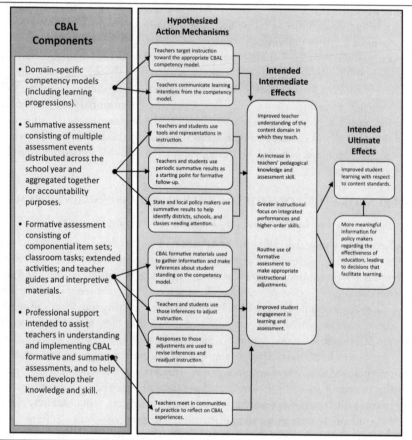

Source. Bennett (2010a). Copyright © 2010 by Educational Testing Service. Reprinted with permission.

program, CBAL (Cognitively Based Assessment *of, for,* and *as* Learning). In their conceptualization, such a system would consist of distinct summative and formative assessment components built in keeping with an explicit, detailed theory of action, where different assessment components were directed at achieving different purposes and where the entire system was intended to function in a coherent way to enhance learning and instruction. Figure 1 shows a logic diagram that summarizes the CBAL theory of action (Bennett, 2010a). That diagram lists the system components, the ways in which those components are supposed to be used, and the intended effects of using those components in the prescribed ways.

FIGURE 2
A Graphical Representation of the Smarter Balanced Theory of Action

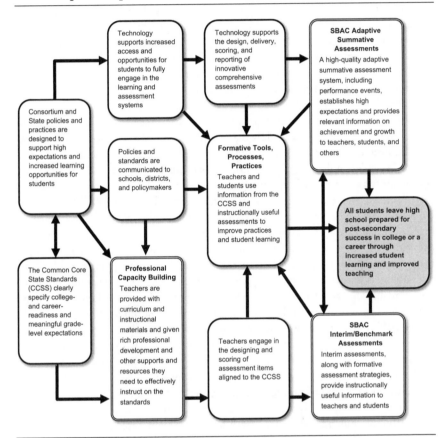

Source. Redrawn from Smarter Balanced Assessment Consortium (2010b). Copyright by Smarter Balanced Assessment Consortium. Used with permission.

In 2010, the U.S. Department of Education (USDOE) issued a call for proposals under the Race to the Top Assessment Program. The Department envisioned the development of comprehensive systems of assessment based on theories of action broadly similar to that described above (USDOE, 2010). The winning applicants—PARCC and Smarter Balanced—proposed systems in which the summative assessments would primarily serve institutional purposes, particularly that of federal accountability and another, *different* set of assessments would be created to serve individual-learning purposes (PARCC, 2010; SBAC, 2010a). In both consortia, this latter set is being conceptualized as comprising interim assessments to help identify where students stand with respect to particular standards at key points during the school year and diagnostic/formative assessments for teachers to use in planning instruction at finer grain sizes than the interim measures might allow. A logic diagram summarizing the theory of action for Smarter Balanced is given in Figure 2 (SBAC, 2010b).

The theories of action proposed for the CCSAs, as well as for CBAL, make a set of explicit, and implicit, claims for the assessment program. Those claims relate not only to the meaning of scores but also, perhaps more important, to the impact of the assessment system on students, teachers, and institutions. These claims become the basis for assessment system validation (with respect to score meaning and use) and evaluation (with respect to effects on individuals and institutions; for more on this point, see Bennett, 2010a; Bennett, Kane, & Bridgeman, 2011).

As noted, in these theories of action, formative assessment is a key mechanism for serving the needs of individuals. How that mechanism should be conceptualized, however, has been the subject of some debate (e.g., see Bennett, 2011c). Since the publication of Black and Wiliam's (1998a, 1998b) classic articles, the literature on formative assessment has characterized the concept as a generic process built around a set of key practices (e.g., goal setting, questioning, feedback; Brookhart, 2010; McManus, 2008; Popham, 2008). That conception effectively discounted the role of the instrument—that is, "formative assessment" was to be thought of not as a test but rather as a process engaged in by teachers and students. The instrument was discounted because of (legitimate) concerns that the term *formative assessment* had been misappropriated by some test publishers for pecuniary gain (Popham, 2006; Sheperd, 2008). That misappropriation arguably distracted teacher and student attention from developing evaluative processes as a routine part of their own instruction and learning. (Why develop such processes if an instrument was already available to perform that very function?) An unfortunate consequence of the adoption of this "process" conception was that it largely ignored, among other things, the centrality of disciplinary substance (that is, the "stuff" of the content domain and of the instruments intended to measure it), as well as the fact that the average teacher did not necessarily have full command of that substance (Bennett, 2011c; Coffey, Hammer, Levin, & Grant, 2011). Without thoughtful instrumentation—that is, well-formed domain-based questions and guidance as to how to interpret student responses—the formative process too easily devolves into a substantively empty exercise (e.g., asking superficial questions and giving uniformed feedback).

In their assessment system designs, the CCSAs appear to have moved toward a more balanced conception that recognizes the legitimate role of the instrument. PARCC includes "diagnostic assessments" for students in Grades 2 to 8, as well as "formative tools" for students in Grades K–1. The latter are described as "curriculum-embedded" and "invisible" to the student (PARCC, 2013b, 2013a), presumably because they are either used by the teacher as part of an evidence-gathering process or built into educational software. In Smarter Balanced, although "formative assessments" are referred to as "practices and strategies," they are accessed through a digital library of professional development materials, resources, and *tools* (SBAC, 2012b). Of course, such tools, when grounded in disciplinary substance, become "instruments." This critical connection between instrumentation and disciplinary substance is the topic to which we now turn.

Designing From Competency Models and Principles Grounded in the Learning Sciences

It was Norman Frederiksen (1984) who perhaps most eloquently argued that the design, format, and content of educational assessment should exemplify the knowledge, processes, strategies, practices, and habits of mind that we wish students and teachers to develop. This idea came from the perception that too much of educational assessment, from K–12 accountability through postsecondary admissions testing, employed item types that predicted standing in the target domain but exemplified only a limited portion of it. Frederiksen's argument derived from his observations of the apparent impact of assessment design on gunnery training during World War II, where he saw dramatic changes in classroom instruction associated with the nature of the test employed to evaluate performance. In short, he observed that the use of a paper-and-pencil test encouraged a focus in teaching and learning on factual knowledge. Once a performance test was introduced, the emphasis shifted to doing repair and maintenance with actual equipment.

For a test to effectively exemplify key competencies, those competencies have to have been codified in a form that can serve as the basis for assessment design. So codified, the design can reflect the key competencies and their structure, calling the attention of teachers and learners to those attributes. Understanding domain structure is, in itself, an important aspect of developing expertise in that experts typically have organized their domain knowledge as a rich network of cross-referenced connections among concepts (Bedard & Chi, 1992; National Research Council [NRC], 2000; Pellegrino, Chudowsky, & Glaser, 2001, p. 73).

Content standards represent an attempt at such codification that, for most states, has been superseded by the CCSS. By many accounts, the CCSS are a significant improvement over the majority of state standards documents, in good part because the CCSS appear to be more demanding, coherent, and focused (Carmichael, Martino, Porter-Magee, & Wilson, 2010; Schmidt & Houang, 2012). However, with the notable exception of text complexity in ELA, the CCSS documents do not clearly ground the standards in learning sciences' research, nor do they make explicit the learning sciences' principles on which assessment design should be based.[5] For these reasons, building so-called *competency models*, or learning maps, has been advocated as a bridge from the CCSS and learning sciences' research to assessment design (Bennett, 2010a). Such models describe a domain in terms of its key constituents (i.e., knowledge, processes, strategies, practices, habits of mind), how those constituents might be organized, and the order in which instruction might best proceed (i.e., a learning progression) for mastering a key constituent or a constellation of constituents. These models are, in essence, a domain theory. Competency models for ELA, mathematics, and science linked to content standards have been proposed (Attali & Cayton-Hodges, 2014; Confrey, Maloney, Nguyen, Mojica, & Myers, 2009; Deane, 2012; Graf, 2009; Graf, Harris, Marquez, Fife, & Redman, 2009; Liu, Rogat, & Bertling, 2013), and in many cases used to create prototype assessments. In these prototypes, every item can be linked to a standard as well as to the domain theory underlying the test. Those linkages can then be evaluated judgmentally through alignment studies. Once alignment is verified, every test administration becomes input to evaluating and refining the domain theory.

In recent years, a focus of research in domain theory has been learning progressions (Heritage, 2008), which may suggest paths toward the achievement of key constituents of the competency model (or of given standards). Well-grounded progressions might, therefore, be of value for assessment design because of their potential implications for instructional planning—see Corcoran, Mosher, and Rogat (2009) for a review of the research on progressions in the sciences, Daro et al. (2011) for a discussion of progressions in mathematics, and Song, Deane, Graf, and van Rijn (2013) for a description of learning progressions for argumentation in ELA.

Deane, Sabatini, and O'Reilly (2012) define a learning progression as follows:

A description of qualitative change in a student's level of sophistication for a key concept, process, strategy, practice, or habit of mind. Change in student standing on such a progression may be due to a variety of factors, including maturation and instruction. Each progression is presumed to be modal—i.e., to hold for most, but not all, students. Finally, it is provisional, subject to empirical verification and theoretical challenge.

Several elements of this definition are worth noting. First, the progression is one of *qualitative* change, where the levels connote cognitive differences in kind and not just amount. Looking at the CCSS, one can see that the path some ELA standards take across grades is indeed one of amount. Reading standards RL.6.1 through RL.9-10.1 (which run from Grades 6 through 9/10) call for the student to "cite textual evidence to support analysis," "cite several pieces of textual evidence," "cite the textual evidence that most strongly supports an analysis," and "cite strong and thorough textual evidence" (CCSSI, 2010, pp. 36, 38). Second, the progression can refer to knowledge, process, strategy, practice, or habit of mind—any qualitatively changing competency central to the development of domain proficiency. As such, a progression relates to a *specific* competency model component. Overall domain proficiency will, therefore, be the result of location in a network of related progressions with no simple correspondence between standing on any individual progression and that overall proficiency. Third, there may be multiple causes for that standing, including (but not only) school instruction. Fourth, the progression describes a path that *most* students are thought to traverse; other students may come to similar levels of development via a different, equally acceptable path. Last, the progression is, at the least, grounded theoretically and, in the ideal case, empirically supported. But even when empirically supported, the progression is still tentative in that it represents a reasoned understanding as to what existing theory and available data suggest being true at a given time.

How much backing is needed before a proposed progression might be useful for instruction and assessment? In principle, both validation and evaluation studies would be required. In terms of validation, an assessment based on the progression should recover it empirically. For example, items meant to measure lower levels should be easier than items mapped to higher levels, and individual examinees should generally get items below their level correct and items above it incorrect. Furthermore, that assessment should place individuals into levels consistently; parallel forms of the test taken at the same point in time should produce the same placement. Finally, placements suggested by the test should generally agree with independent indicators of those assignments (e.g., the judgments of expert teachers).

For a validation study to produce positive results, multiple conditions must be true. Among other things:

- The underlying theory (i.e., the progression) must be a reasonably correct representation of change for most students.
- The test used to verify the progression must contain items that cover multiple levels and there must be enough items per level to reliably measure individual student standing.
- The items themselves (or their response categories) must be correctly mapped to levels and must be free from other, unrelated sources of difficulty that might cause the items to be otherwise harder or easier than their mapping would predict.
- The student sample must contain enough variation in standing on the progression for the test to place students at different levels, and that sample must be large enough to make results dependable.
- The psychometric model used to analyze the data must be sensitive to the level differences inherent in those data.

If validation results support the progression, the second step is evaluation—determining if actions taken on the basis of placement information lead to better learning outcomes than actions taken on some alternative basis. This evaluation must also include documenting exactly what actions were taken because the interpretation of outcomes will be meaningful only if the nature of implementation is understood. Note that evaluation is unnecessary if validation studies do not support the progression in the first place, or if implementation is flawed, because even if learning improves, it cannot have been because of the intended use of the progression.

Given that the number of key competencies in a domain is considerable, and that each competency might have its own learning progression, the logistics of generating empirical verification will necessitate research efforts by many independent investigators conducted over substantial periods of time. The only way to speed up the process might be to develop and identify theoretically grounded progressions, build them

FIGURE 3
Modeling Good Teaching and Learning Practice Through the Use of Key Knowledge Representations Like Conventional Criteria

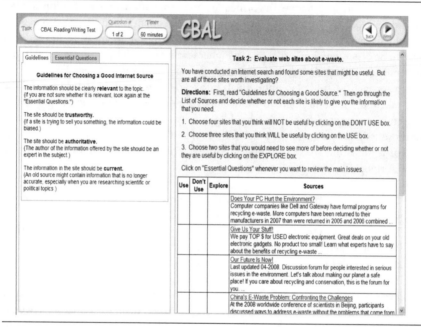

into tests provisionally, use field testing and operational administration to study their validity and impact, and progressively refine the progressions and tests as they are used. Such embedded innovation—carefully planned and continuous—may well need to be a characteristic of the third generation if those tests are to keep up with the rapidly increasing pace of change in education and society.

In addition to competencies and progressions, learning sciences' research offers general principles that might be designed into tests. In particular, those principles can be used to exemplify, or model, good teaching and learning practice. Third-generation tests might attempt to model such practice in at least four ways. First, the assessments might routinely include knowledge representations similar to the ones proficient performers use in their domain practice (Mislevy et al., 2010). For example, proficient performers typically possess disciplinary epistemologies, or epistemic frames (Shaffer, 2006), that include internalized standards and criteria for what constitutes good work in the domain. Skilled performers habitually judge their own work against those standards and criteria, going back and forth between a work product and the criteria more or less automatically. In line with this idea, investigators have created prototype summative and formative ELA assessments that present conventional

FIGURE 4
Modeling Good Teaching and Learning Practice Through the Use of Key Knowledge Representations Like Planning Aids for Writing

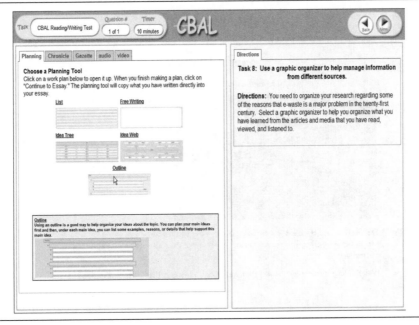

criteria (e.g., for evaluating the quality of a summary, of the information presented on the Internet, of an argumentative essay) and that ask students to apply those criteria *repeatedly* (Deane, Fowles, Baldwin, & Persky, 2011; Deane, Sabatini, & Fowles, 2012). The inclusion of such criteria is aimed at encouraging their use by learners (and by teachers) to the point that they become a "habit of mind." Figure 3 gives an example of an assessment task in which students are asked to apply criteria to the evaluation of web-site summaries.

Proficient performers also often engage in planning behavior (VanLehn & van de Sande, 2009, p. 367), including the use of aids or tools. Figure 4 shows a screen from a prototype writing assessment in which students have access to several such tools for organizing their thoughts. Each tool is built around a different writing structure— the outline, idea tree, idea web, and list—and each tool enforces the conventions of that structure (e.g., the outline tool enforces indentation). A given tool is activated by clicking on the appropriate icon. When the student is done with the tool, he or she can transfer the resulting plan into the response area for use in producing the essay.

An additional way in which third-generation assessments might attempt to model good teaching and learning practice is by presenting reasonably realistic problem

FIGURE 5
Modeling Good Teaching and Learning Practice Through the Use of a
Reasonably Realistic Problem Context

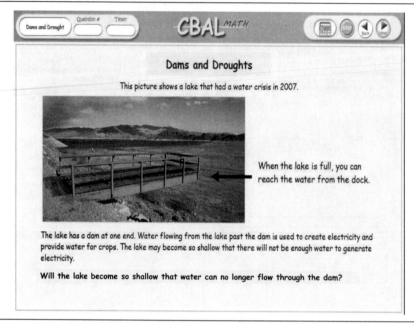

contexts. Such contexts are intended to increase engagement and help students connect solution processes and strategies to the conditions under which they might be used. Figure 5 gives an example of the introduction to such a task. The task revolves around a lake that feeds water through a dam for electricity generation and irrigation of the land downstream. Because of a drought, it is uncertain as to whether the lake will recede to the point that water can no longer flow through the dam. The challenge for the students is to determine if the available data justify instituting emergency water conservation measures. To find an answer, each student must solve a series of problems involving linear functions and then formulate an argument with appropriate mathematical backing.

A third way of modeling good teaching and learning practice is to design assessment tasks to help students (and teachers) connect qualitative understanding with abstract formalism, since a key aspect of conceptual competence is the ability to comprehend and navigate among deep-structure problem representations (Bedard & Chi, 1992; NRC, 2000, p. 243; Sigel, 1993). Such connections with formalism are especially important when using realistic problem contexts, some of which will inevitably be more or less familiar to individual students, especially those who are at-risk

FIGURE 6
Modeling Good Teaching and Learning Practice Through the Use of a Sink Simulation to Help Students (and Teachers) Connect Qualitative Understanding to Mathematical Formalism

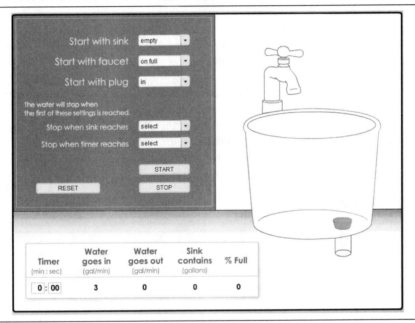

learners. The dam-and-lake scenario in Figure 5 is built around the mathematics of inflow and outflow, the language and concepts of which might not be familiar to all learners in this situation. To ensure that students come to the assessment task with a common qualitative understanding of inflow and outflow that can be connected with mathematical formalism, students are first presented with a simulation of a system known to all—the sink (see Figure 6). In that simulation, the faucet represents the river feeding the lake, the basin stands for the lake, and the plug corresponds to the dam. Students can manipulate the states of the faucet, sink, and plug; understand what happens to the water level under different combinations of states; and mathematically model the relationships among the variables before applying similar modeling to the lake and dam.

A fourth approach to modeling good teaching and learning practice can be realized by structuring extended tasks purposefully. One such structure, described by Deane et al. (2011; Deane, Sabatini, & Fowles, 2012) is built around a unifying problem scenario. The scenario begins with a premise, similar to that shown in Figure 5. That premise is followed by a series of "lead-in" tasks. The assessment closes with a performance requiring the integration of multiple competencies, called a "culminating task." The lead-in tasks have several purposes. First, they are intended to activate prior knowledge. Second, they are used to measure prerequisite competencies needed for the culminating performance. In writing, for example, the lead-in tasks might target specific reading, as well as critical thinking competencies, both of which are required for producing the culminating essay. This scenario-based task structure (i.e., lead-in plus culminating tasks) can suggest to the teacher how the skills required for more complex performance might be decomposed. That decomposition should be useful for planning instruction and as a heuristic for classroom assessment.

How well might assessments function that are built to reflect learning sciences' competency models and to exemplify good teaching and learning practice? The CCSAs are, unfortunately, not informative as of this writing, both because empirical results have yet to be reported and because those assessments were not explicitly designed from competency models or necessarily from the set of principles described above. Some indication, at least in terms of basic psychometric functioning, comes from CBAL, whose prototype assessments were designed in this manner. Among the findings from the first 4 years of CBAL research was that prototypes in reading, writing, and mathematics appeared to function adequately on average (Bennett, 2011b). Taken across multiple test forms and pilot administrations, the median form difficulty was appropriate to the samples tested (implying that test developers might have control of difficulty factors); internal consistency estimates were high enough to suggest that measurement was generalizable across item samples (median coefficient alpha = .88 for reading, .82 for writing, and .92 for mathematics); missing-response rates were low, indicating that students were not put off by the scenario-based structure; and correlations with other indicators of similar skills were reasonably good, suggesting that construct-relevant factors were being captured. In addition, factor analyses of individual forms and of *non*parallel form pairs typically recovered a single dimension, offering the possibility of a principled basis for aggregating scores across test components administered on different occasions.

Although the CBAL assessment prototypes worked well on average, there was considerable variation from one test form to the next on the basic psychometric characteristics summarized above, particularly in writing and mathematics (Bennett, 2011b). That variation suggests that the craft knowledge needed to produce high-quality forms consistently, and to the scale required for an operational assessment, may not yet exist among the CBAL developers. Given the novel nature of scenario-based assessments, it is not clear that the craft knowledge yet exists in the field of educational testing more generally. Although structured development processes such as Evidence-Centered Design (Mislevy, Almond, & Lukas, 2003) and assessment engineering (Luecht, 2009) should help in systematizing the creation of forms that function more consistently, use of those design processes is still very new.

Whereas CBAL research can offer some indication of the basic psychometric functioning of tests designed from learning sciences' models and principles, that knowledge is only a beginning. More specifically, research must address the validation of assessments built from theoretically grounded learning progressions, as well as the iterative refinement of those progressions through that research. As Shepard, Daro, and Stancavage (2013) have noted,

The most significant impediment to implementing learning progressions for any large-scale assessment program is the fledgling state of research . . . Detailed, carefully wrought, and recursively tested progressions are rare, although the few that do exist demonstrate what is possible. (p. 137)

In addition, research must evaluate the impact on teaching and learning practice of basing assessments on learning sciences' models and principles. Earlier work on the effect of assessment design on practice suggests reason for at least cautious optimism. In his review of the literature on performance assessment, Stecher (2010) states,

Tests used for standards-based accountability send signals to educators (as well as students and parents) about the specific content, styles of learning, and styles of performance that are valued. An abundance of research suggests that teachers respond accordingly, emphasizing in their lessons the content, styles of learning, and performing that are manifest on the tests . . . Performance assessment, in particular, has been found to lead to greater emphasis on problem solving and communication in mathematics, and to more extended writing in language arts. (pp. 24–25)

Advances in performance assessment, particularly those made possible through technology, are considered next.

Using Complex Simulations and Other Interactive Performance Tasks

As noted, a key characteristic of third-generation assessments will be the use of complex simulations and other interactive performance tasks that replicate important features of real environments, allow more natural interaction with computers, and assess new skills in more sophisticated ways.[6]

Such tasks are only just beginning to appear in educational assessment, although research has been underway for some time, especially in problem solving and in science. An early significant investigation was the 2003 NAEP Problem Solving in Technology-Rich Environments Study (Bennett, Persky, Weiss, & Jenkins, 2007, 2010). In that study, competency models were posed for the targeted problem-solving constructs and two simulation scenarios were created, one for Internet information search and one for discovering physical relationships through scientific experimentation. Each scenario was administered to a nationally representative sample of ~1,000 eighth-grade students. Both problem-solving processes and end results were used to estimate scores for the population as a whole, as well as for subgroups categorized by gender, race/ethnicity, parents' education level, school location, and eligibility for free or reduced-price school lunch. Results showed that these simulation-based assessments functioned well psychometrically and produced results generally consistent with those from other NAEP assessments. In addition, problem-solving process indicators (e.g., the number and range of experiments conducted) predicted the quality of student answers.

NAEP followed the Technology-Rich Environments study in 2009 with a special study using science Interactive Computer Tasks (ICTs), including simulation, as well as more traditional hands-on performance tasks (National Center for Education Statistics, 2012). This study presented three ICTs to nationally representative samples of about 2,000 students at each of Grades 4, 8, and 12. Performance was reported in terms of percentages of students successfully completing task components for groups categorized by gender, race/ethnicity, and eligibility for the national school lunch program. No analyses related to the functioning of the measures themselves, however, were reported.

Quellmalz et al. (2013) compared the functioning of interactive simulations similar to the NAEP ICTs with that of both traditional tasks and tasks in which the stimuli were dynamic (e.g., animated). Comparisons were made with respect to the ability to measure three types of science inquiry practice: (a) identifying principles, (b) using principles (e.g., to make predictions and generate explanations), and (c) conducting inquiry (e.g., designing experiments). Generalizability, confirmatory factor-analytic, and multidimensional item response theory methodology was applied to data collected from approximately 1,500 middle school students. Results suggested that the simulations measured the "conducting inquiry" practice somewhat more reliably than did the other methods, although the person-by-task interaction was large for all task types, a frequent finding with performance assessment (Linn & Burton, 1994). The presence of this interaction suggests that students who do well on one performance task may not do as well (relative to their peers) on another task measuring the same competencies.

Of special note with respect to interactive performance tasks are the challenges they pose for students from special populations. Kopriva (2009) describes a science simulation that makes very limited use of text so as to reduce irrelevant variance for students who are English language learners or have restricted reading skills. Cayton-Hodges et al. (2012) discuss the accessibility features of a tablet-based task in mathematics that includes a simulation. Two types of features were used to make the task accessible. First, engagement features were included to increase attention and motivation, to limit demands on working memory, and to permit measurement of prerequisite skills, which can provide information about the competencies of low-performing students. These engagement features might be especially helpful for students who are English language learners, or for those with attention deficit disorder and other learning disabilities. Additional features incorporated audio presentation and haptics (e.g., vibration) to facilitate access for students with visual impairments, for whom interacting with a simulation might otherwise be impossible. Audio that presented task instructions in a native language might also be used to make the simulation more accessible for English language learners.

The above studies suggest that it is possible to build and administer assessments consisting of complex simulations and interactive performance tasks, including accessible ones, in research and low-stakes operational testing contexts. These studies say relatively little, however, about the issues surrounding use for making consequential decisions about individuals. Without question, the most highly developed use of these tasks for such decision making is found in the field of professional licensure and certification. From a design perspective, three testing programs are worth noting: the American Institute of Certified Public Accountants (AICPA) Uniform CPA Examination, the National Council of Architectural Registration Boards (NCARB) Architect Registration Examination, and the U.S. Medical Licensing Examination (USMLE) administered by the National Board of Medical Examiners.

The AICPA Uniform CPA Examination consists of four test sections that are to be taken over a maximum period of 18 months (AICPA, 2012). In total, those sections consist of approximately 324 multiple-choice items and 23 performance tasks, including some 20 relatively constrained "task-based simulations" (each designed to take about 10 minutes) and 3 slightly longer written communication tasks (intended to take about 15 minutes apiece). The total testing time is 14 hours and the examination fee (a consequence of the multipart design and use of performance tasks) is substantial. That fee varies by jurisdiction, but for New York, it was about $870 in 2012 (National Association of State Boards of Accountancy, 2012).

The NCARB Architect Registration Examination 4.0 includes seven "divisions," to be taken over a maximum period of 5 years (NCARB, 2012). The seven divisions contain 11 complex performance tasks called "graphic vignettes," which take from 1 to 4 hours each, and 555 multiple-choice questions. The total testing time is 33.5 hours and the 2012 fee was $1,470 (NCARB, 2009).

The USMLE has three "steps" that are meant to be completed at key points over the course of graduate and postgraduate medical education (USMLE, 2012). The three steps contain approximately 1,155 multiple-choice questions and from 21 to 24 performance tasks. Between 9 and 12 of those performance tasks are computer-based case simulations administered in a single 4-hour session, with 10 to 20 minutes allotted to each case. The remaining performance tasks involve interacting with live simulated patients (i.e., human actors) and require the examinee to take case notes on computer. Total testing time is 41 hours at a cost to the examinee in 2013 of $3,165 (Federation of State Medical Boards, 2010; National Board of Medical Examiners, 2012).

Several common features of these three examination programs should be noted because they have implications for consequential educational testing. First, each program contributes to the making of a single proficiency decision: that is, whether the examinee has the minimum level of knowledge and skill to be admitted to practice in the profession. Second, in all three cases, multiple test parts taken over a significant period are aggregated to produce that proficiency classification. Third, complex simulations or other interactive performance tasks are included in each examination program. Those tasks are included because they are intended to measure competencies that a traditional test could not easily assess—for example, for the prospective architect, using computerized tools to create a site plan that meets stipulated design requirements and building code; for the accountancy candidate, manipulating spreadsheets, completing online forms, and producing written communications; and for the physician, diagnosing and managing a patient whose condition dynamically changes in response to treatment. In each instance, the examinee is given access to significant resources that could not be made easily available in traditional form—building codes, tax law and professional accounting standards, and extensive diagnostic results. Fourth, to increase generalizability, at least 11 performance tasks (sometimes relatively short, sometimes quite lengthy), and hundreds of multiple-choice items, are employed. Fifth, the candidate must pass all examination sections to be eligible for licensure (but multiple retakes are permitted). Sixth, the examinations (and familiarization materials) are very expensive to create and maintain. Finally, that expense is passed on to the examinee, and because the candidate pools are relatively small, the costs per examinee are quite substantial.

These three professional certification and licensure programs, then, make extensive use of complex simulation and interactive performance assessment. They justify that use substantively, selectively targeting performance tasks at those job-relevant competencies that would be harder to assess through traditional means. The programs achieve breadth and depth of coverage by employing large numbers of both performance and multiple-choice tasks, far larger numbers than could be administered in a single sitting. To deal with the sitting limitation, they distribute measurement over multiple testing occasions. Because these examinations are mandated for employment, examinees have little choice but to comply with the multiple occasions and to pay the significant fees needed to support these complex enterprises.

What might high-stakes educational assessment programs take from the example of these professional certification and licensure examinations as they evolve toward the third generation? One obvious lesson is that to cover a domain broadly *and* deeply requires both a very long test and a combination of task formats. A small number of performance tasks may measure deeply but, by themselves, produce scores unable to generalize to the broader domain they were intended to represent (Linn & Burton, 1994; Shavelson, Baxter, & Gao, 1993). For consequential decision-making purposes, low generalizability raises issues of fairness and legal liability.

Educational testing programs can justify shorter measures than those used in certification and licensure because the risks to students and to the public of misclassification might for some decision-making purposes be lower than in the job context; also, economic, as well as political, conditions may more strongly limit the time that can be allocated to testing in school settings. Even so, the CCSAs will be used to make important decisions about individuals—about the promotion and graduation of individual students, and about rewarding and sanctioning teachers and school administrators via the measurement of student growth. The CCSAs have taken a significant step to bolster generalizability by incorporating a mix of discrete questions and performance tasks into a notably longer test than typical for state assessment. As of this writing, PARCC's CCSA is estimated to take approximately 8 to 11 hours of time on task across ELA and mathematics, depending on grade level (Strauss, 2014), and the Smarter Balanced assessment will run 7 to 8½ hours (SBAC, 2012a). Second, and perhaps more important, the consortia have distributed these long tests over multiple sessions (nine for PARCC across ELA and mathematics), clustered around two distinct time points (after 75% and 90% of the instructional year have been completed) (PARCC, 2013d). Finally, the consortia have, thus far, managed to keep estimated costs quite low, about $22.50 for Smarter Balanced and $24.00 for PARCC (2014). These low costs (compared to those of the licensure and certification programs) are due to having federal support for initial development, tests that use technology in relatively limited ways, and a multistate membership with huge examinee volumes over which operational expenses can be spread.

More Frequently Sampling Evidence of Learning

Whereas the CCSAs will be distributed over two time points and the professional licensure and certification assessments over even more, third-generation tests are likely to sample with far greater frequency, in some views even continuously. Continuous assessment will be made possible by the emergence of electronic learning environments—e-books, online courses (e.g., massive open online courses), simulations, and games—into which assessment can be embedded. In such environments, every mouse click, keystroke, latency, and resulting event can be recorded, providing an enormous volume of data (Bennett, 2014). To the extent that students do all, or even a significant portion, of their learning in such environments, the collected information (or log file) might constitute a finely detailed record of achievement.

To what extent might that record supplement—or even supplant—formative and summative assessment as currently practiced? With respect to formative assessment, the field of intelligent tutoring has for 30 years been using the real-time analysis of student behavior in electronic learning environments to plan and adjust instruction dynamically (Sleeman & Brown, 1982). Evidence suggests that such tutors can facilitate learning, though this conclusion appears to be more supportable at the university than at the K–12 level (Pane, Griffin, McCaffrey, & Karam, 2013; Steenbergen-Hu & Cooper, 2013, 2014). In terms of extent of use, the most widely employed and probably well-researched of the secondary school applications are the Carnegie Learning Cognitive Tutors (Anderson, Corbett, Koedinger, & Pelletier, 1995; Pane et al., 2013; Ritter, Anderson, Koedinger, & Corbett, 2007). These tutors, which were initially not well coordinated with school curricula, are currently intended to be closely integrated with classroom activity. That integration is consistent with a theoretical shift in the field toward learning as a social activity best fostered through communities of practice (Lave, 1991; Wenger, 2000). Those communities depend on students, peers, and teachers frequently interacting to discuss the following: domain competencies, valued tasks that call on constellations of those competencies, student work done in response to those tasks, the processes used to produce that work, and how that work and those processes might be improved so that domain competencies can be developed. The highly social nature of this interaction can certainly be facilitated by technology (e.g., by broadening the size of the learning community to include members outside the school; NRC, 2000, p. 243), but it is unlikely that technology can supplant the community and the role that a skilled teacher plays in managing it. From this perspective, one could see the learning record that comes from student interactions in electronic environments being used as input to the learning community and to the teacher's decision making about how to adjust instruction (in and outside of the electronic environment). That use would be consistent with notions of formative assessment as a "tool" (provided by the learning environment's analysis of the student's log file), and as "process" (represented by the teacher's and student's use of that information in the broader, community context).

Among other things, to be maximally effective, the above use of log files presumes that the electronic learning environment (be it game, simulation, online course, or e-book) was developed from well-grounded competency models and learning progressions.[7] It further presumes that the types of student behaviors serving as evidence of placement at a given level in a progression have been identified in advance so that the development of key competencies can be facilitated and tracked. Such careful, theoretically motivated design, is likely to raise substantially the chances of making sense of the thousands of events that could conceivably populate a log file. Simply using empirical relationships alone, as in data mining, may not produce results that are either interpretable or instructionally sensible (Harford, 2014; Marcus & Davis, 2014), though it might lead to hypotheses worth testing experimentally (Mislevy, Behrens, DiCerbo, & Levy, 2012). Finally, as with formative assessment generally, judgments about student standing, and the consequent instructional adjustments, must be valid and effective. Ultimately, greater achievement should result from using those judgments to make instructional adjustments than from ignoring them (Bennett, 2011c).

If the log file from an electronic learning environment did prove to be valid for formative purposes, might it not also be valid for summative decisions? Some commentators have, in fact, suggested that analyses of behavior in electronic learning environments could well replace summative assessment (e.g., Bennett, 1998; Gee & Shaffer, 2010; Pellegrino et al., 2001; Tucker, 2012). If a log file kept for formative purposes incidentally provided evidence that a student was proficient in that environment, wouldn't that provision obviate the need for further testing? Although this idea is provocative, multiple challenges would need to be met for it to come to reality.

The first challenge is one of extrapolation (Kane, 2006), or what performance in a given electronic environment says about performance *outside* of that environment. Extrapolation primarily concerns empirical relationships with criterion performance. As such, the interest is not so much in how the student performed in his or her past learning environment but in the potential implications of that performance for achievement in some other context of interest. In the case of the CCSA, the claim centers on "college and career readiness." That claim is a prospective one that, if a student is "on track," proximally implies proficient performance in the next grade (in *any* Common Core–focused school) but ultimately suggests proficient performance at the early stages of college or a career.

In addition to this predictive claim, meaningful extrapolation presumes that the content targeted by a learning environment is acceptably aligned to the CCSS (or some other relevant set of standards). If the environment is, for example, a trivial reflection of the Standards, an extensive log file suggesting that the student performed well in that environment may be of little interest. In addition to alignment, meaningful extrapolation presumes that accomplishment in the learning environment is measured validly and reliably. If the environment is a faithful reflection of the standards but the quality of the environment's embedded assessment is poor, student performance results will likewise be of minimal utility.

Given the philosophy of local control that dominates U.S. education, students in a state or consortium will engage in a multitude of different games, simulations, e-books, and online courses, running into the hundreds, if not thousands. Hence, validating the extrapolation, alignment, and measurement quality inferences for the indicators coming from each and every such environment is unlikely to be feasible.

If we take for granted, however, that performance in electronic learning environments meets the above inferential requirements, a second issue must be addressed. This issue concerns whether performance can be considered to be comparable across the many electronic learning environments in which individuals will work. Even when built to the same set of curricular standards, like the CCSS, learning environments will differ considerably in the distribution, difficulty, and depth of competencies covered; the tools and knowledge representations used; and the problem scenarios and formats employed. The tasks and questions presented by any one environment will necessarily be oriented toward a particular constellation of competencies, tools, representations, scenarios, and formats, making idiosyncratic the meaning of performance results for individuals.

Interestingly, there is a long-standing analogue and a perhaps unexpected solution to this problem. To the extent that the log file represents a student's work for the school year, the summary score generated from performance in an electronic learning environment (or some combination of them) will be analogous to a course grade. It is well established that such grades vary widely in meaning across teachers and schools (USDOE, 1994; Woodruff & Ziomek, 2004) and, as such, can introduce unfairness into consequential decision making. Because of this fact, for purposes such as university admissions, average course grades are usually scaled through the use of a common test (e.g., the SAT or ACT).

The third issue can be expressed as follows: Does the recording of essentially *every* teaching and learning transaction violate common expectations for privacy, especially if employed for consequential purposes (Pellegrino et al., p. 287)? (Note that this recording could go well beyond keystrokes, mouse clicks, and gestures to include eye movements, facial expressions, and vocalizations, which are easily captured by the cameras and microphones routinely embedded in today's digital devices.) Such monitoring would appear to require informed consent, and informed consent implies the right to opt out, an action already being taken by some parents with respect to conventional school testing programs more generally (Reid, 2014). Moreover, a public educational institution is a governmental functionary, and it is not immediately evident whether legal bounds are exceeded should government undertake to monitor an individual's cognition and affect continuously. Generally, public behavior can be so monitored but private behavior cannot (without a court order). Is learning behavior continuously observed, public or private, especially if it is used to affect the life chances of individuals? Finally, if student cognition and affect can be continuously monitored, who will have access to those data? It should be obvious that most school districts will not be able to manage and store such voluminous amounts of data onsite, ceding that responsibility to the learning-environment provider or a data management vendor. Rules for the federal Family Educational Rights and Privacy Act permit schools to share student information with such companies. These rules, a general lack of awareness among school officials regarding vendor privacy arrangements and the reports of vendor misuse of electronically collected student data have further heightened privacy concerns (Herold, 2014a; Reidenberg et al., 2013). In fact, the most visible student data aggregator, created with $100 million in funding from the Gates Foundation and Carnegie Corporation, announced in April 2014 that it would cease operations because of widespread opposition rooted in such concerns (Herold, 2014b; Kamisar, 2014; Singer, 2013).

The fourth issue is one of impact on teaching and learning. Would the benefits of studying for, and taking, a culminating test be lost if only continuously embedded assessment was used? If the test is a faithful representation of content standards, appropriately preparing for it should have a substantial positive effect. There is no shortage of evidence that deliberate practice helps learners achieve proficiency—that is, it helps them develop fluency for basic procedures, acquire qualitative understanding, consolidate knowledge, and connect it to conditions of use (Ericsson, Krampe, & Tesch-Romer, 1993; NRC, 2000, p. 125; VanLehn & van de Sande, 2009). Furthermore, taking a test can, itself, help promote knowledge retention and transfer (Butler, 2010; Hinze, Wiley, & Pellegrino, 2013; Roediger & Karpicke, 2006; Rohrer & Pashler, 2010).

Finally, the most appropriate use of continuously embedded assessment would appear to be for guiding learning. Would using formative results incidentally for consequential purposes undermine the effectiveness of both formative and summative decision making? Good learning and teaching involve experimentation, in essence, sometimes engaging in what has been termed *productive failure* (Kapur, 2010). That fruitful behavior could be stifled by the knowledge that all actions were being monitored and judged. Worse, that knowledge could potentially shift the focus of formative assessment from improving teaching and learning to cynical attempts on the part of instructors and students to game the system.

In short, what might make continuous assessment useful for formative purposes—its intimate connection to context (i.e., being *inside* the content, format, tools, and representations used for instruction)—may be precisely what limits its usefulness for summative decision making, where the need is to make inferences applicable across *many* possible contexts and not to provide information particular to just *one* (Bennett, 2014).

How might the CCSAs (and other state assessments) negotiate these issues as they evolve toward the third generation? One possible scenario follows the "competitive-sports" metaphor, in which continuous assessment is employed, but with a clear distinction between summative and formative purposes—a distinction consistent with the "assessment system" notion described earlier. In baseball, for example, practice and learning—and the formative assessment associated with those activities—occur during spring training and, in regular season, between innings and between games. Formative assessment might also occur secondarily during regulation play, but the primary purpose of that play is undoubtedly summative—to make decisions about what team wins the game, the championship titles, and the monetary rewards attached to those achievements. What counts in terms of team performance, then, is measured *only* during regulation play, and the same holds largely true for player performance. Competition in other sports follows a similar model.

If the CCSAs were to adopt the competitive-sports metaphor, continuous assessment would be employed in those electronic learning environments used in any given classroom but, for the reasons stated, the data from those environments would be used for formative purposes. Because schools would be free to purchase *any* environment they wanted, these embedded formative assessments would necessarily be provided by the learning-environment publishers. For summative purposes, however, the CCSA consortia might continue to provide their own assessments, though they would be considerably different from those of 2014. These new assessments would be built from theoretically grounded competency models and learning progressions, use simulations and highly interactive performance tasks, capture the problem-solving process, and model good teaching and learning practice. The assessments would be designed to be engaging and to be valuable learning experiences in and of themselves. Because there would be many of them, they would be administered at various times throughout the school year, with the results aggregated within-student for purposes of representing achievement (much as teachers aggregate evidence to award an individual's course grade, or the major leagues aggregate wins and losses to determine which team goes to the championships; see Mislevy & Zwick, 2012, for more on the significant psychometric issues attendant to such aggregation). Also due to their number, each assessment would have considerably less influence, in contrast to the onetime test of today, eliminating the problem of a student or class having a "bad day." These new assessments might also incidentally provide tentative formative results, pointing teachers toward a student's placement in a learning progression and how that student's problem-solving processes might be improved, results to be followed up with more targeted, teacher-directed data gathering. The key distinctions between these CCSA-provided summative instruments and the publisher-embedded formative assessments would be that (a) the CCSA offerings would be common, calibrated measures that all students would take regardless of what electronic learning environments they used and (b) students would know when their performance was being assessed for consequential purposes.

Scoring Complex Performances Automatically

In third-generation assessments, the frequent sampling of student learning activity, and the use of complex simulations and other interactive performance tasks, will undoubtedly produce more student responding than can be scored efficiently by human raters. That same problem will face the CCSA consortia more immediately. The CCSAs will generate *hundreds of millions* of answers to constructed-response items and performance tasks annually. From a logistical and financial perspective, using human rating alone is simply not feasible if such questions are to remain part of the CCSAs for the long term. For that reason, some significant portion of student responses will need to be scored automatically. In the immediate term, automated scoring is most likely to be used with elemental questions whose answers take a relatively simple form and which can be judged with essentially perfect accuracy (e.g., numeric entry, clicking on a hot spot, equation entry). Automated scoring also might be used with some performance tasks (e.g., essays) in conjunction with a human rater.

As of this writing, the most common use of automated scoring in educational testing is for essay responses. Such scoring is employed in college placement testing (ACCUPLACER and COMPASS), postsecondary admissions (GRE revised General Test, TOEFL iBT, Pearson Test of English), and in a small number of state assessment programs (WESTEST 2, Utah Direct Writing Assessment). Typically, for high-stakes programs, a human rater also scores each response.

The most extensive study of automated essay scoring in the K–12 context to date was conducted by Shermis and Hamner (2013). That study followed the common practice of attempting to validate the automated scores by comparing their agreement *with* operational human ratings to the agreement *between* operational human ratings (Attali, 2013; Bridgeman, 2013). Nine automated scoring systems were compared on each of nine data sets taken from different state assessment programs. The study results were widely (mis)interpreted to suggest that human rating and automated scoring were equivalent (e.g., Getting Smart, 2012; Quillen, 2012; University of Akron, 2012).

As Bennett and Zhang (in press) have argued, that conclusion can be dismissed on at least three counts. The first count is that the study results did not unequivocally suggest closely similar levels of agreement for human rating and machine scoring—a point also made in a reanalysis by Perelman (2014). In fact, the data tables published in Shermis and Hamner (2013) clearly indicate that human raters were more consistent than were the automated systems in distinguishing small differences in essay quality. Second, the human-rating criterion against which the machine scores were compared was not, itself, evaluated but simply taken to be an accurate representation of student writing skill. As has been repeatedly noted, absent evidence, the validity of operational human ratings cannot be presumed (Bennett, 2011a; Bennett & Bejar, 1998; Bejar, 2012). Operational raters are not typically required to have teaching experience; moreover, they grade under high-pressure conditions, work very quickly, and as a result may be using tangential criteria (e.g., essay length) to maintain adequate levels of agreement. Exactly what criteria operational K–12 raters use is not known because that question has not been well studied. Finally, there are many other dimensions along which automated scoring would need to be evaluated before it could be considered to be equivalent to—or better than—human rating (Bennett & Zhang, in press; Williamson, 2013), none of which the Shermis and Hamner (2013) study explicitly considered.

Bennett and Zhang (in press) cite six additional dimensions to be evaluated (relative to human rating):

- The automated scoring model (e.g., the construct relevance of its features)
- The treatment of unusual responses (i.e., those that are atypically creative or that attempt to game their way into undeservedly high scores)
- Generalization (i.e., the extent to which scores on one task predict scores on other tasks from the domain)
- External relations (i.e., the extent to which expected associations with measures of similar and different constructs are borne out)
- Population invariance (i.e., the degree to which scores function similarly across population groups)
- Impact on teaching and learning practice

In the K–12 context, this last dimension—impact on teaching and learning practice—is of enough concern that some educators have strongly advocated against the use of automated scoring (e.g., Herrington & Moran, 2012; National Council of Teachers of English, 2013). The unease centers on the idea that writing is, and should be taught as, a communicative act—a transaction between writer and (human) audience (Flower, 1994). Writers compose to be read—to affect their audience—and because automated scoring systems do not understand what they read, the mechanisms to achieve that effect are different from what they would be for a human recipient. Not only are those mechanisms different, but the features of writing to which automated scoring systems are least sensitive are the very ones that writing instructors most value, including audience awareness, factual accuracy, rhetorical style, and quality of argument. Conversely, the factors to which machines are most sensitive—essay length and mechanical correctness—are the ones the writing community values least. To the extent that students and teachers adjust their practice to emphasize the latter set of factors over the former, student writing may suffer.

In 2015, the CCSAs will include the largest administration by examinee volume of technology-based performance tasks ever attempted. Among the tasks will be argumentative and informational essays written from given source materials. For the reasons just cited, these question types are not well matched to the capabilities of most current automated scoring systems. However, the availability of such large data sets, combined with the pressing need to find efficient scoring mechanisms, should encourage the development of improved methods. Ideally, those methods will bring scoring into closer alignment with contemporary conceptions of writing competency. That synchronization among competency model, task, and scoring method is central to achieving third-generation assessment.

CONCLUSION

This chapter described the evolution of technology-based assessment as a set of stages. That set consisted of an initial generation of infrastructure building, a second generation of qualitative (but incremental) change and efficiency improvement, and a third generation of reinvention. The CCSAs, as emerging at the time of this writing, appear to be bridging those first two stages, having the characteristics of a first-generation, infrastructure-building activity along with some of the features of second-generation tests (e.g., use of technology-enhanced items calling for valued response behaviors, measurement of such new constructs as writing from sources, embedded accessibility features). In addition, the CCSAs display indications of an evolution toward third-generation tests, particularly in attempting to create systems of assessment that serve both institutional and individual needs and in replacing the traditional single-event test with two measures given at substantially different times.

The evolution toward third-generation assessment is likely to take many years. That evolution includes building out systems of assessment in keeping with the underlying theories of action. It involves designing assessments from competency models and principles grounded in the learning sciences so that the assessments are more likely to have positive impact on teaching and learning. It entails using complex simulation and other interactive performance tasks to measure competencies that cannot be effectively assessed through traditional means. It requires more frequently sampling evidence of learning if the inferences are to be dependable ones about proficiency writ broadly as well as deeply. Finally, due to the huge amount of responding that will be produced through frequent sampling of complex performances, scoring those complex performances automatically is required in ways that are true to the conception of the intended competencies.

Many challenges will need to be addressed in the course of this evolution. One set of challenges relates to generating theory-based competency models and learning progressions, designing tasks to measure standing in them, helping teachers connect student performance to instructional action, and evaluating the measures so as to refine them and the underlying theories. A second challenge will be evaluating the extent to which such measures have the intended positive impact on teaching and learning practice. A third challenge will be in devising frequent sampling schemes that satisfy accountability needs, have educational value, and preserve privacy. Fourth will be creating approaches to automated scoring that are grounded in the important competencies that compose the domain and validated through consideration of a range of dimensions, not simply their ability to predict operational human rating. Finally, and most important, will be the research needed to ensure the validity and fairness of these new assessments for all individuals, but especially those who are at risk. Validity and fairness mean assessments that measure with approximately equal quality, and that have substantially the same positive impact, across demographic groups. In reinventing assessment, we should aspire for nothing less.

NOTES

[1]For a detailed overview of the comprehensive consortia, as well as of the alternate assessment and English language proficiency assessment consortia, see Center for K-12 Assessment & Performance Management at ETS (2014).

[2]For more recent approaches to adaptive testing, see Yan, von Davier, and Lewis (2014).

[3]Comparability questions also arise with respect to computer platform, which may vary materially from school to school and student to student, potentially affecting test performance in unfair ways. See Drasgow et al. (2006) for more on this issue.

[4]PARCC (2013c) organizes its embedded (and other) accessibility features into ones for all students that are available at the time of assessment, ones for all students that must be designated in advance, and accommodations for students with disabilities and/or who are English language learners.

[5]But see Daro, Mosher, and Corcoran (2011) for a discussion of how research on learning progressions influenced the development of the mathematics standards.

[6]In this context, a "complex simulation" is an extended, highly interactive task that presents the examinee with the opportunity to manipulate aspects of a modeled environment, obtain the results of that manipulation, and react as may be appropriate. Scoring may include both the extent to which some correct outcome is produced as well as the path used to achieve that outcome.

[7]The Cognitive Tutors, for example, were based on a carefully developed and extensively studied domain theory (Anderson et al., 1995).

REFERENCES

American Institute of Certified Public Accountants. (2012). *Uniform examination FAQs: Examination content structure and delivery.* Retrieved from http://www.aicpa.org/ BecomeACPA/CPAExam/ForCandidates/FAQ/Pages/computer_faqs_1.aspx

American Psychological Association. (1986). *Guidelines for computer-based tests and interpretations.* Washington, DC: Author.

Anderson, J. R., Corbett, A. T., Koedinger, K. R., & Pelletier, R. (1995). Cognitive tutors: Lessons learned. *Journal of Learning Sciences, 4,* 167–207.

Attali, Y. (2011). *Automated subscores for TOEFL iBT independent essays* (Research Report No. 11-39). Princeton, NJ: Educational Testing Service.

Attali, Y. (2013). Validity and reliability of automated essay scoring. In M. D. Shermis & J. Burstein (Eds.), *Handbook of automated essay evaluation: Current applications and new directions* (pp. 181–198). New York, NY: Routledge.

Attali, M., & Cayton-Hodges, G. (2014). *Expanding the CBAL mathematics assessment to elementary grades: The development of a competency model and a rational number learning progression* (Research Report No. 14-08). Princeton, NJ: Educational Testing Service.

Bedard, J., & Chi, M. T. H. (1992). Expertise. *Current Directions in Psychological Science, 1,* 135–139. Retrieved from http://chilab.asu.edu/papers/Expertise.pdf

Bejar, I. I. (2012). Rater cognition: Implications for validity. *Educational Measurement: Issues and Practice, 31*(3), 2–9.

Bennett, R. E. (1998). *Reinventing assessment: Speculations on the future of large-scale educational testing.* Princeton, NJ: Policy Information Center, Educational Testing Service. Retrieved from https://www.ets.org/research/policy_research_reports/pic-reinvent

Bennett, R. E. (2010a). Cognitively based assessment of, for, and as learning: A preliminary theory of action for summative and formative assessment. *Measurement: Interdisciplinary Research and Perspectives, 8,* 70–91.

Bennett, R. E. (2010b). Technology for large-scale assessment. In P. Peterson, E. Baker, & B. McGaw (Eds.), *International encyclopedia of education* (3rd ed., Vol. 8, pp. 48–55). Oxford, England: Elsevier.

Bennett, R. E. (2011a). *Automated scoring of constructed-response literacy and mathematics items.* Princeton, NJ: Educational Testing Service. Retrieved from http://www.ets.org/s/k12/ pdf/k12_commonassess_automated_scoring_math.pdf

Bennett, R. E. (2011b). *CBAL: Results from piloting innovative k-12 assessments.* Princeton, NJ: Educational Testing Service.

Bennett, R. E. (2011c). Formative assessment: A critical review. *Assessment in Education: Principles, Policy & Practice, 18,* 5–25.

Bennett, R. E. (2014). Preparing for the future: What educational assessment must do. *Teachers College Record, 116*(11). Retrieved from http://www.tcrecord.org/Content.asp?ContentID=17623

Bennett, R. E., & Bejar, I. I. (1998). Validity and automated scoring: It's not only the scoring. *Educational Measurement: Issues and Practice, 17*(4), 9–17.

Bennett, R. E., Braswell, J., Oranje, A., Sandene, B, Kaplan, B., & Yan, F. (2008). Does it matter if I take my mathematics test on computer? A second empirical study of mode effects in NAEP. *Journal of Technology, Learning, and Assessment, 6*(9). Retrieved from http://files.eric.ed.gov/fulltext/EJ838621.pdf

Bennett, R. E., & Gitomer, D. H. (2009). Transforming K-12 assessment: Integrating accountability testing, formative assessment, and professional support. In C. Wyatt-Smith & J. Cumming (Eds.), *Educational assessment in the 21st century* (pp. 43–61). New York, NY: Springer.

Bennett, R. E., Kane, M. T., & Bridgeman, B. (2011). *Theory of action and validity argument in the context of through-course summative assessment.* Princeton, NJ: Educational Testing Service.

Bennett, R. E., Persky, H., Weiss, A. R., & Jenkins, F. (2007). *Problem solving in technology-rich environments: A report from the NAEP Technology-Based Assessment Project* (NCES 2007-466). Washington, DC: National Center for Education Statistics, US Department of Education. Retrieved from http://nces.ed.gov/pubsearch/pubsinfo.asp?pubid=2007466

Bennett, R. E., Persky, H., Weiss, A., & Jenkins, F. (2010). Measuring problem solving with technology: A demonstration study for NAEP. *Journal of Technology, Learning, and Assessment, 8*(8). Retrieved from http://ejournals.bc.edu/ojs/index.php/jtla/article/view/1627/1471

Bennett, R. E., & Zhang, M. (in press). Validity and automated scoring. In F. Drasgow (Ed.), *Technology in testing: Improving educational and psychological measurement.* Washington, DC: National Council on Measurement in Education.

Black, P., & Wiliam, D. (1998a). Assessment and classroom learning. *Assessment in Education, 5,* 7–74.

Black, P., & Wiliam, D. (1998b). Inside the black box: Raising standards through classroom assessment. *Phi Delta Kappan, 80,* 139–148. Retrieved from http://www.pdkintl.org/kappan/kbla9810.htm

Bridgeman, B. (2013). Human ratings and automated essay evaluation. In M. D. Shermis & J. Burstein (Eds.), *Handbook of automated essay evaluation: Current applications and new directions* (pp. 221–232). New York, NY: Routledge.

Brookhart, S. M. (2010). *Formative assessment strategies for every classroom: An ASCD action tool.* Alexandria, VA: ASCD.

Bunderson, C. V., Inouye, D. K., & Olsen, J. B. (1989). The four generations of computerized testing. In R. L. Linn (Ed.), *Educational measurement* (3rd ed., pp. 367–407). New York, NY: Macmillan.

Butler, A. C. (2010). Repeated testing produces superior transfer of learning relative to repeated studying. *Journal of Experimental Psychology: Learning, Memory, and Cognition, 36,* 1118–1133.

Carmichael, S. B., Martino, G., Porter-Magee, K., & Wilson, W. S. (2010). *The state of state standards—and the Common Core in 2010.* Washington, DC: Fordham Institute. Retrieved from http://www.math.jhu.edu/~wsw/FORD/SOSSandCC2010_FullReportFINAL.pdf

Cayton-Hodges, G. A., Marquez, E., Keehner, M., Laitusis, C., van Rijn, P., Zapata-Rivera, D., ...Hakkinen, M. T. (2012). *Technology enhanced assessments in mathematics and beyond: Strengths, challenges, and future directions.* Princeton, NJ: Educational Testing Service.

Center for K-12 Assessment & Performance Management at ETS. (2014). *Coming together to raise achievement: New assessments for the Common Core State Standards.* Princeton, NJ: Educational Testing Service. Retrieved from http://www.k12center.org/rsc/pdf/coming_together_to_raise_achievement_april2014.pdf

Chandler, M. A. (2013, May 20). All Virginia students to use computers for standardized tests. *Washington Post.* Retrieved from http://www.washingtonpost.com/local/education/all-virginia-students-to-use-computers-for-standardized-tests/2013/05/20/e473f924-bd9c-11e2-97d4-a479289a31f9_story.html

Coffey, J. E., Hammer, D., Levin, D., M., & Grant, T. (2011). The missing disciplinary substance of formative assessment. *Journal of Research in Science Teaching, 48,* 1109–1136.

Common Core State Standards Initiative. (2010). *Common Core State Standards for English Language Arts and Literacy in History/Social Studies, Science, Science, and Technical Subjects.* Retrieved from http://www.corestandards.org/ELA-Literacy/

Confrey, J., Maloney, A., Nguyen, K., Mojica, G., & Myers, M. (2009). Equipartitioning/splitting as a foundation of rational number reasoning. In M. Tzekaki, M. Kaldrimidou, & C. Sakonidis (Eds.), *Proceedings of the 33rd Conference of the International Group for the Psychology of Mathematics Education* (Vol. 1, pp. 345–352). Thessaloniki, Greece: PME.

Corcoran, T., Mosher, F. A., & Rogat A. (2009). Learning progressions in science: An evidence-based approach to reform. New York: Consortium for Policy Research in Education (CPRE).

Daro, P., Mosher, F. A., & Corcoran, T. (2011). *Learning trajectories in mathematics: A foundation for standards, curriculum, assessment, and instruction* (Research Report No. 68). Philadelphia, PA: CPRE.

Deane, P. (2012). Rethinking K-12 writing assessment. In N. Elliot & L. Perelman (Eds.), *Writing assessment in the 21st century* (pp. 87–100). New York, NY: Hampton Press.

Deane, P., Fowles, M., Baldwin, D., & Persky, H. (2011). *The CBAL summative writing assessment: A draft eighth-grade design* (ETS Research Memorandum No. 11-01). Princeton, NJ: Educational Testing Service.

Deane, P., Sabatini, J., & Fowles, M. (2012). Rethinking k-12 writing assessment to support best instructional practices. In C. Bazerman, C. Dean, J. Early, K. Lunsford, S. Null, P. Rogers, & A. Stansell (Eds.), *International advances in writing research: Cultures, places, measures* (pp. 83–102). Anderson, SC: Parlor Press.

Deane, P., Sabatini, J., & O'Reilly, T. (2012). *The CBAL English language arts competency model and provisional learning progressions: Outline of provisional learning progressions.* Retrieved from http://elalp.cbalwiki.ets.org/Outline+of+Provisional+Learning+Progressions

Drasgow, F., Luecht, R. M., & Bennett, R. E. (2006). Technology and testing. In R. L. Brennan (Ed.), *Educational measurement* (4th ed., pp. 471–515). Westport, CT: American Council on Education/Praeger.

Durso, R., Golub-Smith, M. L., Mills, C. N., Schaeffer, G. A., & Steffen, M. (1995). *The introduction and comparability of the computer adaptive GRE General Test* (Research Report No. 95-20). Princeton, NJ: Educational Testing Service.

Ericsson, K. A., Krampe, R. T., & Tesch-Romer, C. (1993). The role of deliberate practice in the acquisition of expert performance. *Psychological Review, 100,* 363–406.

Federation of State Medical Boards. (2010). *Medical licensing examination: Generation application information.* Retrieved from http://www.fsmb.org/usmle_apply.html#usmlefees

Flower, L. (1994). *The construction of negotiated meaning: A social cognitive theory of writing.* Carbondale: Southern Illinois University Press.

Frederiksen, N. (1984). The real test bias: Influences of testing on teaching and learning. *American Psychologist, 39,* 193–202.

Gee, J. P., & Shaffer, D. W. (2010). Looking where the light is bad: Video games and the future of assessment. *Edge, 6*, 3–19. Retrieved from http://edgaps.org/gaps/wp-content/uploads/EDge-Light.pdf

Getting Smart. (2012, April 12). *Automated essay scoring demonstrated effective in big trial*. Retrieved from http://gettingsmart.com/2012/04/automated-essay-scoring-systems-demonstrate-effectiveness/

Gierl, M. J., & Haladyna, T. M. (Eds.). (2013). *Automatic item generation: Theory and practice*. New York, NY: Routledge.

Gordon Commission on the Future of Assessment in Education. (2013). *A public policy statement*. Princeton, NJ: Author. Retrieved from http://www.gordoncommission.org/rsc/pdfs/gordon_commission_public_policy_report.pdf

Graf, E. A. (2009). *Defining mathematics competency in the service of Cognitively Based Assessment for grades 6 through 8* (ETS Research Memorandum No. RM-09-42). Princeton, NJ: Educational Testing Service.

Graf, E. A., Harris, K., Marquez, E., Fife, J., & Redman, M. (2009). *Cognitively based assessment of, for, and as learning (CBAL) in mathematics: A design and first steps toward implementation* (ETS Research Memorandum No. RM-09-07). Princeton, NJ: Educational Testing Service.

Harford, T. (2014, March 28). Big data: Are we making a big mistake? *FT Magazine*. Retrieved from http://www.ft.com/intl/cms/s/2/21a6e7d8-b479-11e3-a09a-00144feabdc0.html#axzz2xl8loPdL

Heritage, M. (2008). *Learning progressions: Supporting instruction and formative assessment*. Washington, DC: Council of Chief State School Officers. Retrieved from http://www.k12.wa.us/assessment/ClassroomAssessmentIntegration/pubdocs/FASTLearningProgressions.pdf

Herold, B. (2014a, March 13). Google under fire for data-mining student email messages. *Education Week*. Retrieved from http://www.edweek.org/ew/articles/2014/03/13/26google.h33.html?cmp=ENL-EU-NEWS2

Herold, B. (2014b, April 21). inBloom to shut down amid growing data-privacy concerns. *Education Week*. Retrieved from http://blogs.edweek.org/edweek/DigitalEducation/2014/04/inbloom_to_shut_down_amid_growing_data_privacy_concerns.html

Herrington, A., & Moran, C. (2012). Writing to a machine is not writing at all. In N. Elliot & L. Perelman (Eds.), *Writing assessment in the 21st century: Essays in honor of Edward M. White* (pp. 219–232). New York, NY: Hampton Press.

Hinze, S. R., Wiley, J., & Pellegrino, J. W. (2013). The importance of constructive comprehension processes in learning from tests. *Journal of Memory and Language, 69*, 151–164.

Holland, P. W., & Dorans, N. J. (2006). Linking and equating. In R. L. Brennan (Ed.), *Educational measurement* (4th ed., pp. 187–220). Westport, CT: American Council on Education/Praeger.

Horkay, N., Bennett, R. E., Allen, N., Kaplan, B, & Yan, F. (2006). Does it matter if I take my writing test on computer? An empirical study of mode effects in NAEP. *Journal of Technology, Learning, and Assessment, 5*(2). Retrieved from http://files.eric.ed.gov/fulltext/EJ843858.pdf

Irvine, S. H., & Kyllonen, P. C. (2010). *Item generation for test development*. New York, NY: Routledge.

Kamisar, B. (2014, January 7). InBloom sputters amid concerns about privacy of student data. *Education Week*. Retrieved from http://www.edweek.org/ew/articles/2014/01/08/15inbloom_ep.h33.html

Kane, M. T. (2006). Validation. In R. L. Brennan (Ed.), *Educational measurement* (4th ed., pp. 17–64). Westport, CT: American Council on Education/Praeger.

Kapur, M (2010). Productive failure in mathematical problem solving. *Instructional Science, 38*, 523–550.

Kingsbury, G. G., & Houser, R. L. (1999). Developing computerized adaptive tests for school children. In F. Drasgow & J. B. Olson-Buchanan (Eds.), *Innovations in computerized assessment* (pp. 93–115). Mahwah, NJ: Erlbaum.

Kingston, N. M. (2008). Comparability of computer- and paper-administered multiple-choice tests for k–12 populations: A synthesis. *Applied Measurement in Education, 22*, 22–37. doi:10.1080/08957340802558326

Kopriva, R. J. (2009). Assessing the skills and abilities in math and science of ELLs with low English proficiency: A promising new method. *AccELLerate!, 2*, 7–10. Retrieved from http://www.ncela.us/files/uploads/17/Accellerate_2_1.pdf

Koretz, D., & Hamilton, L. S. (2006). Testing for accountability in k-12. In R. L. Brennan (Ed.), *Educational measurement* (4th ed., pp. 531–578). Westport, CT: American Council on Education/Praeger.

Lave, J. (1991). Situating learning in communities of practice. In L. B. Resnick, J. M. Levine, & S. D. Teasley (Eds.), *Perspectives on socially shared cognition* (pp. 63–82). Washington, DC: American Psychological Association. doi:10.1037/10096-003

Lemann, N. (1999). *The big test: The secret history of the American meritocracy.* New York, NY: Farrar, Strauss, & Giroux.

Linn, R. L., & Burton, E. (1994). Performance-based assessment: Implications of task specificity. *Educational Measurement: Issues and Practice, 13*(1), 5–8.

Liu, L., Rogat, A., & Bertling, M. (2013). *A CBAL science model of cognition: Developing a competency model and learning progressions to support assessment development* (Research Report No.13-29). Princeton, NJ: Educational Testing Service.

Luecht, R. M. (2009). Adaptive computer-based tasks under an assessment engineering paradigm. In D. J. Weiss (Ed.), *Proceedings of the 2009 GMAC Conference on Computerized Adaptive Testing.* Retrieved from http://publicdocs.iacat.org/cat2010/cat09luecht.pdf

Marcus, G., & Davis, E. (2014, April 6). Eight (no, nine!) problems with big data. *New York Times.* Retrieved from http://www.nytimes.com/2014/04/07/opinion/eight-no-nine-problems-with-big-data.html?_r=1

McManus, S. (2008). *Attributes of effective formative assessment.* Washington, DC: Council for Chief State School Officers. Retrieved from http://www.ccsso.org/publications/details.cfm?PublicationID=362

Mislevy, R. J., Almond, R. G., & Lukas, J. F. (2003). *A brief introduction to evidence-centered design* (Research Report No. 03-16). Princeton, NJ: Educational Testing Service.

Mislevy, R. J., Behrens, J. T., Bennett, R. E., Demark, S. F., Frezzo, D. C., Levy, R., . . . Shute, V. J. (2010). On the roles of external knowledge representations in assessment design. *Journal of Technology, Learning, and Assessment, 8*(2). Retrieved from http://files.eric.ed.gov/fulltext/EJ873671.pdf

Mislevy, R. J., Behrens, J. T., DiCerbo, K. E., & Levy, R. (2012). Design and discovery in educational assessment: Evidence-centered design, psychometrics, and educational data mining. *Journal of Educational Data Mining, 4*(1). Retrieved from http://www.educationaldatamining.org/JEDM/index.php/JEDM/article/view/22/12

Mislevy, R. J., & Zwick, R. (2012). Scaling, linking, and reporting in a periodic assessment system. *Journal of Educational Measurement, 49*, 148–166.

National Association of State Boards of Accountancy. (2012). *New York: Applying for the Uniform CPA Exam.* Retrieved from http://www.nasba.org/exams/cpaexam/newyork/

National Board of Medical Examiners. (2012). *USMLE examination fees.* Retrieved from http://www.nbme.org/students/examfees.html

National Center for Education Statistics. (2012). *The nation's report card: Science in action: Hands-on and interactive computer tasks from the 2009 science assessment* (NCES 2012-468). Washington, DC: Institute of Education Sciences, U.S. Department of Education.

National Council of Architectural Registration Boards. (2009). *Taking the ARE*. Retrieved from http://www.ncarb.org/ARE/Taking-the-ARE.aspx

National Council of Architectural Registration Boards. (2012). *ARE guidelines*. Retrieved from http://www.ncarb.org/ARE/~/media/Files/PDF/Guidelines/ARE_Guidelines.pdf

National Council of Teachers of English. (2013). *NCTE position statement on machine scoring: Machine scoring fails the test*. Urbana, IL: Author. Retrieved from http://www.ncte.org/positions/statements/machine_scoring

National Research Council. (2000). *How people learn: Brain, mind, experience, and school* (Expanded ed.). Washington, DC: National Academies Press.

Pane, J. F., Griffin, B. A., McCaffrey, D. F., & Karam, R. (2013). *Effectiveness of Cognitive Tutor Algebra I at scale* (WR-984-DEIES). Pittsburgh, PA: Rand Corporation. Retrieved from http://www.siia.net/visionk20/files/Effectiveness%20of%20Cognitive%20Tutor%20Algebra%20I%20at%20Scale.pdf

Partnership for Assessment of Readiness for College and Careers. (2010). *The Partnership for Assessment of Readiness for College and Careers (PARCC) application for the Race to the Top comprehensive assessment systems competition*. Washington, DC: Author. Retrieved from http://www.parcconline.org/sites/parcc/files/PARCC%20Application%20-%20FINAL.pdf

Partnership for Assessment of Readiness for College and Careers. (2013a). *Diagnostic assessments and K-1 formative assessment tools*. Washington, DC: Author. Retrieved from http://www.parcconline.org/sites/parcc/files/DiagnosticK-1July%202013Overview.pdf

Partnership for Assessment of Readiness for College and Careers. (2013b). *Non-summative assessments*. Washington, DC: Author. Retrieved from http://www.parcconline.org/non-summative-assessments

Partnership for Assessment of Readiness for College and Careers. (2013c). *PARCC accessibility features and accommodations manual*. Washington, DC: Author. Retrieved from http://parcconline.org/sites/parcc/files/PARCCAccessibilityFeaturesandAccommodationsManualNovember2013.pdf

Partnership for Assessment of Readiness for College and Careers. (2013d). *PARCC assessment administration guidance* (Version 1.0). Washington, DC: Author. Retrieved from http://www.parcconline.org/sites/parcc/files/PARCC%20Assessment%20Administration%20Guidance_FINAL_0.pdf

Partnership for Assessment of Readiness for College and Careers. (2013e). *Technology guidelines for PARCC assessments (Version 3.0): Frequently asked questions*. Washington, DC: Author. Retrieved from http://parcconline.org/sites/parcc/files/PARCC_TechnologyGuidelines-V3_FAQ.pdf

Partnership for Assessment of Readiness for College and Careers. (2014). *States select contractor to help develop and implement PARCC tests: Cost comes in under projection*. Washington, DC: Author. Retrieved from http://www.parcconline.org/states-select-contractor-help-develop-and-implement-parcc-tests

Pellegrino, J. W., Chudowsky, N., & Glaser, R. (2001). *Knowing what students know: The science and design of educational assessment*. Washington, DC: National Academies Press.

Perelman, L. (2014). When "the state of the art" is counting words. *Assessing Writing, 21*, 104–111.

Popham, W. J. (2006). Phony formative assessments: Buyer beware! *Educational Leadership, 64*(3), 86–87.

Popham, W. J. (2008). *Transformative assessment*. Alexandria, VA: ASCD.

Quellmalz, E. S., Davenport, J. L., Timms, M. J., DeBoer, G. E., Jordan, K. A., Huang, C.-W., & Buckley, B. C. (2013). Next-generation environments for assessing and promoting complex science learning. *Journal of Educational Psychology, 105*, 1100–1114. doi:10.1037/a0032220

Quillen, I. (2012, May 9). Hewlett automated-essay-grader winners announced. *Education Week*, Retrieved from http://blogs.edweek.org/edweek/DigitalEducation/2012/05/essay_grader_winners_announced.html

Ramineni, C., Trapani, C. S., Williamson, D. M., Davey, T., & Bridgeman, B. (2012). *Evaluation of e-rater for the GRE issue and argument prompts* (Research Report No. 12-02). Princeton, NJ: Educational Testing Service.

Ravitch, D. (2013). *The reign of error: The hoax of the privatization movement and the danger to America's public schools*. New York, NY: Knopf.

Reid, K. S. (2014, February 28). Chicago parents form coalition to promote state test boycott. *Education Week*. Retrieved from http://blogs.edweek.org/edweek/parentsandthepublic/2014/02/chicago_parents_form_coalition_to_support_state_test_boycott.html?cmp=ENL-EU-NEWS2

Reidenberg, J., Russell, N. C., Kovnot, J., Norton, T. B., Cloutier, R., & Alvarado, D. (2013). *Privacy and cloud computing in public schools*. New York, NY: Fordham Center on Law and Information Policy. Retrieved from http://ir.lawnet.fordham.edu/clip/2/

Ritter, S., Anderson, J. R., Koedinger, K. R., & Corbett, A. (2007). Cognitive tutor: Applied research in mathematics education. *Psychonomic Bulletin & Review, 14*, 249–255.

Roediger, H. L., III, & Karpicke, J. D. (2006). Test-enhanced learning: Taking memory tests improves long-term retention. *Psychological Science, 17*, 249–255.

Rohrer, D., & Pashler, H. (2010). Recent research on human learning challenges conventional instructional strategies. *Educational Researcher, 39*, 406–412.

Rudner, L. M. (2010). Implementing the Graduate Management Admission Test computerized adaptive test. In W. J. van der Linden & C. A. W. Glas (Eds.), *Elements of adaptive testing* (pp. 151–165). New York, NY: Springer. doi:10.1007/978-0-387-85461-8_8

Rudner, L. M., Garcia, V., & Welch, C. (2006). An evaluation of the IntelliMetric™ essay scoring system. *Journal of Technology, Learning, and Assessment, 4*(4). Retrieved from http://ejournals.bc.edu/ojs/index.php/jtla/article/view/1651/1493

Schmidt, W. H., & Houang, R. T. (2012). Curricular coherence and the Common Core State Standards for Mathematics. *Educational Researcher, 41*, 294–308. doi:10.3102/0013189X12464517

Shaffer, D. W. (2006). *How computer games help children learn*. New York, NY: Palgrave MacMillan.

Shavelson, R. J., Baxter, G. P., & Gao, X. (1993). Sampling variability of performance assessments. *Journal of Educational Measurement, 30*, 215–232.

Shepard, L. A. (2008). Formative assessment: Caveat emptor. In C. A. Dwyer (Ed.), *The future of assessment: Shaping teaching and learning* (pp. 279–303). New York, NY: Erlbaum.

Shepard, L. A., Daro, P., & Stancavage, F. B. (2013). *The relevance of learning progressions for NAEP*. Washington, DC: American Institutes for Research. Retrieved from http://www.air.org/files/NVS_combined_study_3_Relevance_of_Learning_Progressions_for_NAEP.pdf

Shermis, M. D., & Burstein, J. (Eds.). (2013). *Handbook of automated essay evaluation: Current applications and new directions*. New York, NY: Routledge.

Shermis, M. D., & Hamner, B. (2013). Contrasting state-of-the-art automated scoring of essays. In M. D. Shermis & J. Burstein (Eds.), *Handbook of automated essay evaluation: Current applications and new directions* (pp. 313–346). New York, NY: Routledge.

Sigel, I. (1993). The centrality of a distancing model for the development of representation competence. In R. Cocking & K. A. Renninger (Eds.), *The development and meaning of psychological distance* (pp. 141–158). Mahwah, NJ: Erlbaum.

Singer, N. (2013, October 5). Deciding who sees student data. *New York Times*. Retrieved from http://www.nytimes.com/2013/10/06/business/deciding-who-sees-students-data.html?pagewanted=1&_r=0&adxnnlx=1389978450-gFo%20edDUCpRuRLvjV%20ngMQ

Sleeman, D., & Brown, J. S. (Eds.). (1982). *Intelligent tutoring systems.* New York, NY: Academic Press.

Smarter Balanced Assessment Consortium. (2010a). *Race to the Top Assessment Program Application for new grants: Comprehensive Assessment Systems CFDA Number: 84.395B.* Sacramento, CA: Author. Retrieved from http://www.smarterbalanced.org/wordpress/wp-content/uploads/2011/12/Smarter-Balanced-RttT-Application.pdf

Smarter Balanced Assessment Consortium. (2010b). *Theory of action: An excerpt from the Smarter Balanced Race to the Top Application.* Sacramento, CA: Author. Retrieved from http://www.smarterbalanced.org/wordpress/wp-content/uploads/2012/02/Smarter-Balanced-Theory-of-Action.pdf

Smarter Balanced Assessment Consortium. (2012a). *Frequently asked questions.* Sacramento, CA: Author. Retrieved from http://www.smarterbalanced.org/resources-events/faqs/

Smarter Balanced Assessment Consortium. (2012b). *Smarter Balanced assessments.* Sacramento, CA: Author. Retrieved from http://www.smarterbalanced.org/smarter-balanced-assessments/

Smarter Balanced Assessment Consortium. (2014). *Smarter Balanced Assessment Consortium: Usability, accessibility, and accommodations guidelines.* Sacramento, CA: Author. Retrieved from http://www.smarterbalanced.org/wordpress/wp-content/uploads/2013/09/SmarterBalanced_Guidelines_091113.pdf

Song, Y., Deane, P., Graf, E. A., & van Rijn, P. (2013). Using argumentation learning progressions to support teaching and assessments of English language arts. *R&D Connections, 22,* 1–14. Retrieved from http://www.ets.org/Media/Research/pdf/RD_Connections_22.pdf

Stecher, B. (2010). *Performance assessment in an era of standards-based educational accountability.* Stanford, CA: Stanford University, Stanford Center for Opportunity Policy in Education. Retrieved from https://scale.stanford.edu/system/files/performance-assessment-era-standards-based-educational-accountability.pdf

Steenbergen-Hu, S., & Cooper, H. (2013). A meta-analysis of the effectiveness of intelligent tutoring systems on K-12 students' mathematical learning. *Journal of Educational Psychology, 105,* 980–987. doi:10.1037/a0032447

Steenbergen-Hu, S., & Cooper, H. (2014). A meta-analysis of the effectiveness of intelligent tutoring systems on college students' academic learning. *Journal of Educational Psychology, 106,* 331–347. doi:10.1037/a0034752

Stone, E., & Davey, T. (2011). *Computer-adaptive testing for students with disabilities: A review of the literature* (Research Report No. 11-32). Princeton, NJ: Educational Testing Service.

Strauss, V. (2014, September 28). How much time will new Common Core tests take kids to finish? Quite a lot. *Washington Post.* Retrieved October 1, 2014 from http://www.washingtonpost.com/blogs/answer-sheet/wp/2014/09/28/how-much-time-will-new-common-core-tests-take-kids-to-finish-quite-a-lot/

Tan, S. (2014, May 16). What's the upside to tough, new Common Core tests for schools? Throwing out those decade-old computers. *Hechinger Report.* Retrieved from http://hechingerreport.org/content/whats-upside-tough-new-common-core-tests-schools-throwing-decade-old-computers_15905/

Tucker, B. (2012, May/June). Grand test auto: The end of testing. *Washington Monthly.* Retrieved from http://www.washingtonmonthly.com/magazine/mayjune_2012/special_report/grand_test_auto037192.php

University of Akron. (2012, April 4). *Man and machine: Better writers, better grades.* Retrieved from http://www.uakron.edu/im/online-newsroom/news_details.dot?newsId=40920394-9e62-415d-b038-15fe2e72a677&pageTitle=Top%20Story%20Headline&crumbTitle=Man%20and%20%20machine:%20Better%20writers,%20better%20grades

U.S. Department of Education. (2010). *Race to the Top assessment program application for new grants: Comprehensive Assessment Systems* (CFDA No. 84.395B). Washington, DC: Author.

U.S. Department of Education, Office of Educational Research and Improvement. (1994). *What do student grades mean? Differences across schools* (Office of Research Report OR 94-3401). Washington, DC: Office of Research. Retrieved from http://files.eric.ed.gov/fulltext/ED367666.pdf

U.S. Medical Licensing Examination. (2012). *2013 USMLE bulletin.* Retrieved from http://www.usmle.org/

VanLehn, K., & van de Sande, B. (2009). Acquiring conceptual expertise from modeling: The case of elementary physics. In K. A. Ericsson (Ed.), *Development of professional expertise: Toward measurement of expert performance and design of optimal learning environments* (pp. 356–378). Cambridge, England: Cambridge University Press.

Virginia Department of Education. (2012). *Standards of Learning (SOL) and testing.* Richmond, VA: Author. Retrieved from http://www.doe.virginia.gov/testing/sol/standards_docs/mathematics/parents_students_should_know.shtml

Wainer, H. (Ed.). (2000). *Computerized adaptive testing: A primer* (2nd ed.). Mahwah, NJ: Erlbaum.

Wang, S., Jiao, H., Young, M. J., Brooks, T., & Olson, J. (2007a). Comparability of computer-based and paper-and-pencil testing in K–12 reading assessments: A meta-analysis of testing mode effects. *Educational and Psychological Measurement, 68,* 5–24. doi:10.1177/0013164407305592

Wang, S., Jiao, H., Young, M. J., Brooks, T. E., & Olson, J. (2007b). A meta-analysis of testing mode effects in Grade K–12 mathematics tests. *Educational and Psychological Measurement, 67,* 219–238.

Ward, W. C. (1988). The College Board Computerized Placement Tests: An application of computerized adaptive testing. *Machine-Mediated Learning, 2,* 271–282.

Weiss, D. J. (1982). Improving measurement quality and efficiency with adaptive testing. *Applied Psychological Measurement, 6,* 473–492.

Wenger, E. (2000). Communities of practice and social learning systems. *Organization, 7,* 225–246. doi:10.1177/135050840072002

Williamson, D. M. (2013). Probable cause: Developing warrants for automated scoring of essays. In M. D. Shermis & J. Burstein (Eds.), *Handbook of automated essay evaluation: Current applications and new directions* (pp. 153–180). New York, NY: Routledge.

Woodruff, D. J., & Ziomek, R. L. (2004). *Differential grading standards among high schools* (ACT Research Report Series 2004-2). Iowa City, IA: ACT. Retrieved from http://www.act.org/research/researchers/reports/pdf/ACT_RR2004-2.pdf

Yan, D., von Davier, A. A., & Lewis, C. (Eds.). (2014). *Computerized multistage testing: Theory and applications.* London, England: Chapman & Hall/CRC.

About the Editors

Jamal Abedi is a professor of education at the University of California, Davis. His research interests include studies in the areas of psychometrics and test and scale development. His recent works include studies on the validity of assessments, accommodations, and classification for English language learners. He serves on assessment advisory boards for a number of states and assessment consortia as an expert in testing English language learners. He is the recipient of the 2003 National Professional Service Award in recognition of his "Outstanding Contribution Relating Research to Practice" from the American Educational Research Association, the 2008 Lifetime Achievement Award from the California Educational Research Association, the 2013 National Association of Test Directors: "Outstanding Contribution to Educational Assessment," and the 2014 University of California, Davis: "Distinguished Scholarly Public Service Award." He holds a master's degree in psychology and a PhD degree in psychometrics from Vanderbilt University.

Christian Faltis is the Dolly and David Fiddyment Chair in Teacher Education, Director of Teacher Education, and Professor of Language, Literacy and Culture in the School of Education at University of California, Davis. His research interests include teacher education for emergent bilingual users, Race Radical Vision in bilingual education, and critical arts–based learning. He was the recipient of an American Educational Research Association Distinguished Scholar Award in 2001. His recent books are *The Arts and Emergent Bilingual Youth: Building Culturally Responsive, Critical and Creative Education in School and Community Contexts* (2013, coauthored with S. V. Chappell), *Implementing Educational Language Policy in Arizona: Legal, Historical and Current Practices in SE* (2012, coedited with M. B. Arias), and *Education, Immigrant Students, Refugee Students, and English Learners* (2011, coauthored with G. Valdés). He is an oil painter whose work focuses on issues of Mexican immigrants and education, and his art has been featured in numerous scholarly and art-based literature. He holds an MA degree in Mexican American graduate studies from San José State University and an MA in second language education and a PhD in curriculum studies and teacher education with an emphasis in bilingual cross-cultural education from Stanford University.

Review of Research in Education
March 2015, Vol. 39, pp. 408
DOI: 10.3102/0091732X14558821
© 2015 AERA. http://rre.aera.net

About the Contributors

Alison L. Bailey is a professor of human development and psychology at the University of California, Los Angeles. She is a developmental psycholinguist working on issues germane to children's linguistic, social, and educational development. She has published widely in these areas, most recently in *Language Assessment Quarterly*, *TESOL Quarterly*, *Bilingual Research Journal*, *Language Testing*, *Educational Policy*, and *First Language*, and her books include *The Language Demands of School: Putting Academic English to the Test* (Yale University Press) and *Formative Assessment for Literacy, Grades K-6: Building Reading and Academic Language Skills Across the Curriculum* (Corwin). She is a former Haynes Foundation faculty fellow and is also a faculty research partner at the National Center for Research on Evaluation, Standards, and Student Testing (CRESST). She serves on the technical advisory boards of a number of states and consortia developing next-generation English language proficiency assessment systems.

Eva L. Baker is a UCLA Distinguished Professor, director of the Center for the Study of Evaluation, and codirector of the National Center for Research on Evaluation, Standards, and Student Testing (CRESST). Her research focuses on the integration of standards, instruction, and measurement, including design and empirical validation and feasibility of complex human performance, particularly using technology. She was president of the World Education Research Association, president of the American Educational Research Association, and president of the Educational Psychology Division of the American Psychological Association and is a member of the National Academy of Education. She cochaired the committee that produced *Standards for Educational and Psychological Testing*, published in 1999; was chair of the Board on Testing and Assessment; and was a member of the Edmund W. Gordon Commission on the Future of Assessment in K-12 Education. Among other awards, she received the American Educational Research Association Lindquist Award and the Robert L. Linn Distinguished Address Award. She was UCLA professional alumna of the year.

Review of Research in Education
March 2015, Vol. 39, pp. 409–416
DOI: 10.3102/0091732X14557624
© 2015 AERA. http://rre.aera.net

Randy Elliot Bennett is Norman O. Frederiksen Chair in Assessment Innovation at Educational Testing Service in Princeton, New Jersey. Since the 1980s, he has conducted research on integrating advances in cognitive science, technology, and measurement to create new approaches to assessment. From 1999 through 2005, he directed the National Assessment of Educational Progress (NAEP) Technology-Based Assessment project, which explored the use of computerized testing in NAEP. Three major studies were conducted in *mathematics, writing,* and *problem solving with technology* that were the first to have administered computer-based performance assessments to nationally representative samples of school students and to use "clickstream" data in such samples to measure the processes used in problem solving. He is the author of many publications, including the chapter "Technology and Testing" (with Fritz Drasgow and Ric Luecht) in *Educational Measurement* (4th ed.), *What Does It Mean to Be a Nonprofit Educational Measurement Organization in the 21st Century?, Inevitable and Inexorable: The Continuing Story of Technology and Assessment,* and *How the Internet Will Help Large-Scale Testing Reinvent Itself.*

Alissa Blair is a postdoctoral researcher at the WIDA Consortium at the University of Wisconsin-Madison, where she collaborates on language and literacy initiatives. She holds a PhD in curriculum and instruction from the University of Wisconsin-Madison with a specialization in English as a second language and bilingual education. Her research focuses on the language and literacy learning of emergent bilinguals in and out of school, including language development in academic contexts. She has taught at the middle, high school, and college levels.

Timothy Boals is the executive director of WIDA at the University of Wisconsin-Madison. He holds a PhD in curriculum from the University of Wisconsin-Madison with an emphasis in the education of English language learners (ELLs). His background includes language education, educational policy for ELLs, and Spanish language and literature. As the executive director, he oversees operations, long-range planning, research, and consortium outreach efforts. He is currently collaborating on a teacher handbook for formative language assessment, an edited volume on adolescent literacy development for ELLs, a chapter on how Latinos' school success is influenced by cultural perceptions, and an article on how teachers can facilitate productive language interactions within small groups. He frequently presents at conferences in the United States and internationally on the challenges facing linguistically and culturally diverse learners. He is particularly excited about WIDA projects such as the UCLA/WIDA collaborative to develop language learning progressions for formative classroom assessment, the WIDA Spanish Language Development Standards, and the data-driven school improvement materials and coaching processes within the LADDER project.

Patricia E. Carroll is a joint PhD candidate at the University of California, Los Angeles (UCLA), in the division of Human Development and Psychology, and at California State University, Los Angeles, in the division of Special Education. She is a former English language development teacher and is currently a teaching fellow in Writing Programs at UCLA. Her research interests include the measurement of literacy and language, decision rules governing educational access, and the impact of state and federal policy on data use practices preK–20.

Kirby A. Chow is a Society for Research in Child Development/American Association for the Advancement of Science Fellow. She completed her doctoral work in the Department of Education (Human Development & Psychology Division) at the University of California, Los Angeles. Her research interests are in the areas of family homelessness and children's educational outcomes, human services policy, and children's reasoning about socioeconomic stratification.

M. Elizabeth Cranley is the associate director of WIDA at the University of Wisconsin-Madison. Her responsibilities include directing the development and implementation of WIDA standards, assessments, and professional learning. She also serves as the principal investigator for research related to young dual-language learners, family engagement, and language assessment. Her interest in serving language learners and striving to understand the role of culture and context for learning began as a Peace Corps volunteer teacher in Thailand. She has taught at middle and high school as well as university levels. She earned her PhD in comparative and global studies in education from State University of New York at Buffalo.

Girlie C. Delacruz is a senior research scientist with the National Center for Research on Evaluation, Standards, and Student Testing (CRESST), with over 14 years in assessment, cognitive and learning science, and developmental psychology. Her research goals intersect learning and assessment through the study of various technology including computers, web and mobile applications, video games, and sensor-based networks. In the area of assessment, her research focuses on issues of validity, assessment design, and the use of advanced computational models to support formative assessment and adaptive learning. These interests have guided her projects across educational, training, and military contexts. She is currently the co–project director of a Defense Advanced Research Projects Agency–funded grant to develop and validate games and assessments of young children's understanding of physics and socioemotional learning concepts. She is a fellow with the ETS-Gordon/MacArthur Foundation—a group of emerging scholars concerned with the impact of new technologies, advances in the learning sciences, and the broader impact of assessment and learning in the twenty-first century.

Molly Faulkner-Bond is a doctoral candidate in the Department of Research, Educational Measurement, and Psychometrics at the University of Massachusetts Amherst. Her research interests focus on all things related to English learners, including language assessment, valid content assessment, score reporting, program design and evaluation, and policy development and implementation. These interests recently brought her to Educational Testing Service, where she currently serves as a graduate research fellow in the center for English Language Learning and Assessment while completing her dissertation. In the past she has provided policy assistance and technical support to states, consortia, and the federal government as an associate at edCount, LLC. In all of her work, she strives to bring quantitative tools and methods to bear on real-life problems whose solutions can bolster better, more positive teaching and learning for students and educators. She earned her BA, magna cum laude, as well as a certificate in mind, brain, and behavior studies from Harvard University.

Drew H. Gitomer is the Rose and Nicholas DeMarzo Chair in Education in the Graduate School of Education at Rutgers, the State University of New Jersey. His research centers on the assessment and evaluation of teaching and related policy issues in teaching and teacher education. His current work focuses on a range of constructs, including the quality of classroom interactions, teacher knowledge, teacher beliefs, and student achievement. He and his colleagues are carrying out validity studies of a variety of measures, including classroom observation protocols, classroom assignment protocols, and new measures of teacher knowledge. Through this work, he and his colleagues always strive to make progress on understanding the contextual factors that influence the quality of teaching that is observed. Prior to coming to Rutgers, he was a researcher and senior vice president of research at Educational Testing Service in Princeton, New Jersey. He is currently coediting the AERA *Handbook of Research on Teaching* (5th ed.).

Noelle C. Griffin is associate director of the National Center for Research on Evaluation, Standards, and Student Testing (CRESST) at UCLA. Through her work at CRESST she has led program evaluations in a variety of educational settings, including evaluations of professional development, science instruction, math instruction, and social services programs. She has particularly focused on the evaluation of arts-based education and its integration into the K–12 curriculum, and in addition to her work with the Webplay program, she led the national evaluation of the Leonard Bernstein Center artful learning model. Prior to returning to CRESST in 2006, she served as director of assessment for Loyola Marymount University and has a continued interest in assessment and evaluation issues at the higher education level.

Dorry M. Kenyon has a PhD in measurement, applied statistics, and evaluation from the University of Maryland. He currently serves as vice president, director of assessment at the Center for Applied Linguistics (CAL), Washington, D.C., and as the director of CAL/WIDA partnership activities at CAL. Since joining CAL in 1987, he has gained considerable experience in designing, developing, validating, and operationalizing second and foreign language assessments through many large projects at the state and national levels. Currently he directs or serves as senior advisor on a variety of projects related to developing and researching assessments of the English language and foreign language skills of language learners of preschool to adult age. He has also served as CAL's chief psychometrician, as the leader of CAL's psychometrics/research team. Prior to joining CAL, he taught German and English as a foreign/second language for 7 years in the United States and abroad.

Ryan J. Kettler, PhD, is an associate professor of school psychology in the Graduate School of Applied and Professional Psychology at Rutgers, the State University of New Jersey. He earned his doctorate in educational psychology from the University of Wisconsin-Madison in 2005. His research on data-based decision making in education has been externally funded and has yielded more than 50 publications. Active areas within this program include universal screening, inclusive assessment, and educator effectiveness. He has been a principal investigator or co–principal investigator on seven grant projects, including three funded by the U.S. Department of Education. He is currently a co–principal investigator on the School System Improvement Project, the website editor for the Society for the Study of School Psychology, and the lead editor of *Universal Screening in Educational Settings: Evidence-Based Decision Making for Schools*, a new book from the American Psychological Association.

Rebecca J. Kopriva is a senior scientist at the University of Wisconsin's Wisconsin Center for Educational Research. The author of numerous books, chapters, and articles, including *Improving Testing for ELLs* (2008, Routledge), she investigates accessible assessments and classroom professional development for students with various challenges. She also created an individualized system for differentially accommodating ELs with various challenges and strengths in large-scale and classroom settings. Most recently her team has developed and researched a successful approach to using multisemiotic, technology-based techniques in assessing rigorous mathematics and science. This work allows students to directly demonstrate what they know using simulations, dynamic interactions, and novel response environments and has been found to be especially beneficial for ELs at all levels of English proficiency, struggling readers, and some students with disabilities, including those with select learning disabilities, deaf/hard of hearing, and attention deficit disorder/attention deficit hyperactivity disorder. Furthermore, her work pioneered innovative gamelike methods and algorithmic process and status scoring found to be uniquely suited for measuring academic performances of all students.

Suzanne Lane is a professor in the research methodology program at the University of Pittsburgh. Her research and scholarly interests are in educational measurement and testing, in particular, design, validity, and technical issues related to large-scale assessment and accountability systems, including performance-based assessments. Her work is published in journals such as the *Journal of Educational Measurement, Applied Measurement in Education, Educational Assessment,* and *Educational Measurement: Issues and Practice.* She was president of the National Council on Measurement in Education (2003–2004), vice president of Division D of the American Educational Research Association (2000–2002), and a member of the American Educational Research Association, American Psychological Association, and National Council on Measurement in Education Joint Committee for the Revision of the Standards for Educational and Psychological Testing (1993–1999).

Brian Leventhal is a doctoral candidate in the research methodology program at the University of Pittsburgh. He holds a master's degree in applied statistics from the University of Pittsburgh. His scholarly interests are in measurement, specifically, estimation and application of polytomous item response theory models with an underlying skewed trait distribution, survey development, and psychometric analysis. He is also interested in the use and effectiveness of innovative teaching methods for statistics courses. He has taught statistics and research design courses for both undergraduate and graduate students. He has presented his research at the annual meeting of the National Council on Measurement in Education.

Ayesha Madni is a senior researcher at the National Center for Research on Evaluation, Standards, and Student Testing (CRESST). She has worked in the field of education for over 10 years, and currently works on a broad number of research projects at CRESST. Her research interests span educational games and technology, student motivation, social and emotional learning, and human learning and memory. Her current work involves students' self-efficacy and social and emotional learning within educational games. She also has a strong interest in enhancing performance of students with special needs. Prior to her work at CRESST, she taught at the Rossier School of Education, University of Southern California, and worked as a senior researcher for Intelligent Systems Technology, Inc. She has also worked as a learning specialist providing targeted interventions to facilitate student learning and motivation across a variety of student populations. She received her doctorate in educational psychology from the University of Southern California.

Eduardo Mosqueda is an assistant professor of education at the University of California, Santa Cruz. He completed his doctoral studies at the Harvard Graduate School of Education and was awarded a Spencer Dissertation Fellowship. His career in education began as a middle school mathematics teacher in Santa Ana, California. His research primarily examines the relationship between the English proficiency of language minority students, their access to rigorous courses, and their performance on standardized mathematics assessments. He is the co–principal investigator of English Language and Literacy Integration in Subject Areas (ELLISA): Building Capacity in Preservice Teacher Education, a U.S. Department of Education–funded project. He has authored or coauthored articles in *Equity and Excellence in Education*, the *Journal of Urban Mathematics Education*, and the *Journal of Science Teacher Education*.

Stephen G. Sireci is a professor in the Psychometrics Program and director of the Center for Educational Assessment at the University of Massachusetts Amherst (UMass). His PhD is in psychometrics from Fordham University, and his master's and bachelor's degrees are in psychology from Loyola College. Prior to UMass, he was senior psychometrician for GED Testing Service, psychometrician for Uniform Certified Public Accountant Exam, and research supervisor of testing for Newark Board of Education. His research focuses on educational test development and evaluation, validity, cross-lingual assessment, standard setting, and computer-based testing. He serves on several advisory committees (e.g., National Board for Professional Teaching Standards, Puerto Rico, Texas) and is a fellow of the American Educational Research Association, a fellow of Division 5 of the American Psychological Association, and a past coeditor of *International Journal of Testing* and *Journal of Applied Testing Technology*. He served as president of the Northeastern Educational Research Association and on the board of directors for the National Council on Measurement in Education. His awards include the Outstanding Teacher Award, Chancellor's Medal, Award for Outstanding Accomplishments in Research and Creative Activity, and the Conti Faculty Fellowship.

Kip Téllez is a professor and former chair in the Education Department at University of California, Santa Cruz. He began his career teaching elementary and high school students in East Los Angeles County, where he developed an abiding interest in English language learners. After earning his PhD at the Claremont Graduate University, he began his first academic position at the University of Houston, where he taught courses on methods and theories of second language education, while also initiating several two-way immersion programs in the region. Combining his interests in English language teaching and teacher education, he has published articles in journals such as the *Journal of Teacher Education, Teaching and Teacher Education,* and the *Bilingual Research Journal.* He currently serves as editor for *Teacher Education Quarterly.* A recently published book, *Teaching English Learners* (2011, Paradigm), is designed to help English language development teachers consider the wide implications of their work.

Martha L. Thurlow is director of the National Center on Educational Outcomes at the University of Minnesota. In this position, she addresses the implications of contemporary U.S. policy and practice for students with disabilities and English language learners, including national and statewide assessment policies and practices and state and local graduation requirements. During the past decade, she has been the principal investigator on more than 20 federal or state projects that have focused on students with special needs in state and national policies and in large-scale accountability assessments, including graduation exams. Particular emphasis has been given to how to obtain valid, reliable, and comparable measures of the knowledge and skills of these students while ensuring that the assessments are truly measuring their knowledge and skills rather than their disabilities or limited language when these are not the focus of the assessment. Studies have covered a range of topics, including participation decision making, accommodations, universal design, accessible reading assessments, computer-based testing, graduation exams, and alternate assessments.

Carsten Wilmes is director of assessment for WIDA at the University of Wisconsin-Madison. He oversees the development and operational implementation of WIDA's various assessments. He has conducted research in the area of second language proficiency assessment. His dissertation investigated the validity of a modified C-test procedure for the purposes of a university placement test. Current research interests include the validation of innovative assessments, the adaptation of the Webb alignment model to the standards-to-standards alignment context, and applications of items response theory. He completed an MA degree in Germanic languages and literature with a concentration in second language acquisition, and a PhD in second language acquisition with a concentration in educational measurement at the University of Illinois at Urbana-Champaign. He has received many fellowships and awards such as the Excellence in Undergraduate Teaching Award, Ruth E. Lorbe Excellence in Teaching Award, a research project grant, and university fellowships.

Laura J. Wright is a senior research associate at the Center for Applied Linguistics, where she works on a variety of projects including the National Clearinghouse for English Language Acquisition and WIDA Assessment Services Supporting ELs Through Technology Systems. She holds a PhD in linguistics from Georgetown University, specializing in sociolinguistics and discourse analysis. Her research focuses on how students express understanding through discourse in complex learning environments and assessments, and on language development in academic contexts.

Robert C. Zisk is a doctoral candidate in the Learning, Cognition, Instruction, and Development Program at the Graduate School of Education at Rutgers, the State University of New Jersey. A former middle school science teacher, he currently teaches preservice and in-service physics teachers, as well as elementary science teachers. His research interests include the development and validation of measures of content knowledge for teaching and their relation to other measures of teaching practice. In addition, he develops and teaches professional development for physics teachers across New Jersey.